Ma... 17, ...

..., Dad!

Here's to the beginning
of your collection of
Cornelliana.

Love,
Anne & Andrew

A CENTURY AT CORNELL

The Cornell Daily Sun

A CENTURY AT CORNELL

Published to commemorate the hundredth anniversary of

𝕿𝖍𝖊 𝕮𝖔𝖗𝖓𝖊𝖑𝖑 𝕯𝖆𝖎𝖑𝖞 𝕾𝖚𝖓

Editor
DANIEL MARGULIS
managing editor, 1972-73

Designer
JOHN SCHROEDER
associate editor, 1973-74

Assistant Editor
ROBERTA MOUDRY
associate editor, 1980-81

Coordinators of Written Contributions
PETER COY   MARIE GOTTSCHALK
editor-in-chief, 1978-79   senior editor, 1979-80

Editor at Large
DAVID DAYTON

Published by The Cornell Daily Sun, Inc.
Ithaca, New York • 1980

Library of Congress Cataloging in Publication Data

Main entry under title:

A Century at Cornell

   1. Cornell University – Addresses, essays, lectures.
I. Margulis, Daniel, 1951- II. Cornell Daily Sun.
LD1357.5.C46   378.747'71   80-25542
ISBN 0-938304-00-3

This book was typeset and composed at *The Cornell Daily Sun*
in Kennerley Old Style, Goudy Old Style, ɪᴛᴄ Novarese and
Times Roman.

Printed in the United States of America.

The Cornell Daily Sun, Inc.
109 East State Street
Ithaca, New York 14850

Introduction

This book, I fear, will be as difficult to read as it was to put together. It is hard enough to compile a hundred-year history of anything, let alone a newspaper whose total publications over that time would fill a small library and amount to nearly half a billion words.

How, then, are we to set up, in only one book, a history of *The Cornell Daily Sun*? There is no dearth of fascinating material, and any number of angles to approach it from. A mere history of what has gone on at The Sun's offices over the last century would be hugely interesting, although most readers would find it hard to believe it was non-fiction.

But The Sun's primary business has always been to cover Cornell University. Its pages form the most complete history of Cornell that can be found. It seemed a book about a century at Cornell, written from the perspective of the succeeding editors of The Sun, would tell more about The Sun's past than any mundane chronology. Besides, it would be a lot more fun to read.

Cornell badly needs a new general history of the institution. Morris Bishop's *A History of Cornell* is an excellent book, but it was written 20 years ago, and for that matter, Bishop admitted that he would make no effort to be objective about the tenure of the incumbent president, Deane Malott, who took office in 1951. Cornell badly needs such a history, but it will not get one from us.

Instead, we will hop from decade to decade, backward and forward in time to look at some of the events that have made Cornell what it is today. Naturally, this means that we will ignore many important events. That we lavish 15 pages on the Straight takeover does not mean that we never heard of the much more complex Carpenter Hall takeover of 1972; our coverage of the 1940 Cornell-Dartmouth football game takes nothing away from the 1979 Cornell-Providence hockey game. Then again, we can go into much more detail about the seminal events we have chosen.

If the format is bewildering, it is no more so than Cornell. In addition to our propensity to jump backward in time, there are four different classes of material here, each identified by its own type style.

The type you are reading now is the one used to denote material written especially for this book. Some of these pieces are anecdotes from various former Sun editors; some are full-length essays written by people who have nothing to do with The Sun.

To illustrate the events we are talking about, we have also resurrected a great deal of writing from the past hundred years of Suns. Such reprinted material appears in this typeface, as do essays by Charles Rosewater and Mary Crawford, which are reprinted from our 1930 book, *A Half-Century at Cornell*. The speeches by Robert Cushman, Forrest Hill, and Carl Becker, and the letters by Andrew D. White and Ezra Cornell appeared first in other places, but all have been reprinted in their entirety in The Sun at one time or another. The only piece in this typeface that never has appeared in The Sun is an editorial from *The Cornell Widow*, appearing on Page 185.

These reprints are designed for your entertainment — not for the use of historians. Among newspaper editors there is a pronounced tendency to paint the lily and gild refined gold. The temptation to correct obvious errors proved too strong, and so historians are hereby advised that there may be slight variations from the originals. We have tried to remain faithful to the original style, including spelling and grammar that would not be accepted today, but we have had no compunction about editing out blatant mistakes, such as afflict any publication that has a deadline every night. Occasionally we have eliminated or changed phrases that contained references the modern reader would not understand; we have made some deletions without noting them as such. If, in my opinion, the deletions have a significant impact on the article, it is termed an "excerpt"; if this disclaimer does not appear you may assume that you are reading a complete piece, or one with no deletions of substance. Most of the changes are virtually unnoticeable, but the point is that the originals and what you read here are not in all cases identical.

The third category appears in this typeface. You can call it editorial comment if you like. There is normally a lot of controversy among newspaper people as to just whose view an "editorial" represents. In this case, there is an easy answer. The editorial matter in this book does not represent the opinions of Sun editors, either past or present, or of The Sun's board of directors. It represents my opinions. Sometimes my opinions are very lengthy. At other times I hide them and merely try to make helpful comments. I hope I do not intrude upon the rest of the book's content to an excessive degree.

I also selected and edited all the copy mentioned so far, which is what you might surmise, considering that I am the "editor" of the book. You may wonder, however, what the book's "designer" did to warrant having his name so prominently displayed, so I will tell you. In addition to designing the page layouts, he did the colossal amount of work necessary to collect, identify and credit correctly the more than 300 photographs and drawings that grace the book. He also wrote all of the captions, but if you find fault with any of them, I will have to share some of the blame. He also reviewed all of the text in the book. It was really kind of a joint effort.

We have few recommendations on how this book should be read. We think front to back is a good method, but of course, since it is an anthology, the chapters can be read in almost any order. We do advise a certain sensitivity to dates; Cornell's history is a distinguished one, but its protagonists have not always been as liberal as we might be today.

D.M.

Acknowledgments

This is a big book put together in a small amount of time, so it is not too surprising that we have a lot of thank yous to dole out. It is unfortunate that the language does not provide us with a stronger phrase. Many of the people whose names you are about to read were absolutely crucial to the completion of this project—without them, there might not be a book for you to read.

First of all, we are deeply indebted to all those who responded to our invitation to write essays for us, and to the Sun alumni who so kindly answered our questionnaire. We are sorry that we could not include every single contribution. The names you read in our index of authors do not convey the number of people who were willing to help us.

Among the people who are published in this book, we tip our hats to Bertram Willcox and Harry Case, both of whom supported us with grim determination. Harry Case was the editor of The Sun's 1930 memorial book, A Half-Century at Cornell. The two of us are hoping we will not have to work as hard as he has when The Sun's 150-year book comes out.

There are also some unsung heroes responsible for the fine representation of photographs in this book. It would have been nice to have focused primarily on Sun photos in every chapter, but our historical scope made this impossible. Sad to say, due to the overzealous housecleaning efforts of previous Sun editors and janitors, Sun negatives prior to 1967 do not exist. Because of technical limitations on what newspaper photographers could do and what The Sun could print, Sun pictures prior to the late 1950s would have been of limited usefulness, in any case.

Fortunately, the Cornell University Archives staff offered us the use of their extensive Cornell photograph collection. That this book is as visually rich as we hope to have made it is largely owing to their magnificent cooperation. We were granted permission to cull through files of original nineteenth century photos, and to investigate a score of as yet uncatalogued boxes of negatives and prints. Without this liberty, identifying the people and events seen in each photo and attributing the picture to its original photographer would have been much more difficult—and in many cases, impossible.

Although nearly every archives staff member has assisted us at some point during the last three months, special thanks must be given to H. Thomas Hickerson, who first approved our use of archives materials, to Burton Huth and Charles Rote, Jr., who devoted considerable time to locating boxes and pictures we could not find, and to Julia Crepeau and Geri Solomon, who checked out the endless stacks of photos used in the preparation of this book.

Further thanks must be accorded to the Cornellian, the Office of Sports Information, the Office of Public Information and to John Marcham of the Cornell Alumni News, for permission to use photographs at their disposal.

Many of this book's illustrations have been reproduced from bulky scrapbooks and bound volumes. The task of duplicating pictures and posters from these awkward originals—under extraordinary time pressures as well—fell upon Day Hall's Photographic and Microfilm Services. Their prompt response—due largely to the efforts of Barry DeLibero—aided us immensely.

It should be noted that we have endeavored, whenever we could, to credit the photographer who actually took each photo. Thus, the credit given beneath each picture does not necessarily indicate its immediate source. Scores of photos billed to such venerable photographers of the Cornell landscape as John P. Troy and C. Hadley Smith (and a host of others) were actually borrowed from archives files. And a number of photos attributed to Sun photographers were actually obtained from the archives or the Alumni News.

Finally, thanks must go to four Sun photographers. Carin Ashjian and Hall Hutchison produced numerous new photographs of beautiful quality for the book, and Jan Buskop and Steven Fox devoted many weekend hours to printing stacks of Sun negatives.

We are also grateful to Cornell University Press, for its permission to reprint sections from Morris Bishop's A History of Cornell, copyright © 1962 by Cornell University.

A Century at Cornell was not only edited in-house, but also typeset and composed here. In addition to the persons listed on our title page, we would like to express our appreciation to Carol Cole, who assumed much more than her usual burden of work for the daily production of The Sun while the rest of us were preoccupied with this book; to our proofreaders, Lisa Bloch and Eric Randall, and to John Mikula, The Ithaca Journal's night press foreman, whose camera work is responsible for many of our special graphic effects.

And while we are speaking of the people who put the finishing touches on, let us not forget those without whom we would never have gotten started. Two generations of Sun editors and managers—1979-80 and 1980-81—supported and tolerated the project. It could certainly not have come to fruition without the large amount of time spent by both of the Cornell professors who served as president of The Sun's board of directors over that time, Richard Polenberg and Joseph Bugliari. For that matter, we would like to thank the other senior members of The Sun's board: Harold Bierman, Dale Arrison Grossman, and William Wilcox. These people voted to commit a large amount of the corporation's money to the project without being at all sure what they were getting in exchange, if anything. And we would like to thank The Sun's 1979-80 business manager, John Dowd, for helping with the early financial planning.

But of course, the parties who are chiefly responsible for this book are not listed above, nor even on the title page. The fact of the matter is that most of us who worked on the book did so by accident, in that we were around and available in 1980, when the hundredth anniversary fell. We produced it, but the hundred years of Sun staffers are responsible for it; to them we dedicate this history.

D.M.
J.S.

SYNOPSIS OF CONTENTS

INDEX OF WRITERS

Chapter I: Cornell in the Eyes of the World

The reasonable man adapts himself to the world: the unreasonable one persists in trying to adapt the world to himself. Therefore, all progress depends on the unreasonable man.

— Bernard Shaw

I cannot conceive it to be possible that any man can be more thoroughly identified with the industrial, laboring, and productive classes, than I am, and my ruling desire is to dispose of so much of my property as is not required for the reasonable wants of my family, in a manner that shall do the greatest good to the greatest number of the industrial classes of my native state, and at the same time to do the greatest good to the state itself.

— Ezra Cornell

They say in advertising that image is everything. Cornell is fortunate enough to have an image as one of the world's leading universities, a valuable commodity indeed. If it were to lose this image, in a way it would not matter whether it also lost its excellence in fact. If people *perceived* that Cornell was not first-rate, the best students would no longer apply; leading academic figures would no longer seek employment; funding would be sharply reduced. Any one of these three consequences would be enough to make the perception become reality.

Cornell's history is like that. As we go backward and forward in time over the past hundred years, you will undoubtedly be struck by how frequently the appearance departs from the actuality. The quick impression of what things must have been like often is a superficial one. It takes a much closer look to develop any idea of what the Cornell traditions are.

And for an institution so young, Cornell does have an alarmingly large body of tradition. An enterprising reader might, for example, try to count the number of times the phrase ''freedom and responsibility'' appears in this book. Despite the constant repetition, as we will see, the phrase has not always been particularly appropriate. Or, to take a more positive example, in recent years the University has been criticized for a lack of commitment to racial and sexual equality, and it is popularly assumed that students have always led the administration along the road of righteousness. It comes as somewhat of a blow, then, to learn that Ezra Cornell and Andrew Dickson White held views on equal education that were eighty or ninety years ahead of their time, and that the Cornell tradition is for the administration to be more progressive than the student body, especially on the issue of education of women.

For that matter, who recalls today that Cornell's tradition is one of dramatic innovation? White and Cornell undertook ambitious curriculum reforms, reforms that were eventually pirated by every other university. If we were presenting things chronologically, this book would probably begin with an extended discussion of White's much-misunderstood educational philosophy.

Free from the necessity to consider matters in the order they occurred, however, we will start with the Straight takeover—which, though it took place only eleven years ago, already is surrounded by as much myth as anything Ezra Cornell ever did.

*   *   *

It is almost impossible to overstate the impact of the Straight takeover. In reading Suns from the two weeks following the event, one is struck by the number of appearances of the word *survival*. And people were not just worried about Cornell's future: they actually feared for their lives. The results were severe: some faculty temporarily stopped teaching, and several professors resigned, leaving whole departments in shambles; the president of Cornell was forced out.

Eleven years later, some scars remain. There actually still are some people on campus who will not speak to certain other people, solely because of differences over the handling of the incident. And it still is not necessary to add a date to the event: we just say ''Straight takeover,'' and every-

one knows what we are talking about, even though only a handful of present students and alumni were anywhere near campus when it happened, even though 1980's entering freshmen were six years old or so at the time.

The sight of militant blacks carrying loaded rifles across campus, naturally, excuses a lot of panic and concern. Yet, in looking back to that tumultuous spring, one has to wonder why the Straight takeover became such a seminal event. It did not fall out of the sky, after all: tensions had been building for over a year, there had already been violence and assorted ugly incidents, and it was clear that some sort of confrontation was inevitable.

*   *   *

Still, the nominal cause of the takeover was ludicrous, preposterous, a cause so trivial it defies belief eleven years later. For over a year before the takeover, there had been unpleasant demonstrations by blacks in support of a variety of demands; of these, one on December 18, 1968, came to the attention of the newly-revised campus judicial system. A total of six blacks were accused of offenses against the public order: four were said to have beaten on the tops of cars and waved toy pistols at bystanders. One of these students and two other blacks were also accused of having temporarily removed thirty cushions from Donlon Hall in a second demonstration a month later. The six students announced they did not accept the judicial system's jurisdiction, and refused to show up for several scheduled hearings, despite the judicial board's threat to suspend them if they did not appear.

Finally (having gone for two months through what The Sun called ''a startling and inexplicable oversight'') the board discovered that it had the power to try the defendants *in absentia*, and it did so, two nights before the Straight takeover. It gave no penalty to the students involved in the cushion-stealing; to the others (who were now only three, one having dropped out of school) it issued ''reprimands.''

Now, a ''reprimand'' was not exactly a Draconian punishment. While not absolutely meaningless, its most onerous manifestation was that the reprimandee's parents would get a letter informing them of their child's offense. The difference between a reprimand and no penalty at all, like the difference between vintages of California Cabernet Sauvignons, was noticeable chiefly to connoisseurs.

It may strike you that this was a profoundly foolish issue over which to seize a building and import guns to defend it. Nevertheless, that is what happened; and furthermore the University Faculty had a meeting afterwards at which it did nothing but discuss whether to ''nullify'' the meaningless reprimands; and when it decided not to, another meeting was called for two days afterward, at which, after lengthy and acrimonious debate, the faculty reversed its vote.

*   *   *

In retrospect, it is easy to see that the judicial issue was not a clear-cut one. The new system was having its problems. The black defendants were claiming selective prosecution, and they were plainly correct in this, although it was not the judicial board's fault. The actual cases had gotten so much publicity that it was doubtful that the board could have reached an independent decision anyway.

And yet, when the faculty voted to nullify the reprimands, it was castigated coast to coast. Everybody remembers now that the faculty and administration caved in, capitulated, that they gave in to guns. Such, at least, was the easy description of what they did. To a certain extent, however, here, as elsewhere in the chronology of the Straight takeover, the appearance triumphed over the reality.

–Sun Photo by Brian W. Gray

GUNS AT CORNELL: *A forlorn "Parents Weekend" banner still hangs over the Willard Straight Hall entrance as armed Afro-American Society leaders Eric D. Evans '69 and Edward L. Whitfield '71 spearhead the exit of 110 blacks who had occupied the building on April 19 and 20, 1969. Besides a few makeshift weapons, the protesters carried fifteen rifles and two guns in cases. A score of television and newspaper cameras representing every major American news organization recorded this culminating image of a week that shattered Cornell.*

THE WHOLE WORLD WAS WATCHING: *Associated Press photographer Steve Starr won a Pulitzer Prize for this picture of Eric D. Evans '69 and Edward L. Whitfield '71 leaving Willard Straight Hall on Sunday, April 20, 1969, armed with a shotgun and a rifle. The photograph of the first armed students to be seen during an American campus demonstration appeared the next day on hundreds of front pages across the nation.*

The End of a Bizarre Era

BY ANDREW KREIG '70

Andrew Dickson White would have been surprised that the university he helped found would become best known in its 100th year for an armed occupation of its student union. After all, White—in surveying the violent pranks and student riots that marred the college scene of his youth—had concluded, "I can testify, as can so many others, to the vast improvement in the conduct and aims of American students during the latter half of the 19th Century." He proudly ascribed this improvement to educational innovation, best represented by his own Cornell.

Dramatic photos of armed black students coming out of Willard Straight Hall April 20, 1969 appeared on front pages around the country. One garnered a Pulitzer Prize for an Associated Press photographer. For many bewildered, angry outsiders, the photos of the Ivy League school seemed to sum up a bizarre era of student protest.

Although most attention focused on Cornell's racial problems, the campus was also an important center of Vietnam War resistance and advocacy by Students for a Democratic Society. The SDS Ithaca chapter was its third largest in the nation, with several hundred members by the end of 1969. A dedicated group of activists operated a printing press that papered the campus with material ranging from outright propaganda to thought-provoking and persuasive alternative analyses. The cumulative impact of the Glad Day Press was, for us, at least, as important as that of its legendary neighbor on Stewart Avenue, Jim's Chapter House.

"You can observe a lot just by watching," Yogi Berra once said, with his usual sagacity. Yet during my years as a student from 1966 to 1970, there were unusually strong pressures on the campus community to step down out of the grandstand and choose a team. The draft, for example, was an obvious encouragement to resist the war.

Disputes over the correct degree of political activism split both the student newspaper staff and, in a somewhat different fashion, the University's faculty.

When I first worked for *The Cornell Daily Sun* in the fall of 1967, reporting was expected to meet standards of "objectivity" common to professional daily news organizations. We felt "Ithaca's Only Morning Newspaper" should have the credibility to sustain town readership on a variety of non-Cornell topics. I recall the glee with which Stanley Chess '69, later the paper's editor-in-chief, and I hawked papers on downtown streets in March 1968 as we tried to gain new readers in town with The Sun's late-night scoop on President Johnson's announcement that he would not run for re-election. The speech occurred too late at night for coverage by the Syracuse, Rochester and New York papers sold in Ithaca.

The news operation that year was led by Sam Roberts '68, who was so much a fixture that he seemed to live in the Sun offices. Roberts, who after graduation quickly became a leading political reporter and then city editor of the New York *Daily News*, was regarded as the leader of a faction of competent, industrious Sun staffers who tried to use a noncommittal

6 A CENTURY AT CORNELL

style.

The relatively non-political proteges of Roberts were virtually shut out of Sun offices in an unusually bitter election in the spring of 1968. Edward Zuckerman '70 was elected managing editor as a sophomore despite a tradition of awarding the post to a junior. Zuckerman, who after graduation helped found an alternative newspaper in Harrisburg, Pa., is now a contributing editor of *Rolling Stone* magazine. He recently recalled, with a touch of humor, his perception of intra-office political divisions in the 1968 Sun election: "I didn't think reporters had to wear ties." But for many others the election assumed a more cosmic importance: whether or not the paper would be a forceful voice against the Vietnam War and for minority rights.

The internal politics of The Sun reflected similar self-examination in many parts of the campus, including the faculty.

"A professor is a man who thinks otherwise" was a favorite saying of Carl Becker, who for many years was Cornell's official historian. Becker, who died in 1945, always felt that Cornell acquired a distinct tradition by giving a great deal of freedom to its faculty, which he described as a group of individualistic, eccentric and "otherwise-thinking" scholars. He experienced the essence of this Cornell freedom personally when, upon joining the faculty in 1917, he was astonished at not being given any specific instructions on the subject he was to teach. A colleague told Becker that certain courses had been customary in the past, but that nothing was really required. This colleague added, "We have assumed that whatever you found convenient and profitable would be sufficiently advantageous to the University and satisfactory to the students," Becker recalled.

My faculty adviser, Fred Marcham, said modern faculty still exercised Becker's unimpaired control of course material. But the former boxing coach and history department chairman, who began his teaching career in the 1920s, said modern-day professors, unlike Becker, too often remain distant from students, limiting office hours to four and five hours a week.

Student power activists, taking their cue from the Berkeley demonstrations of 1964, convinced many students at Cornell as elsewhere that faculty members were insensitive to students' educational needs.

In fact, the major internal campus dispute of the late 1960s at Cornell was control by white administrators and faculty over black students. When Cornell established an all-black women's living unit in the spring of 1968, the University served notice that it was taking a big step away from traditional control over non-academic activities of students. However, student demands for an all-black study center met much greater resistance.

Cornell, like most large universities, had in its early years neglected black Americans. A 1946 survey gathered these remarks from the chairmen of Cornell departments on why the University had never hired any black faculty members: "they

EDWARD L. WHITFIELD '71
Afro-American Society Chairman

ERIC D. EVANS '69
Afro-American Society Leader

are better off with their own people...statistically, they are an inferior race...body odors are different." The small number of black students in the past included near-supermen. Jerome "Brud" Holland was an All-American in football who went on to become president of Howard University and chairman of the World Population Council. Meredith "Flash" Gourdine was a silver medalist in the 1952 Olympics who earned a doctorate in engineering physics at Cal Tech after his graduation from Cornell. Even by 1963, the year James Perkins came to Cornell as president, there were only about 25 American blacks on the campus of 11,000 students.

A Rockefeller Foundation grant helped Cornell begin an effort, known as the Committee on Special Educational Projects, to bring minority students in under non-traditional criteria. Its purpose was to seek out members of minority groups and the underprivileged whose college achievement test scores were below what were normally required of Cornell students but whose personal qualities showed they had promise.

Rapid expansion of black enrollment at Cornell under Perkins led the black students to increase their sense of identity and question the University's motives. A black biochemistry major said of the founding of the Afro-American Society, "We've always questioned why we were brought here. I think they want to get us into the mainstream thing. They'd rather have us like that than Malcolm X."

A struggle largely unnoticed outside the black community occurred in November 1968 over control of the University's Afro-American Society. One of the AAS leaders had said, "We're about six months ahead of anyplace else" after Cornell approved the all-black women's living unit and the establishment of an Afro-American studies program. But a growing AAS faction felt the administration's pace was too slow in giving control of the program to black faculty and students. Edward Whitfield '71, who had been an NAACP organizer in Central High School in Little Rock, Ark., was chosen as the new AAS chairman in late November. Soon the AAS was issuing "non-negotiable demands" that charged Cornell's faculty was racist.

Some demands that were reasonable—such as more black-oriented library books, a black psychologist in the health center and more consideration in cafeteria menu-planning—were couched in threatening terms that provoked resistance. In early December, about 50 black students told all white professors on the black studies advisory committee that they were dismissed. The next day the students picked a University-owned building as the site of the studies program, and told professors and secretaries in the building to clear out. Other incidents soon followed in which AAS members scattered lunches in Willard Straight Hall's cafeteria and stacked hundreds of "irrelevant" books into piles on library floors. When a group of black students with toy pistols harassed pedestrians and disrupted traffic, they set in motion a disciplinary process that fueled tensions until the occupation of the Straight.

THOMAS W. JONES '69
Afro-American Society Spokesman

C. DAVID BURAK '67
SDS Co-chairman

Unequal Treatment?
The AAS Buys Bongos

One of the main grievances of moderate white students at the time was that blacks, especially militants, appeared to be getting special kid-glove handling by the administration. The following story, by the then Sun editor-in-chief, tells of one such instance. The story is written in an exceedingly understated way; the author, for instance, does not mention the particular notoriety of the two black protagonists. Gary Patton was the student who had, two weeks earlier, grabbed President Perkins by the collar and pulled him away from a microphone in Alice Statler Auditorium. While Patton was doing so, Larry Dickson was also on stage, brandishing a 2-by-4. Dickson was at the time also facing criminal charges for beating up in December a Sun reporter who had been covering a demonstration.

But, of course, there was no need to mention these things: the readers knew perfectly well who Patton and Dickson were.

BY STAN CHESS '69

Controversy has again entered the realm of student government appropriations. Yet where previously students were up in arms over Drill Team or social protest funding, this year such controversial decisions have been enacted behind closed Day Hall doors.

The most illustrative example, one administration source explained, is the "bongo drums story" that has begun to make its whispered rounds about campus.

Unlike most instances of student requests being choked or at best delayed by the morass of Day Hall red tape, this time a group, the Afro-American Society, legitimately able to receive funds, obtained results in unprecedented time.

Tuesday, Feb. 11, according to Provost Dale R. Corson, Gary Patton '71 approached the vice provost and requested $1,700 for the bongo drums in time for Malcolm X Day, that Friday. The drums, Patton explained, were to be used as part of an informal, student-taught program of black culture that had been first dis-

−Sun Photo by Richard A. Shulman

cussed with and partially funded by Prof. Chandler Morse, who formerly headed the black studies program, in January.

On Thursday morning, the provost said, a meeting was hurriedly called, a compromise $1,000 was appropriated and by 12:30 that afternoon two students were on their way to New York City—in Cornell's airplane—to buy the drums.

"The plane was going anyway," Vice Provost W. Keith Kennedy told The Sun. "Thursday afternoon was the best opportunity for them to make the trip and was the most efficient way to make the purchase."

Yet the appropriation of funds was unusually rapid. "We moved it through channels, so to speak," Kennedy explained.

At 9:30 Thursday morning, Dean of Students Elmer Meyer was called by Kennedy and told for the first time that additional funds were needed to purchase the students' drums. Kennedy explained that he was able to put up only several hundred dollars from his contingency fund and needed additional monies.

The head of the student government finance commission, J.T. Weeker '69, was then called from his morning class and asked whether he could provide additional funds. Weeker agreed to authorize the expenditure of a maximum of $750 from the finance commission yearly budget, Meyer explained; the remainder was to come from Kennedy.

Kennedy, Meyer and Weeker then signed the purchase authorization that had been prepared by Kennedy's office, and Patton and Larry Dickson '70, a former student, left for New York.

But it was not until the following Monday that it became apparent where the additional funds had come from.

"I authorized the student government expenditure," Weeker said. On Monday Dean Meyer and Weeker denied that inquiries were being made as to the propriety of the student government purchase. Meyer ordered a paper transfer of the funds to an unknown and questionable "special activities account."

"I hadn't even heard of that account until it was explained to me that day," Meyer said. But as of yesterday no other student or Day Hall official could be found who knew of it.

"I don't think [the procedure] was unduly irregular," Kennedy said last night. "My office has never had this type of responsibility before."

Kennedy explained that the $1,000 represented a maximum figure. "They felt they could negotiate a considerably more favorable price," he said. And they did.

The two students talked the price down to $630, left the University-approved purchase order and packed the bongos into two University-rented station wagons and headed back for the Cornell plane waiting for them in White Plains, just north of the City.

Both, however, got lost. According to Kennedy, Dickson wound up in the middle of New Jersey and ultimately found his way back to the plane. Patton, however, bypassed White Plains heading north, called Kennedy from Kingston, N.Y., and decided to drive the rest of the way back to Ithaca. He arrived the next day in time for the Malcolm X celebration, Corson said. The University, meanwhile, picked up the rental tab.

"Under normal circumstances," Weeker explained last night, the money would not have been obtained this way. But then, again, he explained, "these were not normal circumstances."

−news story, March 13, 1969

−Sun Photo by Brian W. Gray

UNAUTHORIZED ACTION: *Gary S. Patton '71 grabs President James Perkins on the stage of Statler Auditorium during a South Africa symposium on February 28, 1969. Perkins had just begun answering a question on Cornell investment policy with regard to South Africa when Patton leaped on stage, collared Perkins and lifted him slightly off the ground. Meanwhile, Larry Dickson '70 was standing nearby brandishing a piece of lumber. As Patton let Perkins go, the cry "You just blew it" was heard from the back of the auditorium. The Afro-American Society—which had been planning to beat bongo drums if Perkins' reply was unsatisfactory—quickly repudiated the assault.*

−Sun Photo by N. Eric Weiss

BLACK ON WHITE: *Increasing black frustration with the pace of University action on requests for an autonomous college of Afro-American studies—the administration was instead moving toward final approval of a looser, less independent black studies program—was reflected by the appearance of a "Black Power" slogan on the A.D. White statue in Fall 1968.*

−Sun Photos by Charles M. Leung

PRELUDES: *On December 12, 1968, after President Perkins announced the University's refusal to establish an autonomous black college, a group of blacks carrying toy pistols harassed pedestrians and pounded on car roofs. The next day some 30 blacks entered the Straight Ivy Room shortly before noon and—after upsetting some students' lunches—began dancing on the tables to the accompaniment of chants and bongo drums (above two photos). No charges were brought against the Ivy Room demonstrators, but campus judicial proceedings against the toy pistol protesters helped spark the Straight takeover of April 1969.*

The toy pistol gang was cited under a campus judiciary system created in 1968 to confine punishment by the University to violations of "the special needs" of Cornell as an educational community. The new system was regarded as a reform in that it tended to remove the University from complicity in government prosecution of draft resistance and of drug use. But the toy pistol gang and the AAS refused to accept the conduct committee's jurisdiction over demonstrations.

In February, Perkins was grabbed by the collar and pulled away from the Statler Hall microphone by an AAS member as the president tried to answer a question as to why Cornell held stock in the Chase Manhattan bank, which had South African investments. A second black brandished a two-by-four on stage during the incident.

The AAS immediately repudiated the action and said it would "see that our brother is properly disciplined," adding "It would be wise of the administration to accept" the AAS's jurisdiction in the matter. The administration did.

Meanwhile, in April, the judicial committee finally gave reprimands to three in the non-cooperating toy pistol gang, and absolved the rest. Some expected the move to defuse tensions. But within an hour of the conduct board's decision, a thin, six-foot high cross draped with cloth was ignited on the porch of the black women's living cooperative on Wait Avenue. Safety Division, after conducting a preliminary examination, rushed off to deal with one of more than a dozen false alarms that unknown miscreants set off during the night, routing hundreds from dormitories. A half hour after the report of the cross burning a patrolman was put on guard outside the cooperative.

The next day, a Friday, was relatively quiet on campus after the pandemonium of the previous night. Cornell was preparing for Parents' Weekend, one of those times like Homecoming and Commencement when a university tries its hardest to impress. More than a dozen activities had been scheduled, including home games in five sports plus tours of the campus and debates on educational issues. Students even anticipated that cafeteria food would improve, at least temporarily.

But many blacks were angry that the Safety Division had left frightened women at the black co-op after the cross-burning. The AAS described the police departure as an intentional subordination of black women to the whites in the dormitories. Shortly before 7 a.m. Saturday, I was awakened by The Sun's managing editor, who said, "There's big fat on the fire" at the Straight. Yet little seemed out of place at the student union when I arrived. The iron gates were locked, there was no sign of life inside, and only a few trench-coated figures stood outside in the early morning drizzle.

An hour earlier about 60 black students had evicted parents staying overnight and employees. Later in the morning a picket line of SDS members in support of the takeover began marching around the building near a huge red sign hung by the University that proclaimed, "WELCOME PARENTS."

Parents awaited some official word on the building takeover at an auditorium where Perkins had been scheduled to give an address. Instead of hearing Perkins, the parents were berated by SDS leader David Burak, a graduate student who planted himself in an almost boxer-like crouch on stage and verbally took on all comers. Some parents wandered around the outside of the Straight aimlessly, saying things like "This is communism—this is fascism." Most were completely bewildered. One, the father of a varsity football player living in Delta Upsilon, was critical of the Straight takeover but sympathetic with the plight of blacks integrating an Ivy League school.

Some white athletes, in a reaction common at disrupted schools across the country, regarded themselves as a counterforce. About 25 fraternity men, mostly from Delta Upsilon, put together a commando squad to recapture the Straight.

—Cornell Alumni News

NEGOTIATION AND CONFRONTATION: *Early discussions between Cornell administrators and the blacks who occupied Willard Straight Hall at 5:30 a.m. on Saturday, April 19, 1969 were inconclusive, although an agreement was reached allowing parents evicted by the blacks to retrieve abandoned belongings that afternoon (top photo). Tension had been considerably worsened at 9:30 a.m., when about 25 whites, mostly from Delta Upsilon, headed for the Straight and a dozen entered the building through a side window. The whites later claimed that they had only wanted to talk with those inside, but the blacks regarded the entrance as an invasion. Fistfights broke out, and the whites were expelled. Their exit was followed by a large metal ashtray (bottom left). A megaphone was then thrown to Afro-American Society leader Eric D. Evans '69, who was leaning out of an upper window. In alternatingly threatening and peaceful language, Evans warned whites against further incursion (bottom right). Later in the day, as rumors that whites were planning armed assaults spread, the blacks decided to bring in guns.*

About a dozen were able to get inside through a side window before Safety Division stopped any more from following. During a scuffle inside, three whites and a black were slightly hurt. Whites escaped through the window and a black shouted, "If any more whites come in, you're going to die here!"

Rumors circulated during the rest of the afternoon that whites were organizing a new attack. My Sun assignment was to check these out but I found no such activity. Speakers at a meeting of 140 athletes and fraternity members who advocated some sort of action were silenced by a football coach who said he was ashamed of them. Finally, no one spoke against a resolution "to stand by the administration" and to refrain from unilateral action.

Nevertheless, the blacks in the Straight were worried over rumors that carloads of armed whites were planning to storm the building. The occupiers obtained guns during the night. What had been just another of the nation's many college building takeovers was transformed by the guns into a unique situation. Administration officials, saying they feared violence couldn't be avoided for another day, negotiated a seven-point agreement on Sunday morning that ended the occupation. The agreement's main features were an administration recommendation to the faculty that conduct board reprimands against the three toy pistol gang members be nullified, and that the University press no charges against the Straight's occupiers.

Triumphantly holding their weapons high, the AAS members then left the Straight. Cornell's administrators tried to appear in command of a very difficult situation without irrevocably committing themselves to an action plan. The president delivered a speech about the need for "humane men" to a crowd that was reported to be the largest assembly ever at Cornell outside a football stadium. Afterwards, everyone I talked with felt the speech—which contained no reference to the Straight takeover—could have been a warmed-over version of the previously scheduled Parents' Weekend talk.

—Sun Photo by Richard A. Shulman

—Sun Photo by Richard A. Shulman

A CENTURY AT CORNELL

—Photo by Fenton Sands for *Life* Magazine

THE CRISIS CONTINUES: *Even before Delta Upsilon members entered the Straight, blacks had armed themselves with makeshift weapons, including clubs made from game room billiard cues (above). Late Saturday morning, after having given parents who showed up at a cancelled Parents Weekend convocation a lecture on racism, SDS leader C. David Burak '67 mounted an elm stump used as a "graffiti tree" which then stood in front of the Straight, and addressed the crowd gathered there, which included SDS members picketing in support of the blacks (bottom). The Straight's occupiers watched the milling, sometimes arguing people from windows above the building's entrance (right).*

—Sun Photo by Richard A. Shulman

—Sun Photo by Richard A. Shulman

Chapter I: Cornell in the Eyes of the World

−Sun Photo by N. Eric Weiss

−Sun Photo by Brian W. Gray

THE EXIT: *The first two students to leave the Straight—after the occupiers had arrayed themselves into an armed phalanx inside the lobby—were Eric Evans and Edward Whitfield, as seen earlier in this chapter. Left, Evans' gun casts a silhouette before the south facade of Uris Library, as Whitfield looks in Evans' direction. Above, the last to emerge, Thomas Jones and Larry Dickson, raise their fists. Behind them, wearing weary expressions, shuffle W. Keith Kennedy and Steven Muller, the administrators who had negotiated an end to the takeover. Below, Safety Division officers escort the blacks across the arts quad.*

−Sun Photo by Brian W. Gray

The faculty was not ready to grant the students' demands yet. Immediately after the president's talk, the faculty voted down the amnesty plan, 700 to 200. The faculty said it might nullify the penalties but only under "secure and non-pressurized circumstances."

The AAS and SDS set out to line up massive student support of immediate amnesty. Pressure mounted for another building takeover, and some faculty members moved their families following anonymous telephone threats.

Then came the most unusual and significant aspect of that eventful week: radical speakers at a forum seemed to galvanize several thousand concerned students into the view that the faculty could no longer be trusted, that students had to take power and that the black demand for amnesty had to be granted immediately.

Tom Jones '69, a dynamic AAS speaker, exhorted the crowd to demand that the faculty reverse its decision that very night. Jones told the Barton Hall crowd, so large that it overflowed

the original forum site at Bailey Auditorium, that if the faculty's decision wasn't changed, "This university has half an hour to live."

Then, well over half the crowd of 6,000 stood cheering, with fists in the air in the black power salute. I noticed that one of my roommates, who knew next to nothing about December's disorders or the campus conduct board, was one of the first 10 persons in Barton Hall standing up and shouting for a building takeover. Ten professors joined the troupe of the Barton and Bailey circus that night when they proclaimed they would help occupy a building if their faculty colleagues did not meet the next day and reverse their decision on amnesty.

This stand of the 10 professors was actually a moderating influence. It persuaded about 3,000 in the gym who called themselves "the Barton Hall Community" to take no immediate action. From this time on, initiative passed from radicals to student and faculty reformers. *Continued on Page 16*

−Sun Photo by Larry Baum

ARMED GUARD: *After their march through campus from the Straight, armed students line the crest of a hill at 320 Wait Avenue, which would be the brief home of the Africana Center until the building was gutted by a suspicious fire in April 1970. The remains of the house, which stood near Balch Hall, have since been removed. It was on the cement steps before this building that the occupation-ending seven-point agreement between administrators and blacks was signed by Vice Provost W. Keith Kennedy Ph.D. '47, Vice President for Public Affairs Steven Muller Ph.D. '58, and the Afro-American Society's chairman and vice chairman, Edward L. Whitfield '71 and Zachary W. Carter '70.*

The Sun Is for Nullification . . .

The Sun, a traditional supporter of progressive racial policies ever since World War II, had a difficult time formulating its position on the Straight takeover and the events leading up to it. Basically, it was in sympathy with most of the black demands, although it did not condone some of the more unreasonable demonstrations. The Sun appealed to the judiciary boards for restraint, but urged the blacks to show up, and, the week before the Straight takeover, correctly predicted that any penalties imposed would be light.

It would be interesting to know what The Sun thought of the actual verdict of three reprimands, and what it would have advised the blacks to do. However, the ruling was handed down on a Thursday night, too late for an editorial comment on Friday, and The Sun did not publish on the Saturday of the Straight takeover.

On Sunday, there was an extra edition, but The Sun, like the rest of the campus, was not aware there were guns in the building. Editorially, it called the takeover "an irresponsible action, unsoundly motivated and setting forces in motion that may wreak harmful consequences on black and white Cornellians alike."

As to the judicial proceedings, The Sun commented, "the reprimands leveled against the students in question are minor penalties, that exist on paper only. Yet the Afro-American Society has chosen not to grant them the lack of attention they deserve and instead seems intent on humbling the University before (it hints) it will proceed to discussions on restructuring the imperfect judicial system."

The following day, The Sun came out for nullification.

Today the dean of the Cornell Faculty will recommend to that body that it nullify the proceedings of the student judicial system against five black students, three of whom received reprimands last week and two of whom received no penalty.

The Faculty should accept Dean Miller's recommendation.

The reasons why the Faculty should do so require an insight into the black experience of which few whites are capable. But an effort toward such an insight is crucial, for it is patently clear that blacks have seen differently than whites the events that led to their irresponsible takeover of Willard Straight Hall and the frightening appearance of firearms on the Cornell campus.

Underlying the blacks' perceptions (and misperceptions) of these events has been a predilection to see white racism where others would recognize only incompetence or bureaucratic bottlenecks.

It is clear, for instance, that the blacks were outraged over the burning of a cross on the porch of the black women's co-op and the disappearance of campus police from the scene soon after they arrived to investigate. In fact, the police left the scene only temporarily; they were forced to proceed elsewhere for less than an hour because a massive rash of false fire alarms poured in, not because they were callous about protecting blacks.

The blacks have also made a major point of alleged police complicity in a raid on the Straight by white students during the black occupation. The whites succeeded in breaking into the building, because the police, who have consistently done a sensitive job of serving all Cornellians, did an incompetent job of protection, not because they wanted to see blacks' blood.

These cases of circumstance and incompetence were interpreted by the blacks as racism and led to and resulted finally in their introduction of guns onto the scene. The blacks may have brandished their weapons in a barbaric or juvenile manner, but reports from inside Willard Straight Hall — the target of telephoned threats throughout the night — indicate conclusively that they were borne out of fear.

A similar interpretation is involved in the blacks' view of the key question in the matter — that of the judicial proceedings against five black students. An Afro-American Society statement complained about Cornell's disregard for the mental health of its members who were threatened with suspension for months until a last-minute discovery that they needn't be suspended at all, for a previously unnoticed regulation would allow them to be tried on the relatively minor charges against them in absentia. This last-minute discovery was another innocent event which could understandably be viewed with suspicion through black eyes.

Finally, on an objective level, the blacks have raised serious questions about the judicial system which is, as we have previously noted, new and certainly fallible, since it descended not from Heaven, but from the Faculty.

The blacks have refused to budge an inch on their pride and accept their minor penalties. The Faculty should be more generous, accepting the possibility of faults in the system, accepting Dean Miller's recommendation, and, moreover, examining themselves for tinges of racism, especially in view of the near-hysterical reaction of many faculty members to recent events, even before the introduction of firearms onto the scene.

Acceptance of the proposal will hopefully lead to the construction of a viable judicial system as well as serve as a gesture of good faith that may mollify the suspicions of black students. Rejection of the proposal may lead to bloodshed, and the judicial system, frankly, is not worth anyone's dying over.

—editorial, Monday, April 21, 1969

If the faculty was divided after the Straight takeover, so was the student body. The division reflected itself among The Sun's editors. Editorially, The Sun supported most of the black demands, though not the takeover itself. The Sun's associate editor, however, a thoughtful conservative from Oklahoma, saw the entire affair as the death agony of a once-great university.

Some two weeks after the takeover, he concluded that change must come from the top. In the first column of its kind by a Sun editor, he wrote, "There is a cancer in this community's body, a cancer located ominously close to the head. If this community—both its blacks and its whites—is to be protected in the future from further polarization, from serious violence, that cancer must be removed. It is time that James A. Perkins, the man ultimately responsible for policy, particularly consistent policy, be shelved and that a man of courage, a man of principle devoted to racial justice and to the rule of reason be found to save Cornell from falling from the precipice into the abyss of future destruction we now face."

During the period immediately after the takeover, his columns eloquently espoused the hard-line position and, in fact, were far more articulate than anything else appearing on The Sun's pages. *The End of the Road* appeared in The Sun's extra edition as the takeover continued; *The End of the Beginning* came the day after, as the faculty prepared to vote for the first time on nullification; there was a brief silence after the nullification vote, and then, the brooding columnist emerged the following week with the apocalyptic *The Beginning of the End*.

Standing on his principles, he withdrew from Cornell after the semester, and transferred to Yale. Ten years later, however, he returned—as a professor of history.

. . . *And an Editor Dissents: The End of the Road*

BY PAUL A. RAHE, JR. '70

As the campus knows, early Saturday morning we approached the end of a long road, the culmination of a series of events leading to the destruction of this University as an institution committed to the unfettered search for truth, a series of events involving the use of force by a small minority of students to coerce the University to give into demands which were seldom wholly rational. This use of force has been legitimized by an administration which has consistently responded only to power and most often only to the power of a group willing to use violence to achieve its ends; and which has consistently failed to invoke the processes by which the University community punishes those who, by their actions, constitute a threat to the maintenance of peace, of the order essential to the continued existence of that community.

Anyone with the least semblance of common sense is aware that action rewarded—be it that of a mouse in Cornell's psychology labs or that of a human being—is bound to be repeated. If the reward increases in direct ratio to the intensity of the action, one can expect more intense action. To tolerate, to reward violence is to encourage more violence. And that is precisely the policy Day Hall has followed in the last 16 months.

Last year, a group of students, after their irrational demands were rejected by those in authority, took over the arts college economics office, assaulted two campus patrolmen and made it clear that others wishing to assert their legitimate rights by entering the office would meet a similar fate. The demands were partially met. Judicial procedures were not invoked. No one was punished.

Last year, a group of students took over the campus radio station, threatening destruction and violence if the station manager did not allow them to issue a broadcast. They were allowed to make the broadcast. Judicial procedures were not invoked. No one was punished.

In December, a group of students intimidated others by dancing on Ivy Room tables during lunch and later disrupted the operation of Cornell's libraries, demanding the establishment of an autonomous black college. Had anyone attempted to prevent the disruption, violence would have erupted. The demands were partially met. An all but autonomous Center for Afro-American Studies was set up. Judicial procedures were not invoked. No one was punished.

In March, three blacks backed by many more students and non-students took over the Cornell Symposium on Southern Africa, demanding that this University's President appear and answer their abusive questions. Once again violence was threatened. Once again demands were met. Judicial procedures were invoked only against the student who, in the process, assaulted the University President and, because he withdrew from the University, no one was punished.

In March, a group of students forced their way into a suite of offices in one University building, demanding the ouster of three Cornell alumni recruiting for Chase Manhattan Bank. The demands were met because, to use the words of one prominent University administrator, he "didn't want blood." Once again, despite pacifying Day Hall statements at the time, judicial procedures were not invoked. Once again, no one was punished.

In fact, in the past 16 months, the only students against whom judicial procedures were invoked were a small group who stole some University furniture and a small group who intimidated some members of this community in separate incidents last December. The first group was not punished. They had reportedly been promised some furniture which had not been forthcoming and so had taken some. The second group was given a minimal penalty, a reprimand.

And, yesterday morning, a group of students ejected abruptly awakened parents from Willard Straight Hall and used violent means to prevent another enraged group of students from asserting their legitimate rights to use that building. The students who took over the building demanded that the University "declare null and void all judicial proceedings of the past four months" brought against those mentioned above. Previously, those students had been given innumerable opportunities to discuss their objections to the judicial system with the University Student Conduct Conference and the Faculty Committee on Student Affairs. They refused to discuss the matter until the charges against the individuals were dropped.

The other demand that the University make a "full and thorough investigation of the recent cross burning and the subsequent actions of the campus police" and that a report be made to the Afro-American Society is not unreasonable and would undoubtedly have been met without the threat or use of violence.

There is only one truly significant question facing this University: whether coercive methods are to continue to be tolerated, and encouraged in this community. Use of force to remove the blacks from the Straight is wholly justified, but perhaps unwise—at least at the moment. All other reasonable methods should be tried first. Perhaps the best option is that recently adopted by the University of Chicago, which allowed demonstrators to remain in control of the building, but invoked judicial procedures against them and finally removed those unwilling to accept the ground rules on which the University is based, one of which is the principle of nonviolence, from that community. To reward violence by accepting the unreasonable demand that legitimate judicial proceedings be declared null and void, to refuse to punish those who have used violent and disruptive methods this weekend is only to ask for more and more violence.

If the administration fails to act, Cornell's faculty, who took a backhanded slap at that administration in their recent meeting dealing with judicial legitimacy by deleting a section from one resolution commending the administration for its approach to the problems of recent months, must take the command they technically have over student conduct and act forcefully—soon.

—column, Sunday, April 20, 1969

MARCHING ON THE RIGHT: *Conservative students gather Monday, April 21, 1969 on the steps of Bailey Hall to urge professors to reject the administration's occupation-ending agreement with the blacks. The largest faculty meeting in Cornell's history subsequently failed to nullify penalties given three blacks for December demonstrations.*

The End of the Beginning

BY PAUL A. RAHE, JR. '70

Little need be said about yesterday. In short, Cornell's administration, in the face of a violent takeover of a University building, the harassment of the University's guests, and implicit threats in the form of firearms of a hitherto unimaginable degree of violence, accepted the tyranny of a small minority enraged over slaps on the wrist given to a few members of that minority for intimidating members of this community. In short, Cornell's administration implicitly agreed that violence is a legitimate method of seeking change in this community and has proceeded to encourage the use of such violence.

And, perhaps more significant, the administration agreed to investigate the cross burning incident and the white athletes' attempt to gain entrance to the Straight and to reveal their names to the Afro-American Society, *an act which is a breach of University policy concerning identifying those involved in student conduct proceedings, an act which may spell great danger for the individuals involved.*

However, this time the buck does not stop with Cornell's administration. Today, the faculty which has ultimate control over student conduct will consider the black demands to which the administration has acceded. Today, Cornell's faculty, an amazingly amorphous body normally manipulated by Day Hall—today, that faculty will make what is perhaps the most important decision in Cornell history. Today, that faculty will decide whether violence will prevail on this campus.

Cornell's administration has consistently made it apparent that it is unwilling to defend academic freedom, unwilling to

make sure that coercive methods have no place in this community, unwilling to safeguard the principles its members claim to hold dear.

In a sense, the Perkins administration has placed itself on the line by signing a capitulation agreement with the militants. A faculty rejection of that dictated agreement would be a faculty vote of no confidence in the Perkins administration, an administration which has consistently mouthed platitudes and acceded to the rule of unreason.

The results of a rejection of the black demands are all too clear. Violence would return immediately to the Cornell campus; but reason, not violence, would rule.

The results of an acceptance of the demands is also all too clear. Violence would not return immediately; but, it would return—and return soon.

But, faculty acceptance of that agreement would be a betrayal of this community; a betrayal of those black students unwilling to cooperate with the militants, of those black students who have been the object of substantial intimidation; a betrayal of those professors teaching politically sensitive material who, since last year's economics office sit-in, have grown more and more afraid to speak out; a betrayal of the entire concept of academic freedom and integrity; and an unforgettable betrayal of this student body.

Either way, the faculty decides today, the events of the past 16 months signal the end of the beginning—and perhaps the beginning of the end.

—column, Monday, April 21, 1969

The Beginning of the End

BY PAUL A. RAHE, JR. '70

Cornell is like a woman who took a trip on an ocean liner.

The first day she wrote in her diary that she had seen the captain.

The second day she wrote that he had spoken to her.

The third day she wrote that he had asked her to dinner.

The fourth day she wrote that he had taken her to dinner and proposed oral sodomy, threatening to sink the ship and kill its 600 passengers if she did not consent.

The fifth day she congratulated herself on her virtue and wrote that she had saved 600 people.

—column, Monday, April 28, 1969

−Cornell Alumni News

THE CENTER SPEAKS: *Ten thousand cheering and chanting students jammed Barton Hall Tuesday evening for a mass SDS meeting at which Afro-American Society leader Thomas W. Jones '69 declared that Cornell had one hour to live. Although threats of immediate action were forestalled, the gathering overwhelmingly endorsed the demands of blacks and radicals that the faculty reverse its Monday stand and rescind penalties given to three blacks under the campus judicial system. Barton was declared "occupied" and 2,000 people, including a few professors, stayed all night arguing, debating, sleeping, or playing basketball.*

Continued from Page 12

On the next day, the faculty reversed its vote. Clinton Rossiter, a distinguished government professor, had said on Monday that he would rather work as a janitor than teach at a school that backed down to militants. On Wednesday, he changed his vote but not his job. Some professors, however, felt the vote reversal was a disgrace they wouldn't tolerate. Government Department Chairman Allan Sindler resigned from the faculty, along with his government department colleague Walter Berns, who had been selected that year as the outstanding teacher in the College of Arts and Sciences. George Kahin, a history professor who was a prominent Vietnam War opponent, likened the mob psychology to that of students during the McCarthy years who sought to purge Cornell of professors of Kahin's political stripe.

What altered the faculty vote wasn't the AAS or its guns, but the massive support of white students for the AAS demands.

Many students adopted radicals' jargon that called the faculty a privileged class that oppressed students. Jones, an AAS spokesman who was constantly at a microphone in April, gave an extreme formulation of this view:

> "There was a faculty élite that dictated to their underlings, the Administration, you see, who dictated to the proletariat, otherwise known as niggers, the students.... The reality for most of those faculty up there, if not all of them, has always been a peaceful reality...."

We said, 'You're racist, and you're going to be dealt with. You're trying to destroy me, well, if you believe in your principle sufficiently, if you believe in it to that point, then be ready to die for it.'"

Although I did not at all share the sense of malevolent faculty control at Cornell, I still felt distant enough from the faculty's concerns to see some positive aspects of the building takeover and the resulting clamor. A mass movement focuses attention on new ideas even though it may thrive on unthink-

'POWER TO THE PEOPLE': *Several members of the Barton Hall throng jubilantly raise their fists in support of the black students' demands.*

−Sun Photo by Robert W. Bollenbach

A CENTURY AT CORNELL

ing followers. If the Barton Hall Community resembled a Be-In at times, it shared this characteristic not just with Woodstock but with civil rights demonstrations, Eugene McCarthy's campaign and Vietnam War protests.

The reaction of my brother, Raymond Kreig '68 M.S. '70, to the occupation might explain why so many Cornell students viewed it with more equanimity than the faculty. Raymond, now a consulting engineer in Alaska, generally spent 50 to 65 hours a week on his studies at Cornell. Yet the week of the building occupation intruded enough on his technical concerns to provoke self-criticism of a kind that I've rarely heard from him. I took note of it, in part because he hit on a failure of many of us whites at the University: "I just can't criticize people that know something about these problems of racism and black studies. I've never had the time to read books about them . . . but I guess it's something I'm going to have to do."

ANDREW KREIG '70, Sun senior editor 1969-70, now covers federal courts for *The Hartford Courant.*

−Sun Photo by Richard A. Shulman

PALS: *Afro-American Society leader Eric D. Evans '69 and Students for a Democratic Society co-chairman C. David Burak '67 share smiles with President Perkins before 8,000 members of the "Barton Hall Community" on Wednesday afternoon. Perkins, who had just arrived at Barton after the faculty voted to nullify penalties against three blacks, stepped toward the microphone with the intention of speaking immediately. He instead found himself sitting cross-legged on the floor nervously waiting for Evans to finish an impromptu speech decrying Cornell's treatment of blacks.*

A Radical Recalls How Close We Came

Ten years after the Straight takeover, The Sun ran a 24-page supplement reviewing the events. One of those writing was the most prominent white radical leader of the time—a man noted for his outstanding speaking ability and also, surprisingly, for his always correct and frequently cordial relations with the people one would think would be his blood enemies, the police.

BY DAVID BURAK '67

It's difficult to figure out where to start a story about a series of events which changed my life so dramatically that I have not yet recovered completely, and may not for quite some time. But since my approach to the issues and activities around the seizure of Willard Straight Hall in April, 1969, is going to be different from most of the other articles in this supplement, I might as well accentuate the personal side from the beginning.

Shortly after arriving at the Policeman's Ball, during the summer of 1971, my friend Mary Bates and I were hailed over to a table where several sturdy looking gentlemen and their wives sat drinking Schenley's and ginger ale. At first I didn't recognize them, in part I guess because I'd never seen them in suits and ties. But after an awkward moment of introduction, I realized that I was in the presence of three of Ithaca's finest, Sergeants Joe Rusty, and the brothers Tom and Frank Leone.*

"Sit down and have a drink with us,"

*The author has slightly modified the names here, presumably to protect the innocent.—Ed.

Joe said, making an offer it would have been foolish to refuse. The band was playing a Tommy Dorsey medley.

"What are you up to these days, Dave?" I told them I'd just completed a series of interviews and gotten a job at an experimental school in the Ivory Coast. They wished me good luck, and after a few more casual comments about how surprised they were to see me there, Joe said, "You know, it's a good thing you and your people didn't try to take over Day Hall that night."

"Which night?" I asked quite sincerely, as there had been several situations in which friends and acquaintances had argued that "we,"—meaning Students for a Democratic Society or some segment thereof—should occupy Day Hall to protest about the war in Vietnam or any number of issues.

"That night in April, '69, when you had 10,000 people in Barton Hall," Sgt. Joe responded, his voice becoming very serious.

"Oh, yeah definitely, I agree. In fact it was me who initially proposed that we stay in Barton and declare it occupied."

"Well that was a good move," one of the Leones said, the low rumble of his voice providing a distinct contrast to the smile on his face. "Those 300 sheriff's deputies that were mobilized and waiting down in the Woolworth's parking lot had even us oldtimers a little nervous."

I don't recall which of the officers then came up with the quote that has stuck in my memory like a fishbone too big to swallow but too sturdily wedged in to cough up. One of the sarges said, "Yeah, they were a scary bunch. We watched 'em clean their shotguns, then load 'em up with Double O buck saying, 'Tonight

we're gonna get us some of them niggers and them Jew Commies that are leadin' 'em.'"

Then Sgt. Rusty added, "And you know, the agreement was that if there was any large-scale effort to march out of Barton and seize Day Hall, those deputies were to go to the campus immediately and stop that seizure by whatever means necessary."

One doesn't need much of an imagination to consider how many people could've been shot, seriously injured, killed, and so on. I don't know enough about the administrative decision-making process that was going on at the time to say with certitude what President Perkins did, astutely or ineptly, before, during, and after the crisis.

But after all the critics, second guessers and armchair quarterbacks have had their say, the fact remains that the president, with the help of other administrators like Keith Kennedy, Steven Muller and Mark Barlow, plus the efforts of the Cornell Safety Division, did enough intelligent things to help keep violence to a minimum.

The possibilities of bloodshed at Cornell were so great in April 1969 that it's almost a miracle that nobody was seriously hurt. The volatility of the situation was so incredible that the fact that it didn't explode into mass murder and mayhem is a tribute, in good part, to a sensitive administration. And, despite their understandable resentment, the majority of faculty members reacted wisely and adroitly.

But, at the risk of dwelling on a sore point, I'm compelled to criticize the unfortunate way in which President Perkins was made into a scapegoat and saddled with much of the blame for a situation which was for the most part caused by forces over which he had absolutely no control.

Many of the students involved in the large number of confrontations that took place throughout this country were driven to a state of near-frenzy by the maddening inundation of images of napalmed Vietnamese babies which appeared almost nightly on network newscasts. Almost everybody was painfully aware of the riots which had raged through the last half-decade, when ghettos from Watts to Harlem, from Newark to Detroit, erupted with flaming fury.

This is the context in which the events at Cornell need to be placed if they are to be understood properly. I am not trying to cop a plea of "temporary insanity," either for myself or anyone else who did things then that they wouldn't do now. In fact, I want to emphasize that there were many statements made and deeds done which were pathological and disgraceful under any circumstances.

For example, when one militant leader told the 10,000 people in Barton Hall that "the University has two hours left to live," I was very disturbed. I turned to Chip Marshall, with whom I shared co-chairmanship responsibilities in SDS, and asked, "What the hell did he say that for?" Maybe I should have said that over the microphone, but I didn't feel at the time that it would help keep things peaceful if the debate was directed to such an outrageous, and basically unsupported, threat.

On another, perhaps even more serious note, I feel obliged to stick my neck out a bit further by addressing an issue about which I was not aware in the spring of '69. I don't want to name individuals or point fingers, but I have to say that it makes me sick to my stomach to think about how some militant students contrived political and philosophical justifications for the random beating and robbing of fundamentally helpless and innocent people

—Sun Photo by Ruth Muschel

RESTRUCTURING THE UNIVERSITY: *Students build Tinkertoy castles as the "Barton Hall Community" continues to occupy its namesake in the days following the climactic Wednesday faculty meeting's vote to reverse itself and grant the blacks' and the "community's" chief demand. Some 5,000 attended an SDS teach-in on racism on Thursday and speeches by government and history professors on Friday. But interest began to dwindle after classes resumed. Radicals withdrew to their pet causes, and the remnants of the "community" undertook a long, tedious quest to "restructure" Cornell. The result of their efforts was a faculty-student-employee University Senate, which— crippled by apathy and its own awkwardness—was finally axed by the trustees in March 1977.*

who, as far as I know, never hurt a fly.

*   *   *

I could go on for many pages. When I dwell upon the events of April 1969, sometimes the ten years which have passed collapse into a period which feels more like ten days. But I don't have the time to go into many more details. I have a deadline on this piece, and several other obligations, including the grading of 20 freshman papers.

But before leaving the big meeting in Barton Hall completely behind, I want to praise a few of the other people whose efforts helped keep that gathering peaceful and productive. One of them is Prof. Eldon Kenworthy of the government department. Thank God he had the good sense and assertiveness to urge the 10,000

people to refrain from any militant action until after the faculty had one more meeting. Without his persuasive powers, many other efforts may have been inadequate to prevent the occurrence of a clash which could've made the four killings at Kent State (which occurred over a year later) seem mild by comparison.

Also, people like Prof. Andrew Hacker, another member of the government department, who at the time was also advisor to the Cornell Conservative Club, did something which should not be forgotten. He addressed one of the large Barton gatherings shortly after the faculty had reversed their decision rejecting the Afro-American Society demands. He warned us not to get carried away, and though I don't recall the exact content of his speech, I know that it, combined with the fact that he cared enough to make the effort to speak in relatively hostile territory, helped many of us activists keep a proper perspective on what was happening.

Also, about a month later, profs like Doug Dowd and Bob McGinnis (economics and sociology, respectively) combined with Fr. Dan Berrigan to help the more rational elements in SDS prevail in a very close vote, which, if it had gone the other, "militant" way, would have resulted in a seizure of Day Hall on issues relating to housing, and would've probably forced the administration to allow outside authorities on campus.

Finally, on a level which may be more personal than political and too complex to explain in depth, English department professors like Jim McConkey, Baxter Hathaway and Archie Ammons served, in the long run, like poetic lifeguards, rowing around in the sea of political pathos, throwing life preservers to those in trouble, and occasionally even jumping into the dark and choppy waters to help pull out someone who seemed to be drowning.   —*essay, April 19, 1979*

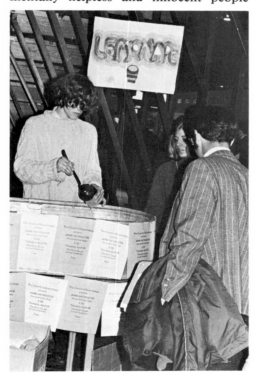

—Sun Photos by John G. Elligers and Ruth Muschel

FORETASTE OF WOODSTOCK: *Members of the "Barton Hall Community" quench their thirst and shoot for the hoops after hearing their fill of political perorations.*

The Things We Know Now

The late 1960s were a time of great bombast. At Cornell, the Straight takeover provoked new plateaus of violent rhetoric even among conservative faculty members, as can be divined from reading these pages. Eleven years later, the Straight takeover lives as legend. Its prime impact on campus was in the early 70s. The first few years President Corson was in office the campus had an administration of fear; an administration so eager to avoid a second Straight takeover, so frightened of bad publicity of any variety, that it plainly achieved the effect opposite to the one it sought. Pressure groups of all persuasions came to realize that the administration would do almost anything to avoid controversy, and they changed their tactics accordingly. The surfeit of political demonstrations that resulted had two important effects on how we think of the Straight takeover.

First, some of the later demonstrations make the Straight takeover seem overblown. In Spring 1969 academic life was disrupted, but not to the extent it was by the political protests of Spring 1970 and Spring 1971. Four people were hurt in the Straight takeover, but there were more injuries in the Collegetown "block party" affair of May 1972. The Straight was damaged by its black occupants, but property loss was nil compared to that during the antiwar demonstrations of May 1972. The Straight takeover issues were interesting but neither as compelling nor as complex as the ones that prompted the student takeover of Carpenter Hall in April 1972. The black demands in Spring 1969 were far more reasonable than some of the demands from assorted radical groups over the next few years. It is true that guns never reappeared, nor did the overwhelming national publicity, but still it is an interesting piece of symbolism that we consider the Straight takeover the granddaddy of all campus demonstrations.

The second consequence of the later demonstrations was that the excitement wore off, the radical leadership declined in quality, and the campus grew more cynical about such activities. All these things combined to create a new view of the Straight takeover.

This revisionist view goes something like this. Once upon a time some wicked black students decided to have some

---

A Week in the Life of a Cornell Student

By Allan J. Mayer '71

It's hard to know where to begin. One gets the feeling that the whole thing should be taken in flashes, a frame at a time. So watch the film and every once in a while turn off the sound and see if you can muster any other thought save "Surreal."

Saturday Night

Saturday night in the Straight parking lot. The temperature is about 25 and you've given up trying to keep warm. Every once in a while you glance up at a window but you see no one. You're cold but you keep wondering how they feel inside.

In Anabel Taylor

In Anabel Taylor it's like a Red Cross station during a flood. People wander around asking for and giving out cigarettes. In one room they're thrashing out a leaflet. Someone once said that, on a campus, whichever group controls the mimeo machines has all the media it needs. Somewhere around 60,000 leaflets were produced in the last six days. Think of it, 60,000 leaflets.

Rumors

The phone rings.

"Hello, rumor clinic."

"I heard that there's fire around the Straight. Is it safe to walk outside?"

"There's absolutely no gunfire at all. Don't worry, it's perfectly safe to go out."

Another ring.

"They say Theta Xi's on fire —"

"Absolutely untrue."

And so on.

Breakfast

The sun is coming up on Sunday and there are thirty dozen eggs which wind up tasting like lukewarm rubber but very few plates are refused. The guitarists have gone home and people begin to arrive for church. In their Sunday best they gingerly step over and around the sprawled sleepers, some of whom spent the entire night outside the Straight waiting and watching for something which very few people could define. Someone scrawls on a blackboard "If H.L. Hunt donated money for a building, they'd call it "Hunt's Hall." Nobody gets it.

Guns

A thousand in front of the Straight as Dave Matthews speaks through a Fender guitar amp that really isn't loud enough. Someone appears at the game room window directly over the banner that proclaims "Welcome Parents." He holds a rifle.

"My God, they really do have guns," someone says as the crowd cheers.

Later that afternoon, as the blacks march out of the Straight and across the arts quad, a white girl, watching them wide-eyed, turns to a friend and says, "I don't know if I have a right to say it, but they make me feel proud."

A Joke?

You walk across campus on Monday and for the first time that you can remember everyone is talking about the same thing. What's going to happen when the faculty turns down nullification? Someone has an idea of how the administration can avert trouble. "All they have to do is announce that next year's hockey tickets are going on sale tomorrow," he says.

10,000

And then it's Tuesday night, and there are 10,000 people in Barton Hall. Tom Jones speaks and it is a gem of a speech. He talks of black and white together, that all students are niggers. He says student power rather than black power and the liberals find themselves clapping.

He also talks of dying but most of the people don't understand him.

Seizure

As it becomes apparent that the prospects for a militant action that night are small, Dave Burak suggests that the crowd stay in Barton Hall until the faculty meets. Two thousand people send out for blankets and McDonald's hamburgers.

Later, someone announces that the University is telling the press that they gave permission for the people to stay the night in Barton. "Is this a teach-in or have we seized Barton Hall?" he asks the crowd. Seizing a building usually makes most people think of cops and getting hurt. Spending the night in Barton looks like it's going to be fun, a giant one-night experiment in communal living. "We've seized Barton!" the crowd roars as twenty guys have two basketball games going on at the east end of the floor.

Connections

The sun comes up grayly at a little after five. Someone is playing a harmonica and it echoes through the hall over a scene that reminds many of a scene in *Gone With the Wind*. They, of course, were Confederate soldiers.

And Now

And now the faculty has nullified the reprimands and several resignations have been sent back and forth and most people, the silent center perhaps, are buoyant, for Cornell isn't dead.

But is it? Is this the same Cornell as the one whch threatened to suspend six black students illegally? Is this the same Cornell which has a judicial system that is student-faculty in name only?

In a sense, the caterpillar has disappeared. Whether the cocoon survives is something we'll know in the fall.

—column, Thursday, April 24, 1969

fun by seizing a building at gunpoint. When they did so, the craven Perkins administration gave them everything they wanted, but the gallant faculty refused to go along. But some evil sorcerers from Barton Hall cast a spell over the faculty, and two days later it caved in. There is no good fairy in this story, nor is there very much emotionalism. Nobody lived happily ever after.

There are two corollaries to this: first, the initial demands that prompted the takeover have been forgotten; probably not one Cornell faculty member in five could tell you that the Straight takeover had anything to do with the campus judicial system. Second, few faculty members can be found today who admit that they voted to nullify the reprimands; that is, that they were capitulators in 1969.

Over the last eleven years, facts about the Straight takeover have come out that cast doubt upon the fairy tale. For example, we have heard from several sources that the takeover was not a spontaneous thing, but had been planned for several months. And we now know that the black leadership planned well, making the best use of its strong points, hiding its weaknesses.

The AAS itself was severely fragmented, although its members agreed on the necessity of appearing united. Accordingly, during the months before the takeover, the AAS adopted a policy of rotating its spokesmen, and not permitting other members to say anything in public. This created somewhat of a mystique, but it also served to confuse the administration and the press. Many of the nominal AAS leaders actually had little to do with formulating policy.

Planning the takeover for Parents' Weekend was another clever move. Tom Jones explained that summer, "to take the action at that time meant that we couldn't be ignored by the University. To seize a vital building in the midst of the weekend when the University is about the job of trying to impress everybody so they can get some more contributions, was something that the University couldn't ignore. So we moved—we moved."

The immediate judicial problem, therefore, was a major cause of the takeover, but not the only cause. The blacks also wanted to reaffirm their demands for faster progress on a black studies program. It appears that the demand for black studies was not just an idle or a nuisance one; much of the AAS membership was in fact doing a sort of independent study project on black culture. If the campus judicial system had accepted the black demand and declared that it had no jurisdiction over black political demonstrators, this might have aborted the Straight takeover. But that clearly was not going to happen; in this way, one can argue that the judicial issue had no bearing on the takeover at all, even though it was the official AAS excuse for it.

For that matter, the AAS almost did not have an excuse. The judicial board had been hemming and hawing for four months; the minutes of its April 16 meeting indicate that it did not want to reach a decision that night and did so *only at AAS insistence*. If the board had succeeded in stalling again, it might well have stopped the building takeover scheduled less than 36 hours away.

The cross-burning later that night also remains mysterious. There was a strong feeling on campus in 1969 that the AAS itself had burnt the cross in an effort to gain sympathy—although this view was never spoken in public by anyone willing to affix his name to it, although The Sun never printed a word about such a possibility. Administrators and editors competed instead to see who could denounce the cross-burning in the most vigorous language.

Those who thought the blacks had burnt the cross had two fairly good arguments. First, Safety Division reports cast doubt on how surprised the women in the co-op were, and questioned how the cross could have been brought to the

house without the inhabitants knowing. Second, some suggested that while burning the cross in front of a women's residence horrified the general public, *real* white racists would have burnt it in front of the black *men's* co-op, to achieve maximum intimidation.

But hindsight provides a much stronger argument. When the cross was lit, the Straight takeover was already planned for 24 hours later. Surely, it is too much of a coincidence for such a dramatic excuse for the takeover to appear at such a propitious time.

Jones, a moderate, later asserted that this was impossible, that an organization as large as the AAS could not have kept it a secret. Although the AAS was able to surprise the campus with the Straight takeover, he is probably right; if more than 100 people knew at the time, something would probably have come out about it in the last eleven years. On the other hand, the AAS had its own radical wing, capable of independent action. Or perhaps the cross-burning really was the work of whites. In either case it had little to nothing to do with the takeover, contrary to what people thought then.

* * *

But if not the judicial system, and if not the cross-burning, and with black studies not being as pre-eminent an issue as earlier, *why*? Writing for The Sun ten years later, Jones, now a prosperous investment analyst, offered this explanation: "Many black students had an emotional need for a 'victorious' confrontation with a powerful white institution. This need was related to the desire to strike a blow against the society and the institutions which had profited from the historical enslavement of black people. Cornell was perceived as an institution which had so profited because all major universities rely on the philanthropy of the wealthiest American families. . . and few of the great fortunes built in America during the eighteenth and nineteenth centuries can claim to have derived no benefit from the socio-economic structure which included black slavery and post-Civil War terrorism against blacks. As such, many black students were emotionally primed for a confrontation even though, in my view, it was quite likely that negotiations with the administration for a substantial black studies program could have been concluded successfully without such action."

This has the ring of truth to it. The popular view in 1969 was that the administration had been giving in to every black demand for some time and so had appeased its way into the Straight crisis. On the contrary: while the AAS had caused a lot of trouble and had gotten away with many things, there was nothing it could point to as a real *victory*—until the administration gave in so abjectly on April 20.

But the appearance triumphed again; given an issue, even the silly judicial issue, to take a stand on, hyperescalation of the stakes set in. And so, the well-spoken and sophisticated Tom Jones, the black who had been most active and most successful in the white-dominated campus government system, who would have been chairman of the judicial board trying the "toy pistol gang" had he not resigned earlier in a dispute over the severity of penalties in a different case—Tom Jones found himself on the stage of Barton Hall, wearing sunglasses, and shrilling, "Cornell has two hours to live."

Furthermore, people took him at his word. One history professor, speaking against nullification at the second faculty meeting, almost carried the day for his side when he declared, "If Mr. Jones says he is going to destroy this University, I say let him try it . . . This University, I believe, can survive the expulsion or departure of no matter what number of students and the destruction of buildings far better than it can survive the death of principle . . . In the nearly 800 years that they have existed, many eminent universities have come and gone and the world has survived their departure. But those that have departed because they stood

A CENTURY AT CORNELL

for nothing have not even been missed."

* * *

By unanimous consent, the administration was guilty of some colossal blunders during the takeover and the months preceding it. Few could compare in magnitude with the blithe and carefree manner in which the administration negotiating team allowed the blacks to come out of the Straight with rifles held high.

Then provost, later president, Dale Corson reflected ten years later that permitting the students to come out carrying guns was "a bad thing to have done," which is like saying Napoleon may have been guilty of an error in judgment when he decided to march on Moscow.

Apparently, the University's negotiating team *did* make the suggestion that the students leave their weapons inside the Straight as they ended the occupation, but did not make it very forcefully. One guesses that, if pressed, the AAS might have agreed to this, on the grounds that all important decision-makers were aware that guns had been introduced, and that enough people knew so that it could not have been kept a secret.

If you assume that the firearms could have been left inside the building, the administration team's failure to grasp the consequences of letting them out becomes, in all probability, the worst public-relations fiasco in the history of United States education. At the time, building takeovers were a very common phenomenon, and so were demands of the sort the AAS was making. But the guns, in addition to being a new twist, were a superbly effective symbol, so eminently photographable, so prodigiously understandable. Millions of citizens saw those guns on television and in newspapers, and were just as frightened as everyone on campus was.

Once the cameras clicked, President Perkins was finished. His tactics after the takeover were frequently second-guessed, but even the second-guessers admitted that other alternatives might have been cataclysmic. The power structure of the time dictated that the faculty take some action, but the only two choices were to give in ignominiously or to stand and fight for a dubious cause. Now it is possible to say that the faculty should have stood and fought; but it is mainly possible to do so as an intellectual exercise, not as actual advocacy. Who knows what demons might have broken loose, if the vote had gone the other way? The prevailing view at the time, clearly, was that there would have been bloodshed. Nothing we have learned since then makes us doubt it. Furthermore, while there was no poll taken of the student body, it is evident that the majority of students favored nullification. It was not unanimous, to be sure, but the faculty would have been treading on shaky enough ground without having to deal with student opposition.

Four Years Earlier: a Warning to Perkins

BY NATHANIEL W. PIERCE '66

Higher education is becoming vastly more complex every year. As each institution expands its operations with a greater demand on financial resources than ever before, the top officers of every university assume greater and greater importance. Because of the very nature of the large expanding university, the president inevitably becomes more powerful than any other individual.

The president of a university plays a key budgetary role. Every request for funds must not only be considered on the basis of eventual destination, but must also be compared and judged along with every other request. As the sources of income become more hard pressed, projects worthy in their own right will be shelved due to a lack of funds. The individual who exerts more influence on the budget than anyone else is the president.

With the control of money goes the power to direct the future course of the university. Every time one request is fulfilled at the expense of another, the university is inevitably affected. It is appropriate that this power should rest with the president. First and foremost, he is in the best position to have all the pertinent information before him. Objectively he can evaluate one project versus another and reach a decision firmly grounded upon the available evidence and his judgment.

Thus, various departments within the College of Arts and Sciences at Cornell have recently made official budgetary requests for additional money for more faculty. It is up to the President to decide whether or not we can afford this luxury. If the answer is no, it does not necessarily mean that the request was without merit. Rather, it probably means that in the opinion of the President there is something else of a greater priority.

Besides the monetary control, the president has two other powerful weapons at his disposal. He has a great deal of prestige, and he is in a unique position to mobilize public opinion. The faculty, acting as a collective body, could undoubtedly override a president, but it would require rare unanimity as well as unrelenting vigilance.

A president of a university can play this game in one of two ways. He can be in the fore of the discussions seeking improvements. He can play a key role in every change, giving the academic community the benefit of his views, based on his opinions and on facts which are often available only to him. He clearly has the opportunity to *lead* his university.

However, he may also choose the alternative of *being led* by his university. He can wait for a consensus to form among the faculty and students, and then act in accordance with that consensus. He can leave the initiative for change and improvement in the hands of others and merely react to proposals that emerge from the labyrinth of the academic community. Inevitably, then, the pressure group that can wield the most power and/or mobilize public opinion will have the greatest chance of success.

Unfortunately, the latter alternative will never produce a great university that is regarded as a leader by sister institutions. Rather, a university that follows will be created, lost in the pack of colleges around the country that refuse to innovate and initiate changes until a *real leading* institution sets the standard for others to imitate. A university that follows will always just be catching up. Does the decision to scrap the five-year engineering program or the recently approved grades proposal establish Cornell as a leader or a follower?

Students are rapidly learning that in order to achieve any of their own educational goals, they must turn themselves into a pressure group, with their only power lying in the threat of campus-wide demonstrations. This must be their course of action when they are confronted with a president who waits for the consensus to form. Students, then, in partnership with the faculty, must assume the responsibility of innovating, changing, and indeed the responsibility of leading the university in the void that has been established.

This is hardly a healthy situation at Cornell, where riots have been narrowly avoided more than once. Unfortunately, the responsible student is left with little choice if he has a real concern for the quality of his undergraduate education.

Mr. Perkins, president of Cornell University, has been heavily involved with Centennial Year activities ever since he arrived in Ithaca. Lacking the services of a Vice-President for Student Affairs, perhaps he has not had the opportunity to exert the leadership that so many people feel he is capable of, leadership that both students and faculty will benefit from. As Cornell completes its first one hundred years, we look toward an uncertain future.

—column, May 24, 1965

Even in a time of inflated rhetoric, the venom directed at President Perkins was out of scale. Two days after the take-over, The Sun's most conservative columnist called for Perkins to quit. No president before or since has suffered this indignity on The Sun's pages, and Perkins suffered it twice: The Sun's associate editor called for his ouster some two weeks later. Now, in light of the events, advocating change starting at the top was certainly a defensible position, and one that a conservative might be expected to espouse. But the columnist, Arthur Shapiro, who was usually one of the most restrained of writers, went far beyond asking Perkins to resign. He said, "There is a stench on this campus. Everyone can smell it. There is something dead and decaying in Day Hall, and its reek has sickened us all . . . There is no way to end the decline of the University without a massive shakeup in Day Hall. We do not need a scapegoat, but we must have a change. We must rid ourselves of the stench on the hill before it fells us all. The handwriting was on the wall, and James A. Perkins did not heed it. It is time for James A. Perkins to go."

Believe it or not, this was not the least flattering desciption of Perkins that appeared. Later, he was likened in print to a sodomite, an eater of excrement, and sundry other unattractive possibilities.

What may seem surprising about the vicious attack quoted above is that it came *before* the faculty had nullified the reprimands. At the time it was written, the penalties stood: the faculty had voted to uphold them the day before.

* * *

One of the distinctive features of the Cornell presidency is that its incumbents tend to hold office a long time. Although Perkins presided over the University's centenary in 1964, he was only Cornell's seventh president. One of the advantages of this is that each man's tenure has been long enough to permit comparision. At first it might seem tempting to liken Perkins to Charles Kendall Adams, who was also forced out of office, but the similarity ends there. When Adams was cast aside in favor of Jacob Gould Schurman, it was almost exclusively because of a personality difference with the chairman of the Board of Trustees.

A much more striking similarity exists between Perkins and Andrew Dickson White. Both men entered their jobs with vast experience in the real world; both were independently wealthy; both kept a high profile on campus; both brought a great deal of enthusiasm and exuberance to the office.

But the most stunning parallels between the two were their willingness to innovate, their vision, and their commitment to equal rights. White's views on racial and sexual equality were quite advanced for his time; many Cornellians are familiar with what he said about admitting qualified black students: "If even one offered himself and passed the examinations, we should receive him even if all our five hundred students were to ask for dismissal on that account."

A hundred years later, the new president of Cornell had this to say: "A university must not only tolerate the expression of opposing and even unpopular ideas, it must show a healthy and lively curiosity about them . . . and . . . even the open and curious mind is not really enough—it must be an informed mind or at least one determined to turn curiosity into solid information and informed judgment." Like White's, this remark would raise few eyebrows were it uttered today. But in the early 1960s, it was a bold and far-reaching statement.

The COSEP program, which brought inner-city blacks to Cornell in sizable numbers, was a Perkins creation from the word go. It was ahead of what other major universities were offering at the time, and in its early years it got real support, not cliches and platitudes, from the administration.

During President White's tenure, Cornell was known for its academic innovations. Perkins, far more than any of the other seven Cornell presidents, followed in White's path. He

—Photo by Sol Goldberg

IN HAPPIER DAYS: *James A. Perkins talks with students in the Temple of Zeus coffeehouse (above) and congratulates one of the few black students to graduate in the early years of his presidency (right). Black enrollment increased dramatically after the Perkins administration established the Committee on Special Educational Projects (COSEP), designed to bring students "disadvantaged by their cultural, economic and educational backgrounds" to Ithaca.*

—Cornell University Archives

hammered COSEP through considerable opposition. He proposed not just a department but a *College* of Biological Sciences (this project was later downgraded into an inter-college "Division.") He pushed faculty salaries higher. He proposed the revolutionary six-year PH.D. program, an interesting idea that failed, and the Society for the Humanities and the Freshman Humanities Program, both of which still exist. He was adept at getting government funds for his many pet projects.

By the late 1960s Perkins was regarded as one of the leading theoreticians of higher education. His 1965 Princeton lecture series, *The University in Transition*, got national acclaim, and from our perspective today what he said in it is truly remarkable. In 1980, the administration follows a course it calls "institutional neutrality," meaning roughly that the University should not take sides on the issues of the day. Various administrators have implied or stated outright that this has always been Cornell's policy. They obviously have never read *The University in Transition*, which blasts "intellectual chastity;" which calls for universities to lead, not to follow; which says the trick is not to *gain* knowledge but to *employ* it.

* * *

Sadly, President Perkins demonstrated he could deal with ideas but not with events. He should have been the most popular president of the century, and for a brief time, he was. What went wrong?

Any conservative support for Perkins had evaporated as he repeatedly took the soft line in dealing with black protests. In 1967 and 1968, the AAS issued a variety of demands, some of which clearly were impossible. One of these was that Cornell create and fund a wholly black degree-granting college that would not be responsible to the administration. Perkins, of course, had to reject this, but when he did the AAS launched a series of annoyance demonstrations and disruptions, including one two days afterward in Perkins' office, where they blocked access, played bongo drums, and read black poetry. When Perkins responded by ordering a cart of soft drinks and snacks sent up to the demonstrators, they knocked it over. After several more such irritating demonstrations, including disruptions in libraries, coffeehouses, and at a varsity basketball game, Perkins, at a press conference called to criticize the AAS, suddenly waffled on the autonomous college. "I am extremely reluctant to accept this idea of a college exclusive to one race," he said, "but I am not finally opposed to it. It would involve a rearranging of my personality."

Response to this comment foreshadowed the uproar when Perkins, after the Straight takeover and after the faculty had nullified the reprimands, told the students in Barton Hall: "There is nothing I have said or will say which will not be modified by changing circumstances."

Perkins also managed to alienate the liberals and the students, his natural constituencies. In 1966, when a prominent antiwar student was physically assaulted by a university official (the assistant proctor) who objected to a political button he was wearing, Perkins after considerable time gave the man no more than an oral reprimand, and that grudgingly. The Sun had called for firing.

A couple of months later, when the Tompkins County district attorney attempted to suppress the campus literary magazine *Trojan Horse* on grounds of obscenity, Perkins did not offer much support, and, furthermore, orchestrated things so that the head of the Safety Division, James Herson, was forced to resign.

Two incidents in the spring term of 1969 raised questions about Perkins' competence and sincerity. First, while defending Cornell's ownership of stock in Chase Manhattan Bank, which was facing charges of racism, he was suddenly hauled away from the microphone by a black student. A few

—Cornell Alumni News

WHO'S IN CHARGE? *President Perkins looks anguished as he sits on the Barton Hall stage on Wednesday, April 23 waiting for student radicals to allow him to speak.*

weeks later it was disclosed that Cornell did not in fact own any such stock. The Sun played this story for laughs.

Also, Perkins gave an informal talk before some students on the theme of the humanities. The Sun reported that he had been sarcastic and critical of Cornell humanities professors. A history professor wrote a furious letter to the editor blaming Perkins for most of the problems in the humanities. Perkins replied by saying that he had been misquoted, and inviting the professor to check with the students who had attended if he wanted to find out what actually had been said. Whereupon, some ten of those students jointly wrote to The Sun and said that The Sun had quoted Perkins accurately!

Undoubtedly the president's worst lapse of judgment came in March and April 1968, when he did not act in the face of a blatant threat to academic freedom. A visiting professor of economics, Father Michael McPhelin, was criticized for his views on race and poverty. Blacks in his class disrupted it and later took over the economics department office, where they demanded that McPhelin be fired and that Cornell allow equal class time to a speaker chosen by the AAS. To end the occupation, Cornell agreed to pay expenses to Ithaca for anyone the AAS chose to discuss the question. A week later, McPhelin canceled one of his lectures, saying he had been "advised to stay off" his proposed topic. Other professors said they had been censoring their own lectures, and there were a few other instances of blacks heckling professors during classes for allegedly racist comments.

If Perkins, then, did not take firm action against the Straight takeover, it is more to the point that he had failed to take firm action in the past when firm action had clearly been called for.

And so, when the blacks marched out of the Straight, Perkins marched alone. This is very significant. The blacks were a different cultural group, they were apparently threatening the community, they were issuing demands that seemed unreasonable. Under these circumstances, one would think that the community's natural impulse would be to unite behind its nominal leader. But just the opposite happened. Like the dog that did not bark in the night-time, the support that did not materialize for James Perkins told its own story. Cornell is very lucky that more faculty did not resign: some ten or twenty were threatening to do so should Perkins not leave. Cornell is also fortunate that an obvious successor to Perkins was available in Provost Corson, who *did* have faculty support.

At any rate, faculty opposition to Perkins grew for the rest of the semester, and when 15 law school professors, almost the entire law school faculty, expressed their doubts in a letter to Perkins on May 28, the Straight takeover claimed another victim.

This is what the law school professors said: "We are not convinced that you have given the highest priority to the preservation of free inquiry and free expression on this campus. . . none of us would be willing to teach in a university where either freedom of inquiry or freedom of expression is seriously impaired. We believe Cornell is perilously close to becoming such a university. Our remaining as faculty members of Cornell University is conditional upon your giving the highest priority to maintaining free inquiry and free expression on this campus."

* * *

James Perkins is certainly a tragic figure, albeit one it is difficult to feel sympathy for. Still, had the Straight takeover not occurred, had the judicial board decided differently, had the administration negotiators somehow managed to keep the guns inside the Straight, had the faculty meetings been more peaceful, then he might possibly have survived and led Cornell through the 70s. Of course, it is idle to speculate on what might have happened in this case, and yet it is a little saddening to look back on his first two or three years and to think what potential went unrealized.

* * *

If Perkins' style resembled that of Andrew D. White, it also has a resemblance to that of our next essayist. President Rhodes, like Perkins, did not have a Cornell background, but was appointed president from another high-ranking education job. Both men, far more so than any other presidents since Livingston Farrand, who left office in 1937, are outstanding speakers who have made extraordinary efforts to make themselves accessible to the community: Perkins was wont to pay unannounced visits to dormitories at night to chat with the students; Rhodes holds office hours, announces he is available to any students who want to invite him to breakfast, says it is his goal to know by name every member of Cornell's thousand-plus faculty. Both committed themselves to academic excellence early in their terms, and both are notorious for their pleasant urbanity.

So that you can see whether the comparison really holds, Rhodes' essay is followed by one by Perkins on the same subject, written three months before the Straight takeover, when matters were clearly getting out of hand. And we close the chapter with a third view of the same topic, this one from 1951.

When Rhodes was inaugurated in 1977, Perkins broke his self-imposed exile and returned to campus, to attend the ceremony along with former presidents Corson and Malott. Naturally, this in itself was big news, and The Sun managed to buttonhole him for an interview. Perkins spoke of the accomplishments of his tenure, said "I wouldn't have given up those six years for anything," and was reluctant to talk about his last crisis. The reporter asked him if, based on his experience, he had any advice to offer President Rhodes.

"Be lucky," Perkins said.

—Office of University Relations

SUMMIT MEETING: *Frank H.T. Rhodes smiles with his three immediate predecessors, Dale R. Corson, James A. Perkins and Deane W. Malott, moments after he was inaugurated Cornell's ninth president in November 1977.*

Old Passions Die Hard

Even now, many years after the Straight takeover, the bitterness has not ended. One of the last examples of this came in a 1977 exchange in The Sun between James Perkins and a popular professor of political philosophy, who had been one of those who had stopped teaching in Spring 1969 after the April disturbance.

In November 1977, Perkins returned to Ithaca to attend the inaugural of President Rhodes, and while here he gave an interview to The Sun, in which he reflected on the Straight takeover, among other things.

"I don't think that the thing that either caused the events before or after was. . .disrespect for the law," he said. "It was the unwillingness to have the law applied to people who were opposing the war in Vietnam or who happened to be black."

Surprisingly, Perkins said he had *not* been in favor of nullifying the reprimands, in spite of the agreement negotiated inside the occupied Straight by his representatives.

When it became clear on that Wednesday that the faculty intended to rescind, therefore, Perkins said, "I came to that whole meeting very reluctantly; I almost decided to resign right then and there before that meeting, because I was opposed to the idea of withdrawing the penalties." This, he said, was "a fascinating decision," and eventually he decided not to oppose the faculty motion and not to resign, on the grounds that it would "break apart the place."

As a corollary, Perkins had harsh words for the professors who did resign: "Those who had opposed the faculty motion on the floor never said anything; all who resigned at that time were silent. I never thought that was a particularly courageous position to take."

These comments provoked the following letter.

To the Editor:
In his interview to The Sun, James Perkins divests himself of a great number of distortions. He also casts aspersions on the courage of men whose shoes he is not fit to shine. These remarks are entirely worthy of him and cause one to appreciate the justice of the reputation he has earned as an incompetent and deceitful coward.

Prof. Werner J. Dannhauser, government
—letter, November 16, 1977

The Spirit of Cornell

By Frank H.T. Rhodes

I welcome the opportunity to join other members of the campus community in congratulating the editors and managers of *The Cornell Daily Sun* on its centenary. For one hundred years, it has carried the varied stories of the day to the campus and the greater Cornell community. The history of The Sun is largely the history of the University, for its existence covers almost the same span of time. It is one of the oldest student newspapers in the country.

I have been intrigued to read the first issue of The Sun, published September 16, 1880. Apart from the "business cards" and advertisements, the topics addressed represented a familiar range of subjects. There was concern at the loss of some faculty members, dismay over rising fuel costs, and pleasure at the return to campus of Andrew Dickson White, after an absence of some duration. The first issue contained "an accurate list of the members of the incoming class that were registered up to 10 o'clock last evening"—a remarkable achievement when one compares it with the time it now takes us to announce our new undergraduate numbers. That class numbered 131. There was a wealth of other material in the "Sunbeams" of the first edition. Topics included painting University buildings, the building of the Psi Upsilon chapter house, reunion plans for the Class of 1880, and some curiosity as to what Professor Fiske meant, "when he wrote from Berlin about June 1, asking that his leave of absence be extended another year, *for the benefit of his health?*"

In comparison with today's Sun, that first number was a modest publication of eight letter-sized pages, announcing carefully to its readers that regular editions would be four pages. It was an inexpensive publication, selling for three cents, so that the present level of 15 cents represents a fine achievement in keeping the price below the general level of a century's inflation.

It was an earnest publication, both in style and in content. "We have no indulgence to ask, no favor to beg," it avowed. "Our principles are those of the institution which we shall endeavor to represent,—liberty of thought, liberty of speech, and liberty of action; but we shall strive earnestly not to allow this liberty to degenerate into license." I believe that The Sun has generally maintained those high aspirations.

My congratulations do not imply, of course, that I invariably find myself in complete agreement with The Sun. On some mornings I find a certain consolation in a statement of Winston Churchill, when he declared, "I do not resent criticism, even when, for the sake of emphasis, it parts for the time with reality." Indeed the relationship between a college president and the student newspaper is likely to be one marked by some ambiguity. But I firmly believe that a strong student newspaper, with the diversity of opinion, and the freedom of expression that it provides, is one of the guarantees of the intellectual health of an academic institution. So I join with the others in congratulating The Sun on its proud record of achievement and in wishing it well as it enters its second century.

So much for the beginning. Equally interesting is the "memorial volume" published by The Sun on the occasion of its half century. This included a letter of congratulation written by President Livingston Farrand from the motor vessel "Vulcania" en route to Italy. Dr. Farrand closed his letter of congratulation with these words, "There can be no doubt at all of the material growth and the creation of an educational monument of surpassing beauty and impressiveness on the unrivalled site which the Founder made available. *The great task for us and for those who come after us is to see to it that the*

−Office of Public Information

Something Old, Something New: *The Great Wall of China winds along hilltops behind President Frank Harold Trevor Rhodes in July 1980. Rhodes headed a ten-member Cornell delegation seeking to reëstablish the close ties between the University and the mainland which had been severed after the Chinese revolution. Several education exchange agreements were signed.*

Cornell of the future shall have a spirit, a quality and a character worthy of its opportunity" (emphasis added).

I want to take Farrand's words and to review the extent to which those who have followed him have succeeded in fulfilling the task that he identified 50 years ago. That task was to ensure that Cornell should have a character, a quality, and a spirit worthy of the opportunity that its inheritance provided.

How do we define the character of an institution such as Cornell? In his recent book *Curriculum*, Frederick Rudolph asserted "Andrew Dickson White, its first president, and Ezra Cornell, who gave it its name, turned out to be the developers of the first American University and, therefore the agents of revolutionary curricular reform." White and Cornell accomplished this by establishing the new university on five distinctive principles; principles which they pursued so effectively that they were later to become characteristics of most major universities in this country.

First, White and Cornell insisted that their new university should contain the most practical sciences and the most liberal arts. They rejected the notion of any hierarchy of knowledge in which one discipline or profession enjoys greater esteem than another. There was to be no restriction of knowledge and no exclusivity of instruction. "I would found an institution where any person can find instruction in any study," declared Ezra Cornell, and though the "any study" has never been true in fact—we have never offered programs in pharmacy or dentistry, for example—it has certainly been followed in principle.

Second, the University from its earliest days stressed equality of opportunity. "Any person...any study" was more than an idle motto. Cornell and White insisted in the first prospectus of the University that those who could not afford to pay their way would be able to obtain manual work in order to support themselves. The *First General Announcement* declared that "...the Trustees are also pledged to try fully and fairly the experiment of allowing students in appropriate departments to do something towards paying their way by organized manual labor, under scientific direction." This pledge has remained a hallmark of Cornell. Nor was student diversity confined to economic background. The desire of Cornell and White to "secure a place where the most highly prized instruction may be afforded to *all*—regardless of sex or color"—as White wrote in an 1862 letter to Gerrit Smith—was already well documented. Despite the University's welcome to all, without regard to race, White's disappointment was evident in his response to an inquirer in 1874 that no blacks were then enrolled. "If even one offered himself and passed examinations," he said, "we should receive him even if all our five hundred students were to ask for dismissal on that account." In actual fact, only a few black Americans were able to obtain the benefits of a Cornell education, though some who did are among our greatest leaders, both in Cornell affairs and in society at large. In 1963, President James A. Perkins founded the Committee on Special Educational Projects (COSEP), whose primary purpose was to increase the number of blacks and other minorities within the student body. Minority students now account for ten percent of the total undergraduate student body.

A lack of living quarters compelled Cornell and White to delay the admission of women to Cornell during the first two years, although women were not actually forbidden entry. The first woman (Emma Sheffield Eastman) to complete the requirements graduated from Cornell with a Bachelor of Philosophy degree in 1873. Morris Bishop records that when Henry Sage's offer to provide funds for a women's college was accepted by the Trustees in 1872, the news brought a "stream of female applicants." In 1873, 16 women were admitted and, in 1874, although the building of Sage College was not yet complete, 37 women enrolled, together with 484 men. Throughout the history of Cornell, women have played an important role as students in the campus community and as graduates of distinction in the nation. To diversity of curriculum, then, was added diversity within the student body.

The third distinctive characteristic of Cornell was that, while it was, on the one hand, an independent institution, it was, on the other hand, to serve as the Land Grant institution of the State of New York. This gave it both an individual distinction and an identity, and also a measure of ambiguity. That ambiguity persists in the presence of four statutory colleges administered and controlled by an independent university, but funded in large part by the citizens of the state. In spite of that apparent paradox, the experiment has been a conspicuous success, and Cornell's Colleges of Agriculture and Life Sciences, Veterinary Medicine, Industrial and Labor Relations and Human Ecology are among the most outstanding in the nation.

The fourth Cornell characteristic, since the time of its foundation, has been a determined insistence upon excellence. That word now represents a currency much debased in some institutions, but it is a word of no small consequence on the Cornell campus. From its earliest days, the University knew no bounds in seeking out the best to join its membership. Andrew Dickson White traveled to England to recruit Goldwin Smith, previously the Regius Professor of History at Oxford, and to Edinburgh to recruit James Law as the first director of veterinary medicine. He traveled to Germany to purchase books and scientific equipment and to Greece to purchase archaeological and artistic material.

The student body was no less diverse and no less committed than the faculty. In an article written for the 50th Anniversary of The Sun, Simon H. Gage, Class of 1877, emphasized both traits, observing that "...there were many who...had been pioneers in the growing west or sailors on the Great Lakes; workers from sunrise to sunset, and later, on the farms, in the factories and mines. There were also a goodly number who knew wealth and leisure as well as labor. To that virile bunch nothing seemed impossible, and they set about with the zeal of crusaders to do something different in education. It was glorious even if at times a little turbulent." Cornell's present community remains "...glorious even if at times a little turbulent."

Those qualities were found in both men and women. In another article for the 50th Anniversary publication, Mary M. Crawford, Class of 1904, praised Cornell and White for their "rare vision" in admitting women on the same terms and in the same classes as men. While asserting that there was no early Cornell type of woman, Mary Crawford indicated that many were poor and in "deadly earnest" because they "had to make sacrifices to get to college at all...."

"But the very qualities," she added, "which made a young woman in the late seventies and eighties go to Cornell insured her fitness and stamped her as exceptional...valiant, strong, able and devoted daughters of their chosen Alma Mater."

Fifth, Cornell has been characterized by great freedom of student choice. Contemporary institutions at the time of Cornell's founding offered curricula as rigid as they were circumscribed. Unvarying in content, they allowed no possibility of student choice in either material to be studied or the pace at which the study was to be undertaken. Cornell broke away from that dominant tradition and placed the responsibility firmly in the hands of the students themselves. White expressed the new freedom in these words in his inaugural address: "You are not here to be made; you are here to make yourselves. You are not here to hang upon an university; you are here to help build a university." The results of that trust in student judgment have justified the boldness of the original experiment. Carl Becker, in prophetic words, has summed up

The Other Presidents of Cornell

ANDREW DICKSON WHITE
President 1866-1885

CHARLES KENDALL ADAMS
President 1885-1892

JACOB GOULD SCHURMAN
President 1892-1920

LIVINGSTON FARRAND
President 1921-1937

A CENTURY AT CORNELL

the history of the average student's experience at Cornell. "If there be any intangible possession that distinguishes this University, it is the tradition of freedom united with responsibility—freedom to do what one chooses, responsibility for what it is that one chooses to do." Not the smallest gift that Cornell has given to its sons and daughters has been that capacity to exercise freedom with responsibility.

These, then, have been the great distinguishing marks of Cornell, the attributes that have given it what Livingston Farrand called its "character." That they are now characteristic of other universities makes them no less significant for Cornell as the institution that gave them birth. The Cornell traditions of freedom, quality, diversity, and service are now to be found in other institutions—but perhaps nowhere to the same degree that they are in our University.

* * *

What of the quality of the University as it now stands? How has it survived the last 50 years? I believe there are several indicators of quality that one can identify in any institution. These include, for example, the distinction of its faculty, the quality of its student body and the adequacy of its library system. In all these areas Cornell has consistently ranked high among the major universities in the nation. David Starr Jordan, Class of 1872, the first president of Stanford, once said that the faculty was the glory of old Cornell. Today's Cornell faculty continues in the distinguished tradition of its early predecessors, gaining recognition and awards in every conceivable area and occupying leadership positions in professional associations related to their fields. To cite but two examples, the Cornell faculty and alumni have produced a total of twelve Nobel Laureates. In 1979, eight members of the Cornell faculty were awarded Guggenheim Fellowships, the third largest number of any university in the nation. In 1980, eleven members of the faculty received these fellowships and again we ranked as the third university in the nation.

But Livingston Farrand stressed the importance not only of Cornell's character and quality, but also of its spirit. That is less easily defined than the other two attributes, but it may, in fact, be the most important quality of all. In what particular aspects of its common life is the spirit of Cornell—its *ésprit de corps*—exemplified? It is exemplified in some of the characteristics I have already mentioned: a deep commitment to excellence and intellectual integrity, an unswerving respect for freedom and an insistent pursuit of equality of opportunity, for example, to name but three. There are, however, other aspects of the spirit of Cornell, and I want to consider briefly the implications of each of them. Some of them, I recognize, reflect the practical outworking of the character of Cornell that I have already described. But it is not so much the theo-

retical commitment to these concepts, as the practical expression of their implications that here concerns us.

Consider, first, the acceptance and welcome given to diversity on this campus. We are not a small regional college, or even a statewide university. Our students and faculty represent every state in the nation as well as some 90 foreign countries. We are, in fact, a microcosm of a global society, and that is a source of great strength. What is important, however, is that we should not only accept that fact, but should capitalize upon it. Our goal should be to nourish that sense of diversity, so that racism, sexism, and parochialism become unthinkable in the larger society of brotherhood and sisterhood that we represent. Idealistic as that may sound, it should have its practical expression in very material ways. It should be reflected in a determined attempt by all of us to build bridges between different cultural and racial groups within our community. It should involve a deliberate attempt to understand and to celebrate the heritage that each of these different groups represents. And it should also involve a patient resolution to make the atmosphere of campus life one which is not only congenial to diversity, but also encourages the preservation of that diversity, while still recognizing an underlying sense of shared goals, common respect, and individual friendship. I want to see that spirit grow, not simply between students, but also between students, faculty, employees and administrators. For too long, boundaries have existed between the various constituencies within our community. We need to dedicate ourselves to the removal of those obstacles, through common understanding, friendship and trust.

Second, the spirit of the University should emphasize personal worth and individual esteem. If this is properly understood, it will mean that everything we do will reflect this basic commitment. The way in which a receptionist or an advisor receives a student will reflect respect for that person's dignity and worth. The way in which we give directions to a stranger we encounter on campus, or write an article, or share our time and interests with residents of our dorm, or devote ourselves to extracurricular activities which we share with others—all these will reflect whether in fact, as well as theory, we accept the supreme importance of personal worth and individual esteem.

Third, Cornell must be a place where equality of opportunity is more than a slogan. It must be a place providing freedom for all of us to grow, and it will be that only by common consent and common effort. No legislation or official pronouncement will guarantee it. It will become a reality only insofar as all groups within our community are represented in every sphere of activity and responsibility.

Fourth, the spirit of Cornell must continue to find expression in a patient but unswerving insistence upon the highest

EDMUND EZRA DAY
President 1937-1949

DEANE WALDO MALOTT
President 1951-1963

JAMES ALFRED PERKINS
President 1963-1969

DALE RAYMOND CORSON
President 1969-1977

intellectual standards and scholarly integrity. The 80s will be a time of erosion of those qualities as colleges compete in an unseemly scramble for a declining number of college-age students. Unless universities are to go the way of many public high schools, there must be a commitment on the part of students and faculty to resist the laxity of standards that now prevails. This will mean that such things as plagiarism, intellectual shoddiness, double standards and doubletalk have no place in the Cornell community. But it will mean more than that. It will also mean the individual determination to exemplify that excellence in everything we do—athletic, social, academic, interpersonal, and societal. The standards of our society will be threatened within the next ten years. It should be part of the spirit of the University to stand against that tide of slovenliness.

Fifth, the spirit of Cornell must continue to be marked by a sense of responsibility and freedom. Of this I have already written, but Carl Becker's epigram will be severely tested in the coming years. It will be tested by the increasingly heavy hand of federal legislation and intervention in every part of our institutional life. It will be tested by the frustration of young people who face bottlenecks in employment and advancement in the light of increasing automation and declining natural resources. And it will be threatened by the shallow cynicism which erodes the underpinning of responsibility, without which freedom is a mockery. Two hundred years ago Edmund Burke declared, "Men are qualified for civil liberty in exact proportion to their disposition to put moral chains on their own appetites. Society cannot exist unless a controlling power upon will and appetite is placed somewhere, and the less of it that there is within, the more there must be without. It is ordained in the eternal constitution of things, that men of intemperate minds cannot be free. Their passions forge their fetters." The freedom and responsibility for which Cornell stands must be part of its spirit in the years ahead.

* * *

Sixth, Cornell must continue to be a place where there is an ultimate respect for the authority of reason, and for the necessity of civility. The universities still bear the scars of the late 60s and 70s. Those years of turmoil took a heavy toll on the integrity of the institution. If there is one thing for which the academic institution must stand, it must be the dispassionate rule of reason in a context of civility. The higher the passions, the more complex the problems, the more opposed the various viewpoints, the greater will be the need for reason and civility. I should like to think that Cornellians might be ambassadors of reason and civility in a world of irrational clamor and intemperate rancor.

But, far as reason and civility will carry us, they are not enough. There is another characteristic which I hope the spirit of Cornell will continue to exemplify, and that is a commitment to the moral and aesthetic faculties, as well as the rational, as being necessary to do justice to the breadth and resourcefulness of the human spirit. This will involve admission that reason alone is not sufficient for the balanced life; that personal freedom and fulfillment are to be found, not in complacency, but in commitment; not in self-gratification, but in service; not in ease, but in effort. This is not an altogether fashionable view today, for we live in an age of timidity, which imposes boundaries upon the largeness of the human spirit, and of despair, which limits the boldness of human hope.

But largeness of spirit and boldness of hope have never been more urgently needed. The problems we face require not only analysis, but also synthesis; not only disciplinary depth, but also multidisciplinary breadth. This means that we must welcome modes of thought and methods of appreciation that extend beyond the narrow rationalism, skepticism and relativism of the contemporary scene.

This expansion of perception and recognition of the expansiveness of the human spirit will not be easy. It will be challenged by those whom Andrew Dickson White called narrow "pettifoggers," whose horizons are constrained by vocational limits, and it will be condemned by those who are captives of contemporary cynicism. But only such a broadened view can ultimately provide context and meaning for the grander aspects of life, giving significance, coherence and motivation to what will otherwise be routine and meaningless tasks, providing new ways of looking at old problems and new resources for old needs.

Is such a spirit characteristic of the Cornell campus today? I believe that, in part, it is, though some aspects exist in weakened form. I should like to think that, 50 years from now, The Sun's commemorative edition will find each characteristic strengthened and the spirit of Cornell raised to even greater heights. Then will the University truly be "a city set on a hill, that cannot be hid."

—Sun Photo by Jan Buskop

—Sun Photo by Matt Sachs

POMP AND CIRCUMSTANCE: *Top, Frank H.T. Rhodes grasps the University mace (tipped with a tiny Big Red Bear) immediately after being officially installed as Cornell's ninth president on November 10, 1977. Below, students protesting the possibility of the University granting some "merit-based" financial aid in addition to "need-based" aid silently walk out of Barton Hall during Rhodes' inaugural address. The aid proposal was discarded, at least temporarily.*

FRANK H.T. RHODES was named Cornell's ninth president in 1977. Previously, he was vice president for academic affairs at the University of Michigan. His academic specialty is geology.

A CENTURY AT CORNELL

—Sun Photos by Larry Baum

DAY HALL UNDER PRESSURE: *The James Perkins administration was increasingly beleaguered as Spring 1969 progressed, first by radical student groups and finally—after the Straight takeover—by professors, alumni and trustees. Left, an SDS picket with a then-novel placard "demands" that Cornell "directly fund the construction of over 1,000 units of low and moderate income housing for Ithaca townspeople." Middle and right photos: students march in support of the May Day 10—Cornellians who were arrested for painting antiwar slogans on a navy practice deck gun then in Barton Hall. The two chaps walking past the construction site for the Campus Store are David Burak and—with a snake twining around his neck—Eric Evans.*

February, 1969: What Each of Us Must Do

BY JAMES A. PERKINS

The time has come:
• to reassert our belief in the university as an enlightened and progressive community that conducts its affairs on the basis of reason and compassion;
• to recognize that individual freedom is one of the hallmarks of the university and that each member's responsibility to respect the freedom of others is the necessary condition of freedom for anyone;
• to reaffirm the university's determination that no one shall be excluded from any university activity because of race, color, or creed;
• to recognize that the financial health of the university is essential to the support of progressive programs;
• to recognize that the social responsibilities of the university must be asserted in a manner that preserves its autonomy and its academic freedom;
• to recognize that the university can be governed effectively only if its members can be knit together into a true community.

To the degree that members of the university community waver in their commitment to the values represented here, the university's ability to perform its central missions—teaching, the advancement of knowledge, and service to society—will be reduced.

The university has discovered during the past few years that if these values are disregarded, the entire university community may be in trouble. It is crucial in our relations with each other, therefore, that we understand how important these values are.

There have been several instances of unreason at Cornell, as at other universities, in the recent past. Demands have been made that clearly could not be granted. These demands have on several occasions been accompanied by threats of disruption. Because discussion and consensus are of particular importance in a university, this kind of demand can never be answered positively. It can only prevent the university from considering matters that may be of great importance.

•

On the subject of individual freedom, we have come to realize that the freedom we demand for ourselves will not survive if we deny the same freedom to others. For this reason, the right to speak must be accompanied by the right to be heard. The right to criticize others must be accompanied by the willingness to accept criticism. The insistence that our views be treated fairly and openly has as its counterpart that we treat others' views the same.

The basis of our relations with each other has to be equal treatment under the rules of the community. Injustice within the university community cannot be excused simply by pointing to injustice outside the university, or else there is no salvation from injustice. If the university practices justice visibly and rigorously, it will help to illuminate and challenge injustice beyond its walls. That is the only way the university can expect to have constructive influence.

The principle of non-discrimination, which has long been given lip-service in the universities as elsewhere in society, is finally becoming more widely practiced. But the principle has now been challenged by those who desire separatism. This is obviously a complication, and it will take time to work out sensible arrangements that can accommodate both the new drive for separatism and the hard-won support for non-discrimination. Doctrinaire stands on either side will be easy; wisdom will require special effort.

On the matter of money, it is clear that the university can be no stronger than its balanced budget. It can live for a few years with expenses exceeding income—but not indefinitely. The university's supply of money, contrary to some of the prevalent folklore, is finite. There is a limit to how much the university can spend during any given year, and the allocation of available funds among the hundreds of competing demands is at times inconceivably complicated, especially when uncommitted funds are such a small part of the total budget. Commitments to personnel, programs and buildings, once made, are generally commitments for a long period of time and cannot be abruptly modified without destroying university morale.

In addition, existing commitments require continually increasing sums of money for higher salaries and for the ever-rising costs of goods and services. Thus new money that can be used for new ventures represents only a fraction of the total budget, and it is the allocation of this small fraction that requires the most sensitive understanding of the total needs of all parts of the university. Those who would threaten disruption of the university to increase their share of uncommitted funds are, in effect, saying that they don't care who else is hurt. It is hard to believe that such a stance represents a truly moral position under any definition of the term.

In addition to financial health, the strength of the university depends on its autonomy. To secure its autonomy, the university must maintain a fine balance between its necessary independence of society and its necessary involvement in society. Since the university is a special institution established to perform specific tasks of teaching and research, it follows that its public policies and public services must be closely and directly related to these tasks.

There are many other important public and social issues with which the members of the community are and should be involved as citizens. It is improper, however, for us to insist that the university be used as an instrument to promote our own special purposes. To accede to such requests would endanger university autonomy and thus its freedom. To accede would also place the university in the position of backing public policies that did not reflect a consensus. There is great danger for any institution to make pronouncements on moral issues in behalf of its individual members.

The detachment of the university from particular positions, be they partisan or religious, is an achievement that has taken centuries of struggle. Detachment has left individuals and groups free to plead and act according to their own consciences without fear of any established institutional policy. It is an achievement that should not be lightly discarded, and one that all the university's members — trustees, faculty, administration and students—must conscientiously maintain.

But these postulates of university integrity—rational conduct, individual freedom and responsibility, racial justice, fiscal stability, and autonomy—will have meaning only if the members of the university are willing to become a cohesive community. This will, in my view, make two demands.

The first is that the governance of the community be considered legitimate by its members. In general, at Cornell, faculty, administration, and trustees have come to an understanding of their respective responsibilities, and we consent to the decisions made by each other as a legitimate exercise of agreed-upon responsibilities. The university is still groping for ways to involve students in university governance so that they will regard decisions in which they participate as legitimate for them also.

While the principle of student involvement is generally accepted, it is by no means clear how this can be best accomplished. Not all students want to be involved in university governance. Many, perhaps most, are content to be passengers on the university ship, and only ask that it give them smooth sailing to port. Some students, on the other hand, want to be involved but are not agreed on the means. Some of these see governance as a tripartite affair in which students, faculty, and administration join forces to reach decisions by discussion and agreement. Others see students as a separate force pressing its views on faculty and administration from the vantage point of a previously consolidated consensus.

Until these widely divergent positions are resolved, every effort should be made to involve as many students as possible in university affairs, whether institutional or academic. In each case the test must be interest, willingness to do the necessary homework, and willingness to accept responsibilities for agreed upon decisions. We now know that when students participate in university activities on this basis the process is improved, decisions in most cases are wiser, and the legitimacy of the university governance is more widely understood and accepted.

•

The second demand on the university community in modern times is that it be progressive in stance and style. Such an attitude would seem to require:

1. That the university visibly stand behind all measures, both public and private, that will support its freedoms and maintain the open campus.

2. That the university oppose all actions, public and private, that would restrict freedom of speech or its converse, the right to be heard. This posture should apply to actions taken inside and outside the university.

3. That the university accept students as citizens first and students second. The doctrine of *in loco parentis* is, therefore, no longer valid. Rules must be based on the notion that the university has a large constituency of citizens who are in the state of being students. Only in certain particular cases is it relevant that many have not legally reached the age when they can exercise the legal powers of full citizenship.

4. That the university recognize that there are deep and critical problems with which society must grapple and that an examination of these problems is part of the responsibility of the university. This does not mean that the university should take a position as an institution on these problems; generally speaking, it should not. But it does mean that faculty and students should be encouraged to study, examine, and debate such matters as national security policy, limited war and Vietnam, racism in America, black nationalism and its place in a democratic society, the control of technology for social ends, the future of the city, the governance of a democracy, and the proper mission and management of the university. A progressive university will recognize the relevance of these questions,

a conservative university will try to stifle them, and a foolish university will accept criticisms as self-evident without careful study and examination.

5. That the university give the question of "relevance" its most careful attention. It is too important a matter to be treated as a slogan, for relevance goes to the heart of the meaning and purpose of the university. To ignore the question of relevance is to deny that there are connections between the university and society, between knowledge and practice, between ideas and their application—something no modern university could ever do.

Relevance too narrowly defined, however, could be destructive. If we insist that only those matters that visibly bear on current problems are relevant to our studies, we will miss crucial areas of research. We will not only cripple our ability to find adequate answers for the immediate problems confronting us, but destroy our capacity to deal with the future.

The university must construe relevance in the widest possible terms. All our past is relevant to the present and to the future. All the peoples of the world are relevant to our concerns; it is just that kind of a world. All knowledge is potentially relevant to current problems and to those future problems we don't even know about. The evolution of the human race, and certainly individual human beings, takes place over time; we must not shrink either time or space to our own immediate and personal interests. The university's concern for knowledge unfettered by the pressure for immediate solutions is the best guarantee that we will be able to deal wisely with new problems when they arise.

6. Finally, that the university community adapt itself to new priorities and new needs. This may in the end be as difficult for students as for many of the faculty, administrators, and trustees. Society's needs and priorities do change. It is important that the university keep pace with them and make the adjustments, major and minor, they demand. Certainly one of the major adjustments for the university will be to make knowledge that is organized on a purely disciplinary basis useful in the solution of live problems that do not fit academia's neat disciplinary lines.

Change in the university should be a constant process, as it is outside the university. Change should be the inevitable consequence of study, rational discussion, and a broad understanding of what is relevant. If the university is not changing, if it is not continually scrapping programs and measures that do not fit and finding new ones to take their place, something is wrong; the university is not doing its job, and disruption is certain to come.

Perhaps the most important thing any of us at Cornell can do in the next few years is to work hard at building a community where reason, compassion, and mutual respect prevail. The university is in many ways a fragile institution, dependent not on its buildings and books for survival but on the attitudes and relations among those who are its members. Cornell's survival, its strength, and its capacity to serve all who need what it has to offer now rests on each of us.

—*essay, February 5, 1969*

The Founders and What They Stood for

The following essay served as the basis of the author's remarks at the 1951 inaugural of President Deane W. Malott. Robert Cushman at the time was Goldwin Smith Professor of Government, having been on the Cornell faculty since 1923.

By Robert E. Cushman

Year by year, Cornell University presents more of the aspects of a huge business enterprise. Most of our newer buildings, planned for maximum efficiency, look like factories or office buildings. We have a large and increasing corps of administrators, whose job it is to keep the University's wheels moving, and to raise and handle the money which is needed to make them move. In many of our classes, student examination papers are now graded, not by professors but by IBM machines, and the student's academic fate is determined by the point which he occupies on a statistical curve. We become steadily more mechanized.

In spite of this, a university remains an intensely human institution. The raw material with which and on which it works is human material, a carefully picked group of boys and girls. Those of us who man the assembly lines and ply the trade of teacher are human beings; though I have known students around examination time who would challenge that statement. Finally, in the post of leadership is a flesh-and-blood man who, as President of the University, imposes upon it his personality, his policies, and his ideals. The constant interplay of all these personalities makes up the daily life of a university.

It is just because Cornell University is a very human institution, that I am sure that you must have a great curiosity about what kind of students we have at Cornell, what sort of men and women make up the Cornell Faculty, what kind of leaders have preceded President Malott in his high office, and what imprint those leaders have left on the life and spirit of the University. I can satisfy only parts of that curiosity. We may, however, properly and very usefully tell something about the Cornell tradition, in terms of the

'A Statue Would Look Nice There': *An elderly Andrew Dickson White stands on the arts quad in front of Goldwin Smith Hall early in the twentieth century. He gazes over land that was a gullied cow pasture when he assumed the Cornell presidency in 1866, two years before the University admitted its first class.*

—Photo by John P. Troy

men who founded Cornell and the principles and ideals which they followed. I think you ought to know these things because the principles and ideals which Ezra Cornell and Andrew D. White built into the new Cornell University which opened its doors 90 years ago still dominate the life of the Cornell of today. And the entire Cornell family gathered here may well profit by being reminded briefly of its own rich heritage.

Cornell University owes its life and its distinctive character to the humanity and generosity of Ezra Cornell, and to the educational statesmanship of Andrew D. White. Each was a remarkable man, and together they made a truly remarkable team.

President White lived the later years of his life on the Cornell campus, and as a result, most Cornellians think of him as a benign old man with a patriarchal beard, living in the memory of his long and distinguished career as an educator and diplomat.

But the Andrew D. White who helped found this University and who became its first President, was a young man of 36, a young man of vivid charm and driving energy. He was superlatively equipped for the task to which he had set his hand. Born in a family of wealth and culture, educated at Yale, Berlin, and the Sorbonne, and for six years a professor of history at the University of Michigan, he found himself a member of the New York State Senate and chairman of its Committee on Literature. He had revolted against the sterile educational program of his own college days, and had formed in his own mind the picture of a great, amply endowed university in central New York which, "by the character of its studies in the whole scope of its curriculum, should satisfy the wants of the hour."

It began to look as though the dream might come true. The newly enacted Morrill Act placed at the disposal of the New York State Legislature some half-million dollars for the establishment of a land-grant college or colleges, in which agriculture, the mechanic arts and military drill were to be taught. There was heavy pressure on the Legislature to divide this half-million dollars amongst several feeble and hungry little colleges, and Ezra Cornell, chairman of the Senate Committee on Agriculture, at first favored this policy since he had helped to establish one of these little schools.

White vigorously opposed this scattering of the Morrill Act funds, and the two men were brought together as opponents on this issue. It is a tribute to White's charm, tact, and skillful salesmanship that Cornell was not only converted to the view that the Morrill funds ought not to be divided, but was also gently led to the conviction that half a million dollars of his own money should be added to the Morrill grant to build the University that White wanted.

Ezra Cornell, 20 years White's senior, is described by Carl Becker as a "tough-minded idealist." Bankrupt at 47, a millionaire at 57, he had in him some of the instincts of a gambler, in the sense that he was willing to take long chances at heavy risks to achieve unconventional ends. He had for education the kind of passionate reverence which only the man who has not had much of it sometimes feels. He could be firm to the point of obstinacy, but he was open-minded and tolerant. Whether he comprehended White's plan for a new University in all of its ramifications is less important than that he had profound confidence in White, liked the fundamentals of the scheme, and was willing to take the plunge. His steady, intelligent and generous support of the new University after it had been opened kept it upon its feet. These were the two men who founded Cornell University.

* * *

The founding of Cornell University was a revolutionary event in the history of higher education in America. The pioneering leadership of White and Cornell has been somewhat obscured by the fact that it has since been so universally followed. Every member of the Cornell family, however, should be clearly aware of the shocking innovations which these intrepid pathbreakers made.

First, the new University was non-sectarian: wholly free from the control of any religious creed or denomination. The Cornell Charter explicitly states that "persons of every religious denomination or of no religious denomination shall be equally eligible to all offices and appointments." Eighty years ago, higher education in this country was largely dominated by religious organizations. College presidents were almost invariably clergymen, as were most college trustees and a generous proportion of college professors. These devout administrators and teachers joined in a pious conspiracy to protect college students from any new or critical ideas which might undermine their faith in revealed religion. Even enlightened professors of the growing science of geology were careful to reconcile their teachings with the Biblical story of the Creation and Flood.

White's independent and sensitive mind resented these arbitrary restraints upon a free intellectual life. He did not want his science mixed with theology. He wanted, to use his own words, "to found a University where truth shall be taught for truth's sake...and where it shall not be the main purpose of the faculty to stretch or cut science exactly to fit revealed religion." And Ezra Cornell, who as a young man had been read out of Quaker meetings because he married a non-Quaker girl, was just the man to back White in his revolt against religious intolerance and domination. At the ceremony at the opening of the University, Mr. Cornell said: "It shall be our aim and our constant effort to make true Christian men, without dwarfing or paring them down to fit the narrow gauge of any sect." The attack upon Cornell's non-sectarianism from the bulwarks of organized religion was immediate, loud, and unscrupulous. Cornell and White were branded as the apostles of atheism and the new University was condemned as "godless." So bitter and powerful was this assault by organized religion throughout the State that Governor Fenton, who had mustered up courage enough to sign the bill granting the Cornell University charter, felt it would be politically safer for him not to be present at the formal opening of the University, so he quietly left Ithaca the night before in order to avoid being a "fellow-traveler."

* * *

A second motivation was the revolutionary broadening of the University curriculum in accordance with White's principle of the "equality of studies." This, again was a move which commanded Mr. Cornell's wholehearted support. A self-made man himself, he believed that a college education should be of practical value, and every Cornellian is familiar with his words on the University's Seal: "I would found an institution where any person can find instruction in any study." White, on the other hand, who had

—Cornell University Archives Photos

FROM LOG CABIN TO ITHACA: *During the summer of 1825, when Ezra Cornell was an eighteen-year-old living with his parents in DeRuyter, New York, he built his frontier family this rude frame house as a replacement for their decaying log cabin. Ezra is pictured at the age of 21, the year he set out to find his fortune, hiking from DeRuyter to Ithaca, where he found a job as a carpenter and what turned out to be a permanent home.*

every educational advantage a man of his generation could enjoy, was in bitter revolt against the intellectual barrenness and snobbishness of the classical curriculum of his own college days.

We are now so accustomed to the hundreds of courses offered in our colleges and universities that it is hard to realize that a college education 80 years ago meant little more than a prolonged and dreary absorption in Greek, Latin and mathematics. These were the studies which a gentleman ought to pursue. In pursuing them he would be exposed to no dangerous or unorthodox ideas; he would not demean himself by studying anything which was in any way practical or useful; and, by an appalling amount of drudgery he would train his memory and discipline his mind.

At the periphery of the college curriculum, was, it is true, a fringe of anemic and subsidiary studies, including history, natural and moral philosophy, and the feeble beginnings of geology, chemistry, and physics, taught without benefit of any laboratory work. And there were also some few schools in which practical vocational, and even professional courses were given; but these were regarded as poor relations in the social caste system of higher education. White himself recalled that while he was at Yale, the boys in the Shefield Scientific School were not allowed to sit in chapel with the Yale boys. Is it any wonder, then, that the conventional educational world of 80 years ago looked with amazement and horror at this queer new University in which mechanical engineering, agriculture, veterinary medicine, architecture, and similar practical subjects rubbed shoulders in the curriculum with Greek, Latin, and mathematics, and in which a student might select any intelligent combination of these subjects.

In the third place, Cornell was the first important Eastern University to open its doors to women. Oberlin, founded in 1833, was the first co-educational college in the country, and by the time Cornell was founded, several of the Midwestern state universities were admitting women. This queer idea, however, had made no progress in the East.

Cornell and White did not run the risk of disturbing the New York Legislature by explicitly providing for co-education in the Cornell Charter, but they carefully saw to it that the Charter did not forbid it!—In his inaugural address, President White spoke with approval of the principle of co-education, and when the next year one of the State Scholarships was won by a girl, she was promptly admitted. As there were no dormitories for women on the Campus, this girl had to live in downtown Ithaca. She stuck it out until winter weather made the long climb up the Hill an impossible hardship and then withdrew. Then Mr. Sage came forward with the gift which made possible the building of Sage College.

Another innovation in the new Cornell University grew very directly out of Andrew D. White's own experience and thinking. This was in the uniquely important place in Cornell's educational program which was allotted to what we now call the social sciences: history, economics, political science, and the beginning of sociology. White had been active in public affairs, both as a member of the State Senate and as attaché to the American Legation in St. Petersburg. He was one of the group of enlightened men who were carrying on the fight for civil service reform. He firmly believed that American colleges and universities should train young men for the public service, and he intended that Cornell turn out a steady stream of men.

At this time, no course in American history was taught in any college or university in the United States. This, White felt, was "monstrous," and he established at Cornell the first chair of American History in this country, a chair held for many years by Moses Coit Tyler. White organized the President White School of Political Science. He endowed fellowships for graduate work in this field, and he made historical research possible by giving to the University one of the finest private libraries in the country. He laid, in short, the foundations upon which Cornell's national and international reputation in the fields of history and economics

has been built.

I have been discussing some of the notable ways in which Cornell University broke new paths, some of the ingredients which went into the making of what we call the Cornell tradition.

I think if one stands off and looks at the composite achievement of these two pioneers, Cornell and White, one sees running through it all a dominating principle which governed all they did. They were driven by the conviction that American college and university education needed a new charter of freedom; and virtually every new idea that went into the founding of Cornell was a plank in that charter.

They were bent upon founding a university devoted to the ideal of a completely free intellectual life. The old restraints, taboos, prejudices, dogmas, and superstitions which had warped and suffocated American higher education were to find no place on the Cornell campus. The free life of a great university is a constant challenge to the teachers to broaden the vision and deepen the understanding of their students, a challenge to the scholar to extend the frontiers of human knowledge, and Cornell and White were determined that the life of Cornell University should be a free life.

It is unfortunately true that the tradition of a college or a university is not always noble or inspiring. It may be narrow; it may be bigoted; it may even be shoddy. There are institutions in which tradition demands that the president be a devout and orthodox member of some religious sect or denomination. There are others in which he must be ruggedly conservative in his political and economic views. In many Southern institutions, he must sympathize with, and administer, rules of racial segregation. In still others, he may go his own way as long as his educational policies do not endanger the success of the football team! In all of these cases, tradition lies like the hand of the dead upon the university.

I have tried to make clear that the Cornell tradition is the tradition of freedom. That tradition does not dictate to President Malott what he must do, or what he must not do. It tells him merely that it is customary for Cornell Presidents to lead and not to follow, to plot their own courses, to defend and cherish their own ideals. The only restriction or limitation which the Cornell tradition imposes upon him is that which is imposed by his own sense of responsibility to conserve scrupulously and to exploit generously the freedom whch is the life-blood of a university.

A university is a community of scholars, teachers, and students in quest of the truth. Its life is the life of freedom, for "the truth shall make you free."

—speech, September 19, 1951

GROWING UP WITH BOOKS: *Ezra Cornell spent his youth in the backwoods, but Andrew Dickson White knew comfort as a banker's son in upstate New York. Ezra did "cyphering" lessons before the hearth on scraps of paper and shingles, while White absorbed Shakespeare and Milton. Above, the library in White's Syracuse home, where his family continued to live until the President's mansion (now the Society for the Humanities) was completed in 1874. Right, White at the age of 47, in 1879.*

—Cornell University Archives Photos

The Accomplishments of Andrew White

Here 'mid the fair fulfillment of his dream
    His statue broods above the busy ways;
Long since on this bare hill he saw the gleam
    Prophetic of these present golden days;

He saw these towers that catch the shafts of dawn,
    These stately hills that crown this hill grown fair,
These arching elms above the shadowy lawn,
    He heard the chimes ring through the vibrant air.

Unmoved through all his statue shall abide
    That men may think of him who saw the gleam,
The seer who toiled; whose toil is glorified
    In this fulfillment of his golden dream.

Twenty-five years ago, upon the centennial celebration of the birth of Andrew D. White, these slightly archaic lines by Albert W. Smith '78 were printed in The Sun. They reflect the feeling of those who knew the University's first president, the man who is largely responsible for Cornell being what it is today.

Today marks the 125th anniversary of White's birth, an anniversary that might well make this campus pause from its gentle cynicism and mild disregard of all those traditional things buried in the University's past. For it is certainly no overstatement to say that what White was, and what White did, has an effect on every Cornellian today.

*   *   *

Andrew White was the man who set the pattern for Cornell's curriculum—a pattern that is now familiar but which was such a revolutionary idea when first presented in the Cornell of 1865. White believed firmly in the humanities and liberal arts, and as a distinguished classical scholar himself, he made sure that his university would give the proper emphasis to what he called "the development of genuine culture." But on the other hand, he was aware of the growing needs of the 20th century, and it was this vision which gave the campus its schools of engineering, agriculture and veterinary medicine, and expanded more than any other college of the time laboratory work in the sciences.

And it was White who built Cornell's early reputation for greatness by bringing to the faculty such outstanding men as

Louis Agassiz, James Russell Lowell, Goldwin Smith, T.F. Crane, Robert Thurston, and George William Curtis. These men, and the revolutionary curricula, were molded by Andrew D. White into a university that would truly embody Ezra Cornell's dream of an institution where any person could find instruction in any study.

*   *   *

White carefully guided the destiny of Cornell from 1868 to 1885. Consider these remarks of his, and then it is perhaps possible to tell not only what kind of man White was, and what kind of university he built, but also why the commemoration of his birth today is important in terms not only of Cornell's history, but the entire history of higher education.

"I would rather be instrumental in sending out into the world one sound-hearted, strong-headed, able-bodied young man to battle for good in any of the various struggles now going on in this country," he said in 1882, "than to graduate a whole legion of fops—of beings born simply to consume the fruits of the earth."

"Our ambition is, as it has been, to increase the number of those who, by manly service in every branch of thought and industry, shall at the same time build up themselves, the University and the country."

"Most of all I have been interested in the founding and maintaining of Cornell University, and by the part I have taken in that, more than any other work of my life, I hope to be judged."

*   *   *

You have been, Mr. White, and it is to signify the vital and ever-present appreciation of this work that the University commemorates your birth today.

—editorial, November 7, 1957

A CENTURY AT CORNELL

On October 7, 1868, Cornell officially opened for business with a magnificent inaugural ceremony, featuring speeches by Ezra Cornell, Andrew D. White, and others. Here, The Sun reflects on the occasion.

−Sun Photo by Tim Foxe

1880:
The Experiment Has Succeeded

Twelve years ago today, Cornell University threw open her doors to the student world, and took her position among the colleges of the land. The theory upon which she was based was a new and broad one. The memorable words of her founder, "I would found an institution where any person can find instruction in any study," were novel to the adherents of the old system of one cast-iron college course. They saw only failure in the experiment, and they were eager to prophesy the early death of the institution.

Many good, conscientious educators were unable to see that a system of education suited for the middle ages was not adapted to the requirements of modern times. They felt that although radical changes had been necessary in every other department, in the college instruction no improvements could be made. Under the plea of *discipline*, they endeavored to maintain the study of the ancient languages, to the exclusion of everything else.

But there was a constantly increasing class who thought that a liberal education could be obtained without the ancient languages, and that the mind could be as well disciplined by the study of science, mathematics and history, as by grubbing out Greek roots. They appreciated the advantages to be derived from the study of the classics, but thought that instruction in other departments was even more necessary.

Among this latter class were the founder and the President of this University; and when Cornell was opened she offered a wider range of studies than was to be found in almost any other college. For 12 years the experiment has been tried, and any impartial person must acknowledge that it has proven a success. Despite the uncalled-for and ungenerous attacks that have been constantly made upon us, the University has continued to prosper; and today affords better facilities for instruction than ever before. Constant improvements have been made in the departments and the buildings, and the work done last year by the students was more satisfactory than ever before. During the 12 years that have just passed, more than three thousand students have received instruction here. The University is no longer an experiment, her success has been demonstrated; and she enters her teens with bright prospects for a long and useful life.

—editorial, October 7, 1880

1974: Where Are the Dreamers?

The Cornell campus had one-and-a-half buildings to its name on October 7, 1868 when the University first opened for operation. The labor and high hopes of two men gave birth to this infant institution: Ezra Cornell, gaunt, humorless, frugal and obstinate; and Andrew Dickson White, an eloquent, wealthy and brilliant academic. Dreamers both, they laid foundations for a university that was intended to last for centuries.

Ezra Cornell saw the need for an institution where young men and women could learn agriculture and mechanics (he had taught himself basic science and technology by long hours sitting in the Library of Congress); Andrew White fostered in him a lasting respect for history, literature and the classics. This country could boast of no high quality University in the mid-19th century, and these men vowed to create one.

* * *

Nothing breeds cynicism quite so well as watching the erosion of high ideals. Anniversaries are stopping places by the side of the road, times for looking forward and back. This birthday, Cornell University's 106th, hardly calls for candles or cakes. A stern sermon might be more appropriate.

Academic matters are the muscle, blood and soul of a University; the founders knew this, and sought to build "a center from which ideas and men shall go forth to bless the nation during the ages."

Today it seems the men in charge of Cornell are in danger of whitewashing their concern for academics with a kind of corporate mentality—the primary concern of which is money.

Now that the national economic forecast has blackened, the administration has begun to wail of our "financial plight" and speak of cutbacks in academic areas. As yet they have not specified where such cutbacks might come. There is talk of combining courses which are duplicated in various departments: which might serve a valid purpose, but which is more likely to add to the list of Cornell's onerous, oversized lectures.

Beyond this there are only rumors, which breed rumblings of fear and uncertainty. Will class size increase and course offerings drop? Might it be deemed necessary to jack up enrollment past the overcrowded levels currently predicted? Might entire departments be slashed from the University? Nothing has been said to still these fears, and suspicions have begun to swarm angrily.

Can we expect the superpowerful Board of Trustees to show more than a peripheral concern for academics? Unlikely. Their membership reads like a roster of corporate managers and big businessmen. The Board's major committees deal with state relations, investments and buildings and properties, all of which, while essential, are secondary to the business of teaching, learning and research.

In all Cornell University's 106 years the trustees have never seen fit to create a Committee on Academics. Which is quite an ironic omission. We note that Oxford and Cambridge, the great universities of Britain, have no "trustees" *per se*. There the faculty serves as the governing body.

If only we could call upon the fiery eloquence of Andrew White, or the tough, persistent idealism of Ezra Cornell, to fight for the academic quality of this University. Without men of strength and convictions to rival theirs, Cornell University might become a pretty spot on top of East Hill with all the intellectual worth of a junkpile.

—editorial, October 7, 1974

INTERLUDE: The Tribulations of the Student Life

Problem #1: The Weather

BY CHAD GRAHAM '51

We had been hoping we might get through the winter just once without feeling the necessity for fulminating on the quality and temperament of Ithaca weather. But yesterday afternoon's performance shattered that rosy little dream once more. So pull up a chair and lend an ear. We are preparing to expound a few deathless truths.

No Cornellian can truthfully claim he came to Ithaca unprepared. The weather in these parts is the subject of all kinds of sly remarks and warnings in the voluminous printed matter shipped out in bales to the entering freshmen each summer. The deskbook, for example, usually contains a chatty little section on the latest fashion trends for coeds, which points out the ever-present need for ski suits, galoshes, and raincoats. The Inter-Fraternity Council's pamphlet shows pictures of the houses wreathed and draped in dribbling festoons of snow. As often as not, the Student Council will send out a little poop-sheet containing a passing reference to "the frigid uplands of the Ag school." All in all, even the greenest frosh gets a pretty clear notion that all is not sunshine and violets in Ithaca when the gray days of November close in.

But mere words cannot describe the catastrophes which plague the campus dweller all through the eight-month winter. Let the reader cast back in his memory to the Colgate games of years past, when sheets of icy rain sluiced down on the Crescent, all the long afternoon. Or recall the Syracuse game this very fall, when snow and wind plagued spectators

—Sun Photo

and players alike.

Hearken to the first day of fraternity rushing this year, as the grim dawn saw little bands of prowling brothers splashing through the mud and rain around the temporaries* in the do-or-die struggle to "fill the quota."

Count up the number of times that snow and sleet and rain and hail have begun to fall on the Thursday afternoon before vacation—any vacation—and continued until Sunday morning, so that nobody could get home with any degree of promptness, facility, or comfort.

And, most of all, examine the treacherous and evil-hearted way in which a howling blizzard yesterday crept up upon an unsuspecting population beaten into a semi-stupor by a solid week of snow, hail, and bitter cold, and wreaked its bitter vengeance upon these helpless mortals. Clearly, there is no justice. And just as clearly, the perverted genius who designs and produces Ithaca weather should be sentenced to walk the limits of the quadrangle in T-shirt and shorts for the remainder of eternity.

—*berry patch, February 25, 1951*

*Quonset Huts—Ed.

An Obsession and a Scapegoat

BY ALLAN J. MAYER '71

There is a great, almost instinctive suspicion that lurks in all of us concerning the weather. I suppose it comes down to us from the days when lightning and thunder were supposed to be the rumblings of a series of remarkably moody Olympians who thought nothing of throwing celestial hammers and other divine implements of destruction at each other at the slightest provocation. And so, the poor fellow whose hut was destroyed by a poorly aimed heavenly bolt could always sigh and, rather than gnash his teeth, conclude, "Those damned Fates are at it again."

Today, of course, we have dentists and think nothing of teeth gnashing, which we, like the gods of old, engage in at the slightest provocation. We still, however, like to think of the weather as being something more than a system of up-drafts, warm fronts and isobars—Dr. Frank Field (himself a dentist by degree) notwithstanding.

This peculiar facet of human nature is not really surprising, although after even a little study, one finds that there are hardly any facets of human nature that one can label surprising. In any case, per-

—Photo by Sol Goldberg

WIPE OUT: A Libe Slope tray slider careens into bales of straw roped around a tree trunk as his lunch tray explodes in mid-air and another slider glides by. Until the middle 1970s, the University padded the slope's trees with straw in tacit recognition of the officially discouraged undergraduate tradition.

haps because it is one of the few remaining phenomena over which we can claim no control whatsoever, we have a tendency to impute higher motives to the most significant of thunder-storms.

Weather, more than any other single phenomenon, affects our moods, our actions, our very thought processes. Rather than controlling it, it firmly controls us. To what subject does the stammering beau invariably address himself to alleviate the embarrassment of being thrust into the singular company of his latest blind date? Why, the weather, of course. On what topic does the postcard from the more fortunate fraternity brother or roommate in Miami or Bermuda for the holidays inevitably dwell upon first? Yes, how the sun shines and the breezes blow, how the temperature lingers somewhere over 75, how the rain clouds float far off, never daring to cross the horizon—in short, the weather.

*   *   *

We are obsessed by it. Our plans are determined by precipitation probabilities and we have reserved a special place in the Inferno for the mortal who dares call himself weather forecaster. But, like it or not, it is a force with which we must reckon. To a large part, the history of the Straight takeover last spring was played out in accordance to the weather's designs. And who knows how many battles, sporting events, even political campaigns had to kowtow to its demands? Just mention the word "snow" to Mayor Lindsay and you get an indication.

Nevertheless, with our singular propensity for turning the tables to our advantage, we humans have assigned the weather a most necessary function. In talking about it, and talking about it alone, we have indeed done something about it. We have made the weather a scapegoat. If things are going wrong, if we feel out of sorts, if we flunk a prelim or lose a girlfriend, we go no further than the nearest nimbo-stratus and "blame it on the weather." Needless to say, the weather, like any responsible scapegoat, doesn't talk back. It merely rains.

Aristotle had a word for it, though it can't be repeated here. His advantage, of course, was that, after uttering his nasty imprecation, he could go off to Delphi and receive the latest 30 day forecast. We have no recourse beyond 30 Rockefeller Plaza, the east coast home of the U.S. Weather Bureau, an organization that would be more aptly named the Weather-or-Not Bureau.

Of course, the weather does not always have the last laugh, as the Minnesota Vikings learned when they were so thoroughly trounced by the interlopers from Kansas City. Or perhaps it does, for it invariably lets you down when you make your plans based on its cooperation. A persnickity acquaintance who accosted me in Barton Hall last April 22 took great joy in reminding me of a column of mine called "Weather to Blame" that appeared on this page late last March. In it, I advised all who would listen that this campus would see no disruptions because the weather was too depressing.

"Ha," he said. "Ha."

—*column, February 9, 1970*

Interlude: The Tribulations of the Student Life

A Vote Against December . . .

—Sun Photo by Elizabeth Werner

Some may insist that April is the cruelest month, but as far as we're concerned, nobody can hold a candle to December. It's not simply that December is a cold, nasty, brutish fellow; we hear tell that he's a regular good time Charlie in Tierra del Fuego and Kuala Lumpur. And it's not just that a lot of swell things are finished in this month. After all, for every school semester, calendar year, and meaningful relationship that winds down to a wintry end, the odds are good that new ones will flower and pollinate (so to speak) next January (more on January next month).

What it comes down to is this: all that glitters is not gold, and it's going to take more than a pretty frost to placate our suspicions about *this* month. Sure he talks a good game, his wind whistling in your ear, his slush sliding between your toes, his holidays and ho ho hos. But let's take a look at the record. Beethoven was cursed with a December birthdate, and it hardly comes as a surprise to note that this great composer went deaf, and that he never even married, even though he seems to have been very nice looking.

Also, many terrible things have happened in December. On December 30, 1922, the USSR was established. Who can deny that the world would be a lot less complicated, if not a happier place altogether, without the USSR? Probably not too many can.

And so, for all of the above reasons (and others too numerous to mention here), The Sun has decided not to endorse December this month. We realize that this action may seriously inconvenience some people (department store Santas and impatient skiers to name a few), but there comes a time when considerations of crass expediency can no longer be entertained. What's right is right, and December is wrong. Right? Right!

—*editorial, December 7, 1972*

. . . And Against Energy Conservation

When, some time ago, a sudden change in the temperature found the janitors unprepared for its reception, the students shivered in silence, and, in most cases, uncomplainingly, but now, that an apparently settled period of cold weather has commenced, there seems to be no reason why comfort should be longer rendered impossible and health further endangered.

This brings us back to the old subject so often discussed, yet never settled by removing the root of the evil. It is claimed for Cornell that she teaches the latest thought and science of the age; that no sooner is an advance made in any department of knowledge, than it is at once incorporated into her work. And such is the case. In the Anatomical Lecture Room we are taught the injurious effects of impure air, and in the course upon Physics, we are shown the best methods of heating and ventilating, yet all winter we are compelled to sit for hours each day in rooms lacking all ventilation, varying many degrees in temperature according to the time and place of observation, and loaded with the sickening and unhealthy gases which poorly constructed stoves are constantly emitting.

Is this in accord with the boasts and principles of Cornell? Better get along with one less new building, and have those we now possess comfortable and healthy; better devote less money to predicting weather, and more to adequately providing for it when it does come; better forestall a hospital, by removing the causes which render it necessary. In the anxiety for new buildings, an enlarged library, for art galleries, and all other desirable improvements and additions, we beg those in authority not to forget that far more important than all these to young men and women preparing for life is sound, perfect health, and that the time spent here may prove, to many young people, a blessing or a curse, according as the evils now existing are remedied or neglected.

—*editorial, October 11, 1881*

The Devil You Say

Oh, what fun in hades, now that winter's
    here;
The coal supply in hades will last through-
    out the year.
We don't get up at five o'clock to monkey
    with the furnace;
The angels never come around to blow
    their horns and spurn us.
We're not thrown out when rent comes
    due, our grace is more than seven —
I'd rather roast in hades now than freeze
    up there in heaven.
    —*berry patch, December 14, 1926*

The Wisdom Of the Founders

As we spent yesterday morning, and yesterday afternoon, and yesterday evening struggling through the snow and the drifts and the wind and the traffic and the mountain byways, munching on our cold turkey sandwiches as we cursed our return to Ithaca, a certain old story about the founding of Cornell kept running through our mind.

It is related that Ezra Cornell got together one day with Andrew Dickson White to describe his dream of a great university of which White would be the first president.

"I would found an institution where any person can find instruction in any study," rhapsodized Ezra.

"But that's ridiculous," sputtered Andrew. "It would have to be the biggest university in the world. It will be flooded with an impossible number of students."

"Don't worry," counseled wise Ezra. "Just wait until you see where I'm going to put it."

—*editorial, December 1, 1969*

—Photo by Russ Hamilton

BECAUSE IT'S THERE: *Mark Spitzer '81 climbs a frozen gorge waterfall with the aid of mountaineer's equipment.*

−Sun Photo

'Ithaca Rain'

Last year it first snowed in Ithaca on October 10. This year October 4 marked the first fall of what has come to be known as "Ithaca rain." As one student with a perverted sense of humor remarked yesterday, next year it will probably snow during orientation, which will give incoming freshmen a better insight into what they will have to face in the following four years than any other orientation activity could.

—editorial, October 6, 1965

It's the Weather

Do you ever have that feeling
That everything is right?
That the Profs are really human,
And the work they give is light?
That the prelims aren't really bad,
And not too often, too?
That the meanest blues you've ever had
Are really caused by you?
That next-door folks aren't all so slow,
But some are quite O.K. —
Now I ask you like a pal, old bo,
Do you ever feel that way?

—berry patch, April 15, 1920

March: In Like a Pigeon

Pleasant old platitudes notwithstanding, our friend the third month has come in not as a lion, nor even as a lamb, but rather as a pigeon, merrily dumping her fluids onto unwary passersby and into awaiting pots prudently placed beneath leaks dotting the roofs of lovely Collegetown. This would not be so distressing (after all, "into each life...") except that such aviary antics are particularly unbecoming to noble March, normally a most dignified month.

March's distinguished calendar career dates back to classical times, when it was named after Marc Antony in recognition of the latter's invention of the famous word "honorable," now archaic. The name for the fifteenth of the month — the Ides — also dates from Greco-Roman times, and is taken from a bowling alley located in ancient Ithaca, which was famous across the Aegean for its middle-of-the-month wine-and-goat cheese blasts.

March continued its leading position among the months, marking through the years the discovery of rice by Marco Polo, the invention of the eye gouge by Attila the Hun, and the development of door-knobs by Benjamin Franklin. It marks a period of celebration after the births of both Lincoln and Washington, and of course does yeoman service as a buffer and important stall before April Fool's Day. It also provides an eager and grateful world with spring (or fall, if you're born on the wrong side of the equator), and ecumenically abides, at times, both Easter and Passover. All in all, it's been real keen.

Which only serves to bring home with special poignance the disgraceful performance of this year's scion of a formerly noble line. Coming as it does after a predictably foul February and a singularly noxious January, March has a special responsibility to its constituents to be, if not leonine, at least muttonous — and this pigeon nonsense is an insupportable abdication of that responsibility. We urge the University Senate, which has jurisdiction over the calendar, to take whatever steps it deems proper with a view toward correcting this untoward turn of events. And we hope April takes the hint.

—editorial, March 7, 1973

Get Your Act Together, Sun!

To the Editor:

I can stand it no longer! I must protest! In this beautiful weather, in these days filched from paradise, I have been tricked into wearing a raincoat and rainhat. And the fault lies with the SUN.

The fact is that my room is a little dungeon deep in the bowels of the Baker Dorms. There are no windows. When I get up each morning, I look at the SUN weather report on the front page of the SUN.

Invariably the prognostication is "Wind and Rain" or "Cold with Showers." Being a prudent sort of chap, I climb into my raincoat, cover my head, and emerge into the "rain and cold." I look at the sky! But it is too late. I must carry my raincoat for the rest of the day and endure the sneers of the merest Freshmen.

What little humor there is in reading such monstrous predictions is not enough to compensate for the public ridicule which I must endure. In the words of the Bard, "For pity's sake, cut it out!"

JERRY SHAFFER '50
—letter, October 13, 1949

−Sun Photo by Elizabeth Werner

Out of Misery, Art

CLOCKWISE, FROM UPPER RIGHT: *An 1880s snow bust of William Shakespeare built to the south of Central Avenue; a seven-foot-tall caricature of then trustee chairman Henry Williams Sage shaped by Prof. H.D. Williams on February 3, 1894; "King Winter," the winning entry in a snow sculpting contest held during Junior Week of 1939; Seal and Serpent fraternity's appropriate entry in a similar contest of 1936; a kneeling elephant and an emerging passenger before Theta Xi fraternity; and— in a change of taste—a commodious commode created by North Campus residents in March 1970.*

A CENTURY AT CORNELL

Problem #2: The Social Life

Few creatures on this earth have been so consistently and unjustly traduced and maligned as the Cornell coed. During Cornell's early years most of its male population was opposed to coeducation. Later, many fraternities shunned coeds, and socializing with them was taboo in some quarters until as late as the 1940s, the men preferring ''imports.''

Even after dating coeds became not only possible but desirable, Cornell males slapped a variety of offensive stereotypes on their schoolmates. Coeds were supposedly ugly, swinish, and frigid by nature. The only reason one would date a coed, so went the story, was the ''Ratio''—about 4 to 1 male in 1950; about 3 to 1 in 1970; about 2 to 1 in 1980. Naturally, coeds had their own opinion of these matters, and when one freshwoman wrote about her grievances in a letter to the editor in 1950, it provoked one of the greatest torrents of correspondence in The Sun's history. So many usable letters were received that the Sun editors decided to make a book of them and sell it for its salacious appeal. The administration vetoed this on grounds of embarrassment (this was 1950, remember) but some of the editors bootlegged the book anyway.

As a matter of linguistic interest, the word *coed* is no longer used, at least not at Cornell. It died out in the mid-60s when it was realized that the word itself implied the primacy of male students. It had a brief renaissance as a pejorative in the late 60s and early 70s; a man might refer to a particularly offensive female student as a *coed*. Even this meaning has died out now, however.

In 1950, though, the word was still in full flower; and here we present some of the correspondence on the nature and habits of the elusive coed, prompted by that one letter from the freshman who will go down in Cornell history as ''Miss Name Withheld.''

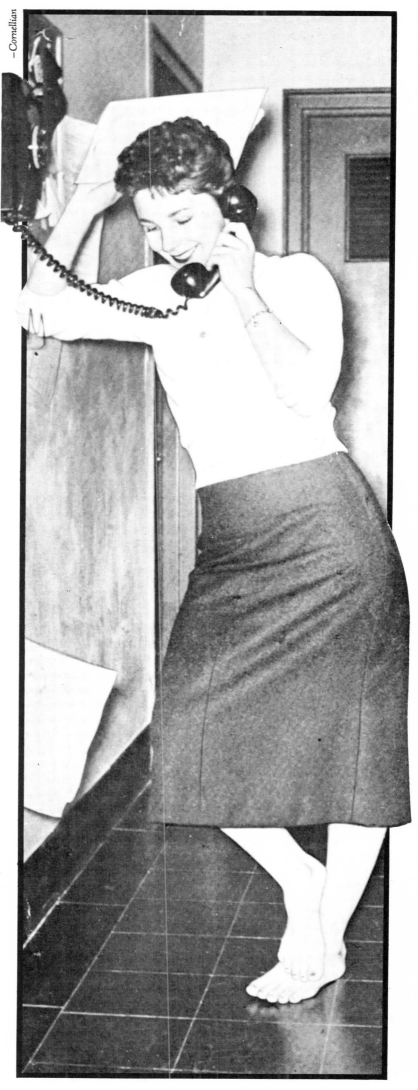

—Cornellian

O Mighty Ratio . . .

To the Editor:

Many's the gripe I've heard from Cornell men on the dating situation and coeds in general, but as a frosh coed, I would like to offer a few complaints from the better fifth of the student body. It is high time that a popular Cornell tradition receive a well-deserved squelching from one of the group that has long borne the brunt of its abuse. The tradition in question is the ignoble status of the Cornell coed, the myth of popularity which surrounds her, and the resulting behavior of Cornell men toward us.

Far and wide, Cornell coeds are known as "dogs" or "pigs." Years before I came here, I had heard that they were not only by far the world's ugliest women, but that they further disgraced their sex by their scandalously loose morals. On campus we are told that we are conceited, spoiled snobs, prudes, or frigid women, who are getting away with repeated outrages, who are living in an ideal set-up, and who are taking unfair advantage of an unfortunate situation—namely, the Ratio.

Proof of our fabulous popularity and the desperate shortage of girls may be seen in the large number of girls who stay home on weekends in Dickson (Home-of-the-Freshman-Rush) Hall alone. These coeds are not just the "ugly 30 percent," but include an amazing amount of cute and "popular" girls. Several weeks ago, one of my "rushed" corridor-mates held a formal funeral for her telephone, complete with candles and epitaph. "It died," she mourned solemnly as I passed her darkened room.

The hardest thing to grin at and bear, however, is the assortment of low, vile tricks commonly employed by the male population hereabouts in dating techniques.

The most lovable of these is used by the smoothie who selfishly attaches himself to a new coed to tide him over the rush season, leaving her with scanty dating prospects. Closely related to him is the type who also goes practically steady with a coed, then shows

The Import Strikes Back

To the Editor:

Saturday night is the most important night at Wells College because dates from Cornell, Colgate and other schools flock to Aurora. Many boys like those who travel 30 miles for blind dates regard Saturday night as the night for conquest. They arrive in uniform with their coat of arms blazing proudly on their chests. The knights from Cornell all intend to bring honor to their houses. The weapons are designed to overwhelm their adversary completely.

To confuse the girl the Cornellian has a complete battery of witty and appropriate comments upon the world situation and his dissatisfaction with it. By impressing a Wells girl with his intelligence he diverts her attention from the main objective. To exhaust her energy the fraternity man usually engages in a series of preliminary skirmishes at the house. Through the use of such tiring dances as a "twist," jitterbug, and lindy, combined with the stupefying effects of whiskey sours, seven and seven, and beer, he launches his frontal attack.

* * *

At the end of the evening after the Wells girl has been safely returned to Aurora, I wonder what the Cornellian thinks, or if he does think? I wonder, what has he really accomplished? What has he really proved?

He lives in an unreal world without any standards. The Cornellian has rejected society's moral rules. He has reverted to a realistic or pragmatic philosophy. He will take whatever means will accomplish his ends. It seems impossible for the average Cornellian to comprehend any but the most base objectives.

A Fighting Freshman
Wells College
—letter, April 4, 1961

Bleeding Heart

To the Editor:

Our hearts bleed borscht for the "Fighting Freshman" from Wells College who sobbed her way into The Sun on Tuesday (April 4). She actually complains of the Cornellian's "battery of witty(?) and appropriate comments upon the world situation" as being part of his ammunition in diverting her attention "from the main objective(?)." Well, we wonder what kind of a fellow she would like to date—someone with no comments to make on any subject perhaps, or maybe a mute.

She has illimitable(?) disdain for his witty conversation, and deplores his "base objectives" too. We suggest that this "Fighting Freshman" curl up with a good book on Saturday nights where she'll be most happy. And as a matter of fact, we doubt whether she'll have any choice.

—Indignant Cornell Coeds
—letter, April 6, 1961

—Wells College

FROM WELLS FARGO TO WELLS COLLEGE: *Wells students study on Macmillan lawn. By 1866, Henry Wells—of Wells Fargo express fame—had decided to found a women's college in his home town of Aurora on Cayuga Lake. His friend Ezra Cornell, who was doing some founding of his own, urged Wells to reconsider. "Instead of building a Female Seminary at Aurora," wrote Cornell to Wells, ". . . build at Ithaca 'The Wells Female Department of the Cornell University,' and thus aid us to engraft female education upon what I trust will become our highest educational institution in America." But Wells replied that women must be educated separately, to allow "American girls to fulfill the duties and take the position that a kind Providence has assigned to the better half of our race in this broad land. . . ." Wells College was officially established in 1868, the same year Cornell opened.*

'Shocked and Amazed'

To the Editor:

We were shocked and amazed at the obvious lack of morality of the "Fighting Freshman" of Wells College (Sun, April 4th). It is apparent from her letter that she is governed by certain preconceived notions concerning the Cornellian's "objective." Certainly if she had taken the trouble to listen to her date, she would have found that he was only trying to stimulate her intellectually. We would theorize that it would have been a mutually more enjoyable evening if she had forgotten the malicious and biased tales circulated by her gullible friends. We sympathize with the Cornellian who had to put up with her base suspicions.

On the other hand, it is unfortunate that the attitude of the "indignant Cornell Coeds" (April 6th) is not typical of the majority of campus women. Indeed it is true that a guy will find a warmer reception at the hands of the "prudish" Wells girls than at "broad-minded" Risley.

It is a sorry situation.

—Annoyed Cornell Men
—letter, April 10, 1961

More From Wells . . .

To the Editor:

You know, some people find it very difficult to tell the difference between a freshman and a senior. I'll go along with this, up to a point—when he or she opens her mouth and begins to expound on some subject or other, particularly when the subject concerns the opposite sex.

Frankly, quite a number of us feel that one Wells freshman over-stepped her bounds. What right has anyone to get up on a moral pedestal and shake her finger at people? The article in The Cornell Sun was an obvious manifestation of immaturity, naïveté, and selfishness. What does this freshman want and how does she have the right to come forth with such broad generalizations concerning human nature? Are the "knights" of Cornell the only ones who employ such "weapons?" Anyone knows that it takes "two to twist." Certainly a bit of reasoning will show that these "tiring dances" and "stupefying drinks" are not mandatory for anyone.

Perhaps the "fighting freshman" doesn't realize that it takes more than just the male to make the evening enjoyable for them both. This girl can quickly be reminded of the fact that it is the girl who sets the pace, and it is she who can squelch or encourage advances as she desires. We hardly expect that this freshman is going to find a moral utopia anywhere she goes. She might even try looking around on her own campus, if she is so inclined toward criticizing the morals of others. We are not advocating free love, but it is our opinion that morals are everyone's own business and that she should have thought just once more before she caused the readers of this article to believe that hers might possibly be a case of sour grapes. Some day she will look back on her endeavor and will kick herself around the block. We also wonder who is laughing harder, Cornell or Wells.

—a group of salty Seniors
—letter, April 11, 1961

up at a houseparty with an import. Imports, we note bitterly, are given sickeningly special consideration over coeds at every opportunity. This is usually to "teach her a lesson."

Still griping, we are especially repelled by the tender lover who carries on an elaborate courtship, with or without a line, then reveals with a sheepish grin after several months that he's really engaged. This leaves us speechless with laughter.

Then there's the lad (often a first date), who after wearing an unmasked leer for half the evening, suggests to his date that they spend the remaining two hours of a cold and windy night on the bleachers of Hoy Field, "to talk." Should the girl display any doubts as to the conversational conduciveness of a snow-covered wooden bench, he becomes mortally wounded and bitterly disillusioned as to the moral simplicity of women.

The third thing that a freshman coed is told by the helpful upperclassmen who are eager to orient her (after she has been warned about the Sophomore Slump and the size her legs will be in two years), is that she has got to "give." Not only does everyone else "give," but if she doesn't, she is doomed to social failure. Plainly we are expected to be sex-machines for the satisfaction of adolescent male libidos. Nobody bothers to mention how such generosity is received by fraternity bull sessions and bulletin boards. "Kiss and tell" may not be a practice exclusive to Cornell men, but it is not the less obnoxious for its popularity.

I'm tired of drying the tears and patting the crew-cuts of men on this campus who are heaped with abuse from coeds. If the social situation is not ideal, let them consider the possibility that it is not all our fault. They can learn to live with the Ratio and like it.

Name Withheld
— letter, April 7, 1950

—Photo by Wesp-Buzzell

—Photo by Via Wynroth

DEATH OF A WORD: *In 1948, when female student leaders met in the Dickson "ballroom" to pose with dolls as Santa's Helpers (top photo), the word "coed," meaning "female student," was used every day by both sexes. By the late 1960s, however, when its implicit subordination of women was increasingly recognized, "coed" became an epithet used to ridicule excessively fashion-conscious and make-up caked women, such as these students photographed before a Willard Straight Hall restroom mirror in 1968. Now the word has died altogether.*

Interlude: The Tribulations of the Student Life

—Cornell University Archives

CORNELLIANS OF THE GILDED AGE: *"The Coed is the Quaint Creature that Students make fun of in the Daytime and take to the Crescent at Night."*

On Sexism in Language

Messrs. Editors: — Why are young ladies of Cornell University called "co-eds"? I think that a term that conveys an idea of inferiority, and, in deference to the ladies, should be speedily abolished.

E.M.

Like a thousand other words in the language, this one is sadly out of place. Co-education is, of course, the education of the sexes together. The fact that, at its establishment, the University admitted only gentlemen and afterwards admitted ladies, gave to the latter the name "co-eds," but the gentlemen of the University may be as properly denominated "co-eds" as the ladies. In its restricted sense, however, contrary to our friend's belief, the word "co-ed" is not used to manifest disrespect.

— letter and reply, January 18, 1881

The Anomaly of the Coed

There are commonly alleged to be two kinds of Women — Ordinary Women and Coeds. This Dire Distinction is principally made in the Effete East. In the Wild West they have become Resigned to the Presence of the Extra-ordinary Women and the Distinction has become Obsolete. Here, however, a Woman is a Woman until she starts to attend a University, and then she is no longer a Woman but a Coed.

The Male Majority find Dreadful Difficulty in establishing in their own Alleged Minds the Social Status which should be rightfully and duly accorded the Extra-ordinary Woman or Coed. Regardless of her Status, however, the Many Males agree that she is Unusually Useful as the Object of Funny Remarks. After all, when there is Nothing Else to smile at, it is Quite Convenient to have a good old Standby to fall back on. The great Wonder is that the Coed likes it, as testified to by the Immoderate Increase in Feminine Enrollment Figures.

The More Perceiving say that the Male Majority renounce their affiliation with the Cute Coed in word only, and that to act as Earnest Escort is a Daring Disgrace only in Round Table Discussions and Inter-lecture Parleys by the Goldwin Smith Columns. Indeed it is a Doubtful Assertion that the Male Majority live up to the Traditions of the Tongue.

Which only goes to prove the worth of a Remark let slip by a Wise Person the other day when he stuck his head around the Corner of Sage and sighed: "The Coed is the Quaint Creature that Students make fun of in the Daytime and take to the Crescent at Night."

—editorial, October 20, 1920

Coeds: Hard Workers...

President Schurman is alarmed. He said so in his last Report while commenting on the work of the new Sage College Examining Physician, Dr. Emily Dunning Barringer. The latter finds the average "coed's" health, such as there is of it, is poor. The former says: "Dr. Barringer also confirms the opinion often expressed by the President, that the women work too hard, sometimes from love of learning or excess of ambition, sometimes also from the necessity which circumstances are supposed to impose. Dr. Barringer's conclusions afford matter for serious reflection, if not indeed for positive alarm."

Now that President Schurman and Dr. Emily Dunning Barringer have proclaimed that the "coeds" are enjoying poor health, we would say that the large majority of us have suspected it for some time and that the cause of it is the fact that the women students are inveterate studiers. Those men who have encountered them in the classroom usually realize this to their own mortification and exasperation. The "coeds" are raising the standard in the academic department above the heads of the men. Already they have captured Phi Beta Kappa *in toto* and only permit mellow-hearted professors and one or two students of the Socrates stamp to join the defunct organization. And three years ago, they almost succeeded in obtaining membership on the *Era* Board. It is, indeed, a matter for "positive alarm."

And therefore, we are really solicitous for the welfare of the poor women students who are ignominiously undermining their future health and happiness (and that of some one else) by their unremitting and riotous application to books. Let them exercise a little. We suggest that a Rules Committee be appointed to make it "unfair" for "coeds" to study more than 20 hours a day.

—editorial, January 16, 1907

...or Harmless?

The times are alive with a renewed interest in the vigor of our nation's educational institutions. Here at Cornell we have a new President. Yale and Williams are likewise inaugurating new leaders. Oberlin, America's pioneer in co-education is celebrating its centenary. Avoiding the obvious opportunity for jesting, let us consider Oberlin's experiment in co-education, an institution which is now accepted with a careless shrug of the shoulders.

Judged intrinsically, co-education is neither good nor bad. It often happens that anxious editors and students complain that co-education is detrimental to any school's prime interest, education itself. It has very often been said that the continual presence of the other sex at a large university detracts from everyone's interest in study. It has been bemoaned that co-education transforms schools into country clubs and fashion shows.

Surely there is a measure of truth in these assertions, but we do not believe that co-education is responsible for any widespread influence on education one way or the other. Rather it appears that when the vitality of the students' pursuits for education is on the wane, then does co-education abet academic failure. But it is never a cause of deep perversion of intellectual activity.

If we would search out the cause for the fluctuation of interest in studies, we should have to look past the coeds.

We do not profess to know why large universities undergo sporadic periods of "collegiatism" and genuine intellectual concern. That the coeds are not to be blamed for any large motion one way or another we are certain. If it were suddenly decided that Cornell's coeds should leave our campus immediately there probably would be no difference in the attitude of the men toward their academic pursuits. Perhaps there would be a slight change in the manner of some students' dress. But that is merely external adornment; internally most students, and particularly Cornell men, would be indifferent. Coeds are harmless.

—editorial, October 9, 1937

—Photo by Marion Ilsa Wesp

'CHERRY PINK AND APPLE BLOSSOM WHITE': *Before visitation rules gradually melted away during the 1960s, men were permitted to visit the downstairs living rooms of the women's dormitories on North Campus at certain hours on certain days, but were always forbidden to enter women's personal rooms. Here, a couple makes the best of the situation in 1955 at a piano in Dickson Hall.*

A Sickening Pride

To the Editor:

Now that Miss "Name Withheld" has rid herself of her bitterness and has "blown off steam," I would like to comment on several points expounded in her letter.

The incidents that she resents could have and have happened to many other young women, regardless of whether or not they are Cornell coeds and victims of the Ratio. I cannot see how the examples that she places forth of Cornellians taking advantage of the "fairer" sex can be restricted to the situation on this campus, and why she sees fit to apply them only to that situation. She has no right to make generalizations based on a few insignificant things which have happened to her.

It is her opinion that men unjustifiably complain of the dating situation. She claims that 30 percent of the frosh coeds, including cute and popular girls, spend all their weekends in solitude in Clara Dickson Hall. Is not their loneliness largely the result of their own doing? Many coeds, if asked out less than a week in advance, refuse dates, though they have no previous engagement. They do not want the men to consider them leftovers or girls who can be asked out at the "last minute." They are afraid of ruining their social reputations. Are the males to be blamed for this foolish pride on the part of the coeds? If so many women are available, where are they when one desperately tries to get a date at least two weeks in advance? To add insult to injury, the negative replies are so perfume-scented, that the coeds' attempts to keep the men on the string are obviously sickening.

Many is the man whom she feels should be sorry for the way he has treated his female companion on a date, though in nearly nine out of ten cases I am quite certain that the coed engaged wholeheartedly in the endeavor that the male should now be ashamed of. What she considers that the male mercilessly

—Photo by Marion Ilsa Wesp

'SHAKE, RATTLE AND ROLL': *A man picks up his date in August 1955 at an entrance to Dickson Hall. At the moment this photograph was taken, the Number One record in America was "Rock Around the Clock" by Bill Haley and the Comets—the first unmistakable rock 'n' roll single to top the charts. The changing values of the "rock generation" of the 1960s would lead to the total elimination of mandatory dormitory curfews in 1969.*

—Photo by Via Wynroth

'DAYDREAM BELIEVER': *An abstracted "athletic supporter" manning a table in the empty lobby of Willard Straight Hall gazes at the plastic legs of a mannequin standing on a "pedestal" behind a chain barrier.*

demands from the coed is merely what society today considers to be a part of the natural sexual instinct. Are not necking and kissing outlets for the inhibited sexual desires of mature, unmarried males and females?

I suggest that Miss "Name Withheld" read the Kinsey report on the American male and the one which is now in the stages of being written on the American female.

Name Withheld
—letter, April 10, 1950

Not to Be Confused . . .

BY GEORGE HANO '51

In a genuine effort to clarify a clouded situation which is rapidly gaining widespread attention, we hereby offer authentic definitions of terms which are vital to any proper understanding of that situation.

The definitions are based upon informal studies and polls. Any similarities between persons either living or dead is purely co-incidental.

Dog—flesh eating domesticated animal related in some manner to wolf, jackal and fox. Sometimes confused with the Latin word "doll," as in the sentence—She is a real doll, d-o-g, doll.

Pig—A swine; especially a young swine. From the French word *donner*—meaning to give. Not to be confused with the old English—prude. Synonym—beast.

Ratio—Proportion; especially as between male and female. Found in its most exciting form at a school in upper New York State.

Import (verb)—to bring (goods) from another country into one's own country in commerce. Generally arising from highly competitive conditions. Thus the free trade theory is in some way involved.

Import (noun)—good or goods imported. Not to be confused with the Greek word "coed." Commonly used as a curse word among women.

Give—(verb)—to deliver; to furnish or provide; sometimes to grant or permit. Common around Christmas time or in the spring. From the biblical phrase—"'Tis more blessed to give than to receive." Not to be confused.

Libidos—a psychological term from the Freudian school. See a psych major.

Prudes—Those who affect excessive modesty in speech and behavior. Commonly confused with the word prune, a variety of dried plum. A species gradually disappearing from the American scene. From the Latin word *prudibus*, meaning unhealthy.

Hoy Field—scene of many and varied athletic events. Better known for its exceedingly damp and cold benches. Until recently a badly neglected spot on the Cornell campus. From the Latin phrase *hoi-polloi*. Not to be confused with Sunset Park. The word was saved from extinction by action of the Board of Trustees.

—berry patch, April 10, 1950

Bravo, Miss Name Withheld!

To the Editor:

To you, Miss Name Withheld, fellow friend-in-the-fight, a hearty "Bravo." As a Graduate Student in Engineering I really have had very little time during the last four years to go out with girls; and so, for me this alarming ratio question is far from a problem. But as far as its anthropological and sociological implications are concerned, this subject has occupied my interest to some degree.

I think it is just terrible—no, that is not a strong enough word —I think it is perfectly abominable, scandalous that such behavior be perpetrated. I am sure there are a lot of nice boys on campus—in fact I have been able to locate several. I find it too bad that these fellows must alter their personalities when girls are around, and act like boors. Sex seems to have become the password of college "society." Without it you just simply aren't anybody. After all, its purpose is to keep alive the race, and should not be a short-cut to Damnation.

And so I welcome you as "one of Us." It is an entirely misleading concept that life is all "give" and "take." That is a communist viewpoint, and we must jealously guard against all inroads in that direction.

So go forth unto the world. Carry the torch—and like Diogenes seek an Honest Man. Be a Splendid Woman—and as for Hoy Field, if you think that's cold, wait till you've tried the Crescent.

Name Withheld
—letter, April 10, 1950

Girl of My Dreams

BY BOB BEYERS '52

I think that I shall never see
A coed lovely as dear thee;

A coed that looks at men all day
And lifts the telephone to pray;

A coed that may in summer claim
A list of sweethearts to her name;

A coed who is really keen—
Something more than a machine;

A coed who will never yield
Despite the benches on Hoy Field;

A coed who will always live
Without being asked to "give."

Poems are made by hacks like me,
But only God can make someone like thee,
Dear Name Withheld.

—berry patch, April 11, 1950

—Photo by C. Hadley Smith

AT THE CROSSROADS: *A student phones a friend from between two corridors of the newly opened Mary Donlon Hall women's dormitory in 1962. This was the year senior women won freedom from dorm curfews and the in loco parentis walls began tumbling down.*

Imports Get Better Mileage

To the Editor:

Despite my exclusion from the "better fifth of the student body," I would like to offer a few comments.

First, I'm sure Cornell coeds are not the ugliest women in the world. Although there is no proof, I can truthfully say, of all the males I know, only a small group (not even half) consider them the ugliest in the world. I can suspect the reason for the "far and wide reputation" of Cornell coeds as "dogs and pigs," but regardless of the reason, these words are decided misnomers. I personally think there are very many coeds who look just like girls.

The statement that a larger number of popular coeds stay home over the weekends seems self-contradictory; however, if there are any coeds languishing in the dorms on Saturday nights, they must be the "cute" ones, for it is painfully obvious that the "ugly 30 percent" are not in their dorms. The blame for this unfortunate situation (dateless coeds) is clearly due to men who aren't capable of planning their social life more than four weeks in advance.

Secondly, the "low, vile dating tricks" so vehemently condemned appear to result from a fellow failing to marry a coed after he has dated her a few times. Surprisingly, there are some fellows who like to decide for themselves whom they'd like to date and when. And, callous creatures that they are, they hardly ever cry when they "calmly stop dating" a coed.

It is abundantly clear that the male's preferential sexual selection of imports for house parties stems from the fact that imports are not only more appreciative and more deserving, but their lack of shallow sophistication is refreshing. Some males have heard enough "fabulous" stories about "fabulous" professors in "fabulous" classes along with shrill, monkey-like chatter about "Japes," "the Quad," "Beeb," "Cayug," "G-S," "the Libe," and a hundred other crummy, phony abbreviations.

Thirdly, I would like to remark on a subject termed "giving," which apparently means acting like a sex-machine. Actually the word "offering" should be substituted for "giving" in the interest of strict accuracy and honesty. Women should not object to being called baby-machines, for this is a term of endearment, like Fido or Pal.

In conclusion, I'm sure there'll be hundreds of fellows lost without anyone to dry their tears and pat their crew-cuts now that Miss Name Withheld has resigned her job. May I respectfully suggest, Miss Name Withheld, that the next time a fellow "calmly stops dating" you, you write Doris Blake. She's ever so understanding.

Larry Heptig
—letter, April 11, 1950

For Companionship

To the Editor:

Throughout this campus from one end of the year to the next there is always talk of some kind concerning dating and social life on campus. Often such talk consists of complaints, about the Ratio, the coeds, the fraternity boys, the beer-parties, or the dark vastness of Hoy Field. Sometimes the talk turns to spoofing and joking in an attempt to make the social situation appear ridiculous or over-rated. No matter what form the talk takes it still indicates the importance which Cornellians and, indeed, all Americans attach to dating and its concomitants.

One of the complaints recently voiced on the campus is that there is little to do on a date except go to a beer-party or a movie. The further objection was raised that only a few people enjoy beer-parties, the remainder of the drinkers being present because they can find no better entertainment. One of the possible causes for this attitude is that the speaker (who is apparently a fraternity boy) entered his fraternity quite soon after arriving at Cornell and thus never had a chance to become acquainted with the more varied non-fraternity activities here. Another possible cause is that he has had a rather narrow range of interests and is not attracted by the possibilities of the music room of the Straight, the many dances sponsored by the Straight and other campus clubs, or any other events such as basketball games or theatre productions.

Complaints that coeds are ugly, or not pretty, or are beasts are also heard. The cause for this is that too many boys here and about the country expect to find movie actress glamour in a large percentage of women. They refuse to accept the fact that starlets populate Hollywood and not the Cornell campus. Thus, after looking for dream glamour women, in their disappointment they call the coeds beasts.

Another complaint is that the coeds have a shallow type of sophistication and are addicted to a trite, over-worked slang. The percentage of sophisticates is unknown; however, there are undoubtedly a few, if not a sizable number, of coeds who do not act pseudo-sophisticated. Those boys who complain about slang and such probably have not looked far, or carefully enough to find the coeds without these traits. It is perhaps possible that some coeds talk slang and act sophisticated because they think it appeals to the boys. Certainly most girls are not going to waste their time acting blasé and sultry, or chattering coyly merely for the benefit of their Dickson or Risley hallmates. Thus, the fault may lie partially with the boy. If he treats his date, not as his equal, but as a mental babe, what right has he to expect anything save murmurs about "fabulous professors," "Japes," and the "Libe."

As for over-all reasons for the general discontent, perhaps the trouble comes from looking upon dates solely as a method of removing, temporarily, the pent-up sexual urges of the preceding week. If as much thought were devoted to having a good time through companionship and being together at interesting events, social and otherwise, as is devoted to finding the quickest way into a dark, semi-private place, then perhaps there would be more people on the Hill who were satisfied with their social life.

Name Withheld
—letter, April 25, 1950

Hang It Up, Men!

To the Editor:
'Twas the eve of a prelim
And in our snug dorm
We were tucked in our beds
All comfy and warm.

My roommate and I,
Our books put away,
Expected to sleep,
Until the next day.

At the ungodly hour
Of midnight plus ten,
The telephone rang once,
And then rang again.

From my top double decker,
I sprang to the floor,
Breaking three ribs,
And an ankle or more.

The voice on the phone
Asked if Sandy were there
And said that he'd seen me—
I wouldn't know where.

"Just wanted to chat
For an hour or so"
His name was fictitious.
His buddies I'd know.

He asked for a date
Between giggle and groan.
I growled, "Go to hell"
And slammed down the phone.

But alas for the torture
I went through that night!
Wond'ring is he a dreamboat
Or is he a fright.

I beg you, dear men,
I'm weary and worn.
If you find yourself bored
The wee hours of the morn,

DON'T MAKE THAT PHONE CALL!
Think, for my sake,
How unpleasant it is
To be jarred wide-awake.

And not even one of you,
Dreamboat or creep,
Is half as important
To me, as my sleep.

S.R.
—letter, December 19, 1949

—Sun Photos by Ruth Muschel and Robert W. Bollenbach

DREAMBOATS OR CREEPS? *One bygone hindrance to women's sleep was the Panty Raid, an annual spring ritual until the early 1970s, when the distinction between the men's dorms of West Campus and the women's dorms of North Campus was at last abolished, and individual buildings became coëducational. Above left, Donlon women—one of whom is about to drop a pair of panties—cluster around a window during a raid of March 1969. Above right, the freshmen raiders strain wildly for underwear floating earthward. Bottom, frenzied men, who had been gazing peacefully at the aurora borealis from the West Campus "dust bowl" before the cry of "Panty Raid!" was heard, vie for possession of an undergarment.*

—Sun Photo by Robert W. Bollenbach

Interlude: The Tribulations of the Student Life

The opening of the North Campus dormitories in 1969 temporarily alleviated Cornell's housing shortage. However, it was a difficult life for many of the first North Campus residents. Bathrooms were incomplete, there was not sufficient electricity, and during the second winter of use, the heating system broke down entirely, prompting some studies purporting to show that North Campus denizens had more of a sex life than other dormitory residents, as they had to do *something* to keep warm. The situation grew so desperate that the University was obliged to move some students into the as yet-unfinished High Rise dormitories. With all the confusion that ensued, it was difficult for the new high-rises to be used properly; but eventually this difficulty was overcome, as we shall see.

Strippers in the Night

BY JOHN SCHROEDER '74

The ghost of Rose La Rose is haunting the halls of North Campus, luring scores of excited undergraduates to witness a new dorm phenomenon: the Late Evening Strip Tease.

On any weekday night about eleven o'clock, the stillness before Dorm 5 is shattered by the shrill cries and whoops of an impresario.

"Everybody out," he screams to the surrounding dorms. "It's showtime!"

Books are shut and the crowd pours out. They come from all directions. They trek from University Halls.

Within 15 minutes the courtyards and balconies of North Campus are jammed with between 300 and 500 whistling, stomping, shouting spectators, staring *en masse* at an obscure curtained window in the high-rise edifice.

Behind this window, at precisely eleven o'clock, a high-intensity stroboscopic light begins pulsating rhythmically to the beat of David Rose and "The Stripper," revealing the shadowy forms of numerous feminine and quasi-feminine dancers in the process of disrobing.

In the well-honored strip tease tradition, the gray phantoms wriggle and bend, stretch and titillate, as articles of clothing slip from sight or drift out the window.

"More skin!" they clamor below. "Take it off!"

An underclassman beams. "That's a real girl!" he enthuses. "Oh, I can't believe it. That girl is fantastic!"

A passerby scowls. "It's exploitation of women," she grumbles. A companion adds that "those guys are really sick."

Amid the confusion, two bottles smash to the pavement from nearby dorms, and the Safety Division arrives. "Someone called and said there was a little demonstration going on," explains Sgt. E.J. Smith.

Investigation has revealed that the mastermind behind the nightly mayhem is a group known as the "North Campus High Risers," a group of theatrical neophytes directed by Fred A. Levine '73 and Mark L. Wurzel '73, with choreographical assistance from Jessica L. Bram '74.

Most of the strippers are male and female volunteers, attracted by the mystery of a vanishing art form. One of these is Nancy.

"Not many people have the nerve to strip," she observes, "but it's good for the ego, especially when they can tell it's a girl."

"We belong to the public now!" exclaims Ken, another of the exhibitionists. "They don't want it to end—they were going wild over us!"

The daily stripping event had its origins about two weeks ago when the impresarios began playing renditions of "The Stripper" every night. "Then we started choreographing," says Wurzel, a member of the 1971-72 University Senate executive committee.

"People don't have any fun any more at Cornell," explains Levine. He said he hopes the High Risers' act will help to resurrect some of the frolicsome spirit of the vanished goldfish-swallowing days.

"We're just trying to get people together," he adds. "It's like a communal feeling."

"Dorm stripping is an institution already," concludes Susan M. Sussman '76, as the last pair of perfumed panties wafts softly to the earth. "It's part of North Campus."

—*news story, September 20, 1972*

—Sun Photo by Elizabeth Olmsted

THE SCENE BEFORE THE STRIP: *Laura, a volunteer stripper of the "North Campus High Risers," perfects her form prior to a well-received performance before 500 cheering students on September 18, 1972.*

The Show Closes

BY JOHN SCHROEDER '74

The Dean of Students Office has finally responded to the North Campus stripping phenomenon, and the message is "No more shows."

The message was delivered to Mark L. Wurzel '73, a representative of the loosely knit "North Campus High Risers" stripping organization, during an impromptu 45-minute conference conducted at 1 a.m. yesterday morning in the apartment of Larry Feheley law '73, the head resident of Dorm 5.

Over 1,500 boisterous students attended the final stripping performance at 11 p.m. last night.

Present at the conference were Wurzel; Feheley; Robert Johnson, residential area coordinator of North Campus; and James L. Palcic, assistant dean of students, director of North Campus.

"They expressed their concern about the goings-on," said Wurzel. "They saw that the crowds were getting bigger and bigger, and if they got any bigger there might be a security problem."

"It's true that things do happen in crowds," admitted Jessica L. Bram '74, choreographical assistant to the strippers. Two bottle-throwing incidents were noted during the performance Monday night, and the Safety Division has been on hand every night since.

"All we're asking is that they stop the show," Johnson explained. "We've had numerous complaints from people claiming they can't study—some made to me, some to the head resident [Feheley], and some to the Dean of Students Office."

The early morning stripping conference produced a compromise agreement between Wurzel and the University emissaries. The officials conceded one final striptease to Wurzel, which took place last night, and in return Wurzel agreed that it would be the last.

The University officials seem adamant.

"If they continued to have the show we'd have to take further

More on Strippers: A Columnist Calls for Revolution

BY JESS WITTENBERG '74

So those crypto- (or maybe not so crypto-) fascists in the Dean of Students Office think they can get away with this one, do they? So they figure the student as nigger can be sent a' sprawlin' into the cotton fields again, do they? So we're supposed to sit back and relax as they alienate all those inalienable rights, huh? Well, we've had enough! Bad weather or not, it's time for we students to fight back.

Sneaks as always, the fat cats met at 1 a.m. yesterday morning to stew up their latest oppressive potation. Probably drinking cocktails and undoubtedly smoking cigars, an impromptu *junta* decided that *they*, not the students, would determine what is suitable entertainment; that *they*, not the students, know what is right and moral and proper and the rest; that *they* and not the hard-working students who pay those creeps' salaries, would **end a legitimate act of expression** by the people!!

That's right: they think they can end the People's Guerrilla Theatre, which has provided such right-on proletarian entertainment to the people of North Campus. And they think they can do it by fiat — the old story of a stroke of a bourgeois pen or a gesture of a chubby hand having vast and cataclysmic repercussions on the lifestyle and freedom of thousands. It may have been that way in the past, in the old days, but we tell you it will be that way no longer! We will strike back, Elmer Meyer! We will strike back, James L. Palcic! We will strike back, Larry Feheley!

How do we plan to free the North Campus Five? How do we plan to bring back those brassy strains of "Love Potion Number Nine" and that other tune, the name of which I've forgotten but the tune of which Noxema and we both recall? How do we plan to achieve justice in the unjust and immoral University power structure?

Simple. We will mount a massive campaign of resistance, of retaliation. **We will hit the University where it hurts!** The decadent anti-ecdysiasts will be stopped by the might of the people.

The People's Anti-Bluenose Resistance League calls upon all committed students to:

—join in a massive Panty Raid on Balch Hall, at 8 p.m. today, to show our solidarity and support for the High Risers. Bring cameras, plenty of rope, beer, and enthusiasm. We must be prepared in the event of an onslaught by the lecherous Safety Division.

—demand that professors either teach in the nude or devote class time to discussions of the historical role of burlesque in the class war. Emphasize that puritanism is the opiate of the masses.

—help us out in our massive leafletting campaign. If you have old copies of "Monsieur" or "Nugget," bring them to our desk in the Straight.

—join in a vigil to bear silent witness against the latest persecution. Meet at 12 noon today outside of the Helen Newman locker room.

The Dean of Students Office must be stopped. A crimson beacon must be set out atop every high-rise, as a warning to oppressed peoples all over the globe. Cornell and its ilk must not be allowed to turn the lights out on our brothers in other nations. We will not be emasculated.

Power to the Voyeur! Free the North Campus Five!

—column, September 21, 1972

A Reader Finds It Degrading

To the Editor:

I am very much saddened by the recent striptease business on campus. All those who hold that the combination of nudity and sexual suggestion ought to be a private and spiritually expressive side of human behavior should share my distress. I can characterize the whole affair in no other terms than degrading to human beings and human sexuality.

Allen Morrison '76
—letter, September 22, 1972

action," Palcic said with an amused smile. "I'd like to keep my options open, but I feel that referral to a judicial administrator would be a possibility."

More pointedly, Johnson stated that "If there's a disturbance tonight I think the people putting on the show should know they are responsible for it."

For one and one-half weeks crowds of up to 500 students have been gathering every weekday night in front of Dorm 5 to witness stripteases conducted behind the curtains of an internally lit second-floor window.

But it appears unlikely that the "High Risers" will ever strip again.

"We've got to consider our original purpose," said Fred A. Levine '73, one of the leaders of the group, "you know, fun, some kind of party.... It won't be fun for us anymore if we have to start bucking Day Hall."

"That's the way things work around here," sighed Bram resignedly. "You find a good thing, and somebody finds a reason for you to stop it."

In the biggest night the North Campus Living Complex had ever known, over 1,500 chanting, hollering, horn-blowing students packed the courtyard in front of North Campus Dorm 5 to witness the final performance of the "North Campus High Risers" stripping exhibition.

"Go, go, go!" bellowed the crowd, in fond remembrance of bygone high school pep rallies. Flashbulbs flickered in the blackness and tin cans pounded out an expectant beat.

And over the home-assembled public address system of room 5264, the announcement came: "On behalf of the North Campus High Risers, we'd like to welcome you to our show. We hope you will like what we have to offer as this will be our very last performance."

—Sun Photo by Kirk A. Shinsky

LET ME ENTERTAIN YOU: *Over 1,500 students gathered "one more time" to watch the final presentation of the North Campus strippers. The Dean of Students Office, citing potential security problems, ordered a halt to the shows, but permitted the "High Risers" to stage a farewell performance. Louie's lunch truck positioned itself amid the crowd to dispense hamburgers and soft drinks.*

A loud disapproving roar issued from the multitude.

The light came on and the strippers appeared: Ken, Jim, Nancy, and Laura, swaying and contorting their bodies to the pounding of David Rose and the dissonance of Offenbach.

"Give them a side view!" they coaxed in the shadowy room above, "Kick! Kick! Throw them a kiss!"

As balloons cascaded from Dorm 5, the highlight of the evening was reached, as seven pantless men displayed their rear extremities to the cheering crowd below. "Dorm 6 salutes Dorm 5," proclaimed their banner.

"That's all, folks," blared the loudspeaker, and the crowd melted away.

The show was over.

—news story, September 21, 1972

Interlude: The Tribulations of the Student Life

'Gathering Wild Fruits'

While breezing through a few old constitutions the other evening in sad preoccupation over a term paper, we were surprised and pleased to come upon the Constitution of Bavaria. We had just finished reading involved clauses under the USSR Constitution, all of which seemed to begin with: "The Supreme Soviet of the Union of Soviet Socialist Republics, in order to maintain the struggle of all working classes against...." We would read on through the tremendous collections of titles, and sweeping statements of the glory of the masses, gathering momentum as we went—only to go down for the third time as we bypassed magnificent verbiage in search of one humble verb.

We turned then, in confusion and frustration, to the Bavarian Constitution, Article 143, and we read it in stunned delight: "All citizens can enjoy the beauties of nature and rest in the freedom of nature, walking in the meadows, sailing on the streams, and gathering the wild fruits of the forest as permitted by local customs."

Nobody ordains this right. Nobody is forced to participate in it because of racial, political, or sexual equality. It is merely granted, in all its stark simplicity—something like an anonymous birthday present that was just what you wanted. We promptly went all funny inside, and wired the State Department about visas.

Our fore-fathers, we are told, fled Europe to escape from persecution and oppression. We think it is time to repay the visit. Whatever may be going on in the rest of Europe, persecution and oppression surely can't happen in Bavaria, once her constitution comes into operation. Anyway, we can't think of a moment when we'd rather be oppressed than while we are gathering-the-wild-fruits-of-the-forest-as-permitted-by-local-custom.

—berry patch, January 15, 1948

—Cornell University Archives

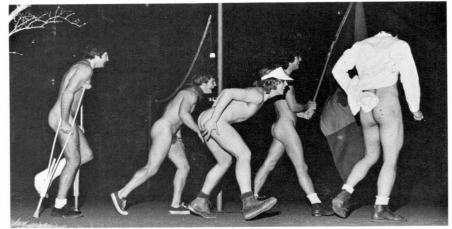

—Sun Photo by Bill Howard

SPIRITS IN THE NIGHT: *Neither crutches nor crippling cold deter these 1974 West Campus streakers. The short-lived streaking fad had arrived at Cornell a week earlier, when thirty men raced about campus in the altogether. A mass streak-in was then scheduled for March 13, but 23-degree weather discouraged all but the hardiest from disrobing. Left: this unusual photo is filed in a University archives picture folder laconically labeled "Uris Library, Exterior Views."*

—Sun Photo by Liza Jones

A PUFF... AND A MAGIC DRAGON: *An exhaling, 48-legged Green Dragon pokes its horned head out of Goldwin Smith Hall while celebrating the architecture college's one hundredth anniversary in 1971. The beast has appeared annually since architecture student Willard Straight '01 dreamed up the dragon as one colorful way to vent undergraduate frustrations.*

—Photo by Kenneth Gruskin

'WE WANT A WEEK!': *After an especially gloomy fall of incessant rain and an abnormal influx of calls to the mental health clinic, West Campus erupted with spontaneous glee on November 14, 1977. Over 500 freshmen demanding that Thanksgiving vacation be extended to a full week marched across campus, gathered on and around the Andrew White statue to chant (above) and—somehow or other—broke into Day Hall for a brief and good-natured 1:30 a.m. "occupation" of the building.*

A CENTURY AT CORNELL

Problem #3: Where to Live

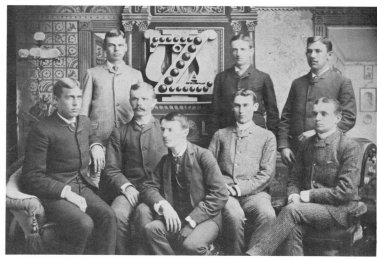

—Cornell University Archives

FIRST ON THE HILL: *These students established Cornell's Zeta Psi chapter in 1868, the year the University opened. Though Zeta Psi was first, the local chapters of Chi Phi and Kappa Alpha also date from 1868.*

—Scrapbook of James Irving Clark '12

GIBSON GIRLS? *Members of Delta Chi, then located at 503 Buffalo Street, enjoy a house party with their dates in 1912. The requisite chaperone sits staidly in the center of the group.*

Innocent and unsophisticated, hundreds of freshmen come to college intent on winning a letter, a few keys, and enjoying the opportunities and bearing the encumbrances of a fraternity. By the time you read this a score or more of the most prominent, best dressed, and neatest appearing kings of the Greek Letter world will have pleaded and beseeched you to favor them with your company and most august presence.

Be neither overjoyed nor flattered! The upperclassmen are just rushing you, and if you are lucky, wealthy, a good athlete, and a prep school hero, you will be asked to wed into the most complicated social life in the University. For the next ten days your time will be jammed with lunches, dinners, movies, golf, tennis, and motor car rides and, worst of all, long confidential sessions in a rear room learning of the great advantages and the hoary traditions of the "leading Cornell fraternity." Don't be misled! Each and every

fraternity has an axe to grind. For the time being you are the prize, and though a fraternity wants you now, in two weeks you will be all but forgotten.

Rushing at Cornell is a hectic experience for all concerned. Sooner or later you may wear a pledge button, but don't make the fatal mistake of jumping at the first little lapel decoration that is thrust upon you. Take your time, regardless of

FRATERNITY...

the entreaties of the men who desire you to decide in a hurry. A mistake at this particular point of your college career may ruin your four years at Cornell. It is best to wait until you have found the group of men with whom you think you will be most congenial and who will offer the best opportunities for being of service

to Cornell. You are the prize, and if a fraternity wants you, it will keep after you.

Many of you will experience all types of rushing. Avoid the mud-slinging species that knocks and decries another group. The mud may fall around your ears, too.

You will become intoxicated by the temporary presence of luxury in its best and worst forms. Rushing banquets soon

turn into hash and pork chops. Limousines give way to flivvers. And the finery soon becomes drab on second inspection.

Do not forget that it is you who are making the decision and you who are going to live the next four years with it, so Stop, Look, and Listen.

—*editorial, September 26, 1927*

—Sun File Photos

'AND WE'LL HAVE DRINKS...' *Crew-cut fraternity brothers crowd the Zinck's bar on Aurora Street. Founded in the 1880s by the kindly but proper German saloon keeper Theodore Zinck, the establishment was a favorite watering hole for members of the fraternity culture until it closed its doors in Spring 1967.*

—Cornellian

RETURN OF THE NATIVE: *Members of Cornell's social élite whoop it up at their house. Believe it or not, this photograph is only one generation old.*

Interlude: The Tribulations of the Student Life

Guess What's Substandard

A traditional debate among independent men at Cornell is whether living conditions are worse in off-campus apartments or in Cornell dormitories, particularly the notorious University Halls. In 1966, the administration seemed to come out for the former when it announced that henceforth all off-campus apartments would have to be inspected before Cornell would allow students to live in them.

The Sun was very opposed to this policy, which did not last long; and in the process of researching the following editorial, the editor found a rather compelling reason in his support.

Amid the campaign paraphernalia that adorns the campus this week, a terse letter from the Director of Housing and Dining is to be found. It tells the story of Cornell's solicitude for the living quarters of all students and announces what most knew before: that the University has adopted an Approved Housing Code and that under pain of suspension or complete banishment, all had better shape up to its standard.

While we do not question the University's good offices, certain features of the Code ought to be re-examined—and quick—before their full rigor takes effect. According to the University's Student Residence Standards and Regulations (1966 edition): "For student rooms, there must be...at least one shower or tub...and one water closet for every eight persons or less."

Given the serious nature of the ruling it is quite a scandal that University Halls do not meet this requirement. The following statistics have been uncovered. There are 1,286 student and counselor beds in University Halls and only 130 showers, yielding a ratio of 9.89 persons per shower. Without further comment, let it be noted that to bring U.H. up to Cornell standards, 30.75 showers must be added if students can be permitted to reside therein next September.

The matter of water closet sufficiency is even more grave. It is debatable whether a urinal is a water closet. Webster's Dictionary does not give much help. But as well meaning students, we must give Cornell the benefit of the doubt in this area. Otherwise, some 53.25 water closets will have to be added. The facts are: 106 toilets, 111 urinals, 12.1 persons per toilet; 11.6 people share a urinal, and 5.93 per urinal or toilet.

The Regulations tell us further that "A student who continues to reside in unapproved premises shall be called before the Proctor for consultation." And if a student persists in his obstinacy, the appropriate judicial committee "may direct the registrar to deny the student permission to re-register."

As things now stand 1,286 students ought to consult the Proctor about the showers and toilets in their dormitories. (After all, Proctor George, what is your definition of a toilet?) Or, more in the spirit of the times, an appropriate sit-in or rent-strike might produce some concrete results. While 1965 may be remembered for the housing shortage, 1966 may yet be remembered as the year of the toilet crisis. And if the University's own residence standards are not enforced in Cornell's own dormitories, what will the situation be like in off-campus dwellings?

Perhaps the most inexpensive and therefore most probable way for the University to add the required showers is to build a single, central structure on the mud flats in the middle of the University Halls complex. In keeping with the rest of the area, this structure would be inefficient, inconvenient, and of course, unapproved.

—*editorial, March 10, 1966*

—Cornellian

...DORM...

FROM GOTHIC GRANDEUR TO BLAND BOXES: *The model below shows how West Campus was originally intended to appear, according to a development plan of 1925. The Baker dorms (upper corner) and Lyon and McFaddin halls (along model's top edge) were actually built. But enormous pressure to expand caused Cornell to abandon English Collegiate Gothic magnificence and construct the cheap, boxlike, brick-and-cinderblock University Halls instead. They are seen above, under construction during the winter of 1953-54.*

A Movable Lease

BY ROB SIMON '76

Then came the bad weather and it would rain and the rain would cover the cobbled streets and carry leaves down the gutter and the trees would strain with the weight of the rain and I would sit in my flat and watch the rain drip down the window till it would wet my soul and my socks which filled the crack in the window. I would pick up *le Journal Ithaca* and circle the ads for flats to rent. It would be wet walking from flat to flat for when it rained everything was wet, but I didn't mind the rain and looking for apartments then because I was in love and young and poor and a writer.

The first ad was for a three room flat on Avenue College, an avenue both evil and tragic, evil for its dark steamy cafes full of drunken young women and men with loose blouses and shirts, playing out their sad lives and where the toilets, full of urine, stank and made it difficult to walk, and tragic because I could not get in these crowded cafes. The flat was over a liquor store and as I walked in, the lady who owned the store recognized me and gave me a broad smile which made me happy and I promised myself to put her in a story. I walked up the uneven stairs and thought that perhaps these were the stairs that Nabokov or Pynchon or Fariña

our conversation.

"You came for the apartment?" she said.

"The flat, yes," I said.

I looked around and the three rooms advertised were a hall, a foyer, and a larger foyer with a bed in it. The water closet and kitchen were in the next hall and shared, she told me, and at once I decided this flat was not for me as a writer. It was too clean. She asked me if I would like a drink and smiled with her head tilted to one side and I realized what this drink was mixed with, so I said something in French and she gave me a funny look so I let her walk me to the door which I then opened and stepped through, but I was sad. I had disappointed her. So I walked sadly down the steps and picked up my finished story and put it in an envelope and outside, I mailed it to my publisher so that in four weeks when I would be running out of money and eating only cheese and bread and wine, I would receive a check in the mail so I could buy some fancy cheese and bread and wine or maybe use the money for a vacation skiing in

–Cornell University Archives

ROOMING HOUSES ON HUESTIS STREET–NOW COLLEGE AVENUE–ABOUT 1880.

of this," she said and we both left.

This flat was below a laundromat on Rue St. Eddy, a street of singular charm and ugliness, punctuated with garbage cans and parking meters and ended with a fine ivied arch. The landlord, an unfriendly and unshaven man with an apron, showed me into the flat which had a bedroom, kitchen, and water closet and all slanting ten degrees off the horizontal. The table was nailed to the floor and the landlord told me the only problem with the flat was when Sally upstairs washed her 12 blue jeans and washing machine B overflowed, but there was plastic in the closet to catch the drippings, and the flat was renting for $150 a month plus utilities. That was over 600 francs a month so I excused myself and walked up to le Deli to think about this unfair man and have a cheese cake and rum St. James to cheer me up and I got the cheese cake and another funny look in place of the rum St. James. I decided to try one more flat.

This flat was on le Boulevard Buffalo and the flat was in the attic of an old Gothic house. The landlord led me up the stairs and the stairs creaked with the poverty that makes a great writer and my heart beat faster and my pencil weighed heavy in my pocket. The door to the flat led to the kitchen which led to the bathroom which led to the bedroom where the light from the gabled window lit all three rooms because they were in a straight line. The floors were bare and the bedroom was naked except for a bed which stood squarely in the middle of the room and the cupboards were clean but I could fix that and the window had a crack in it where I could stuff my socks. Bad apartments make good writers so I signed the lease and I was happy.

. . .OR COLLEGETOWN?

walked and I felt excited and inspired and pulled out a pencil and paper and started to write about Maine and the lady who owned the liquor store below, but as I wrote, the story started to write itself, so I put down the paper and pencil and decided to come back when the story was done. I knocked on the door and a beautiful woman appeared. She bade me enter and I did and I was inside. I can still remember

–Sun Photo by Carin Ashjian

ROOMING HOUSE AT 209 COLLEGE AVENUE, 1980

the mountains with my lover or maybe instead go to a racetrack and spend all the money on one lean horse and order a rum St. James. My spirits lifted and I forgot about the beautiful woman in the flat and I walked up to Café Zeus where I was to meet my lover.

I was late. But she didn't mind because when you are in love, waiting increases your desire like alcohol, but when you are in love with alcohol, waiting for your drink is intolerable and inexcusable. She was sitting in the same corner of the Café where Ezra used to sit and sip sherry. The cafe had a light and brown atmosphere of good food, good liquor, old friends and fine talk, and the high windows let in beams of light which fell on the many small checkered tables and played with the cigarette smoke as it snaked toward the ceiling. I felt comfortable and good when I came in here, like slipping into a warm tub. I sat down next to my lover and ordered two rums St. James but instead got a funny look from the cashier and I turned to my lover and said,

"I thought I'd look at another flat and then meet you and then we could go for a walk and maybe if it rains, take off our shoes and hold hands and when we are numbed and hungry, find some nice cafe to sit in and warm ourselves with wine and cheese and a plate of oysters and maybe a pastrami sandwich and then go home and make love on the floor and it would hurt."

"It was good and right of you to think

That night I met my lover and we walked along le Commons and nodded to other lovers and stopped to dip our feet in the fountain and our feet got wet so we took them out of the fountain and we walked into le Diner Rosebud and I ordered two les especialities de la maison and two rums St. James and the waiter, an old friend, brought us two turkey clubs and two cokes and a funny look instead, but it did not matter because I was young and in love and poor and a writer, and what's more, I finally had a movable lease.

—column, October 6, 1975

S. S. ANDREW D. WHITE

Chapter II: The World in the Eyes of Cornell

Intricate are the steps! Intricate are the mazes of this labyrinth! Intricate are the troubles which the pursuit of this bewitching phantom, KNOWLEDGE, will bring upon thee.

—Sterne, *Tristram Shandy*

We are at last, and lately, coming to recognize that the function of society is to serve the needs of the people who are members thereof, and that an unjust society has within it the seeds of its own destruction.

—James A. Perkins

THE MAINE REMEMBERED: *Cornell members of the First Regiment of U.S. Volunteers pose in full regalia during the Spanish-American War. First row, kneeling or sitting: A.S. Downey '96, Noah Cummings '94, C.M. Smith '91, Major L.L. Seaman '72, Captain I.A. Shaler '84, G.E. Waesche '95, D.H. Dixon '96. Second row: W.M. Purman '94, H.C. Nelson '92, Lieutenant F.R. Slater '94, W.V. Kelley '93, J.R. Rand '98, Lieutenant H.C. DeLano '95, C.J. Heilman '97, C.W. Marsh '94. Back row: Swindells '94, C.G. Rainey '87, R.H. Keays '95, A.B. Rider '98, J. Burns '92, B. Stevens '97, L.H. Ireland '96.*

The Campus Through Five Wars

BY MARIE GOTTSCHALK '80

With the exception of the Spanish-American War and the Korean War, every major war in the past century has forced drastic changes and upheaval on the Cornell campus and in the University's view of the world. Cornell's acquiescence and opposition to war and the military has been a mixture of farce and tragedy.

During the Spanish-American War, students studied and caroused without interruption. When World War I erupted nearly two decades later, the University once again seemed oblivious to the conflict overseas. Describing the average American student in 1916 as "thoroughly

FAR BEYOND CAYUGA'S WATERS: *The University's sweeping World War II mobilization was symbolized on both coasts in 1943 when the S.S. Andrew Dickson White (pictured) and the S.S. Ezra Cornell were simultaneously christened. The White was launched into the Pacific on January 28 from a Sausalito, California shipyard, while the Cornell—sponsored by the wife of one of Ezra's descendants—slid into the Atlantic from South Portland, Maine. Both were "Liberty ships," mass-produced vessels commissioned to transport war matériel and troops.*

hidebound, as provincial, as narrow gauge, as a colorless and uninterested mind can make him," The Sun charged that most students scarcely knew that there was a problem of sorts in Europe. Once the United States declared war on Germany the following year, however, nearly half the University went off to enlist. Students were ambivalent and pessimistic about U.S. intervention in World War II. Following the Japanese attack on Pearl Harbor in 1941, The Sun said, "The question 'Will a better world result even if we win?' is one which we should be foolish to ignore in the moment when we take up our arms." The *Cornell Bulletin*, the weekly wartime replacement for The Sun, was just as ambivalent and somber when the war ended four years later. "The war is over, the Atomic Age has begun..." the *Bulletin* declared ominously in one of its final editorials.

By the late 1960s, many students had become convinced that war would never go away. But they resolved that the current war in Southeast Asia would have to continue without their consent and participation. "So long as Thanksgiving and human nature continue to exist, there will continue to be a contradiction. Only this year the contradiction is more

apparent and more pronounced," The Sun said at the height of U.S. involvement in Vietnam in November 1968. Two years later, when there was no hint that the situation had improved any, the editor declared, quoting a poem by Cornell's Daniel Berrigan, that America had become "hard to find."

"Harder still is reconciling our roles as students, faculty and Ithacans with our roles as people; most difficult will be the peace every one of us must make with the war; and with America's adventures . . ." he concluded.

* * *

In 1898, Cornell did not have difficulty accepting adventures overseas. The University revelled in them. After Congress declared war on Spain in the spring, students rallied to adopt a series of resolutions commending President McKinley. With a chorus of students singing "America" in the background, a leader of the rally declared, "We feel like our forefathers in '61, who from Maine to California rent the air with the mighty shout, "We are coming, Father Abraham, 300,000 strong!" The captain of the football team proudly predicted that the training his men had received in practice would serve them well at the front and anticipated that the team would be back

−Cornell University Archives

THE BLOOD-RED BLOSSOM OF WAR: *The ladies and townsfolk have all turned out to watch the entire Cornell Reserve Officer Corps parade on the arts quad in 1917. This photo was probably taken in the spring, about the time the United States officially entered the war on April 6.*

in time for the fall season.

Despite the patriotic fervor, few Cornellians actually served in the War of 1898, about 150 in all. The Sun took what we would now call an elitist stance. "There are plenty of men lying idle throughout the country, who are willing and anxious" to go to battle, the paper asserted, and only when such types have been depleted "should the students, whom we are convinced are the most patriotic of men, don the blue, go to the front and help uphold humanity's and the country's honor."

The Sun's primary concern at the time was the performance of the Cornell crew. The newspaper finally concluded that

the war would probably not "prevent the men from training conscientiously for the important races next summer."

At the outset of World War I, The Sun mixed its traditional concern about the performance of the athletic teams with a new concern, the fate of Europe. Students returned to campus in Fall 1914 in time to read headlines about the outbreak of war in Europe. The Sun chastised students for their "habitual, self-centered complacency" in the face of a war that promised to be the "most fearful in the history of the world."

As students began signing up in record numbers that October for drill courses in the Cadet Corps, The Sun was cynical

about their motives. The editor suspected that the renewed interest in matters military had nothing to do with the possibility that the U.S. would enter the European conflict. Paraphrasing Jonathan Swift, he said, "Down deep in its heart, the world loves war." He doubted that the surge in the drill enrollment was due to any sincere political commitments, but thought it was instead a symptom of "martial fever, the most contagious disease ever omitted from the curriculum of a medical college." A reader had high praise for these remarks. In a letter to the editor, he commended "the word of our genial 'Sun,' who leans back in his office chair, at peace with the gods and men, and assures us that human nature tends in quite another way."

While The Sun took a cautious position on the European conflict ("It has never been within the field of The Sun to discuss national issues from a partisan viewpoint," explained an editor) Cornellians took an inattentive one. The newspaper presented itself as advocating neither pacifism nor militarism. Instead, it encouraged students to get a thorough grasp of world affairs. The Sun pushed for increasing the number of lectures on international events and encouraged support for the Belgian Relief Fund.

As U.S. entry into the war became more likely, student interest increased and The Sun gradually shifted from its position of informed neutrality. Following the German sinking of the *Lusitania* in May 1915, a group of students circulated petitions declaring that "the events, such as the sinking of the *Lusitania*, have no legal or moral significance in the national or international situation." The Sun condemned these petitions, saying they "aggravate the situation," and

−Photo by John P. Troy

SHOCKS OF RIFLES: *Cornell student cadets, laden with canteens and field gear, pitch bivouac tents on the arts quad in April 1916. After completion of the exercise the entire southern half of the quadrangle was filled with neat rows of tents, rifle stacks and saluting soldiers. Crowds gathered to watch the drill from beside their cars.*

A CENTURY AT CORNELL

defended President Wilson as a man of "high ideals" who was trying to maintain neutrality amid bursts of jingoism. The newspaper also attacked the "peace at any price pacifists," who showed up at Cadet Corps drills and created confusion by mocking the officers' orders. The newspaper began extolling the virtues of military preparedness and admitted that "physical force must for some years remain uppermost in practical world politics."

Days before Wilson sent his war message to Congress in April 1917, the editor of The Sun exclaimed, "How calmly we go to war!" and once again charged students with having no ideas of their own on the "present day vital issues." He said the appearance of calm on the campus was "a mask for ignorance."

Four days before Congress declared war on Germany, more than 300 Cornellians enlisted at recruiting stations on campus. The Athletic Council cancelled all intercollegiate contests in case of war and the faculty agreed to grant special academic privileges to those entering the armed forces.

The declaration of war came while Cornellians were on their spring break, and even though President Schurman urged students to "return promptly to the University and studiously pursue their work," over 650 did not do so. By the close of that semester, 45 percent of the male undergraduates had joined various branches of the military. The Sun advocated military service and categorized this war as "largely one of quiet, unselfish, unrecognized devotion to duty."

−U.S. School of Military Aeronautics

THE HUN HALTED: *World War I biplanes used by the United States School of Military Aeronautics fill Barton Hall shortly after the armistice of 1918. A lone guard stands at attention.*

Each World War had far more of an impact on Cornell's history than did the Spanish-American conflict. The insulation characteristic of 1898 was no longer possible. The World War required overwhelming quantities of manpower and drew heavily from Cornell. Thousands of Cornellians went overseas, and hundreds never returned. Nearly 9,000 Cornellians donned uniforms in the First World War, over half of those in active service. Two percent of all the commissioned officers in the military were Cornell alumni. Students "witnessed a greater change in Cornell than any two terms since the founding of the University," The Sun declared months after the United States entered the war. In September 1917, only 3,800 students returned to the campus, compared to over 5,200 the year before. For the first time in Cornell's history, women outnumbered men on campus. Cornell helped to keep itself afloat by turning much of the University into a military training center for future officers.

Cornell went to war in 1917 with most of its students and faculty excited and united by the belief that the promise of an Allied victory was worth the cost in men and anxiety. During the warfare, few questioned the correctness of U.S.

As Another War Looms, Some Thoughts on the First One

Just 18 years ago today, guns that had been belching death and destruction for four long years were silenced. The whole world went wild with joy at the prospect of a war-torn existence finally at an end. In every town and city in the country people went hysterical, business was at a standstill, women cried in the streets for joy, men shouted themselves hoarse to give vent to their feelings.

And after the momentary excitement had died down, nations and statesmen promised each other that never again would such an inhuman episode as the World War take place. Plans were immediately under way for a League of Nations, pacts of peace and disarmament were made by the dozens, the watch cry of the decade, yes even of the century, seemed to be peace at any price. There was not a statesman in the whole of Europe who dared to say that war would ever again descend on the peoples of the world. Even Germany was crying for everlasting peace. War was outlawed forever.

And now, just 18 years after millions of men sacrificed their lives to show the futility of war, and millions more were permanently crippled to drive home the point to all those who saw them daily, the world seems once more on its way to a bigger and better deal of death. What 18 years ago was going to be a century of disarmed countries now appears to be one of constant expenditures for preparations to kill fellow-beings.

It seems a bit hypocritical to stop for one minute during one day out of the whole year to respect those millions who lost their lives in the last war and then turn around to go back to manufacturing better flame throwers, bigger bombers, heavier battleships, and more rapid-firing machine guns.

We were supposed to make the world safe for democracy. It seems that all we did was fertilize fields for dictators with the blood of 10 million men. It doesn't take people long to forget the terrors of former days. No amount of looking at row upon row of white crosses or pictures of men suffering can change their minds. They won't be content until they repeat the whole fiasco, until they

see their brothers and loved ones come home without arms or legs.

This may be all very well for the nations of Europe to do. But let us pray that the blaring of bands, the sound of marching feet, and the roar of airplanes, will not allow the people of the United States to lose their reason once more. It may seem less courageous, but it is a whole lot saner. For the sake of one or two violations of rights, we entered the last war and sacrificed hundreds of thousands of our youth. What it did for us was make the world safe for democracy. It was certainly worth it.

Let us hope that after this short period of less than two decades, the American public has not forgotten what it means to enter another war, what it means to see its men slaughtered for an intangible right. It is far better to permit a humiliation of our fair name than to throw away unwarranted the lives of our citizens. A little less vanity and a little more common sense is all we need to keep us from another bloody chaos. Better a living dog than a dead lion.

—*editorial, November 11, 1936*

The Meaning of Pearl Harbor: Two Later Views

This day marks the end of a decade, a decade so cluttered with violence, emotion, and eruptive transition that one cannot hope to understand its years in more than a limited sense.

It began on a Sunday in December, 1941, when swarms of Japanese aircraft droned in over Pearl Harbor, raining death and destruction on a shocked, surprised garrison of servicemen, civilians, and natives. The stage was set for an empty decade, one in which men would war against men for year after year, conclude their warring in hope of a permanent peace, and begin another war before the last one could be declared officially at an end.

This decade ends today—nowhere. It ends in the midst of major conflict, a conflict whose full meaning is known to no one, including the purveyors of communism. It may be the first step in another chain of world struggles; it may be the signal for armed neutrality.

Hope, that magic, frightening word, still springs eternal from the hearts of men, but those men number not as strong as once they did.

We, as a generation, have known little but violence and impending disaster in our time. The prospect for permanent peace dims considerably when we view the good intentions down the drain in the past ten years.

The "infamous" Sunday shibboleth that is raised again today impresses us with the confusion and heartbreak of the road since 1941. Positive purpose is hard to create for the ten years to come, but whether we want to face them or not, the ten years will still be there.

The dawn of civilization has been obscure before, on many occasions, and each time, man has found his way into the light.

We cling to history, and to God.

—editorial, December 7, 1951

—Cornell University Archives

THE WORLD WAR II S.S. CORNELL VICTORY

Yesterday was the 28th anniversary of the Japanese sneak attack on Pearl Harbor that propelled the United States into the Second World War, armed to the teeth with moral outrage against the sneaking Japanese imperialists and the sadistic German Fascists.

In those respects, it was a black-and-white war. We knew what we were fighting for and that it was valuable. We knew what we were fighting against and that it was hateful. The American soldier was, at the least, a decent Willie or Joe, and he could even be John Wayne. The enemy soldier was, at the least, a dupe, and could be a vicious criminal.

Now that we are engaged in another war, it would serve us to remember what we once fought for and how we once felt about our battle. It would appear that wars were easier then, but it would also appear that they were just.

—editorial, December 8, 1969

---

policies, which was a good thing, for those who opposed the war effort at other colleges found they were not tolerated; free speech was at its all-time low in this country.

* * *

Almost 18 years to the day after the United States entered World War I, Cornell joined 16 other colleges in the first of a series of student strikes for peace. Weeks before the first strike Adolf Hitler had announced Germany's rearmament and withdrawal from the League of Nations. Over 2,500 students attended the first demonstration for peace, held in Bailey Hall in April 1935. Speakers at the rally attacked the "appalling ignorance of international issues among the faculty as well as the students," and called upon the University to abolish Cornell's ROTC program. In an editorial urging students to attend the rally, The Sun argued that the "peculiar American susceptibility to idealistic motives" had made "every one of our foreign wars possible." *The Ithaca Journal* commended those attending the rally, but was jaded about their sincerity. Ithaca's other daily warned that "those of us who lived through the hysteria of the World War" must admit that "once the war fever crept upon us, many of those very students would be rushing to the colors, and Cornell professors would be making three minute speeches." The

Journal predicted that the young men would fight, once again "convinced the country was in danger or her honor besmirched."

The Journal was partially correct. Attendance at the spring peace rallies dwindled as U.S. entry into the war became more likely. 1,200 attended the rally in Spring 1937, while only 800 showed up a year later. "While some 1,000 apathetic capitalists crowded the Willard Straight bar yesterday, about 800 students went to Bailey Hall to see what they could do to prevent the next war," D.W. Kops commented in a Sun editorial the day after the 1938 rally.

Kops, like many students, apparently did not have any illusions about peace. After Britain, France and Italy agreed at Munich in September 1938 to give Germany the Sudetenland, Kops was skeptical about the sudden "sharp rise" in the "peace stock" which took place after the four powers reached agreement. "Armageddon has been postponed for a while," he remarked.

"A while" turned out to be less than a year. Britain and France declared war on Germany three weeks before classes started in Fall 1939. In the first issue of The Sun that year, the latest war news, not the traditional banner headline of welcome to the new freshmen, was at the top of Page One. FRENCH TROOPS PUSH ATTACK ON SAAR FRONT; BEGIN

OFFENSIVE TO HALT NAZI THRUST IN WEST greeted students.

As Nazi troops marched through Belgium and the Netherlands the following spring, the "American resolve" to stay away from the war was "dying to a mere whisper," according to J.C. Jaqua '40 of The Sun. "Where are the resolves of yesterday?" he asked that May. "Where is the triumphant and comfortable majority that only last year pointed out the folly of our last European venture?"

Blind patriotism did not rush in to replace pacifism, which had fallen out of vogue by this time. Few hurried off to enlist. Most just waited, wondering when the U.S. would enter the battle, and how soon after that they would be required to follow the flag to the battlefield. When the first students registered for the draft in the fall of 1940, as required by the new draft law, The Sun said, "When our children look back on this occasion, they will do so with greater assurance than those of us who register today..." A week before the Japanese bombed Pearl Harbor, The Sun described the American people as "amazingly calm in the present crisis in our relations with Japan."

The waiting period, in many ways, did not cease even after Pearl Harbor. President Day advised students not to enlist hastily, and most students heeded his call to stay "at their jobs" until more definitive news about what to do came from Washington. Day called war "by its very nature a direct nullification of the basic purposes of higher education." A week after the Pearl Harbor raid, The Sun said "the hostilities have been received rather quietly and without the intense feeling characteristic of 1917."

Many tried to sustain a sense of humor amid the prevailing atmosphere of apprehension and pessimism. The students waited for the government's first draft call. After the student government voted to eliminate the Ice Carnival and to reduce Junior Week to two days, Moe Feil heralded the moves in his column in The Sun. Now there was "no need for freezing or getting tired of your date," he pointed out. Anticipating Ithaca's first test blackout, Sy Deitelzweig predicted it would be an "entertaining affair," adding, "What intrigues us most is the thought of all lights being turned out in the library as hundreds of Cornellians are busily cramming for finals."

The pressure of war did not prevent The Sun's Kurt Vonnegut from instituting a new fad during finals week that term. Vonnegut attended final exams given in courses he was not registered in. He waited until the "*bona fide* brow-mopping students had quieted down,

and then with a roar of disgust he strode down the aisle, tearing exam and exam blank to shreds—shreds which were thrown into the befuddled instructor's face." Word got around about Vonnegut's prank, and in one course seven students ripped up their exams. It became so "commonplace that instructors who did not have it happen to them felt that something vital was lacking."

Interspersed between the joking and the attempts to be roseate, The Sun produced some of its most articulate and impassioned Cassandras. There was no ritualistically upbeat editorial for the first seniors to graduate after the bombing of Pearl Harbor. "Inevitably our thoughts turn now and again to death. Two years ago seniors little considered the subject. Today seniors who don't are incapable of profound thought on any subject," the editor wrote.

The anxiety and dread had not lessened by Christmas vacation in 1942. Anticipating the second term, the editor of The Sun said, "Some of us will return and hit the books as hard as ever. Some will throw up their hands and fill a chaise lounge or empty a bottle until called. Some will not return at all."

The dreaded call to arms came in March 1943, right before what imme-

diately became known as the "last civilian binge"—Easter vacation. On March 23, Cornell's Enlisted Reserve Corps was finally called into service, with all recruits required to report for active duty within two weeks. Days before the call came, S. Miller Harris commended the college student "who stuck by his books until he was given a gun to stick by. That is as it is, and that is as it should be. The act of killing is important today; the act of living, every day." After the call to service came in, The Sun anticipated the impact. "Our attitudes, our habits, our thoughts will become hardened. It will not be easy to return to the liberal studies, to the intangible after we have seen the gross material aspects of life which military service and total war bring about."

The military call-up that thrust the role of soldier on most men also forced the role of leader on women. Women who "hitherto had been subjugated in higher education," The Sun predicted, "would provide the connecting link between liberal education of today and the higher pursuits of the post-war world." The newspaper could not understand the "obvious apathy of the co-ed to take the responsibility for which she had so long and so often cried."

—Cornell University Archives

PROPAGANDA PICTURE OF PROPAGANDA POSTERS: *Two Cornellians pretend to "paint" patriotic broadsheets in this World War II publicity photo. The picture may never have been used, however, since a note scribbled on the back reads: "Not Approved. Obviously faked. Posters not made this way."*

As the World Goes to Hell

BY EDWARD D. EDDY '44

There can be little doubt about the conjecture that student morale on the Cornell campus at the present time is at a new low. Each day brings forward a batch of disillusioned Cornell men who say, "What the hell!" and promptly go forth into the Army. Each day brings forward more evidence of the mental and moral confusion of thousands of students. It is so very easy now, without the slightest conscientious hesitation, to drink quarts of milk punch on a Sunday morning, to interrupt concentration frequently for nonsense and horse-play, to spend many valuable hours during the week preparing for a few hours of week-end fun.

The whole problem seems to revolve about the question: Where are we going? The whole world may be going to hell, and the confusion that faces us now is whether to worry about the details of that voyage or to plot the course in another direction, or just to climb aboard and enjoy the trip.

We have heard recently of a young wife, two months married, who received a letter from her Selective Service husband now in Ireland. He hoped she would understand when he told her that, for once in his life, he was really and completely happy. He had a goal ahead, but one goal. He knew his job. He could forget now about the petty details of life—about crabbing because his train was late, or his feet were wet, or his soup was cold. He knew where he was going. He was happy.

Perhaps this is the answer for us. Perhaps military life with a definite goal is best. Certainly we are not happy without some future—whether it means dying in a bomber over Tokyo or working 18 hours a day in order to ship another bullet to a dying bombardier over Tokyo. It would seem now as though anything with some sense of security and direction in it is the thing.

Perhaps in today's world there can be no spiritual security. But there is direction, that kind of direction that came to the soldier in Ireland. It is high time we find our bearings, chart our course and start forth in the right direction. Maybe we can yet overtake the s.s. World on its way to hell before it sinks into a whirlpool of complete chaos.

—*column, October 23, 1942*

About this time, The Sun appointed its first female news editor and combined its women's and men's news boards into one. Ironically, Guinevere Gloria Griest '44 became The Sun's first female editor-in-chief days before The Sun temporarily folded in Fall 1943, the victim of dearths of money, newsprint, and personnel. Griest was named editor-in-chief of the *Cornell Bulletin*, the weekly wartime replacement for The Sun put out by the University.

The *Bulletin* continued the assault on women who refused to claim their opportunity. It charged that "while their sweethearts were being mowed down by...enemy machine guns, Cornell's women felt no compunctions about whiling away their spare time gossiping about next Saturday's dances."

World War II accelerated the maturation of those who were of college (and thus, fighting) age in the 1940s. As Germany's collapse appeared imminent in May 1945, the *Bulletin* officially repudiated the guiding slogan of World War I,

something the campus had been doing indirectly over the previous decade. "All of us have learned that there is no such thing as a war to end wars. We know that there must be a peace to end wars."

* * *

In the 1940s, it was the blood spilled overseas which disrupted the campus at home and which matured University students. During the 1960s it was the blood that was spilled at home which brought upheaval to the universities. In the 1960s, students attempted to use protests and violence at home to promote peace abroad. Unlike those in preceding wars, the peace movements did not dissipate as the United States became more committed to the war.

At first, students were prepared to dismiss Vietnam as a "nasty and bloody, but minor wound" and a "Punch-and-Judy" scale war. The first demonstration against the war in Ithaca, in February 1965, drew 59 protesters and 20 members of the campus and city police. After the march, the local chapter of the Veterans

of Foreign Wars appointed a panel to investigate the "subversive students" who "abused tax money by protesting against U.S. policies while receiving government loans for their education at the same time."

Students protesting against the war soon began to number in the hundreds, and shortly thereafter in the thousands. The Sun, like many of the students, no longer feigned neutrality. In May 1970 its editors, along with the editors of nearly a dozen other campus newspapers, helped coordinate and promote the student strike that closed hundreds of universities across the country. After President Nixon's announcement of the U.S. invasion of Cambodia, The Sun suggested war crimes trials.

The Sun's position on Vietnam became very black-and-white. After President Johnson announced in March 1968 that he would not be a candidate for renomination, it commented editorially, "'Thank God' is an understatement." The day after Nixon was reëlected in 1972 over peace candidate George McGovern, the newspaper ran a black editorial page.

The opposition to the war was so complete that even President Corson got in the act in 1969. Speaking at an arts quad rally on the occasion of the national "moratorium" against the war, which cancelled classes for a day at Cornell, Corson announced his opposition to the war, the first time he had done so in public.

Corson may have had a special aversion to wars. A physicist by training, he worked on the Manhattan project, which developed the first atomic bomb. He said, "The war's impact on our colleges and universities threatens to impair their effectiveness for years to come. The war demoralizes our students, polarizes our professors, and diverts from higher education the financial support which only the federal government can provide."

Corson scraped and bowed in the general direction of institutional neutrality by saying that those views were his own, not Cornell's and adding "The University is not an espouser of causes because it is a place where faculty and students must be free to pursue, advocate and criticize different versions of the truth." But few paid any attention to this.

After nearly a decade of protests yielded a suspect peace agreement in 1973, The Sun put the campus role of wars and peace movements in proper perspective: "...we must never forget...there are few of us who could not have done more in attempting to end this war, and we must be ashamed of what we did not do if we are to recognize all we can do, both for our country and for each other, in the future."

MARIE GOTTSCHALK '80, Sun senior editor 1979-80, plans a career in government.

Of Guernica and Vietnam

On April 26, 1937, 29 years ago today, German planes flew over the Basque town of Guernica dropping incendiary bombs and high explosives. 1,654 men, women, and children were killed and 889 others were wounded out of a population of 7,000.

We do not mention this just to drag up old history. Instead we hope that this will serve as a reminder that the practice of bombing civilian populations is a relatively new one, less than 30 years old. It was during the Spanish civil war that the fascists and their German allies introduced this method of modern warfare. The bombing of Guernica was soon followed by air strikes at Madrid and other strongholds of the Loyalists.

Most of the world cried out at the slaughter of the people of Guernica. Such bombings were considered highly inhuman and Picasso's painting caught much of the outrage that was shared by most civilized people. But they soon got used to such bombings. Nazi bombings of London were followed by the saturation bombings of German and Japanese cities by the Allies, culminating in the mass slaughter of the people of Dresden. Soon after that the idea of the annihilation of whole cities and countries by the use of nuclear weapons was meekly accepted.

We mention Guernica as a reminder that we have become cold-hearted with regard to "the necessities of war." Today the United States is carrying on extensive bombings of civilian populations in South Viet Nam. This is accepted, along with the ruining of crops in Viet Cong-controlled areas, as the necessities of war.

Bombing civilian areas has never won any war. Military experts tell us that Hitler's worst mistake was the

bombing of London. It drew off his strength from where it should have been focused and it strengthened the will of the British people. The bombings of Dresden did not aid the Allied victory over the Nazis. Arguments will go on forever as to whether the bombing of Hiroshima was necessary to end the war quickly, but certainly America would have won the war anyway. The bombing of Nagasaki in retrospect also seems needless. In a conventional war, the arguments for the "necessity" of such methods are highly dubious.

Friendly populations have never been the victims of bombings. Thus, French cities under German control were not subjected to repeated bombings, whereas German cities like Hamburg and Dresden were. Guernica was a stronghold of antifascist opinion. Perhaps the bombings of peasant villages in the sections of South Viet Nam controlled by the Viet Cong show us what kind of war our government is waging.

We are fooling ourselves if we think that the Vietnamese respond to American bombings of their villages in a different manner from the way the British responded in World War II. It is ridiculous to think that a Vietnamese peasant will be kindly disposed towards America after he has seen his village and perhaps his family destroyed by American bombs. They are, after all, people like the rest of us.

Perhaps remembering the original horror and revulsion that was felt in 1937 after the bombing of Guernica will remind us that the bombing of civilians is a hideous and immoral practice of eliminating helpless and innocent people whose only crime is living in a war zone.

—editorial, April 26, 1966

A CENTURY AT CORNELL

Confessions of a Jaywalker

The huge antiwar rallies in Washington, D.C. during early May, 1971 attracted more than a thousand Cornell students—and thousands of riot-equipped police, National Guard, Army and Marine squads. Worried about possible violence, and also about a radical threat to sit down in the middle of Washington's busiest streets and so paralyze the city's traffic, the chief of police instructed his men to arrest potential trouble-makers on any pretext. This resulted in more than 10,000 arrests, many of them apparently unprovoked, and lengthy court proceedings later.

One of those arrested was the outgoing editor-in-chief of The Sun, who certainly *looked* like a troublemaker. The police no doubt found this arrest meaningless; but the editor, a frustrated English major, found it not only meaningful, but a metaphor for his existence.

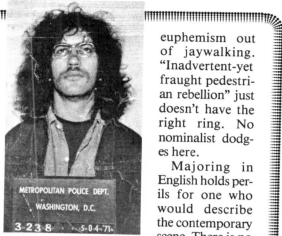

– Washington, D.C.
Police Department Photo

By Howard A. Rodman '71

On my sixteenth birthday, on a visit to Los Angeles, I crossed Wilshire Boulevard against the light. I was arrested and appeared in court later that week. The judge let me off with a lecture on account of my age, and because I had come from New York, where people don't know that laws are to be obeyed.

I have kept my record clean since then. On May 4, though, I found myself at Washington's DuPont Circle, taking notes on a hardhat talking to a demonstrator. A policeman told me to move on. I crossed the street to a traffic island. I was told to move on once more. I took three steps across the street, where the walk and don't-walk lights were flashing simultaneously. Then I felt a hand on my elbow escorting me across the street. "You're under arrest," said the policeman to whom the hand pertained.

"Sir, with what am I charged?" I asked in my best yes-sir-sir-officer-sir voice. "Jaywalking," he replied. I had become a two-time loser.

As he took me to the police buses I fingered the chain around my neck. The chain held my new laminated press-pass, my amulet, my get-out-of-jail-free card, my mark of objectivity, my reportorial rosary. "Officer," I recited from the memorized litany, "I am a member of the working press who has been mistakenly arrested. I firmly but politely request that you get in touch with Paul Fuqua, head of the Police Information Unit, 626-2871, and with Mr. Eastman, Mayor Washington's press officer, 626-6000 or 629-5151 if the demonstrations are severe. They will require my immediate release. I am to make sure you understand that this is not to be counted as my customary one phone call." The officer looked at me. "Oh," he said. I was frisked, up against the wall of the bus, just like in *Dragnet*. The policeman actually said, "up against the wall." It was the day's one great moment. Then we posed for a Polaroid snapshot. This was attached to my arrest form, on which I requested that my status as working-press be noted. It wasn't. To them I was just another jaywalker.

Now jaywalking is one of those crimes that somehow don't make it. "Cross at the green and not in between." To be arrested for it is ignominious. Jean Genet would scoff and George Jackson would probably laugh his head off. It's even lamer than disorderly conduct, which can mean anything. Arlo Guthrie's littering is a capital crime by comparison. It's the Marv Throneberry of illegal activities.

And so the dilemma with which I was faced assumed three-fold proportions as I entered the converted-schoolbus Black Maria. Should I continue to assert my exempt status as working press, and thus be open to charges of elitism and non-solidarity with my fellow jaywalkers? Should I shut up and go to jail for a crime I did not really commit, burning objective reportorial detachment on the altar of jaywalkers' liberation? And how could I face the hardened criminals I was bound to meet in jail with the mark of the wimp on my arrest form?

The crisis's canon assumed dimensions of a great theological debate. It finally boiled down to how many jaywalkers can dance on the floor of a one-man cell. An objective determination was possible in this instance: fifteen, counting the two standing on the toilet. While I had silently pondered the implications of my act I had been escorted from the bus and thrown in the slammer.

*   *   *

Consider an *acte gratuite,* a gesture performed just for the hell of it. Consider an existential act by which one finds oneself in an assertion of personal good faith against the meaninglessness of it all. Consider a Sartrean project, an attempt to make one's will felt in the least alienated fashion possible in the realm of the *practico-inerte.* And then consider my arrest, which could not be horned into any of the above philosophical shoes. I had not even the grace of good style. I had plodded my way through my first jailing with the élan of a Nixon gesture. We both are prone to the abortively overdetermined. The President, however, can get away with it via *post facto* redefinition of intention—cf. Laos and Cambodia. But there was no way my arrest and incarceration could be made a victory for anything. One cannot pull a "protective reaction" and make a semantic

euphemism out of jaywalking. "Inadvertent-yet fraught pedestrian rebellion" just doesn't have the right ring. No nominalist dodges here.

Majoring in English holds perils for one who would describe the contemporary scene. There is no jail that can compare to Genet's, no bureaucracy that can vie with William Burroughs', no logic that can beat Joseph Heller's. And so I won't tell you what it was like in jail because it palls before any exciting and meaningful representation. The cops were neither excessively brutal nor particularly nice. The processing was no more absurd than almost any processing in America today. My civil liberties were denied, but no more than anyone else's. My fellow prisoners consisted of English majors, clergymen. Even Howard Zinn was there, busted for asking an officer why he was beating a kid. The one genuine *lumpen-figure* was a 16-year-old kid who shouted "pig" at the cops and who claimed to be an anarchist. He was a bore and an asshole.

At one point I was called to a phone. A man from Fuqua's office wanted to know if I would "forget everything" if he were to get me released. I pondered the ethics of collaboration vs. expediency. By the time I capitulated it was too late, and the guy retracted the offer. He said a man from his office would meet me in court. He didn't.

*   *   *

Well. I finally got out of jail at 11:30 that night, after 15 hours of incarceration. The jaywalking was changed to "blocking a public thoroughfare" at the arraignment, but that's still too lame. I want to be able to light wooden matches with my thumbnail, mumble like Marlon Brando, have a jail record like Tom Hayden's, be as degenerate as Dorian Grey. I would also like to get a Ph.D. in English, be regarded as scholarly, say things like James Reston. But like a major portion of my generation, I am a jaywalker. We go to demonstrations to write about them. We get busted but not badly. We work for the revolution with one eye on the cut of our Adidases. We are jaywalkers without the minimal dignity of knowing that jaywalking is the best metaphor for our Condition. We cross streets against the light except when alone. It could be worse but even that might be better. If the jaywalkers of the world were to unite we would probably hate each other's guts. And yet we are there, with a wink and a limpid skip, thinking about thumbing our noses as we depart the curb in the middle of the block.

—column, May 7, 1971

In Which Cornell Attends a Nazi Festival

As World War II approached, The Sun's editorial stance was consistently isolationist, albeit with a strong anti-Nazi tinge. In those days, it was unusual for The Sun to criticize the Cornell administration directly, but it did so in strong terms in March, 1936, when the German press announced that for a forthcoming celebration of the 550th anniversary of Heidelberg University, prominent universities from around the world, including Cornell, were sending delegations. In an editorial entitled "R.S.V.P." The Sun asked President Livingston Farrand why he saw fit to accept the Hitler-inspired invitation, when Oxford, Cambridge and other great universities had refused to attend to protest the lack of academic freedom under the Nazis. The same day, The Sun received a telegram from one of Cornell's most famous and popular alumni, the prize-winning author of *The Story of Mankind*, and followed it with a rare front-page editorial.

To the Editorial Director:

I get my information from the daily papers and therefore I may be slightly misinformed, but if it is true that Cornell University intends to dispatch a representative to the Heidelberg celebrations then I sacrifice a couple of hard-earned dollars telegraphing you my loudest squeak of disapprobration, disapproval, and for the rest see Roget 932. The Germans, being free, white and twenty-one, at least within their own lights, are of course entitled to any form of government that happens to please their Teutonic fancy and it is none of our business to what lengths they may go in offending the decent opinion of the rest of mankind. But it seems incredible that Hitler's bright boys would care to be associated with the representatives of a university founded by the eminently broadminded Quaker, Ezra Cornell, and afterwards made into the very champion of tolerance by Andrew D. White and George Lincoln Burr. Indeed any representative that Cornell University might send to this Heidelbergian jamboree would be just so much dirt, for dirt, if I remember my definitions correctly, is "matter out of place" wherefore we might call such a representation "direct with a vengeance." This was not written by order of the Elders of Zion, but because as a 100 percent Aryan and now almost one of the oldest graduates of Cornell University and therefore perhaps a little more conscious of our origin and hence our sacred obligations, than most other Cornellians could be, I feel that such a step as that of sending a Cornell delegate to a German celebration in the year of grace 1936 would be a direct and insufferable insult to the memory of the man who founded us and to those who succeeded in turning a random farm somewhere in a forlorn part of upper New York state into one of the few academic communities that not only have preached but that actually have practiced the eminently intelligent ideal of tolerance.

Hendrik Willem van Loon '05
— telegram, March 3, 1936

The Sun Calls for Reconsideration

Mr. van Loon's telegram protesting Cornell's acceptance of the Heidelberg invitation is the voice not of one man but of all those great scientists, professional men, educators and men of practical affairs who refuse to believe that Cornell has abandoned those standards of liberalism, tolerance, and freedom which made her one of the foremost universities of the world.

No one will deny that Nazi Germany has suppressed every word and every doctrine contrary to its own National Socialist ideology. It has subjected its whole educational system to the rule of its government. It has expelled its most brilliant scholars and professors. It has restricted intellectual research to a narrow field. In effect, the educational institutions have become the instrument of the Nazi state for the promulgation of its own doctrines.

THE SUN unqualifiedly favored American participation in the Olympic Games at Berlin. These Games are purely international in character, and they are directed by an international committee for the promotion of sport. Now we oppose Cornell's participation in the Heidelberg festival because it is preëminently a cele-

bration by the fascist government for its own edification. Heidelberg has lost every characteristic and feature that once distinguished it as a prominent university. How can Cornell send representatives to such a celebration, when the very men who have carried on the traditions of Heidelberg and the very spirit which once permeated that university will no longer be present? Cornell will join not with the true scholars and students of Germany if its representatives go there in June, but rather with the representatives of the National Socialist government who have perverted the spirit of Education into their own creed of power, war, and blood.

Arturo Toscanini has just refused the greatest honor that has ever been accorded to a conductor, an invitation to conduct at the Bayreuth Festival, an honor which has been granted to only one other foreign musician, himself. This greatest of modern musicians was motivated by no desire to repudiate the immortal Richard Wagner because he was a German, nor because he felt that the Wagnerian operas had suddenly acquired the taint of Nazism, but simply because he felt he could not morally accept the hospitality and honor of a nation that shamefully repudiated so many of his fellow musicians and cast them out of Germany because they refused to ascribe to Nazi beliefs.

Oxford and Cambridge have already refused to attend the Heidelberg festival. We can not believe that President Farrand has said his last word on this matter. It is unbelievable that Cornell, steeped in the great liberal traditions of Ezra Cornell, Andrew D. White, and countless others should partake in the ceremonies of a university where students are permitted to study only those theories consistent with National Socialism, where professors are allowed to teach only that which conforms with those doctrines, and where those who disagree or dissent are expelled from their homeland. We can only hope that President Farrand, the Chairman of the Committee for the Aid of Displaced German Scholars, will seriously re-consider his acceptance of the invitation in the light of Cornell's past and present history as a champion for liberalism in education.

—front page editorial, March 3, 1936

Dr. Farrand's Silence

The President is silent. Dr. Farrand has declined to comment on the criticisms of THE SUN and alumni of Cornell's acceptance of the Heidelberg invitation. Harvard University, so long a defender of liberal principles of education and one of the Nazis' most bitter critics, has accepted the German invitation. Thus it is probable that the issue as far as Cornell is concerned is finished, though not forgotten, as numerous letters from anxious alumni will attest.

Coincident with Cornell's gesture is the news of a new outbreak of Jewish persecution in Germany. The peace of the last few months in Germany, enforced that visitors to the Winter Olympics might not be offended, has been broken. Sadistic Julius Streicher announces in his *Frankische Tages Zeitung* that "Whoever thought National Socialism's enlightenment campaign had gone to sleep cruelly deceived himself. It was only a short pause which must come from time to time. This is over and a new wave begins."

Can President Farrand and Harvard reconcile their undoubted contempt for cruelty of this sort with acceptance of the Nazi-issued invitation to come to Heidelberg? Their strongest argument is that long after Hitler falls from power, Heidelberg will go on as it has in the past as a center of culture and learning. Can this argument, true though it is, justify an action that cannot help but create the impression of endorsing the present regime? We must remember that it is not the voice of the Heidelberg of yore but the voice of the Nazi government speaking through this invitation. With "Nordic" arrogance the German government will regard the acceptance of Cornell and Harvard as tacit approval of its present system of education.

It seems inevitable now that Cornell's acceptance will stand. There is only the faintest hope that a retraction will be made. Perhaps the solution would be reached if the German government withdrew the invitations to America, even as it did to England, because "the academic character of Heidelberg University's invitation to its 550th anniversary celebration has, to our regret, been publicly confused by a number of" Cornellians.

Certain it is that a great many Cornellians are militantly opposed to Cornell's action, and not only Cornellians but believers throughout the world in the liberal ideas upon which our University is founded. But the President is silent. The issue is closed.

—editorial, March 4, 1936

We Cannot Afford to Accept

Dear Sir:

I have to thank one of your editors for his courtesy in sending

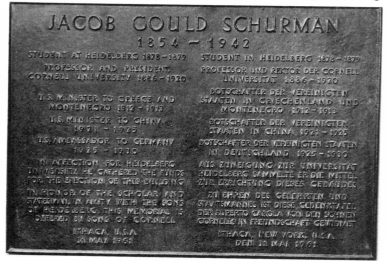

—Cornell University Archives

VON DEN SÖHNEN CORNELLS: *From 1925 to 1930 Jacob Gould Schurman, Cornell's third president, was U.S. ambassador to Germany. In fond remembrance of a year he studied at Heidelberg University in 1878, Ambassador Schurman solicited funds for the building of a classroom building on Germany's oldest campus. An original plaque in this Schurman Hall was sawed in half during the Nazi years because it mentioned the names of Jews who responded to Schurman's fundraising drive. On June 1, 1961 the replacement plaque pictured above was unveiled during ceremonies attended by Cornell's sixth president, Deane Malott.*

me a copy of the *Cornell Alumni News* which devoted considerable space to the Heidelberg affair. Its news comment ends with the words: "No further word has come from the President's-Office." Under the circumstances, I fear that I must once more impose upon your kindness and ask you: "Has the debate been definitely closed?" and does the Presidential Office, by its silence, indicate that this matter is too much for the *beschränkte Unterthanen-Verstand* of Cornell's former graduates?

Once having obtained a definite answer to that question, I shall consider it my duty to continue the discussion, even if it cannot be done on the official premises.

I am sorry to write in so bitter a fashion. But that happens to be exactly the way I feel. I disagree, and I disagree with all the 285 pounds of disagreement at my present disposal, with the statement of President Farrand that "an exchange of courtesies between two institutions of learning does not involve an expression of judgment as to the present political regime in Germany."

If I accept a man's invitation to his home, that acceptance tacitly implies that I approve of him as a fellow-citizen, for otherwise (in case I consider him utterly unworthy of my attention) I plead a headache or I suddenly discover that my spare shirt has failed to come back from the laundry or something. For I know that if I am seen in his parlor, the neighbors will say, "Oh look! There is van Loon! He must like that fellow or he would not be drinking his beer and eating his pretzels."

I repeat what I have said before. A University pledged to the ideals of Ezra Cornell cannot afford to accept an invitation from a University which by its treatment of a great number of its most distinguished scholars has given concrete evidence of having complete contempt for aforementioned Cornellian ideals.

I repeat what I have said before: Cornell should not send representatives to the Heidelberg celebration.

I have no personal axes to grind. I am a noble, upstanding 100 percent Aryan without even a drop of Slavic blood and my name is my own and has never been changed for the sake of patriotic convenience. What I liked best about that name (until this present and most regrettable incident) was the fact that I could identify it with something considerably more important than my own little ambitions or such worldy vanities as are the share of all us poor mortals, and that I could do so by the very simple expedient of signing myself

Hendrik Willem van Loon, Cornell '05.
—letter, March 21, 1936

A Sun Editor Recalls the Heidelberg Affair

The amusing part of the story of the editorials was the sequel. My passionate words aroused no response from the University at first, but several cocktail invitations from the German Department so that I could hear the argument "it's not as bad over there as the Press pretends" and "after all, you don't make an omelette without breaking a few eggs." I was taking a German course or two, and if memory serves me a veiled threat about my marks in one case followed my failure to accept some pro-Hitler sentiments. I believe this happened, but at my age memory is faulty and maybe I just dreamed it to dramatize a bit. I don't think so.

Suddenly I got a message to report one morning to President Farrand's office. I had never met him, but knew his reputation for urbanity. I was determined not to be won over by any persuasive powers. When I entered his office he was indeed courtly. He said that he had been reading my editorials in The Sun and wanted a word with me. I replied brashly that I hoped in view of what had been written and said by a number of students, faculty and alumni the University might withdraw its acceptance.

No, said Dr. Farrand, we will not. We had a full discussion of the matter among the Trustees. We are agreed that it is purely an academic matter, and that we must pay tribute to Heidelberg's five and one half centuries as a seat of learning. Indeed we at Cornell have special reason to thank Heidelberg for its help to us after our founding and its influence on our intellectual growth. We have very strong ties to Heidelberg.

No, said he again, we will not now change our minds... but in view of your interest I thought it would be proper to tell

you among the first the name of the alumnus we have chosen to represent us at the Heidelberg Jubilium this summer. Can you guess who it might be?

No, Sir, said I. I haven't the slightest idea. I can only hope that it is someone who will show no sympathy for National Socialist ideas.

Cornell's representative, said Dr. Farrand, will be your father. I received a letter of acceptance from him this morning. He apparently has no idea how you stand in the matter.

A postscript to this story is that my father (Class of '00, who had done a bit of graduate work at Heidelberg after his Cornell law degree) had a marvelous time in Germany that summer. On arrival he was greeted and entertained by Putsy Hanfstängle (Hitler's pet Harvardman and PR rep). He got a great kick out of trailing in the academic processions behind such medieval characters as the Rector of Prague in bright scarlet and others of that ilk. He was courted and deferred to; and finally given a couple of tickets for the Olympics in Berlin (he invited me to join him, but I was chasing some Danish girl down the Rhine on a bicycle and hoped I was gaining). But when we met again in the fall he admitted that Goebbels and his office had stage-managed the whole Heidelberg event, and suggested that I had best stop messing around with the Cornell Peace Council and spend more time at ROTC. He shortly thereafter began writing some articles to say that Germany would expand by force unless immediately opposed by France, Britain and America (I don't think he knew anything about Russia).

—James Nolan '37
assistant editorial director, 1936-37

Waiting for a War to Happen

By Frank Curtis Abbott '42

As *The Cornell Daily Sun* marks its 100th anniversary, the proportion of the folks who run the country who recall the debate in 1940 grows smaller and smaller. Of the people living today, only one in three had even been born in 1940. Indeed, it strains the memory of a substantial percentage to recall how we got into that mess in Vietnam. World War II? That was back before Vietnam and, yes, before Korea—but *after* Versailles, wasn't it?

Reflecting back over more recent years when campus life was more activist than it had been before or has been since, one must marvel at the impact that student activism had in forcing the wider public to confront the cost and meaning of Vietnam. If it is true that many forces led to our ultimate withdrawal from that tragic event, surely the interest, concern, and action of students on a thousand campuses across this land was a major force.

How was it on the campus as the American people were forced by world events to move beyond debate and to confront war in the early 1940s?

* * *

It was a different day in a great many ways. It was different in ways both superficial and profound:

•The Sport Shop was offering 100 percent virgin wool suits at $29.50.

•Down on Taughannock Boulevard ethyl gas was going for 12.5 cents a gallon plus tax, at Hambledon's.

•Students arrived in Ithaca each fall and left (on the few occasions when they could) on the square-wheeled flyer, sometimes known as the Lehigh Valley Railroad; the coach ride to New York City cost $7.50.

•Arts college and hotel school men wore jackets and ties to class. (Perhaps we should add: so did the faculty.)

•Engineers were identifiable anywhere—they came with slide rules.

•It was a male-dominated, Anglo-Saxon, Protestant community. Blacks and browns were seldom recruited and even less frequently came on their own. Throughout New York State, quotas ruled the admission of Jewish students on many a campus. In campus affairs the Cornell coed was second-class at best. Witness the production of *The Cornell Sun*—no women on the editorial board, all women relegated to the women's news and women's business boards, both of which were engaged in gathering not *news* and *ads* but *women's news* and *women's ads*.

•Student affairs were *student* affairs. There was an admissions office and there was a placement office, but until September 1941 there was no dean of students or of student affairs nor anything of the sort. It was a momentous development when Don Moyer and Thelma Brummett took up, that fall, duties in new offices as "Counselors of Students."

•It was a time when statesmen met on warships because there were no jets to take them quickly and safely to far-away places.

•It was a world without television.

•It was a world in which it still was possible to feel, even to believe, that people in other walks of life, and certainly in other lands, and most certainly in *certain* other lands, were less vigorous and less intelligent, or more cunning and more corrupt, and altogether less human beings, than we.

* * *

The heritage of World War I was, not a new world order within which America would play a leading role, but a renewed and pervasive isolationism that in the early 30s infected even some liberal supporters of the New Deal. Seeking

the presidential nomination in 1932, even Franklin D. Roosevelt had eschewed American participation in the League of Nations. In 1935 and 1936, as Italy invaded Ethiopia, as Hitler began to rearm Germany in violation of the Versailles treaty, and as the Rome-Berlin axis was formed, the reaction in America was to be sure to stay out: Congress enacted Neutrality Acts that embargoed shipments of arms to belligerents, denied protection to Americans traveling on ships of belligerents, prohibited loans to nations at war.

But world events in the late 1930s produced a different reaction in substantial sectors of the public and in Franklin Roosevelt. In October 1937 he warned, "War is a contagion, whether it be declared or undeclared. It can engulf states and peoples remote from the original scene of hostilities. We are determined to keep out of war, yet we cannot insure ourselves against the disastrous effects of war and the dangers of involvement. . ." In January 1938 he asked Congress to appropriate a billion dollars toward development of a two-ocean navy.

It was on Sept. 1, 1939, that Hitler invaded Poland, just two weeks after he and Stalin signed the Russo-German pact. England and France declared war. The Germans advanced with terrrifying speed; Poland was subjugated and a six-month lull ensued before, in the spring of 1940, Hitler's forces rapidly subdued Denmark, Norway, Belgium, Holland, even France. That summer Great Britain was alone in battle against forces that seemed overwhelming. In the United States the debate went on, but the authority with which the interventionists spoke was increasing and the nation was responding more actively. Roosevelt's Republican opponent in 1940 was not Senator Robert Taft or Senator Arthur Vandenberg, both notable isolationists, nor even Tom Dewey, an attorney who leaned toward an isolationist position, but Wendell Willkie, a former Democrat who believed in increased preparedness and assistance to the remaining allied forces in Europe.

In June 1941 the German-Russian Pact evaporated; Der Führer unleashed his armies against the Soviet Union.

* * *

The initial issue of *Cornell Daily Sun* Volume LXII rolled off the presses on Sept. 22, 1941. Its lead story reported that the Russians had admitted abandoning Kiev, their third largest city, capital of the Ukraine. Leningrad was under siege. Three weeks later Moscow itself was threatened. Germany prevailed over virtually all of Western Europe and North Africa. It was a high-water mark in the Nazi quest for world domination.

Editorial comment acknowledged the crisis in free-world affairs and in that first 24-page issue attempted to draw lessons from the "Cornell tradition of freedom and responsibility," which had been articulated by Prof. Carl Becker just two years before. "Freedom remains freedom only so long as it is limited by the sense of responsibility of every man and woman," said The Sun. "Dirty rushing, 'fraternity politics,' destruction at the dormitories—examples of freedom combined with responsibility? The malady that has killed France shows certain symptoms much nearer home than the rocks of Brittany."

In late September and early October as the college year began, the news from Europe and from the North Atlantic was more of the same—all bad. Yet the war did not dominate editorial comment as clearly as it did the news columns. The Sun took the lead in pointing out deficiencies in a new fraternity rushing system that had been approved by the Interfraternity Council the spring before, and in a week, after two front-page editorials and a series of meetings, the Interfraternity Council, by a vote of 42 to 1, adopted a plan of preferential pledging, advanced by The Sun, that promised to ensure the fair shake for rushees that had been the intention but not the effect of the changes IFC had made too hastily the spring before.

It was necessary, too, to get Carl Snavely's new football team launched. Right under the banner headline on Page 1 that Friday, Oct. 3—DON'T MISS THE RALLY—7:30 P.M. BAILEY HALL—appeared the headline for the lead story: NAZIS STRIKE AT 'INTERNAL FRONT' EXTENDING FROM PRAGUE TO PARIS; RUSSIANS UNDERGO AERIAL ATTACK. Student life was indeed a mix. The war was a backdrop; but it was War Pre-Atom Bomb. We lived in the knowledge that whether and when the war would engulf us were decisions that would be reached in the established American fashion.

* * *

In 1941-42 editorial policy at *The Cornell Daily Sun* was, purely and simply, established by the editorial director. True, there was an editorial board. The board did not meet. The role of its members was to write editorials for review by the editorial director, who determined what would be printed. It was a small board, containing in addition to "VTY" (Very Truly

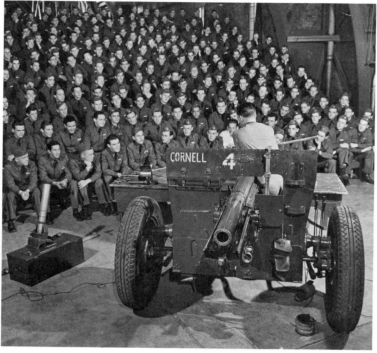

—Photo by Bernard Hoffman, *Life* Magazine

HOW TO USE A MORTAR: *World War II Army ROTC students receive instruction in Barton Hall.*

Yours, the editorial director, who also was the editor-in-chief that year), an assistant editorial director, Fred Jaqua, and two associate editors, Bob Plantz and Jock Harwood.

So centralized, not to say dictatorial, an editorial policy and practice seems, 40 years later, incongruous from the standpoint of typical patterns of campus governance—and also from what VTY knows about VTY's style of administration. Perhaps it was the tradition—I wish I could remember. But for certain it was the only way a consistent editorial policy could have been effected. On the four-man *(sic)* board were two interventionists and two isolationists. Fortunately from my point of view, VTY had the vote that counted.

So, editorial policy of the board that moved in at 109 East State Street in March 1941 was consistently interventionist. The editorials that were printed during the following year, when much of the free world was overrun by the Nazis and the Russians were brought close to defeat, were *almost* consistently interventionist. In the spring of 1941 VTY fell to an attack that might be attributed to the Germans, namely, German measles, and for four or five days was incarcerated with a good many others at the Infirmary.

While he and his colleagues did battle with Doc Norman Moore and his staff (who objected to their intricate and wily schemes for lifting beer and munchies to the ward on the top floor), Assistant Editorial Director Jaqua took charge of

the store. Fred had suffered in the face of an interventionist policy that he found misguided, stupid, and dangerous. During those few days there appeared to be a remarkable change in editorial policy, something that newspapers no more than nations can countenance without gross loss of face. As it happened, I escaped the Infirmary and arrived at the Sun office on a day when indeed the editorial then set to go simply could not, if printed, have been overlooked. It would have had to be repudiated and explained, a public confession that, as perceived by the editor-in-chief, would have destroyed the aura of authority carefully developed over months of six-day-a-week effort. Ironically, during the couple of days following Fred's fling we received virtually the only letters we got all year that applauded the wisdom of our views—views that seemed illogical and short-sighted to the man with the vote that counted.

But by no means was the interventionist view either a campus or a national exclusive. A student opinion survey taken by The Sun in early November found a shade under a majority of Cornell men (49.4 percent) favoring repeal of the Neutrality Act; a substantially larger proportion of women in favor of repeal pushed the campus average to 51.9 percent while 35.9 percent opposed and 12.2 percent were on the fence. The proportions weren't much different in Congress, where the Senate vote for amendment in early November was 50 to 38 and the House approved by 212 to 194. Almost on the eve of Pearl Harbor a nation-wide survey of student opinion by 165 student newspapers, including The Sun, posed the question whether "the United States should at this time send part of its air force, with American pilots, to Europe to help Britain." The response: Yes, send the air force: 19.8 percent. No, do not send it: 80.2 percent.

* * *

Pearl Harbor was a surprise. There is no reason it should have been.

Secretary of the Navy Frank Knox had stated publicly on Oct. 24 that the U.S. had abandoned hope of coming to terms with Japan and that a collision in the Orient seemed "inevitable." Special Japanese envoy Saburo Kurusu was dispatched to Washington, November 5, "probably...the last stab which Japan and this country will make toward discovering a peaceful solution to the almost irreconcilable aims of the two nations," The Sun editorialized.

By the beginning of December the crisis led Roosevelt to cut short a brief holiday at Warm Springs and return to Washington. Secretary Knox was announcing that "the greatly strengthened United States Navy is ready for any emergency in the Atlantic or Pacific." Peace talks with Kurusu and Ambassador Nomura continued. But Japan's concentration of troops in Indochina was very much on the minds of Roosevelt and the American military. "Foreboding statements at Tokyo and significant developments here [in Washington] tonight indicated an imminent major break in the Far-Eastern crisis—one upon which may hang the question of peace or war"—so read the opening paragraph in the lead story of December 5.

* * *

The news reached us by radio that Sunday afternoon. It was a hellish early morning at Pearl Harbor, that much was clear; but the first details were scant. Managing Editor Bob MacFarland decided that there would be an Extra and the wheels began to turn. I remember walking down State Street early that evening, the editorial for the morrow having been finished, hawking (for a nickel) the first Sunday Sun in years. The Extra was a mostly-Saturday edition: only the outside pages were new. In the tabloid size, Saturday's Page One was consumed by two rows of four-inch high capital letters: JAPS START WAR ON U.S. There was barely enough news to fill the bottom half of the sheet—Saturday's Page 8.

The lead reported, from the Associated Press wire, that "Japanese bombs killed at least five persons and injured many

—Photo by James H. Fenner

THE RIGORS OF TRAINING: *If the Nazis had built "jungle gyms" to halt the advance of Allied troops through France, these Cornell commando trainees would have risen to the challenge. The site is Lower Alumni Field, an alumni gift to the University for use "in perpetuity" as an open athletic and recreational space. "In perpetuity" lasted precisely seven decades, since—as this book goes to press—the field's grass is giving way to a new biology complex.*

The Birth of an Extra Edition

I went to Cornell from Indianapolis for the excellent reason that my Uncle Tony was a great quarter-miler there in the Class of '06 or thereabouts. I was told by my father that I could go to college only if I studied something useful. He said chemistry was useful, so I set out to be a chemist. The subject annoyed and bored me, and I had no gift for it. I was flunking everything when I departed in my junior year to become an infantry private. I was glad to leave. All I ever found to like about the place was The Sun. All my fraternity brothers were engineers, so my only contact with the liberal arts was through my colleagues at The Sun. I never got close to getting a degree, and would have quit or been thrown out, if it weren't for the war. I eventually took an M.A. in anthropology at the University of Chicago.

As for the extra we got out after the bombing of Pearl Harbor: I was night editor. I heard about the bombing while I was sitting in a bathtub. I tore down to the office, and we laid out a new first and last page, keeping the stale insides of the previous issue, as I recall. We took whatever was coming off the AP machine, slapped it in, and were, I still believe, the first paper in the state to hit the streets with an extra.

Then we stayed up all night, getting out a more responsible issue. Drew Pearson, to whose column we subscribed, sent us a telegram listing all the ships that were sunk. This telegram was followed almost immediately by one from the Department of War, saying that it had no power to prevent our publishing whatever we pleased. It asked us as patriots to suppress Pearson information. We suppressed it. Were we wrong?

— *Kurt Vonnegut, Jr. '44*
assistant managing editor, 1941-42
associate editor, 1942-43

others, three seriously, in a surprise early morning aerial attack on Honolulu today." There was a report from Pearl Harbor that "one ship there was lying on its side in the water and four others were on fire." Manila was reported also to be under attack. Secretary Knox gave a more complete though still guarded report when, a week later, he returned to Washington from an inspection of the damage. Lost: the battleship *Arizona*, three destroyers and two other vessels; damaged: the battleship *Oklahoma* and several other ships not identified; killed: 91 officers and 2,638 men. It was an awkward moment for Knox, who had to concede that U.S. forces were not on the alert and that a formal investigation would be ordered.

But at least, the great debate was over.

Of all the courses of action which have been available to Japan, she has, from the point of view of her own interests, chosen the most foolish one. In no conceivable way could Japan have more completely insulted American pride, more thoroughly aroused American anger, more instantaneously produced a condition of complete unity of thought and purpose in the United States...

The world scene today is vastly changed from what it was yesterday forenoon. American hopes that non-interventionist aid to Britain and Russia would suffice for the defeat of the Nazis are suddenly swept aside. America today is involved in a conflict being fought by all of the major powers in the world. We are in; it is Britain *and* Russia *and* America against Germany and Japan—this *de facto* if not yet *de jure*. We do not today face the immediate future with joy, or even with great hope. There are black days ahead—blacker for us Americans than at any time since the Civil War. The outcome of the struggle is uncertain...

But whether the world of tomorrow will be a better one is a question which will be answered by our actions—the actions of our government, of groups within our nation, of every last citizen of this our country—from this moment on until tomorrow's world is a *fait accompli*. What we think and what we do—these are the factors out of which tomorrow's world will grow. Right now, at this moment, and in succeeding moments, do we determine our future. So this is not a moment when "it is all over." At this dark moment, we are but starting on a task. Our children will be the judges of how truly we loved our democratic way of life.

(Dec. 8)

There's a saying, "The rest is history." There was a lot of history that winter and spring, as there has been in every one of the years that stretch from 1941 to 1980. In the years immediately ahead there was tragedy for hundreds of Cornellians, along with the opportunities. And it has been so for Cornellians, and for the rest of humankind, in every year. Crisis, with its combination of threat and opportunity, seems to be the rule of life.

Our problems matched, and they seem with no trouble at all to continue to match, the best talents that human beings can bring to bear upon them. The annual Sun banquet was held at the Dutch Kitchen on March 19; the last editorial expression of the outgoing gang appeared that morning. We acknowledged that "the temptation to reminisce" was overpowering. But 40 years thereafter the element that lifts the spirits is the forward-looking optimism.

The past year has been a great time to be alive and kicking. Our history lessons yield no tales of times past when the process of living was so intense—when it was possible to live so much in so little time, when one could do so much good or so much bad in the space of so few moments. The past has been a time of opportunity, just as the present continues to be, just as the future will be, increasingly.

What greater joy could a student or any group of students ask than the opportunity of living, of having a job to do, in times like these?

FRANK CURTIS ABBOTT '42 MPA '49, Sun editor-in-chief 1941-42, is now assistant commissioner for the professions in the New York State Department of Education. He previously had a career as an academic administrator, including a stint as assistant to Cornell Provost Arthur Adams and President Edmund E. Day.

A CENTURY AT CORNELL

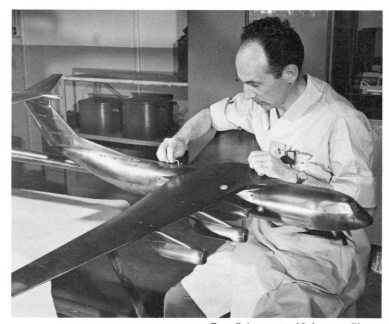

—Cornell Aeronautical Laboratory Photos

CORNELL COMPLICITY? *One of the major targets of local antiwar protests during the late 1960s and early 1970s was the Buffalo-based Cornell Aeronautical Laboratory (CAL), a not-for-profit outfit which frequently conducted weapons, aircraft and counter-insurgency research for the Pentagon. Right, Army personnel and CAL technicians wearing "CORNELL" uniforms ready a CAL-designed Lacrosse missile for test-firing at the White Sands Proving Ground in New Mexico. Above, a laboratory employee finishes a 1961 test model C-141 military transport plane. Cornell finally sold its controlling interest in the lab in 1977, after years of gradual disengagement.*

Cornell in the Age of Student Protests

BY DOUGLAS F. DOWD

I arrived at Cornell to begin teaching in the economics department in 1953, on the lam, so to speak, from the University of California at Berkeley. U.C. had instituted the first academic loyalty oath in 1950, against which we had fought long, bitterly, and hopelessly. By the time Cornell placed a contract in front of me for signature, the oil stain of Mc-Carthyism had already spread over the land to New York. No place to hide.

The Cold War had begun in 1946, and was by 1953 much hotter: the United States, in one guise or another, was fighting a major war (calling it "a police action") in Korea; was in the process of deposing the Mossadegh government in Iran in order to reinstall our shah; was already paying 80 percent of France's expenses in the Indochina War and was preparing to take over the whole endless, bloody, cruel, and unconscionable operation in the next year, when France got booted out; had already ringed China with naval, land, and air forces, using Japan and Okinawa as very large aircraft carriers—while using Turkey (and later, Iran) for the same purposes against the USSR; and on and on and on, in the global arena. By the 1960s, the U.S. had well over 2,000 military bases dotted over the globe, and over three and a half million people in our military uniforms. *La mission civilisatrice*, as the French used to call their imperialist policy, doesn't come cheap, not in money terms, not in terms of social and human deformation; not cheap at all. In money terms, after 1946, the U.S. has spent more than two and a half *trillion* dollars on military garbage/poison/waste, conservatively estimated; and if present contracted military budgets are fulfilled, from the beginning of the Carter Administration up through 1984 we can add another trillion. (Why not? It creates jobs, doesn't it? No, it doesn't. But that's not why not.)

Anyhow, despite all, Cornell was, for me, a good place to

come to; in 1953 it was relatively one of the better homes of academic freedom. Its president then, Deane Malott, was a dyed-in-the-wool conservative, but not a reactionary, nor, about certain things, a damned fool. He believed that without unfettered academic freedom the University would deteriorate into a sandbox, a mere training school for technicians (by whatever name). For Malott there was *no* academic freedom if there were political tests of any sort for hiring or retention. He got a lot of heat from alumni, trustees and faculty, but he stood fast, and in the 1950s Cornell was the beneficiary.

Cornell was a quiet place in the 1950s, like the rest of the country. I became known as a socialist soon after my arrival, and gave what came to be an annual lecture on "Why Socialism" at the University (and, subsequently, also at SUNY Binghamton). The lectures were of little if any consequence. There were few who wanted to hear any positive answers to that question, and many of them were afraid to be seen in public when such matters were discussed. Quiet were the times, quiet and full of fear.

It all began to change in 1958, a change more than symbolized by the brouhaha over social rules.* I believe this was the first "student upheaval" of the post-World War II era. Although its focus was seemingly distant from the subsequent student struggles over racial and military (etc.) issues, that appearance is deceptive. The students were then, as later, contesting the authority of the University to behave in unjustifiable ways, contesting, then as later, the presumed moral authority of the University, an authority deeply compromised by a persisting combination of inconsistency, corruption, dishonesty and complicity in processes standing in opposition to the proclaimed ideals of The University. Not for the first (and let us hope, not for the last) time, an emperor was seen as naked—and ugly.

The substance of the 1958 arguments did not have to

*See Chapter V.—Ed.

Chapter II: The World in the Eyes of Cornell

change much when it came to "issues" having to do with the presence (or absence) of black students and faculty at Cornell, or University military requirements (ROTC), contracts, and subservience, its cooperation with the draft, its South African investments, its treatment of women, or any other items on the ever-lengthening laundry list of obviously political issues. Through it all the powers that were and are at the University have clung to the notion that self-created and -styled elites take to as fleas do to a dog's hide: that they are the purveyors and the arbiters of truth, and beauty, and justice, and the sooner the great unwashed see that, the better off we'll all be.

Just as the dust from the 1958 social code fight was beginning to settle, the nucleus of what was to become an ongoing left protest movement took shape at Cornell. It began with a campaign (with roots and branches elsewhere, of course) to end nuclear testing. Two Texans, new to Cornell, sparked the effort, Joe and Patricia Griffith. They were likable, talkative, energetic and determined. They had three kids, lived in voluntary poverty on Joe's grad student stipend from the chemistry department, and before long they had facilitated an active movement of students and a few faculty at Cornell. That was not a bad place for such a movement, for Hans Bethe of the physics department was also a prime adviser on nuclear policy to more than one president; it seems clear that when he began to support a nuclear test ban he had been significantly influenced by the persistence and warmth of the Cornell effort—a major participant in which was his colleague and co-author, Phillip Morrison (now at MIT), one of those protected by President Malott in the 1950s when he refused to testify at McCarthy-type hearings.

From there it was an easy step for essentially the same (if now larger) group of people to run a peace candidate for Congress, in 1962, Harrop Freeman. He was a prof in the law school, a Quaker, and a pacifist. (I was his campaign manager.) The campaign failed miserably if the measure is votes received; but it succeeded nicely if the measure used has to do with the level and content of political life in Ithaca. In 1963 and 1964 there was a quantum leap in the political life at Cornell.

Of all places, Fayette County, Tennessee, became the focal point of the struggle. In that county, the fourth poorest in the nation, with a population two-thirds black, and half of them unable to find work, there had been a voter registration campaign going on for some time. Charlie Haynie, a good friend of the Griffiths (and of me), himself a graduate student, had spent the summer of 1963 assisting in the voter registration fight. (That it should have to be a *fight* told much about the U.S. then, as so many other counterpart instances do still today.) Charlie came back in the fall impressed, horrified, and angry; one consequence was the formation of the Cornell-Tompkins County Committee for Free and Fair Elections in Fayette County, Tennessee, which hoped to have 50 or so students (and perhaps faculty) spend the summer of 1964 in Fayette County. For that, money was needed. Many ways of raising the money were utilized; what shook up the campus was the request for $1,000 of student funds, a request argued about with an intensity, spread, and persistence unique to Cornell; a request, finally, approved by the student Executive Board. That very evening, a referendum to overturn the grant was announced, with a three-week period of debate to ensue. In retrospect it is difficult to believe how much tumult and shouting occurred over the matter; suffice it to say that few corners of the University were left untouched, that there were countless (and endless) public, dorm, fraternity and sorority meetings, that for three weeks the pages of The Sun knew little else (and its editor, Dick Denenberg, finally talked himself into signing up for the summer, so eloquent were his editorials); and, finally, the referendum lost; we won.

The background to this movement at Cornell was of course the growing civil rights movement that had been sparked by young blacks in the South—a movement that had attracted two Cornellians, Andrew Goodman and Michael Schwerner, to work in Mississippi, where they were murdered

The Isolation of the Ivory Tower

To the Editor:

This is a minor challenge to the major part of the campus. You are all aware that Cornell University has a reputation as one of the most liberal, intellectually forthright, and forward-looking (I can't use the word "progressive" for fear of getting the University in trouble) universities in the country. We have an outstanding faculty, reputed to be almost independent of trustee domination, and we have a fine publicity staff. We also have a leading fraternity system, a blue-ribbon IFC, and innumerable other organizations, clubs, and honoraries.

But you also know that most of this is a sham. We know that we have tried to set ourselves apart in an ironclad community on the hill, away from the corruption and evils and strife that now grip world government and politics. Most of us plead that college is a time for study and technical grooming—strife (and prosperity, we assume) will come later. So we bury ourselves in the pettiness of campus organizations, campus elections; we involve ourselves in the intricacies of fraternity and sorority management, or we plunge ourselves into erudite study or trade school.

* * *

There is another kind of corruption here at Cornell, and it permeates all our lives. It is the corruption of isolation. We are self-styled liberals, and we erect monuments to our liberalism in the form of bureaucratic organization, advanced seminars in technical studies, football cheering sections, fraternity rushing, and Saturday night beer brawls. We try to make a miniature democratic world of our university, actually talk ourselves into believing this is possible.

We preach the twin religions of the academic life and social growth—but books and professors and study are not sacred when they turn in on themselves and create pedantry, isolation, and decadence of the real community. Isolation turns into pettiness, of action and of thoughts. Anything vital that we learn in the classroom, we leave in the classroom, for it contradicts the rest of our lives.

What we will not admit is that we are children—some of us playing with ideas, words, books, as children play with toys, the rest of us playing party-party like little girls play house, or vain men play politics.

Outside the campus, the world seethes on. In Egypt 11 are killed and 100 wounded, in Asia thousands die every week. This has nothing to do with us. For a brief moment, we glimpse a hint of tragedy when a poor freshman kills himself in the gorge. Many of us are shocked, for the ivory tower has been dented, the world of reality intrudes. But death and annihilation are spreading over the earth's surface, and our isolation here is poor training to meet the onrushing forces of war and violence.

* * *

Does it seem senseless, a cheap trick of journalism to end this with a plea, an announcement of a public discussion here on campus? Can you see the connection? Or is the challenge meaningless? Sunday night at 8 p.m. in the Memorial Room a distinguished panel will speak on "The Future of Asia and the United States: War or Peace?" This is a personal invitation to you, asking you to be there.

This forum is an effort—just a small candle burning in a wilderness—to bring the outside world into the campus. You might not want to give up your movie or your evening of study or your trip to Zinck's. We are getting out of practice, it seems, in asserting our famous rights of free speech and assembly. Perhaps the campus doesn't want this sort of thing, maybe you prefer to loll in the false and fleeting world of isolation. But anyway, here is a small challenge.

— **Cliff Irving '51**
— *letter, October 19, 1951*

A Real, Live Rip-off

Not all antiwar protests were serious. One that the administration took more seriously than it should have is described below, with an accompanying editorial. A brief introduction: in Spring 1970, the dining department introduced what it called "fast food." This concept mainly consisted of removing more than half the items from the Ivy Room menu, with the result that the other, more popular items, would be served more quickly and students would not have to wait. Or such was the theory, at any rate; the service did not seem any faster to most students and so there were many irate Straight patrons.

One day, crudely printed flyers appeared on campus, supposedly from the "Yippies." The Yippies announced that at a certain hour a "rip off" would be held in the Ivy Room.

It is an interesting commentary on the English language that while this word is today completely standard and known to all (although it is usually written rip-off) in 1970 it was a neologism and only a very small percentage of students, even those active in radical groups, actually knew what it was supposed to mean. So half the fun of watching the Yippies was that few people knew exactly what they had in mind.

By Aric J. Press '70

The rip off never came off.

For days, Cornell's underground had been alive with plans for a disruption of the Straight's fast food operation. The planning, done under the label of a Yippie action, temporarily united the fractured Left here. The strategy was to charge the noon hour clogged fast food area, take a sampling of food and flee. Hence, a rip off.

The planning for this action was as careful and precise as usual. Day Hall people say they found out about it Tuesday and promptly decided to attend. Therefore, as the Yippies, Left, et al, entered the Ivy Room yesterday, they found a fanned out stake out in progress.

Assistant Judicial Administrator Hartwig E. Kisker, who, unimpeachable sources say, has fingered student protesters in the past, was leaning against the wall. Safety Division Lt. Ralph J. Coskey and four of his patrolmen plus a camera were spread out. Supervisor of Public Safety Lowell T. George was there and Elmer Meyer Jr., assistant vice president for student affairs, walked among them.

The stake out was obvious to the two dozen protesters. It was obvious to the ten Sun staffers there, as a tall Ivy Leaguish senior kept saying, "Jesus, *The Ithaca Journal* is here. Jesus, WHCU is here. Jesus, everybody knows about this." It was also obvious to them because people began sitting on the wooden tables facing the check out lines waiting for the drama to unfold.

The Leftist types milled around for a while then met near the jukebox and decided to change the rip off to a put-on. It is yet to be determined whether this change was then made clear to the official observers who were having their pictures taken during the jukebox meeting.

The Left left the jukebox and came marching toward the cafeteria. Kisker, very dapper in his pale blue blazer, moved forward. Alan Plofsky '71 started to yell. Meyer moved into the line of march and everybody entered the food area together.

"Arrrrgh!" somebody yelled as he fondled the bananas and apples.

"Thump," went the "Bologna .30" sandwich sign.

Everybody milled around. Meyer grabbed a tray.

"Let's get out of here," somebody yelled and some ran out as the put-on started to die.

"Cheese it," somebody else yelled and they ran out. Everybody was laughing. "Hurry up," Meyer called, tongue in cheek. "Hurry up."

Somebody swiped two folded paper plates and ran out.

—Sun Photo by Ruth Muschel

Do It! *Two self-styled Yippies, otherwise known as "freaks" or "crazies," attend a May 1970 "Free Bobby Seale" rally at Yale. Three hundred Cornellians joined 20,000 others—including Youth International Party leaders Abbie Hoffman and Jerry Rubin—in support of the Black Panther chairman and eight other blacks facing murder charges in New Haven. Yippies were known for their flamboyant posturing and absurdist humor, such as running a pig for president in 1968 or appearing in court dressed as Uncle Sam.*

"We're just here to prevent trouble," George said later. He didn't stop to eat lunch in the Ivy Room because he had to prepare for Arthur Goldberg's speech.

The Left returned and passed out a prepared ironic statement (see editorial on Page 4) linking their action to needs for legalized abortion, onion rings, ending worker layoffs and keeping the Rolling Stones.

"It's symbolic," Meyer said, shrugging his shoulders over an Ivy Room snack. "They have to do something." He picked up his tray with the potato chip wrapper, plastic salad bowl and milk carton, dropped it off at the conveyer belt and walked out.

—news story, March 26, 1970

For Responsibility

"We claim total victory."
—Unidentified Yippie Spokesman

Admittedly abortion should be legalized. Admittedly onion rings should be restored to their rightful place on the Ivy Room's menu. Admittedly Bobby Seale should be freed. And certainly, something must be done about the cookie situation.

But even granting the justness of the above propositions, which constituted the hard core of the Yippie demands, their demonstration yesterday was violent, obscene, and uncondonable; their actions constituted a serious breach of the Regulations for the Maintenance of Public Order, and were detrimental to the educational environment.

In judging a demonstration, there are several criteria to be considered. The justness of the demands is but one of them. Others include the conduct of the demonstrators, the determination of whether *all* official channels had been exhausted *first*, and the appropriateness of the action to the situation. The Yippies, while probably acting in good faith in accordance with their consciences, fail to pass the test. Good intentions cannot be construed as a *carte blanche* for wholesale anarchy.

It is not the traditional role of The Sun to make non-negotiable demands. But given the gravity of the situation, the Yippies must be made aware, in no uncertain terms, that certain forms of protest are not and never will be tolerated on this campus. Immediate steps on their part are required.

Director of Dining Shaw must be returned *now*, unopened. Kidnaping is no joke. And the demand for ransom is totally out of hand considering the tightness of the University budget.

The ten thousand dollars' worth of food stolen from the Ivy Room must be given back at once. Especially the hamburgers. This must be done soon. If they are kept for more than a week without refrigeration, they will become inedible.

And finally, the Yippies should pay for the cost of calling out the Dean of Students' Office and the Safety Division. These are men with many important things to do. It is a disgrace to make them waste their time keeping under surveillance a bunch of scruffy scoundrels. More importantly, the men from Day Hall should never be forced to mingle with (shudder) students in the Ivy Room.

It is hoped that the Yippies will make their reparations and return quickly to the sanity befitting an educational environment.

—editorial, March 26, 1970

in that same summer of 1964.

In retrospect, the years from the late 1950s into the mid-1960s at Cornell may be seen as a microcosm of the larger developments that came to be called "the movement," or at least of that part of it involving university-based people. At Cornell, by the mid-1960s, that movement was emerging into its best-organized, most self-conscious, most powerful, tumultuous, and effective years; it was quantitatively strong and qualitatively admirable, and not only by comparison with other universities. Cornell had what may have been the largest SDS chapter in the country; it was certainly the first SDS chapter to combine draft resistance with its other concerns—not least of all because of the numerous and tough draft resisters among its students—best known of whom were, perhaps, Joe Kelly, and Chip Marshall, and Mike Rotkin, and Larry Kramer, and among many others (including my own son Jeff by 1968), Bruce Dancis, probably its most effective leader at Cornell and elsewhere, sent to prison, finally, for his pains. Bruce knew what was most important about those years of the mid- and late-1960s—and he knew the fun and dignity and grand spirits that were generated also on the non-student side, by Dan Berrigan, and Jay Shulman, and Eqbal Ahmad, and some others. It was a tough world, that world of the 1960s, but by God, it was good to work with all those people to keep it from getting worse, and, just perhaps, to make it a bit more livable.

—*Cornell Alumni News*

'I'D HAMMER OUT THE LOVE BETWEEN MY BROTHERS AND MY SISTERS': *Then graduate student Fred Weaver urges a Fayette County, Tennessee, resident to register to vote. Weaver was one of 30 Cornellians who spent the summer of 1964 promoting civil rights causes in this poor, rural, predominantly black county just north of the Mississippi border. The drive was supported by some $50,000 raised in Ithaca.*

On Mr. Dowd's Resignation

To the Editor:

I find myself greatly distressed by Prof. Douglas Dowd's comments explaining his reasons for leaving Cornell, as quoted in your article of February 2. Taking for granted that his criticisms of Cornell were justified, I still find that he has revealed in himself a trait for which I can find no respect.

Professor Dowd, as his title indicates, should be first and foremost a teacher, yet his method of combatting apathy and indifference at Cornell by withdrawing to another school seems to be unlike any method a true teacher would use. If we are apathetic, it should be his goal as a teacher to stimulate our interest and concern.

Even though this is only my first year here at Cornell, I appreciate the efforts Mr. Dowd has made in the past to raise interest among Cornellians. However, it seems that he has found the going a little rough and so has decided to quit. He is not needed at Berkeley. Berkeley has enough activists. We at Cornell need Prof. Dowd and men like him if we are to progress in the future.

Scott A. Neslin '74
—*letter, February 8, 1971*

Be that as it may, by the mid-1960s, the recognition had grown and was growing that the university (Cornell and the others) reflected and supported all that's worst, as well as only some of what is best, in the society: institutionalized racism and sexism, imperialism, militarism, and the whole run of attitudes and efforts comprised in capitalist ideology. All this had a long history; it had been characterized neatly and gently by Thorstein Veblen (in his *The Higher Learning in America*, 1908) long before, after he had studied and taught at, among other places, Cornell, Chicago, and Stanford. Speaking of faculty, he wrote: "...their intellectual horizon is bounded by the same limits of commonplace insight and preconceptions as are the prevailing opinions of the conservative middle class. A large and aggressive mediocrity is their prime qualification...."

It may be put differently, if not better. If, around 1960, before all hell had begun to break loose, one were to have asked the faculty at Cornell to characterize itself on the political spectrum, it probably would have seen itself as predominantly liberal, especially, of course, in the arts college. Indeed I recall well the scorn heaped on the "aggie" and "hotelie" faculties (and on President Malott), among others, by my elegant colleagues in Goldwin Smith Hall, scorn directed against their presumed conservative/reactionary attitudes in comparison with the Olympian liberalism of the keepers of all that was seen as holy on the hill. Well, all that began to change very rapidly when students and a handful of faculty began to turn over the rocks in the larger society and also at Cornell, to reveal the slugs, scorpions, and other odious/poisonous forms of life constituting a supporting stratum for the higher dandyism of our betters. It was enough to bring to mind the behavior of whites who saw themselves as "liberal" on "the Negro question" until, that is, they found blacks trying to live in "their" neighborhoods, and/or have their children going to "their" schools. Tawdry, man; tawdry.

I spent about 17 years at Cornell, some of the best and some of the worst years of my life. I enjoyed and thrived on the teaching, the politics, the friends, the fights; but by the last year or so the life had gone out of it all: too many friends fired, jailed, mistreated; too many former friends who had become enemies; too much fear and loathing. No place to be, not for me.

The very last faculty meeting I attended was in the early winter of 1970. It was to debate—once more!—the role of ROTC at Cornell, a debate that had taken place first (at least for my years there) in 1955. From the beginning, those of us who saw ROTC, or anything military, as being poison in a university, had been accused of being "political" in our insistence that it be removed from the campus; that it was equally political to wish it to stay never seemed to be able to penetrate the ideological lead casings within which the minds of ROTC's supporters presumed to function. Anyhow, I had begun to believe I no longer belonged at Cornell when, before that meeting, some of my liberal friends (and opponents of ROTC) asked me, in the friendliest way, to keep my mouth shut, letting me know that good intentions or not, I had become Judas. Sitting through the meeting, not hearing any meaningful arguments against ROTC, I spoke; I said my piece, and I left Bailey Hall. As I crossed the parking lot, a professor I had not seen before screamed at me: "Dowd, when are you going to leave us alone?!!!" Unbeknownst to me, at that moment, the answer was: From that day forward. I returned to a visiting spot at Berkeley the next semester and upon due reflection decided I was wrong for Cornell and Cornell was wrong for me. There is work to be done, but the likes of me can't do it there. It, and all that it so fully represents, I miss not at all. But I do miss some of what it was, and those who made it that way, at its best, at their best. *Sic transit....*

DOUGLAS F. DOWD, a professor of economics at Cornell in the 1960s, was considered the most prominent "radical" on the Cornell faculty.

JANUARY 1967: *Although Cornellians had joined civil rights struggles in the South in 1963-64 and slowly awakened to the Vietnam War in 1965-66, a mass protest of 1,500 students involving an allegedly obscene student literary magazine called* The Trojan Horse *was the "first big blow-up" of the 1960s at Cornell. The incident is fully discussed in Chapter V. Left to right above: reporter George Fisher; a city police officer; District Attorney Richard Thaler; Police Chief Herbert van Ostrand; and activist Burt Weiss. Students later avenged themselves on Thaler's car, seen in the foreground, by deflating its tires and writing obscenities in the dust on its hood.*

APRIL 1967: *Campus opposition to the Vietnam War would soon be virtually unanimous, but a significant minority still supported the war in Spring 1967. Here 100 neatly dressed members of STOP (Students To Oppose Protest) stage a sit-in in front of three buses chartered to take Cornellians to a peace rally in New York City's Central Park.*

APRIL 1967: *The colorful, carefree spirit of San Francisco's Haight-Ashbury phenomenon arrives at Cornell as costumed revelers express their "love of love" to the accompaniment of flutes and guitars at a "be-in" on the arts quad. Pastimes included "ring-around-the-rosie" and a parade behind a Scottish bagpiper. Posters announcing the event, which drew 500 people, requested everyone to "bring bells and flowers."*

A Portfolio of Protests, 1967-1980

SEPTEMBER 1967: *Daniel Berrigan—the "Antiwar Priest" whose poetry and vehement pacifism would soon capture national attention—had begun serving as Cornell United Religious Work's associate director for service when students returned to Ithaca in the fall. Here Berrigan, wearing a dark jacket and beret, leads a peace march downtown shortly after his arrival.*

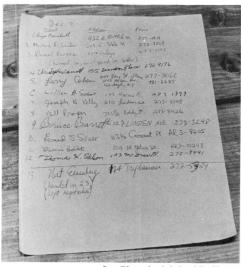

DECEMBER 1967: *Following the example of SDS member Bruce Dancis '69, who eventually went to prison for tearing up his draft card in December 1966, a dozen Cornellians signed this list and turned in their cards to Ithaca's Draft Board a year later. Joining eleven students was Prof. Leonard S. Silver, mathematics.*

—Sun Photo by Harry LeVine

MARCH 1968: *With U.S. participation in the Vietnam War reaching its peak, Cornell architects abandoned their traditionally festive and brightly painted Green Dragon. Instead, a somber Black Dragon—seen here behind a tree and its dialectical sign—slithered across the arts quad on a rainy Monday.*

—Sun Photo by Justin R. Rattner

APRIL 1968: *A picket in front of the Straight supports SDS and Afro-American Society demands that Cornell sell its stock in banks investing in South Africa. The sign reflects an increasing polarization of political attitudes, and the contempt felt by many for any show of moderation.*

—Sun Photo by John G. Elligers

APRIL 1968: *The interior of the Anabel Taylor Hall Chapel and its elaborate carved wooden altar stand blackened the morning after a midnight blaze ignited by an arsonist. A charred remnant of the altar now decorates the Cornell United Religious Work director's office as a poignant reminder of the years of dissent.*

—Sun Photo by Charles M. Leung

APRIL 1968: *Pictured is Stanley R. Jonas, the happily panting winner of the Bertrand Russell Award for the Most Peaceful Dog at an arts quad dog show. Leaflets reported that Jonas had burned his rabies vaccination certificate after being scheduled for induction into the Canine Corps as a police dog.*

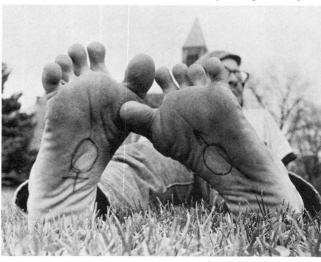

—Sun Photo by Charles M. Leung

APRIL 1968: *A student lying on Libe Slope symbolically demonstrates the "New Morality" of the late 1960s.*

—Photo by Via Wynroth

APRIL 1968: *By now, leafletters were a daily sight at the entrance to the Straight—and marches to the Ithaca draft board sometimes seemed almost as frequent.*

A CENTURY AT CORNELL

—Sun Photo by Larry Baum

APRIL 1969: "U.S. soldiers" toting toy machine guns and rifles demolish a "Vietnamese peasant hut" during an April 18 guerrilla theater performance in front of Ezra Cornell's statue. The conviction of several black students by a University judicial board earlier that same day would usher in the April 19 Straight Takeover—and real, loaded guns. What had the convicted blacks done? They had waved toy guns on campus.

—Sun Photo by Brian W. Gray

MAY 1969: SDS demonstrators who would become known as the "May Day 10" chant slogans and paint graffiti on a Navy ROTC practice deck gun then contained in a restricted area of Barton Hall. The gun was sold for scrap only days later. Several of the ten arrestees eventually pleaded guilty to third degree criminal trespass, while charges against others were dismissed for insufficient evidence.

Left: Photo by Sol Goldberg

—Sun Photo by Brian W. Gray

Moratorium Day, 1969

OCTOBER 15, 1969: *Above, thousands of Cornellians march from Barton Hall to the arts quad on Moratorium Day, when Americans from coast to coast were to suspend normal activities to protest the war. Left, a precocious Jan Peterson flashes the peace sign in Barton, where antiwar Senator Charles Goodell urged 7,500 listeners to support his "Vietnam Disengagement Act," designed to bring home all American troops by December 1970. Right, the Rev. Jerome Travis of the Snyder Hill Baptist Church and his steed observe the occasion in their own fashion on the arts quad, where President Corson condemned the war and decried its "disastrous effect on education." Hundreds of students spent the afternoon and evening canvassing Ithaca neighborhoods on behalf of Goodell's bill.*

—Sun Photo by Leilani Hu

—Sun Photo
by Peter
Cartwright

NOVEMBER 1969: *With the meager comfort of a wooden crate to sit on and a cellophane package of leaflets to sort through, a student participates in an arts quad peace vigil on a late fall afternoon. The campsite was occupied around the clock by various individuals on single eight or twelve hour shifts—even throughout nights when the temperature dropped below freezing. Daytime passersby were occasionally handed leaflets reading, "I am sitting here in the name of peace. What are you doing?" Explained vigil organizer Jonathan Miller '71: "We can never have too many reminders that we are committing murder in Vietnam at the rate of 100 people a day."*

—Sun Photos by Peter Cartwright

MARCH 1970: *Demonstrators at an anti-draft rally in Syracuse display late 1960s styles. Over 100 people, including 45 Cornellians, were arrested for bodily preventing a bus of potential inductees from entering the U.S. Army Induction Center.*

—Sun Photo by Leilani Hu

MARCH 1970: *A shrouded "Spectre of Death" haunts the Ithaca Draft Board office on Aurora Street.*

—Cornell University Archives

APRIL 1970: *Right, an early morning two-alarm fire set by an arsonist guts the Africana Studies and Research Center, then located at 320 Wait Avenue, during Spring recess. In response, blacks staged a series of angry protests during the week students returned. Books were overturned in the new Campus Store; windows were smashed in Olin Library, Donlon (above) and many other buildings; phones were ripped out in Balch; and a Volkswagen was overturned on East Avenue.*

—Photo by George Clay, Ithaca Journal

A CENTURY AT CORNELL

> . . . Dear friends
> I choose to be a jail bird
> (one species is flourishing)
> in a kingdom of fowlers
> Like strawberries good bread
> swans herons Great Lakes
> I shall shortly be
> hard to find
> an exotic inmate of the
> NATIONALLY ENDOWED
> ELECTRONICALLY
> INESCAPABLE ZOO . . .
>
> —from "America Is Hard to Find,"
> by Daniel Berrigan

—Ithaca
Journal

America Is Hard to Find

APRIL 17-19, 1970: On May 17, 1968, Cornell United Religious Work's Daniel Berrigan and eight others removed 1-A files from a Catonsville, Maryland draft office, and immolated them with homemade napalm in a parking lot. The "Catonsville 9" were convicted in federal court, and—their appeals having run out—several faced jail in Spring 1970. However, Berrigan, along with four others, failed to keep an April 9 appointment with a Baltimore federal marshal. In honor of the nationally prominent fugitive, Cornellians sponsored an "America Is Hard to Find" weekend featuring music, speeches and political workshops. Among the guests were activist David Dellinger, folkie Jerry Jeff Walker and the rock group Rhinoceros. The festival's climax came on the first evening when Berrigan appeared in Barton before 15,000 wildly cheering people . . . and a handful of utterly helpless FBI agents. Berrigan had been disguised in a motorcycle helmet and visor before he doffed the costume and walked on stage, just after the celebrants of a radicalized "Freedom Seder" invoked the spirit of the prophet Elijah. "I'm here at your service," Berrigan declared. Friends later smuggled him out of Barton inside a huge guerrilla theater dummy. He eluded federal agents for four months, before being apprehended in a Rhode Island home and serving 18 months in prison. Upper right: a star-spangled Richard Nixon opens the weekend by leading a procession to Barton, accompanied by cymbals, drums and a brass band. Below: tall, ghostly forms of the Bread and Puppet Theatre wind through a hushed crowd towards the stage, where the troupe's 16-foot-high effigies satirize American justice. Top: the triumphant Berrigan and Dellinger meet in Barton.

—Photo by Russ Hamilton

Right: Sun Photo by
Richard A. Shulman

Above: Photo by
Russ Hamilton

—Cornellian

MAY 1970: *An attack by U.S. and South Vietnamese troops into Cambodian territory and the shootings of four Kent State University students triggered the most widespread and spirited campus protests in the nation's history. The Associated Press reported effective student strikes at over 130 colleges, and sit-ins, marches and cancelled classes at many more. At Cornell, contingents of strikers—brandishing placards emblazoned with red "Strike!" fists and waving wooden crosses symbolizing the Kent State deaths—marched from quad to quad amid May snow flurries. Others built barricades at various campus entrances and intersections. Above, strikers man a mound of logs, garbage cans, bicycles and chain link on the Collegetown bridge.*

—Sun Photo

APRIL 1971: *As so many times before, Cornellians joined hundreds of thousands of demonstrators in a peaceful march from the White House to the Capitol on April 4. Students favoring more militant tactics returned to Washington one week later to attempt to shut down the federal government by blocking morning traffic heading into the city. Individual bridges and highways were assigned to specific regional Mayday groups; the Upstate New York Region, for example, was expected to halt traffic entering over the Francis Scott Key Bridge. The Washington police—who would arrest 12,614 people in just three days—kept the streets open. But Cornellians and other upstaters scored an isolated triumph when they pushed an abandoned garbage truck over a bluff overlooking Canal Street. The wreck blocked the out-going lanes of this major thoroughfare until police managed to move the hulk aside with a forklift.*

—Sun Photo by David Krathwohl

APRIL 1972: *Safety Division officers use heavy tools and a crowbar to gain entry into Carpenter Hall by smashing its front plate glass windows. Some 125 students protesting "Cornell's complicity in the war machine"—they cited defense research, ROTC programs and stock holdings—had begun a five-day occupation of the building and renamed it "Giap-Cabral Hall" in honor of two third world military leaders. Sympathizers camped outside, watching revolutionary movies and chatting with Safety officers beside campfires.*

—Sun Photo by Gary Benzion

APRIL 1972: *Peace marchers fill an entire block of State Street between Tioga and Cayuga Streets. This area is now the western half of the Commons pedestrian mall.*

A CENTURY AT CORNELL

-Sun Photo by Gary Benzion

MAY 1972: A dog slumbers outside Carpenter Hall after the "Giap-Cabral" protesters, facing a state court injunction, marched away in song, raising their fists and carrying two banners.

-Sun Photo by Dan Brothers

MAY 1972: An Ithaca police officer and a Safety Division lieutenant stand guard over a handcuffed student at a corner of College and Dryden Road during what must surely rank as the most ridiculous and needless clash in Cornell history. City officials—made nervous by the Carpenter Hall takeover and a subsequent antiwar window smashing spree on campus and in Collegetown—mistook a wholly non-political rock music block party for a disguised protest rally. Formations of Ithaca police in full riot gear, augmented by county sheriffs and Safety Division officers, marched up College Avenue. Their appearance immediately transformed the party into a political confrontation, whereupon the police began firing tear gas into the crowd and sallying with raised billy clubs against the amazed students. "We're going to rip you freaks apart," one officer reportedly shouted. Mayor Edward Conley later acknowledged that this absurd fiasco, which resulted in 29 arrests and minor property damage, was the result of a misunderstanding.

-Sun Photo by Jack Frost

APRIL 1978: President Rhodes glares at Africana Center director James E. Turner after 200 students forcibly detained Rhodes and top trustees in the Johnson art museum. The students feared a possible re-evaluation of the center and sought University divestment of stock in firms operating in South Africa. The museum blockade was one of a number of 1970s protests in support of strong minority programs.

-Sun Photo by Jonathan Rosenblum

MARCH 1980: A procession of 30,000 students, including 150 Cornellians, marches past the White House to protest peacetime draft registration proposed by President Carter. But the "Draft Sucks" banner sounds facetious and sophomoric, as though it were a parody of the tactics and passion of an earlier generation.

-Sun Photo by Jeff Earickson

NOVEMBER 1979: John F. Raposa '83 waves the Stars and Stripes in solidarity with the American government several weeks after revolutionary Iranians in Tehran seized fifty U.S. embassy staffers as hostages. Other Cornellians joined Raposa in singing "The Star Spangled Banner" during this counter-demonstration which stole the show from a rally called in support of Iranian militants' demands. The counter-demonstration was probably the loudest and most enthusiastic pro-government Cornell protest since 100 conservatives blocked a peace bus in April 1967. In a sense, the clock seemed to have come full circle.

Chapter II: The World in the Eyes of Cornell

Sixty Years of Presidential Endorsements

It being summer 1980 as this book goes to press, The Sun is preparing to endorse, perhaps, someone for president, and it looks like a rough choice. Endorsing presidential candidates is not particularly long-standing as Sun traditions go, but the history of Sun political thinking provides an interesting insight into student political awareness in the last 50 years or so.

Sad to say, The Sun's influence on national elections does not appear to be as pronounced as on elections for campus government, where Sun endorsees have historically done well: of the eight presidential candidates The Sun has endorsed, five went the way of William Jennings Bryan.

Basically, pre-World War II The Sun was isolationist, and solidly Republican; after the war the liberals took over and Democrats have always gotten the endorsement, with the degree of enthusiasm depending upon more or less the participation of Richard Nixon.

* * *

The Sun's first presidential endorsement was plainly the most interesting, not only because of the endorsee, but because of the endorser. In 1932, at the height of the greatest depression in the country's history, Americans faced a choice between the discredited Republican policies of President Herbert Hoover, and the unknown potential of the attractive, charismatic governor of New York, Franklin D. Roosevelt.

The editor of The Sun that year, who had to make the choice, became quite a politician himself. Henry S. (for Schoellkopf) Reuss, the Sun editor, is now chairman of the House Committee on Banking, Finance and Urban Affairs, one of the most prominent Democrats in the country, well known for his progressive views on the nation's financial structure.

At this point, readers should recall what they doubtless learned in an introductory government or history course: that American politics is a strange creature, not easily understood: it is a system whereby Woodrow Wilson, Franklin Roosevelt, and Lyndon Johnson can each be nominated president on a peace plaftorm and not only be elected but be elected in the same century; where a Republican party with not only a Herbert Hoover but a Cornellian like Charles Evans Hughes available, could instead nominate for president the likes of Harding and then Coolidge; where it is actually conceivable for a former B-movie actor and either one of two former football players to run on the same ticket; where two men of such undoubted merit as Al Smith and Franklin Roosevelt can be the warmest of friends in one election and as bitter enemies as Prince Hal and Hotspur eight years later; where a Theodore Roosevelt can be so incensed at the man he installed as president four years earlier that he runs himself as an independent, destroying both of their chances; a system of which Tocqueville could say that "mountebanks of every sort show themselves able to please the people, whereas their truest friends cannot obtain a vote of confidence."

It is a system of which Mencken observed, "Has the art and mystery of politics no apparent utility? Does it appear to be unqualifiedly ratty, raffish, sordid, obscene and low down, and its salient *virtuosi* a gang of unmitigated scoundrels? Then let us not forget its high capacity to soothe and tickle the midriff, its incomparable services as a maker of entertainment." With Mencken's sentiments in mind, let us commence our journey by recording, gentle reader, that in 1932 Henry Reuss came out for Hoover.

1920: Harding vs. Cox

As was the custom in those days, The Sun had very little to say on national politics. The day after the election, however, The Sun's editor, E.B. White '21, commented as follows:

At the time of this writing, every indication points to Mr. Harding's election to the presidency. Two things stand out prominently, now that some of the much-tossed mud has been cleared from the arena.

The first is that the poor old solemn referendum, so dear to many a trusting heart, was completely and irredeemably immersed in the deep and turbulent waters of the political whirlpool. As expected. The second is that anti-Wilsonism has accounted for a vast amount of ostensible pro-Hardingism.

Which has nothing to do with the prospects for the next four years, during which time the country is again to resume its state of normalcy.

—*editorial, November 3, 1920*

1928: Hoover vs. Smith

The Sun finally began to make a practice of commenting on national politics during this year, and it is apparent that the editors favored Hoover over Smith, whose economic policies they feared. Nevertheless, early in the fall semester The Sun staked out the following position:

We Pass

Any newspaper, commencing publication in the midst of a political furor such as now harasses this country, ought to define early the stand which it proposes to take. The Sun will be non-partisan.

We grant that the majority of self-styled non-partisan newspapers have quite obvious leanings in either one direction or the other. We grant further that partisan readers are apt to distinguish partisan intentions where they do not exist. It will be our purpose, nevertheless, to comment on the happenings of this presidential campaign without intent in any manner to influence the votes of the readers. We take this position with some assurance, for in all probability very few students will take the trouble to vote, and in all certainty no professors would be persuaded by our arguments.

If this is to be our stand, we are not privileged to take sides on the various issues of the campaign, but we are privileged, we think, to attempt to state the issues. To our mind they are: farm relief, prohibition, ownership of power companies, Republican corruption, Republican prosperity, inland waterways, and immigration. If a voter could make up his mind on these issues and determine in his own mind their importance, he could at least know what he was voting for, whether or not he voted intelligently.

Concerning farm relief, both have promised definite action, and it is simply for the voter to decide which, to the best of his knowledge, would be most effective. Concerning prohibition, which we think is overemphasized as an issue, we would only say that Smith's election, in view of the normal Republican majority, would indicate decided dissatisfaction with the Volstead law, but that Hoover's election would not necessarily indicate satisfaction with that law.

The attitude of the men toward ownership of power companies is clearly contradictory: the one favors public ownership, the other private. Concerning Republican corruption, we think that the only question can be that of the relative importance of this issue. The same is true of Republican prosperity. We believe that both of these problems have been too much stressed, for we are not convinced that corruption and prosperity are closely associated with party. The problem of inland waterways is one which demands more intimate knowledge, and probably will not influence the layman.

Religious tolerance is not an issue. We have no more sym-

—Photo by John P. Troy

BATHTUB BUSTER: *Above, former President William Howard Taft smiles with University President Jacob Gould Schurman in front of what is now Uris Library in May 1916, when Taft delivered a series of lectures at Cornell. During this period Taft was teaching law at Yale, prior to being selected Chief Justice in 1921. Right, a freshman captured during an interclass "battle" with the sophomores holds a placard with a caricature of the incumbent president.*

—Scrapbook of James Irving Clark '12

pathy with the man who is voting for Smith because he thinks that he must do so to prevent bigotry from ruling the nation than with the man who is voting for Hoover because Smith is Catholic.

And then of course there is the matter of the men themselves. Both have shown themselves unusually able men in the fields in which they have been active, the one as a state administrator, the other as an engineer.

—*editorial, September 27, 1928*

1932: Hoover vs. Roosevelt

We now return to the melancholy saga of Henry Reuss, and although it is not possible to assert that Herbert Hoover was the most enthusiastically endorsed candidate in the history of The Sun, he was certainly the most *thoroughly* endorsed. Throughout the month of October, Reuss hammered away at his typewriter, coming up with reason after logical reason to stay with the proven man. Some of his arguments sound suspiciously like they belong in articles about the 1980, not 1932 election, but then again, as they say in politics, the more things change, the more they stay the same.

Seldom since the days when the rabble cursed the locksmith king, Louis XVI, has there been such widespread and seething hatred of a government head as is now President Hoover's lot. The very banana peddlers heap his name with dark oaths in the same breath that they say "good morning" to their customers. Every little shopkeeper from Maine to California whose business teeters on the verge of bankruptcy mutters ugly things about Hoover whenever anything goes wrong, whether it be the bursting of a water pipe or the failure of a debtor.

Right on the face of it, it is obvious that Mr. Hoover is being

made the scapegoat for ills that are absolutely remote from his sphere. Even if he were the blackest Judas that promoted a Class D mining stock, he could never cause all the evil that is being laid at his door today.

Our argument is with those unthinking persons who simply blame all their troubles on the most convenient peg, and positively refuse to inform themselves. It is hardly fair to lambast blindly a man who is trying his hardest to do justice to a big job and who is probably more capable than any of the other candidates seeking to take it away from him.

Admit that Herbert Hoover is no knight in shining armor who can stir the masses to enthusiasm. Admit that he has signed one of the worst tariff acts in history, and bungled the government into the price stabilization business which cost it literally millions of dollars and didn't get to first base with the disgruntled farmers. Admit these facts and a score more that could be dug up to stultify almost any president from Washington right down the line, yet it is crystal clear to any intelligent observer that the complications of the past two years have been far too complex for any one man to solve to the satisfaction of one hundred and twenty million persons.

His achievements in the Caribbean and the reduction of the standing army of marines there, his conduct in arranging the MacDonald visit in 1929 and the Five Power Naval Conference at London in 1930 are no mean feats. He has been as busy as a bee with child conferences, home planning commissions, and commerce conferences which have borne some fruit.

After getting tangled up with a Democratic Congress and some of his own understudies he finally has rigged up the Reconstruction Finance Corporation, a formidable offensive against the depression. While far from adequate, his plan of reconstruction is sounder than that promised by Candidate Roosevelt. For more detailed catalogue of Mr. Hoover's achievements we would refer to the recent addresses of Messrs. Hurley, Brown, and Wilbur, where, underneath a mass of superlatives and glowing eulogies, any keen eye can detect some of the really praiseworthy efforts of the incumbent.

It is not easy to say whether Hoover deserves reëlection or not. Another man could have made much less headway against the troubles that kept piling up during the air-tight regimes of Harding and Coolidge.

One way of looking at the situation is this: the country has already paid dearly for educating Mr. Hoover in the ways of battling with economic depression; should it now fire him and take on Roosevelt in the pious hope that he can go on from where Hoover leaves off without losing out on the count of inexperience?

—*editorial, October 12, 1932*

Roosevelt: Vague and Hazy

A name to conjure with, an ability to smooth over ticklish situations, and a propitious time for a Democratic victory, give Franklin D. Roosevelt a better chance of election at the moment, than any Democratic candidate in many campaigns. He has not the religious bugbear to battle against, nor is he butting his head against the stone wall of solid Republicanism. He has done nothing as yet to antagonize possible voters. Perhaps Chief Optimist Farley's glowing predictions have an element of truth at their base.

Roosevelt's record in politics is a long one, and one which may be quoted to his credit and to his discredit. His eight years as Assistant Secretary of the Navy, made him to some extent responsible for the condition of the Navy at the outset of the War. And yet he handled his position efficiently and conscientiously.

His record as Governor of New York is open to inspection. Many sadly needed bills were passed during his administration. Handicapped by a hostile Legislature, he still fought courageously for state development of power, for regional planning in the dairy industry, for unemployment relief. His period in office was marked by progress and perspicacity to no small extent.

When the presidential campaign began to peek around the corner of the years, Governor Roosevelt underwent a metamorphosis. Positive statements no longer were to be found in his vocabulary. Progressive became a noun instead of an adjective. Legislation gave way to nebulous ideas and frenzied forensics. Attacks on a Republican Legislature dwindled off to nothing and emerged from the haze in the guise of baby-kissing and handshaking. Roosevelt's campaign has not been startling in any way, except possibly through its lack of positiveness.

Beginning with his farm plan at Topeka, which experts have

denounced as utterly ridiculous and impossible, Governor Roosevelt has suffered from a bad case of "politichosis," a disease which prevents the victim from offending anyone over the age of 21. He has said nothing definite or striking on the prohibition question, other than supporting the Democratic plank. He has urged closer regulation for railroads without bothering to explain how close. Such has been his attitude on almost every important question. He has promised, yes; but his promises are vague and hazy.

— editorial, October 14, 1932 (excerpt)

The Voice of Experience

We believe that this country will benefit more, will recuperate faster, and will remain more stable under the guidance of President Hoover than under the leadership of Challenger Roosevelt. A judgment must be based on externals, of course, and on externals, the incumbent promises more to the nation than does New York's Governor.

The Republican slogan, "Don't swap horses in mid-stream," is not quite as foolish as it sounds. Herbert Hoover has done a capable job in his four years of travail and heartbreak. He has been faced with an unconquerable situation, by circumstances which would make any of his actions seem wrong. And yet he has labored and striven mightily. The results have certainly·done more good than harm; few men in his position could have done more.

The nation in these years has had a taste of what Mr. Hoover wishes to do. He has his finger on the pulse of the situation; his ideas and plans have been formulated. To elect a new and inexperienced leader as President would require an entirely new organization, would destroy everything Dr. Hoover has struggled to build. In addition, what proof have we that Roosevelt will do anything? His campaign has been marked by the exercise of an astounding gift of evasion and persiflage. Vast quantities of nothing have come from his mouth and heart. And promises are not quite sufficient for the country to pay its taxes on.

— editorial, October 17, 1932 (excerpt)

The Day of Decision: Will Man Bite Dog?

When some of the big boys put their money on the street at five to one on Roosevelt, they were frankly fishing for suckers. Every indicia of political direction during the past months has pointed unveeringly to the judgment that is to be pronounced this day.

The medieval trial by ordeal would probably elect President Hoover just as nicely as the ballot process which today must take him off the firing line. It is merely a question of how completely pent-up anger and resentment will cancel out reason and logic.

It was too much to expect that any combination of flesh and blood could sit in the President's chair during the hell of the past three years and escape being made the scapegoat at the polls. One shudders to think of the tragedy that Al Smith so reluctantly was spared.

When things start to go wrong and when money becomes scarce the average American voter reacts in about the same way that a Congo tribesman reacts when the fleshpot stays empty and bad luck stalks the village. He never thinks of blaming himself, but points his finger accusingly at the most prominent person in sight, the chief headsman.

Every ruler since the days of the Pharaoh has taken that gamble. Every president of the United States has taken the chance in the same breath as the inaugural oath.

Of course, there will be many who, after talking Roosevelt all fall, will get just a little scary when it comes to pulling down the gadgets and switch over to Hoover. It will be interesting to see how far this sort of thing goes in contradicting the pre-election prognostication of the Digest, New York Times, and other professional soothsayers.

On the whole Hoover's addresses have been on a higher plane than those of the Governor. He has dealt more concretely and comprehensively with the economic impasse. Probably this was political suicide.

What the masses wanted to hear was the news about a change, not detailed review of the laborious measures that had already been taken. Inevitably the popular mind was bound to identify a change in the national pocketbook with a change in administration. With excellent political sagacity Roosevelt capitalized on this sentiment and patly epitomized it in that euphonious bit of nonsense, "a new deal."

For the most part we are in agreement with Professor Carl Becker and Norman Thomas when the former says: "The chief difference between the two major political parties in the United States is that the party in power is trying to stay in, while the party on the outside is trying to get in."

Our support of Hoover springs from our conviction that, man for man, he is head and shoulders above Roosevelt. We have had no compunction in seizing upon his many blunders and in throwing the spotlight on some of his prize aberrations. Other agencies have specialized solely in this chopping down work.

Today will tell the story of how well they succeeded.

— editorial, November 8, 1932

1936: Landon vs. Roosevelt

It is somewhat amusing to note that the 20th century provided the two greatest landslides in the history of American presidential politics, and The Sun each time found itself on the wrong side of the mountain. During this campaign, The Sun officially returned to its traditional posture of neutrality—but it was clear throughout that there was a strong undercurrent of unease with President Roosevelt. Shortly before the election, a poll was taken of Cornell undergraduates, with Landon narrowly winning. On election day, The Sun offered this speculation on the future:

According to advance reports, today's election returns will show the largest number of Americans voting in the history of this country. The interest this year in the choice apparently surpasses that of any campaign in this century. Recriminations have been more bitter, campaign tours more intensive, epithets, perhaps, less frequent, and prophecies much more dire should the wrong man be elected, than at any time during the memory of the great majority of this year's voters.

Why should there be such unprecedented fervor in the 1936 campaign? Can it be true that the election of one man will throw the country into the hands of the Wall Street brokers—or the other candidate's success will mean that the United States will become an out-and-out Socialistic or Communistic state? Obviously any sane thinking person can see the absurdity of either of these two positions. We have had Republican administrators before and the country managed to survive, even prosperously, under their rules. Franklin D. Roosevelt has not yet put *every* working man in the nation on the federal payrolls.

No, the election today will rather be a referendum of the people. It will be their chance to show their opinions regarding what sort of government we should have in the future. If the majority of people believe that in these so-called trying times a pure Jeffersonian Democracy is unworkable, they will show it by reëlecting Roosevelt. Governments, as well as everything else, change. It is quite possible that the American people feel that the time for such a change is imminent.

On the other hand there are many who feel that the Constitution, *per se*, is still the one and only means of governing the United States. These voters, rightfully believing that Roosevelt has in several instances completely disregarded this document, will turn to Landon at today's polls. True, they do not know what he will do if elected, but they have a fairly good idea of the Socialistic trend of the present administration, and are willing to take a chance that the Kansan will abide by the older principles of democracy.

So the outcome of this highly contested election will prove which way the United States wants to go—back to the tried and tested democratic principles or toward a socialistic dictatorship. The question is not whether one is right and the other is wrong, it is *which* the country's voters desire.

— editorial, November 3, 1936

1940: Willkie vs. Roosevelt

The editors this year lost little time in announcing they would not endorse anyone, and the reasons they cited were:

1. The editors feel that on such delicate and controversial issues as politics there can be no absolute right or wrong. Since this newspaper is not in any way affiliated with any partisan movement, no motive, other than the various opinions of its

editors, could dictate a favorite in the election. The editors are not prepared to foster their personal beliefs and prejudices on the reader.

2. The editors further feel that this stand of impartiality will be a pledge of sincerity, designed to increase the effectiveness of what comments we do make. It is our hope that the reader will accept us in good faith, and not feel inclined to read non-existing motives into our articles.

3. Last, we feel there is nothing to be accomplished by aligning ourselves with either faction. The Sun's support has never in the past been known to vitally affect the outcome of a national campaign. Its enthusiastic endorsement did not reëlect Mr. Hoover in 1932; nor is it commonly asserted that its "Hands Off" policy materially altered the size of the Roosevelt landslide in 1936.

—editorial, September 23, 1940 (excerpt)

Again, however, throughout the campaign the editorials had a pro-Willkie tinge. One guesses that there may have been strong sentiment to break the earlier pledge and come out with a Willkie endorsement; at any rate, the editors solved the problem on election day by running, believe it or not, one editorial endorsing each candidate.

For Roosevelt

With seven years of experience behind him, Franklin Roosevelt has based his campaign on the grounds that the present situation requires an experienced administrator with an inside knowledge of governmental affairs.

Following a program of social reform, President Roosevelt has dedicated his administration to the "greater good of the greater number." In doing this he has fought "special privilege" enjoyed by the few, and tried to return the reins of government to the people.

In seven years he has spent a record sum of money, but in return has almost doubled the national income. The ranks of organized labor have swelled; farm prices have risen; millions of unemployed have been fed; new social legislation has been adopted.

With recovery well underway

For Willkie

Today the people of this nation will cast their votes in one of the most important elections in the history of the United States. They will vote for or against the breaking of time-honored precedent—that no one man is so indispensable to the United States that he should hold the office of president for more than two terms.

Aside from the third-term issue which in itself is one of the most important of the campaign, the voters of the nation will have the chance to elect a man who has proven himself to be something which President Roosevelt is not—an efficient executive who can conduct a business on a sound economical basis. And after all, what is government but a business? Surely a man of proven administrative ability can assemble a well-coördinated government which can function with more efficiency

and most of the New Deal adopted and even accepted by the opposition, Mr. Roosevelt was ready to retire. But the strained international situation and the desire to complete the rearmament program he had begun in May prompted him to seek reëlection.

During his brief campaign, hindered by duties of state, he defended New Deal objectives, and denounced the "Unholy Alliance" of Republicans as designed to sabotage social reform. He pointed to the records of "Martin, Barton, and Fish" as examples of what might be expected from the GOP.

For his own, Mr. Roosevelt pledged to "keep on fighting" for the same things he had advocated in the past. He pledged his faith in private property, and an intent to retire "after seeing things through" these next four years. Finally, he promised no entanglement in foreign wars, and declared he would continue the foreign policy of his able Secretary of State, Cordell Hull.

than the New Deal jumble. The people do not want an economic theorist who veers from pillar to post trying to discover a successful policy. They want a man who can settle down to a consistent policy for economic recovery.

If this country is to survive the attacks of its enemies from without, it must first cure the ills which are gnawing at it from within. The roots of these ills are to be found in the economic fallacies which have predominated during the last seven years. These have bred class hatred, destroyed the confidence of the American business man in the government, increased taxes and plunged the country into debt.

To cure the country's ills, we must have a leader who not only understands the theories of economics, but also has a deep insight into the practical problems of American industry. Such leadership is to be found in Wendell L. Willkie.

—editorials, November 5, 1940

1944: Dewey vs. Roosevelt

The Sun was spared the ignominy of failing to endorse Franklin Roosevelt for the fourth successive time by the fortuitous circumstance that it was not publishing due to the wartime shortage of paper and manpower.

1948: Dewey vs. Truman

The first postwar election posed a challenge to the editors. They again announced a policy of neutrality early in the term, but showed a certain admiration for the policies of a third-party candidate, former Vice President Henry A. Wallace. By election day, however, Wallace had slipped from serious contention; The Sun called his domestic program "thought-provoking," but added, "Whatever good be embodied in the domestic program, it is snowed under by the new pacifism of appeasement and timidity, which Mr. Wallace so zealously enunciates."

The Sun was no happier with the major candidates, which may account for the lack of an official endorsement. President Truman, it wrote simply, "has proven himself inadequate in the office . . . it will be a blow to good government if his defeat should drag down other able members of his ticket in the various states." Of Governor Thomas Dewey, it added, "He has alienated voters by his foppish campaign for unity, for he seems incapable of frankness and honesty in his political talks."

"Thus it is," The Sun concluded, "that the voter cannot enthusiastically vote for any of the candidates, unless the person is a rock-ribbed party supporter."

—Photo by Sol Goldberg

NEVER BELIEVE THE CHICAGO TRIBUNE: *Then New York Governor and two-time Republican presidential candidate Thomas E. Dewey (right) ponders a portrait of Ezra Cornell with newly inaugurated University President Deane W. Malott in Statler Hall on September 19, 1951.*

1952:
Eisenhower vs. Stevenson, I

It was a very special day last June when General Dwight D. Eisenhower stepped out of his plane in Washington, D.C., leaving the relative safety of European battlefronts and the cold war with Russia to enter American politics.

We had known this awesome fellow as Allied Commander in North Africa, and Commander-in-Chief of SHAEF and SHAPE, but never as a politician. The only inkling we had of his political philosophy was a statement he had made earlier in the spring, in which he noted a disturbing trend toward the left in his country's policies in recent years.

* * *

So when Eisenhower started out his political career with plain statements on the virtues of American life and a number of broadly worded comments on foreign policy, we hoped he was merely laying the groundwork for a searching analysis of America's problems.

We were slightly thrilled by his forthright statements of faith in the American way of life, and his ready admission of his own shortcomings. Mixed with a sufficient quantity of fighting statements such as "Graft and incompetence [are] the inevitable consequence" of a party's remaining too long in power, these remarks made us await the General's nomination with a good deal of relish.

In pre-convention days, Eisenhower showed signs of developing some good political arguments, and turning out an intelligent, fighting campaign. While Senator Robert Taft tried to destroy the principal issue separating himself and the General—foreign policy—Eisenhower shrewdly pointed up the real difference between his thinking and the Senator's.

In an off-the-record statement (which somehow found its way into most of the nation's newspapers) Eisenhower said flatly on June 17, "Taft is an isolationist."

And while the militant Senator was claiming that the Truman administration had sold China down the river just to satisfy a whim, the military candidate-to-be made the logical, if obvious, statement:

Wittman for President

To the Editor:

The time has come to rid the University of bureaucracy and stuffed-shirted control. Join me and my followers and we shall reinstitute a system first conceived by your colleagues at Bologna more than 700 years ago.

Allow me to appeal to your reason. For nearly 100 years students here have groveled at the whims of old men on committees. They do not understand your problems. Their economic views are tailored to their own benefit. Their views on morality are outdated. They claim students are given Freedom With Responsibility, yet they hesitate to allow members of your own government to step into areas of discipline and curriculum. They have a wonderful campus, but they institute such programs that students cannot enjoy it. They have a conspiracy with the town so that students may be economically exploited. I have worked with these old men and I know.

Students, coeds, help me. Join ranks behind me, that we may rid ourselves once and for all of grey flannel suits. Join the townspeople, who would like to take your money directly instead of having it go through channels. Help me institute a foundation where any instructor may find students in any subject.

Students, coeds, we will lead a valiant struggle. We will fight in the gorges, we will fight on the quads, we will fight in the Co-op, we will fight in the Straight and in G.S. and in Statler. We will never retreat, and if this University and its affiliates last for a thousand years, students will say, "This was their finest hour."

Jack Wittman '64
Candidate for Senior Class President
— letter, May 11, 1964

"I do not know who is to blame for the loss of China. I do know that the diplomatic triumphs of that period, if any, were claimed by the party in power. The party in power has to take some of the responsibility for any losses we have suffered."

Some of Eisenhower's other generalities seemed like logical foundation for a campaign based on an intelligent political philosophy.

He said he had no ready-made prescription for ending the Korean War, but declared that we were in Korea to uphold a principle, that we should stand fast, not extend the War to China, and seek "a decent armistice."

He said in his first political press conference, "Every American has a right to decent medical care."

* * *

In the face of such high-sounding declarations, we hardly noticed a fellow in Illinois who was saying, "[I] could and would not be a candidate for presidential nomination." A little later he answered a question about a draft at the Democratic convention simply, "That remains to be seen." By the end of June, he professed to be thoroughly bored with conjectures about his political future, and shortened his answer to the perennial "no comment."

Governor Adlai E. Stevenson had little of real significance to say until after his campaign was officially kicked off on Labor Day. Until that time he remained something of a mystery man. He had a good record as governor of Illinois and an unusual display of humility combined with determination to recommend him, but his specific views on important issues were as little known as Eisenhower's.

* * *

It was virtually impossible to make an intelligent choice between the two candidates at that stage of the campaign. We waited expectantly for the two nominees to clarify, explain, and support their views on significant matters.

We were a bit surprised, shortly thereafter, when Eisenhower spoke before the American Legion and again brought up the question of our policy toward Europe, dropping it with a remark so vague and misleading that John Foster Dulles spent several days trying to explain that the General had not advocated an armed invasion of eastern Europe.

Our surprise grew to dismay when the Republican candidate left foreign policy long enough to express, in the good old American tradition, his opposition to "socialized medicine."

The most encouragement he could give those Americans suffering from inadequate health services was, "the usefulness of federal loans or other aid to local health plans should be explored," for special cases of permanent disability.

But Eisenhower's latest remarks on Far Eastern policy have been the most disillusioning part of his campaign. After several generalities about the inadequacy of our Far Eastern policy to date, the General has not formulated a consistent criticism of our action in the Korean War, much less any plan for the future.

* * *

While Eisenhower has been demonstrating his inability to discuss political issues in a rational, consistent manner, Governor Stevenson has been developing detailed, objective treatments of many of these same topics. Starting off with little of the reputation or popular appeal which blessed his opponent, he has built himself up to be a figure of far greater stature in the field of politics.

The treatment which the two candidates gave the problem of economy in government illustrates the difference in their approaches to such major problems. Each outlined several things which must be done to reduce defense expenditures. But while Eisenhower based his argument on the election of Republicans to carry out these reforms, Stevenson emphasized the quality he would require in his defense program administrators. He advocated such specific measures as giving the president the "item veto" over defense appropriation bills.

On foreign policy, Stevenson adopted the same objective attitude, as contrasted with Eisenhower's contradictory assertions about the conduct of our relations with China and the Korean War. "Many Americans in both parties made the same mistake," Stevenson asserted. "America did demobilize too rapidly and too severely."

Stevenson, who has been criticized for his lack of experience in foreign affairs, has further shown his ability to cope with foreign problems by pointing out the dangers of restricting trade with foreign nations.

The governor has shown that he is not afraid to stand by his

QUEMOY AND MATSU: *Crowds in Schoellkopf Stadium witness the precision marching pyrotechnics of Band Day, 1960. Local residents who heeded the combined bands' patriotic call the following November carried Tompkins County for the Republicans for the twelfth straight national election. Lyndon Johnson was the first Democrat to win the county since Woodrow Wilson in 1912. Franklin Roosevelt never even came close.*

beliefs even when so doing may cost him votes.

The campaigns of the two presidential candidates have tended in opposite directions. Eisenhower, who started out with a great deal of prestige and popular appeal, has not shown us that he can think clearly or progressively on important issues. He has sacrificed objective commentary for pure partisanship.

Stevenson, on the other hand, has developed his campaign along logical, well-thought-out lines. He has shown himself to be capable of formulating independent views which look to the future rather than the past. While his opponent has faltered in the obstacle course of presidential politics, Stevenson has shown himself to be exceptionally well qualified for the job of president.

We hope to see him in the White House January 20.

—editorial, October 14, 1952

1956:
Eisenhower vs. Stevenson, II

The editors had a lot to say in their endorsement this year. Not only did they require the entire editorial page for their views, when two columns normally suffice, but they also reduced the size of the type so as to fit more in. For all the verbiage, the arguments were largely the same as in 1952, and the candidate was the same. The rationale was basically anti-Eisenhower rather than pro-Stevenson, and yet the editors said, "Both men, obviously and certainly, are the best their individual parties have to offer."

Eisenhower was attacked for a lack of leadership; for a lack of action in foreign affairs; and a "big-business slant." But the most interesting aspect of the editorial, to the modern reader, was its treatment of a subject that would get a great deal of further attention in the succeeding 24 years.

Finally, on the debit side of the Eisenhower ledger must also go the presence of that somewhat controversial figure, Vice President Richard M. Nixon. Ignoring for the moment the substance of the charges that have been made against him, we feel safe in saying that a significant majority of the American people, with or without reason, have a distrust of Nixon. In many cases it goes deeper than his smile and outward expression; in some, it is dependent on what they know of his past smear campaigns, and in others, it is based on the feeling that Nixon's actions in the last four years have indicated only a costlier brand of "McCarthyism." Whatever the reasons, and we can agree with most of them, the American people do not feel the proper confidence and respect for a man who is so close—in several ways—to the presidency.

This feeling about Nixon is a dangerous one, especially at a time when there is some question—no matter what disclaimers either party makes—as to whether a man of Eisenhower's health and age can survive the terrible rigors of the presidency. And it seems significant to us that this feeling against Nixon does exist— it proves that the American people aren't as easy to fool as some people think. And it is our stand that the closer Nixon gets to the presidency, the more unfortunate it will be for the nation.

—editorial, October 23, 1956 (excerpt)

1960: Nixon vs. Kennedy

This year was one of those in which Richard Nixon was perceived as shifting toward the left. This did not prevent The Sun from endorsing Kennedy, but it did cause the editors to remark that either candidate would be better than Eisenhower. The Sun perceptively criticized Kennedy's hard line on Cuba: "He should realize, as all Americans eventually will, that the government Castro built is not going to collapse soon. But he and the Democrats are right in demanding that the United States pay more heed to Latin America."

Kennedy's domestic proposals were praised; The Sun called some of them extravagant and correctly predicted that Congress would not pass them. Very little was said about Nixon and his policies—quite a contrast to future years.

1964: Goldwater vs. Johnson

This was a suspenseful election. Not, of course, because of whom The Sun endorsed: with 90 percent or so of the student body for Johnson, that was a forgone conclusion. Rather, the question was, how could one possibly endorse Johnson without lapsing into cliches and tired one-liners? After all, Johnson had an enviable domestic record; Goldwater was seen as an irresponsible warmonger by nearly everyone; virtually every newspaper in the country supported the President.

After lengthy consideration, The Sun, which had taken a full page to endorse Stevenson in 1956, dispensed with this election in three paragraphs plus a headline.

For President: LBJ

There has been much written about the current presidential election. We feel we can add little to the mountain of verbiage that has already spewn forth. However, we would like to remind the campus of the following exchange.

Mr. Goldwater said, if Matthew, Mark, Luke and John were like the current gentlemen of the press, Christianity would never have gotten off the ground.

And Mr. Lippman replied, Mr. Goldwater is forgetting that Matthew, Mark, Luke and John had a slightly more inspiring subject.

—editorial, October 26, 1964

—Photo by C. Hadley Smith

—Sun File

PRESIDENT MEETS PRESIDENT: *Top, Cornell President Deane W. Malott greets Dwight D. Eisenhower at the Tompkins County Airport in May 1963, with Eisenhower aide Robert Schultz, a retired brigadier general, in the background. Bottom, Cornell President James A. Perkins stands between Lyndon Baines Johnson and Health, Education and Welfare Secretary John Gardner at a conference on international education at Williamsburg, Virginia in Fall 1967. Johnson had considered naming Perkins to a cabinet position.*

1968: Nixon vs. Humphrey

Banquo asks, after seeing the witches, "Were such things here as we do speak about?/ Or have we eaten on the insane root/ That takes the reason prisoner?"

The late 60s were not so long ago, and yet it is almost impossible to comprehend the complete turnabout in political attitudes that took place in only four years. From complete confidence to a near-total despair; from optimism to physical fear, particularly in college communities like Cornell, where the shadow of the draft was everywhere; from the most unswerving loyalty to any president since Roosevelt to a perception that the same president might be a war criminal.

The Sun tried to solve its problems by endorsing two liberals for their parties' nominations before the conventions, but in the end it was forced to choose between two candidates it clearly despised.

The Vietnam issue was so all-pervasive, it must be noted, that it almost completely demolished support for Humphrey, who had impeccable liberal credentials otherwise.

The following editorial is the only presidential endorsement that has ever appeared on Page One of *The Cornell Daily Sun.*

We, too, are tempted to sit this one out.

It was only last spring that The Sun endorsed two candidates who represented the direction we saw best for their respective parties and for the country. Senator Robert F. Kennedy, we then argued, could "best handle the American social and economic tinderbox and, at the same time, dig this country out of its Big Muddy brand of foreign policy." Likewise, we endorsed New York's Gov. Nelson Rockefeller as providing a healthy perspective and a reasoned alternative.

Concomitant to these endorsements were our criticism and disdain for the two front-runners, the two gentlemen who copped their parties' top nominations this summer. Vice President Humphrey we praised for his civil rights stands and social foresight, while we blasted him for his sycophantic support of Johnsonian myopia. We treated, and dismissed, former Vice President Nixon in fewer words.

But in between last spring and next week's elections two mammoth disasters have occurred in American politics—Miami and Chicago. The death of Robert Kennedy only served as a harbinger for the greater tragedy that tore apart his party. The reünification of the Grand Old Party under that Grand Old American Richard Milhous Nixon was equally as tragic.

So now we are faced with several alternatives. We may support a particular major party candidate, cast a protest endorsement or abstain completely from the process. We choose the first option and the candidate for whom we plan to vote is Hubert Humphrey, the Democrat from Minnesota.

We shall not present our argument in detail for it has already been belabored by the news media. What it boils down to is a modified form of the simplistic "lesser of evils" deduction based on complex contingencies. The difference in our argument is that while we find it hard to accept any of the three candidates there is only one candidate whom we would not classify as an "evil."

His name is Humphrey. We question his pussyfooting and kowtowing to Johnson on the war issue—but we fear Richard Nixon. Hubert Humphrey may be bending his stance out of political expediency—but Richard Nixon is as rigid as Gen. Hershey's draft calls.

We've been frustrated by talk of the old Humphrey—but all we've seen is the Public Relations Nixon, not the frightful one with whom we may have to live for the next four years. For while we may question the manner in which Humphrey would direct this country in foreign affairs, we fear for the rashness of a Nixon or a Wallace in his simplistic dogmatic *Weltanschauung.*

Thus, our primary basis for supporting Humphrey is a negative one. Richard Nixon and Gov. Spiro Agnew of Maryland, we feel, would be disastrous. Mr. Nixon is pre-occupied with the arms race and shows a lack of understanding and appreciation for domestic strife and social and economic priorities.

We realize that a victory for Richard Nixon might be the best thing that ever happened to the Democratic Party. But we fear it might also be one of the worst things that ever happened to this country.

For the next four years may be perhaps the most critical the United States has faced since the Civil War. What we do not want to see is a reälignment of economic priorities and the possibility of a re-directed Supreme Court. The spectre of a robed Strom Thurmond would be laughable were it not for the pre-Miami chances of a Spiro Agnew.

And in this realm we find a large plus for Mr. Humphrey's candidacy—his vice presidential choice. Our support of Edmund Muskie is strong and enthusiastic. The comparison with his Republican counterpart is lopsided and serves as a makeweight in the Humphrey camp.

We've thought of supporting a fourth-party candidate but we feel this would be reneging on our responsibility. For the last thing we want for the next four years is the albatross of Richard Nixon and Spiro Agnew or of strengthening the percentage vote and potential of George Wallace.

—*editorial, October 31, 1968*

—Reni Photos

1972: Nixon vs. McGovern

This year provided 1) the most enthusiastic endorsement of any individual, ever; 2) the most vicious denunciation of any individual, ever; 3) the most lopsided defeat ever handed by one presidential candidate to another. Needless to say, the remainder of the country did not view the election the way The Sun did.

Every editor of The Sun since 1969 had kept up a bastinado of protest against President Nixon. The editors elected in March 1972 kept this pattern up; but in April, long before the Democratic convention, they announced their choice.

—Sun Photo

Media endorsements are too often the products of personal whim and empty ritual, the third ring in a circus of polls and primaries. But the educated guesses must be made, and in some elections more than others. The 1972 Presidential race is one of these, for two complementary reasons: 1) Never have the stakes seemed quite so high, and 2) Rarely have we had a candidate so capable of placing the right bets.

That candidate is Senator George McGovern, and we endorse him without further philosophizing and with no reservations.

George McGovern was the first U.S. Senator to speak out against the war, and his opposition is as dedicated today as it was courageous eight years ago. He calls for an immediate termination of all American military operations in Southeast Asia, and has worked toward that goal with such legislation as the Mc-Govern-Hatfield Vietnam Disengagement Act.

A long-time enemy of bloated military expenditures, he advocates a $31 billion cut in the Pentagon's budget within three years. The liberated money would be shunted toward such causes as mass public transportation, pollution control, a federally funded welfare program, more schools and hospitals, urban renewal, etc.

McGovern is a respected crusader for equal rights and opportunities for all Americans. He was the only Senator to support the Congressional Black Caucus Program, and is a major ally of the Southern Christian Leadership Conference. He actively opposed the Haynsworth and Carswell nominations.

McGovern co-sponsored the Equal Rights for Women Amendment, the Women's Equality Act, and the Comprehensive Child Care Development Act. He has pledged to appoint women to high-level government positions: to the Supreme Court, the United Nations, the National Security Council, the McGovern Cabinet.

McGovern has engineered major political reforms as chairman of the Democratic Party's Commission on Party Structure and Delegate Selection. His efforts have insured that this year's Democratic Convention will be open to unprecedented numbers of women, minority people, and voters under 30.

Rather more subtly, a McGovern Presidency would signal a refreshing new style at the White House. Imagine candor replacing evasions and lies, press conferences replacing Ronald Ziegler, Walter LaFeber replacing Henry Kissinger, William Sloane Coffin replacing Billy Graham, anyone at all replacing Melvin Laird.

All too good to be true?

All too crucial not to be.

—*editorial, April 20, 1972 (excerpt)*

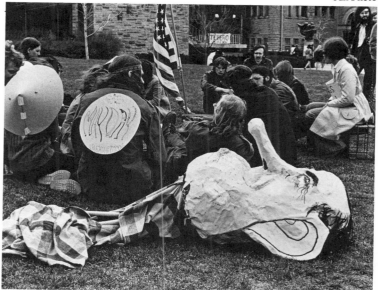

—Sun Photo by David Krathwohl

POPULARITY, TO RIDICULE, TO DISDAIN: *Top, Vice President Richard M. Nixon and Attorney General William P. Rogers law '39 chat with Cornell President Deane W. Malott (far right) and former faculty dean Robert S. Stevens (far left). In the 1950s Nixon was sufficiently popular to attract 2,000 greeters, including banner-waving members of several Cornell organizations, to Tompkins County Airport. The vice president arrived on October 17, 1956 to face a nationally televised student press conference in Bailey Hall. Middle photo: Jubilant but tongue-in-cheek students display "Dickie" signs on the arts quad in April 1968. By this time, presidential candidate Nixon was already a student nemesis. Bottom photo: an abandoned Nixon effigy lies in the grass before Vietnamese peasants about to be "killed" by flag-bearing Americans, as the Guerrilla Theatre Wing of a local antiwar coalition seeks to drum up support for a May 1971 demonstration in Washington. Nixon planned to be out of town.*

In September, The Sun made more explicit the nature of its objections to the incumbent.

Put simply, Richard Nixon is a threat. The first four years of his Presidency have been uncomfortable at best and murderous at worst; another four, without the damper of an impending re-election campaign, could easily spell disaster.

When Nixon entered the White House in 1968, he found himself in the perfect spot to end an unpopular war engineered by his Democratic rivals, to allow the proper self-determination of a proud Asian people, to stop the wholesale slaughter of soldiers and civilians. He chose, instead, to expand the Vietnam war into Cambodia and Laos. He chose, instead, to drop more than 3,550,000 tons of bombs on the villages and fields and dikes of Indochina. He chose, instead, to allow the killing of over 15,000 Americans, and of countless thousands of Cambodians and Laotians and Vietnamese.

And all for what? To prop up the sickly Saigon regime of one Nguyen Van Thieu, a man who has jailed, censored, and murdered his way to political supremacy within a hated dictatorship. The President tells us we must support this man to avoid "dishonor, surrender, and the destruction of the ability of the United States to conduct foreign policy in a responsible way." No number of jaunts to Peking can redeem this kind of vicious sham.

On the domestic front, Nixon's demagoguery has been no less shameful, just a little less bloody. The last four years have witnessed the repeated abuse and politicization of the conspiracy law, an alarming increase in electronic surveillance, the calculated intimidation of the press, and a dubious string of appointees to the Supreme Court. The Nixon administration has made its intentions perfectly clear: lots of defense, lots of secrecy, very little welfare, very little aid to the cities, no busing, no amnesty, no tax reform, and absolutely no "policy made in the streets."

And so, the choice in 1972 is much less between two evils than it is between a certified evil and an uncertain good. We therefore urge you to vote, and to vote for George McGovern.

—editorial, September 13, 1972

Agnew and What He Stands for:

If Richard Nixon was seen as a sinister figure, The Sun portrayed Spiro Agnew as the Clown Prince of Satanity. Agnew's pseudo-intellectualisms grated on the academic community, and his constant assaults on the press naturally did not sit well with The Sun. Things got so bad that one Sun editor admitted in print, "We tell Agnew jokes the way he tells Polack jokes. We condemn him in editorials when we can't think of much else to say."

The editor continued, "Agnew-baiting is incorrect for two reasons. First, it is an easy way of sidestepping a phenomenon we cannot fully comprehend. But more importantly, we have made Agnew into a symbol for 'what's wrong with America.' And by doing so, we have not only ignored our root problems, but we have also failed to deal with our own inability to solve those problems."

Here are two of The Sun's spicier assaults on this perplexing and contradictory figure. "Fooled Again" was the response to Agnew's forced resignation; the other one requires a little more explanation.

In 1970, the vice president went on a tear against campus radicals. In the midst of a tirade, which included several examples of the kind of thing he objected to, Agnew referred to "the score of students at Cornell University who, wielding pipes and tire chains, beat a dormitory president into unconsciousness."

Agnew's reference to this incident was entirely accurate but for one detail. It took place at the University of Connecticut, not Cornell. President Corson, forgetting that

Agnew's Rhetoric

Vice President Agnew's speech on campus disorder was factually inaccurate. But more, the rhetoric in which the man engages has the effect of preëmpting reasoned, logical response. He has created a condition where the use of a term like "irresponsible" becomes an inadequately understated reaction. He has so defiled with excess the language called English that one can only deal with him via invective: his speech was idiotic, obscene, absurd, reprehensible, uncomprehending, slanderous, repressive, ridiculous, politically inane, and a vile disservice to his office. Agnew should be replaced by a dog. The dog should be shot.

The two and a half sentences following the colon in the preceding paragraph sound like overkill. To be asked, though, is the question, what kind of language have they left us strong enough to deal with madness? Reagan says, "no more appeasement." Agnew talks about separating the rotten apples from the good ones so that society will not be contaminated. Nixon says that he is not dealing with the New Left, but rather with "the criminal mind." Given the above, are we able to effectively say anything other than that there can be no appeasement for known fools like Reagan, that Agnew must be separated from America lest he spoil us all, that we are not dealing with the Administration but with the criminal mind; that the greatest cause of campus unrest today is our Vice President?

It is fifth-grade to say, "I'm rubber, you're glue, anything you say bounces off me and sticks to you." Yet how far are we from the truth of the matter when we say that if ideological criminals exist they reside not on our campuses but in the Justice Department? To say that the real eunuchs are not the commentators but the newsmakers? To advocate the end of open door admissions policies for unqualified presidents? To eliminate amnesty for our atrocities in Vietnam? The Sun, unlike Reagan, is not in favor of an immediate bloodbath. Yet when high officials make impassioned pleas for reasoned argument, we can only say that they

Cartoon by Susan Brennan
October 17, 1973

have made a society in which rational discourse is impotent. And when they call for an end to violence, we can only say that *their* minds are like Swiss cheese.

Escalation begets escalation, and we are locked into a situation where we have no choice but to up the ante, to make more powerful our words and more felt our actions. We wish for a return to that early-60s era when it was still possible to sing "We Shall Overcome," when it was still possible to petition with the hope that things would change. That time is past. The old songs are out of tune, the old tactics grossly inappropriate. Making the best of what our government has left us with, we must find words both effective and sane, actions both viable and non-suicidal.

The task is hard, the line we must tread quite thin. If the Administration continues its intransigence, the thin line may disappear. The result would be self-defeating street-fighting which would be tragic and, in a strange sense, inevitable.

—editorial, April 30, 1970

Of course, in the end, the support of The Sun and every other student newspaper had about as much impact as King Canute's attempt to command the tides. But even after it became obvious that McGovern could not possibly win, the Sun editors made one last gesture: on the right, The Sun's editorial page the day after Nixon's reelection.

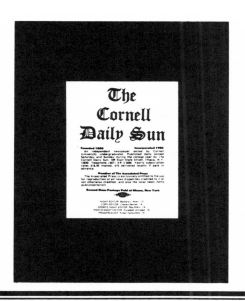

1973-74: Nixon vs. Nixon

As one might expect, The Sun stridently advocated impeaching Nixon, dating from the moment he fired the special Watergate prosecutor, Archibald Cox, in the "Saturday Night Massacre." Since Nixon's resignation eventually came during the summer, there is no editorial reaction to it. But we do have this remarkable piece, from shortly after the "Massacre," a couple of days after The Sun and all the other Ivy League newspapers came out for impeachment. It's called "Sympathy for the Devil."

Try watching Nixon's next press conference twice, first live and then again at the 11 p.m. rebroadcast.

The first time through, if his next performance is at all similar to last Friday night's, you'll react with a very predictable anger and—psychologist Nixon's comment on the dynamics of anger

A Nattering Nabob of Negativism's View

Cornell had some dirty linen of its own, fired off a furious telegram to Agnew demanding that he make amends.

This proved unwise. Agnew's office issued the following apology: "The beating of a dormitory president by students wielding tire irons and chains occurred this month at the University of Connecticut rather than Cornell.

"It was at Cornell University this month that the Africana Studies and Research Center was destroyed by fire, probably arson, that small groups of students vandalized the bookstore, that University authorities had to obtain restraining orders to prohibit violence, that these orders were tested by SDS and the Black Liberation Front with no action taken against them.

"It was at Cornell University this month where numerous bomb threats were received by campus authorities, where a Molotov cocktail was thrown through a window of the University library and where Molotov cocktails were discovered in other buildings.

"The Vice President regrets that he misplaced the location of the beating of the dormitory president at Cornell rather than at Connecticut."

This time, Agnew was, alas, accurate.

"Agnew's Rhetoric" was The Sun's response-in-kind to the vice president. In 1980, it is also interesting to note the references to the then-governor of California, who was advocating a hard line against student demonstrations in that state.

Fooled Again

"There can be a mystique about the man. You can look him in the eye and know he's got it. This guy has got it."
— Richard Nixon on Spiro Agnew, 1968

What can you say about a 54-year-old crook who resigned?

You might start by wondering why he's making out so well. America has a possibly fatal soft spot in its heart for big-time criminals: we hear how Lee Harvey Oswald had a domineering mother, how poor old William Calley was just doing his chores, how even the Godfather has grandchildren. Richard Nixon, that blackguard author of several impeachable offenses, is still sitting pretty. It's only when we're picking on foreigners that this country takes off the gloves.

Spiro Theodore Agnew, Vice President of the United States, made a habit of receiving cash pay-offs from assorted criminal types. He actually sat in his Vice Presidential office and accepted regular bribes, occasionally going home to his hotel to collect the money. He didn't discontinue this brazen outlawry until after the investigations of his past thievery began—in January of 1973. Early this very year, this man who was so trusted by so many was using his office to line his pockets, and, almost as despicably, continuing to rail against "this morbid preoccupation" with Watergate. And this is the man who made himself the darling of the flagwavers by pontificating about law and order.

What does Mr. Agnew get for his lying, his thieving, his hypocrisy, his wholehearted disrespect for the law and for the people of this country whom he so blithely hoodwinked? A fine that comes to a fraction of his extorted earnings, an unsupervised probation, a long-overdue exit from an office he never in any sense merited, and the saccharine sentiments of political heart-throbs who talk of his "personal tragedy," his "profound dedication to the welfare of the nation," his "courage and candor." Please kick us again, Ted.

In simpler days, criminals were punished—even big political fish. Albert Fall, Harding's crooked Secretary of the Interior, wound up in the pokey, and Charles Forbes, the head of the Veterans Bureau, joined him soon thereafter. No one has been able to discern any related precipitous drop in respect for the Cabinet or for the Veteran's Administration: the only ones who lost the country's good will were the jailbirds themselves. The Vice Presidency is hardly going to suffer any more opprobrium if Spiro Agnew is given a little time to think over the baseness of his conduct.

Similarly, the cry that he's been punished enough becomes an empty one when you consider what would happen to any other American (save, of course, the sacrosanct Mr. Nixon) charged with multiple counts of bribery, extortion and tax evasion. Anyone else would have a rough time plea-bargaining his way down to a five year stay in Leavenworth: yet Agnew gets the chance to trade in an office from which he'd have been hastily booted anyway right after conviction, for a suspended sentence and a far-from-hefty fine. And then Agnew and Nixon and Mitchell wonder why people think that justice is not equitably meted out around here.

Let's not, in our national sympathy for the underdog (a sympathy that often indiscriminately applies even to an underdog with great big canines and an instinct for democracy's jugular vein), forget that Agnew's relinquishing an office he never deserved is no greater punishment than a burglar's losing that stolen TV set upon being collared by the cops. It doesn't matter *how* many votes he got: a man who uses the Vice Presidency as a bribe-collection agency does not merit the office.

Nixon, it seems, mistook that gleam in Agnew's eye for the gleam of character, when it only signified a lean and hungry greed. The whole country was fooled—yes, even The Sun, which spoke with respect about the man's forthrightness, just as he was lying most egregiously. It is a shame that Elliot Richardson and Judge Hoffman, and all those who prate about Agnew's basic nobility, have conspired to fool us once more.

—editorial, October 12, 1973

−Sun Photo by Philip Lee

TWISTING SLOWLY, SLOWLY IN THE WIND: *With hands on "telephone" and feet on "intercom," two students await the next move in the "Rose Mary Woods Contortion Game" at a Richard Nixon Impeachment Fair held in the Straight Memorial Room in early 1974. The game spoofed the nearly impossible posture supposedly assumed by Nixon's private secretary when −according to Administration spokesmen−she accidentally erased 18½ minutes of a key White House tape recording.*

and respect notwithstanding−a wholehearted disrespect. A bitter and belligerent man, the President divided his free TV time between boasting of his international prowess and griping about the news media, managing also to twist and distort the circumstances of the firing of Archibald Cox. All the old and despicable stunts were there, a little worse for wear but as crudely bizarre as ever: the last time you guys picked on me I brought peace with honor to Vietnam; sure there's pressure on me, but my mandate says not to listen to it but to stick to my guns and defy it; even if all those charges are true, my understanding with Leonid Brezhnev shows what a great President I am; the American people respect me for my control of inflation and my determination to get to the bottom of Watergate, even if the underhanded press doesn't.

Particularly galling was Nixon's energetic obfuscation of the special prosecutor issue. "The special prosecutor will have independence, he will have total cooperation from the executive branch.... It's time for those who are guilty to be prosecuted," said one side of the presidential mouth; "we will not provide presidential documents to a special prosecutor," who will not find it "necessary to obtain evidence from [my] files" anyway, said the other. And of course Congress will not find it necessary to duplicate the Executive's efforts and appoint its own investigator. And of course Elliot Richardson approved of the Stennis compromise, Nixon fudged and fibbed and made it fully clear that if there's any way to commission a bogus investigation at this late date, he'll give it the ol' college try.

This sort of slapstick is not likely to calm people who believe Richard Nixon to be the most corrupt and arrogant leader in American history; neither is heatedly and fitfully jabbering about how "the tougher it gets the cooler I get," and how "I have what it

After the Nixon Pardon: Unclean Hands

BY CHARLES ROTHFELD '77

President Ford seemed very disturbed yesterday. He kept pacing up and down the White House halls rubbing his hands together. Finally Mrs. Ford asked him what was the matter.

"I seem to have some kind of spot on my hand," said the President. "It won't come off."

Mrs. Ford put down her knitting and went over to the President and looked. She told him that she didn't see any spots on his hand. "I think that you've been working too hard putting an end to inflation, dear," she said. "And it must be very tiring getting up early in the morning, so that you can get the paper in your bathrobe. I think you need a rest."

The President said no, there really was a spot on his hand, and anyway if she got up earlier to make breakfast for him in the morning, he wouldn't be so tired. But there really was a spot. "In fact," he said, "when I walked downstairs this morning I saw all those reporters pointing at me and snickering, and I looked down and saw this ugly spot. It was very embarrassing. After all, I am the President."

"Maybe your fly was open," said Mrs. Ford.

The President said that President's flies are never open. Presidents might wear bathrobes sometimes, but their flies were never open. The American people wouldn't stand for it. The President said that he wasn't a Democrat, he couldn't do something like that. Maybe John Kennedy could have done it, but the President was a Middle American. What

would the VFW have said if he'd addressed them with an open fly? Then the President looked back down at his hand. His mouth fell open. "The spot is growing!" he shouted.

Mrs. Ford said that there was no spot, and that if the President didn't believe her he should ask someone else. "Why don't you call Dr. Kissinger," she asked. "If anyone can help you, he can."

The President said yes, Secretary Kissinger was indispensable to world peace and domestic tranquility, and he called him up and told him to come right over to the White House.

Secretary Kissinger came right over. He was wearing black leather gloves.

"Secretary Kissinger," said the President, "my Administration is facing its first great crisis of confidence. There is a spot growing on my hand, which is threatening my ability to govern. How can I sign a major bill with a spotty hand? How can I go before Congress or the press in this discolored state? They would never take seriously a President who changes his colors like this. Please, Mr. Secretary, only your great intellect and tremendous reputation can help me."

Secretary Kissinger looked at the President's hand with a frown, and asked him whether he had had any close contact with ex-President Nixon recently.

Mrs. Ford gasped.

The President said yes, just the other day he and the ex-President had gotten together for a friendly game of golf, and when the ex-President had left, the President had given him a pardon or two

to take home to the family.

"Oh tell us, doctor, what is it?" cried Mrs. Ford.

"Just as I thought," said Secretary Kissinger. "It is the stain of Watergate."

There was a painful silence.

"The ex-President should be quarantined in California," said Secretary Kissinger. "He seems to be the center of infection. Almost anyone who comes into contact with him for any length of time seems to get it. In fact, this winter you'll see a lot of people wearing gloves, trying to cover it up." Secretary Kissinger put his hands in his pockets.

The President asked what he could do.

"You'll just have to hope that it rubs off on to someone else, like draft evaders," said Secretary Kissinger. "But be careful−in some cases the stain of Watergate has been almost totally debilitating. You'll just have to pray, and buy a pair of gloves. If worst comes to worst, you could write a book."

The President said that he had never been the type to go the cover-up route.

Secretary Kissinger said that he had to go check on detente and excused himself.

The President and Mrs. Ford went to sleep. Later than night Mrs. Ford woke up to hear water running in the Executive washroom. "What's the matter, dear?" yelled Mrs. Ford.

"I'm trying to wash it off," said the President. "Out, damn spot, out I say!"

Mrs. Ford sighed and went back to sleep.

−column, September 11, 1974

takes." Even Gerald Ford thinks Nixon may now regret some of his seamier statements. On the first run-through, anger is the natural — the only — response.

The second time through, the picture changes in a profound way. It's a few hours later, and the anger cools. You feel deeply, genuinely sorry for Richard Nixon.

That's not meant sarcastically; our President is a sad and lonely man, a fundamentally pathetic figure. That's not said for polemics' sake, either; if anything, a little sympathy will cool the ardor of the impeachment seekers. It's said, perhaps, to hint at the strength of our conviction that Nixon must go: justice must outweigh sentiment.

It was difficult to agree with that last during the Nixon rerun; let the thing slide, you wanted to say, leave this unhappy old man alone. Nixon would smile and, palpably, no one grinned with him; he tried to joke, and no one laughed. Beset by ideas he certainly cannot agree with, ideas presented with a vehemence he cannot fully comprehend, he resorted to bravado and pathos, speaking in the third person of the President's virtues, trotting out international crisis in a desperate and transparent attempt to divert the flood. Doing his damnedest to bear up and look Presidential, Nixon's human abilities failed him when he needed them most, and he looked ragged and tired and bitter and weak. It was a sad and sobering scene.

Impeachment is not a lark; as necessary and promising as it is, there are very real human costs and personal tragedies involved, human factors that we should only ignore in so far as we are willing to imitate Richard Nixon in his decisions to bomb and burgle. But as much as the second viewing of the press conference brings home the pathos of the situation, the first watching establishes its utter necessity. Richard Nixon, for the record, is a sad and sorry man; Richard Nixon, for the good of the country, is a man who must be disgraced.

— editorial, October 29, 1973

1976: Ford vs. Carter

In 1968, The Sun began its endorsement of Hubert Humphrey with the words, "We, too, are tempted to sit this one out." It is symptomatic of the uninspiring national leadership provided this country in recent years that the sentiment applies equally well to the election of 1976.

Both major party candidates have been running for the presidency for close to two years now, but neither has managed to inspire the nation with his policies or his vision of the future. Thus, as in 1968, the choice reduces largely to the lesser of two evils. As The Sun observed then in anguish and some indecision, "we may support a major party candidate, cast a protest endorsement or abstain completely from the process." It is with similar feelings this year that we find ourselves supporting the candidacy of Jimmy Carter.

For all his recent issue straddling and campaign gyrations, President Ford comes to the electorate as a given, with two years of proven blandness behind him. In that sense, the election has largely become a referendum on the character of Carter, a question of whether his progressive promise balances the risks and inconsistencies of an ominous unknown.

Despite the cries of Democratic stalwarts that only issues should count and that the excesses of this year's lackluster campaign should be ignored, it is clear that after the political traumas of the last decade character itself should be an issue. It is up to the electorate, then, to decide how far he will go and what he will compromise to make himself a salable commodity; the burden of proof is on him.

James Reston, in his meditations on American electoral folly, has suggested that Carter represents the force of movement in the political system and is therefore the man who can again interest the young in political life. But if the polls are to be believed it is the young who are most resistant to Carter. This is, perhaps, because the political consciousness of those in their early twenties was formed in the crucible of the Johnson and Nixon presidencies, a time of illusion when voters seeking peace and progress were presented with something quite different.

And Carter carries on one of the most disturbing trends of the imperial presidency by wanting to lead the nation — and in apparently thinking he is the only one who knows where the nation ought to go. As he wrote in *The New York Times*, "A national leader, to be effective, must have the ability to lead this country and the vision to know where it must be led." And, in dangerous combination, he seems convinced he is in communion with the

American people: "I have a direct relationship with hundreds of thousands of people around the country."

Given the excesses of recent years, it was particularly disturbing to find Carter tinged with touches of the Johnson and Nixon paranoia when dealing with the opposition, and to see his campaign take on an acid and occasionally frantic tone when confronted with criticism. It was equally disturbing to hear a candidate during his campaign espousing high ideals and the intention never to deceive his listeners, while he would clearly rather be president than be right.

So what is the real Carter? Or is there a real Carter? He is undoubtedly a driven man — he has been running for the presidency since the age of 30 — but his past gives little clue. There is no way, in this age of enemies lists, for the voter to know how the candidate will act when confronted with determined opposition. Carter is a risk for the voter; the question is whether taking that risk is justified by the quality of his opposition.

President Ford, in contrast, is above all things safe; he will deliver the nation intact in four years for someone else to mold. And there is a tremendous appeal in having as president a man who doesn't have a visceral need for the job. Ford's happiest quality is his predictability, a quality the nation has clearly taken to heart.

Nonetheless, Ford has proven himself a man of limited potential and little vision, with an insensitivity to the basic needs of the poor and underprivileged. His negative record, after two years in office, is clear to all: he has done little of note to upgrade the nation's cities, economy, or social and physical environment.

Here — in his vision of the future and of what America can be — lies Jimmy Carter's appeal. Hearing Carter speak to the issues makes one realize just what potential is there, and just what one is throwing away with a vote for Ford. Carter presents at least the hope of decent health care, a comprehensive energy policy, tax reform, help for the environment and education, and above all employment for all Americans.

Ford has provided valuable service in calming America after the turmoil of Watergate and Vietnam. But he has shown no talent for taking the nation beyond where it is, or for achieving progress towards social justice. That is what Carter offers despite his flaws, and, after years of social stagnation, it is an offer that is difficult to reject.

— editorial, November 1, 1976

— Sun Photo by Dan Clement

'And You Can Depend on It': *Presidential candidate Jimmy Carter squeezes out yet another grin at a Station Restaurant luncheon meeting of the local Democratic Party on November 19, 1975, when he was still considered a longshot for the nomination. Then Ithaca Mayor Edward Conley sits at a table behind.*

INTERLUDE: Reminders of Better Times

A Turn-of-the-Century Cornell Childhood

Time present and time past
Are both perhaps present in time future
And time future contained in time past.
—T.S. Eliot, *Burnt Norton*

Part I — A Boy's View

By Bertram F. Willcox '17

"See you in whiskey!" "Meet you in beer!" "Cider, after school!" These calls, across the campus, are not from a gang of young alcoholics. They are from members of our gang of young faculty off-spring, often referred to by our adults lovingly, or venomously, as the "Campus Tigers." In clement weather we swim, at random, in certain pools of Cascadilla Gorge to which we have attached those names. There are also pools more dangerous and thus more challenging—some forbidden—in Fall Creek, under the foot bridge and at the upper end of Beebe Lake which we visit less routinely.

I am ten years old. The year is 1905. I stand in the entrance gateway to the campus built by Andrew D. White of sandstone and limestone to mimic the Cornell colors. According to Prof. Bishop's excellent *History of Cornell*, bluff Prof. Hull called it "frankly hideous" but "the world," more tolerant perhaps, dubbed it "Andy White's layer cake." I walk between Cascadilla Gorge's edge on my left and a grey, rather ugly building on my right. (Cascadilla Building, where I was born, will still be standing in 1980. This structure began its life as a health spa, but by the time I began my life, it had been turned into apartments for young faculty families.)

From there I walk toward the arched stone bridge over the Gorge, another changeless feature in an ever changing landscape. Trolley tracks come up from Eddy Street on the far side of Cascadilla Building, passing in front of Sheldon Court, an expensive residence for students, and then plunging into the woods just beyond the Bridge. I follow these tracks; they lead me across a trestle-bridge of open ties, over the Gorge. (This

—Cornell University Archives Photos

—Main Photo by Wesp-Buzzell,
Inset Photo by Carin Ashjian

THE ARCH OF HEAVEN: *Until the arrival of Dutch elm blight, Central Avenue was lined with splendid American elms whose boughs met overhead, forming a continuous leafy tunnel through which students and professors strolled to class. The large photograph was taken about 1940 between Barnes Hall and the Straight, facing the Tower and the arts quad. Sage Chapel can be seen through elm trunks on the right, and several windows of Uris Library are partially visible on the left. The inset picture shows the barrenness of the same area in 1980, as viewed from precisely the same vantage point.*

'CLANG, CLANG, CLANG WENT THE TROLLEY!': *Top: As a little boy looks on from the lower right, an Ithaca Street Railway Co. trolley car glides past Andrew Dickson White's Eddygate, known in 1905 as "Andy White's Chocolate Layer Cake" because of its alternating red and white stones. Middle: Rails curve toward a trolley bridge over Cascadilla Gorge, as a sign warns away passersby. A pedestrian span now crosses the chasm at the same place, just east of the Collegetown stone arch bridge. Bottom: Turn-of-the-century conductors and passengers pose at a trolley stop on the south end of the arts quad. In the background are Sibley Hall, Lincoln Hall, and the Dairy Building (now incorporated as one of the wings of Goldwin Smith Hall).*

Interlude: Reminders of Better Times

THREE SOUTH AVENUE: *Above, the yellow and white Willcox home stands prominently in the distance behind Sage and Barnes halls. The gully before it has since been filled in to form part of the engineering quad. Left, the roof of the Willcox residence glows with late evening sunshine. The house and the hydrangea bush in front of its porch are gone, but the large oak tree guarding it to the left is still alive, rising from a hillock at the northwest corner of Upson Hall.*

will be a firm footbridge in 1980 with no more than a distant memory of trolley cars.) The trestle-bridge is close to my family's house, and I always enjoy the adventure of crossing it, knowing that a streetcar too speedy to allow escape from the bridge may meet or overtake me. If it does I will have to select one of the long ties that jut out, here and there, farther than the others, and thereby offer refuge; one walks out on it and clings to the post at its end while the trolley clangs nervously past. If you are a romantic small boy you blow up the thrill by pretending that the solid wire-net casing that surrounds the ends of these ties would not be strong enough to hold against an accident. The car passes; there is no accident.

I continue to follow the tracks north (passing through what will in 1980 be the gap between Hollister and Bard Halls). On my right, dense woods that hide our house and others. On my left, a complex of red brick buildings comprising the University's heating plant, with its tall chimneys, and the University's Armory, with its vast open hall (predecessor of the far vaster Barton Hall). Piles of coal for the furnaces of the heating plant stand below the tracks on this side. The tracks soon come to South Avenue, the most southerly of the streets of the Campus. (By 1980 this part of South Avenue will have vanished without a trace.)

Now my trolley tracks turn square right, so suddenly that their rigid little four-wheel cars screech fiendishly in turning. Occasionally a car comes off the rails here, and has to be jacked and eased back into place. The conductor of each car knows his passengers, who use Ithaca trolleys almost daily in place of the automobiles that are still far in the future. When an elderly lady and her conductor happen both to slip up on where she should have gotten off, the trolley will back up to the proper spot.

We children knew little and speculated less, I think, about how our elders lived and were cared for. We supposed that by the laws of nature much was done to make their tasks easier. Although our fathers had to walk to

ONE WHISKEY, ONE BEER: *The pool above the waterfall is the swimming hole "Beer," where a bar of "Violet Island" (now the Cascadilla tennis courts) is visible. Beneath the falls lies the more turbulent "Whiskey." The water is cascading over Otis Eddy's stone dam, which—in the 1820s—supplied water for his cotton mill near the present site of Cascadilla Hall; traces of this 150-year-old dam can still be seen at the end of the Goldwin Smith Walk. Besides providing a convenient name for Eddy Street, Eddy gave the young Ezra Cornell his first full-time job after the Founder arrived in Ithaca in 1828.*

KNICKERED TIGER: *"Campus Tiger" Bertram Willcox '17 wears his Sunday best at the age of ten.*

A CENTURY AT CORNELL

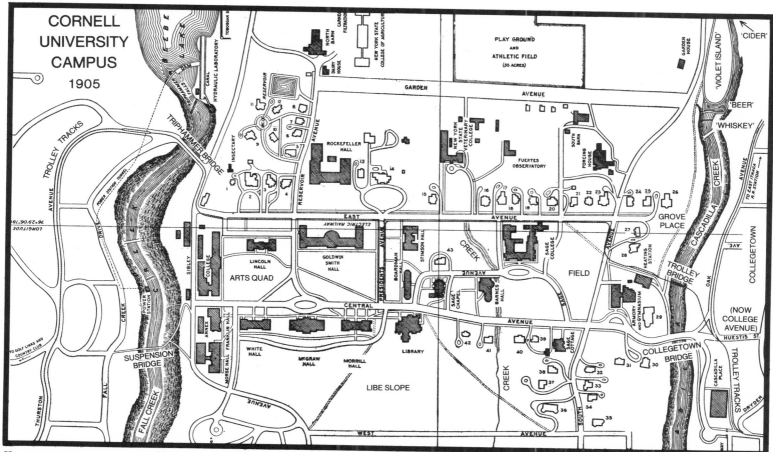

CORNELL UNIVERSITY CAMPUS 1905

KEY TO THE PROFESSORS' HOMES AND FRATERNITY HOUSES ON CAMPUS IN 1905: (1) Prof. John H. Comstock, entomology; (2) President Jacob Gould Schurman; (3) Prof. Ernest Merritt, physics; (4) Prof. Thomas F. Hunt, agronomy; (5) Prof. James M. Hart, English; (6) Prof. Henry H. Wing, animal husbandry; (7) Prof. Carl Thomas, marine engineering; (8) Prof. Henry S. Jacoby, civil engineering; (9) Prof. James E. Creighton, philosophy*; (10) Prof. Lucien A. Wait, mathematics*; (11) Prof. James Law, veterinary medicine*; (12) Prof. J.E. Trevor, chemistry*; (13) Prof. William A. Hammond, philosophy; (14) Former President Andrew Dickson White; (15) Mr. Duncan C. Lee; (16) Widow of Prof. Robert H. Thurston, mechanical engineering (this house was soon to be occupied by Prof. Albert W. "Pete" Smith, mechanical engineering); (17) Prof. W.L. Drew, law; (18) Prof. Willard W. Rowlee, botany; (19) Prof. Henry S. Williams, geology (In 1906 Prof. Frank Thilly, philosophy, moved into this house, which was donated to the University by Henry Williams Sage, as a residence for the Sage Professor of Christian Ethics and Moral Philosophy.); (20) Prof. Wilder D. Bancroft, chemistry; (21) Prof. George F. Atkinson, botany; (22) Prof. John Craig, agricultural extension; (23) Prof. Ralph S. Tarr, geology; (24) Prof. Charles E. Bennett, Latin; (25) Librarian George W. Harris; (26) Prof. George P. Bristol, Greek; (27) Prof. Frederick C. Prescott, English; (28) Prof. Walter F. Willcox, economics; (29) the original Kappa Alpha Lodge; (30) the original Psi Upsilon Lodge; (31) the original Sigma Phi Lodge; (32) Prof. Edward L. Nichols, physics; (33) Prof. Evander B. McGilvary, ethics; (34) Prof. Irving P. Church, civil engineering; (35) Delta Kappa Epsilon Lodge (where it still stands); (36) Delta Upsilon Lodge (where it still stands); (37) Prof. Simon H. Gage, zoology; (38) Prof. Jeremiah Whipple Jenks, economics; (39) Prof. Ralph C. Catterall, history; (40) Prof. James McMahon, mathematics; (41) Prof. Thomas F. "Teefy" Crane, romance languages; (42) Prof. George C. Caldwell, agricultural chemistry; (43) Prof. Charles Babcock, architecture.

*The houses of Professors Creighton, Wait, Law, and Trevor were originally located where Rockefeller Hall stands.

their classes and their other work, our mothers—who ran them and us and our houses—enjoyed as a matter of course one or two full-time servants and some other occasional helpers. Grocers and butchers solicitously took orders over the telephone, made selections calculated to please, and sent them by their wagons to our doors. The iceman brought staggering great cubes of ice and hoisted them into our back-porch iceboxes. Any residual need for local transportation was met, as I have said, by the streetcars, forever creeping up and down the fearsome hills that connected the campus with the town below.

For more extended journeys one would hire a horse and buggy. I remember that we hired one on April 18th or 19th, 1906, to visit the devoted, imaginative, and controversial George Junior Republic near Freeville. We took all day for this visit, although our distance was only about 15 miles. When we got back to Three South Avenue at about six o'clock, I ran up the steps to our front porch and found an *Ithaca Daily News and Journal* lying on our doorstep

with giant headlines announcing the San Francisco earthquake. Incidentally, I can still hear the cries of the newsboys of Ithaca hawking that paper; they put all the emphasis of their young voices on the word *and* in its name as though that were the only important part of their announcement.

Now, back to the campus. I am still standing on the trolley tracks where they turn east on South Avenue. On my left, the brick complex houses (in addition to the heating plant and the Armory) a wretched smelly little gymnasium with an indoor running track circling it on a shelf above our heads, and with an even more inadequate swimming pool tucked into a long narrow building lower down. (This will, in 1980, occupy a part of the site of Hollister Hall.) The pool's only appeal, even for youngsters, is that one can swim in its unappetizing lukewarm waters even in winter. Profiting by some arcane knowledge of a half-hidden window that lacks a lock, some of us are wont to steal stealthily in on winter Sundays when the building is closed and deserted. I remember that one such

group, of mixed sexes, engaged in a spirited debate on the morality *vel non* of skinnydipping in these circumstances. The decision is affirmative, based on the questionable logic that because the group consists entirely of sisters and brothers, each of whom has seen her or his opposite number in the altogether, there can be no impropriety in the whole group's going in together. In the gymnasium later on we exercise on all the apparatus and run endlessly and joyously on the small track. But we take no such liberties in the great hall of the Armory. Its size is far too awe-inspiring for that.

Outside, in front of the impressive façade of the Armory, there is, in good weather, another much larger wooden running-track, with ends banked to facilitate the turns: a quarter-mile track if I remember correctly. This one is taken up every winter. Here also, close to the Armory, stands a noble totem pole: strange carved creature above strange carved creature. It was brought from Alaska near the turn of the century, at vast effort. A circular protective fence, of iron piping, surrounds the base of the pole.

Interlude: Reminders of Better Times

On this fence we children delight to climb. (Now, in 1980, the old pole can be seen at Cornell's Arnot Forest, some 18 miles south of Newfield, having been re-erected there after many years of neglect in some barn or warehouse.)

Back to our trolley tracks again. In the short easterly block they pass two of the houses of what I think of as "Professors' Row." These two stand back in the woods nearer to the Gorge. The first is Three South Avenue, already mentioned, a large yellow and white house with a big hydrangia bush close to its porch; it is the house in which I have been growing up. An oak stands on the lip of a little hollow and close to the house. (In 1980, it will still be standing near the site of the house. The oak now commands the top of a shapely little knoll, considerably left when excavation was done for the nearby Upson and Kimball-Thurston-Bard Halls.) So dramatic is its position that our father has had a long swing made—two ropes and a board seat—to hang from a horizontal northwesterly branch that sticks out far overhead. Here we children savor the delight of swinging out over what

seems to us a fathomless abyss. Stevenson's ecstatic child in his *Child's Garden of Verses* could not have been more thrilled than are we.

Our next-door neighbors to the east are the Prescotts, Prof. Prescott of the English department, a soft-spoken, gentle, Lincolnesque scholar whose investigations into the nature of dreams and poetic inspiration brought him, I am told, honor in France that never came to him in his own country. But I must not wander; my business is with the campus scene and, more particularly, with the professors' houses and the professors' children.†

Except for a special situation or two, such as the donated house of Prof. Thilly to be noted later, each house in Professors' Row has been built or bought by a Cornell faculty member, but the land on which the house stands remains the property of the University, rented to the tenant for one dollar a year. (Although a dollar has some real value in 1905, it is still not much for a house-site for a year.) So long as the owner of the house continues to be a member of the faculty, this arrangement can go on, and whenever he

leaves the faculty he may sell it to some other faculty member. But there is one big *quid pro quo*: whenever the University may need the land for a University purpose, it has the power to acquire the house for demolition, paying its owner an appraised value or $5,000, whichever is the greater.

In the early literature and letters, and even in Bishop's *History of Cornell*, these dwellings were usually referred to as "cottages." In actuality they were for the most part full-blown houses such as faculty members might have been expected to build upon their own land, of varying sizes and degrees of elegance.

The outstandingly distinguished Prof. James Law, a famous Scottish veterinarian, was one of the first of Andrew D. White's triumphant appointments for his burgeoning little institution where every person was to find instruction in every subject. It is Elizabeth Law, his wife, who is credited with having persuaded the University to adopt the foregoing rather unconventional plan for housing its small faculty on its ample acres (adapting the plan, perhaps, from one utilized at Oxford).

(By 1980 Professors' Row will have disappeared completely. Kimball and Upson Halls, Phillips, The Statler, Uris — alias "Old Rusty" — Rockefeller, Clark and Baker will have swept it clean away, except, of course, the Andrew D. White Mansion, which was never a part of it anyhow. Willard Straight and the Gannett Clinic will have done the same for Central Avenue south of the old

—Cornell University Archives

PROFESSOR'S ROW, SOUTH: *The homes of Prof. Evander B. McGilvary and Prof. Edward Leamington Nichols commanded a breath-taking panorama of Cayuga Lake, Libe Slope (seen to the far right), and the distant McGraw-Fiske mansion (right), which burned spectacularly in 1906 to be replaced by the present Chi Psi Lodge. The McGilvary and Nichols homes stood on a vanished segment of South Avenue, on a site now occupied by Myron Taylor Hall and its lower parking lots.*

†This sketch does not pretend to be local history. It is a distillation of recollections of a dreamy small boy, about things three quarters of a century ago: things he remembers or thinks he remembers, or has been told of enough times so that he seems to remember them. My co-author, with a younger and far more precise memory, has kindly pointed out some half dozen or more spots where the boy's memory must be at fault. If time allowed, for me and for the editors, revisions would surely be in order. But seeing that the time *is* short and that, after all, my purpose is not a photographic reproduction so much as a recapture of an overall impression, I let it stand as it is. With this warning no historian will be misled. —B.F.W.

—Photo by W.P. Allen

RUINED COTTAGES: *The professors' cottages which lined the southern half of East Avenue until the middle of this century were all bulldozed to make way for Statler and Phillips halls. This 1889 view, photographed from a meadow north of Sage College for women, shows five cottages which would be respectively occupied in the early 1900s by (left to right) Prof. Albert W. Smith; Prof. W.L. Drew; Prof. Willard Rowlee; Prof. Frank Thilly; and Prof. Wilder Bancroft.*

A CENTURY AT CORNELL

Library—now the Uris Library. The old "Circle" of some half dozen faculty houses close to the 1980 site of Bailey and Clark Halls, has also vanished, together with the nearby reservoir with a mountainous wooden roof, on which we were sternly forbidden to play lest we fall through, 70-odd years ago, and on which we, knowing better, played whenever we thought we would not be caught.)

Return now to our walk in 1905 past the Willcox and Prescott houses. We reach East Avenue and Grove Place, its short southerly spur to our right, containing the Bennett house (of Bennett's *Latin Grammar*), the house of University Librarian George Harris, who is reputed —perhaps unfairly—to take such loving care of his books that he defends them against all readers. And deepest into the woods on this dead end, the Bristol house.

From this corner of East and South Avenues a dirt road continues the line of South Avenue eastward until it snakes around a hillock on its left (which in 1980 will buttress Schoellkopf Field) and, following Cascadilla's valley on its right, passes a lovely wild island far below, well named "Violet Island" for its luscious carpet of especially large ones, and having a pool at its foot, "Beer" I think, and a somewhat more turbulent pool beneath a lovely waterfall at its head, "Whiskey" I'm pretty sure. (If we look into a crystal ball we shall see its violets replaced by a girls' playing field and, later on, by 'varsity tennis courts.) Higher upstream, where our meandering road crosses, there is a small dam above the bridge, and behind it the less potent pool, appropriately called "Cider." Whether I have remembered the names correctly or not, I can assure you that all three pools were lovely on a hot summer afternoon.

—Cornell University Archives

TRIPPING HITHER, TRIPPING THITHER: *By 1915, the Campus Tigers' "Violet Island" near the "Beer" and "Whiskey" swimming holes in Cascadilla Gorge had become a women's playground. Here nearly all the women of Cornell would participate in annual spring pageants, dancing and prancing about dressed as faeries, forest queens, water nymphs, and other mythological creatures. The townsfolk of Ithaca would trek up the Hill to sit in folding chairs and watch the gamboling sprites. "Violet Island" is now covered with tennis courts.*

Now for the eastern side of East Avenue, the right hand side where the sidewalk is. The trolley tracks are on the left hand side, with an open field beyond as we start north. East Avenue itself, like Central Avenue, is a road of extraordinary beauty, for it runs between a double row of great elms that meet overhead in a benison of greenery. These trees were planted, first on East Avenue, in 1877, by a hard-working farmer, one Mr. Ostrander, who had told President White that he wanted to help the new university; that he had no money; that he would like to contribute instead by planting on its campus some fine elm saplings which were growing on his farm. White, who loved trees with a fine passion, accepted eagerly. Thus came the Ostrander Elms, one of our early glories until the Dutch elm disease annihilated them.

The first house on our right as we go north is that of Prof. Ralph S. Tarr (geologist; great explorer; co-author of the Tarr & McMurray Geographies); then the house of Prof. John Craig (agriculture, and first Extension teacher thereof in America); then the house of George Atkinson (botany); next, that of Prof. Wilder Bancroft (chemistry) featuring a great copper beech tree in his front yard.

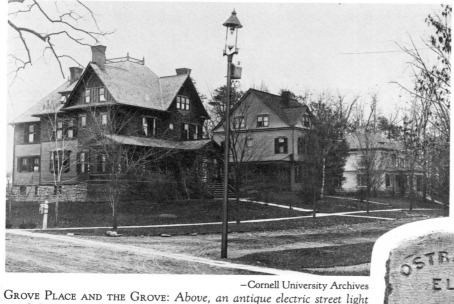

—Cornell University Archives

GROVE PLACE AND THE GROVE: *Above, an antique electric street light stands before the Grove Place homes of Prof. Charles Bennet, Librarian George Harris, and Prof. George Bristol. Phillips Hall occupies this strip of land today. Right, the famous Cornell elms, some of which were donated in 1880 by the poor Danby farmer John B. Ostrander, flank East Avenue behind Goldwin Smith Hall at their maturity. All the elms are now dead, but—almost like tombstones to their memory—two tablets (inset) in honor of Ostrander remain, one in front of Phillips Hall and another before Stimson Hall.*

—Cornell University Archives

Interlude: Reminders of Better Times

It still graces the front of the Statler in 1980. The large green Bancroft house contains a wonderfully jolly but combative family of children of all the age-levels that mattered to us. The Bancroft children's motto was "Why work while Mother's strength lasts?"

Next is the house of Prof. Frank Thilly (philosophy; history of philosophy), one of whose lovely daughters is my sister's age and—to my great joy—my co-author in this resuscitation of campus memories. The Thilly house was donated to the University by Henry Sage and so may differ somewhat from the others in Professors' Row. Next door to the Thillys is the W.W. Rowlee family (professor of botany and in addition a highly creative superintendent of the Cornell grounds). Next, I think—I may be missing one—the house of Ruby Green Smith and Albert W. Smith (dean of mechanical engineering, the beloved "Uncle Pete," who would become Cornell's acting president in 1920). Here a large open field intervenes extending from East Avenue to the yellow Veterinary Building far back from the street. We have just passed Sage Dormitory for girls on the left across the street. (It will be complemented by Prudence Risley, across Fall Creek to the north in 1913—did the two names suggest that the girls were expected to behave themselves? The field in front of the Veterinary Building will in 1980 be partly occupied by "Old Rusty"—Uris Hall.)

In this field we like to play baseball. With some feeling of *noblesse oblige* blended with more than a bit of condescension, we boys send an invitation, or challenge, to a team of lads we have heard of as living down near the Inlet. Our baseball equipment—gloves, bats, mask, even uniforms! wrung from parents—is superb. Our baseball, however, is ragged. Their equipment is ragged; their baseball, however, is

−Cornell University Archives

END OF THE LINE: *Seen through the arches and stone carvings of the entrance porch to Boardman Hall, a trolley pauses before returning along a spur of track on the south side of the arts quad. In the background are Uris Library, Morrill Hall, and the tower of McGraw Hall. Boardman was demolished in 1959 to make way for Olin Library.*

superb. They win, 11-1. We pretend, shamefacedly, that this must have been because they are a little bigger than we are.

So, swimming, baseball, tennis and bicycling in summer; sledding, skating on Beebe lake when the ice was both firm and cleared, and tobogganning in winter. Our amusements were varied enough. One other sport flared like a comet, became the rage overnight, and died. Diabolo. You held two sticks in your two hands. Their ends were joined by a string. On that you could spin a sort of double-ended top shaped like an hourglass. The string passed under its slender waist. You can throw it high, high in the air and catch it on the string again, many times, without dropping it. Campus records, reaching to over a hundred times, were made only to be broken the next day; and the latest record was hot campus news.

Back again to East Avenue. Farther along, we see the beautiful and lofty Andrew D. White Mansion high on the right (later to become for some years the University's museum of art, and by 1980 the home of its Center for the Humanities). Beneath the eminence on which it stands our little trolley car steps out of its monotonous progression for a side trip. At a three-way switch it clangs to the left and glides downhill on President's Avenue between another two beautiful rows of trees, passing on its left Stimson Hall, the home of the cadavers, and Boardman Hall, the home of the Law School. (By 1980 Boardman will have vanished, except for a few sculptured heads preserved within and without the new Olin Library, which will have replaced it.) On its right, the site of what will be Goldwin Smith Hall. So we reach the old Library

−Cornell University Archives

A DAY IN THE LIFE: *The Andrew Dickson White mansion, decked with colorful summer awnings, bustles with family activity. Boys and girls lounge on the front yard grass and a horse and buggy waits before the front entrance, where a woman sits with child on lap.*

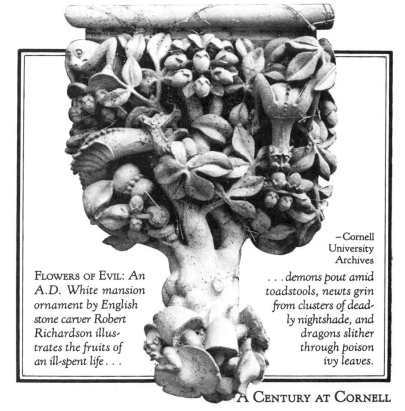

−Cornell University Archives

FLOWERS OF EVIL: *An A.D. White mansion ornament by English stone carver Robert Richardson illustrates the fruits of an ill-spent life . . .*

. . . demons pout amid toadstools, newts grin from clusters of deadly nightshade, and dragons slither through poison ivy leaves.

-Photo by James H. Fenner

JACOBS' LADDER: *Three generations of President Jacob Gould Schurman's family pose. Top row: Mrs. Schurman, President Schurman, and Jacob Gould Schurman Jr. '17, who was Bertram Willcox's classmate and friend. Bottom row: Bernice Wilson Schurman, Robert Schurman '07, Jacob Gould Schurman III, and George Munro Schurman '13.*

-Cornell University Archives

WHEN 'COTTAGES' WERE MANSIONS: *President Schurman's East Avenue home crowned the hill where Baker Laboratory now rises. Although called a "cottage," it was a massive edifice with overhanging gables and stained glass windows. The architect was William Henry Miller, Cornell's first architecture student, who also designed Uris Library, Risley College, Barnes Hall, and many of the finer fraternity houses near campus.*

and its famous Tower. Here the trolley car pauses. The conductor descends deliberately and, pulling down the cord of the trolley proper, swings it in a half circle to the other end of the car. He helps it find its overhead wire again, setting off an exciting shower of sparks. The motorman changes places with him, meanwhile, and unleashes his controls. The car moves backwards up the hill, turns left at the three-way switch and continues, without further reversal, north along East Avenue.

As we again glimpse the aura of the great White Mansion above us, I am reminded of a silly little story. Andrew D. White has retired from the presidency, but his patriarchal figure, with flowing white beard, is a familiar sight on the sidewalks of his beloved campus. He loves small children, too, just as he loves trees. Whenever he meets a little girl he

raises his hat in courtly, formal manner and asks after her welfare. My sister, aged seven or eight, and four other girls of her age, have a very secret club, as small girls will. They elect four of the five girls: president, vice-president, secretary, and treasurer; but they fear that the feelings of the fifth may be hurt by having no office. So, after some discussion, they elect the fifth ex-president.

Now, back to our trolley car. On our left Goldwin Smith Hall is building, and incorporating an earlier dairy building as its northern wing. Goldwin Smith is opened in 1906. Beyond it is Lincoln Hall. On the right is the house of Prof. Law, which was the first house of Professors' Row proper. The house of Prof. Hammond (philosophy) may, however, have been between the Law house and the White Mansion—the evidence is confusing. In any event, the Law house

was removed in 1905 to make way for Rockefeller Hall, opened in 1906. The Hammond house survived to become the home of Prof. Kinkeldey (musicology) who came here in 1923 from the New York Public Library.

Prof. Hammond's son, Donald, although a coeval and playmate of mine, is obviously more sophisticated than I. Mischievously he once persuaded me that great elm trees occasionally reach down with their branches and capture people. I tremble still to think of my half-believing homeward trip, at dusk that evening, and the half-circles out into the middle of East Avenue which I made to keep at a distance from the towering Ostrander Elms—utterly benign, I am now persuaded, and not at all interested in capturing a small boy.

After Rockefeller Hall comes the large green house of our reigning president,

-Cornell University Archives

ENGLISHMAN AND ANGLOPHILE: *As an umbrella shields against bright sunshine, an elderly Goldwin Smith removes his bowler and Andrew Dickson White doffs his top hat during the October 19, 1904 cornerstone laying ceremony for Goldwin Smith Hall.*

-Cornell University Archives

WHEN DREAM BECOMES FACT: *In 1862, Andrew Dickson White first fully expressed his desire to help found a new kind of modern university "from which ideas and men shall go forth to bless the nation during ages." Here he stands on the arts quad half a century later, looking out over the fulfillment of his goal. Behind him is the stone bench donated by Goldwin Smith, inscribed "ABOVE ALL NATIONS IS HUMANITY."*

Interlude: Reminders of Better Times

Jacob Gould Schurman, the father of my best friend (not at this time only but also in boarding school, in college, in law school and in the practice of law). Incidentally, my father, who was a member of the Cornell Faculty for 73 years—including 33 as emeritus—thought White and Schurman Cornell's greatest presidents, in part at least because each of them was an experienced teacher and understood the points of view of a faculty. The Schurman house, spacious and elegant, stands high on a bluff looking out over Beebe Lake and the Thurston Avenue bridge. (In 1980 Baker Lab will occupy this site.)

The faculty of this young university is still small, and the Schurman house, with its friendly president, gracious wife and lively family of dynamic children is a center of hospitality and activity.

On the hither side of Beebe Lake a wooded road winds off toward Forest Home, where there is a general store that sells particularly fine, durable all-day-suckers. Should you set out by yourself on a spring evening you may notice a strange and colorful procession of about a dozen bicycles propelled by very young riders starting out along this road. In about half an hour, if you wait and watch, it will return with every rider hard at work on an all-day-sucker. If the hour should happen to be that of one of the Senior Sings, with clusters of senior men sitting on the steps in front of Goldwin Smith Hall and singing their hearts out, then you may perhaps see the strange troop of cyclists ending its Odyssey here by riding circles in and among and around the listeners, getting ourselves heartily cursed for the brats that we are. We feel deeply and indignantly, however, that this outrageously inconsiderate behavior is our right, because the entire university is *our* university. It is not wickedness, I believe, so much as the utter lack of comprehension on the part of the young. The name, incidentally, of our bicycle troop is "The Tonawanda Limited Express." God alone knows why. Our leader, and first bicycle, is a tomboy a few years older than I, a masterful girl named Jean Stanton whose overlordship was romantically enhanced when she fell from her bicycle and broke her leg.

In winter the Forest Home road leads to nearer and more exciting thrills, when the weather is propitious and the ice on Beebe is clear. Within sight of the Schurman residence, I think, an open-work tower rises above the shore on the nearer side of the lake. A steep approach, cleated for the benefit of snow-clogged boots and having railings on both sides, leads to the top of the tower. Up this we drag our long toboggans. An attendant presides there. When he gives us the go-ahead signal, we lift our tobog-

—Cornell University Archives
LIGHTLY GLIDING O'ER THE SNOW: *One of the highlights of a Cornell winter prior to 1940 was the toboggan slide which slanted down the south bank of Beebe Lake. A trip along the icy ramp on a frosty day sent a four or five person toboggan gliding all the way to the far side of the lake. Tobogganing is just one of many outdoor pleasures the University has officially or unofficially banned in recent decades. Others include Beebe Lake swimming and skating, Libe Slope tray sliding, and unobstructed gazing at nature's beauty from the Fall Creek Suspension Bridge which was lined with bars in the summer of 1977.*

A CENTURY AT CORNELL

—Photo by John P. Troy

VANISHED FUN ON BEEBE LAKE: *Above: Students swim in fresh water at the head of the lake, where a small stone bridge now connects the banks. The pool is now befouled with soap scum. Below, top: Skaters swirl over the ice above Triphammer Falls, prior to warming themselves before the fireplace of the Johnny Parsons Club seen in the distance. The clubhouse was demolished to make way for Noyes Lodge. Below, middle: Turreted pavilions and strings of electric lights decorate Beebe for a Junior Week carnival celebrated by the Class of 1908. Below, bottom: A six-man toboggan team demonstrates proper gliding posture, with the tail-end rider extending his legs to sway to and fro as a human rudder. Below, right: Third Cornell President Jacob Gould Schurman wears a ski cap and pulls a toboggan across the lake.*

—Skating Photo by John P. Troy, others Cornell University Archives

Interlude: Reminders of Better Times

gan upon a sort of see-saw, and pile aboard. A girl tucks her boots under the curling front; then a boy puts his legs around her waist and his feet on her lap; then a girl does the same to him; and so on. Thrilling postures! The attendant tilts the see-saw a few inches, and our vehicle starts its accelerating slide down one of the two parallel, ice-lined slides. The rearmost rider, usually a boy, kneels at the back holding the side-ropes with his hands. Faster and faster we rush, first aloft and then through bare-branched woods (where the traces of the slide's route can still be noted, I think, in 1980), straightaway, faster and faster until we level off on the smooth ice of the lake at, I should guess, about 45 miles an hour; but we are so close to the ice—about one inch—that it seems much faster. Here the boy at the back swings brass-capped toes out behind him and puts his weight upon them, swinging his body to right and left as a rudder to keep the toboggan from slewing out of line. On a good day the toboggan will cross the greater portion of the lake and end its flight in the snow banks on the farther side. (In 1940, according to Bishop's *History*, the slide was abandoned because it had caused 21 injuries that winter, including seven fractured vertebrae.)

Now our trolley clatters over the Triphammer Bridge and follows Thurston Avenue, passing the Titcheners' and Fuertes' houses and many more. It will recross Fall Creek by the Stewart Avenue Bridge. It will pass above the house of Prof. and Mrs. Henry Ogden (civil engineering) and their delightful children. There are many more professors' houses on Cornell land than I can enumerate, and some I probably enumerate wrongly. It is likely, for example, that there are quite a number on Fall Creek Drive and on The Knoll.

The majority of the faculty's children and some outsiders attend a remark-

99

able one-room school, the Miss Hitchcocks' School, or, more officially, The Campus School. It will move next year, 1906, from a room in Barnes Hall to a Model School House behind the Andrew D. White Mansion and its great Red Barn. Miss Martha Hitchcock is a superb and redoubtable teacher of the old no-nonsense kind. The gentler, and perhaps even more lovable Miss Mary is her sister. Her we call "Singing Miss Hitchcock" because she teaches us that subject; the other is always just simply Miss Hitchcock. These two wonderful ladies are sisters of Professor Bennett. They began the School in 1896 in the Bennett House, at Number One Grove Place. After a year there, the school attendance grew too large for the house, and they moved to a room in Barnes Hall. For recess, while at Barnes, we play in the brook nearby. (It still passes Barnes in 1980 but its pollution in the intervening years has earned it the sobriquet of "Wee Stinky.")

One other aspect of our education may be briefly mentioned, in concluding this sketch. Dancing school. This was not held on the campus, but many of the Campus Tigers have been dragooned into going downtown for it. We are reasonably well-behaved, I believe, during most of the sessions. We learn to do what passes for a two-step, each with a partner chosen by him or her or—otherwise—decreed. Each such couple "two-steps," without turning, solemnly and silently, down one long side of the rectangular hall, the boy pushing or pulling a hapless little girl. At the corner we rotate once—clockwise. Then we march again, trying ineffectually to keep time to the music, across the short side of the hall, with one more releasing spin—clockwise—at the next corner. And so on, and on, until the long music mercifully ends. Conversation is usually frozen like a winter brook. Hester Bancroft, however, after suffering a tongueless youth for 20 minutes, once earned some local fame by sweetly saying, "Chatter brightly."

Somewhat later there comes, what I still remember as quite a profound revelation, that in a two-step one should be twirling all the time, not only clockwise but counterclockwise as well.

One session is memorable because in it we were promoted to learning what I am fairly certain was called a "barn dance." The teacher's instructions for it were

—Cornell University Archives

RETURN TO ITHACA: *After passing through campus and looping through the suburban streets of Cornell Heights on the far side of Fall Creek, a trolley car wending its way back downtown crosses the Stewart Avenue bridge, dwarfed by Ithaca Falls far below.*

"One, two, three, kick." Chaos, of course, was foreordained: it engulfed us, kicking and shouting with joyous release. Order was never restored. The "barn dance" vanished from the curriculum.

Looking back from 1980, I incline to think that the "Campus Tigers" were a quite delightful company, friendly and congenial, probably somewhat overprotected, brought up in a highly moral and often romanticized atmosphere. On the whole we were, in spite of our escapades, well-behaved children, and well-intentioned. We were a bit naïve and starry-eyed. And life seemed good to

us—or so it seems in retrospect. We flowed in and out of one another's houses with easy familiarity. There was no formality. The grown-ups who lived in these remarkable houses we did not know very well, except in a few cases; they all seemed happy to their offspring who led what seems in 1980 to have been a halcyon existence.

BERTRAM F. WILLCOX '17, a Cornell emeritus professor of law, is a member of one of Cornell's most distinguished families. His father, the late Walter F. Willcox, was a well-known economics professor and student of Cornell who served as dean of the arts college in the early 1900s and remained active in the faculty into his nineties. Bertram Willcox's brother, the late Alanson W. Willcox '22, succeeded E.B. White as editor-in-chief of *The Cornell Daily Sun* before going on to a career as a government lawyer, and another brother, William B. Willcox '28, is a professor of history at Yale, where he is now editing the Benjamin Franklin papers.

—Photo by C. Hadley Smith
FATHER AND SON, EMERITUS: *After July 1, 1963, Bertram F. Willcox (left), then 68, and the late Walter F. Willcox, then 102, were both emeritus professors at Cornell, a situation unique in the University's history. Walter was one of the nation's first social scientists, and his son taught law.*

Part II – A Girl's View

By Margaret Thilly Raynolds '21

How sorry I am for the professors' children who came after us and never knew the joys of growing up on the Cornell campus! The campus to us in the early 1900s was bounded by South Avenue, East Avenue, Grove Place (the three-house place at the south end of East Avenue) and Central Avenue. Reservoir Avenue and The Circle were also parts of it. It was a small area with professors' houses standing elbow to elbow and teeming with childen of closely matching ages.

We came, my father and mother—Prof. and Mrs. Frank Thilly—with three children ranging from ten years to two, from Princeton University in 1906, and moved into Number 9 East Avenue. It was the house given, as the plaque* read, "by Henry Sage in memory of his wife Susan Linn Sage for The Chair of Christian Ethics and Philosophy."

We found that our back yard was fenced in with six-foot high chicken wire to keep the neighborhood children from running across the land of our predecessors (Prof. and Mrs. H.S. Williams). It took us very little time to break it down, throw it away, and become friends of those children for life. We were welcomed by our neighbors—Rowlees to right of us and Bancrofts to left of us—throwing pears at us from our own pear trees. Gertrude, my older sister, and I

*Rym Berry '04 was very critical in his column in *The Ithaca Journal* of the fact that the plaque was thrown out when the house was torn down for the coming of the Statler Hall about 1937.—M.T.R.

threw them back with a will and thus began years of happy comradeship.

On South Avenue lived the Willcoxes with three children (the fourth, Bill, to come later). Next, the Prescotts who contributed no children to the pack but kindness and charm galore. On Grove Place the Bristols, no children. The Harrises—he was Cornell's Librarian—gave us their daughter, Dorothy, with lovely red hair down to her shoe-laces. The Charles Bennetts, four children, too old for some of us but they had their group. At the start of East Avenue, Professor and Mrs. Tarr, a son and daughter; Professor and Mrs. Craig, one son; the Atkinsons, who left Cornell soon after we got there, were replaced by Professor and Mrs Benjamin Dugger with three, then later by Professor and Mrs. Augustus Sill with three (I think) young children. Then Professor and Mrs. Wild-

THE CORNELL UNIVERSITY FACULTY, 1916

—Photo by John P. Troy

1. M.W. Sampson	28. A.R. Mann	55. H.L. Jones	82. F.O. Ellenwood
2. W.F. Willcox	29. H.E. Dann	56. W.A. Hurwitz	83. G.B. Upton
3. S.H. Gage	30. J.L. Stone	57. J.H. Tanner	84. M. Dresbach
4. G.W. Harris	31. Alexander Gray	58. E.N. Burrows	85. H.W. Edgerton
5. I.P. Church	32. A.C. White	59. K.B. Turner	86. Cornelius Betten
6. C.L. Crandall	33. M.C. Burritt	60. G.W. Cavanaugh	87. Paul Fenton
7. G.L. Burr	34. W. N. Barnard	61. E.M. Chamot	88. J.Q. Adams
8. E.E. Haskell	35. C.L. Durham	62. G.G. Bogert	89. W.M. Sawdon
9. J.E. Creighton	36. H.H. Love	63. C.K. Burdick	90. G.R. Chamberlain
10. J.G. Schurman	37. T.L. Lyon	64. S.S. Garrett	91. S. Stevens
11. W.A. Hammond	38. F.W. Owens	65. Miss Flora Rose	92. C.M.S. Midjo
12. Frank Thilly	39. G.W. Herrick	66. Miss A. Warner	93. A.B. Recknagel
13. E.H. Woodruff	40. Arthur Ranum	67. Miss B.E. Hazard	94. J.K. Wilson
14. L.M. Dennis	41. C.T. Stagg	68. F.M. Blodgett	95. H.A. Sill
15. Nathaniel Schmidt	42. W.L. Williams	69. A.P. Mills	96. L.A. Maynard
16. Abram Kerr	43. C.D. Albert	70. J.B. Sumner	97. S. Simpson
17. E.L. Nichols	44. W.B. Carver	71. Lane Cooper	98. O.L. McCaskill
18. G.P. Bristol	45. J.T. Parson	72. A.W. Browne	99. J.I. Hutchinson
19. D.S. Kimball	46. J. McMahon	73. O.M. Leland	100. G.S. Hopkins
20. George Young, Jr.	47. A.P. Usher	74. A.C. Beal	101. Earl Sunderville
21. J.T. Quarles	48. C.E. Bennett	75. D.C. Gillespie	102. B.B. Robb
22. H.S. Jacoby	49. H.N. Ogden	76. D.J. Crosby	103. R.C. Carpenter
23. H.H. Wing	50. F.A. Barnes	77. C.E. Hayden	104. A.J. Eames
24. C.H. Hull	51. A.C. Phelps	78. H.S. Gutsell	105. L.W. Sharp
25. A. W. Smith	52. C.S. Northup	79. J.F. Putnam	106. T.R. Briggs
26. V.A. Moore	53. W.W. Warsaw	80. J.G. Pertsch	107. A.A. Young
27. G.S. Moler	54. A.E. Wells	81. C.W. Hamm	108. W.D. Bancroft

109. G.C. Embody	136. P.A. Fish	163. E.A. White
110. V.R. Gage	137. E.W. Benjamin	164. Virgil Snyder
111. G.R. McDermott	138. M.A. Pond	165. W.E. Lunt
112. Vladimir Karapetoff	139. C.H. Berry	166. A.B. Faust
113. John Bentley	140. R. Matthews	167. P.R. Pope
114. G.H. Collingwood	141. G.B. Muchmore	168. W.W. Comfort
115. M.F. Barrus	142. J.A. Winans	169. Royal Gilkey
116. A.A. Allen	143. C.P. Fitch	170. W.H. Rankin
117. R.W. Curtis	144. Charles Gregory	171. R.H. Wheeler
118. Laurence Pumpelly	145. C.H. Myers	172. E.M. Pickens
119. H.D. Reed	146. A.W. Boesche	173. C.A. Peirce
120. R.M. Ogden	147. J.F. Mason	174. A.H. Wright
121. G.F. Warren	148. B.S. Monroe	175. V.B. Stewart
122. H.A. Hitchcock	149. J.G. Nedham	176. R.A. Emerson
123. R.S. Saby	150. A.C. King	177. H.W. van Loon
124. Heinrich Ries	151. H.A. Hopper	178. C.E. Thompson
125. G.E.F. Lundell	152. H.C. Troy	179. W.S. Foster
126. E.O. Fippin	153. H.E. Babcock	180. H.J. Davenport
127. G.N. Lauman	154. J.R. Schramm	181. E.H. Wood
128. J.E. Rice	155. M.A. Lee	182. S.G. George
129. H.C. Davidsen	156. E.E. Barker	183. H. Hermannsson
130. E.S. Guthrie	157. R.P. Anderson	184. W.M. Wilson
131. E.G. Davis	158. E.W. Schoder	185. E.G. Montgomery
132. O.D. von Engeln	159. S.N. Spring	186. J.A. Bissell
133. Donald English	160. P.H. Underwood	187. L.D. Hayes
134. Bristow Adams	161. M. Robinson	188. L.N. Broughton
135. D. Lumsden	162. R.S. Hosmer	189. Lt. T.H. Tweston

Interlude: Reminders of Better Times

er Bancroft with a count of five. The Thillys, three; Rowlees, three; Professor and Mrs. Drew, no children but a cat, Sylvia, and bees complete with beehives and honeycombs. Next, "Uncle Pete" and Mrs. Smith with three, including Alpheus, onetime editor of *The Cornell Daily Sun*, the Dexter Kimballs, who later moved to Central Avenue, three; then the Andrew D. Whites, one; Professor Hammond, three sons. President and Mrs. Jacob Gould Schurman came next with seven, and the Charles Durhams with five. Thus, even without counting the more distant Catteralls and the Jenks on Central Avenue, or Stockings, Wings, or Lyons on Reservoir Avenue, or the Trevors on The Circle, the count of Campus kids on what we thought of as our part of the campus was around fifty. Is that all? I wonder.

We fell naturally into age groups, equal but separate, and we preëmpted the campus as our domain. We invaded the University buildings, often bicycling or roller skating through Goldwin Smith Hall, especially through the lower corridor passing Gene Andrews' Greek statues.

McGraw Hall had its own fascination. It had monkeys, one "Jocko" who used to spit at us; and a stuffed two- or three-headed calf. (It gets more heads as I get older.) McGraw also had pigeons in its Tower. During a phase of collecting birds' eggs, Hester Bancroft and I climbed up a rickety ladder into the Tower and were so fiercely attacked by pigeons that we abandoned the enterprise in a hurry.

We jumped in the hay at the University Barn behind the Schurmans' (site of Baker Laboratory today); sampled the fruits and vegetables in the University gardens behind East Avenue (where Barton Hall is now) and served collations on the very slanty roof of our back porch. We were often chased out of fruit trees, shooed off the "Sage girls'" and faculty's tennis courts (behind Rockefeller), banished from the running tracks both

MYTH OF THE 'UGLY' COED: *Freshmen Delta Gamma sorority pledges of the Class of 1902 pose in a downtown photographer's studio. Left to right: Ina Scott, Helen Brown (above), Grace Gibbs (below), Esther Swift, an unknown freshman, Ruth Bentley, Katherine Buckley, and Elsie Singmaster (lower right).*

inside and outside of the old Armory.

We had clubs galore, to include or exclude others and mainly because we fancied a certain club-pin in a catalogue of pins. A good many shards and artifacts were buried in the woods behind the Willcoxes, and I have often wondered what was unearthed when they built Thurston-Kimball Hall. We had the Nature Study Club (pretty pin), the Industrious Workers Club (membership, Hester Bancroft and I, but we never went on with that one—must have gotten too industrious in something else). The C.A.S. was the longest lasting. We had sales in the Schurmans' ballroom. We sold items that we (or mostly our mothers) made, and sold them to the other mothers. We had two names for C.A.S. in case the campus boys guessed it. C.A.S. was the Children's Aid Society (hence the sale at the Schurmans) or the Campus Athletic Society.

Which brings us to our passion for baseball. We played in an open field

behind the Smiths' next to the original Veterinary College. My sister Gertrude had to be our pitcher because she could get the ball quite near the plate. We ran up astronomical scores—68 to 17, etc. Most of the brothers ignored us, but we challenged them to combat and even the girls who lived in Sage Dormitory across the street from our house. The "Sage girls" never accepted our challenge—lucky for us. The boys did. They won.

We swam in the Sage swimming pool when invited. When there was the annual Sage Circus, Hester and I dived for pennies in the pool all evening until we were so soaked and puckered that they had to get us out, loaded with pennies for the till.

Winter in Ithaca was marvelous with what seems now mountains of snow. We skated on Beebe Lake, often with music, tobogganned, and came home at twilight through banks of snow with the lovely sound of the evening chimes wafting on the cold crisp air—unforgettable. We skied down the Library Slope, rarely getting to the bottom on our skis. But the most exhilarating was coasting down "Ghost Hill" (a westward extension of South Avenue). At the top was the hazard of cars coming out of fraternity driveways; at the bottom an unexpected meeting with the Stewart Avenue streetcar.

As we grew up, and we did, we devoted a great deal of time to tennis and golf and dancing.

But this reminiscence could go on forever! Let it be said it was the most glorious growing up any children could have had.

'MUSIC WITH THE TWILIGHT FALLS . . .': *Half a century ago, seniors would gather on the steps of Goldwin Smith Hall during the last weeks of their college lives to sing the songs of Cornell. Undergraduates, professors and townspeople would gather on the arts quad to listen to the melodies in twilight.*

MARGARET THILLY RAYNOLDS '21 *is the daughter of the late Prof. Frank Thilly, philosophy, and is also the stepmother of Sun editor-in-chief Harold Raynolds '48, whose writing appears elsewhere in this book.*

When Cornell Was a Smaller Place

By Paul M. O'Leary

Today, when as an agéd emeritus professor I walk through Goldwin Smith and speak to young faculty members hurrying through the corridor, more often than not they will merely stare as much as to say, "Who is this old codger?" The place is simply so large, many of the faculty so new and so keenly in competition with their colleagues for promotion to tenure or for "outside offers" that much of the easy-going friendship of collegiality has gone from the place. It's too bad.

The Cornell that I first saw 55 years ago was about a third its present size. The faculty was probably less than a third the size of today's faculty, teaching loads then being heavier and federal research funds being almost unknown. I quickly found the faculty to be a friendly group. The first day I walked into Goldwin Smith Hall two fine-looking elderly men spoke to me cordially. Subsequently I learned that one was Nathaniel Schmidt, a genuine polymath of the widest learning. The other was Charles Hull, a distinguished economic historian.

The campus 55 years ago had many open spaces and 30 or so faculty homes. At 3 Central Avenue, just south of where the Gannett Clinic is now, stood what was called the "University Club." It was a four-story shingled monstrosity which had been condemned as being unsafe for a women's dormitory but was assumed to be safe enough for unmarried faculty members of all ages. On its top three floors in comfortable but plain rooms lived a dozen or so congenial fellows of whom I was fortunate to have been one. Woodford Patterson, Julian Bretz, Freddy Smith, Halldor Hermannsson, Donald English and the young Morris Bishop were among them. The rest of us were young instructors.

The first floor of 3 Central Avenue was the University Club's dining and social area. Good luncheons and dinners costing as much as 75 cents were served. Lunchtime drew such well-known faculty members as Othon Guerlac, Carl Becker, Walter Willcox, Alec Drummond, Lane Cooper and Frank Thilly.

After lunch there was often a "smoke-in" (mostly cigars and pipes) with spirited conversation in the library lounge, one large room with a few books. Here we younger fellows listened and watched. Here I saw the authoritarian Lane Cooper set back on his heels by a young entomologist. Cooper was holding forth on the wonders of Aristotle as a scientist. The young entomologist suddenly spoke up saying: "Aristotle may have been quite a philosopher but he certainly was not much of a scientist." To this, the outraged Cooper answered: "Young man, have you read (so and so) on Aristotle as a scientist?" To this the young man replied: "No, but I've read Aristotle." Exit Professor Cooper harrumphing.

One evening a well known British political scientist, a high League of Nations official, Sir Alfred Zimmer, lectured in Bailey Hall, drawing a large audience that did not include the sardonic Prof. Donald English. After the lecture a group of faculty members came down to the Club for a social discussion on the lecture. As Carl Becker entered, English asked: "Well, Becker, what did he have to say?"

In his gently weary voice Becker replied: "The world is disturbed."

The faculty was almost completely in charge of things at Cornell 55 years ago. Its meetings in old Boardman Hall were well attended and spirited. There were a number of good faculty orators. The President usually presided and always got an earful. George Lincoln Burr, the tiny but brave and sometimes emotional professor of European history, made many impassioned speeches in defense of liberty. Once he was queried by an opponent in a rather tortured and involved way. Burr fixed him with an icy stare and said: "Sir, were you to ask me, 'If the world comes to an end will the sky rain larks?' I shall be compelled to answer, 'I do not know.'"

The administrative apparatus at Cornell before the Second World War was simple and spare. University officials fitted easily into Morrill Hall with room left for other activities. In the arts college Dean Robert Ogden and Assistant Dean Sibley occupied one room. Across the hall the administrative secretary, Miss Ashton, with two or three young women to help her, kept *all* student records on large white cards. On them grades, disciplinary actions, leaves of absence, etc., were entered by hand. Remember, this was for a college in which the total number of students taught was at least one-third of what it is today. Have a look at the administrative group in Goldwin Smith today!

Before the great expansion of student enrollment following the Second World War the care and nursing of students at Cornell was minimal. The students simply didn't seem to need or want much attention. There was a dean of women but no dean of men. There were many specific rules of conduct for the women students both in and out of dormitories and sorority houses. There were almost none for men. Student conduct was expected to be that of "a gentleman and a scholar." A faculty committee on student conduct defined what that meant in specific cases. Hearings were simple and direct. There was no elaborate "code of student rights." The attitude of the conduct committee was that of a stern but not unfriendly parent. Most student offenses were really minor. But on one occasion eight students were summarily dismissed from Cornell for stealing books from the library and the Campus Store. This was regarded as a most serious "offense against the academy" and was punished as such. There was no appeal. The eight offenders were simply "dismissed from the academy" and sent out into the world at large. Their thieving activities were a rarity at Cornell. Would that it were so today.

In the 1920s and 1930s Cornell's several college faculties held students to tough standards of academic performance (as measured by end-of-term grades). Poor records resulted in students being: (a) Warned, (b) put on Probation, or (c) Dropped —"busted" as the students called it. Compared to what I am told is the case today the number of students dropped for poor records was large. There seems to be some reason to believe that "grade inflation" at Cornell like "price inflation" throughout the world is real. But after 12 years of retirement I should probably not push this matter too far.

—Cornell University Archives

TRANSMOGRIFICATION: *When Sage Cottage was the Central Avenue home of Prof. Albert N. Prentiss (about where Anabel Taylor Hall is now), it was a simple, cheerful structure. Then additional floors, turrets and towers were added, resulting in the formidable bachelor faculty rooming house seen above.*

The standards of student journalism at Cornell have usually been high. They were certainly so in the 1920s. I have in mind the following Sun editors: E.B. White, Harvey Gerry, Jerry Thompson, Jimmy Austin, Jervis Langdon, Charles Howland, Stanley Krusen and Charles Kades, who 20 years later as a colonel on General Douglas MacArthur's staff wrote most of Japan's post-war constitution.

There was at least one ridiculous aspect of student life and behavior at the Cornell I first knew 55 years ago. This was the anti-coed attitude or tradition of the "leading fraternities." To a young middle westerner this seemed like arrant nonsense in the presence of so many very attractive and bright young women. Its passing is not to be regretted.

Three interesting characters of my early Cornell days were:

1. Jack Moakley, Cornell's great track coach whose assistant I was for six of my early years. A genuine master of his profession, he was a delightfully straight and simple person. Once when it had been proposed to give all coaches some kind of professorial status Jack said to me, "Why should I want to be called 'Professor Moakley'? I'd rather be called 'Jack Moakley, Cornell track coach.'"

2. Proctor Twesten, a handsome old ex-cavalry officer who had served with General Custer but missed the "last stand" because he had been sent away on a special detail and was late in reporting back to the main forces. Once he was heard to shout at freshmen who were rushing down State Street to attack the sophomores in a class fight: "Boys, boys slow down! Never be in a hurry to get to a fight." He had learned his lesson well 50 years before. Twesten was Cornell's whole Campus Patrol even though he was in his 70s. He was regarded with respect and affection by most undergraduates.

3. George Hamilton, professor of romance languages. A basically lovable fellow, he barked and snarled his way through life, damning the numerous "fools" he met along the way. With a fierce demeanor and blazing eyes, he was actually a delight to visit with and listen to. He once wrote a learned paper on The Eyes of Alexander the Great in History and Myth (or some such title) but his greatest pride was in his knowledge of "the illegitimate sons of Presidents of Harvard College"—his alma mater. Quite a man!

The long depression of the 1930s put the whole country

under great strain. It was amazing how well the University held together. In 1934 salaries were cut 10 percent across the board. For those of us who kept our jobs, and most of us at Cornell did, this was no great hardship. The cost of living declined more than 10 percent. Unemployment was the great scourge. For at least 15 million Americans it was a terrible fact of life.

President Roosevelt and his New Deal attacked the Depression with gusto but not with much success. The Roosevelt administration called many academic people to Washington to assist in the assault. Moreover, as the World War approached Washington's demand for academic people accelerated. When the United States entered the war in December 1941, my own department, economics, had sent five of us to various defense and war agencies.

I had met the vigorous and gifted Leon Henderson in 1939 while serving on the staff of the Temporary National Economic Committee, a joint Congressional and executive agency committee set up to examine the whole structure of the American economy. Outbreak of war aborted the committee before any real consequences could follow from its activities. The war effort took over. Unemployment melted away. When Leon Henderson was put in charge of price stabilization he called me to Washington to assist him. Ultimately I became his deputy in charge of all the wartime rationing programs in the Office of Price Administration.

John Hutchins left the economics department for distinguished service in the War Shipping Administration. Paul Homan joined the research division of the War Production Board. Frank Southard went to the Treasury and then into the Navy in charge of money programs in occupied areas. Later he was to become for many years the United States' top man at the International Monetary Fund. Julian Woodward joined Elmo Roper in the Office of War Information. The young George Hildebrand, just finishing his graduate work, moved at once to a high post in the War Labor Board.

Outside the economics department, especially in chemistry, physics and engineering, similar drafts were made by the war agencies on the Cornell faculty. Some of us returned after the war. Others did not.

What did come to Cornell after the war were several thou-

MORRIS BISHOP '14 (1893-1973)
Cornell's Historian

LANE COOPER (1875-1959)
Professor of English

"TEEFY" CRANE (1844-1927)
Professor of Romance Languages

"DAVY" HOY '91 (1863-1930)
University Registrar

JACK MOAKLEY (1863-1955)
Half a Century as Track Coach

PROCTOR TWESTEN (1852-1928)
Missed Custer's 'Last Stand'

GEORGE HAMILTON (1874-1940)
Professor of Romance Languages

GEORGE LINCOLN BURR '81 (1857-1938)
Andrew Dickson White's Protégé

sand veterans under the G.I. Bill of Rights. They were fine, mature, highly motivated young men and women. The University had to strain and expand its facilities to accommodate them. Some of us felt that the great bulge in enrollment must be accepted but should be shrunk back as the veterans finished their studies. But this was not to be the case. Pressure from Albany, fear at Cornell of what the newly projected State University might become, and the local desire to use the new "temporary" facilities, bad as they were, whch had come with the war and the veterans' bulge, carried the day. Cornell "stayed big" and grew bigger from year to year. This has put great pressure on our endowment base. The financial results have not been good. Nor, in my opinion, have the educational consequences. The place is simply too damn crowded! The University, which "loses money" on every student, takes more students every year to get their tuition, fees and room rent. It has behaved like the merchant who said that he lost money on every sale but made it up on the turnover.

In closing I offer these comments on the deleterious consequences of the deep post-war intrusion of the federal government into the affairs of Cornell and other American universities.

Grabbing eagerly for federal money, the universities have come to find themselves beset by a horde of bureaucrats demanding this report and that action, threatening to cut off the flow of money for any of a variety of peccadillos, even going so far as to harass the universities in such matters as: the confidentiality (or lack of it) attached to letters of recommendation, the living arrangements of ethnic groups in dormitories, and the apportionment of non-federal physical education and athletic funds between male and female students. For far too long American administrators have failed to organize and fight back against the follies of Health, Education and Welfare and other federal agencies. It is not too late. The University of North Carolina has tried to show the way. It has not had much support from its fellow universities. That has been a shame.

PAUL M. O'LEARY, a Cornell emeritus professor of economics, served as dean of the College of Arts and Sciences, and was also the first dean of the School of Business and Public Administration.

—Cornell University Archives Photos

POSTWAR EXPANSION: *After the return of the veterans of each World War, Cornell's enrollment reached new peaks. The 1919-1920 total of 5,765 full-time students was the largest ever, and in fall term 1946 over 10,500 students jammed the campus compared to the pre-World War II high of about 7,000. Below, Barton Hall is filled with hundreds of World War I era cadets exercising in unison. Above, representatives of several military branches operating at Cornell during World War II cluster around A.D. White's statue. Left to right: Frederic H. Deutsch '47 of ROTC, William F. Hunt '45 of the Marines, and Richard W. Jordan of the Navy V-12 program listen to Army Student Training Program Corporal Leonard Cautela relate stories of service in England and Ireland.*

Interlude: Reminders of Better Times

FIRST LADY: *Eleanor Roosevelt greets girl scouts during Farm and Home Week at Cornell in 1934. She regularly attended this annual agriculture college event, and once even served husband Franklin a "Depression lunch" of prune pudding and eggs stuffed with tomato sauce that had been recommended by Cornell nutritionists.*

HISTORY'S DARLINGS: *Der Führer, il Duce and friends share a convivial moment on Schoellkopf Field during one of the "McNaboe rallies" staged by late 1930s students to ridicule State Sen. John McNaboe, who had called Cornell "a hotbed of Communism"* *(for more on these rallies, please turn to Page 198).*

An Age of Activism

BY AUSTIN H. KIPLINGER '39

They were depression days. Franklin D. Roosevelt was in the White House. Unemployment reached 25 percent and most of those 25 percent were sole bread-winners in their families. The right of labor to organize was still being tested. On the campus, we were wired into the social and political turmoil of the times—or at least a part of the student body was. The bulk of the undergraduate body, as always, was chiefly concerned with pre-lims, term papers and final examinations. But for those attuned to public affairs, it was a heady time.

For monetary policy, we could visit the classroom of Prof. George Warren on the ag campus and hear the anti-gold views that he was urging on President Roosevelt, then sit in on the classes of Prof. Reed in arts and sciences when he denounced them as the prelude to rampant inflation. The Supreme Court was page one news, as it struck down much of the early New Deal legislation. The constitutional law courses with Profs. Robert Cushman and Max Shepard were like being in the front-line trenches.

The political activists divided into identifiable camps—the hard-line disciplined members of the Young Communist League, the free-thinking radicals of the American Student Union, the Trotskyite anti-Stalin bloc, the Jay Lovestone anti-deviationists, and the hard-put conservatives (whose life was made miserable by the fashionable idea that all Republicans and all defenders of business were, by definition, enemies of humanity). Then there were the middle-of-the-road liberal-conservatives (or conservative-liberals) among whom I counted myself. We were viewed with suspicion by all camps, because we wouldn't come down unequivocally in any of their territories —naively insisting that our position was,

indeed, the right one and that *they* were the ones out of step.

So it went. I knew all the *dramatis personae* on the campus political scene and could usually predict how each of them would react to any political stimulus. When 1938 came, and a truce pact was made between Stalin and Hitler, the disciplined party-line Communists finally were exposed for everyone to see. Literally overnight, they switched from being vociferous anti-Nazis to pragmatic pacifists, preaching a cynical doctrine that it didn't matter how brutal and de-humanizing Hitler was, he wasn't any worse than the leadership of the western democracies. *Then*, Hitler attacked Russia and things immediately swung back to the opposite pole: Hitler must be destroyed at all costs. As, indeed, he had to be, and as, indeed, we moderate, quiet-spoken namby-pamby liberals had been saying all along.

At Cornell, some of us had formed discussion groups and seminars. As editor of the monthly magazine, *Areopagus*, I was active in these efforts, and in the fall of 1938, when war threatened in Europe, we got in touch with like-minded students at Penn and Dartmouth. Bill Remington, a bright young student of economics, was chairman of the Dartmouth host group. (After World War II, he was convicted and sent to jail for perjury in denying a period of underground Communist affiliation.) The Penn chairman was Reginald Jones, now chairman of General Electric. I was chairman of the Cornell delegation. We discussed and debated and agreed that Democracy *could* be made to work, although we disagreed on the changes necessary to bring this about.

Student protest centered on compulsory military training, which then was *de rigueur* for all freshmen and sophomore males. I led the movement to make the

training optional, on grounds that it really wasn't very good military training anyway and the only purpose it served was to give the upperclassmen some bodies to practice on while qualifying for officer commissions. The Student Council, on which I sat, endorsed the protest and sent me to New York to meet with the Board of Trustees at the home of Neal Dow Becker, chairman of the Executive Committee. In trepidation, I bearded the august lions in their den—which was actually the library of Mr. Becker's Park Avenue apartment. I presented the case strongly (I thought) and respectfully (I am sure) and retired to await the verdict. In time, the board said no, on the ground that the perilous condition of the world did not support such a move at that time. I suspect they were right. War broke out in September of that year.

What was different between the protests of that time and the student demonstrations of the 60s? Basically, it was a matter of spirit. In the 30s, the fabric of respect between students and faculty, faculty and administration, students and board, students and administration, was not ruptured. Strained, yes, but there remained a sense of mutual respect. There was still a mood of shared goals, of everyday human courtesy, of civility, however different the individual views happened to be. Missing was the spirit of contempt that later soured relations between the extreme antagonists in the turmoil of the 60s. Behind the front, however, I suspect the spirit was much the same—a love of the institutions and an intense desire to have our university do the right thing as each of us saw it to be. If we hadn't cared, we wouldn't have put ourselves to the trouble of protesting in the first place.

AUSTIN H. KIPLINGER '39 now publishes a variety of financial periodicals in Washington, D.C., and is a member of Cornell's Board of Trustees.

The Once Most Beautiful University

BY JOHN SCHROEDER '74

". . . [T]he Cornell campus is beautiful. Beautiful, not merely as pretty, but in a way that inspires one with a profound conviction of the entire appropriateness of the scene and its setting. . . . Where else, pray, may there be found a plateau with its summit crowned by a score and more of pleasing buildings, . . . attractively grouped and set about a campus and quadrangle dotted by noble trees in groves and avenues? At every turn the structures and trees frame and furnish the content of a beautiful landscape picture. . . . Where else can one find a campus bounded by profound chasms that impress one by their immensity with the greatness of the works of nature, and are decorated in their length with a hundred waterfalls large and small? . . . What pleasure to lift the eyes and sweep a horizon enclosing long hill slopes and deep valley furrows, forest and farm in unending succession; a town, the busy habitat of man; and the solitary ribbon of blue lake waters continuing many miles and lost to sight only in the distance. . . . Such is Cornell."

—Prof. O.D. von Engeln '08, describing his University in a guidebook of 1924.

"Why do you want to stay here? It's such an ugly campus."

—Louise M. Perkins, a University of North Carolina zoology major, visiting Cornell in August, 1980.

—Cornell University Archives
BEFORE THE ARCH: *Young elms line Central Avenue at the turn of the century.*

cold barrenness of the inset picture—to believe that both photographs capture the same area from the same vantage point. The elms, along with the impressions of warmth, softness and harmony they fostered, are all dead, victims of Dutch elm disease. Inexplicably, they have never been replaced with a different species that might yield similar effect. Indeed, the only major landscape element that has been replaced is the shaded lawn that formerly separated Sage Chapel and Barnes Hall (seen in the background to a picture on Page 71). Today's student sees instead the sterile concrete bunker and gaudy red-striped doors of the Cornell Campus Store.

The present dilapidation of Central Avenue will not endure. Plans for its total redevelopment are being drawn up as this book goes to press, although no final decisions have been announced. It appears, however, that a partially underground addition to Uris Library will eliminate through traffic, and that the area bounded by the library, Sage Chapel, the Campus Store and the Straight will become a "pedestrian enclave." Banishing cars from this heart of Cornell has been a planners' dream since the 1920s, and its fulfillment *could* stand among the finest aesthetic decisions in the University's history.

Unfortunately, some of the redevelopment ideas being mentioned give one pause, and the precedents of other Cornell "pedestrian plazas" that have been contemplated or built further the uneasiness. It seems that planners will not seek their inspiration from Central Avenue's own rich visual heritage, or even from the timeless Romanesque and Gothic dignity of the older nearby structures. Instead, the aesthetic prototype of the new enclave may be the suburban American shopping plaza—or, as one Sun letter writer put it, the "downtown-brick-and-redwood-bench-mall craze."

And so it seems that the newly roadless space in front of Gannett Clinic will not become a tree-lined path, flanked by open lawns and devoted to the students who daily trek in from Collegetown. Instead, it will be devoted to the automobile, the newest in an ever-expanding number of University parking lots. Indeed, if the most ambitious plans are ever adopted (two proposals suggest paving over grass in front of the Straight for an outdoor café and paving over a corner of Libe Slope for an amphitheatre), there may well be less grass to lounge on than there was before Central Avenue closed.

More disturbing are hints of commercialism: possible minibus tours for alumni and prospective applicants, and a "Memorial Road" extending from the library addition to the Johnson museum, providing wealthy donors with the opportunity to honor themselves with plaques and benches. Meanwhile, to allow construction of a "Memorial Road" traffic loop, one of the oldest and foremost Cornell memorials, a bench at the crest of Libe Slope dedicated to Cornellians by first president Andrew Dickson White and his second wife, may have to be uprooted. The bench is inscribed:

> To those who shall sit here rejoicing,
>   To those who shall sit here mourning,
>   Sympathy and Greeting;
> So we have done in our time.

One wonders if White would be pleased.

Only one generation ago, the notion that any visitor to Cornell could seriously call the central campus "ugly" would have been ludicrous. In 1980, the characterization is still untrue, but—sad to say—it is no longer ludicrous.

The decline in the University's appearance over the past thirty years—as distinguished from its still magnificent surroundings of gorge, valley, hill and lake—has been dramatic, and pervasive. No longer may Cornellians stroll across "the most beautiful campus in America"—a reputation Cornell earned during its first fifty years and upheld for the better part of the twentieth century.

The stretch of Central Avenue to the south of McGraw Tower epitomizes this passing from glory to visual devastation, and the potential dangers in the aesthetic future Cornell is designing for itself. When today's undergraduates were infants, this avenue was the very symbol of the University's beauty. Two unbroken rows of massive American elms lined its sidewalks; multiple limbs swooped heavenward and met overhead to form a long, leafy tunnel of green through which professors and students meandered to class. On sunny, windy days, a gentle rush was heard above and dappled light played upon sidewalk and street. The elms' grand trunks and rustic, hanging boughs nurtured feelings of permanence and tranquility. Whether they bore summer green, autumn yellow or winter snow on black branches, the elms unified the surrounding buildings and open lawns into a delightful, picturesque whole.

Two pictures on Page 90 show the astonishing contrast between the Central Avenue that was and the Central Avenue of 1980. It is probably difficult for today's Cornellian—familiar only with the battered curbs, jumbled pavements and

'...O'er the Dreaming Lake and Dell...': *Above, the campus about 1920, photographed from the tower of Sage Hall, showing the Central Avenue elms, a park beside Sage Chapel and Barnes Hall in the foreground. Below, students cross the arts quad at mid-century. Olin Library has not yet replaced Boardman Hall, whose graceful form echoes the style of Uris Library.*

The Vision Sought

That Cornell should be beautiful—beautiful in a grand, enduring, ennobling sense—was a principle of both Cornell founders. Ezra Cornell, the flinty, utilitarian telegraph man, delighted in leading the University's visitors through Cascadilla gorge; he was frequently found with pickax in hand helping student crews grade campus avenues. Nineteenth century Ithacan William L. Bostwick wrote that Cornell "had a peculiar love for the picturesque and beautiful in nature; any wanton destruction of plants and trees, or the disfigurement of natural scenery was an abomination in his sight."

But it was White who took the lead in transforming Cornell's barren cow pasture into a handsome seat of learning. For White, sensitivity to beauty, both in nature and in architecture, was not a frill or a luxury, but an essential element of education. He stated his ideals best in 1885, in his final presidential report to the trustees:

...[T]he atmosphere of sentiment which gathers about the University is a most powerful factor in its real success. If all be hard, dry, and unattractive, its buildings mere boxes, its grounds a mere plot of earth for such boxes to stand upon—if all this be as devoid of interest as an attorney's office in a city block, then the University will fail in one of the highest parts of its mission. Fortunately all its surroundings are such as to create love for the place even in hearts least susceptible to natural beauty....The chimes, the memorials, the bits of carving here and there, the walks among the groves and along the ravines and streams, have their value in creating an atmosphere which shall make our students something more than machines. I would lay stress again upon the educating value of all these things.

White was not content to harbor ideals; he insisted upon bringing them to fruition. In the 1850s, while a young professor at an unadorned University of Michigan, White planted scores of elms at his own

−Photo by Ralph Baker, *Ithaca Journal*

'. . .'Tis an Echo From the Walls of Our Own, Our Fair Cornell': *Above, Willard Straight Hall, framed by a Central Avenue elm and other trees, glows invitingly after a 1964 snowfall. Below, a class meets beneath a towering arts quad elm, probably during the 1950s. Note Ezra Cornell's statue between Morrill and McGraw Halls.*

expense along campus walks. And when—with the addition of Ezra Cornell's and the Morrill Act's money—White's dream university became real in 1865, he sought to endow it with the dignified quadrangles and Gothic spires he had imagined since his youth.

Whenever White returned from one of his frequent trips to Europe, he brought back crates of illuminated manuscripts, original and reproduced sculptures, abandoned medieval carvings, paintings and engravings. All were eventually donated to Cornell libraries, museums, dormitories or lecture halls. Another precious "import" was the English stone carver Robert Richardson (recruited by Prof. Goldwin Smith). White put him to work embellishing Sage Chapel, Sage dormitory and his own mansion (for a fine example of Richardson's work, turn to Page 96).

During White's presidency over 200 elm saplings were planted along campus avenues and before the first Cornell buildings. Scores of other trees, including evergreens and flowering species, were scattered about the grounds. By 1910 Cornell's reputation for matchless beauty was firmly established. The University's rugged gorges and rustic landscape—with opportunities for skating, swimming and hiking—seemed to express Cornell's tradition of scholarly and personal independence for faculty and students.

The Vision Attained

Why was Cornell special? Its spectacular East Hill site was part, but not all of the reason, for the University boasted an exceptional harmony between its grounds, its buildings—and its famous vistas.

Everywhere Cornellians were delighted by careful aesthetic balances between the formal and the casual. Heavily shaded groves balanced grassy meadows, and

−Photo by C. Hadley Smith

Interlude: Reminders of Better Times

dense, regular rows of street trees balanced the wilder foliage and scenic drama of the gorges, Beebe Lake and Libe Slope. At the same time, the geometric arrangement of the stone buildings enclosing the arts quad balanced the irregular placement of other campus buildings, which were mostly brick. No building felt cold or impersonal, both because of limited size and because of their decorative styles. An intimate equilibrium between people, buildings, trees and lawns gave Cornell its special charm.

Beauty increased steadily between 1910 and mid-century. This was the era of uncompromising quality in the best campus architecture. The Baker dorms, the Lyon and McFaddin towers, Willard Straight Hall, Balch Hall and Myron and Anabel Taylor halls all date from these years. Each is constructed of stone quarried from Libe Slope or West Campus, and each is excellently adapted to a sloping terrain. Numerous carvings and ornaments embellish their picturesque forms.

By 1952, with some 800 elms in their mature glory, with the grounds meticulously groomed, and with harmony maintained between architecture and landscape, Cornell was more beautiful than it ever had been before, or is likely to be again.

The Vision Fades

Uris Hall, dedicated in 1972, seems like a sad symbol of the aesthetic misfortunes that have eroded Cornell's beauty during the past twenty years. The building is powerful, and forces its presence upon passersby. It is also the ugliest building on campus: boldy, insistently, and proudly ugly.

With chill urban hauteur, it ignores Day Hall to its west, the White mansion to its north, Ives Hall to its east, and Statler Hall to its south. The materials of its exterior hulk are doubly inappropriate to its Ithaca setting; rusty girders mar Finger Lakes beauty, and extensive sheet glass squanders energy throughout the year. How did Cornell arrive at the point where such an unfortunate structure could be erected?

The first signs of decline became apparent in the early 1950s. Given Cornell harmony of landscape and architecture, it was fitting that the slow deterioration should spring from both natural and human sources.

Nature's blow was the arrival in Ithaca of Dutch elm disease, which began to ravage the trees so essential to the University's legendary beauty. Some survived until the early 1970s, when a second blight, phloem necrosis, finished off the remaining specimens. Cornell's last elm—a tree near Warren Hall—died in 1977.

But human causes predominated. Foremost was the dramatic post-war expansion of enrollment (only 7,000 students attended Cornell before World War II). The administrative staff, too, was expanding rapidly, though not yet at the bewildering pace of the 1960s. More people, more traffic and demand for more buildings began—slowly at first—to take their toll on the campus.

The first crucial aesthetic gaffe occurred in the early 1950s, when the splendid Gothic West Campus development plan pictured on Page 52 was officially abandoned in favor of the faceless University Halls. That Cornell could not continue to build with "Gothic magnificence" is perfectly understandable. But this does not excuse the erection of such utterly mediocre and unimaginative structures. The University Halls are perfect examples of the barracks-like "mere boxes" President White loathed.

Though less bland than the U-Halls, the sterile 1950s buildings of the engineering quad also lack any attempt at original form or ornament. From now on, the unadorned modernistic box would reign supreme.

But the 1960s were truly the disastrous years for the Cornell landscape. Now all re-straint was cast aside. "Unplanned, ubiquitous growth," as an administration report would later phrase it, became the University's chief imperative: growth of enrollment, growth of staff, growth of programs, and enormous, unprecedented growth of the physical plant. Concurrently, budgets for maintaining older buildings and the still beautiful grounds were repeatedly slashed.

The most visually ham-handed and tasteless building project ever endorsed by Cornell—a $30 million "Science Center," the centerpiece of a 27-building, $82 million construction drive—was proudly unveiled by Vice Provost for Planning Thomas W. Mackesey on October 29, 1964 (see photo below). Included in Mackesey's model of the center were three structures that would actually be completed: the highrise Chemistry Research Building, the sprawling Clark Hall (then already under construction) and the Space Sciences Building. Also proposed, but never built, were two linked biology buildings—one a soaring tower—behind the Andrew Dickson White mansion and a ponderous replacement for Rockefeller Hall with huge round protrusions facing East Avenue. Planners defended the introduction of skyscrapers to Cornell as a necessity and lauded the new structures' sleek impersonality as a "reflection of the architecture of our time." But the aesthetic insensitivity of the plan was appalling.

Simply examine the biology tower envisioned behind White's Victorian mansion. All regard for architectural decorum has been jettisoned; the tower relates neither to its landscape nor to its neighbors. Indeed, the proposed edifice is so wildly out of scale as to invite suspicions that it was consciously intended to ridicule the home of the University's first president. For a host of historical, stylistic and spiritual reasons, raising a skyscraper on White's back lawn would have been a monumental blunder. Fortunately, it never materialized.

Cornell planners almost seemed proud of their disrespect for traditional architecture. Why else would the Chemistry Research Building—one of the first highrises to clutter the campus skyscape and smash the sense of scale that related earlier buildings to their environment—be given long *vertical* strips of windows, as if to emphasize the structure's height? Why else would the designer of Clark Hall wholly ignore the style of both Baker Lab to the north and Rockefeller Hall to the south, even while joining all three structures into a ground-gobbling superbuilding? Completion of the Chemistry Research Building in Spring 1967 prompted an "ugly-in" attended by 100 students, and a reviewer dubbed Clark the "coldest building on campus" within two years of its 1965 completion.

—Photo by Fred Mohn

THE MACKESEY TOUCH: *In October 1964, Vice Provost for Planning Thomas W. Mackesey stands beside the model of a proposed $30 million "Science Center" above East Avenue. The model includes (left to right) the soon-to-be-built Chemistry Research Building behind Baker Lab; Clark Hall (then under construction); a replacement for Rockefeller Hall (never built); a Space Sciences Building to its rear (soon to be built); and two looming biology buildings behind the Andrew Dickson White mansion. The site of biology construction was later shifted to Lower Alumni Field.*

And so it went throughout the 1960s and early 1970s. Helen Newman Hall was built so near Beebe Lake that a broad swath of the forest circling the lake had to be removed (the trees have not been replaced). Bradfield Hall became the University's tallest building, exceeding the height of the library tower (couldn't Cornell's symbol have been granted the same respect Paris accords the Eiffel Tower?). And the artificial hill raised to house the "underground" Campus Store destroyed the visual relationships between the coördinated brick of Sage Hall, Sage Chapel and Barnes Hall.

The attitude of the administration toward campus development in the 1960s is perhaps best summed up by a remark made by William Littlewood '20, the 1967 chairman of the trustee Buildings and Properties Committee, when the proposed site of the high-rise biology building was shifted from behind the White mansion to Lower Alumni Field. "There isn't enough room to do the job artistically," remarked Littlewood, "so the only thing we can do is go up in the air."

By 1972, after a decade of not doing the job artistically, Cornell's claim to being "the most beautiful campus" had been severely undermined. The bucolic "institution in the woods," whose delightful vistas and rural intimacy had attracted scholars and students for generations, increasingly resembled a cold, crowded urban space, whose skyline was jammed with buildings of unrelated styles and volumes. Even the one superlative structure built during those boom years, the Herbert F. Johnson museum, contributes to the skyline's confusing profile.

A Doubtful Future

How has Cornell's appearance been affected since the early 1970s, when financial problems forced an end to the era of "unplanned ubiquitous growth"? And what will be the aesthetic future of the once most beautiful campus? There have been many hopeful signs, but the portents of danger are at least as numerous.

The most positive omen was Day Hall's 1973 report "Cornell in the 70s," which for the first time officially recognized limits to Cornell's expansion. Enrollment had continuously risen throughout the University's history, but now the administration decreed an upper limit of 16,500 students. But the bad news is that his limit has proved illusory. Year by year—due to "misjudgments" and sleight-of-hand counting techniques—enrollment continues to creep upward. In Fall 1979, 17,090 students jammed the campus, 415 more than the administration's "adjusted" goal and 2,000 more than a decade earlier.

Another bright step was a large-scale tree-planting and re-landscaping project launched in 1972 to replace the 1,000 trees Cornell had lost to old age and disease during the preceding decades. Under the auspices of this Campus Beautification Program, concerned alumni have funded the planting of some 300 new trees, including rows of red oaks and Japanese zelkovas and groves of tulip trees and maples. Unfortunately, though, this program's emphasis now appears to be shifting from grass, bushes and trees to unnecessary benches and brick-and-concrete plazas. If this trend continues, the beautification program will, ironically, further urbanize the University's already strained landscape. "Beautification" and beauty are not equivalent words.

Other signs are also mixed. Cornell's gorges are still splendid, but a drive has begun to cage their scenic wealth behind suicide prevention bridge barriers (garish silver bars were actually installed on the Fall Creek suspension bridge in 1977). There has been a national reäwakening to the charm of ornate architecture and individual craftsmanship, but this has not been reflected in a single Cornell construction project. Environmental concern is growing, but Fall Creek and Casca-

dilla Creek are increasingly befouled with soap scum. The pace of University building has slowed, but incongruous additions—like a new concrete wing to the stone Gannett Clinic — are still undertaken.

* * *

If Cornell is to preserve the beauty it retains, and (one can dream) retrieve the beauty it has lost, several changes are essential.

First, Cornellians must become aware of their own aesthetic heritage. How many people, for example, are aware of the

–Sun Photo by Carin Ashjian
Manhattan in Ithaca: *With its rusty steel girders, energy-wasting plate glass and coldly impersonal monumentality, Uris Hall symbolizes the worst aesthetic mistakes of the past two decades of campus planning.*

artistic impact of the recent renaming of Franklin Hall, home of the art department, to "Tjaden Hall"? Built to house electrical engineers and named after Benjamin Franklin, "The First American Electrician," the edifice is emblazoned with medallions in honor of Newton, Galvani and Franklin himself. Almost certainly these decorations originated with President White. By acquiescing in the renaming of the structure to "honor" a wealthy alumna, Cornell's artists have not only clouded University history, but obscured the meaning of art on their own walls!

Second, the University must restrain its public relations impulses. A quiet, simple, grassy and tree-shaded replacement for Central Avenue, echoing the former magnificence of this important hub of campus life, would do more to enhance Cornell's appearance and prestige than any number of Memorial Roads, mini-bus tours, concrete plazas, alumni plaque and bench areas and outdoor cafés. It is well for Cornell to honor its most generous and faithful donors. But the University's eager attempts to please wealthy alumni by laying down unneeded cement and by renaming gardens, quadrangles and buildings verges on insult. It is as though Cornell assumes its alumni are so vainglorious that they will give more money the more times they see their name.

Cornell may need funds from the J.N. Pew Charitable Trust, but was it really necessary to name the engineering quad after Pew, replace grass with three concrete bench areas announcing the fact, and replace more grass in the quad's direct center with concrete topped by a "mechanical sundial"? One hopes that the arts quad, which belongs to every Cornellian, and the arts college, which belongs to scholarship, will never be named after individuals.

Finally, the key to maintaining and restoring Cornell's beauty is a final, binding acknowledgment by the University of the limits to its human and physical expansion. Additional enrollment boosts, or additional construction projects on remaining open spaces can only further mar the campus environment. Concern for quality must replace incessant groping for quantity.

Should this take place—and should the worst construction mistakes of the past two decades be supplanted by lawns or buildings of architectural merit—the "most beautiful University" may once again be Cornell.

John Schroeder '74, Sun associate editor 1973-74, now works full time in The Sun's composing room.

Chapter III: In Quest of Excellence

So much cries out to be done
And always so urgently;
The world continues
Time goes on
Ten thousand years is too long:
The time is now!
                    —Mao Zedong

Liberal education has lived too long on its reputation. It is time
it undertook to regain its prestige through renewed
demonstration of specific educational achievements.
                    —Edmund Ezra Day

In a recent speech, President Rhodes inquired why it was that Harvard, Yale and Princeton are considered the class of the Ivy League and people assume that Cornell can only aspire to a kind of second-rate status. He said he hoped Cornell would be number one some day.

For the time being, that is wishful thinking, but it represents the kind of thinking that has made Cornell as good of an institution as it has been in such a short lifetime.

In this chapter, we will look at some more of this type of thinking. The authors write on a variety of topics, most of which have nothing to do with one another. But they are held together by the theme of making Cornell a better place, even if only slightly. You may not care about the quality of care Cornell's art collection gets, or whether a few hundred more students are admitted, or how our alma mater is sung. Or perhaps you have your own pet grievance. Excellence is a state of mind.

It is appropriate to begin a chapter on the quest for excellence with the most famous series of correspondence The Sun has ever run. The letter from the "Five Bewildered Freshmen," and Carl Becker's response to it, are reprinted

in The Sun nearly every year. Most people have forgotten that the subject brought forth many other letters, some of them of pretty high quality, as well as a lengthy series of editorials.

It is too much to ask that a book put out by journalists should not have a "scoop." So here is ours.

There were no five bewildered freshmen. They were as fictitious as Frankenstein's monster. The letter was actually written by The Sun's editor-in-chief, Jervis Langdon Jr. '27, because he wanted to write a series of editorials on the subject and lacked a sufficient excuse to do so.

In an exclusive interview with A *Century at Cornell*, Langdon admitted . . . ah, pardon me. This is a book, not a news story. At any rate, Langdon said he was as surprised as anyone at the reaction it got.

Incidentally, Langdon went on to head both the Baltimore & Ohio and Penn Central railroads. We reprint four of his many editorials about the bewildered freshmen here; you will have to judge for yourself whether he should have chosen journalism for a career instead.

Five Bewildered Frosh Seek Some Answers

To the Editor of The Cornell Daily Sun:

We are five freshmen who live in a boarding house together. We are students in the College of Arts and Sciences, and as Christmas draws near, and we are about to pack up and go home for the holidays, we've been wondering just what progress we could report to our parents. We are all taking about the same courses—the regular ones for incoming students, but in a bull session we had last night we all discovered that we were suffering from a common ailment. We hadn't found out what it was all about. And by that we mean that we don't see why we should be taking the courses that we are, we don't see any connection between them, we don't see where they are going to lead us, we are just fulfilling certain hour requirements, it seems. What's it all about?

And as a last resort we decided to write The Sun in an appeal to discover just what all these courses mean and how they fit together in what is generally termed this educational process.

Five Unhappy and Bewildered Freshmen.
—*letter, December 6, 1926*

Five Hundred Bewildered Freshmen

To the Editor of The Cornell Daily Sun:

The letter of "five unhappy and bewildered freshmen" and your editorial in answer were especially interesting to me, both as a freshman and as one who likes to view the actions and reactions of persons ensconced in a new environment, with new problems and new issues.

Your suggestion is, as many of your suggestions are, sound. However, I should like to add to your remarks on this subject, which means so much and interests so few.

Have you ever asked the average freshman why he has come

to Cornell? The obvious answer, so esoteric and meaningless, is, "To get an education." And yet, upon hearing this sentiment, you know deep down in your heart that the fellow is either giving the lie to himself or else saying something so general in its scope that it connotes nothing in particular.

If every man entered college with a complete understanding of the reasons for his so doing, there would be no plaintive wails such as were emitted by five of my fellow classmen. The crux of the matter lies in that most "frosh" don't know why they come, and, most unspeakable, some don't seem to care. "The old man," sometimes in desperation, sometimes in stultified anticipation, sends his son to college. The boy, in many instances, realizing that he doesn't really care about educating himself and further realizing that four years of "raising hell" face him, packs his trunks and off he goes. Then comes the sad plight of not five but generally 500 newcomers wondering where they are and, occasionally, why they are.

This state of affairs is clearly shown by the attitude taken by the freshmen, and freshwomen, if you please, towards the essays, from one of which you admirably quoted, which are studied in the first few weeks in the freshmen English courses. The instructors try hard enough to inculcate the excellent educational ideas of Ruskin, Newman, Emerson, and Huxley. But the ignorant freshmen, with hides like rhinoceri, evidence no interest, but, slumped down in their seats, look the picture of lethargic stupidity.

Your espousing of the cause of transcendentalism is worthwhile, but to attempt to make freshmen, who do not even realize what the word means, understand and utilize its ideas and ideals is ludicrous. One does not learn overnight to put everything in its proper sphere. Years and years must elapse during which the individual must be constantly thinking of things in their relation to himself and to the world. The freshman knows so little that putting his knowledge in its place would be like picking up a chair and putting it in its place.

And so, Mr. Editor, although I respect your ideas, nevertheless I feel that the fault lies not so much with the college as with the individual freshman.

GEORGE SIMPSON '30.
—*letter, December 8, 1926*

A Map of the Road Ahead

The postman still is bending low under the weight of the correspondence pouring into this office anent the "five bewildered freshmen." Some would tender helpful advice to the distressed members of the entering class. Some would indict the Arts College for its scholastic procedure, notably in respect to its freshman year. Some would blame the American educational system as

—Cornell University Archives
'I LOVED BOOKS': *Andrew Dickson White sits in the library of his East Avenue mansion, perhaps in 1886. White was an avid bibliophile, spending endless hours in European bookstores—the shops of leading dealers and obscure antiquarians alike—in search of the rarest and finest volumes. White's proudest possessions were his fifteenth and sixteenth century first editions of scholarly works, and his hand-painted medieval illuminated manuscripts. The massive spiked volume supported by a bookstand in the left middle foreground is a precious choirbook of the late Middle Ages, now housed in Olin Library's rare book room. Produced about 1445 by northern Italian artists, it contains twenty-seven superb miniatures of religious scenes, as well as other decorations. This book might fetch half a million dollars at auction in 1980. White bought it in 1885—along with three other embellished manuscripts—for a grand total of $820.*

ANKLE-DEEP IN THE BIG MUDDY: *In the early decades of this century, the rivalry between the freshman and sophomore classes was intense. Rigid frosh rules promulgated by upperclassmen proscribed many actions, and sophomores—freshly liberated from such rules themselves—were especially zealous in ensuring their enforcement. The culmination of a year of half-joking, half-serious antagonism occurred each spring, when the two classes would meet on a field of mud and battle it out in the quagmire (above). After a suitable interval of warfare, the frosh would typically be "captured" by the sophomores, who would accouter their prisoners with ridiculous signs and costumes (left).*

decently and in order." The newcomer should not be forced to approach this new world blindfolded. One cannot very well "take the edge off learning" by seeing a map of the road ahead.

—editorial, December 10, 1926

'Where Are We?'

To the Editor of The Cornell Daily Sun:

I was interested in the letter of Five Bewildered Freshmen, and in the discussion it gave rise to. The freshmen say they have been engaged in the intellectual life for more than two months and don't know what it's all about. This is bad, but who is to blame? Some say the students are to blame, and some say the professors. What is to be done about it? You suggest a foundation or an orientation course such as is given in other universities.

For my part, I don't blame any one—not the freshmen, certainly. It's not especially the student's fault if he doesn't know what it's all about. If he did, he wouldn't need to come to college. That's why, I have always supposed, young people come to college—to get some notion, even if only a glimmering, of what it's about. They come to get "oriented." But why expect to be oriented in two months, or a year? The whole four years college course is a course in orientation. It isn't a very satisfactory one, indeed. Four years isn't enough. Life itself is scarcely long enough to enable one to find out what it's all about.

Neither do I blame the professors—not particularly. Many people appear to think that professors possess some secret of knowledge and wisdom which would set the students right as to the meaning of things if they would only impart it. This, I do assure you, is an illusion. I could write you a letter on behalf of Five Bewildered Professors which would make the five bewildered freshmen appear cocksure by comparison. The professors are in the same boat. They don't know either what it's all about. They tried to find out when in college, and they have been trying ever since. Most of them, if they are wise, don't expect ever to find out, not really. But still they will, if they are wise, keep on trying. That is, indeed, just what the intellectual life is—a continuous adventure of the mind in which something is being discovered possessing whatever meaning the adventurer can find in it.

This effort to find out what it's all about is, in our time, more difficult than ever before. The reason is that the old foundations of assured faith and familiar custom are crumbling under our feet. For 400 years the world of education and knowledge rested securely on two fundamentals which were rarely questioned. These were Christian philosophy and Classical learning. For the better part of a century Christian faith has been going by the board, and Classical learning into the discard. To replace these we have as yet no foundation, no certainties. We live in a world dominated by machines, a world of incredibly rapid change, a world of naturalistic science and of physico-chemico-libido psychology. There are no longer any certainties either in life or in

a whole. Some confess that they are in the same mental condition as the five newcomers and seek some relief for their bewilderment and their lack of interest in their work.

As The Sun pointed out Wednesday morning, an Orientation course was proposed "as a possibly efficacious means for supplying the Arts College with a rudimentary implement for performing its undeniable duty of stimulating those who can be stimulated." The difficulties of the American educational system, the generally unintelligent family and secondary school trainings which prospective college undergraduates receive, were taken into full account. In view of these basic facts, the proposal was made that the Arts College, when financial arrangements made it possible, should equip itself more thoroughly with those attributes which might serve to dispel what our friend, Mr. Simpson, calls "the picture of lethargic stupidity manifested by 500 freshmen." This state of apathy was shown in the original letter from the "five freshmen" when they said "we are just fulfilling certain hour requirements, it seems."

Should such a course be installed in the scholastic procedure of the Arts College its purpose would not be to convey any false sense of omniscience to the newcomers nor would it give them much satisfaction in discovering what it is all about. But as we stated in the original editorial of Monday last, "such a course as this would lay a blank form which the student will fill in with ideas and information as he goes along, with increasing discernment and widening horizon taking in the details and the bearings of the great subjects of which in this course he gets only the street addresses and the telephone numbers."

The great problem in college education, as we see it, is the stimulation of the individual students who possess all the requisite attributes, but who, under the present regime, are left untouched and unaffected by the cold educational process which at present obtains in the Arts College, notably in respect to its freshmen routine. As has been said before, under the strictest entrance requirements there still would be present in any institution of learning those undergraduates upon whom any attempt to evoke intelligent interest, any effort to bring forth a deep individual self-realization would be a waste of time.

But any media which might be adopted for fighting apathy, for combating lethargy, for stimulating students should meet with the highest favor. A bird's-eye view of education should bring zest to the student's work. Education, as has been suggested, is not a cryptic ceremony of which the sacred "ritual must be observed

thought. Everywhere confusion. Everywhere questions. Where are we? Where did we come from? Where do we go from here? What is it all about? The freshmen are asking, and they may well ask. Everyone is asking. No one knows; and those who profess with most confidence to know are most likely to be mistaken. Professors could reorganize the College of Arts if they knew what a College of Arts should be. They could give students a "general education" if they knew what a general education was, or would be good for if one had it. Professors are not especially to blame because the world has lost all certainty about these things.

One of the sure signs that the intellectual world is bewildered is that everywhere, in colleges and out, people are asking for "Orientation" courses which will tell the freshmen straight off what it is all about. If we were oriented we shouldn't need such courses. This does not mean that I am opposed to an orientation course for freshmen. I would like an orientation course for freshmen. I would like one for seniors. I would like one for professors and trustees. I would like one for President Farrand and President Butler. Only, who is to give it? And what is it to consist of? I asked Professor Hayes, "What about your orientation course at Columbia?" He said, "It's a good thing for the instructors who give it." I asked a man whose son had taken the course, "What did he get out of it?" The reply was, "He read three books in three unrelated fields of knowledge and got a kick out of one of them." Who knows the "background" or the "general field of knowledge?" If the course is given by many professors the student will be taking several courses as one course instead of several courses as separate courses. If one man gives it what will it be? It will be as good as the man is. If we could get a really top notch man to give a course, no matter what, and call it an orientation course, I should welcome it. H.G. Wells might give such a course, and it would be a good course. I doubt if it would orient any one or settle anything, but it would stir the students up and make them think. That would be its great merit. That is the chief merit of any course—that it unsettles students, makes them ask questions.

The Five Bewildered Freshmen have got more out of their course then they know. It has made them ask a question—What is it all about? That is a pertinent question. I have been asking it for 35 years, and I am still as bewildered as they are.

CARL BECKER.
—letter, December 10, 1926

When Progress Seems Slow

To the Editor of The Cornell Daily Sun:
Have you ever watched a builder at work erecting a house?

For a long time there's nothing to indicate that he's done anything except to make a hole in the ground. Even after he has started to lay the bricks, it's hard to see any progress. A layer today and a layer tomorrow do not raise the walls enough to be noticeable. It is only when you wake up some fine morning and find the roof being put on that you suddenly realize that the house is almost complete.

So it is with education. You study a little of this and a little of that; you lay the foundation for this subject; you dig a little into the preliminaries of that, but as far as having anything to show for it is concerned, you feel pretty much like the builder with his hole in the ground.

Don't let that discourage you. The foundations are there, unseen though they may be. And if you will lay your bricks on them faithfully, painstakingly, you'll wake up some fine morning to find that you've been erecting the solid edifice of a thorough education—an edifice that will stand you in good stead the rest of your days.

New York City.
ROBERT COLLIER.
—letter, December 11, 1926

A Reply to Professor Becker

To the Editor of The Cornell Daily Sun:
I have read with interest Professor Becker's brilliant letter to you on the Five Bewildered Freshmen, and enjoyed the style very much. Since that is doubtless the important part, he will perhaps pardon me if, in default of a better, I suggest a reconsideration of some of his statements which can scarcely be allowed to go unchallenged. After granting that "young people come to college

to get some notion of what it's about" he relieves them of all need of worry on that score by confiding to them that it is impossible to reach their goal since "there are no longer any certainties either in life or in thought." Still they should remain here for they are very promising students. Have they not in two months succeeded in becoming almost as learned as the professor could in 35 years? Are we to rest content with an intellectual life which is "a continuous adventure of the mind in which something is being discovered possessing whatever meaning the adventurer can find in it."

The most interesting idea in those remarks of the Bewildered Professor is that apparently there is for him a distinction between the fields of thought and life, and practically the only one with which he is concerned is the field of thought. In his mind the Five Unhappy and Bewildered Freshmen become simply the Five Bewildered Freshmen. Assuming that they are like himself, primarily interested in thought for thought's sake and the continuous mental discovery of rubbish or treasure as the finder may elect, he gives them the encouraging picture of their future. I am happy to state, however, that I have yet to discover in any of my classes any Freshman who reaches, or apparently has any ambition to reach Dr. Becker's standard. They all seem to retain some interest in life as well as in thought, and are taking an intellectual training, if for any motive, apparently the better to prepare themselves for lives devoted primarily to the ordinary social, economic, religious, or artistic pleasures. Even as a side-line few will be interested in a ceaseless search for truth. Of my own college class-mates I can think of only one who has any such spirit, and he is teaching Philosophy.

Now if one considers the actual lives college graduates lead, and accepts the historical axiom that human nature does not vary

Slip swine into your dark and slimy holes,
Crowd Off the earth you maggot covered moles,
Oh you hopeless Pests off to your gruesome fate,
Or beat it hairy homely Hogs till late at night,
To-morrow you foul vermin, we Shall show our might.

—Scrapbook of Richard Evett Bishop '09

FUNERAL TONIGHT: *A notice of Spring 1909 announces mortal combat between the sophisticated Class of 1911 and the fledgling Class of 1912. A similar poster proclaimed that the "Snivelling Order of Phmph Ya-Ya Hellish Steweds" (known as SOPHS, for short) would be interred in "infinitesimal fragments" in the Ithaca Dumping Ground. During one previous year, a sophomore prank had resulted in the death of a non-combatant, when the clever "sophs" had released chlorine gas into a room where the frosh were enjoying a traditional banquet. The freshmen survived, but one middle-aged cook did not.*

greatly from age to age, within a certain restricted field of choice it becomes pretty certain what life is all about. It becomes the pursuit of the particular value which may be chosen. Let them, then, be explained as clearly as possible to Freshmen, and let them take their choice. To a few unfortunates, it is true, life will have for its absorbing end the continuous nocturnal search for the hypothetical black cat as "something possessing whatever meaning the adventurer can find in it." To many others, however, it will be the pursuit of the maximum physical, social, economic, or artistic pleasure in the next 40 or 50 years. To a third group it will be an interesting and important preparation for a far better future life.

It is amusing to read the statements by the Modern History professor that "the old foundations of assured faith and familiar custom (i.e., "Christian philosophy and Classical learning") are crumbling beneath our feet," and that "for the greater part of a century Christian faith has been going by the board." However it may be with Classical learning, he will not have to look far in his French Revolution period to discover that Christianity's opponents knew it to be at death's door then, and if he should care to approach the field of Classical learning he would find that the enemies of the Christian religion in the third and fourth centuries were also certain of its early demise. Having survived a lingering death for 16 centuries it would not seem to be in immediate need of such self-appointed pallbearers as the Bewildered Professor. In an age of specialization the intellectualists who refuse to look far beyond the borders of their particular fields may have temporarily excluded Christian philosophy from a few colleges, but people were complaining about that a hundred and fifty years ago. Since religion is not a philosophy, and depends, therefore, as was also pointed out long ago, not so much on the intellect as on the emotions and will, it cannot be driven out by arguments which move only the mind. Few people are swayed by pure reason alone.

It might be suggested then, that the Arts College first orient its faculty before starting on the Freshmen. Why should more or less amateur philosophers be supposed to "inculcate the excellent educational ideas of Ruskin, etc.," in an English class, or teach a bewildering philosophy of life under the guise of a history or language course. And if the Philosophy Department cannot undertake to give a sympathetic interpretation of the different values in life or the explanations of what it is all about which have already satisfied millions of people like the Freshmen, why not tell the students to look elsewhere for the purpose of life, and be content with a little intellectual sharpening from us?

It is now time, before someone else does, to quote Dr. Becker's statement that "those who profess with most confidence (what it is all about) are most likely to be mistaken." I am therefore condemned in advance, but I shall survive, and it will be understood that it is difficult to remain silent when that which is more than life to you is calmly bowed out of consideration before such a large audience by one who apparently has no first-hand experience of it. And it is barely possible that the Bewildered Professor may be bewildered even in making that statement.

Very truly yours,
M.M. KNAPPEN.
— letter, December 13, 1926

Making Victims Victors

Whether the Five Unhappy and Bewildered Freshmen still retain their mental confusion of a few days ago, despite the spirited controversy which is being waged for their comfort and their despair, is, of course, a matter which they alone could tell. It is to be hoped that the recent intellectual outburst has not served to plunge them more deeply into the depths of the "damp of hell." But, as has been said, despair sometimes makes victims victors.

It will be admitted that the liberal arts college is essentially neither a place of the body, nor of the feelings, nor even of the will. It is, above all, a place of the mind. But it seems fair to ask, "Are the teachers of the present day and generation always faithful to this intellectual mission of the college?" The popular mind too often is befogged and confused by our teachers and scholars who seem in league, as it were, to mystify the average student of the practical value of intellectual activities. The intellectuals appear as if content to live in a world of themselves, keeping aloft the intellectual banner, proclaiming the intellectual gospel, yet demanding public adherence to the faith. Results and benefits of

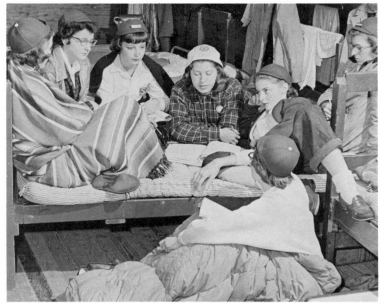

'FOUND A PEANUT, FOUND A PEANUT, FOUND A PEANUT, JUST NOW': *Beanie-clad freshmen of the 1950s sit on a bunk at Freshman Camp. These coëducational camps, sponsored by Cornell United Religious Work at various wooded sites near Ithaca, used to be a special feature of the University's orientation program. Upperclass counselors introduced the frosh to Cornell life, traditions and songs. By the late 1950s, though, the camps were extinct.*

intellectual work seem to them to be inconsequential. They give little satisfaction to their students except to those who are their sworn disciples. And because of this very common professorial attitude, the great majority of Americans has little understanding of the intellectual work of the liberal college.

The families of the Cornellians who are now registered in the College of Arts and Sciences readily can see the very distinct advantage which the "education" will give their progeny. They understand how the democratic give and take of a college community is valuable in itself. The chances for physical development are not discounted. The opportunities of friendship, of social contact are placed high on the scale of the values of a college education. Most families, moreover, perceive that their sons may acquire some training for their future life-work, some information which will make them more efficient bread winners. Some even are inclined to appreciate the advantages which result when a boy is kept at some sort of thinking for four years; that his mind may become more efficient, more acute, more systematic and hence more useful than it was before. But the average citizen, it seems safe to say, is at a loss when asked to relate the utility of a course in Philosophy, Psychology, the Classics, History, or Literature. He may see some professional usefulness, but beyond that he is in the dark for an explanation.

Our educational system is out of order when the teachers say that "the effect of knowledge" upon the life and character of the student must always be for the college a circumstance remote from its main function, a mere accident with which the college has no intimate connection or deep interest. There is no excuse for liberal instruction if there is no relationship between knowledge and life, except in so far as the acquisition of wisdom is a pleasure in itself.

As one eminent college professor has put it, "Give us your boys, give us the means we need, and we will so train and inform the minds of these boys that their own lives and the lives of the men about them shall be more successful than they could be without our training. Give us our chance and we will show your boys what human living is, for we are convinced that they can live better in knowledge than they can in ignorance."

Knowledge is, indeed, justified by its results.

— editorial, December 13, 1926

Go Home, Five Freshmen

To the Editor of The Cornell Daily Sun:

I would like to say a few more words as a commentary on the argument of those "Five Bewildered Freshmen" and on your very sensible editorial "A Challenge to the Arts College."

The whole question revolves, first, on the standing of these five men; second, on their innate intelligence. If they are at the bottom of their class and likely to flunk, then their argument is not worth mentioning. It explains itself. If they are well up in their class — speaking of numerical grades and not of their ability, since the two are often wide apart — then there is something wrong with their mentality. Because, no person with an average intelligence could possibly be in such a mental quagmire after one college term taking up advanced work and at the same time express his inability to understand what it is all about.

The fault — as it is often so misstated — does not lie with the college or the professors, but with the individual himself who does not happen to know what he wants and whose brain has not yet reached a sufficient maturity to differentiate the relative values of the subjects taught and their adaptation in practical life. The best and wisest thing for those five men to do is to be frank and honest enough to state the facts to their parents and confess their temporary inability to grasp the meaning and purpose of advanced education.

In that case it would be worth their while to leave college and set out for a year or two in the world until they have found out the extent of their capacity and their natural adaptability. Then they can return to college and appreciate the value of those courses that bewildered them so terribly in their first term.

G.W. LLOYD '28.
— letter, December 14, 1926

A Sixth Freshman Wants to Transfer

To the Editor of The Cornell Daily Sun:

While I am not one of the "Five Bewildered Freshmen" I agree entirely with the ideas which they have expressed, and have followed the controversy in The Sun with interest. The idea of an orientation course seemed so logical that I have expected it to be received with open arms by the faculty.

As yet, however, the only person who has supported you is an assistant in history, while the influential professors with whom I am acquainted are opposed to the idea. If such is the case and the majority of the faculty are against the idea, then I think that the view of scholarship at Cornell is so limited that a man of practical ideas who expects to make his way in the world as I do is out of place here at Cornell.

I, like many other freshmen, am working my way through the University and until now I have thought it worth-while, but now I think that I am wasting my time here and am planning to transfer to some other university at the end of the term where I can find a more real attitude toward life out in the world. I have made many fine friends here but I cannot help but feel that the system is still under the influence of old ideas too much for me and many others of my class.

R.S. '30.
— letter, December 14, 1926

Becker Redivivus

To the Editor of The Cornell Daily Sun:

May I take a little space to say that Mr. Knappen has apparently misunderstood me in two important respects. First, as to "certainties in life and thought," and Christian philosophy "going by the board." Of course there are certainties in life and thought, for the individual. I have many of my own, although Mr. Knappen appears to think not. Of course there are many people who have an assured Christian faith and an assured Christian philosophy. But which of these so many and conflicting certainties in life and thought, which of these so many and diverse versions of Christian faith and philosophy shall the college teach? Formerly the educated and learned world was fairly well agreed as to what a college should teach in order to give the student a "general education." It should teach Latin, Greek, Mathematics, and the Evidences of Christianity. Is it not evident that there is no longer any agreement, either in college or outside it, that those are the essentials of a college course? My point is only that Christian Philosophy and Classical Learning are "going by the board" as the commonly accepted foundations of a "general education." This seems to me merely the statement of obvious fact. Personally, I am strong for the teaching of Latin and Greek, and mathematics, and I think that a philosophy of life, whether Christian or other, is what a student should mainly seek in his college courses.

The second point. Mr. Knappen appears to think that I wish students to accept my "findings" — my ideas, my point of view, my philosophy of life. Heaven forbid! The main point of my letter was that college offers the student an opportunity (not so good an opportunity as we all wish) to enlarge his experience, extend his knowledge, to be initiated into many points of view, many philosophies of life. I would not have the student tamely accept any professor's "findings." He cannot accept all that are offered. The student must, with whatever aid he can get from professors, work out his own philosophy. The college does not offer all these various and conflicting points of view in order to confuse the student. It offers them because they exist in modern thought, and the college necessarily reflects the conditions of modern thought. In any case, a philosophy which the student accepts on authority, whether the authority of a professor or of a faculty, is not in my opinion worth much. The student who manages to work out any sort of philosophy of life during his four years has got the most a modern college can give him. Mr. Knappen has obviously done just that. It is what I wish every student to do.

CARL BECKER.
— letter, December 15, 1926

Becker Upheld

To the Editor of The Cornell Daily Sun:

Mr. M.M. Knappen's reply to Professor Becker's letter has interested me greatly, despite its polemical style. His reply is interesting, rather for the light that it throws upon the personality of the writer than for any intrinsic worth in thought or composition. At the risk of appearing disdainful of whatever comfort or solace Mr. Knappen might have brought to the many, anxious readers of The Sun, I might say at the very outset that I found his conclusions both irrelevant and superficial. On the other hand, through some perverse instinct, I enjoyed following him in his troubled search for truth. It is difficult to escape the logic of Mr. Knappen's inference in his concluding paragraph, that whereas Professor Becker has had no first-hand experience of "that which is dearer than life" to Mr. Knappen, he, Mr. Knappen, has experienced it to the full. For which reason, no doubt, he strenuously objects to seeing it bowed out of consideration before a large audience.

Professor Becker should unquestionably have been more considerate of Mr. Knappen's feelings before a large audience. I am not sure, however, whether Mr. Knappen would be relieved if there were a smaller audience, or no audience at all, if only he and Professor Becker were present when "that which is dearer than life" were bowed out of consideration. I assume that he refers to faith; I assume that what he means to say is that Professor Becker has attacked the foundations of his faith. In that case, a large audience of Five Bewildered Freshmen and five thousand other perplexed students is as inconsequential a consideration as the presence of an exclusive audience of Mr. Knappen alone. The only thing that matters is the fact that Professor Becker has disturbed Mr. Knappen. But may I carry indelicacy to the point of reminding Mr. Knappen that he himself has had no first-hand experience of the faith in which Professor Becker has rejoiced and suffered, as he says, for more than 35 years, a faith which may conceivably mean as much to Professor Becker as Mr. Knappen's does to him.

But Professor Becker's faith is not founded upon the fundamentals of "Christian philosophy and Classical learning," a sorry state of affairs which prompts Mr. Knappen alternately to pity and denunciation. In his pity, he undertakes to put Professor Becker right and explain to the "Modern History Professor" that Christian philosophy is still valid for Mr. Knappen. In his denunciation he points out that religion is not a philosophy, that "it cannot be driven out by arguments which move only the mind." All of which is very true, of course, but why trouble Mr. Becker with it. I should not be at all surprised if he had been aware of it for many years, certainly for many more years than Mr. Knappen could possibly be. Nor does Professor Becker's letter anywhere so much as suggest his disagreement with it. The letter merely states an opinion of Professor Becker's — that there are a great many hidden mysteries in a thoughtful existence which neither Christian faith nor classical learning have fully explained to him.

If, for Mr. Knappen, Christian faith and the directing of his mind towards "the pursuit of the particular value" that it chooses, give meaning to life and bring him tranquility and confidence, he is to be congratulated. Indeed, he is to be envied by a poor unfortunate like Professor Becker who finds that his intellectual pursuit of any value of life leads to no earthly paradise of certainty and surcease from further inquiry. Perhaps it is true that Professor Becker sets too high a standard for the freshman in Mr. Knappen's classes who, he is happy to say, lacks the ambition to soar to such heights. Perhaps he even sets too high a standard for Mr. Knappen himself, but then Mr. Knappen's interest is in life as well as in thought.

Here, indeed, is the very crux of his difficulty. It is he and not the author of the letter in question who makes the conceptual distinction between life and thought. For my part, I thought that far from making the career of life distinct from that of thought, Professor Becker would put thought—active, continuous mental speculation—into the very value of life, whether it were the pursuit of the maximum social pleasure or even the maximum physical pleasure which Walter Camp's thoughtful system promises to every American home.

I fear that Mr. Knappen has read the letter with too much ardor and too little meditation. If Professor Becker finds that ever since the 17th century science has developed counter to the long-prevailing premises of Christian philosophy, or if he concludes that the transformation of all our human values, partly through that development, partly through the application of that scientific knowledge, has made the former touchstones of education inadequate and obsolete, he merely states what is common knowledge to all thoughtful persons. He seems very remote from implying, as Mr. Knappen needlessly fears and by anticipation resents, that Mr. Knappen or anybody else should rush and renounce his faith, and with it all his hopes. He implies, it appears to me, no more than he explicitly states—that the rewards of thinking are those of finding "something possessing whatever meaning the adventurer can find in it."

What has all this discussion to do with Five Bewildered Freshmen, university education, Mr. Knappen, or even myself? Simply this, that any system of teaching which turns its back upon what is happening to thought and life is doomed to sterility. If, like the Schoolmen's our goal is the preservation and rigid handing on of supposedly established truth, we can do no better than by holding tight to what our fathers learned and their fathers before them. But in that case we must be prepared to accept the fate of the Schoolmen.

LEO GERSHOY '19.
—letter, December 15, 1926

Not a Cure-All, But a Stimulant

It seems as if the Five Bewildered and Unhappy Freshmen (though there is a sixth now) will go down into Cornell history as symbolic of unconscious genius. In all probability, it was without willful premeditation or malicious intent that they started the storm of discussion about orientation, or foundation courses.

Our correspondents, however, appear to have wandered rather far afield in the more recent letters brought by the postman. They are putting the entire matter on a philosophical basis. The issue raised by The Sun in its endeavor to aid the Bewildered Five is not whether, or not, life has a purpose; it is not whether, or not, the function of college is to give a student a purpose in life; it

—Sun Photo by Dan Brothers

is not whether, or not, an orientation course will be the means by which a college may fulfill this function; in fact, The Sun does not for one moment suppose that any orientation course will "orientate" a freshman.

Our stand is this: Lost in the maze of his various subjects, a freshman sees no relation between one and another; they are all merely subjects to him. A course, such as suggested, may be helpful in showing him the essential unity of knowledge. It will not give him any philosophical system of life, nor will it be a panacea for the ills of an Arts College. In helping to orient him as regards the broad expanse of learning, the professor, or professors, giving the course may perhaps stimulate the freshman to genuine study, and not merely the preparation of assignments. If it does this, if it arouses intellectual curiosity in minds that otherwise would lie unused, any orientation course, whether it be known as Contemporary Civilization, Foundation 1, or Unity 101, will have achieved its end.

—editorial, December 16, 1926

Whose Fault Is It?

The Arts College has been attacked many times for its failure to fulfill one of its primary functions as a liberal college—that of stimulating a certain intellectual curiosity in those who are potentially receptive and who, under the present system, are allowed to pass into the world without ever having experienced even a mild stimulation provoked by the college. The Sun, moreover, has pointed on numerous occasions to the dearth of any educational processes in this college which might be employed to combat undergraduate apathy and lethargy.

Only the exceptional student exercises his intellectual curiosity by nature. It is only these few exceptions who ever manifest any great interest in the Arts College curriculum. But the great majority of the Arts undergraduates just drift aimlessly along the path of point collecting, accumulating sufficient credits at the end of four years for graduation, and then go out into the world with the very serious illusion that they are "educated," or at least, are well on the road. It is almost safe to say, furthermore, that this great majority spends more time at the start of the term in selecting from the long array of courses announced in the college bulletin those classes which are not scheduled for afternoons, eight o'clock or Saturdays, then it does in preparing the actual work in the courses.

Such indifference, such stoicism, such insensibility—all hold full sway in the Cornell College of Arts and Sciences. There are no manifestations of intellectual curiosity except from those whose sparks have been touched off before they entered the college. To these ranks are added each year a few more converts—those who have seen the light as a result of intelligent professorial direction. But the great majority, many of whom have the potentialities—what of them?

Even the Dean of the College, Prof. R.M. Ogden, admits the sad state of affairs when he says in his annual report, which is printed in abbreviated form in the *Alumni News*: "The plan of informal study has not met with great favor. Despite the fact that more than 200 upperclassmen met the requirements, only 32 availed themselves of the privilege. The problem of inducing more students to engage in informal study is coupled with that of providing a staff in English and in Public Speaking and in Economics, Government, and History sufficient in size and properly qualified to supervise the work of the students."

Imagine it! One-seventh of the total number who were eligible for informal study cared to bother with any reading on an interesting subject for which they would have received scholastic credit! And from the testimony of those few who have "availed themselves of the privilege" of informal study, it is evident that it has been no fault of the system that so few have been interested.

No, there is no student apathy in the College of Arts and Sciences. Of course not! The undergraduates prefer to snooze in dry lectures and then hastily to prepare for final examinations. It's so much more valuable, you know. There is genuine interest in intellectual activities. The students are desperately in earnest. For proof, examine the zest and enthusiasm with which the golden opportunity of informal study has been seized upon!

And yet, what has the Arts College done to interest its potential students in the curriculum, in the informal plan of study, in the infinite possibilities which a liberal education has to give?

What has it done? Nothing.

—editorial, December 17, 1926

—Photo by
Fred
Robinson

What Cornell Women Owe to the Founders

By Mary M. Crawford '04

Whether Ezra Cornell knew it or not, his famous "any-person-any-subject" slogan carried along with it as a corollary the entire women's movement since 1868. The whole trend of the woman-invasion of the economic and professional fields is epitomized in the 60-odd years of Cornell history. From the moment that Mr. Cornell settled the moot point as to whether women were "persons" or not, and admitted them on the same terms and in the same classes as men, it only remained for enterprising women to come forward and blaze the trail.

Every Cornell woman must feel a thrill of gratitude to Ezra Cornell, and his collaborators, Henry W. Sage and Andrew D. White. They were not only men of rare vision and still more rare practical idealism; they were made of the stuff that does not bow to condemnation or ridicule. Probably the men who could create a non-sectarian university in an age of rigid sectarianism and enunciate the principle that higher education is not the exclusive prerogative of class or wealth, did not very much mind the criticism of the multitude on admitting women to the hitherto masculine sphere of knowledge. But their faith has imposed a great obligation on Cornell women. They laid the foundation of a new tradition, and every Cornell woman should from time to time think of the obligation placed upon her and consider how she has followed this tradition, how handed it on.

With all her mistakes, and eccentricities, the pioneer-woman of the 60s and 70s remains a noble figure. She was aggressive because she had to be. She went to institutions of higher learning because she desperately needed tools to hew her way. She dared masculine disapproval and defied the conventions of her day. There were not many of her at Cornell but the few who came succeeded in establishing the precedent that women belonged there.

The second generation proved what the pioneers had believed, namely, that women could absorb education as well as men. They were in deadly earnest; their outlook was necessarily narrow; and their way was hard. They made the natural mistake of over-emphasizing high marks and passing of examinations, because in that accomplishment there was objective proof of mental ability. But there was a practical side to this viewpoint too. The great majority of Cornell women of this time were poor; they had to make sacrifices to get to college at all, and they were obliged to prepare for their life work while there. Thus evolved the popular legend of the feminine "grind."

There was no early Cornell type of woman, but the very qualities which made a young woman in the late 70s and 80s go to Cornell insured her fitness and stamped her as exceptional. Cornell women of today may look back with pride at the roster of their earlier sisters. In every Cornell women's club today these older women of an earlier Cornell stand out — valiant, strong, able, and devoted daughters of their Alma Mater.

Somewhere in the early part of the 19th Century men had gracefully conceded *belles lettres* to women, and the demand for

—Photo by J. Beardsley
EMMA SHEFFIELD EASTMAN '73
Cornell's First Female Graduate

teachers had thrown open the doors of that profession to large numbers of them. Men said generously that a woman's mind could gain a superficial mastery of elementary subjects and of classics and it was quite right and fitting that women should busy themselves with the education of youth, up to a certain point. But of course, the technical field remained a masculine domain.

It was the third generation (the granddaughters of the women of the 60s) who took up this challenge. Among this generation of women themselves a reaction had set in against the traditional "grind" and against teaching as the only profession open to them. Girls began to apply for admission into the colleges of medicine, law, engineering, architecture, and others. Thanks to the positive and unmistakable attitude of the Founder, there could arise no question of exclusion at Cornell.

The Cornell woman of this era reasserted her right to feminine charm. Her social life expanded and her interests widened. She welcomed the first national fraternity for women to open a chapter at Cornell in 1881. This was soon followed by three more. The chapters were small, meetings were held in dormitory rooms and the relative number of women students initiated was few. She began to develop athletics for herself. Tennis and rowing were the favorite outdoor sports and basket ball was played in the winter. Competition was only between classes. Nothing intercollegiate had yet begun. She also began to attend mass-meetings, to go to football games, and generally to participate in the life of the University. She acquired student self-government, asked for an Adviser of Women, and finally obtained a Dean of Women. Gradually her sense of isolation from affairs Cornellian disappeared. She came to realize that she was missing something. She found too that she was needed, that she had something to give as well as to receive; that Cornell, in fact, was hers. Ironically enough, as she was learning this, Cornell men had been becoming "coed-conscious." Just why and when the Cornell man became "coed-conscious" is open to conjecture. There is little record of it in the earlier classes. Perhaps the increasing athletic contacts with the older universities of the East prompted him to neutralize ridicule and to counteract the humiliation of going to college with girls by out-Heroding Herod. The mythical "coed," so unlovely in comparison with her non-collegiate sisters, became a campus joke, while in actual fact the drawing-rooms of Sage College were crowded. This myth was undoubtedly inspired by the early "grind" who had stamped her peculiarities on the masculine mind; even in recent years she is occasionally revived in the form of an ephemeral spectre. Any observer of Cornell life today may well wonder what has become of the old prejudice and may note in passing that while the older universities have been fostering a European tradition, Cornell has been creating an American one toward which Europe is now looking.

Since the third generation, pioneering has not been so obvious or so painful. The rough trail has been widened and macadamized, and traffic is far greater and more unrestricted. Every year women are qualifying for new technical and professional positions, and more of the professional schools have women in their classes. Yet Cornell is still pioneering. One of the latest schools to be established has grown out of the development of new sciences unknown at the time of Cornell's founding. The Science of Nutrition, the chemistry of foods and textiles, economics of consumption and psychology of unknown relations have resulted in the establishment of the College of Home Economics. Here in the great home of joint education of men and women has arisen a fine modern school. Its scientific training is based on woman's traditional sphere but it has elevated that sphere to the plane of scientific research. While preëminently for women and women's training, this is in no sense a retrogression from the ideal of coeducation. It is rather a deepening and broadening of Mr. Cornell's inspired statement.

Indeed as year after year sees more men seeking special courses and whole sections of the training given in this college, it is demonstrated again that all knowledge is sought by both men and women. There is no sex limitation in the quest for truth.

What of the Cornell woman of today? How does she appear when measured by the standards of the past, set up so ably, even nobly by the earlier generations, with all their faults admitted? What would the pioneer of the 60s who dreamed of a free world for women, where each could attain the highest she was capable of, think of the progress made? After the first faint shock occasioned by the superficial aspects of today,—the scantiness of clothes, the casual informal manners, the rushing around at such a terrifying rate of speed,—she would breathe a sigh of relief and contentment, for here she would find what she had dreamed of, consciously or half-consciously,—a world where women stood on their own feet, did what they would and could, and abided the judgment of their times, on their own merits as individuals. She would see a group of a thousand young women going about their complicated University affairs with efficiency, studying hard,

Andrew White on Coeducation: A Success. . .

—Scrapbook of Richard Evett Bishop '09

'A Blessing From Every View': *The fresh smile of this Cornellian of about 1909 melts away the intervening decades.*

Sir:

Referring to your letter of Jan. 17, I answer your questions as follows:

1. Young women have now been admitted to this University for about 11 years.

2. The present number of women students is about 50 out of a total of 563.

3. We have never experienced any difficulty in the way of discipline arising from the admission of women to the classes, and nothing has happened to warrant the inference that mixed classes tend to lower the moral sentiment or injure the character of any of the students. On the contrary, the general feeling, even among those members of the Faculty who were opposed to their admission, is that the tone of conduct among our young men has been improved thereby. Young men cannot glory in the same things or talk in the same way when even a small number of ladies are present among them as many would do without such restraint. We all know perfectly well that a public room full of men alone is pretty much at the mercy of any blackguard who chooses to indulge in unbecoming conduct or foul speech. When a woman enters, all that is changed.

This fact asserts itself with the admission of women to the lecture rooms and laboratories of the University, and there is something of the same difference between the rooms where they are not and where they are, which we observe between a smoking car and the car back of it.

Nor has scholarship suffered. While young women are not, as a rule, the very best scholars in our classes they are very rarely poor scholars. As a rule the great majority of them stand in the first third or first half of their classes. A natural quiet emulation stimulates and strengthens both sexes. Nor is this elevation of the tone of the young men at the expense of the young women. It is a mere superstition to suppose that they become less womanly in universities where young men are present; both at the University of Michigan and here it has been noted that their best womanly characteristics are developed and strengthened. They see as by instinct that a certain reserve must be maintained, and if in any case any one of them should break over such proper reserve there are none who would resent this more quickly than the other lady students.

As to the effect upon young men, I think that the history of our recent civil war is sufficient to prove that "co-education" does not cause them to deteriorate in manly qualities. As a simple matter of fact from no colleges did young men volunteer to serve in the army more generally than from those to which women were admitted; and the willingness to take up a musket for one's country is about as good a test of manliness as the world knows.

To sum up on this point. I think that by the admission of women to university classes men become more manly and women more womanly.

4. My observation and experience in this system have discovered no valid objection to it. When the admission of women was proposed here I had seen so many good results arising from the presence in our high schools and normal schools of young men and young women of marriageable age from distant homes that I had little fear of any evils so generally prophesied. There was only one thing which aroused my apprehensions, and that was the possibility of injury to the health of the young women. I feared that emulation and eagerness in study might undermine their constitutions and

playing hard and training themselves effectively for life in the world of today.

She would see 14 chapters of national sororities at Cornell, with a much greater proportion of the student body enrolled in them—owning their own chapter houses where most of them live, and managing the business of these houses on the whole effectively. She would see the dormitory life developed in importance, the center of the woman's life at Cornell. Here she would note how the training of Student Self Government teaches the girls to cooperate, to discipline themselves and to organize. She would find junior and senior honorary societies selecting the leaders of their classes and these leaders setting the tone of the entire student body. Perhaps the greatest change which the pioneer of the 60s would see is the development of sports and athletics. This is one of the most promising things in the life of the modern girl at Cornell. The range of activities is great. There is now at Cornell organized work in baseball, archery, track, rowing, tennis, soccer, fencing, field hockey, basket ball and rifle shooting. The last three have intercollegiate meets, while the others have intramural contests. The whole subject of physical development has been taken out of the indoor gymnasium and is now based largely on outdoors sports, carefully supervised and medically protected. The result is a fine body of strong healthy young women.

Non-athletic activities are also contributing to the development of the Cornell girl of today. Glee and mandolin clubs are maintained. There is a successful debate team, and a weekly paper is published. *The Cornell Daily Sun* has five or six girls in editorial and business positions and many girls annually go out as "compets" for these places. Dramatics are popular at Cornell. The men and women work together in this and the plays given frequently during the year show hard work and real ability.

The comment is sometimes made that girls of today enjoy a freedom which they did nothing to secure. They pay no heed to the women who won it for them. Why should they, after all? Did the older Cornell women waste much time on the opinions and advice of those who went before them? Not consciously, certainly. They were too busy building for themselves and the future, and that is how the world moves on.

As new freedoms are won, we must learn how to use them, and that is one of the lessons of the past which girls of today should study. The older Cornell woman should turn this page too, from time to time. If she feels that she did well, and was helpful, should she not trust her younger sisters, in the same general environment, to do and be the same?

Cornell women are going out from the University in far greater numbers than in the past, and they are going out to positions of trust and responsibility where they acquit themselves well. They are also making successful homes for themselves and for the men of their choice and are rearing healthy, intelligent, valuable children to whom they impart the lessons of life learned at Cornell.

There is little need for pessimism in the present outlook. Mistakes are being made and too hasty steps are being retraced, but all in all the Cornell girl of today is justifying her existence at the University as ably as did the earlier woman who came there. One great duty lies clearly before her and all Cornell women,—to

. . .Men More Manly, Women More Womanly

that we might in this way render the very opposite of a service to the country.

I feel that there is, under ordinary circumstances, some danger of this sort. As a rule women are more conscientious and earnest in study then men, and are likely to throw themselves into it more eagerly. This fact has to be taken account of and especial care exercised in regard to it.

In this view we have insisted that they shall attend lectures on hygiene, and that certain simple rules of health shall be steadily observed. A special gymnasium has been established where all lady students are required, under the direction of our Professor of Physical Culture and his assistants, to take a certain amount of exercise every day. They are also encouraged to take much exercise in the open air, and a lady of high character and large experience is especially appointed to act in a general way as a sort of "guide, counselor, and friend" to the whole body of lady students. Should any one of them show signs of declining health it is insisted that she give up her studies temporarily or permanently. The general testimony of these students is that their health under this system is better than at home, and I believe that in the great majority of cases this is the fact.

5. The experiment of co-education at various institutions in this country, and especially at the State University of Michigan and at Cornell, has proved, as we fully believe, a success. I see no signs of its losing the confidence of the people; on the contrary it is slowly gaining in public favor as it becomes more and more understood. I am not especially an apostle of the system, have no desire to establish any propaganda in its behalf, and am perfectly willing that results shall decide the matter. Confidence in this, as in other important reforms, is a plant of slow growth; and I am far from advocating the training of all young women, or even the majority of young women, in universities with young men. Such training demands great definiteness of purpose and earnestness of effort. It is only a comparatively small minority of young women who ever will or ought to take advantage of university privileges. The great majority of young women will continue to be educated in women's colleges and ladies' boarding schools; those who will enter our universities will be the select few who are animated either by a great love of learning or by the desire to fit themselves for teaching. Here is one of the great safeguards of "co-education," so called, namely, that only young women of most earnest and definite purpose will submit to the sacrifices involved, — the thorough preparation to enter, the giving up of the best four years of their lives to hard work, and the passing of the examinations requisite for certificates and degrees. The idea that the ladies' boarding schools of any country or town are to be emptied into the university classes is simply absurd.

As to one point more which has troubled many, — the possibility of attachments springing up between students of the two sexes which would interfere with work, — we have never suffered in the least from that cause. The experience of the University of Michigan, Oberlin, and other institutions where young women are admitted is, I am informed, like our own. Very few such attachments have been formed and in these rare cases where they have existed, they have but increased emulation in study and made work more serious.

In conclusion allow me to say that the experience of 11 years under this system here and elsewhere, leads me to believe it a blessing from every point of view, and my observation of the same system at other American universities strengthens me in this opinion.

I remain, dear sir,
Very truly yours,
Andrew D. White.
—*letter to E.G. O'Connor, January 26, 1885, reprinted in Sun, January 30, 1885*

Another Founder, Another Letter

April 28, 1874

Miss Marietta E. Parker

Your favor Apr. 14 came duly to hand.

The "Sage College for Women" will be treated as a component part of the University, and not as a "boarding School for girls." It will therefore not be equipped with a separate corps of teachers but the girls will receive instruction from the professors and Asst. Professors the same as the boys do in the same class and same lecture rooms.

Your application should be made to Presst. Andrew D. White for a professorship in such department as you deem yourself qualified to fill.

There is no law or usage that will prevent the appointment of a woman to a professorship—Merit as a teacher will be the only test.

We must have the best professors we can obtain without reference to sex, religious belief, politicks, nationality, or color.

Yours Respectfully,
Ezra Cornell

PS—Sage College for women will be ready for use at the commencement of the next college year in September next.

share in the responsibility of directing the finest and most promising of the young people of today to Cornell. Here, as elsewhere, large numbers apply for admission far beyond the powers of Cornell to accept. The question arises, what qualities in a girl justify her admission to Cornell—how shall we now without betraying the very principles which are the pride and mainstay of Cornell, restrict Cornell women numerically and yet secure the best individuals? Sound scholarship she must have first and foremost, sound principles of life and a healthy vigorous body with which to do her work; and there should be in her that gleam of the spirit which means the forward looking person who wants to be and insists on being in the van of progress, steadied by the balanced judgment which will know how to choose between the true and the false. Young women such as these will justify the pioneering of the past and hold fast to the good which was found in the past. They will justify their present training by sound accomplishment and they will give back to their world, especially their Cornell world, full value for the priceless gifts received.

from A HALF-CENTURY AT CORNELL, *1930*

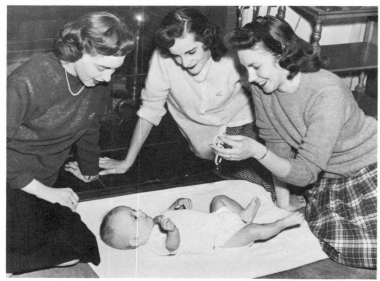

—Cornell University Archives

BAUBLES AND BANGLES TO BANNERS AND FISTS: *Above, home economics students of a generation ago coo over a "practice baby" as part of their child development and family relations training. These babies were burdened with names like "Dickie Domecon" (for Domestic Economics). Below, a feminist march of Spring 1970 proceeds from the Straight to President Corson's office, where 150 men and women demanded that Gannett Clinic introduce "competent contraceptive and gynecological" care. As this book goes to press, the protesters' wish has come to full fruition: Gannett has just opened a new Contraceptive, Gynecology and Sexuality Service.*

On Sexism in Advertising

To the Editor:

This letter is in protest against the type of advertising solicited by your newspaper as of late. THE SUN has always been conservative in such matters. Why the awful change?

We refer specifically to an ad appearing on Page 7 of Tuesday's SUN. It pictures a young woman with her mouth open, about to kiss an elderly gentleman. (At least he's elderly.) The dastardly implications of this are all too obvious, considering that this paper serves a coed college. We protest this affront. You're always making fun of coeds, but sometimes, SUN, you go too far.

Above these rapidly approaching heads is the vulgar command, "Make the Kiss Test!" What kind of women do you take us to be? What's wrong with the old Kleenex test? If you don't want your paper boycotted by the few but determined right-thinking coeds, you had better change your tactics.

F.V.L.T.
F.D.S.

Editor's Note: Patronize SUN advertisers.

—letter, March 5, 1948

To the Editor:

The ad placed in Tuesday's Sun in an attempt to encourage freshwomen to sign up for sorority spring rush is very insulting. The ad consists of a cartoon representation of a man, ostensibly John Hancock, signing various papers with a quill pen. The caption reads, "FRESHMEN WOMEN — Give us your John Hancock. Sign up for sorority spring rush . . ."

How can a woman give a "John Hancock?" More to the point, why should she?

I can see how such an ad might have been developed; a publicity committee is looking for clever ways to attract signatures: what famous signatures can we think up: John Hancock! I am surprised and horrified, however, that no one took the thinking a step further to realize how grossly inappropriate and sexist this ad is, especially for an ad directed at women.

Too bad there were no women signers of the Declaration of Independence to lend their names to sorority ads today. But whatever inequalities might have existed in 1776, the position of women now will not be improved as long as men and women fail to think past clichéd, sexist references, like the one displayed in Tuesday's ad.

Wendy Zomparelli
—letter, December 5, 1974

—Photo by Russ Hamilton

ANDROCLES' LION? *Amid a splendid profusion of Greek and Roman casts and ornaments, staid students in an old Sibley Hall freehand drawing room seek to capture a snarling lion's head on their pads of paper. Although most such drawing models owned by the University in the late nineteenth and early twentieth century were plaster reproductions of classical originals, some were the real article. For example, while passing through eastern France about 1870, Andrew Dickson White came across a medieval stone carving of "the grotesque face of a monk in the midst of a mass of foliage supporting the base of a statue," which a so-called architectural "restorer" had wrenched from the walls of Troyes cathedral. White rescued this discarded corbel, and donated it to "the museum of the Architectural Department at Cornell." Does anyone know where it is now?*

The Rise and Fall of Cornell's Art

By Elizabeth Baker Wells '28

One hundred years ago visitors to Cornell would find only a few of the works of art we see today in many buildings and on the campus. The only buildings at that time were Cascadilla Hall, Morrill Hall, White Hall, West Sibley, McGraw Hall, Andrew D. White's house, Sage Chapel, and Sage College.

The University was young and few members of the faculty or administration had any interest in art objects or funds to enable them to acquire them. One exception was the University's first president, Andrew D. White, a collector of pictures, furniture, art objects, and books. He possessed taste and discrimination in selecting the best, and fortunately he had ample means to purchase them, not only for himself, but also, during his later years, for the University.

Soon after Risley Hall was opened to women students in 1913, Mr. White gave several paintings, a set of Arundel prints, several etchings, some furniture, and statuary for the reception areas, all of which, according to the *Cornell Alumni News* in 1914 gave a "cheerful atmosphere to these rooms." Many of these objects are still there.

When the lowest of the West Dorms were completed in 1916, he presented a collection of 15 reproductions, in color, of famous European paintings for the lounges. He felt, again quoting the *Alumni News* of that time, that "pleasant surroundings would contribute to the students' well-being." These reproductions have all disappeared.

In 1917 Jacques Reich, a well-known engraver, gave the University a large collection of portraits of American worthies, including most of the presidents, statesmen, writers, etc. There were some 30 engravings, many by Mr. Reich. These were hung in the Reading Room on the top floor of Goldwin Smith. Now the Reading Room has been divided into several small offices and most of the pictures lost. A few of them, tattered and dusty, were found recently in the attic of Goldwin Smith and are now in the Department of Manuscripts and Archives in Olin Library.

In 1929 Balch Hall was dedicated as a residence for women students. The donors, Mr. and Mrs. Allan C. Balch, hoped that by providing elegant housing, they would stimulate an appreciation of fine arts and furnishings among the residents and visitors. The Balches gave several Chinese paintings, examples of Indian silks, and some antique furniture. Most of these are now in storage.

Myron Taylor Hall, 1930, possesses the most beautiful furnishings of all our campus buildings. These were provided by Mr. and Mrs. Taylor. Several of the portraits of famous jurists in the Law Library Reading Room were given to the law school by Andrew D. White when the school occupied Boardman Hall, now demolished and replaced by Olin Library. Some of the portraits of law school deans, also in the library, were given by individuals or classes.

Many outstanding Cornell faculty members, deans of colleges, and all presidents have been memorialized by portraits, portrait busts and/or portrait plaques. Some of the notable teachers represented by portraits are James Law, professor and dean of the College of Veterinary Medicine, 1868-1908, in the foyer of the James Law Auditorium; Charles Babcock, first dean of the College of Architecture, 1871-1897, in the college office; Estevan A. Fuertes, professor of civil engineering, 1873-1890, and director of the College of Engineering, whose portrait hangs in the stairway of Hollister Hall; Isaac P. Roberts, dean of the College of Agriculture, 1874-1903, whose portrait is in the Reference Room of Mann Library.

The portraits of the University presidents hang in the main reading room of Uris Library, the deans in or near their college offices except those of the College of Agriculture which are in the Reference Room of Mann Library; and faculty members in their departments or in the smaller reading rooms of Uris Library. There are portrait plaques and portrait statues of Cornell notables in Sage Chapel. And of course we all know that Ezra Cornell and Andrew D. White grace the arts quadrangle. There are many more representations of faculty and staff scattered about the campus, about 260 memorial portraits in all.

BEHEADED PHILOSOPHERS: *Cornell was once proud of its collection of some 500 plaster casts made from original Greek and Roman sculptures of deities, athletes, statesmen and philosophers. The statues—painstakingly assembled by Andrew Dickson White during European travels in the 1880s—were prominently displayed in a Goldwin Smith basement gallery (above) complete with friezes, columns and hanging draperies. The collection, which included an almost complete set of sculptures from a pediment of the Parthenon, was probably the finest in America. By the mid-twentieth century, however, such reproductions had fallen into acute disfavor. Removed into attics, storerooms and obscure tunnels—or lost or stolen—the artifacts were utterly neglected for several decades. Many were spray-painted, dismembered or battered. One statue (below), which still stands near a Goldwin Smith stairwell, lost its head to the swing of a baseball bat (or similar weapon) in the mid-1970s. A professor of the 1960s actually boasted of bashing the casts, claiming they were nothing but "fakes." Of course, molds from original Greek statues of Athens, Pergamon and Olympia could not be made today at any price. Recently, Prof. Peter Kuniholm and his classics students have rescued many of the plaster heroes from abuse, and begun identifying and restoring them (one group of casts was removed from a tunnel behind the Temple of Zeus coffeehouse just minutes before a broken water main flooded the area). But despite Kuniholm's best efforts, Cornell's gods and goddesses still await a permanent home.*

GRACIOUS LIVING: *Some of the most elaborately furnished and decorated Cornell interiors once graced the older North Campus dormitories, which housed only women until a decade ago. Balch Hall, built during the 1920s, was especially luxurious. Different period styles—English Georgian, English Jacobean, Early American and Gramercy Park—distinguished its original four separate living units. An early description of the Early American unit mentions "maple furniture in the dining room whose yellow tones are repeated in the paper and relieved by the soft green of the china, glass and hand-loom fabric of the chairs." The furnishings consisted exclusively of antiques or authentic reproductions, and residents dined using genuine china and silver-plated utensils ("Balch" was engraved on the handle of each piece). While traces of former opulence remain, the china, silver and elaborate glassware have disappeared, and much furniture and artwork is now in storage. Risley Hall—the above photo dates from its early years—has fared better, and still retains much of its intended English charm. This is probably because so much of its interior embellishment was incorporated into the building itself. It is difficult to remove overhanging, carved mantlepieces or sculpted dwarves dwelling beneath ceiling rafters. Still, some of Risley's original statues and paintings are gone, and those that remain—such as the reproduction of Michelangelo's Moses seen below—are not always accorded the highest respect. The same could be said of much of Cornell's art.*

A CENTURY AT CORNELL

In recent years photographs of faculty members have replaced the types of portraiture just noted. We see many of them in hallways or near department directories. One wonders why this change has come about. It may be simple economics, since carved and painted portraits are costly. Perhaps this change also reflects our hurry to achieve quick results. The earlier portraits may reflect times of more leisure and certainly deeper appreciation of fine arts. In any event, it is sad to see this change and I believe we are in some way poorer.

During the last 10 years we have witnessed another change. There are now on the lower campus many examples of contemporary sculpture, and perhaps it is only a matter of time before there will be some scattered about the upper campus.

This brief summary of art works at Cornell would not be complete without a mention of the Herbert F. Johnson Museum of Art, opened in 1973. Its permanent collections include examples of many periods and various media. Travelling exhibits provide works by present-day artists as well as those of earlier periods.

The collections of works of art at Cornell enrich our living and learning environment. They also bring problems of preservation, restoration, and security. On several occasions departments have moved (engineering from Franklin, Sibley, and Lincoln to the south end of the campus; architecture from White Hall to Sibley, for examples). In these moves some paintings have been damaged and are in need of restoration, for which the University has not made adequate funds available. In some cases portraits of earlier professors recently located have not been rehung because the present staff members are not interested in them or their work. It seems to me that those portraits should hang where the individuals did their work. Those worthies are part of our Cornell heritage and should be visible even though few of us today knew them, and as time goes on fewer will recognize them or remember their contributions. Most of them are labeled; those that are not are still known and should be properly identified before they too are forgotten.

Paintings have suffered when classrooms or offices were redecorated. At such times they were shifted about in hallways, often not rehung, and finally put by custodians in the nearest broomcloset or attic, where they have been victims of leaking roofs or cleaning water, and usually forced to share a limited space with broken furniture. Eventually they slipped into dusty oblivion. Of course occasionally accidents occurred. Once an over-zealous janitor dusted a large portrait too vigorously and it fell off the wall, landing on him, and his head went through the canvas. He was shifted to another type of activity.

Finally, our art collections are security risks. Since the 1960s some portraits, paintings, and art objects have been put in storage (as noted). Once this would have not been thought necessary. These works of art belong to all of us, so to speak, for all of us to enjoy.

The University needs a focal point, a center staffed by individuals familiar with Cornell history and with Cornell's collections (except those connected with the art museum, whose holdings are all catalogued). Such a center should have a list of art works on campus, including all furnishings of historic interest—tapestries, desks, tables, etc., and should keep an up-to-date register. It would be desirable for such a center to have its own exhibition area in which to display what can best be described as "Cornelliana." And what a wealth there is of objects (aside from portraits) associated with Cornell history: the president's chair, given by Andrew D. White; the Dean of Agriculture's top hat, etc. Each year the list grows longer and our responsibilities greater. We should know where our treasures are and be sure that they are safe.

ELIZABETH BAKER WELLS '28 is author of *Catalogue of Art Works at Cornell University.*

—Photo by Eagles

—Photo by J. Beardsley

—Collection of Gustav J. Requardt '09

A CASTLE ON THE RHINE? *It was once hoped that the McGraw-Fiske mansion, a fairytale "castle" of spires and pinnacles which stood below the current site of the Johnson museum, would become Cornell's first art museum. The edifice was built by Jennie McGraw Fiske, donor of the McGraw Tower chimes, who saw it once from a carriage before her 1881 death. She willed the mansion to Cornell along with an enormous sum for building a library, but her husband, for a number of complex reasons that have never been fully sorted out, contested the will. After years of acrimonious litigation, the University lost the money—and the hoped-for museum. Actually, the edifice was a museum of its own, for its chambers (one interior view is seen in the top photo) were filled with bits of classical sculpture, Egyptian and Chinese artifacts, tapestries, grotesque German furniture and unbelievable expanses of carved wood. On December 7, 1906 the mansion—which by then had become Chi Psi's lodge—was gutted by a spectacular fire that claimed the lives of four students and three firemen. Above: The structure's northwest facade is seen before and after the blaze.*

We now turn to the problem of what is euphemistically termed "academic integrity," and what is more popularly known as cheating. On a campus as idyllic as Cornell's, it seems a shame to bring up such a topic. But it exists none-theless, and, to judge by The Sun's writings on the subject over the past century, it always has, and always will. Like the last digit of the square root of two, it is an insoluble prob-lem, insoluble for a number of reasons.

First, there are the grade pressures. Throughout most of Cornell's history, it was fairly easy for a student to bust out if he did not do well academically. Nowadays it is much more difficult, but even so there is a new deterrent to honesty: the greater selectivity of the various professional graduate schools, especially medical and business schools. Cheating among premeds is reputedly so widespread that it occa-sions no comment any more. The only time professors are outraged is when it degenerates into actual sabotage: when other students' experiments are deliberately ruined, for example, to lower the grade curve. There have been well-documented instances of this happening, unfortunately.

Second, the grade system, in every permutation that has been tried, has been proven to contain gross unfairnesses. Today, as always, some professors mark easier than others; during the Vietnam War days, some professors announced that as a protest they would give out only A's. Grade infla-tion has been rampant. The law school newspaper in 1976 proposed that the present A,B,C,D,F system be scrapped for lack of utility, and be replaced by an A++,A+,A,A−,A−− system. There has also been an increase in the number of credits for a given course: four credits is standard for a course today whereas three was the rule 20 years ago. The

credit inflation was a gradual process, as one course after another would go from three to four. Now, we are seeing the next logical step: some courses are awarding five credits for the same amount of work that would have justified three in 1960.

Some professors have resisted this trend, and in so doing have created more problems than the grade-and-credit inflation itself. What is to be done with a faculty member who refuses to allow the standard number of credits for work done in his courses, and who will not mark on a par with his fellows? It is irrelevant to students whether the holdout professor is wrong, or whether the inflationary system is.

The decrease in the faculty-student ratio and the increase in the number of large lecture classes have had a couple of unpleasant side effects. More and more graduate students are doing the grading, and the graduate students have proven even more inconsistent than the professors. Also, more and more emphasis is now placed on performance on a few papers or examinations.

All of these factors do not constitute a defense of cheating or plagiarism, but they do explain to a certain extent why it occurs. In an institution as large as Cornell, the unfairnesses cannot be removed. The grading system will always play favorites; a few institutions have even aban-doned the Scylla of letter or number grades for the Charyb-dis of pass-fail, but this has not been an answer either. At Cornell, for example, some students have recently been permitted to elect to take certain courses "S-U": that is, to have their course work graded only as Satisfactory or Unsatisfactory, the idea being to reduce the pressure in such a course. Some professors have managed to defeat this sys-tem by setting their standards for "Satisfactory" work so high that none of their students will elect the S-U option; others, unwilling to dole out the U, have asked for a third possible grade, "Low Pass." The fourth and fifth possible grades for the S-U option, one supposes, would be along presently.

In short, it is easy enough to become so annoyed with the system that one is tempted to cheat, and if one decides to give in to temptation, it is preposterously easy to suc-ceed. It is conceivable that there may be an infallible method of preventing cheating and plagiarism, but if there is, the Cornell faculty has so far failed to unearth it.

Cheating on examinations has never taxed students' ingenuity too heavily, but nowadays it is even easier to hand in non-original papers. Students frequently hand in the same paper, modified slightly, in different courses. Sometimes they borrow such a paper from a friend. More interesting is the advent in the last ten years of the professional term-paper service: a company that retails finished papers. These fascinating companies, for fear of violating laws, like New York's, against selling term papers, now advertise only "research assistance," but the assistance comes in the form of a paper that could easily be handed in as a finished pro-duct. Some of the companies have extensive catalogs of the available papers, which usually range in price of $50 to $1,000. The more sophisticated companies also keep records of where each paper has gone, to guard against the possibility of the same paper being handed in twice to the same professor. They also keep staffs of freelancers who are able to custom-write papers for those who cannot find a suitable topic in the catalog. The commercial papers are generally of a good quality; they normally get A's or B's, but they are not so brilliantly done that they would arouse suspicion. Unless a professor has either seen a paper before or is familiar with a student's writing style (which is extremely uncommon today), the purchased product is undetectable. The Sun's board of directors, spitting in the ocean in an effort to create high tide, banned "research

For a New Exam System

Perhaps a well meant suggestion might arouse a little consideration on the part of the Faculty in regard to examina-tions. At Amherst at present a system is being tested of having no examinations at all. The students are supposed to be men with true manly spirit and enthusiasm mixed with a *desire* to learn, and character enough to work and do their ordinary duty without a continual goad to urge them on, or examina-tions to scare them. In case a student does not do his duty, the professor may impose upon him an examination which, if he fail to pass, he is conditioned and has to make it up. But if the professor be satisfied that a student is doing the right and proper amount of work in his branch, *no* examination is imposed and the student goes on: learning all the time to rely on himself. The system thus far has given very eminent satis-faction, and we write this to urge a trial of the same or a similar system here. Were the examinations here fair tests, we should say nothing, but in many, and, we are sorry to have to say, *too* many cases of dishonesty, for such it is though often not so looked upon enters to such a degree as to be positively unfair and unjust to the honest and perhaps better student. Especially does this come into play when the comparative merits are taken into account. A poor student may by skill-fully cribbing write a paper which will be much better than one written by a good student who has worked honestly. Not only is this unfair toward the honest and good student but the mere presence of the good paper shows the professor that his examination was not too difficult when, if all had been honest, the professor would be able at once to see that the examination was too hard for the class. It is exceedingly discouraging for the good honest student, and it has now reached a point when there is quite universal student com-plaining. We are sure our professors wish to be just and impartial and we are so confident of their sense of honor and integrity, that we should be perfectly willing to be judged by them. We then beg a trial of the system, at least, and should it fail to give satisfaction, then let us return to the old way, or any other that the Faculty sees fit to adopt.

—editorial, April 29, 1881

assistance'' advertising in 1972—over the objections of most of the student members.

Faculty and student views on how to control cheating have come full circle several times. Every so often a total honor system is put into effect, where the faculty completely ceases to supervise examinations and students are responsible for reporting malefactors. When this does not work, as is customary, the faculty beefs up its presence, increases security, and threatens offenders with harsh punishments, thereby irritating almost everyone and creating an incentive for students to tolerate cheaters. In 1969 a professor boasted to one of his classes that he would have six teaching assistants monitor a forthcoming examination (among other security measures) and that cheating would be *impossible*. It wasn't. Five or six enterprising students managed to steal a copy of the examination from the department office a day in advance. And, not being content with this, they also stole official examination booklets, wrote out their answers beforehand, hid the completed booklets under their coats, and adroitly substituted them for the real booklets upon handing them to the professor. At least ten people in the class were aware of what was happening, but nobody tattled.

How to punish transgressors has proved nearly as abstruse a question as how to catch them in the first place. If punishments are too severe, many will not cooperate with the system. If they are too light, cheating and plagiarism are encouraged. There are frequently mitigating circumstances. Few students are so depraved that they take pleasure in cheating *per se*; frequently they are driven into error by personal difficulties that make it impossible for them to devote the requisite time to their schoolwork. Cornell's present enforcement system, in which students play an important part, is imperfect because it has to be, but it has shown a willingness to take such circumstances into consideration—a willingness that some consider excessive.

There is also the question of unequal enforcement. Certain faculty members, especially untenured professors afflicted by the publish-or-perish syndrome, have been known to use outside help themselves. Some books and articles carrying the names of faculty members have been written by other than their putative authors; some professors are accused of never looking at papers they are supposed to grade. Nothing teaches like example.

Unequal treatment is not just confined to faculty members. A notorious case arose in the early 70s, when a student handed in a term paper that had been turned in to the same professor one semester earlier. The evidence was overwhelming, the offense was severe, but the punishment was not—the defendant, a star athlete, did not miss a single game.

That case, however, was trifling in comparison to the one we will look at next: the most spectacular case of plagiarism in Cornell history.

* * *

In 1951, Cornell finally got its sixth president. President Day, in poor health, had retired in 1949; he died in March 1951. Cornell's trustees were for a time unable to find a suitable successor. Consequently, the provost, Cornelis W. de Kiewiet, served as acting president for more than a year. He was quite unpopular, and it rapidly became clear that he was not being considered for the permanent presidency. He was, however, offered the presidency of the University of Rochester, and he left Cornell in January, 1951. This forced the Cornell trustees' hand, and on the day de Kiewiet's resignation took effect, they announced that Cornell's next president would be Deane Waldo Malott, chancellor of the University of Kansas.

Malott did not seem a likely president. He was the first Cornell president inaugurated in this century not to hold a doctorate; he will surely be the last. His background was basically in business, not education. A native Kansan, he was a former vice president of a pineapple company in Honolulu, but, as he observed, ''I decided long ago that I would rather deal with young people than pineapples.'' In the early 30s, he went to Harvard Business School as an associate professor. He became K.U.'s chancellor in 1939, and compiled an impressive record as a fundraiser; this was not lost on Cornell's trustees.

At any rate, Malott took over in Summer 1951, and immediately began to reorganize the administration, hoping for more efficiency. He also announced a major break with tradition—instead of the spectacular, long-winded ceremonies that had characterized the formal inaugurations of all past Cornell presidents, he proposed a ''family affair''

Only the Undergraduates Can Banish Cribbing

The dust has cleared away from the cribbing farce and reveals 106 victims "found guilty." Eight more cases are still to be tried. The scandal is without doubt the largest in the history of the University, and no good can come from trying to hush it up. It needs to be talked about and not dodged.

In spite of the things that might be said about the psychology of the mob spirit which must have prevailed, or about the thoughtfulness of youth, or about the susceptibility of young males to any venture that smacks of excitement, there remains the bald fact that more than 100 seekers after higher learning deliberately perpetrated a fraud and one seeker committed an ordinary theft. This fact stands out above any argument.

Nothing in the way of a penalty can ever stop cribbing in this or any other university. All the preventive measures in the world cannot stop it. If the students want to crib, they will; if they do

not want to, they will not. For that reason we believe that the committee chose the right course in delaying the sentence of suspension upon good behavior, thus allowing the guilty parties, except the thief, to return to the University.

The issue of cribbing and fraud in examinations has been usually argued from a purely moral standpoint. That is the vital point of the issue. And yet, there is one phase of the whole question which many students have never considered. It is a direct appeal to good sportsmanship, which is itself a little code of honor.

Look at it in this way. A professor maintains a certain standard in his course. If there is cribbing going on, all he sees is that certain poor students are passing his examinations. He immediately takes it for granted that his standards are not high enough, and proceeds to make his examinations more difficult. Then the result is that the hard-working, mediocre student — the plugging type —

does not stand a chance of making the grade. That is the greatest of the purely physical evils of cribbing — it makes a goat out of the plodder who is playing a straight hand. Any man who is party to a game like that is just a sporting tyro, regardless of whether or not he is rated as a gentleman and a scholar. That particular brand of rottenness works more injustice than is commonly believed. Any one who has seen a toiler handed a bust notice while a slippery-fingered gentleman receives a B in his work knows what cribbing really amounts to.

Cribbing will exist here until it is banished by the undergraduate body. The introduction of a so-called Honor System will avail nothing where there is no honor to be systematized. But let the undergraduate sentiment become strong against unsportsmanslike procedure such as that which ended in the grand finale last June, and the word crib will become obsolete in Ithaca.

—editorial, October 4, 1920

on Libe Slope.

As a piece of symbolism, this was not a bad idea. Cornell had been growing rapidly; both Day and de Kiewiet had been perceived as inaccessible. Despite the formality protocol would seem to require—even Governor Thomas E. Dewey would attend—Malott decreed that there would be no academic costumes, and that the audience would sit on the grass. If you are unimpressed, consider this: all of Malott's three successors have elected to be inaugurated in cap and gown. Also, previous inaugurations had always featured addresses by many other college presidents; Malott limited the speakers to two: himself and Robert Cushman, whose speech on the occasion is reprinted in Chapter 1.

Malott's speech was the poorer of the two. He did not speak of Cornell directly, but presented a great number of tired allusions to what various historical figures had thought about education and its virtues. He then turned to academic freedom, speaking of "the great forces of liberal and professional education which fear neither truth nor heresy," and condemning "the old fraidy-cats who . . . never suggest any additions to the store of human knowledge, but only subtractions." He closed with a variety of overdone references to the solemnity of the occasion. All in all, it must have been as boring to listen to as it is to read.

The Sun, which had applauded the idea of an informal ceremony, objected to Malott's speech on different grounds. The new president had called for government not to be "an end in itself but a servant of free enterprise," because "otherwise an unseen paralysis sweeps over the nation, and we sink slowly from the free republic of decentralized government, to the welfare state, to the handout state, to the police state." The Sun called this view simplistic and historically unjustifiable. Meanwhile, it gave Cushman's address a rave review.

Within a few weeks, however, it became distressingly clear that there was much more wrong with Malott's speech than tiresome phraseology and conservative politics. In fact, parts of the speech were outright plagiarism. Rumors of this

had spread around the campus, but the first official word of it came from, of all places, *The New Yorker*, home of former Sun editor E.B. White '21. The source of some of Malott's remarks was shown to be "The Student as a Responsible Person," by President Harold Taylor of Sarah Lawrence College, an article that appeared two years earlier in the Harvard Educational Review. You may find it difficult to believe that a Cornell president would plagiarize; if so, read the two side by side.

Even more embarrassing to Cornell than the plagiarism, Taylor was one of the main candidates whom the trustees had passed up in selecting Malott for the presidency.

If a student, in 1951, had handed in a paper with a fraudulent passage like Malott's, that would have been the end. He would have been expelled. Today, the punishment would not be so severe; he would probably get a reprimand and a failing grade in the course. We do not have enough experience to say what would have happened to a faculty member either then or now, but presumably he would have walked into a pile of trouble.

The president of the university, however, was not held to such a standard. Indeed, what can be done to punish a man who is responsible only to the trustees? As a matter of fact, several faculty members formed a delegation to the trustees for the purpose of getting Malott fired, but nothing came of it, of course.

In fairness to Malott, it should be pointed out that, as is common in such cases, there were mitigating circumstances. He was having family problems of a personal nature at the time (this never was made public) and one can readily believe that he did not have as much time as he should have to prepare such an important speech.

The Sun's situation after the plagiarism was discovered was almost as ticklish as President Malott's. If such a thing were to happen today, The Sun would be all over the story, gleeful in its ability to expose a mini-Watergate. In common with most other 1980 journalists, Sun reporters secretly hope that some high official will do something outrageous, so that the big story can be written.

More important, in 1980 The Sun is independent of the administration in fact as well as theory. In the 1950s, suppression was all too conceivable, as we will see in Chapter v. In 1953 Sun editors actually faced University judicial proceedings as a result of what the paper printed. Furthermore, the strongest trend of Malott's young administration had been, as it continued to be, the centralization of power. Malott was already mentioning the possibility of moving control over student discipline from the faculty to the administration, a step the trustees would later approve with catastrophic results.

Another frightening factor for The Sun was Malott's own background as a journalist. Really, the president's experience was only in the 1920s, but the subject had remained an interest with him. More than any other president before or since, Malott knew how newspapers work, and how to deal with them.

As if Malott personally were not frightening enough: he is repeatedly described as a dangerous man to cross. Six-foot-three, vigorously self-confident, for most of his term he dictated to the faculty, and he was backed up by the board of trustees. Undoubtedly, he had the most personal power of any of the nine Cornell presidents.

And again, things were different in 1951. The Sun, while not an arm of the administration, treated it with respect. Things that were supposed to be confidential were kept confidential. Acting President de Kiewiet's departure for Rochester was known to The Sun weeks before it was announced, for example, and the editors sat on

−Photo by C. Hadley Smith

Dᴇᴊᴀ Vᴜ: *Newly invested president Deane Waldo Malott delivers his inaugural speech during an informal September 1951 ceremony at the base of Libe Slope. Sitting behind Malott and before the West Campus war memorial cloister is Prof. Robert Cushman, whose fine address that day is reprinted in Chapter I. Unfortunately, Malott had lifted an entire section of his remarks almost verbatim from a 1949 article by Dr. Harold Taylor of Sarah Lawrence College in the* Harvard Educational Review. *Malott did not acknowledge his source.*

the story. Deane Malott was never mentioned in the pages of The Sun before his selection as president became official. By contrast, in 1977, another presidential selection was taking place in great secrecy and The Sun named Frank Rhodes as the winner days before the trustees did; The Sun also called Rhodes the most prominent candidate weeks before that, and for good measure it also ran a secret list of the six top rejected candidates.

But in 1951, The Sun had a problem. On the other hand, there was probably never a staff better equipped to face it. The 1951 staff, under editor-in-chief Alvin Friedman '52, was liberally sprinkled with serious people who wanted to make a career of journalism. It produced the most distinguished editorial writing since E.B. White, especially on national matters. The Sun's statements on the menace of McCarthyism were consistently thoughtful and well-written, in addition to being considerably ahead of their time. The editors correctly gauged the significance of several seemingly trivial national events. They advocated recognizing mainland China. And they ran a stinging reply to *Time* magazine, which had coined the phrase "Silent Generation" to describe that year's students.

Malott delivered his speech on September 19. *The New Yorker* exposed the plagiarism on November 8. But before that time, The Sun knew. Reporters went to Malott, who

decided to stonewall it. He refused to comment on the record, saying that it would do him no good. And The Sun decided not to print anything.

The Sun and Malott faced their next major decisions when the *New Yorker* item appeared. Malott chose to continue his silence, and The Sun again had to decide whether to defy the president by printing a story.

By this time, Malott's gaffe was the talk of the campus; the very statues on the arts quad were gossiping about the affair. But The Sun was not. The editors finally saw their way clear to reprinting the *New Yorker* item, verbatim, which they did without comment on November 9, at the bottom of Page 4, below a cartoon and a letter to the editor on other subjects. Not one word appeared on the news pages. The editorial and letters columns were silent.

The next break *was* the result of action by a student newspaper—but it was *The Daily Kansan*, not *The Cornell Daily Sun*. The Kansas newspaper called Malott up for comment, which he gave, and thereby hosed down a swarm of hornets. Malott later claimed that his remarks were off the record, and judging by his earlier posture, one can well believe this. Apparently *The Kansan* missed the boat, however.

It is more difficult to believe Malott's second claim about the *Kansan* story: that the quotes themselves were inaccurate. For Malott was quoted as implying that Taylor was

Finally, Mr. Malott Responds

In view of conflicting opinions and widespread discussion on campus of the "Funny Coincidence" item printed in the Nov. 10 issue of *The New Yorker*, President Deane W. Malott last night told The SUN that the controversial material used in his installation address came from random notes in his speech file.

The President remarked that the quotation, "which proved to have originally appeared in an address by Dr. Harold Taylor of Sarah Lawrence College," came to his attention in the form of "some educational handout or filler paragraph in a weekly newspaper which was printed with no reference or authority."

Mr. Malott went on to say that he had never seen Dr. Taylor's speech, so he had no way of crediting Dr. Taylor with the authorship of these particular thoughts, which he would of course have gladly done had he known the source.

Discussion on the issue of Mr. Malott's installation address arose out of the *New Yorker* article which printed, side by side, nearly identical quotations from an essay by Dr. Taylor in the *Harvard Educational Review*, printed in 1949, and the Sept., 1951, installation address by Mr. Malott.

Reached by The SUN yesterday afternoon, a reliable authority at Sarah Lawrence reported that Dr. Taylor's article in the Harvard magazine was a follow-up on a speech given at the University of Wisconsin.

Later in the year, Dr. Taylor used the quotation in question in another speech at Boston University and this in turn was published by the *Community Relations Service Pamphlet*, a magazine circulated to educational institutions over the country.

Until last night, President Malott had refused to give The SUN an official statement "because he felt that there was no purpose to be served by a refutation of the implication that the material had been taken by him from Dr. Taylor."

On Nov. 23, however, *The Daily Kansan*, student newspaper at the University of Kansas, printed an article concerning the incident which contained a statement by Mr. Malott. The story was obtained by Joseph Taylor, city editor of *The Kansan*, through telephone conversation with the Cornell president which Taylor considered to be a normal newspaper interview.

Apparently, there was a misunderstanding between the student editor and Mr. Malott, since the latter had not thought of his remarks as meant for publication.

Since Nov. 8 when the *New Yorker* story first appeared, The SUN had contacted President Malott three times for a public statement and was refused each time.

The same day that *The New Yorker* magazine appeared on newsstands in Ithaca, The SUN telephoned President Malott and requested an explanation. Mr. Malott refused to comment on the issue and when asked whether "the *New Yorker* material is all we have to go on," the President replied "yes."

The Nov. 9 issue of this newspaper reprinted the *New Yorker* material on its editorial page.

President Malott left the campus the same day the incident occurred and was absent from Ithaca far into the next week. He attended a meeting in New Jersey and then flew to Houston, Texas, for the annual conference convention of the nation's land-grant colleges.

Since his return to Cornell, President Malott twice has been requested to comment in personal visits by members of this newspaper. They received nothing more than consent to publish "no comment."

Although Mr. Malott made several comments at those times—comments which have now been made public—he did not consent to having them printed.

The incident was not again mentioned in the columns of this newspaper until last Wednesday when an article described Student Council interest in the situation. Council adjourned before any discussion began, however, and then discussed it informally.

Talk among alumni and secondary school circles concerning the *New Yorker* incident has been neglible, stated officials of the Alumni and Admissions offices yesterday. To date, the Alumni Office has received no letters asking for an explanation, although alumni representatives have been questioned in their travels around the country.

The fact that there was so little said about the issue, according to two officials in the Alumni Office may be attributed to the fact that the story broke just prior to the Cornell-Michigan football game. That same weekend, there was a meeting of the Federation of Cornell Clubs in Ithaca at which, to the knowledge of the Alumni Office, only three comments were made.

One official expressed the view that he thought the issue would just die out of its own accord but he could see now that it wasn't pursuing such a course.

—news story, November 30, 1951

Why We Printed the Story

Yesterday, The SUN in its news columns fulfilled one of its functions as a newspaper, painfully unpleasant as it may have been. That was to report the news. Today, we undertake to fulfill a second function of a newspaper—to comment editorially on the news.

*   *   *   *   *

The printing of a story that appeared in the Nov. 27 issue of the Kansas City Star, together with the facts leading up to a statement and the statement itself from President Deane W. Malott, has been misinterpreted by many people to be the reflection of a value judgment—by this newspaper—of Mr. Malott himself. This, however, was not our intent—nor is it the case.

The articles in yesterday's news columns explain factually, and in Mr. Malott's own words wherever possible, the background of the *New Yorker* incident, including:

1. The authorship of the paragraphs printed in the Nov. 10 issue of the *New Yorker* magazine.

2. How these paragraphs came to be included in the President's inaugural address.
3. Why the President had previously made no public statement explaining this.
4. How the stories in the Daily Kansan, Kansas University student newspaper, and the Kansas City Star originated.

No attempt has been made at any time to make an issue of this incident; the attempt has only been to get at the facts. Furthermore, it is not pertinent at this time that we disagreed with Mr. Malott's judgment and that of his advisors in his decision not to make a statement at the outset.

Coupled with our feeling that the Cornell community is entitled to know the full factual story is a deep, considered conviction that it is to the best interests of the University to make that story known. It is rumor and gossip, and not truth, that degrades and makes fools of men and of universities.

With the publication of a full report of the *New Yorker* incident, the incident, in our opinion, becomes a closed one. In simple terms, the occurrence was the result of an unfortunate chain of circumstances. It was an incident which never would have been carried to such a sorry pass had an open, public statement of the facts of the case been issued immediately.

Those facts became public to the campus yesterday. The tardiness of their publication has not in the least lessened their effect. We believe them to be a full, thorough and competent explanation of an unhappy situation.

This newspaper's decision with regard to any aspect of the printing or not printing of a news story, editorial or letter to the editor on a topic as liable to misinterpretation as the *New Yorker* incident comes only as a result of thorough consideration of all the factors involved. In this, we are not above reproach, no more than anyone else would be. In this particular instance, however, we feel strongly that the test of time will bear us out—as it will bear out Mr. Malott.

—editorial, December 1, 1951

also a plagiarist! *The Kansan* wrote that Malott "stated he thought that he had first come across the information in a routine handout of some educational organization. He said that he had used ideas from it several times in speeches and articles while still at [Kansas] and prior to its use by President Taylor in 1949."

Now the fat was in the fire. The national wire services picked up the story, and The Sun was being scooped all over the country. Taylor indignantly denied the charges of plagiarism.

Finally, The Sun moved. On November 29, it ran a major editorial entitled "Commentary on Closed Doors." The editorial was played at the top of Page 4, a highly unusual layout maneuver in those days, so it was obvious something was cooking. The editorial purported to be a criticism of campus secrecy. It criticized the faculty's stand on academic freedom, a closed investigation by Student Council, a closed meeting by the Interfraternity Council. Its final example was President Malott's refusal to comment about his inaugural speech, the controversy over which still had never been mentioned on the news pages of The Sun. The end of the editorial made it clear that the news blackout would not continue much longer, however. "We would rather have a reputation for being honest and fearless in admitting and discussing our actions openly than cover them up and appear to be pure," the editor wrote. "In an academic community, especially, suppression of unfavorable news is hypocrisy; boasting favorable news is conceit."

As it was obvious that it would, the news story appeared the next day. Or, rather, the *Kansas City Star's* news story appeared: The Sun could not screw up the courage to write its own. It did run a summary article on what Malott was now saying publicly, as well as another major editorial called "The Campus Newspaper," which, without ever men-

tioning by name either Malott or his speech, defended The Sun for writing about the issue, using the following rationale:

"We realize that the occasion may arise when the truth may be used to better advantage at some later date, in some new context, or in combination with other truths. There is in this case rationality for suppressing the news when such suppression is in the interest of a more comprehensive analysis at some future date.

"But in the case of the open *fait accompli*, which is fully realized within itself, there can be no excuse for mollifying, tempering, or hiding the truth. If facts such as these exist, and are obtainable and verifiable, then it is our duty to print them in these columns."

The Sun's last editorial comment on the issue came the following day. Now anybody who would give a moment's credence to Malott's explanation that the whole affair was a "perfectly innocent inadvertence," was also capable of believing in the tooth fairy. However, The Sun professed itself convinced, and swore it would never mention the incident again: read the editorial for yourself if you don't believe it.

And so, Malott survived the gravest charges of personal misconduct ever leveled at a Cornell president, although, to be sure, certain members of the faculty never forgave him. The Sun's total contribution was one news analysis and one editorial.

Amid all the controversy, shortly after the *New Yorker* article appeared but before Malott commented publicly, a Student Council report on academic integrity was banished to The Sun's inside pages. It was based on a survey of 500 randomly selected students. 10 percent said they cheated frequently or occasionally. 10 percent said they believed that more than 50 percent of Cornellians cheat. And 47 percent said they themselves had cheated in the Fall 1950 term.

E.B. White on Campus Language

Sun editor-in-chief E.B. White '21 went on to fame and fortune as an essayist for *The New Yorker* and as the author of the children's classics *Charlotte's Web* and *Stuart Little*. Students of composition, however, may be more aware that he is also a minor authority on the English language. *The Elements of Style*, which White wrote based on the teachings of Cornell's William Strunk, is still a best seller. The rules in that book are somewhat rigid and doctrinaire, and it is sharply critical of some of the modern trends of the language.

White held many of the same views when he was an undergraduate. Here is a 1920 precursor of *The Elements of Style*. Naturally enough, White titled this editorial *The King's English*.

Except for the Bowery brogue, there is probably nothing that can compare with the undergraduate vernacular when it comes to setting a standard for English "as she is spoke." Persons coming from foreign parts are astounded at the strange tongue, and are somewhat embarrassed at having to ask for interpretations.

There are several very remarkable things about the everyday speech of the average undergraduate. One is that it can run along with ease on a minimum number of words; and another is that it is quite expressive within the limited student circle, and quite unintelligible elsewhere. It consists in the main of ten or twelve coined phrases and a certain number of high explosives, built upon the foundation of the usual grammar school verbiage. Add to this the fact that it is rendered with very little motion on the part of the organs of enunciation, so that five words very easily merge into one, and a passing conversation

sounds something like this:
"Jevvernoim?"
"No, jew?"

For these reasons the undergraduate tongue has limitations. Although it may be entirely adequate upon most occasions, when put to the test it is often found wanting. Once in a while the student finds himself in a situation where a ban is put on the high explosives. Robbed of these he falls back in disorder on the ten phrases and the verbiage. And then, mayhap, there comes a time when even the phrases have to be forsaken, and he finds himself groping for a word. Little delicacies of expression are entirely beyond his reach. He is unable to express the shades of meaning which are in his mind. Bereft of his one means of conveying an impression forcefully, he listens to his prattle in dismay, and marvels at its weakness and childishness. It is only in such a position that he realizes what an elusive thing a word can be, and wishes he had taken a course in public speaking — his idea of the way to learn to speak.

It is unfortunate that in a university community very little attention is paid to the acquisition of a universally acceptable power of expression. Any one can develop a code of expletives with a little practice, and the unique phrases can be picked up within 24 hours after their inception. So the undergraduate goes blithely along on the strength of these flimsy subterfuges, occasionally remarking that he would like to have a good vocabulary and never taking the trouble to acquire one.

Fluency of speech is a distinct asset to any man, and the college man that graduates without having gained even an orderly method of expression has taken stock neither of himself nor of his opportunities. There is too great a tendency to say the easy thing, too little to say the accurate thing.

We have a good language — why not use it?
—*editorial, May 18, 1920*

Administering a Changing Cornell

BY ROBERT W. PURCELL '32

Fifty years ago I was an undergraduate in the College of Arts and Sciences. The nation was in a deep depression. Admission to the University was easy. Cornell needed students. Once admitted, a student found the curriculum not very difficult—at least that is my recollection. My concerns seemed principally about the fate of the football team, social arrangements for the weekend, various extracurricular activities and then getting by with grades. This was certainly not a very admirable attitude, but one that seemed to prevail, at least in the circles I frequented. Naturally, we did bone up for exams and one way or another most of us would successfully finish each semester.

There was a great deal more formality at the time. At the fraternity house jackets and ties were required at dinner under upperclass discipline. Recently, I was glancing through a publication of that period and I came across a picture of the people attending the Junior Prom in Barton Hall. The ladies were all in long evening gowns and the men (perhaps I was among them) all in white tie and tails—quite a difference from

Far Above Cayuga's Waters . . .

Every Cornellian has a deep feeling of reverence toward our song, "Alma Mater," yet we have allowed a mistake made by a miserable printer about twelve years ago to remain in it all this time. We sing,
> "Far above Cayuga's waters,
> With its waves of blue,
> Stands our noble Alma Mater,
> Glorious to view." etc.

Why should we sing "waters" when we mean "water." The plural is not necessary it being simply a wrong usage, besides spoiling the rhyme with "Mater," in the fourth line. It is unfortunate that we have learned Alma Mater with this error. But we need not continue to make the mistake any longer.
— *editorial, November 17, 1906*

. . . There's an Awful Smell

EDITOR CORNELL SUN:

Sir:—Some days ago you took exception to the use of the form "waters" in the first line of "Alma Mater," saying, "The plural is not necessary; it being simply a wrong usage, besides spoiling the rhyme with 'Mater' in the fourth line." The form "waters" was ascribed to a typographical error.

The authors of the original words, A.C. Weeks, '72, and W.M. Smith, '74, wrote "waters," as will appear by consulting their letters, with the complete words, as first written, in the *Cornell Era*, xix. 171. "Waters" is necessary, as indicating not the substance water, but the moving body of water, possessing individualilty and action. "Beside the still waters;" "cast they bread upon the waters;" "the mighty waters rolling evermore;" "like music on the waters." The odd-numbered lines of the poem (which has twenty-four lines in all) are not intended to rhyme. Finally, "water" itself does not rhyme with "Mater." Properly, "Mater" rhymes with "later" and similar words, but even if one adopts a class-room pronunciation, giving the "a" the same value as in "father," this is still not the vowel sound that occurs in "water."

Incidentally, it may be noted that in the course of years the words of the song have actually been changed. The authors wrote, "Ever free and true," not "Glorious to view," and "Far above the distant humming of the busy town." The changes here concerned may be regarded as sanctioned by long tradition, but it would be unfortunate if others should be permitted to creep in.

S.
— *letter, December 5, 1906*

today, but better or worse? I don't know.

I never heard of anyone using drugs, soft or hard, even mild stimulants or sedatives, but there was plenty of alcohol around.

There were no protests, no building occupations, no confrontations, nobody was trying to interfere with the governance of the University by its administration. No one could drum up any enthusiasm for supporting a social cause. Everyone was broke by the depression, and maybe this contributed to the lethargy. But don't think we didn't have a good time. We did. I'll say we did!

When I entered law school, things changed. I knew I had to buckle down to work. The period of relaxed, easygoing fun was over.

I was appointed a trustee in 1958 and elected Chairman of the Board in 1968, a position from which I retired in 1978.

My chairmanship covered the most turbulent decade in Cornell's history. It was a period of student protest, a phenomenon which originated in academic institutions outside of Cornell,* but which eventually deeply involved Cornell as it did many other universities. The history of student protest at Cornell has been the subject of much comment and its events well documented. Therefore, I shall not try to describe what happened. But to be Chairman of the Board during that period was indeed traumatic for me. I had personal concern for the physical well-being of the students and others who became embroiled on one side or another. Some people were hurt, but fortunately no one was killed. I was worried about the buildings on the campus and whether they would still be able to serve their several functions. Some were damaged, but none irreparably. I was also worried that factionalism between various campus entities might become so bitter and the healing process take so long, that the entire Cornell community would suffer. I think it did—for a while.

In the late spring of 1969 President Perkins called me and asked that I take whatever steps were necessary to set the wheels in motion for the selection of a new president. Throughout the summer of that year, with the involvement of many other dedicated trustees, we set about this task. Fortunately for Cornell, Dr. Dale Corson, who had been serving as provost and who was totally familiar with the Cornell situation, was available. He was unanimously elected to the presidency at the beginning of the fall semester. We embarked on a program of remedying the differences that had developed and by patience, hard work and understanding, we made steady progress, although not without occasional setbacks. I have the greatest admiration for Dr. Corson and the hard working members of his administration for how they handled this exceedingly difficult period.

Many other matters during that time required a lot of thought and attention.

Budgetary problems were always before us. The University had earlier enjoyed several years of balanced budgets with even an occasional surplus. Unhappily, our financial situation commenced to deteriorate and we began to experience deficits. These were partly caused by inflation and rapidly increasing expenses which we could not control. Partly, also, the problems were the products of changing circumstances on campus. Measures were taken to protect people and property. The Safety Division was increased considerably. Campus lighting was improved, as were other security provisions. These were all both expensive and unproductive. Cornell undertook to improve minority education—certainly a laudable objective. It did, however, place new strains on the budget. As total expen-

---

*Many people would disagree with this last statement. See the last part of Chapter v.—Ed.

A Christmas Carol for Cornellians

BY LINC REAVIS '55

fter having indulged in our usual repast of smoked oysters and milk shakes made with creme de cacao, which we are often wont to do in one of Ithaca's many romantic little night spots (whose name the business manager won't let us mention), we tried to lull ourselves with Dickens's "A Christmas Carol."

But even with Dickens, sleep didn't come too easily, and when it finally did it was immediately shattered by two strange looking individuals who appeared, rather rudely we thought, on either bedpost.

"Are you Eb Scrooge?" asked the taller of the two, on the right.

"No, he graduated last year," we replied, rubbing sleep from our eyes. "Who are you?"

"Doom, doom, Ebenezer Scrooge," said the other, shaking his finger. "Oh, doom!"

"I'm not Ebenezer Scrooge," we replied, "and what's with this doom business?"

"My good man," said the one on the right, "if you were at all versed in ghosts you would realize that the expression 'Doom' is one of our favorites. Some other popular expressions, if you are interested, include 'Ooooh' and 'Boooo,' as we have found the soft O tone to be most conducive to..."

lease, please!" we interrupted. "Just who are you?"

"I am the ghost of Cornell past," said the ghost of Cornell past.

"And I am the ghost of Cornell future," said the ghost of Cornell future. "Glad to meet you, Mr. Scrooge."

"Charmed, I'm sure," we replied. "What are you fellows doing here?"

"Oh, we just decided to drop around, see how things were shaping up on The Hill," said the ghost of Cornell future. He added, "You were the only one with smoked oysters and creme de cacao in his stomach."

"An honor, sir, an honor," we replied. "If I can be of any service..."

"Well, for one thing," said the ghost of Cornell past, "you can tell us just what the Ithaca Gun Company means by moving its plant on to the Cornell Campus?"

"Oh no, those are just the new men's dorms," we explained, trying not to let our pride be too apparent.

"You mean people live in those things?" our friend exclaimed. "Now, in my day, sir..."

"All right, just simmer down, Steve," said the ghost of Cornell future. "As Mr. Scrooge can assure you, your day has gone for good. Progress, that's the word! Right, Mr. Scrooge? Yes, sir! Of course, these new dorms of yours are built with too much emphasis on aesthetic values to be really practical..."

"Erp," said Steve, leaning over a wastebasket.

"...but at least they—shut up, Steve—are a step in the right direction. Mr. Scrooge, just wait until you see the 1990 model! There, sir, *there* is efficiency and practicality carried to the last degree. They were designed by a chap who had already made a fortune in sardines; there was a man, sir, *there* was a man who really understood the meaning of living!"

ell, well, well," said the ghost of Christmas past. "Well, well, well. There certainly have been a lot of new buildings put up since my time. Are they new dormitories, too, or new liberal arts halls?"

"Neither, sir," we smiled. "Those buildings are for the hotel school, the home economics school, the industrial and labor relations school, the schools of mechanical, electrical, civil, chemical and aeronautical engineering, the law school, the business school..."

"My, my, my," said the ghost of Cornell past. "My, my, my. And, uh, what about arts and sciences?"

"Oh, we still have that," we admitted.

"And a poor commentary on so-called higher education it is, let me tell you!" said the ghost of Cornell future. "It didn't—hah!—take us long to get rid of that, I can assure you. Who ever heard of making money out of a—a—a—degree in classic literature, for example. The idea!"

"You mean to say that Cornell is made up of nothing but trade schools?" asked his friend.

"Oh, no, we kept some art school courses. We still carry some economics, public speaking, accounting and all. It seems to pay off. But as for those others—bah!"

hy," we asked, "did you drop all those other courses?"

"It's so obvious," said the ghost of Cornell future. "With all your graduates engaged in nothing but the

—Sun Photo by Rob Simon
IN THE SAGE CHAPEL VAULT...

most profitable professions, think of the money that comes in. We have more than we know what to do with."

"How do you use all this money?" asked the ghost of Cornell past, looking bewildered.

"Why, we use it to build new buildings, start new schools, turn out more graduates so we can get more money. Don't you see?"

"Not at all," we replied.

oung man," said the ghost of Cornell future, "it is quite apparent that you do not understand the meaning of a college education."

We had to agree, blushingly, that we didn't.

"Then put it this way," he concluded. "All our efforts go towards turning out the Good Cornell Alumnus." While saying this, he really looked quite noble.

"The Good Cornell Alumnus?" asked his companion.

"The Wealthy Alumnus," he explained.

At that moment the sounds of the Jenny McGraw Rag came drifting in through the window. Our two ghosts drew up in panic, and disappeared back into the bedposts.

—berry patch, October 25, 1954

ditures increased, endowment income, which had been so important to Cornell's well-being since its founding, became an even smaller percentage of total income. It seemed that we were always pleading with alumni, foundations, corporations and every conceivable potential source (including the state and federal governments) for more money.

We annually struggled to determine the proper level of tuition charges. On the one hand, we wanted to be able to provide the best possible education, and that is expensive. On the other hand, we did not want to charge tuition so high that it would exclude many qualified students, or cause Cornell to lose students to competitive institutions. Fixing student aid levels was always a factor to consider. Those who paid full tuition were in fact paying a part of the cost of educating other students, who (usually through no fault of their own) were unable to pay their own way.

Cornell's endowed colleges are private, and yet, there seemed to be ever-increasing involvement of both the state and federal governments in the management of the University. I frequently felt that this was an unfortunate and unhealthy trend. Compliance with the many directives from the Department of Health, Education and Welfare was both troublesome and costly. Furthermore, it limited the freedom of the administration to handle University affairs as it felt best.

The relations with New York State became complicated at times, because when state financial problems developed, the competition for limited funds between the State University and the statutory colleges at Cornell resulted in tensions which were detrimental to the institution.

Those were some of the problems which commanded my attention as Chairman. Certainly they were difficult, time consuming, and frequently frustrating and unpleasant.

However, if I were to end this essay on that note, I would be leaving a wholly erroneous impression.

All of my years of association with Cornell—seven as a student, 20 as a trustee and now as trustee emeritus—have been richly rewarding. To be associated in this work with a wonderful group of hard working trustees and able administrative officers was stimulating and gratifying to me. Working together with others dedicated to a noble cause is one of life's most satisfying experiences, and Cornell has provided that in large measure.

As the end of my chairmanship approached, and President Corson decided to retire, it became necessary to select a new president. Cornell is most fortunate that Dr. Frank Rhodes was available and accepted the responsibilities of the office. He is a great president, and under his wise and stimulating leadership, Cornell can look forward to the future assured that it will continue as one of the nation's leading universities.

ROBERT W. PURCELL '32, a financial adviser to the Rockefeller family, was chairman of Cornell's Board of Trustees from 1968 to 1978.

For the Man Who Has Everything, 'Honor'

BY PATTY CALHOUN '77

For those new graduates whose names have never graced more than the Willard Straight Hall bad check list, Cornell University offers a unique, if costly, way to be remembered by their alma mater.

"Enduring Honor," a booklet published by the Office of University Development, Cornell's alumni-milking office, is chockful of suggestions for ways ex-Cornellians may achieve fame and immortality.

The booklet lists "named gift opportunities" at Cornell, a selection ranging from funding scholarships to becoming the new patron saint of the College of Arts and Sciences.

As the booklet suggests, "A name joined to Cornell becomes a permanent part of the institution, its growth and progress." The money joined to the name also becomes a permanent part of the University.

Of course, "while every gift is deeply appreciated, unrestricted gifts are the most welcome of all." The University will find a "suitable way" to recognize this generosity.

Because this vast range of donation possibilities may bewilder the seeker of immortality and enduring honor, the booklet says officers of the University will ensure the donor proper consultation.

Most generous, not to mention ostentatious, of the gifts listed is the purchase of a college by name. The booklet implies that the University is quite ready to sell the title of a school to any Tom, Dick or Harry.

"At present, most schools and colleges at Cornell are known by their generic names—the College of Engineering, the Law School, the College of Arts and Sciences, and so on. The administration is prepared to consider the naming of individual colleges in recognition of gifts ranging from $5 million to $50 million," states the booklet.

So far, there have been no takers, although it is possible that when seniors return to their alma mater, that school may have been signed, sealed and delivered to the highest bidder.

* * *

Less ambitious donations include the endowment of a chair, where the donors can obtain their very own professor, in the department of their choice. Only a modest $500,000 to $1,000,000 is needed to endow a chair for a full professor.

The chair can be named for the donor or a friend.

The faculty can also benefit from research funds and new lecture hall equipment. Fellowship funds for graduate study are compiled from gifts of $75,000, important to all those graduating seniors who need patrons with "enduring honor."

Moving down the scale, the booklet suggests options for providing scholarships for undergraduates, because "there is a steadily rising need for financial aid." Various happy students are shown in various happy poses as the beneficiaries of such gifts in the booklet.

The booklet lists some specific bargains. A gift of $20 million would "per-mit the renaming" of the entire Division of Biological Sciences with the name of the donor's choice.

Putting a name inside a name is also possible. A graduate may steal a little glory and enduring honor from Uris or Johnson by endowing a room in the buildings of the same name.

The activity rooms in the North Campus Union may be equipped and yours, in name only, for $10,000 and up.

As the booklet rhapsodizes, the possibilities for gift-giving are endless. One page lists named gift opportunities at Cornell. The "Endowment for Gardenership, Plantations" is going for a sprightly $200,000. Endowments for acquisition to the Herbert F. Johnson Museum of Art also are listed at $200,000. The endowment of the directorship of athletics runs a whopping $750,000. And for those who never wrote honors theses and missed their own carrel, a study carrel in the library goes for only $1,000.

The booklet concludes, "a named gift brings health and vigor to Cornell and enduring honor to the donor or to the person remembered. A name so honored becomes part of the life of the University and lives in the minds and hearts of generations of Cornell men." The number of generations is variable, depending on the size of the gift.

Finally, the enduring honor "is lastingly linked with the quest for knowledge, one of the highest goals of mankind." If you have thus far failed to become linked with this quest, Cornell offers the ultimate solution.

—*news story, May 30, 1975*

Throughout its history, Cornell has been a growing place. When The Sun was founded, there were about 400 students. A hundred years later, there are more than 17,000. The increase has been a gradual one. What's more, since about 1950 most people have been saying it should stop.

Indeed, the place is crowded. With the present construction of a biology complex on what was Lower Alumni Field, there is no longer any space anywhere on central campus where a new building could conceivably be located; it is now necessary to tear down old ones if new ones are desired. This is what is happening today on the ag quad, where three buildings are slated to come down soon.

The glut of incoming freshmen has been unable to find a place to live ever since 1972, when a significant number of freshmen found Cornell would not house them except in dormitory lounges, barracks-fashion. This deplorable scene has been reenacted in each succeeding year, the number of homeless freshmen ranging from 100 to 700, and the amount of time they must spend in makeshift accommodations (for which Cornell actually charges rent) varying from two weeks to nearly a full semester. The University could end this idiocy in an instant by merely reserving more rooms for incoming students. This policy was abandoned in the early 1970s when it was decided that it would be better to have some freshmen homeless every year than to lose money by having empty dorm spaces any year. You may or may not agree with this rationale; in any case, it is certainly no longer valid. Cornell has grown by nearly two thousand students since it was adopted, with no new housing built to absorb the increase. If not enough freshmen arrived to fill the dorms, the empty spaces would be snapped up immediately by upperclassmen and Cornell would be no poorer.

The campus dining halls, the parking lots, library study space, all are overtaxed. Meanwhile, the faculty-student ratio declines. Enrollment increases have clearly been perceived as undesirable for a long time; the administration has defended them by saying they were necessary to get more income from tuition.

Interestingly enough, this is exactly, absolutely, the opposite of what the administration said in the 1950s. President Malott spoke vigorously against enrollment increases, which he said were forced upon Cornell by state pressure to accept more of the burgeoning college-age population. He consistently blamed tuition increases on enrollment rises, saying that Cornell took a financial loss on every student accepted, because of the extra faculty, administration and facilities needed. Here, you can read what the 1954 provost thought about enrollment increases.

Nevertheless, enrollment hit 10,000 in the early 50s, and 15,000 in the late 60s. President Corson, to his credit, realized that the line had to be drawn somewhere. He ordered a study to determine whether Cornell could support an enrollment of 20,000. When the answer he got was no, he referred the question to his hand-picked "Committee on Long-Range Planning"—which embodied its recommendations in the much-maligned 1972 "Cranch report." The committee coined an attractive phrase to summarize Cornell's postwar history: "unplanned ubiquitous growth." It also, however, recommended an enrollment increase of 2,000, to 17,500, blaming financial necessity.

After a year of furious campus reaction, Corson overruled this and announced that Cornell's "final" enrollment would be 16,500. This concession was not enough for some; the Sun editorial reprinted here fairly summarizes the response. Despite Corson's promise, changes in the method of counting students and "unexpected" factors have resulted in an enrollment well above the 16,500 ceiling.

* * *

Among many other recommendations, the Cranch report

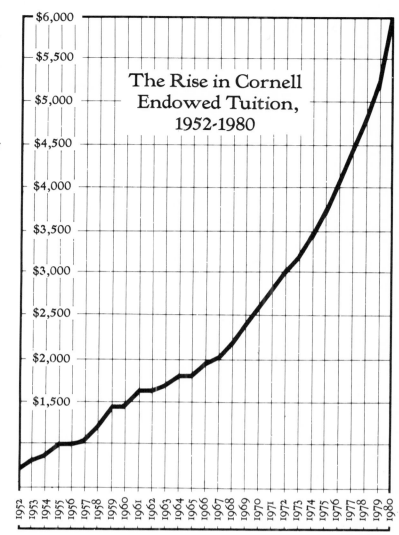

The Rise in Cornell Endowed Tuition, 1952-1980

also advocated continuing Cornell's policy of raising tuition each year "by at least six percent." As this book goes to press, President Rhodes has announced that tuition in 1980 for Cornell's endowed colleges will be increased for the 15th consecutive year, to $6,000.

In 1952, endowed tuition was $700, about one-ninth what it is today. A look at Sun advertisements of that year shows that Cornell tuition has increased far faster than most other things: rents for apartments were $40-$50 a month, about a fourth of today's price; a good man's suit was $50 to $75, more than a quarter of today's prices. Roast beef was 70 cents a pound, a third to a fourth what one pays today. A good pair of men's shoes was $10; today's prices are five times that. Butter has not even doubled: it was advertised at 79 cents a pound in 1952. Most other foodstuffs appear to have tripled in price, roughly. And some prices have even gone down: a round-trip flight to London was advertised in 1952 at $486. It can be bought at $400 today. Even gasoline, an irritating subject to 1980 Americans, costs only about six times as much as it did in 1952, when it could be had for 19 or 20 cents a gallon. It is true that the price of gold has gone up faster than Cornell tuition, but still the administration's record is not one to be proud of.

A number of excuses have been offered over the years for this sorry performance, often contradicting previous excuses. Tuition is raised because of enrollment increases; to prevent further enrollment increases. It goes up faster than disposable income in order to keep pace with inflation one year; faster than inflation so as to keep up with disposable income the year after. Tuition has gone up every year since 1966, despite a more or less continually improving financial picture. While demand for Cornell's services appears to be inelastic, and although Cornell's tuition never varies significantly from that charged by other Ivy League schools, The Sun's arguments in 1966 (when it became clear that the administration had embarked upon a policy of yearly tuition increases) look pretty accurate today.

What Size Cornell?

By Forrest F. Hill

It is clear that during the next 10 to 15 years, institutions of higher education in the United States are going to be confronted by unprecedented problems—problems of providing additional classroom, library and laboratory facilities, problems of housing greatly increased numbers of students and, most important, problems of staffing.

In considering the need for additional college and university facilities in the years ahead it should be kept in mind, of course, that enrollment has declined between eight and nine percent since the post-war peak was reached in 1949. In other words, we presumably have some unused capacity at the present time, although many temporary facilities used in the late 1940s and early 1950s have long since disappeared.

There was also a degree of over-crowding and under-staffing during the years of peak enrollment immediately following the war that should not be tolerated as a long-term policy.

I do not see how private colleges and universities, including Cornell, which are largely or wholly dependent upon income from tuition and endowment to finance their operations, can possibly take on their pro rata share of the anticipated increase in enrollment in the years ahead. Barring public assistance to private institutions, which at the moment appears to be an unlikely approach to the problem, the greater part of the job is going to have to be done by publicly supported institutions.

This does not mean that there will be no increase in enrollment in private colleges and universities. Assuming a continued high level of business activity, the number of persons applying for admission to private institutions will no doubt increase substantially in the years ahead, despite relatively high tuition costs. Until the point is reached where existing facilities, particularly physical plant, are used to capacity, it will pay under most circumstances to take on additional students.

Whether or not it will be to the financial advantage of a given institution to expand in a particular direction, however, involves careful consideration of much of the same questions as those which confront a private business firm contemplating expansion. I do want to emphasize, however, that on financial grounds alone, I do not think we can look forward to an increase in enrollment in private institutions in the years ahead beyond the number of students that can be accommodated in the existing facilities of these institutions plus modest additions to round out the present plant.

Tuition income probably covers no more than one-half to two-thirds of the total cost of educating a student in most of the better private institutions of the country. The balance of the cost is paid in other ways—from endowment income and gifts from alumni and friends of the institution. Doubling enrollment, with no increase in endowment, obviously reduces endowment income per student by half.

Unless an increase in enrollment materially reduces unit costs, including overhead, or unless additional funds are forthcoming from other sources, a private institution which materially increases its enrollment without a corresponding increase in endowment may find itself worse off financially than before.

Estimates made during the past year of attending such publicly supported institutions as California, Michigan, Illinois, Wisconsin, and Minnesota, show a typical cost for four years of $5,500-$5,600. These are all good institutions. In contrast, the estimated cost of four years at such institutions as Cornell, Harvard and MIT is between $8,300 and $8,400 or $2,800 higher than at the five publicly supported institutions referred to above.

These figures bring sharply into focus a question which private institutions such as Cornell are going to have to face squarely. What has Cornell, Harvard, MIT, Columbia, Princeton or any of our major private institutions got that is worth $2,500 to $3,000 more than the kind of education that can be obtained at a good publicly supported institution?

What happens to enrollment at Cornell in the event of a sharp business recession if a student can go to a publicly supported institution in his home state for $2,800 to $3,000 less for a four-year course, and for $3,500 to $3,700 less for a five-year course, than the cost of attending Cornell? Your guess is as good as mine. There will always be a demand, of course, for better-than-average education just as there is a demand for Cadillacs and Lincolns as well as less expensive automobiles. The point is, I don't believe a private institution, even in a beautiful setting, can long continue to sell a Chevrolet or Ford education at a Cadillac or Lincoln price.

If, in the long run, Cornell's endowed colleges are going to charge more for an education than is charged by publicly supported institutions, then Cornell has got to provide something that cannot be obtained at a typical public institution. Emphasis must, in my judgment, be placed on quality rather than quantity—on the quality and organization of the curricula, the quality of teaching and academic advising, and on the level of required academic standards rather than on the number of curricula, the number of students or the size of the physical plant.

"What Size Cornell?" It is clear that there are so many "ifs" in the picture, so many questions of policy yet to be decided both by our own Board of Trustees and the State of New York, that one cannot be very specific. It seems to me, however, and this is a purely personal opinion, that the odds at the moment favor some increase in size; perhaps a fall enrollment of 10,000 to 12,000 students on the Ithaca campus by the late 1960s, compared with approximately 9,500 at the present time.

I would express the hope that we would not exceed this number. In fact, so as mere size is concerned, I would personally favor a somewhat smaller institution than we have at present but I am of the opinion that this is wishful thinking. The pressures, as I see them, are in the otherwise.

In closing, I should like to try to summarize the outlook for Cornell as I see it:

1. The cost of attending a privately endowed school or college at Cornell seems likely to continue to be high relative to the cost of attending a publicly supported institution.

2. The prospective number of persons of college age during the next 10-15 years is certain to result in a substantial increase in the capacity of publicly supported colleges and universities. State colleges in such states as Pennsylvania, Massachusetts and Connecticut have been converted to state universities since World War II with greatly expanded facilities; and they are planning further expansion. The State of New York undoubtedly will have to provide for state support of higher education in the years ahead on a hitherto unprecedented scale.

3. The foregoing developments are likely to raise more sharply in years gone by such questions as "Why Attend a Private College or University?" "What Have They Got That One Cannot Get at a Publicly Supported Institution?"

4. Private institutions are going to have to carefully reappraise their role in modern society and organize to effectively play that role. In this connection it would appear that a private institution is likely to be most effective if it concentrates on doing a quality rather than a quantity job. This means carefully worked out curricula that emphasize basic subject matter, good teaching, good student advising and insistence upon standards of academic performance. This, in turn, means a carefully selected and well-paid teaching staff, carefully worked out admission policies and reasonably good physical facilities. Care must be exercised not to spread available resources too thinly.

5. Unless Cornell is prepared to liquidate certain existing departments with attendant staff and facilities, we need $500,000 to $1,000,000 of additional income annually to maintain a high quality program. This is not for expansion but for professors' salaries, library and laboratory expense, heat, light, janitors' wages, clerical salaries, etc. In addition we need more scholarship funds, especially in certain fields, to attract outstanding all-round students from medium and low income families in all parts of the country.

6. In closing, may I say that I think the really important question is not so much "What Size Cornell?", although this is a question with which we must deal, but "What IS Cornell to Stand for Educationally in the Years Ahead?"

—*speech, October 1, 1954 (excerpt)*

Tuition Increases Are All Too Rational

Word flashed through the East. This year the "prestige" schools charge a minimum of $1,900. If you're below that you're not really prestigious. If you're below that you're not milking the students as much as is possible.

"We regret to announce...Faculty salaries are rising... Improvements in undergraduate education are costly...Scholarship aid will be increased..." It almost sounds respectable. Almost but not quite.

"We regret to announce...unending spiral that must be stopped...solution must be found, but for this year we must..." It almost sounds convincing. Almost, but not quite.

"Gentlemen, the students will be unhappy with a $2,000 tuition. $2,000 sounds too formidable and ugly. Better $1,995.98. Or even better $1,950. And to soothe the students we'll call a meeting of student leaders a week before we tell it to the public, show them what a bind we're in, lay in on thick, make them feel privileged to have inside information so they won't squawk."

It is, after all, completely rational. Costs are rising, undergraduate education is improving (perhaps more slowly than tuition rises, but then it is easier and less complex to make tuition changes as opposed to educational changes), aid to students is increasing, and Cornell, at $1,950, will be charging less than other schools.

It is, in the end, completely logical. Cornell doesn't desperately need the extra income for next year. The problem is a long-range one. If you don't raise tuition now and next year and the year after you are not short a million dollars, but a few million dollars. At that point the effects might begin to show. At that point things might be tight.

So in order that in 1975 the tuition can be increased to $3,000, tuition this year goes up to $1,950. It is necessary; it is arbitrary, but it is just; actually, it may not even be just, but it is necessary. Protest is futile, ineffectual, meaningless, beating your head against a wall.

We protest. We insist on futilely beating our heads against the wall. Tuition should not be $1,950 next year and $2,000 a year later. We are not satisfied by apologies from administrators and trustees saying, "We're sorry, but there is nothing we can do about it." We are outraged by the semi-facetious, but nevertheless revealing remark of the administrator who, when asked how the tuition rise is determined, said "whatever the traffic will bear." At MIT somebody decided the traffic would bear a $200 increase, and there ensued a snowball throwing shouting march on the presidential mansion. Cornell students are more docile. The traffic *will* bear a $150 increase.

Why do we protest if the rise is logical, rational, and unavoidable? On principle. And on practical considerations. Because American higher education is rapidly becoming polarized, with high-priced, prestigious schools at one end of the spectrum, and mediocre schools at the other. Because excessive tuitions are making this country's better universities purely middle-class institutions. Because by raising fees twice as much as tuition (in order to get at the state schools' students) Cornell is perverting the original ideal of a free or inexpensive state system of higher education.

It is all very well for those responsible for the tuition increase to bemoan its necessity, to decry the ever increasing spiral, to prophesy the necessity of a change. But is that enough? Are they preparing themselves and the faculty for the rapidly approaching day when federal aid to higher education will have to be a massive enterprise, not just a small trickle through the Defense Department? Are they preparing the federal government for the opening of the debate, and the ensuing outcry from the public and the universities about control, that will inevitably lead to huge federal spending?

We doubt it. And until we have no reason to doubt it we will protest when the administration and trustees charge "what the traffic will bear," and then sit back placidly saying that something should be done about such an unfortunate situation.

—editorial, January 17, 1966

Cornell, 1984

BY RONALD G. THWAITES '67

The Red Chinese news agency recently announced that the settlement of the New York City transit strike marked a "victory for the working class." It has long been their custom to interpret conflicts of whatever sort in the United States as being symptomatic of a squashed proletariat struggling against repressive capitalists. We would like to suggest that while up to now much incredulity has greeted their tortured rationale, the day is not far off when right here at Cornell, to their glee as well as that of *Tass, Izvestia* and their cohorts (not to mention our own Young Socialists) an authentic class war will be waged. And to be even more specific, the battleground will most probably be in the vicinity of the traffic lights at the intersection of East Avenue and Tower Road.

This, of course, will be the logical climax to the cost of learning hike announced on Monday. Since we have been warned to expect further tuition increments every odd year or so, one can only conclude that sooner or later the bulk of students in the endowed colleges will represent the financial and intellectual élite of the nation, those scions of American nobility who will be the only ones able not only to afford the three to six thousand dollar tuition per annum but also to qualify academically for the super education which all this money had better produce.

Financial aid will continue to allow a few middle-classers to "pass" into the ranks of this nobleman-gentry group. These, however, will soon shape up to the mores of the arts or engineering quads, become uppity and aware of their own superiority. Who can deny the unmistakable signs of this attitude even now?

The crux of the revolution will lie in the comparative poverty of the average Aggie, ILRie and Home Economist. Given the continuance of the present ratio of difference between the two sectors of the University, the state-schools will always be paying more than fifty percent less than their well-endowed counterparts. It may therefore be reasonably concluded that the lower middle class plebs will comprise the major proportion of these divisions.

*   *   *

And there you have a ready made class struggle on your hands, the likes of which will put a red twinkle in every Marxist eye. Conflict there must inevitably be; all that will be lacking is a catalyst, and we can suggest many of them. As the social and cultural differences between students, incidental to greater or lesser wealth, are underscored, the fissure separating the endowed "haves" from the socially supported "have-nots" will, we predict, yawn as wide as Cascadilla Gorge.

Many things could snap the slender cords of the existing suspension bridge of toleration between the two opposing sides. For example, fraternities and sororities will dramatically decide to abandon their traditional selectivity criteria and adopt standards of discrimination by college. It needs no Jeremiah to foresee that the ensuing purges might well signal a Cornellian Sarajevo.

Then again, Armageddon could just as easily come when, for obvious reasons, the economic now being allied with the social, the Agriculture students are excluded from their favorite Artsie gut course, or when the Labor Relations students decide to unionize themselves and picket their elimination from Goldwin Smith.

And what a tussle it will be too. Right at the traffic lights, that amorphous middle field between privileged Stimson and plebian Ives. We predict that the I&LR infantry will lead the attack reinforced by cavalry from the vet college. The Home Economics coeds will be there too, dashing their messes of porridge in the faces of the proud artsies brandishing their gilt-edged treasurers slips.

The iron plowshares of the Farmers will clank viciously with the tin spoons of the Hotel Administrators. And when it's all over they will adjourn to the Straight where, while the rebel women from Martha Van knit ominously, the leaders of the endowed-dominated Executive Board and assorted other worthies will be hanged from the flagpole. Their regimes of taxing all students while representing only the few will be ended for good.

Being at last aware of the limit "the traffic will bear," the administrators will recite their *Nun Dimittis*, wait out the siege and arise to a dawn of socialist control and a student Board of Trustees.

—column, January 19, 1966

President Corson and the Cranch Menace

"If they're...enterprising...they'll solve the problem."

—University President Dale R. Corson
•

"The problem," for all the casual air with which the University Administration suggests that it can be easily solved, is not a petty one. What President Corson was talking about at his Saturday press conference was the housing crisis at Cornell—and it is no exaggeration to call it a crisis. Asked if there is room around the campus to house the overflow of Cornellians, Dean W. Donald Cooke admitted that "around the campus the answer is no." Asked this month whether last fall's deplorable situation—300 students, many of them freshmen, living on cots in lounges—is likely to be repeated this fall, Associate Dean Ruth Darling said "yes." Asked where the 300 extra incoming students to be admitted this fall will sleep, President Corson could only note that "the system certainly can't respond to these short-term changes in living preferences." The callousness with which the Administration's reply to the Cranch report treats the problem of bedless freshmen makes a total lack of response certain.

It is incredible that after a two-year effort devoted to long-range planning, seemingly dealing in depth with factors such as student enrollment and housing costs, purportedly containing wide input from numerous staff studies and community reactions, all the Administraton can come up with in response to the housing problem is an admission that the problem is a difficult one—a conclusion any one of those 300 lounge-dwellers and every one of the participants in this year's housing lottery could have volunteered a long time ago. "Planning," in the Cornell context, seems to mean a process whereby officials responsible for a large number of problems decide they will feel free to neglect totally. Housing and over-crowding seem to be this year's unanimous choices.

Some of the contradictions in the Administration's *laissez-faire* outlook on housing were brought up in questioning during the weekend's press conference—and to those contradictions, more than once President Corson could only say "I have no reply." For instance: there is not enough room for all entering freshmen to live on campus; by the time they are notified (the summer), almost all Collegetown apartments are already rented out for the

next year; the freshmen therefore must look for housing in the surrounding towns; freshmen are not allowed to have cars. President Corson's response: he had a freshman friend this year who was "enterprising" enough to solve the problems decide which they will feel free to neglect totally. Housing and over-crowding seem to be this year's unanimous choices.

There you have it. No attempt to meet the problem squarely, no apparent effort to help out freshmen who, even if they do find a place to live, will be missing an important and perhaps crucial part of the Cornell experience: the chance to live in a dorm with friends, to develop some sense of community. The introduction to the Administration's draft report pays lip service to the need to develop a community feeling once again; the body of the report makes this impossible.

The Administration's attitude is caused less by "let-them-eat-cake" arrogance than by the simple-minded belief that if you can't iron out all the wrinkles, you can usually wear the suit anyway and ignore the mess. The result, of course, is that you look like an idiot—and the wrinkles stay there or even get worse.

—*editorial, April 23, 1973*

After Cranch: The Ethics of Journalistic Theft

I always regretted coming to Cornell after the days of student activism. By the time I was an editor, the preprofessionalism kick was big. Everybody wanted to get into med school. Other than the usual COSEP demonstrations, there was little to catch the students' attention. So, believe it or not, our big story was the quality of a Cornell education. In the aftermath of the Cranch Report, I headed a staff of about five people, and we interviewed hundreds of professors over Christmas break. A five-part series slugged *Decade of Decline?* was the result. We found dissatisfaction among the faculty, particularly those in liberal arts, who feared cutbacks. The things the Cranch Report advocated—bigger classes, a weeding out of courses—were already actually happening, and these things were demoralizing to everyone. As usual, the administration turned a deaf ear. That series sparked other stories throughout the year and even became the topic of a top-secret trustee Executive Committee meeting. But change was slow, when it came at all.

While on the subject of the Cranch Report, here is a little tale that shows how far people at The Sun were willing to go to get a story. The Sun crusaded against the Cranch Report's recommendations. It had obtained a secret copy of the report before it was officially released in October, 1972, and this was always a coup. The then managing editor, Dan Margulis, never did say how he got it. The following spring, when the administration's official response to the Cranch Report was due, Chuck Sennet and I were determined to get it in advance. Chuck at the time was assistant managing editor, and one of the great Sun characters. He approached everything in legalistic fashion, expounding for hours on such critical questions as, where does Central New York end and Upstate New York begin? He was the copy editor's copy editor, our own Theodore Bernstein. He also loved a prank.

As the University Senate reporter, I knew that a small special senate committee had access to the response. There

were a couple of students on the committee. We knew they were nerds and would never give us the report. We followed them around anyway. One day I got a call from another reporter saying she had met one of the students in the library and had seen he had the report on with him. He was premed or something and would study for hours in Uris, off the Kirby Room.

We considered theft. I got to the library and sat nearby, figuring that sooner or later he would have to take a break and leave the report on his desk. Hours went by. He didn't move. I called Chuck, who was at The Sun, and had him drive up a staffer named Barbara Elkin, who knew this student. Barbara came into the library and got the student into a hallway on the pretext of having trouble with a mutual course, a reading assignment or something. But then the student said he had to leave. He went back to get the report. When he came out, Barbara introduced him to Chuck, who began discussing the senate and offering some coverage to the student's committee. The conversation continued in the Uris Library men's room. While the student was preoccupied, Chuck lifted the manila envelope from the student's pile of books, opened the men's room door, and passed the report to Barbara. I grabbed it and ran to Olin, where I photocopied it. Meanwhile, Chuck walked the student to his destination, keeping him so busy that he never noticed he didn't have the report. Later that evening, Barbara returned it to the Uris lost and found. A few days after, the story broke, with much hoopla. Chuck got a call from the student's committee chairman. Chuck was so righteously indignant at the charges hinted at that the chairman never pursued the matter. Both Barbara and Chuck are now lawyers. I think the incident raises an ethical question they would cringe about now.

—*Cathy Panagoulias '75*
managing editor, 1974-75

The Motivations Of the Faculty

To the Editor:

A recent letter to The Sun raises the question of faculty incentives but never comes to grips with it. Since this question is central to the hostility currently greeting the recommendations of the Cranch committee, a discussion of faculty motivation at Cornell may serve to clarify the lines that separate the faculty, the administration and the members of the Cranch committee.

Certain assumptions seem to me permissible. Cornell is a first-rate university. It has a first-rate faculty. This faculty has been recruited and tested by standards that, generally, guarantee that a tenured member of this faculty has demonstrated his ability to do and to publish first-rate research. The level of undergraduate teaching at Cornell, by and large, is probably as good if not better than at any other first-rate university. The tenure system, like any other system devised by human beings, is not perfect and there are a number of tenured members of the Cornell faculty who ought not to be here. This number is small.

If these assumptions are granted, and there is a great deal of evidence supporting them, then we can ask what it is that makes a first-rate academic mind and what makes it continue to function in a first-rate way? The answer, I believe, is simple: it is a compulsive curiosity and drive towards the acquisition of knowledge coupled with an intellect that makes such an acquisition possible. This drive and talent makes all other supposed sources of motivation pale by comparison. Money, fame, peer pressure, Distinguished Professorships or free U parking permits simply don't enter into the question on this primary level. Every first-rate scholar and teacher is driven by the need to know, to pursue that will o' the wisp of truth whose image he or she can see only dimly in the mists of the mind's eye. This pursuit leads to exciting scholarship and inspiring teaching. The myth that good teaching can be done without good research is simply that—a myth. The enthusiasm that comes from the discovery of new ideas cannot be matched by the regurgitation of someone else's, no matter how devoted a teacher may be to teaching. I think one need only look here at Cornell at the list of Clark Teaching Award winners: they are overwhelmingly scholars whose teaching has been drawn from their research. No amount of gimmickry, neither increased pay nor special privileges, can create the essential flame of curiosity that lights the scholar's way.

It is a well-known fact that most academic administrators are former academics in whom, it may be surmised, the drive to know has been either seriously weakened or killed. They could not become administrators if they were still possessed. If they have never known that drive, they cannot really understand it in others; if they have known it and it has died, they cannot believe that it is as intense still in others as it is. And so they tend to discredit it and reduce its importance in their own calculations. They look for other motivations because they are "realists" not romantics, and know that men and women do not act for noble reasons. Well, they are wrong and it is time that they were told so in a blunt fashion.

What, then, is to be done? No one, I think, can object to setting standards of scholarship and teaching that will maximize the probability of selecting permanent faculty who are devoted to teaching and scholarship. Perhaps we shall have to cut back in our faculty, but the humane way to do this is to leave vacancies unfilled when a faculty member retires or leaves Cornell, not to revert to some vaguely defined "shape up or ship out" philosophy. The main point is that the majority of the Cornell faculty want to do nothing more than pursue truth and teach the facet of it they believe they have captured. These people should be left alone to do just this. There will be abuses and we can all name someone whom we feel is or has been coasting and who should never have been given tenure. This, however, is the price of leaving unfettered one of the strongest and best urges of human beings.

We may all sympathize with administrators who feel that they have to do something and who see the Cranch report as a call to action on their part. It would be fatal to Cornell as a great university if the administration acted along the lines suggested by the Cranch committee, for enthusiasm and passion cannot be legislated or called into being by administrative fiat. What the administration can and should do is concern itself with the conditions in which scholarship and teaching can thrive. Policies to create such conditions are not difficult; they consist, in the main, of a kind of benevolent *laissez-faire* that allows scholars and students to get on with the task of learning. The temptation to over-organize and over-supervise must be resisted. As the great Chinese anarchist philosopher, Lao Tse, put it (only slightly amended by me), in governing a great university, one should use the same principles as in cooking a very small fish: one must be careful not to overdo it.

Prof. L. Pearce Williams '48, history
—letter, November 27, 1972

—Cornell University Archives

VIVAT ACADEMIA, VIVANT PROFESSORES: *During the University's first major general gift campaign in 1919, marching students urge a substantial increase in professors' salaries.*

This letter provoked the following response from the arts college dean:

A Sense of Duty

To the Editor:

I have had some difficulty interpreting a sentence in the letter from my usually lucid fellow-administrator, Professor L. Pearce Williams, Chairman of the History Department.

"It is a well-known fact," he asserts, "that most academic administrators are former academics in whom, it may be surmised, the drive to know has been either seriously weakened or killed."

This sentence can have at least three possible meanings:

1. "It is a well-known fact that most academic administrators are former academics."

I don't know that this is a fact, or that it is well-known, but if confined to people like Presidents, Provosts, Deans and Department Chairmen, as distinguished from people involved mainly in the business operations of universities, it is probably correct.

2. "It is a well-known fact that...it may be surmised..."

It is a well-known fact that *anything* may be surmised. OK.

3. "It is a well-known fact that most academic administrators are former academics in whom...the drive to know has been either seriously weakened or killed."

This is the meaning Administrator Williams probably intended; at least it is the one that many readers will infer. But if *that* is such a "well-known fact," why does the usually forthright Professor Williams qualify it with "it may be surmised?" In fact, I do not know it to be a fact, well-known or otherwise.

My experience has been that most academic administrators, like Chairman Williams, have undertaken these responsibilities, often at considerable personal, professional and even financial—yes, financial—sacrifice, because they have been importuned to do so by their fellow professors, and out of a sense of duty and loyalty to Cornell, and not because they have lost the "drive to know." But I suppose Mr. Williams will have to speak for himself.

Alfred E. Kahn
Robert Julius Thorne Professor of Economics, and Academic Administrator
—letter, December 5, 1972

INTERLUDE: Of Football, Fans, and a Fifth Down

—From *Frank Leslie's Illustrated Newspaper*

CREW 1875: *After winning a major regatta for the first time in their young University's history, the victorious Cornell crew is carried on fellow collegians' shoulders past the grandstand at Saratoga.*

Coaches come and coaches go, great teams fade in and out, but the Cornell tradition of excellence in athletics has been one thing that has not changed much in a century. A hundred years ago, Cornell came to the attention of the civilized world as much for the prowess of its crew as for its academic innovations. Cornell remained a major rowing school for more than a generation, to the great excitement of its student body. In its first 30 years, for example, The Sun put out a host of extra editions on rowing events, most of which were eagerly snapped up.

In 1980, the athletic frenzy remains the same, but now it finds a different outlet. Cornell's hockey and lacrosse teams have been national powers for more than a decade; the exploits of Cornell hockey fans are notorious. They stay overnight outside Teagle Hall to buy tickets; they throw fish at opposing teams; they are the noisiest, and most sophisticated, fans any team could ask for. A few months before this book went to press, a spectacular reconfirmation of this took place in Boston Garden. The Cornell team, in a shocking upset, had just won the Eastern hockey championship, to the screaming approval of the thousands of Cornellians who had made the long trip. At such a time, it is considered good form for the captain of the winning team to skate a lap around the ice and drink in the applause. When Cornell won, the whole team took the lap, then stopped underneath the Cornell cheering section, where the fans were chanting the traditional, ''We're Number One!'' The non-Cornell crowd must have thought it was seeing a preview of some Grade B movie when the Big Red team closed ranks, pointed fingers at its fans, and began to chant along with them, ''*You're* Number One! *You're* Number One!'' Corny, perhaps, but sensationally emotional, and it could only have happened with a Cornell team.

Cornell has had greatness in other sports: the basketball team was an Ivy League contender once, for example; and tennis fans will recall that Cornell once boasted a Wimbledon champion, Dick Savitt '50.

But during most of this century, football was dominant, the major event on campus, The Sun's constant lead story in the fall, the pride of all Cornellians. Nowadays the sport is considerably reduced in importance; the play is frequently not of a high caliber; the crowds are smaller; the games do not get as much publicity. Fraternities do not play as large a role as they once did, and no doubt this has also dampened student enthusiasm for the game.

But winning is cathartic, and in those rare years when Cornell contends for the Ivy League title, the fans come back, although they realize that the Ivy League contains no ''football factories,'' and that even the best Ivy team would be utterly demolished if it had the effrontery to schedule, say, a Big Ten squad.

In a way, this is the Cornell tradition too. As football became a prominent sport in the 1870s, the Cornell team requested University backing for a trip to neutral Ohio for a game with the University of Michigan. President White scotched this idea with the remark, ''I refuse to let forty of our boys travel four hundred miles merely to agitate a bag of wind.''

And yet it has not always been so. Today it is merely a pleasant daydream to imagine Cornell a national football power; but it actually occurred once. Imagine 33,000 fans packed into Schoellkopf Field, waiting for a confrontation between Cornell, ranked Number One in the country, and the underdog team, *Ohio State!* That fantasy is true, I swear it. It happened in 1940.

It is plainly out of the question here to write a history of Cornell athletics, or even of Cornell football. Instead, we will go back to 1940 for a closer look at this greatest of all

—Cornell University Archives

WHEN THE BIG RED WERE BIG: *In the golden years of Cornell football, when it was still possible for the Red to receive banner headlines in New York City newspapers and be ranked Number One in the nation by The Associated Press, Schoellkopf Crescent was frequently filled from tip to tip. In this photograph—probably dating from the bittersweet 1940 season recalled on the following pages—temporary bleachers accommodate excess crowds and a movie camera to the lower left records the action.*

—Photo by Jeff Earickson, *Cornellian*

HOCKEY 1980: *"You're Number One!"*

Interlude: Of Football, Fans, and a Fifth Down

Cornell football teams: a team now renowned more for a single defeat than for all its victories—for this was the team that took part in probably the most talked-about college football contest ever, the legendary Fifth Down Game.

* * *

The story of the 1940 team actually began in 1935, the year that control of intercollegiate athletics was transferred from the undergraduate student body to an athletic director appointed by the Board of Trustees. This action was prompted by large sports deficits, particularly during the Depression years. The trustees appointed an experienced, dynamic businessman, James Lynah '05, to head the athletic program.

The 1935 Cornell football team welcomed Lynah by failing to win a single game. As might be expected, that was the end for its coach, Gil Dobie. Lynah replaced him with Carl Snavely, who had been coach of the University of North Carolina, and Snavely set about to upgrade the program. By 1938 he had a national power, noted for its powerful front line, its All-America end, Brud Holland '39, and its propensity for unexpected strategic moves. Writers started to call Snavely "the Grey Fox."

One of Snavely's priorities was to increase the difficulty of the Cornell schedule, which had previously consisted of nearby schools like Clarkson and St. Lawrence as well as the ·tougher Syracuse and Colgate. The Penn game in Phila-delphia was always the highlight of the year. Cornell usually had games with Columbia and Dartmouth, and the rest of the schedule consisted of imported nonentities such as Western Reserve of Ohio and an occasional away game at Harvard, Yale or Princeton.

Upgrading the schedule was more of a chore than it sounds, as Cornell was not a big gate attraction and most major schools refused to play in Ithaca. Lynah tried to negotiate home games with several major teams, notably the Big Three of the still-mythical Ivy League, but to no avail. In desperation, he somehow wangled a home-and-home series for 1939-1940 with Ohio State, the perennial Big Ten champion.

If the 1980 Cornell athletic director suggested a football game with Ohio State, he would be sent to an asylum: Cornell would rate to lose such a game by six or seven touchdowns. People felt the same way about James Lynah in 1937, and there was a strong move by alumni, including members of the Board of Trustees, to cancel Lynah's agree-ment with Ohio State—and possibly his employment with Cornell. The new president, Edmund E. Day, himself a rabid football fan, tried to reason with Lynah and force an abroga-tion of the Ohio State contract, but Lynah faced him down.

By the start of the 1939 season, however, Ohio State was merely one of many problems facing the Cornell football team. For some reason, almost all of the teams on the schedule looked to have much better teams than usual. Cornell would be

The Sun vs. THE Coach

–Photo by McGillivray
GLENN 'POP' WARNER '94
He Helped Invent Football

One of the major irritants in Sun coverage of athletics has traditionally been the fawning adulation that the writers heap upon the coaches, particularly of football. Stories that would cast the athletic department in a negative light are held or suppressed altogether; the coach's post-game remarks are treated as gospel; blatant botches are glossed over. Such is The Sun's melancholy tradition of boosterism, although there have been some exceptions.

In consequence, notorious incompetents are protected in print (until they are fired, when they become fair game), and there is no way a reader can know which coaches are doing a good job, other than by reference to their won-lost record, which can be deceiving.

When Cornell was a national football power (and it has been many times, most recently in the 40s) the editors of The Sun were a little tougher on the coaches, as the follow-ing correspondence indicates. It appears that The Sun was a little rash, not only in the nature of its criticism, but in whom they sought to criticize: no less a personage than the legendary "Pop" Warner. (The legend came later.)

Then again, The Sun *did* have cause for annoyance: the team had lost a game, a comparative novelty. The last time Cornell had defeated Princeton was in 1900; in 1901 the Tigers were Cornell's only loss. In 1904 Cornell went 7-5; in 1905 7-4; and there were high hopes for a better result in the 1906 season. It started off poorly enough with a score-less tie with Colgate, but Cornell reeled off the next five games by a combined score of 122-17. A highly rated Bowdoin team came to Percy Field the week before the Princeton game; Cornell won by the shocking score of 72-0 and The Sun exulted. "The 1906 eleven has at last a great opportunity before it. As regards material we have as good as can be found anywhere; in Coach Warner we have the best football strategist in the country; and in our other alumni coaches we have splendid individual instructors and inspiring enthusiasts; in the undergraduates we have a body which, as the team knows, agonizes at defeat and fully appreciates victory; and in our eleven we have as strong a fighting spirit as can be found in the intercollegiate world."

it rhapsodized.

But, alas, how quickly we forget. Princeton defeated Cornell, 14-5, before 20,000 people in New York's Polo Grounds, and a few days later The Sun ran the following editorial, en-titled *A Frank Criticism of Our Football Methods.* Remember, at that time the team's record was 6-1-1; it is doubtful that this record would provoke such an editorial today.

The question has been asked frequently this fall, "Why have our football elevens not been as successful in the past as our other teams?" It is true that the same body of undergraduates, which cheers our crews to traditional victories, which applauds our track team to consecutive triumphs, which urges our baseball nines to repeated conquests, also supports the elevens.

It is true that Cornellians give the football team their most enthusiastic encouragement, that their support cannot be criti-cised, that it must be highly praised. And then, it is true that the same kind of men, who make-up our nines and crews and track teams, also compose our elevens.

And yet, to put it mildly, we have not been very successful in football. There are probably many reasons for our deficiency in this sport, but two of them are quite evident. First, Cornell Uni-versity demands hard work of its students and the majority of its courses require afternoon periods. Hence many football players are unable to report afternoons at Percy Field, while oarsmen can practice after 5 p.m. and track men at any spare time during the day.

A more important source of our deficiency, however, can be found in the fact that our teams scrimmage at the field *only occa-sionally.* It would seem that to learn football, actual football playing and only actual playing can accomplish results. Our methods savor of the "don't-go-near-the-water-until-you-have-learned-to-swim" rule.

It is not generally understood how seldom scrimmages have been held at the Field. Since the import of these remarks cannot be understood until this fact is known, we have collected data of

playing no less than four teams that had a chance to be in the top ten in the country: Syracuse, Penn State, Ohio State, and Pennsylvania. Three other teams, Princeton, Columbia and Colgate, were not much weaker: each school reportedly had its best team of the decade. Of the eight games Cornell would play, only Dartmouth looked easy.

By contrast, most people thought Cornell would have a weak team. Coach Snavely was an expert at badmouthing his squad's chances, but this time it seemed he was right. The interior line, which had been the strength of the 1938 powerhouse, had graduated; so had Brud Holland. The new team had virtually no seniors. It was smaller than it should have been, and none of the players had exceptional speed. Many players were shifted to new, unfamiliar positions; Snavely remarked that this was part of his coaching philosophy of "bringing chaos out of confusion."

For these reasons, 1939 was looked at as a rebuilding season: before it began, Cornellians were already thinking of 1940, when the junior-dominated 1939 team would have had a year of experience. The Sun prepared for the expected losses by making plans to liven up Schoellkopf Field. The Sun-dominated Sigma Delta Chi journalism honorary acquired a bear cub with a view to making it the team's mascot. The last real bear to attend a Cornell game had done so in 1919. This may sound like a touching piece of school spirit; in actuality it was more of a political statement. James Lynah, of whom The Sun was not a great fan, was

known to have a particular prejudice against bears. Cornell's past ursine mascots, Touchdown I, II, and III, had caused some injuries, Lynah claimed, and if The Sun's cub, Touchdown IV, wanted to see a football game she would have to claw her way in over his dead body.

The Sun bought a steel muzzle for Touchdown, and two pairs of leather gloves to prevent any clawings. She made several campus appearances without these accoutrements, however, as tame as the football team was supposed to be. The subject was definitely a bugbear with Lynah, though; he even tried to restrain the press from referring to the Cornell team in the traditional way as "the Bear."

But we are digressing from the remarkable story of the two seasons of the Class of '41's football team, which began, remarkably enough, with a stunning 19-6 upset of Syracuse. It was not a close game at all, and it offered the first look at the distinctive style of play that would characterize the Cornell team for the next two years.

The team's weaknesses had been apparent at the start of the season, but now some strengths were equally obvious. It was the kind of team everybody likes to root for. It had no superstars, like Michigan's Tom Harmon or Penn's Frank Reagan. An astounding quickness was its trademark. The Cornell defense was small, but aggressive. It took chances and got away with them; it anticipated every move of the slower opponents. Syracuse, with a highly-rated offense, was completely unable to move the ball until the Cornell

---

the year's practices to date, which anyone may verify by recourse to newspaper files.

Since September 24, Varsity men have been in only ten scrimmages at Percy Field, exclusive of the games themselves. The following is a summary of the fall's practices, containing a list of the Varsity men present in each scrimmage.

It shows but *ten* scrimmages in five weeks, with an average of only *six* Varsity men in these, and not a *single complete line-up*, *eight* Varsity men being the maximum, and *four* the minimum present in the scrimmages counted....

Of course, we undergraduates do not presume to know how to develop a football eleven. But we yell hard for the team and sorrow deeply at defeat. We consider the eleven a part of us; its failure is our failure.

And therefore, since we are heart and soul for the team, we criticise the football methods frankly and earnestly. We do not understand how *pampering* the Varsity with leisure can be beneficial. While we are not complaining of our present eleven, and while we are proud of its achievements thus far, what could that team not do if it were, with all the Varsity *together*, put through *frequent* vigorous *scrimmages* and welded under fire into a *unit*? It could then defeat any eleven in the country!

—*editorial, November 1, 1906*

To the Cornell Sun and its Readers:

In order to partially counteract the demoralizing influence of the editorial in this morning's Sun, in which the editor endeavors to create the impression among the student body and the football squad that the team is not being properly handled by the coaches and trainer, I deem it advisable to point out wherein I think the said editorial is wrong in some of its conclusions and in its spirit.

Of the two reasons suggested to account for Cornell's past weakness in football, the first one mentioned, lack of time to practice because of so much afternoon work, is to my mind by all odds the main one, while the reason given that the team does not scrimmage enough is all bosh. If I was to give any reason than that of lack of time for practice, I would say that it is a lack of support given those in charge of the teams — a tendency by undergraduates, the college daily and newspaper correspondents to criticise the team and especially those in charge during the season after every defeat, thus fostering and building up a lack of confidence in the coaches and trainer, not only among the student body, but among those trying for the team. The editorial in The Sun this morning was a fair example of this very spirit and I fail to see wherein the editor could expect any good to result from his ill-timed criticism.

I am firmly of the opinion that our football team was in as perfect physical condition for the Princeton game as it was possi-

ble for any man or any number of men to get them in under the conditions under which we labored, and if the Princeton team was in any better condition, it was simply because they have more time for practice at Princeton and the team is composed of more mature men, and they had a much shorter distance to travel with a night's rest in their own beds before the game.

The only football team that I ever had anything to do with which scrimmaged every day, or nearly every day, was the Cornell team of '93. We scrimmaged almost every day until we were bruised and crippled, and all the life and ambition and spirit we had was pounded out of us, and the following record was the result: —

Cornell 16	Penn. State 0	Cornell 0	Harvard 34
Cornell 18	Union 0	Cornell 0	Tufts 6
Cornell 0	Princeton 46	Cornell 0	Lehigh 14
Cornell 10	Williams 10	Cornell 0	Pennsylvania 50

Cornell had two of the best teams in her history the year previous and the year after this disastrous season with practically the same calibre of material.

* * *

When it mentioned the fact that afternoon work interfered with the development of Cornell's football teams, The Sun hit it correctly, as there is no doubt but that is the paramount reason for our short-comings in football. To illustrate just how much afternoon work interferes, I will give each regular player's afternoon schedule....

When the students realize the amount of afternoon work the players have, it seems to me they should wonder that some of them can get into condition and play as well as they do, and certainly these players are deserving a great deal of credit for coming out for the team and doing the best they can with the amount of afternoon work so many of them have. At Princeton I understand all university work is suspended early in the afternoon, so that all the football squad can get out at a certain time every day, and this is an enormous advantage the Princeton football team has over Cornell.

In closing allow me to say that while The Sun is loud in its protestations of loyal support to the team and the coaches, the kind of support and backing indicated in the editorial this morning is not the kind we are in any great need of, and its inconsistency and unreasonableness is best illustrated by a quotation from the editorial itself.

"Of course, we undergraduates do not presume to know how to develop a football team. . . and therefore since we are heart and soul for the team, we criticise the football methods frankly and earnestly."

GLENN S. WARNER '94
—*letter, November 2, 1906*

TEDDYBEAR PICNICS: *"The Big Red Bear" is more than an idle nickname, for on at least four occasions living bears—all dubbed "Touchdown"—have served as Cornell football mascots. Left, an early Touchdown literally holds a football in its paws (the "1915," however, was added to the photograph). Above, the last of this ursine royal house, Touchdown IV, frolics on campus in October 1939. Within a few weeks she made a final triumphant appearance in Columbus at the Cornell-Ohio State game.*

substitutes came in with the score 19-0 in the fourth quarter.

Offensively, the Bear was just as impressive. Like most college teams of the era, it attacked from the single-wing formation, but Snavely introduced a bewildering array of shifts and variant formations. Not physically strong enough for a power running game, the Cornell offense relied on finesse. Its execution of the end around and the reverse was spectacular, and these two plays set up the enemy line for cross-bucks and off-tackle runs.

But Cornell would be primarily a passing team; this much was clear immediately. Halfbacks Hal McCullough and Walt Scholl (the nominal quarterback in Cornell's attack was a blocking back) were not classic passers, but they were accurate and each threw a ''soft ball,'' easy prey for Cornell's formidable corps of receivers. Cornell was far and away the most skillful passing team in the nation. Some opponents were able to adjust to this; others were utterly routed.

The second contest of the season, an away game at Princeton, was a much tougher one. The Cornell offense was held to two first downs the entire game (Princeton had 11.) But games are not won by such statistics, and this Cornell team could strike at any time, with cobra-like speed. In the first few minutes of the game, Cornell scored on a 25-yard reverse and again on an 87-yard end around; in the second period another end around was good for 49 yards and the third touchdown. Meanwhile, the defense was doing its usual job, so Cornell won 20-7. Although Princeton had a good team, Cornell's victory was unimpressive, and The Sun was more concerned about Lynah's refusal to let Touchdown IV make the trip. Princeton officials had said the little bear would be allowed in Palmer Stadium—but only if Lynah approved. He did not.

What was expected to be the toughest

The Making of an All-American

'BRUD' HOLLAND '39 *Future Ambassador to Sweden*

Not the least of leading men with whom Sun men of my years worked was "Brud" (known to his Class of '39 teammates as Jerome Heartwell) Holland. During the 1937 football season, some of us decided to try to make "Brud" an All-America. I then was acting managing editor (the original electee having busted out due to having spent more time in the newsroom and at Wells and Elmira Colleges and the Dutch Kitchen than at the textbooks—although later to more than redeem himself by ascending to the monsignori), so I wrote the first draft of a front-page editorial "nominating" Holland for the mythical award; we "pulled" dozens of galley-proofs, attached a release-date of some days hence and dispatched a copy to each of the nation's leading newspapers, wire services, news magazines, sports columnists, and radio networks.

* * *

Came the release day, and the published results far exceeded even our wildest hopes; and "Brud" got that honor and many others, whether what we had done was in any part to contribute or not.

But moments after the bombshell of our publicity broke, on the telephone to me was Cornell's publicity man, almost tearfully asking why had I done this awful thing. At age 19, of course, I had difficulty understanding his travail, but he made it clear he feared his job might be jeopardized by the arguments our editorial had used.

No wonder university presidents, deans and other administrators age prematurely: Our editorial's main thrust had been that each year there are many players worthy of All-America designation so honors go to those whose qualifications are most impressively publicized, and, as we had put it, Cornell's publicity office was undermanned and weak (if not scandalously incompetent and a joke) and so, therefore, to assure justice we students had "nominated" "Brud." At the time, I wondered why Cornell's public relations director could be so insensitive, unappreciative, and unrealistic as to take exception to our ingenious style of promotion.

—Fred Hillegas '38
editor-in-chief 1937-38

A CENTURY AT CORNELL

home game of the season was next, against Penn State, which had destroyed its first two opponents, including a 33-6 shellacking of Syracuse. Snavely, who had predicted a loss to Princeton, refused to say much about this game, but allowed that his offense would have a few surprises for Penn State.

No surprises were necessary. Cornell won, 47-0. Penn State, headed for the Cotton Bowl, would not lose another football game for nearly three years. It was the Class of '41's most impressive achievement in its two years of football dominance. The AP football poll ranked Cornell seventh in the nation on the strength of it, just behind Oklahoma and just ahead of Southern Cal. Ohio State was ranked fourth, and would be the next opponent, in Cornell's first trip to the midwest in memory. A Sun editorial even implied, although it did not say so outright, that the squad actually had a chance against unbeaten Ohio State. "*Cornell Victorious* rings clear and true this football season," the editors wrote. "[Ohio State is] the highest hurdle. But this team has given us good reason to be confident; the guard must be against that beatable 'over-confidence' . . . it will take more than crossed fingers to beat the Buckeyes."

More important to the editors, Touchdown IV was finally going to get to see a football game. At the invitation of the Cornell Club of Cleveland, the cub was being shipped to Ohio, and the Ohio State Athletic Association had promised to let her in no matter what Lynah thought, noting that the stadium had previously hosted "goats, geese, lion cubs, wildcats, turkeys, wolves and a snake."

A nervous Cornell team invaded Columbus on October 30; one wonders what Ohio State felt like. Bob Kane '34 suggests that they were complacent, but this is plainly absurd; the Buckeyes may have been stupid, but they were not illiterate. A glance at the newspapers would have told them that Cornell was easily the best team in the East; Penn State was known to be extremely strong, and Cornell's 47-0 win did not exactly seem like an accident.

The game, played before 60,000 fans, was a classic. Cornell kicked off, and after one exchange of punts, the Ohio State running game began to grind it out. Starting from their own 15-yard line, they moved slowly down the field, as unstoppable as a flow of lava, finally scoring on the 19th consecutive running play. Cornell could do nothing on the ensuing series, and when it was forced to punt, the Buckeyes put together another long march and led, 14-0, early in the second quarter.

In those low-scoring days, this would seem an insurmountable margin, but Cornell showed why it was noted for its volatility. On the first play from scrimmage after the second Buckeye touchdown, Scholl ran 79 yards for a touchdown; three minutes later he hit Speedy Bohrman with a 63-yard touchdown pass. Meanwhile, Snavely had told the Cornell defense to be more aggressive, to hit more—and when they did, Ohio State could not move the ball. The first half ended with the Buckeyes ahead 14-13, but Cornell dominated the second half and won 23-14, setting off the greatest football celebration in Ithaca history. 2,500 fans met the Cornell team at the Lehigh Valley train station; when the Big Red Band arrived after 11 p.m., "a spontaneous demonstration of mass hysteria" broke out, according to The Sun. The band marched through Ithaca, trailed by a procession of honking cars, and arrived on campus at midnight, at which time "from all over the campus awakened students streamed in night clothes to join the rally just in time to take part in the last triumphant march to the Drill Hall."

Among those who celebrated a bit too much was Touchdown IV. Some drunken Cornell supporters kidnapped the bear from the victory train and took her into what The Sun called "a more or less snooty Cleveland entertainment resort." When the under-age Touchdown climbed a potted palm and resisted efforts to get her down, the Animal Protective League was summoned, and that was the last Cornell fans would see of the would-be mascot. The league wound up releasing her in a Pennsylvania forest.

The gloomy Snavely attributed the Cornell win to sheer luck, but, as he noted to The Associated Press, "all the fellows like to block."

Yes, sir," Snavely continued, "we've been lucky enough to get off a couple of long runs for touchdowns in each game. You see, with the fellows liking to block, once they get a play started the runner is able to pick up interference. That helps."

Meanwhile, Lynah announced that in 1938 the football program had made enough money to pay for the deficit of the rest of the athletic department with nearly $10,000 to spare.

The Cornell team was so busy congratulating itself that it almost forgot to defeat Columbia in Ithaca the following week, trailing 7-6 at the half and scoring on a blocked punt in the third quarter to gain a 13-7 win. The following week, the Bear had its closest call yet: the kicker for a strong Colgate team missed what would have been the winning field goal on the last play of the game, and Cornell escaped with a 14-12 victory. Cornell then took the 20-hour trip to Hanover, N.H., and defeated Dartmouth 35-6, more or less as expected. This paved the way for the final showdown with Penn in Philadelphia, a game Snavely said would be more difficult than the Ohio State affair.

The Big Red tornado—to use The Sun's term—destroyed

—Photo by James H. Fenner

'TOWN GOES BERSERK': *Some 2,500 Cornellians and townspeople jam Ithaca's Lehigh Valley station on a Sunday afternoon in October 1939 to greet the Big Red team after its stunning 23-14 triumph over Ohio State. The Lehigh Valley Railroad had added special red and white cars to its Black Diamond express for the occasion, and planned to convert the entire train to Cornell's colors.*

Penn, 26-0, before 69,000 spectators. The team that many had said would win only one game had gone undefeated and untied. The Big Red Band did a snake dance on Franklin Field to the tune of *Cornell Victorious*. Snavely, who had been denigrating his team's ability all year, finally admitted it was "the greatest eleven I ever coached." To that, a Sun columnist retorted that for Snavely to say such a thing was more surprising than all of the team's upsets put together.

* * *

Was the 1939 Cornell team the best in the country? Yes, if you ask Cornellians who were around then; No, if you ask the Associated Press. It ranked the team third, no doubt swayed by the close games with Columbia and Colgate, and probably not paying enough attention to the ease of the victories over the four superpowers.

There was, however, one thing all agreed on. The 1940 Cornell team, not facing significant graduation losses, would be the nation's best. Its schedule was certainly easier than the 1939 one. Ohio State would come to Ithaca seeking revenge, and Penn would be tougher than the year before, but no other opponent was in the class of these two. Syracuse, Colgate and Columbia would be competent this year, but for any one of these three to beat mighty Cornell would be a huge upset. Furthermore, there were three push-overs on the schedule: Army, Yale and Dartmouth.

In short, it looked like a very boring season, with the exception of the Ohio State rematch, which was being bally-hooed as the game of the century. At the beginning of practice Snavely made so bold as to predict his team would win at least two games that year; but once the season opened his weekly jeremiads about how badly Cornell would probably be beaten on Saturday were missing. Even he realized they would be favorites in every game.

The season opened with Colgate and only 15,000 spectators at Schoellkopf Field, a measure of how lightly the fans took it: by contrast, the Ohio State game, a month away, was already a 30,000-plus sellout, although tickets were priced at $3.30, the equivalent of perhaps $20 today. Colgate was supposed to be a strong passing team also; it had beaten its first opponent, Akron University, 44-0, and some people even thought it had a chance against the Bear —er, the Big Red, as Lynah now insisted the team be called.

The game itself proved only that Cornell was not over-rated. The Big Red filled the air with passes, completing 11 of 16 of them (McCullough was 6 for 8); the passing game gained Cornell 239 yards, more than double Colgate's total offense. It was typical of Colgate's futility that they were able to complete only 4 of 18 passes—Cornell intercepted 5 of them. For the record, the score was 34-0, but who was keeping track?

The next Friday, as the Cornell team left by train for West Point, a weird scene took place in front of the Athletic Association offices. Distribution of Ohio State tickets to AA book holders was slated for the following Tuesday, and although Assistant Athletic Director Kane promised plenty of tickets for all, some fraternity members did not believe him. So the line formed four days in advance. The AA made several efforts to chase it away, to no avail.

On Saturday, a record crowd of 28,000, including Herbert Hoover, packed into West Point's Michie Stadium and watched another record set—the worst football defeat in Army history. Cornell won 45-0, again with a remarkably balanced attack: all seven touchdowns were scored by dif-ferent players.

The following week the first AP poll of the season came out. Cornell was easily ranked Number One, getting 90 of a possible 156 first-place votes. Meanwhile, a writer for the New York *Herald-Tribune* charged in a column that the famous Cornell end around play was actually against the rules, since

it involved what he called an illegal forward pass. Nothing came of this. A second potshot came from another Ivy League newspaper. *The Harvard Crimson*, egged on by the Harvard athletic department, accused both Cornell and Penn of having "professional" teams and said that Harvard would refuse to play either of them again after 1942, which was as far ahead as games were scheduled. The most shock-ing charge: Cornell and Penn had "teams which have more or less openly recruited for the purpose of winning games."

This was 1940, remember.

The Big Red tuned up for Ohio State by burying Syra-cuse, 33-6, behind 309 yards passing. The Syracuse coach, Ossie Solem, who before the game thought his team could win, called it "the greatest passing attack I've ever seen," possibly the greatest passing team of all time. Asked whether he thought Ohio State could beat Cornell, Solem effused, "I don't see how the Buckeyes can stop them. I don't see how anybody can. They sure are wonderful."

One could tell that Cornell was going to enter the Ohio State game as a heavy favorite: when asked for a prediction, Snavely said, "You can quote me as saying that we have a chance. Yes, say that we have a chance."

And so, Ithaca prepared for the greatest football game the town had ever seen—and Lynah announced that the football team of 1939 had had a budget surplus of $150,000. The enthusiasm for the upcoming intersectional classic was not diminished by Ohio State's disappointing year: they would come into the Cornell game with a miserable (for them) 2-2 record. For that matter, one of the Buckeye wins had been tainted. They had beaten Purdue, 17-14, on a field goal in the last minute of play. But that marvelous modern invention, film, had proven that the Ohio State kicker had entered the game illegally. The kicker should have been thrown out of the game, the field goal should not have counted, Ohio State should have gotten a penalty instead of three points. But the referees had been asleep; the field goal stood, and both coaches agreed that it was a shame to have tainted victories and a greater shame to have incompetent officials in the Big Ten. We will hear more about the Ohio State-Purdue game later, but now it is time for Ohio State-Cornell.

Lynah's department prepared for the great rematch by constructing temporary bleachers to increase the stadium's capacity to 33,400. It also took out full-page ads in The Sun to urge fans, due to the unprecedented crowds expected, to walk to the game, as there was not expected to be sufficient parking. On the day of the game, The Sun ran its front page on its side, combining it with the back page to create a mammoth Page One, on which every story had to do with the big game. There was a full page of pictures of the Ohio State team and its All-America quarterback, Don Scott.

The game was another exciting one, and it resembled the first one fairly closely. Ohio State kicked off, and Cornell, with breathless ease, short-passed its way in 11 plays to the Buckeye 35, where it had to punt. Starting from its own 11-yard line, Ohio State marched down the field with 19 con-secutive running plays, finally scoring, and the Big Red was behind for the first time all season. The Ohio State drive had consumed most of the first quarter, and the turning point in the game came when Cornell fumbled away the ensuing kickoff and Ohio State failed to score. Thereafter, Cornell justified its rating. Starting from its own 16, the Big Red drove to the Ohio State 16 before running out of downs. But the next Cornell series drew blood on a 33-yard McCullough touchdown pass to Jim Schmuck, and at the half it was 7-7 with Cornell holding a large yardage edge.

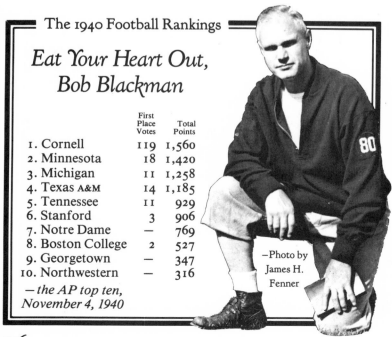

The 1940 Football Rankings

Eat Your Heart Out, Bob Blackman

	First Place Votes	Total Points
1. Cornell	119	1,560
2. Minnesota	18	1,420
3. Michigan	11	1,258
4. Texas A&M	14	1,185
5. Tennessee	11	929
6. Stanford	3	906
7. Notre Dame	—	769
8. Boston College	2	527
9. Georgetown	—	347
10. Northwestern	—	316

—*the AP top ten, November 4, 1940*

—Photo by James H. Fenner

CARL SNAVELY
He Led the Red to Number One

Cornell was simply devastating in the second half, especially on defense: the vaunted Buckeye attack managed only two first downs, both late in the fourth quarter with

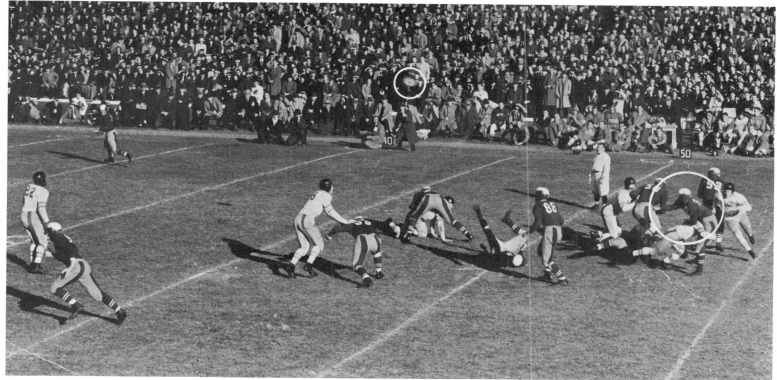

GOODBYE, COLUMBUS: *The long-anticipated rematch between Cornell and Ohio State took place on October 26, 1940 at Schoellkopf Field, before a record 34,000 people and the nation's press. The Buckeyes, having thoroughly outplayed the Red early in the game, led 7-0 after the first stanza. "It was against this background of futility and seeming helplessness in the grasp of a foe tackling and running with berserk fury," The New York Times would report the following morning, "that Cornell exploded a series of bombshells that brought bedlam in the stands." The first shell thundered when Harold McCullough '41 threw a touchdown pass to James Schmuck '41, and the Red was on its way to a 21-7 victory. Concluded The Times: "It was the . . . ability to strike for home with a few stabbing plays, rather than with Ohio State's tremendous grinding power of sustained marches, that carried the day for the wonderfully game and vigilant Ithacans." Above, with the score tied, McCullough (circled) hurls the ball again late in the second quarter—this time incomplete.*

the game out of reach. Having established the passing game, McCullough and Scholl began to run; the new strategy resulted in two fourth-quarter touchdowns and a 21-7 Cornell win, in a game not as close as the score indicates.

Ohio State, apparently unable to accept that such a small upstart team could defeat them twice in a row, then joined with *The Crimson* and the *Herald-Tribune* in accusing Snavely of sharp practice. This time, the charge was that Snavely was calling his team's plays from the sidelines by means of illegal signals. According to an Ohio State press release, the Cornell coach used a small, light-colored cylinder, "grasping it by the end for a pass play, in the center for a sweep, in both hands for a line smash, and then crossing his legs and swinging one foot when he wanted a kick." The Ohio State coach added, "It was a crime, but it was so obvious and so amateurish that we had to laugh. We finally got to the place were we could call practically every play, Snavely's actions were so bald-faced." OSU directed an official protest to the Office of Eastern Intercollegiate Athletics.

Now, these charges were preposterous, but they did show something about the mystique Snavely had started to build around himself. What other coach in the country could win against a team that knew in advance what plays were going to be called against it? If Snavely had indeed been signalling, surely Ohio State's best course would have been to intercept the signals and adjust its defense accordingly. The referee, William "Red" Friesell, said he saw no illegal signals, and noted that the Buckeyes had not protested during the game. The Eastern athletics office overruled the Ohio protest.

The short-lived Cornell-Ohio State series did give Cornell one new tradition. The rule at the time gave the home team the choice of what color jerseys to wear, and Cornell wore white at home. But Ohio State, in an effort to gain a psychological edge, "inadvertently" brought only white uniforms with them, thus forcing the Cornell team to play in its red jerseys. The Cornell players, thrilled by the sweep of the two Ohio State games, voted to continue to wear red at home—and they still do today.

* * *

With Ohio State out of the way, Cornell prepared for the easy three-game prelude to the big game with Penn, which was holding third-ranked Michigan to a two-point win while Cornell was thrashing the Buckeyes. The Big Red opened the second half of its season with an aerial avalanche, snowing Columbia under, 27-0, with four touchdown passes. The score might have been higher, but it started to rain in the second half, and this closed down the Cornell passing game.

By now the invincible Cornell team was assuming mythic proportions, especially in the New York City press, which had come *en masse* to Ithaca two weekends in a row. "They are so perfectly co-ordinated a unit that it is simply impossible to single out individuals," the *New York Times* reporter covering the Columbia game wrote. "They were all good, and that goes also for the third and fourth stringers who saw action near the finish."

That Penn was now the only obstacle to a second undefeated season was a foregone conclusion: Yale would be the weakest team Cornell had played yet, and Yale had beaten Dartmouth, which Cornell would play the week after. The Big Red badly needed an impressive win over Yale to retain its Number One national ranking; the second- and third-ranked teams, Minnesota and Michigan, were playing each other that weekend. But Snavely got a warning of things to come when his team played its poorest game of the year. Cornell won 21-0, but looked dismal offensively: only 54 yards passing, only two first downs in the entire second half. Yale, which had been a 10-1 underdog (this was before the days of the point spread system of betting) treated the game as a great victory, as did *The New York Times*, which said, "Cornell took the football game and Yale took the glory . . . [Yale] sent out an inspired team that lost only because Cornell was much too good for it." The following day, a *Times* columnist suggested, "If Dartmouth can hold Cornell in reasonable check, the Hanoverians will have a real chance to haul Cornell from the unbeaten ranks."

Dartmouth had a chance indeed, but only because of the weather. It had been snowing and raining in Hanover for a week; the field was in such atrocious condition that Dartmouth had to practice indoors. Snavely countered by creating muddy conditions on Alumni Field and having his team practice there. This did not do much good, however. Teams with Cornell's type of offense were still sufficiently scarce that neither The Sun nor the national press realized that the weather would hurt the Big Red far more than Dartmouth. Cornell's passing game and tricky backfield plays required sure footing—and that would be hard to find in Hanover.

This turned out to be the game that all the nostalgia is about. Cornell came in as the second-ranked team in the country, with 18 wins in a row, with a combined 1940 score against its opponents of 181 to 13. Dartmouth's record was 4-3 against very moderate opposition. It had lost to two teams Cornell had crushed: to Yale, 13-7, and 20-6 to Columbia.

On the surface, the game had to be one-sided—but there was no surface: the field was a quagmire. Snavely realized quickly that neither team would be able to generate an offense, and decided to play conservatively, hope for a score, and rely on the defense to record its fifth shutout in seven games.

It was the right strategy, but the Indians foiled it with some good kick returning. A less-than-capacity crowd of 10,000 watched Cornell elect to kick off, hoping to bog Dartmouth down in its own territory. But the kick was returned all the way to the Cornell 45, and a punting contest ensued. The first time Cornell got the ball, inside its own 20, Snavely ordered a kick on second down, a stratagem he would employ once more in the period.

Trying to run through the mire was an impossible task. Not only did neither team score in the first quarter, neither had a first down. When the game was over, each team would have punted eleven times.

Cornell did get one scare in the quarter: its third punt was run back to the Cornell 28. But for the third time in the four times it had the ball, the Dartmouth offense lost yardage. In desperation, the Indians even tried a pass on third and 14—it would be their only pass attempt of the game, and it was incomplete. On fourth down, Bob Krieger tried a long field goal, but it went wide.

The second quarter was more of the same. On its first series, Cornell actually picked up a first down, but that was all. Dartmouth, starting in its own territory, then produced a march of sorts, but fumbled the ball away on the Cornell 27. Two series later, they did better, driving inside the Cornell 10. Surprisingly, though, they did not try a field goal, instead losing the ball on downs.

So the first half ended scoreless, but scoreless in favor of Dartmouth. The Indians had had three good scoring opportunities; Cornell had not advanced past its own 35. The unstoppable Big Red offense had only one first down, and had not attempted a single pass. It looked as if the game might end in a scoreless tie—or a Dartmouth win.

In the locker room, Cornell decided to start passing again in spite of the conditions—it had started to snow again—and the move paid off. On its first possession, the team marched 50 yards, but, rather than try a 30-yard field goal against the wind, threw an unsuccessful pass into the end zone on fourth down. Neither team threatened again in the quarter, but on the last play Cornell had a disaster: a slip in the backfield on an attempted end around, caused by the muddy field, and it was second and 23 from the Cornell 5-yard line.

So the final quarter began, still scoreless but with Cornell in trouble. The Big Red immediately kicked, but it was run back to the Cornell 26. Dartmouth picked up one first down, then broke the ice with a 27-yard Krieger field goal.

An interception ended Cornell's next possession, but the defense held, and Cornell got the ball again on its own 26 with less than ten minutes left in the game. McCullough and Scholl engineered another long drive, but again it was stopped, inside the Dartmouth 20, by an interception. It looked like the game would end at 3-0, but, of course, this would not be the greatest team in Cornell history if it could not overcome such odds. The defense held once more, and Dartmouth had to punt again. Cornell's last chance, with four minutes remaining, would start at its own 42.

And the Red moved leisurely upfield. Run; short pass, first down; incompletion; pass, first down; run; and then a costly Dartmouth penalty for pass interference gave Cornell a first down on the Indian 19. The Red tried another running play, and then Scholl hit Bill Murphy on the 5-yard line. The Big Red had created hysteria in the stadium by moving to within one yard of the winning touchdown when captain Walt Matuszak made an uncharacteristic mental error: he called time out—one time out more than the rules allowed. The penalty moved Cornell back to the 6—but it did not matter. Some said there were six seconds left, some that there were three, but everyone agreed that Walt Scholl had completed a touchdown pass to Bill Murphy, and the undefeated season was still alive. Back in Ithaca, the campus, its collective ear glued to the radio, exploded when the announcer stammered out "t-t-touchdown!" *Cornell Victorious* was ringing on the chimes before Nick Drahos kicked the extra point to make the final score 7-3.

The final gun sounded in Hanover, but the game was not over. Minutes after the teams left the field, Dartmouth made a sensational accusation: that in the final seconds, in the general din and confusion, the referees had lost track of the number of plays Cornell had run; that the winning Cornell touchdown had been scored on *fifth down*. Reporters frantically pored over their scoresheets, with inconclusive results. Cornell had indeed run five plays from the time of its final first down, but there had been at least one penalty called and some reporters swore they had seen another. The stadium had been a madhouse that final minute; the only ones who could have said what actually happened were the referees, and they were nowhere to be found. So the Dartmouth coaches could only congratulate Snavely and Lynah, gnash their teeth, and mutter something about next year.

But the story did not end there. Astoundingly, Lynah and President Day issued a joint statement to the effect that if it could be shown that the officials had made an error, Cornell would give the game back to the Indians!

Now, this was entirely unprecedented. Errors by referees are fairly common. They had changed the outcome of games before; you may recall that such an error had done so that very year in the Ohio State-Purdue game. But nobody had ever suggested that the result should be changed *ex post facto*. Asked his opinion of the matter, the head of the Eastern Intercollegiate Athletic Association said

The Kane Half-Century

BY KENNY VAN SICKLE

-Photo by Sol Goldberg
ROBERT J. KANE '34
Cornell to Mount Olympus

The story of Bob Kane is a page of Cornell history.

As a "townie" he developed an early fascination in Cornell athletics, was a full-fledged participant as an undergraduate, administered them for 37 years, and still possesses vast interest as an alumnus.

He has been a leader in virtually every area, going back to his Ithaca High School days, when he became a state sprint champion.

Bob played some baseball before turning to track, and he also did well in football and basketball. He turned full attention to track at Cornell under Coach Jack Moakley, especially after football coach Gil Dobie suggested that the sport might be better suited to him. In fact, at one of his famed closed practice sessions, Dobie made it official, exclaiming, "Kane. Stick to track."

So Kane did, and it led to one thing and another. There was the Big Red competition, then after a brief whirl in business, returning to campus and working a short time as a freshman track coach, becoming an aide to athletic director James Lynah, then assuming command.

Kane's Cornell administration overlapped that of Lynah as director of athletics. After taking over for Hank Godshall in 1939 he became acting athletic director when Lynah busied himself with government business in Washington. He took over full command in 1944 and served until 1976 when Dick Schultz took over. He had the title of dean of athletics from 1971 until his retirement.

While there have been good times and bad times in Cornell sports, few moments could compare to the period of renascence in the late 30s.

"Everybody seemed to be for us and the advocacy came right from the top," Kane recalled. "Success came electrifyingly fast. It didn't come unprogrammed, however, any more than it does in any enterprise.

"Lynah was a hard-headed and innovative business man. He hired a brilliant football coach in Carl Snavely, and our alumni worked hard to persuade football talent to come our way. In fact, this started before Lynah or Snavely arrived. One of the finest freshman squads in Cornell history preceded by a year Coach Snavely's arrival in 1936.

"Talented athletes received a sympathetic and gracious reception on campus which helped in the wooing process. That is not to imply that special consideration was given them at the admissions office and in financial aid. No more than there is today. No, these were representative students on those football teams and they are extraordinarily successful men today."

The Big Red eleven was unbeaten in 1939 and continued that way until 1940, until the ill-fated trip to Hanover and the Fifth Down game with Dartmouth.

"It was an unforgettable event as time has proved," Kane said.

"As acting athletic director then I was in charge in the absence of Jim Lynah, who was in Washington on business. About a half hour after the contest the first knowledge of a fifth down came to me while we were relaxing at the Hanover Inn," Bob recalled.

"We telephoned President Day," Kane added. "And the football world still recalls the turn of events, the switching of a 7-3 Saturday Cornell victory on Monday to a 3-0 Dartmouth victory after films showed that the Cornell touchdown was on a game-ending play that it didn't deserve."

President Day visited the practice field and told the players, "We have done the right thing, and this will live with us. We shall not have to spend the rest of our lives apologizing for a tarnished victory."

Kane felt that Day's remarks were very prophetic.

"No victory or bundles of victories have or will ever bring the glory this loss with honor has," he said.

* * *

During Kane's tenure some $8.5 million worth of athletic facilities have been built: Teagle Hall for men; Helen Newman for women; Lynah skating rink; Collyer Boathouse; Grumman Squash Courts; the 18-hole golf course; Moakley House; Paul Schoellkopf House; artificial turf on Schoellkopf Field; a Poly-Turf track; and hard-surface tennis courts. He was also instrumental in cutting of a flood relief channel in Ithaca's West End that provides for a 2000-meter rowing course.

While many individuals had a hand in encouraging and bringing to completion these gifts, Kane's own talent as a writer and speaker cannot be discounted.

In addition to his service to the University and its athletic program Bob has been a leader in amateur athletics nationally and internationally.

He has held numerous other top positions in intercollegiate athletics. He was vice president of the NCAA in 1947; president of the ECAC in both 1950 and 1959; and president of the Intercollegiate Amateur Athletic Association of America (IC4A) in 1944, 1948 and 1952.

Bob's first association with the Olympics was as an usher in 1932 at Los Angeles. He would have liked to have competed in 1936 but was denied the chance when ruled to be a professional. The approximately $400 he received as Cornell's assistant track coach while in law school put him in that category.

Since becoming a member of the Board of Directors of the U.S. Olympic Committee in 1951 he has been very active in the Olympic movement. He had key management roles with the U.S. teams in the 1952 Olympic games at Helsinki, at Rome in 1960, Tokyo in '64, Mexico City in '68 (when he was secretary) and at Munich in 1972 (when he was second vice president). He was chief of mission in 1976 at Montreal.

Some of the highlights in Cornell sports during Kane's administrative career were:

• 1939 football team (8-0), ranked No. 2 in the nation behind Texas A&M.

• 8-1 football seasons in 1948, 1949 and 1971 when they figured in Ivy titles.

• NCAA hockey championships in 1967 and 1970. A perfect 29-0 record in 1970. Eight Ivy champions.

• IRA champion crews of 1955, '56, '57, '58, '62, '63, '71. 1957 crew undefeated, won world title at Henley Royal Regatta.

• NCAA lacrosse champion in 1971.

• Ivy League basketball champion in 1953-54.

Bob Kane, now president of the U.S. Olympic Committee, is gone from the Cornell scene, you might say. Or is he?

Although Olympic commitments normally keep him far from the heights above Cayuga he still gets back occasionally. He has a cottage on the west shore and retains an office in Moakley House.

And his thoughts are ever here.

KENNY VAN SICKLE, sports editor of *The Ithaca Journal*, has covered Cornell sports for The Journal for nearly 50 years.

Interlude: Of Football, Fans, and a Fifth Down

that the Cornell victory would have to stand; that no one, not even the referee, had authority to alter a score once the game was over. And yet Cornell insisted: if and when the referee could be found (and he could not be found as of the night after the game), if he admitted the mistake Cornell would forfeit the game.

Still waiting for the referee's report on Monday morning, The Sun endorsed Cornell's position, saying, "Cornell has nothing to be ashamed of in its athletic record, and there is no reason for blemishing ourselves by winning a game on questionable grounds. If the officials should find that there was a mistake in the ruling Saturday, then we shall declare Dartmouth the winner. In this decision, every Cornellian will concur, and in concurring will not lose one bit of respect for our team. For its inspired play of the final minutes cannot be cancelled, nor can its record of sportsmanship, and honorable competition."

And now, what really happened in that climactic and chaotic minute.

The Scholl-to-Murphy pass play had given Cornell a first down on the Dartmouth 5-yard line. Cornell then had tried

---

---

to run the ball in—three times, without success. That made it fourth down on the one-yard line, which is when Matuszczak attempted to call his ill-advised time out. For this, Cornell was handed a five-yard penalty, but it remained fourth down. The referee (the hapless Red Friesell, who had also had problems in the Cornell-Ohio State game in Ithaca) realized this, but a linesman did not: he assumed that the penalty had nullified the preceding play, which would have made it *third* down again.

In any event, on the succeeding play Scholl passed incomplete into the end zone, and Friesell started to do the correct thing, which was to give Dartmouth the ball on the 20-yard line. But as he trotted out, the linesman stopped him to tell him that it was still Cornell's ball. And now there was even more confusion, which is understandable, given the noise of the frenzied crowd. Somehow, Friesell thought the linesman was telling him that both teams had been offside on the fourth down play. If that had been so, the penalties would have offset one another, and the play would not have counted. It would have to be run over again. So Friesell gave Cornell the ball, pushing away the protesting Dartmouth captain as he did so. And thus, indeed, Cornell scored on fifth down.

Friesell emerged that Monday with a full report, blaming himself for the whole fiasco, and expressing the view that the score still could not be changed. Nevertheless, Lynah telegraphed the Dartmouth athletic director: "Cornell relinquishes claim to the victory and extends congratulations to Dartmouth." His opposite number, William McCarter, wired back, "Dartmouth accepts the victory and salutes the Cornell team, the honorable and honored..."

Acclaim poured in for the noble gesture. *The New York Times* said in an editorial, "The result probably deprived Cornell of the mythical championship of the East, yet the Cornell authorities accepted it without a quiver... If we were Cornell, we shouldn't trade that [concession] telegram for all the team's victories in the past two years. It proves that sportsmanship hasn't died in intercollegiate football. It proves that this sport which is too often described as a 'struggle,' a 'battle,' and even a 'Blitzkrieg,' is just a game for all that."

And the *Herald-Tribune*, calling the concession "magnificent," wrote, "There seems again to be hope for the world." The editor added perceptively, "What the once-defeated Cornell team of 1940 has done for amateur football will be remembered long after the dozens of unbeaten and untied wonders of this decade are completely forgotten."

Not everyone was so pleased. Even fifteen years later, Coach Snavely was unconvinced. Writing about the 1939-40 teams for The Sun's 75th anniversary issue in 1955, he said the 1940 team was the better of the two, despite the record, and added, "This team did the unexpected so often that perhaps it should not be surprising for it to become the only team in history to lose a game on Monday which it had won on Saturday. But don't try to tell the members of the team that they were licked in that game. They think that the officials made more than one mistake in that encounter."

* * *

In 1954, Cornell was involved in a similar football game. It lost to Harvard, 13-12, but the officials had disallowed a fourth-quarter Cornell touchdown pass on the ground that the receiver was out-of-bounds when he caught it. The films proved that the catch had actually been legal. The Sun suggested that Harvard should concede the game, in fifth-down fashion. Robert Kane, now athletic director, pooh-poohed the idea because he said Harvard had outplayed Cornell and deserved to win. (In the 1940 Cornell-Dartmouth game, Cornell had 11 first downs to Dartmouth's 4; 181 yards total offense to 116.) Kane also pointed out that if the touchdown had counted, Harvard might have altered its

---

strategy and won the game anyway. That is certainly true; for a much better example, let us go back to Hanover, 39 years after the Fifth Down Game, for another contest having an impact on the national championship.

The game was ice hockey, which had replaced football as the most exciting Ivy League sport. The time was March 1979, and it was a quarter-final Eastern playoff game between Dartmouth, still wearing green but no longer called the Indians, and Clarkson. Dartmouth was the favorite, but regulation time expired with the score tied 1-1. As the rules decreed, the teams then played overtime, with the winner to be the first team to score a goal. And the first goal went to Clarkson. It was a beautiful, classic goal, a hard shot over the goaltender's shoulder, bulging the back of the net and bouncing out again. There was only one problem with it. Everyone in the rink saw it—except the referee. He said it had never gone in. Play continued, and, as the devil would have it, Dartmouth scored, to "win" the game.

The phantom Clarkson goal was the talk of the post-game interviews, and both the Dartmouth coach and goaltender freely admitted that it was an obvious goal, and said it was unbelievable, and an astonishing piece of good fortune, that the referee had not seen it. The films confirmed this.

What happened next? Did the college that had so graciously accepted the Cornell concession in 1940 now concede the game to Clarkson? Did Dartmouth, the honorable and honored, offer to let Clarkson advance in the playoffs instead of its own team? Of course not. It was not 1940, you know.

* * *

In explaining why Cornell had chosen to forfeit the Fifth Down Game, President Day said, "If we hadn't made that decision, we'd have been explaining that game as long as football has a place in intercollegiate athletics." Obviously, that is ridiculous; if Cornell had retained the victory, we would no more remember it today than we do the 1940 Ohio State-Purdue game, or the 1954 Harvard-Cornell game, or the 1979 Dartmouth-Clarkson hockey game; or for that matter, any more than we remember that after the Fifth Down Game the mighty 1940 Cornell team also lost to Pennsylvania. But as long as football has a place in intercollegiate athletics, Mr. Day, the story of the Fifth Down Game will not be forgotten.

The record books now tell us that in 1940 Dartmouth defeated Cornell 3-0, and the sons of guns don't even put in an asterisk. They also record the great two-year winning streak that preceded it, and make it clear that the 1939 and 1940 teams were the best Cornell ever fielded, probably the best in Eastern college history, clearly teams that had a claim to the national championship. A Cornellian today looks back on those teams' 14 wins with awe. But he looks back on the first loss with a song in his heart—and the song is:

From blue Cayuga,
From hill and dell,
Far rings the story and the glory of Cornell.
From east and west, the crashing echoes answ'ring call,
"Cornell victorious: the champions of all."

The Sun's Farewell to a Princess

The suspense is ended now, and after two days we finally know that Dartmouth has broken the Cornell winning streak, and that the Indian Princess, our guest for two years, must make the long trip to the cold White Mountains.

Referee "Red" Friesell admitted yesterday that he had erred, and that Cornell had scored on an illegal down. And though there was nothing all football officialdom could have done about it, Cornell has conceded the game to Dartmouth, and our honor and good name remain unstained.

Cornellians in general will support the move of the administration in giving the Green this tactical victory in the game of last Saturday. No one here wants to claim an undefeated season if there is a shadow to mar it.

With the move of yesterday, we crate up the Indian Princess and ship her to Hanover, where the happy Dartmouth people can rally to their heart's content at her unveiling. They have a right to be proud of their team, and all reports are that they are not stinting in displaying their joy.

But that does not finish the business here. We have yet to think of another party in this affair, the Cornell team which, notwithstanding the inspired reporting of so-called "experts," gained a lot of glory for itself last Saturday.

This 1940 Cornell football team, which a few weeks ago was riding the heights, presents a curious enigma today, for everywhere sportswriters who prodigiously lifted it to the top of the heap, are busy nailing down its coffin

lid. At this point, more than one player is pondering the fate of a team that has been subjected to one of the most grueling campaigns of any team of any time. Not only was the Cornell team badly over-rated on the basis of its early season prospects, but even worse, the cruel publicizing that the national high pressure publicity machinery heaped on this team resulted in so many unpleasant adventures that even in its moments of victory, the Cornell team was robbed of the taste of sweet fruits.

The ungrounded charges of professionalism from the so-called gentlemen of Harvard, the bad taste of the Ohio State athletic authorities, and even the bitter sarcasm of the *Yale Daily News* all contributed to making the Cornell team know that it was never to have a minute of peace.

In our present situation, with the Penn game yet to come, it is well that at least we, the Cornell students, get this team of ours straight. Those metropolitan newsmen who yesterday were writing sneering comments on our showing of last Saturday will begin the build up again later in the week. We at least must never be fooled by them.

The Cornell team is not made up of super-stars and master players. It is made of boys who play good football, because they take their work seriously, and try sincerely. At times they have done remarkably well. At other times, they have failed, like anyone else.

Yet they have fight, as that last-second scoring effort of the past Saturday shows. They are a great team today, not-

withstanding the remarks the "experts" will make at their expense.

When they meet Penn this Saturday they will be fighting again, as the Cornell athletes they are. And they can be bolstered this Saturday, sure that their record is spotless clean, and that all decent people will respect them for what they are. There will be no more undefeated record to defend, no more elaborate build-ups to justify, nor slurs to take.

It has been announced that Dartmouth beat Cornell 3-0, and that the Indian will go to Hanover.

We are glad to give Dartmouth the symbol of victory.

—*editorial, Tuesday, November 19, 1940*

The Cornell Sun.

PUBLISHED DAILY (SATURDAYS EXCEPTED) DURING TERM TIME.

Vol. I. No. I.　　　　ITHACA, N. Y., SEPT. 16, 1880.　　　　Price Three Cents.

Business Cards.

AURORA HOTEL, opp. Tompkins House. Cor. Aurora and Seneca Sts. Rooms and Board at lowest rates. Temperance House.

B. MINTZ, Dealer in New and Second-Hand Clothing. The highest cash price paid for Gentlemen's cast-off Clothing. N.B.—Clothing cleaned repaired and exchanged.

C. L. GRANT, JR., Dealer in Drugs, Medicines and Toilet Articles. 76 East State St.

C. W. MANCHESTER, Manufacturer of Red Line Cigars, No. 4 Clinton Block.

CITY BOTTLING WORKS, B. Schwartz, Proprietor. Bottler of the P.H. Best Milwaukee, & Bartholomay Brewing Co.s Rochester Lager. Manufacturer of Belfast Ginger Ale, Birch Beer, Lemon and Sarsaparilla Soda. Also Greenway's Syracuse XX and XXX Ale. Imported Bottled Bass Ale for sale. All orders will receive prompt attention. Basement Old Ithaca Bank Building, Ithaca, N. Y.

DAY & ROBINSON, Importers and dealers in Wines and Liquors. No. 9 North Aurora street.

D. H. WANZER, Dealer in Teas, Coffees and Spices. Clubs furnished cheap for Cash No. 3 North Aurora Street, Ithaca, N. Y.

EAGLES, Photographer of University Crew of '80. Cards, $2 : Cabinets, $4 ; Bon Tons, 25 c. 74 and 76 East State.

E. J. MORGAN & SON, Surgeons and Homeopathic Physicians, Offices, 2 and 4 East State Street. Office hours, 2 to 4 and 6 to 8 p. m. N, B.—Piles cured permanently. Special attention given to diseases of the throat and chest. E. J. Morgan, M. D. E. J. Morgan, Jr. M. D.

F. C. FOWLER, Guns, Fishing Tackle, Ammunition, Sporting Goods, a full line. 56 State.

FOOTE & THATCHER, Dentists, Morrison Block, Ithaca, N. Y.
P. L. FOOTE, D. D. S.　　　F. E. THATCHER.

F. S. HOWE, DENTIST.
1 and 11 Bates Block, Aurora Street, Ithaca, N. Y. Particular attention given to the Preservation of the Natural Teeth.

HILL & GOLDSMITH, DRUGGISTS, Corner State and Aurora.

HATS, CAPS, FURS and GLOVES. LATEST STYLES, At WILLSON'S, the People's Hatter.

HUCK'S NEW BATH AND HAIR CUTting Rooms, under Finch & Apgar's Bookstore. No more waiting. Six first-class barbers employed. The best conducted establishment in the city. Hair cutting a specialty.

THE SUN

is published during term time by the Students of Cornell University. On sale at Miss Ackley's, Finch & Apgar's, Spence Spencer's, and Andrus & Church's, or will be forwarded to subscribers at the rate of 40 cents a month, $1.00 a term, or $3.00 a year. All communications should be addressed to

THE CORNELL SUN,
Ithaca, N. Y.

PRINTED BY ANDRUS & CHURCH, 41 E. STATE STREET.

WITHOUT any apology for our appearance, we make our bow to the college world, and especially to that part of it in which Cornell, her students, friends and alumni are most interested. We have no indulgence to ask, no favors to beg. Believing that the interests of the University and of the students would be subserved by the publication of a daily paper, one which should present news not only from the various colleges, but whatever was of especial interest to students wherever it occurred, we determined to publish the CORNELL SUN. Its financial success is already assured ; and we can announce unhesitatingly that it will make its appearance every day during the term time of the coming year. Our principles are those of the institution which we shall endeavor to represent,—liberty of thought, liberty of speech and liberty of action ; but we shall strive earnestly not to allow this liberty to degenerate into license. That there are many obstacles in the path of a college daily we fully realize. The labor required to edit such a publication will be no small addition to our college work ; and though we undertake it willingly, it is not without some misgivings as to our ability to perform the extra duties in a suitable manner. We expect to receive severe criticism at the hands of many, but we ask that it be deferred until a fair trial shall have shown that we deserve it.

OWING to the press of matter for the first issue, we are compelled to publish a double number to-day. It would have probably been considered a mark of prosperity, if we had published an enlarged number later in the term ; but we prefer to give the news when it is fresh than to win congratulations by issuing supplements. It shall be the endeavor of the SUN to be a *news*paper, and whenever occasion demands enlargement, additional pages will be added. The regular size of the SUN will be four pages, of the size of this sheet. We make this announcement so that none may be deceived by this issue , or be allured into subscribing for a four page paper by seeing an eight page issue. We want the support of the students, but we will take no underhand method to obtain it.

BY the changes in the Faculty which have occurred during the past vacation, Cornell loses some men whose loss she can ill afford. Men who have grown up with the University, who have helped to mould its character and give it its reputation have been allowed to go away, and in their places new ones will stand. Whatever may be the cause of the resignation of one or two of our professors, we sincerely regret that anything should have rendered that step necessary or expedient. While the reputation of this institution rests upon no one man, yet there are members of the Faculty whose withdrawal from the University would seriously injure it, and by the recent changes, one, at least, of this kind has gone. The places made vacant have been filled, and we hope by the right men. They certainly come here highly recommended, and we hope that the change may prove for the best. Cornell may not be able to secure the services of many new men of established reputation, but it can at least obtain good men, and those who give promise of future greatness. Of this kind are those who have been obtained to fill the positions made vacant by the recent changes.

Chapter IV: The Growth of a Newspaper

A newspaper is a game
Where his error scores the player victory
While another's skill wins death.
A newspaper is a symbol;
It is feckless life's chronicle,
A collection of loud tales
Concentrating eternal stupidities
That in remote ages lived unhaltered,
Roaming through a fenceless world.
　　　　　　　　　—Stephen Crane

I think that almost everyone
Admires The Cornell Daily Sun.
While other papers rise and fall,
The Sun does not descend at all.
Where is today the New York World?
Its pages are forever furled.
The New York Sun does not exist;
It's deader than *The Federalist*.
And who, of all the men who scan script,

Recalls the Boston Evening Transcript?
And yet The Cornell Daily Sun
Will never bow to anyone.
It scorns the censure of the city
And every Faculty Committee;
It does not heed the discontent
Evidenced by the President;
"Sic semper," says The Sun, *"tyrannis!"*
So *floreat Sol Cornellianus!*
　　　　　　　　　—Morris Bishop '14

Ezra Walked Here: *Staffers crowd around the desks of the night editor and copy editor in the Cornell Daily Sun newsroom beneath the rafters of the 150-year-old Colonial Building on the downtown Commons. In the 1850s, Ezra Cornell attended meetings of his farmers' club in this very room. More recently, young Ithacans learned to jitterbug and foxtrot at a dance studio which had rented the space. The Sun, cramped in its second-floor offices, added this third floor to its domain in 1967.*

The occasion for this book is the hundredth anniversary of *The Cornell Daily Sun*, so few can object if we include a word from our sponsor. In *A Half-Century at Cornell*, which The Sun published on its 50th anniversary in 1930, there was a lengthy section on The Sun's history. Such an epic is not really necessary in this book. The earlier one consisted entirely of essays about Cornell written especially for the occasion; essays similar to those interspersed throughout this one. Our format, however, is different. We have included a lot of Sun writings on the various events and concepts we have looked at; these do a much better job of recounting The Sun's history than any writer could. The business of The Sun, after all, is and has been to cover and comment on the news.

It would be pleasant, on such an occasion as this, to report that The Sun's past is entirely spotless and that it has always been graced by writing of the highest standard. Unfortunately, the reader could easily determine the falsity of such a statement by perusing the remainder of this book. In the next chapter, for example, we will look at how, in 1921, a student was driven from Cornell for the heinous crime of refusing to wear a freshman cap. There is simply no denying that The Sun's role in this affair was disgraceful. Thinking back to the last chapter, we recall with little gusto The Sun's timorous coverage of the issues raised by President Malott's inaugural. The Sun's coverage of the Straight takeover was adequate, but it cannot be called inspired.

Also, although there is no mention of it elsewhere in this book, let it be recorded that in the post-World War II era The Sun has twice committed errors so ghastly and inexcusable in its news coverage that it has had to run a correction on the front page; and that on two other occasions similar errors in editorials required complete retractions.

So much for full disclosure. The Sun has lasted a hundred years, and is thriving now: it must be doing some-

thing right. As you read through this volume, you will come across many other noteworthy student publications: the *Cornell Era*, *The Cornell Widow*, *Trojan Horse*, *The Cornell Writer*. All have made significant contributions to the University. And all are deader than Andrew D. White.

One of the prime reasons for The Sun's longevity has nothing to do with merit. Thanks to Ezra Cornell, The Sun serves a large student community in a small town. It has had many competitors over the years, but always the business community has seen it as the most effective way to reach the student market, which it is. And, as student patronage is vital to most Ithaca retailers, a strong advertising base has been guaranteed. This is an advantage our counterparts in Cambridge, Providence and Philadelphia, for example, do not have.

Taking this a step further, while *The Ithaca Journal* has usually been an outstanding newspaper, considering the size of the community it serves, it does not compare favorably with the local newspapers in the above-mentioned large cities. Also, The Journal is an afternoon newspaper, so The Sun does not face head-to-head competition.

The more advertising a newspaper has, the more space for news will be available. Consequently, since The Sun gets much more advertising than its Ivy League counterparts, its "news hole" is also much bigger, which presumably translates to happier readers.

But there is something more—the closest word I can find is "consistency," which is inadequate. Can we say, "The Sun is the best newspaper in the Ivy League?" No, certainly not, at least not always. Sometimes The Sun is run by incompetents; sometimes some of the other newspapers get outstanding groups of editors. When this happens, the other papers are more interesting to read, more important to their communities, than we are. But The Sun is never one of the worst newspapers; and if the question were which was the best newspaper of the 60s, or of the 70s, there would be no debate; The Sun simply stands head and shoulders above all its Ivy League counterparts.

Now this is not a blanket claim of superiority over the rest of the world; for example, there are those who would

So Floreat Sol Cornellianus! *Volume I, Number 1 of* The Cornell Sun, *dated September 16, 1880—the word "Daily" would not be added to the masthead until two years later. A front page editorial proclaimed the paper's principles to be "those of the institution which we shall endeavor to represent—liberty of thought, liberty of speech and liberty of action."*

say (I am one of them) that *The Michigan Daily* is consistently a better newspaper than The Sun is. The point is that only a few college newspapers have the same kind of tradition of professionalism—of excellence, if you like.

This hypothesis is supported by a closer look. There have been several periods, for example, when the quality of writing in The Sun would make one ponder how such a newspaper could have produced an E.B. White or a Kurt Vonnegut. The Sun has a grand and glorious tradition of verbosity, tedious writing style, and dubious grammar. On at least one occasion during the 70s, The Sun was arguably the worst-written newspaper in the Ivy League. There is little tradition can do to improve writing if the editors and reporters are poor writers by nature. Sun feature stories have also been lamentable, as a rule, probably because assigning good features has required more imagination than most editors have.

As against that, The Sun's story selection is *almost always* superior. The editors seem to know what to assign: how to play all angles of a story, how to see through obfuscation, how to follow a continuing story from day to day. As a newspaper of record, The Sun has been reasonably complete. It would be fatuous to say that The Sun always covers all the important areas of Cornell, but you should see how incomplete the other newspapers are.

Not too surprisingly, a high percentage of Sun graduates go on to careers in journalism. Nowadays, about half a dozen a year go on into newspaper work, normally without going to journalism school; The Sun is, in effect, Cornell's journalism department. It is represented on most major national newspapers and magazines; particularly large pockets of Sun graduates are found on the New York *Daily News*, *The Wall Street Journal*, *Newsweek*, *Newsday*, and both major wire services.

Later in this chapter, essays by three former Sun editors, ranging in class year from 1929 to 1964, give a good idea of what the Sun tradition is all about. Here, we will take a brief look at that history in hopes of finding further clues.

* * *

In 1880 the main source of Cornell news was the *Cornell Era*, a literary and journalistic weekly. The name was not facetious: Cornell students took seriously their place as heirs to the novel educational ideas of Andrew D. White and Ezra Cornell. Editors were generally selected by the University's secret societies; intrigues were common, and the student body as a whole expressed considerable interest in Era elections. In the 1890s, when the Era editors chose a law student as business manager, some 600 undergraduates held a mass meeting to protest the naming of a

non-undergraduate.

In March 1880, an ambitious *Era* editor, William Ballard Hoyt '81, decided that Cornell could support a daily newspaper. He enlisted the aid of the *Era's* graduating business manager, George Francis Gifford '80, and both signed a scrap of paper, still preserved in the University Archives, committing themselves to publishing a daily in Fall 1880. Soon the two were soliciting bids from all area printers, including the University Press. They settled on the State Street firm of Andrus & Church, which also printed the *Era*, and secured there a shared office in a back room.

Hoyt, who was to be editor, assembled ten other men to be the paper's first staff, and Gifford, who was to be business manager, agreed to spend the summer in Ithaca soliciting ads and taking care of the paper's finances.

First, of course, the enterprise had to have a name. The final choice was between the *Sun* and the *Star*, and the editors decided on the former on the ground that the paper was supposed to appear before 11 a.m.

On September 1, 1880, two weeks before the fall term began, The Sun sent a circular to all Cornellians asking for subscriptions. The letter said, ''The paper will be devoted to the collection and dissemination of Cornell news, together with a brief daily epitome of the doings of other universities, both in America and Europe. It will be the pleasure and pride of the editors in charge to gather and print every item of interest to Cornellians, while foreign news will be contributed from time to time by the alumni, other former students, and correspondents selected from the undergraduates of other colleges. Among our letters, weekly, fortnightly or monthly, will be those from Harvard, Yale, Princeton, Columbia, Michigan, and Cambridge, England, the latter from a young lady who was last year at Cornell.

''Among the features of the paper will be A COMPLETE HISTORY OF COLLEGE BOATING IN AMERICA, written as a serial, from notes gathered by graduates of this and other boating colleges; and short biographical sketches of Professors and persons who have graduated from Cornell, together with personal mention of all others who have pursued a course here, and who will be acquainting us briefly of their doings.

''The subscription price of the paper will be 35 cts. a month, $1.00 a term, or $3.00 a year.''

On September 10, the editors sent a further postcard to faculty, advising them how to get notices printed in the projected newspaper.

It was just after the Cornell chimes struck midnight, on the morning of September 16, 1880, that the first few issues came off the press. And that morning—registration day for

THE ORIGINAL STAFF OF THE CORNELL SUN, 1880-1881
(Founder Hoyt Stands at Top Center)

—Photo by
J. Notman

WILLIAM BALLARD HOYT '81
Founder of The Cornell Daily Sun

the University—*The Cornell Sun* made its first appearance on campus. The first issue was eight pages, 9"x12", but the editors were quick to add, "the regular size of the SUN will be four pages, of the size of this sheet. We make this announcement so that none may be deceived by this issue, or be allured into subscribing for a four page paper by seeing an eight page issue. We want the support of students, but we will take no underhand method to obtain it."

One thing the editors were not willing to announce was their own names. These did not appear until two issues later, once matters had settled down.

The opening editorials were properly feisty. "We have no indulgence to ask, no favors to beg," the editors said. "Believing that the interests of the University and of the students would be subserved by the publication of a daily paper, one which should present news not only from the various colleges, but wherever it occurred, we determined to publish THE CORNELL SUN."

And, in an important aside, they added, "Its financial success is already assured; and we can announce unhesitatingly that it will make its appearance every day during the term time of the coming year."

Now, this was quite an achievement. Cornell at the time had less than 400 students. Today, colleges ten times that size cannot support *weekly* newspapers. Yet Gifford had sold enough advertising to bankroll a daily, and, what with the rather high newsstand price of three cents, The Sun made a tidy profit. For the first few years, the editors were reputed to make more money than faculty members did, but there is no proof of this.

The first issue was a smashing success. It hit the streets at about 11 a.m., and was a quick sellout, whereupon more were printed. Complimentary copies were sent to freshmen and faculty members. In all, some 900 papers were printed, rather a shock considering that this was more than double Cornell's enrollment.

Not everyone was pleased. The *Era* commented, "One day last week as we went down the hill, we were set upon by a band of boys who looked like youthful highwaymen, each carrying a number of diminutive papers . . . these are not robbers, we ejaculated, but an advance guard of the Salvation Army distributing tracts. We extended a hand, expecting to have it filled with interesting literature, but instead were greeted with the shriek, 'CORNELL SUN 3 cents.' We bought one and soon learned by a glance at the little sheet, which we had mistaken for a tract, that a half-fledged daily was trying its wings in the University." The *Era* saw it all as a plot by Gifford, and charged that the sole purpose of the paper was to line his pockets.

And so, America's third college daily (*The Yale Daily News* was first; the *Harvard Echo* is defunct, so The Sun is now the nation's second oldest daily college paper) began its existence, even though, given Gifford's presence, it could not strictly be called an undergraduate publication. On the other hand, it was, as it is today, completely independent of the University administration, and it lost no time in delving into campus politics. In the first issue, the editors noted with apprehension the loss of some prominent faculty members, and reading between the lines of later editorials one can detect a call for higher faculty salaries.

A major controversy erupted that January when the Board of Trustees forced the resignation of Cornell's acting president, William C. Russel. President White was at the time United States ambassador to Germany, on leave from Cornell, his second extended absence from the presidency. Russel had served almost three years as acting president; according to Morris Bishop, he was unpopular because he did not control the pursestrings and so was not able to propose new programs. He was also perceived as anti-religious, which was a bad thing to be at a university

that was already being condemned nation-wide as infidel.

At any rate, The Sun jumped in on Russel's side with more zeal than accuracy: the acting president's name was misspelled as *Russell* the first few times it appeared. The trustees were condemned; it would be 75 years before The Sun would use language this strong about the administration again. As a matter of fact, a few years later The Sun began to style itself an "official University organ." It was not until 1913 that it repudiated this phrase and again asserted it would follow its own line instead of the administration's.

The financial success continued, and the second generation of editors, writing in June 1882, was able to say, "As we hand the SUN over to our successors, we do so with a pardonable amount of pride in the thought that it now stands upon a firm basis, and is as much a fixture of Cornell as any of her more aged institutions. We expect to see such improvements in the next and succeeding volumes that we shall be proud to proclaim the fact that we were among those who watched over its tender years."

One such improvement came in the very next issue, the first of Fall 1882. The Sun expanded its page size to 10"x14", and introduced a new masthead, in which the word *Daily* appeared for the first time. The new mast was a great piece of rococo, including adornments of Ezra Cornell's motto,

---

oars, vines, a lamp upon a book, and an owl. In 1887 this overembellishment was scrapped, and after a year of traditional Old English lettering, a new monstrosity appeared: a mast designed to look like a rising sun.

In the late 1880s there was a considerable turnover of editors, and one contributing factor was that some editors were selected by vote of the student body as a whole, rather than by outgoing editors. During the 1887-88 publication year, no less than five different men served as editor-in-chief at one time or another.

To end such instability, The Sun in Spring 1891 made the momentous announcement that from then on it would choose its own editors, who would comprise a board of four seniors, two juniors, one sophomore and one law student. Elucidating, the editors said, "In taking this action The Sun is placing itself in the same position regarding the student body as the other college dailies, and although to a few it may seem that an injustice is being done the classes, those who understand the effect that class politics have had on The Sun will readily perceive that it is for the interest of The Sun and 'Varsity which it represents, that the board should be made up of men of experience. Competition is now open for places on next year's board, and the board hopes that all interested will begin work immediately."

And, for a time, it appeared that the new system would produce excellence. The page size grew again; the ugly "rising sun" mast was discarded in favor of Old English lettering, similar to that in use today, although the The was no longer included in the paper's title; and in Fall 1892, The Sun ran its first pictures, beginning, appropriately enough, with one of the new president, Jacob Gould Schurman.

The framers of the new board system were probably so busy congratulating themselves on their own cleverness that they did not notice a fatal flaw, which evinced itself in spectacular fashion in June 1893.

With eight people on the board, it was possible to have an irreconcilable tie, and, as Murphy's Law would have it, this is exactly what happened. The newly-constituted board unanimously elected a new editor-in-chief, but deadlocked 4-4 on business manager between John L. Ahern '94 and Samuel Scott Slater '94. The board took 147 futile ballots over several weeks before the Slater faction, which included the new editor-in-chief, Charles C. Rosewater '94, decided to stage a *coup de gazette* and publish The Sun without the other four! The Ahern faction refused to accept this, and arranged to publish their own version. And so it came to pass that there were *two* newspapers called *The Cornell Daily Sun*, each claiming legitimacy, and each devoting a considerable quantity of ink every day to denouncing the other.

After two chaotic weeks, the situation was resolved by President Schurman, who decreed that there would be a binding campus referendum on which of the two would survive. After a tempestuous "campaign," the Ahern group triumphed.

One major, lasting change came out of the schism: the

In 1883 some reports of smallpox caused the Cornell administration to require all students to be vaccinated. To judge by the Suns of those days, painful complications were common: the editors printed suggestions on how to deal with aching arms and other consequences. And in the beginning there was the editorial page.

The Parable of the Sacred Bovine

And lo, when the first month of the eighty-third year was but half spent, a decree went forth from the ruler over people that dwelt in the land of Ezra the Cornellite.

For there was an exceeding rumour of great sickness in the land; and sore were the elders affrighted.

So the decree went forth that on a certain day all the children of Ezra the Cornellite be gathered together unto the doctors and magicians that they might look upon the sacred cow and be healed.

And all the people of that land, yea even the Seniorites and the Juniorites, the Sophomorites and the Freshmanites were gathered unto one spot, but the Coeduites were gathered together in a place apart to look upon the sacred bovine that they should not be sick.

And behold a vaccinator went forth to vaccinate, and as he vaccinated some fell upon sterile places that it did not take, and great was the joy of those thus vaccinated. But others fell upon ripe places with an exceeding take, and great was the take thereof. For it is an exceeding taking thing.

Then went the Cornellites joyfully homeward, for it was promised that whoso had looked upon the sacred cow should not be sick, but be infernal sore:

And there was joy and feasting in all that land for the space of one week.

But when one week was spent all the people of that land were again gathered unto the magicians. And when they beheld the magicians all the people groaned aloud, and they presented arms, and exceeding sore were their arms.

And when they beheld the chief of the magicians they murmured and said, Who is this who hath done this thing unto us and what preventeth us that we do not slay him. And when he opened his mouth to speak unto them their anger waxed hot and they spat upon him, and they rolled up his coat sleeve, and they took of his hat. And when the people saw what things were done unto the magician they were glad.

And one of the chiefs of the people spake unto them and said, What shall now be done unto this soothsayer which hath so vexed this people. And the people opened their mouths and cried, Vaccinate him, vaccinate him. And they did even so. And the last state of that man was worse than the first.

And the sacred bovine was avenged.

—*editorial, January 23, 1883*

Ahern half-Sun, as a competitive gimmick, began to publish on Saturday, the first time in Sun history this had been done. The experiment was successful, and The Sun continued to publish six days a week for 60 years.

Meanwhile, The Sun's bitter rival, the *Era,* had in effect conceded defeat after ten years of editorial wrangling. It was an unequal struggle from the beginning: a weekly cannot compete with a daily for hot news, and the type of in-depth analysis that typifies good weekly newspapers today was unknown in the 1880s.

The *Era* tried desperately for nearly a generation to find some kind of identity for itself. In 1891 it started to stress humor, drawing a series of condescending editorials from The Sun, which termed it "pitiful." In 1898 the *Era* merged with the *Cornell Magazine* and began life anew as a literary monthly, but that did not last long either. It became a muckraking newsletter in the 1900s, returned to literary affairs in the teens, and had a brief stint as a picture magazine before finally expiring in 1923.

In 1896 a further election wrangle resulted in The Sun losing a considerable talent. Frank E. Gannett '98, the defeated candidate, quit The Sun, but went on to acquire *The Ithaca Journal-News, The Elmira Star-Gazette,* and a host of others on the way to producing one of the country's foremost newspaper chains.

* * *

The nineteenth-century Sun bore little resemblance to its present-day counterpart. The line between hard news and editorial comment was hazy, when it existed at all. Sports was the big news item, there was no national news, and extra editions to cover major sporting events were fairly regular. Strangest of all to the modern reader, The Sun would hit the streets between 11 a.m. and 2 p.m.

This changed along with the century: in Summer 1900 The Sun opened its first full-fledged offices, at 202 North Tioga Street, and began to be printed at night, on the press of *The Ithaca News.* This finally allowed papers to be delivered before classes, even as they are today.

The ambitious Sun Class of '00 tried one other experiment that was not as successful: they raised the price of the newspaper from three to five cents, but when circulation dropped drastically, they were forced to rescind the increase. By this time, The Sun had a circulation of over a thousand. At least in terms of newsstand price, The Sun has coped with inflation well over the years: the price went to a nickel again in 1910, but after World War I the price went back to three cents. It was raised by a penny during World War II, and to five cents again in 1948. In 1959 it went up to a dime, and a further price rise in 1975 brought The Sun to its present level of 15 cents an issue.

Sun profit statements have always been kept confidential, but the 1910 editor-in-chief later claimed that he had made the princely sum of $3,000 during his term. The

editor, Stanton Griffis, became an investment banker. His partner as business manager, Jansen Noyes, also achieved financial success and became a major donor to Cornell. One of the things he donated was his son, Jansen Jr. '39, who is now chairman of Cornell's Board of Trustees.

The increasing complexity of the financial operation provoked The Sun to incorporate, under the watchful eye of the administration, on March 25, 1905. Previously, it had been the custom for the editors either to divide the profits among themselves, or to pay the losses out of their own pockets.

Buy Your Own, Dammit!

The "fiend" who borrows his neighbor's paper or in some way manages to read it through every day without ever buying a copy himself, seems to be quite as numerous about Cornell as elsewhere. The Sun does not need to go begging for subscriptions, and persons who pretend that it does not pay to subscribe for a college paper are respectfully requested not to read the paper. They, however, are the very ones who seem to be most interested in it and on every occasion endeavor to peruse it as before mentioned. All who think it is worth reading at all ought to be willing to help support it, and it needs all the support it can get from the student body. The great majority of our students we are glad to say are, however, imbued with a spirit of fairness and understand that it is their duty as well as to their advantage to subscribe for the college papers. For such of its readers The Sun endeavors, and we believe succeeds, in giving bountiful return for their subscriptions. In justice to them and in justice to ourselves we submit this to the good sense of the numerous third parties for whom this gentle hint is intended.

—editorial, October 28, 1885

Thus, at the start of each year, The Sun would have no assets but its name. The incorporation agreement replaced a wild stock-selling scheme proposed by the Class of '04.

Also in 1904, The Sun began to carry national news, the result of an agreement with Joseph Pulitzer's New York *World,* which sent the news by telegraph to The Sun every evening. In 1912 the paper became the first collegiate member of The Associated Press. Since that time The Sun and The AP have had a close relationship. The Sun added United Press International photo service in the 1960s.

In addition to their financial acumen, Griffis and Noyes made a major contribution to Sun history when they hired a full-time secretary, Jessica Holland. Miss Holland kept her post for an incredible 45 years; she provided corporate continuity, was the permanent alter ego of business managers, and was the force behind The Sun's quick resumption of publication after each world war.

Many tears were shed and resolutions of gratitude passed when Miss Holland retired in 1955, but The Sun would miss her more than anyone knew. Her successor as office manager proved to be an embezzler, and was fired in 1958 following the discovery that she had squirreled away a five-figure sum. She died soon afterward and The Sun never recovered most of the money.

The iron-willed Ruth Hartwig then took over—with some temporary assistance from Miss Holland—and she continued until her sudden death in 1970. The job then fell to Martha Howe, who had been The Sun's second secretary since 1961. Norma Sullivan, hired as a second secretary in 1973, became office manager in 1977 when Mrs. Howe, upon reaching retirement age, became a part-time Sun employee. Sun office managers, then, have a longer average term than even Cornell presidents.

* * *

A disastrous financial decision in 1917 led to the awarding of the Sun printing contract to a printer who was unable to do the job. The first six issues of the year were never delivered. The contract was broken, and The Sun was thereafter printed at the Cayuga Press, at a new size, 17" × 22". It would stay with these Brobdingnagian dimensions for 20 years.

Should Sun Editors Get Academic Credit?

The members of the *Sun* board do not ask or desire University credit in hours to reward their labor. In this particular, we disagree with the *Cornell Era*, which states in its last issue, "We see no reason why the labors of those chiefly concerned in bringing forth the *Sun*, the *Countryman*, or the *Sibley Journal* should not be rewarded by a proportionate amount of University credit, if, say, their editors fall respectively under the jurisdiction of the English, the Agricultural, or the Sibley Engineering departments in their University course."

As for other publications, we believe their desire for University credit is a just one, provided they want this concession. But, as for ourselves, we recognize that our first obligation is to the undergraduates and we do not care to be subsidized by any faculty connection which could possibly interfere with our freedom of expression.

—*editorial, January 12, 1907*

Two other events in 1917 are worth noting. First, The Sun condescended to permit women to work on the newspaper, for the first time since Jessie M. Boulton '83 served briefly as literary editor in 1882. A women's editor and a women's manager were named; later, there would be a complete women's news board. Men, however, continued to control the paper.

Second, an interesting piece of vegetation known as the Berry Patch sprouted on the editorial page. The editor in charge of this column, A.W. Smith '19, who used the alias "C.D.," filled his space with jokes, poems and other light entertainment. The Patch remained one of the most endearing features of the newspaper until it was weeded out in the late 1950s. As can be gleaned from a cursory reading of this book, some of The Sun's best writing has germinated in the Berry Patch.

During the Patch's first 20 years, its editors honored the first one by continuing to use his pseudonym. When CDII made his appearance in 1919, it is unlikely that he imagined there would be a CDXXXVIII in 1941.

But when World War I broke out, The Sun's growth came to a sudden end. At first, the editors advocated closing the University so that all could contribute to the war effort. Cornell remained open, although it was surely not business as usual, but The Sun announced it would not publish in 1918-19.

"The War Department's order creating a branch of the Student Army Training Corps at Cornell virtually transforms the University into an Army training camp," The Sun effused. "In this camp, each individual will pledge his most sincere efforts to help win the war. Any diversion from the work of preparation to enter officers' training camps to undertake student activities becomes unpatriotic. So The Sun will not even attempt publication.

"Until the war is won, The Sun can only ask its advertisers, subscribers, and friends to remember that The Sun will come back the moment conditions permit."

Conditions permitted sooner than the editors thought. Publication resumed December 30, 1918.

E.B. White '21, who had previously played in the Berry Patch, was elected editor-in-chief in 1920, and in addition to contributing his fine writing style to the editorial page, he

—Scrapbook of Richard Evett Bishop '09

ADOLESCENT SUN: *Left, a Cornellian of about 1910 holds several copies of The Sun in front of a friend. Below, James Irving Clark, a member of the 1912 Sun board, sits at his desk in the third-floor, back-room Sun office in the Ithaca Trust Building at 110 North Tioga Street. The Sun would become the first collegiate member of The Associated Press later in 1912 and therefore move its office to the Ithaca Journal building, where it would have easy access to the AP wire.*

—Scrapbook of James Irving Clark '12

A CENTURY AT CORNELL

ALMOST AS OLD AS ITS NAME: *Though not quite as ancient as its title might indicate, the Colonial Building at 109 The Commons—home of The Sun since 1936—is indeed one of the oldest structures in the Fingerlakes region. Erected about 1829 as the Bank of Ithaca, the edifice later served as the Post Office, as Atwater's grocery store, and finally—after the bottom halves of its once imposing Greek Ionic columns had been hacked off by a tasteless owner—as home for a succession of ground floor storefronts. The Sun's newsroom occupies the whole third floor, and its business office and composing room part of the second. The composing room exists where Atwater's once cured meats and prepared specialty foods.*

also indulged in a spot of meddling in campus politics. President Schurman had finally retired after 28 years in office, and the enormously popular director of Sibley College, Albert W. Smith '78, known to one and all as "Uncle Pete," was named acting president. White carried on a vigorous editorial campaign to have Uncle Pete named as permanent president. He pointed out that Smith was near retirement age and deserved the honor; he also noted that it would be a good tradition to have the Cornell presidency occupied by Cornell alumni. White did not get his way: the presidency went to Dr. Livingston Farrand; and, as of 1980, not one of Cornell's nine presidents has been an alumnus.

The Sun showed little change during the Republican prosperity of the 20s, and during the Great Depression, the editors celebrated its 50th birthday. Both the editor-in-chief and the business manager from the Class of '29 stayed in town to produce *A Half-Century at Cornell*. This book, which contained advertising and sold for $3.50 hardbound, produced enough revenue for the two to pay themselves the lavish wage of $15 per week. The editor, Harry L. Case, has also offered considerable help with the present book, in addition to his essay appearing in this chapter. Sun people stay together.

The 1930 book made money, and, despite the Depression, so did The Sun. 1929-30 showed the best profit in many years, and both the editor and business manager pocketed some $2,500, a huge sum in those days of deflation. As the national financial blight continued, however, The Sun's profit dwindled; in 1934, the editor and business manager had to be content with $25 apiece. Also, like the University, The Sun was forced to cut the salaries of its full-time employees.

Two momentous changes occurred later in the decade. After moving from office to office for several years, The Sun took space in the Colonial Building at 109 East State Street in Summer 1936, and has occupied it ever since. The building is one of the oldest in Ithaca, dating from about 1829, and Ezra Cornell attended meetings of his farmers' club on

its top floor during the 1850s. This third floor—which had later been converted into a dance hall, complete with a balcony from which earlier generations of parents could observe their close-dancing progeny—was turned into a newsroom in 1967.

The second change had even more impact. After nearly 30 years as a broadsheet newspaper, The Sun changed over to tabloid size in January 1938. There is no doubt that this made the paper easier for readers to handle, but the editors seemed excessively proud of all the changes, especially the typographical ones. They boasted of their sans-serif headlines and their "streamlined" format. They proclaimed that "after a thorough study of different types, a form has been chosen which experts describe as the easiest to read and most attractive in appearance."

The experts were evidently wrong in at least one area, however. A new masthead was introduced. The *The* was again dropped from the newspaper's name, and *Cornell Daily Sun* appeared in huge, bold square letters. It was a prodigious feat of ugliness, and it lasted just 21 issues, the shortest-lived mast in Sun history. It was quietly replaced by the traditional Old English lettering, again without the *The*.

Both new mastheads, however, incorporated an innovation which had first made its appearance, again without comment, in the issue of Tuesday, October 25, 1935. Underneath the newspaper's title was the small legend, ITHACA'S ONLY MORNING NEWSPAPER.

The 1939-40 editor-in-chief, Robert W. Storandt, later

—*From A Half-Century at Cornell*

THE SUN LOOMS LARGER: *The page dimensions of The Sun grew steadily through its first 50 years from the three-column, 9-by-12 inch size of the inaugural issue to the seven-column, 17-by-23 inch proportion of 1930. The latter unwieldy broadsheet size was abandoned in January 1938, when The Sun changed over to its current tabloid format. The caption accompanying this illustration from A Half-Century at Cornell alleges these papers of 1880, 1887, 1911, 1916 and 1926 represent the "chief aspects" of The Sun's physical evolution. Apparently no one wanted to admit that the "sunburst" mast of 1888, reproduced earlier in this book, ever existed.*

became president of the Sun corporation, and also Cornell's director of admissions. On the same page of the yearbook of the Class of 1940 were Neal Stamp, who would become University Counsel, and Charles Stewart, now vice chairman of the Cornell Board of Trustees.

Throughout the late 30s, as war drew nearer, The Sun had espoused an isolationist line. By 1940, the editors had become convinced of the evils of Hitler, although they continued to hold out some hope for peace until Pearl Harbor. On December 7, 1941, The Sun put out an extra edition on the bombing. The night editor for the issue was Kurt Vonnegut '44, who finished the war as a German prisoner, and witnessed the horrible firebombing of Dresden. The book that came out of his experience, *Slaughterhouse-Five*, stands as one of the great antiwar statements in any language.

It did not take long for the war to have an impact on The Sun. Newsprint was put on allocation, and this, coupled with an increasing shortage of manpower, forced the newspaper to suspend Monday publication in November, 1942 and to ration news and advertising space. Still, The Sun was a five-day-a-week paper, as Saturday publication continued.

War conditions caused accelerated study, and the University stayed open during the summer. Accordingly, The Sun announced plans to publish three days a week beginning in July, 1943, the first and last summer publication since 1914.

But it soon became clear that there would be neither sufficient newsprint nor personnel to resume publication in the fall on a normal schedule, and on July 31, the word *Daily* was removed from the mast.

Nevertheless, issues continued to appear three times a week into the fall. And, miraculously, they were of fair quality. The news was written concisely and accurately; the editorials, while supporting the war effort, never degenerated into hysteria. The Sun changed editorships in October, in line with the University's accelerated schedule, and in his final editorial, outgoing editor-in-chief Edward Eddy '44 wrote, "We would like to spend paragraphs being grateful to those we leave here, naming one by one the kindhearted and the helpful. But there are other men and other times which occupy our thoughts. And those men are the ones who have gone before us into the torn world. Those men are the ones who, at a time when they should be marching in cap and gown, are marching in jungle brush and over sand. It is not easy to speak of them, for, no matter what is said, it will sound overly patriotic and full of sentiment. But we hope with all our heart that they are fully conscious that their courage and conviction have not gone unrecognized."

With Eddy's departure, and the tremendous burden of military training, The Sun ended 63 years of male domination by electing Guinevere Griest '44, then women's editor, as editor-in-chief. In her first editorial, she stressed the necessity of "constructive thought" as a counterweight to the predominantly technical training Cornell undergraduates were getting, adding, "It is essential that we retain our capacity for appraisal and criticism. Only thus can we retain our identity as individuals; only thus can Cornell retain its identity as a great liberal institution; only thus can America retain its identity as a democratic nation."

As for The Sun, she had this to say: "We are taking over the reins of Ithaca's Only Morning Newspaper at one of the most critical periods in its history. In 1918 the exigencies of war caused a temporary setting of The Sun for the first and only time in its history. Though the war we fight today reduces that struggle to the stature of a mere pre-view, circumstances have happily allowed us to keep our heads safely above the horizon, if below the zenith attained in the past."

But Miss Griest was mistaken. Her first editorial was also her last. The Sun, going out not with a whimper but a bang, would not publish again for three years.

* * *

For the remainder of the war, The Sun was replaced by the *Cornell Bulletin*, an undistinguished weekly sponsored by the administration and edited mostly by former Sun staffers.

Among the veterans who returned to Cornell after the conflict were some veterans of The Sun. Harold "Ron" Raynolds, formerly '46 but now '48, became the first and only person in Sun history to serve two terms as editor-in-chief. The University had expanded to a record 9,000 students, and many traditions were dying: it was preposterous, for example, for veterans to be asked to wear freshman caps, but they were. The Sun's first editorial upon resumption of publication October 11, 1946, said, "We presuppose an adult community at Cornell. We will defend it as such and we will criticize it as such." This statement proved an apt prediction of The Sun's role over the next 15 years.

During the first year of its return, The Sun published Tuesday through Saturday, as had been the case early in·the war. The Monday edition was then reinstated, and The Sun issued six editions a week until Fall 1953, when the Saturday edition was dropped for want of support.

During the first few postwar years, The Sun was a bland product, seldom offering criticism of the administration. In 1951 it almost completely refused to cover the scandal caused when part of President Malott's inaugural address was found to have been stolen from someone else, as recounted in Chapter III.

Nevertheless, the paper was beginning to look more and more as it does today. Bylines on news stories became more frequent, the newspaper became more consistent in its style of writing and layout, and it assumed a more activist editorial stance. President Farrand had been loved, President Day had been sacrosanct, but it soon became obvious that The Sun did not care for President Malott. The fracas over his inaugural was one factor; so was his high-handed way of dealing with people; so were his conservative views on morality, and his preoccupation with enacting needless rules.

In the early 50s both The Sun and the Student Council waged war on local landlords who practiced racial discrimination; Malott refused to cooperate. Later in his term, The Sun also found fault with his handling of academic freedom cases and his alleged neglect of the humanities.

The climax was a housing rules insurrection in 1958, led by a former Sun editor-in-chief, who was temporarily suspended for his actions, and whose exploits are chronicled in Chapter v.

Even that editor, Kirkpatrick Sale '58, was halting and euphemistic in his criticism of Malott. Throughout the 50s, it was The Sun's practice to praise Malott by name, but to use "the administration" or some other less invidious phrase when, in reality, criticizing him personally. President Perkins was popular with The Sun up until his last year, and even then he was not castigated in the editorials; of all Cornell's presidents, only Dale Corson has really been attacked personally by Sun editors on a regular basis.

The Sun took on a slightly more strident tone in the 60s, becoming more interested in both campus and national politics, especially after thousands of young men started to be sent to Vietnam. The last major change in the masthead took place: one year's editors, not convinced that *Ithaca's Only Morning Newspaper* was a sufficiently tacky slogan, changed it to *Ithaca's ONLY Morning Newspaper*. The first day after the next generation of editors took over, the *Only* was pointedly returned to upper and lower case, but in the meantime, the entire slogan had grown a set of quotation marks. So, "*Ithaca's Only Morning Newspaper*" it remains.

Internally, a long-standing dispute between the news and business departments was settled by the Sun board of directors in 1967, when an amendment to the corporation bylaws was passed setting up a procedure by which the news department could overrule any decision by the business manager.

This amendment was an anachronism in a way, in that it emphasized the role of the editor-in-chief. One of The Sun's main trends over the last thirty years, one that accelerated in the late 60s, has been an increase in the power of the managing editor at the expense of the editor-in-chief.

Traditionally, the editor-in-chief controls the editorial page, and the managing editor the news pages. Before The Sun switched to tabloid size in 1938, the space available for editorials was almost twice what it is today.

Normally, a staff of at least three people wrote the editorials; recalling the Heidelberg University controversy of 1936 described in Chapter II, for example, an "assistant editorial director" wrote the main editorials. Somehow, this system faded away. By the mid-50s, it was clearly established that the editor-in-chief personally wrote almost all editorials.

Meanwhile, the editor-in-chief, who used to be the managing editor's superior, began to lose control over the news pages. And the news pages began to take on much more importance in the paper's style. For 90 years, a recurring pattern was that a junior would be managing editor, and would be promoted to editor-in-chief for his senior year. This happened as recently as 1969. And during the Straight crisis of that spring, when the new editor-in-chief, who had been managing editor a month before, tried to exercise some control over news, the new managing editor rebuffed him. If one has to pick a time for the emergence of the managing editorship as the most important position on the newspaper, this would be it. While the managing editor continues to be listed below the editor-in-chief and business manager on the mast, during the last decade at least there has been no doubt that the managing editor runs the news operation and the editor-in-chief is confined to Page 4. And as this book takes shape, the final contortion in the standing of tradition on its head has taken place: the 1980-81 managing editor was "promoted" from his 1979-80 position, editor-in-chief.

*   *   *

A woman finally served more than three days as editor-in-chief when Elizabeth Bass was elected in 1971. In 1974-75 not only was there a second female editor-in-chief but also the first female managing editor in 20 years, Cathy Panagoulias. During the 70s, there were three women editors-in-chief—all of whom defeated qualified male opponents—and two women managing editors, one of whom defeated another female, the other emerging as a compromise candidate when the two top candidates, both male, killed each other off.

Nearly parallel to the rise of the managing editor has been the vast increase in the amount of space devoted to news. The main reason for this is financial. The newspaper had money problems in the early 70s, largely due to high production costs at *The Ithaca Journal*. The editors were forced to squeeze as many ads into as few pages as possible, with the result that papers had pitifully little news space. And this merely allowed The Sun to break even, not

very good news for editors and managers who received no compensation other than their share of the profits. With no other typesetters or printers in town capable of producing The Sun, the newspaper's management began to consider purchasing typesetting equipment and a press of its own.

Faced with this planning, in 1972 The Journal reduced The Sun's printing charges by 22 percent, a saving of about $20,000 a year. Not surprisingly, 1972-73 became the all-time record year for profits, and the editors responded by sharply reducing the percentage of advertising and abolishing eight-page papers, which had been appearing at least once a week.

Advertising continued to increase, and 1974-75 established another new profit record, which has not been approached since. It seemed an optimal time for the most important financial decision since incorporation: the purchase of a complete composing room, at a cost of some $50,000. Presswork continued to be done at The Journal.

—Sun Photo by Steven Fox

This move saved a lot of money, but more important in the long run, it made larger papers feasible. The results were dramatic: the average Sun in 1979-80 was about 19 pages compared to about 14 a decade earlier, and the pages themselves were 14 percent larger, due to a 1976 decision to increase the depth of the page to 16 inches, the same size as when The Sun became a tabloid in 1938. Meanwhile, the quantity of advertising had stayed roughly constant.

What this all means is that in a 1980 Sun there is, on the average, twice as much room for editorial matter as there was in a 1970 Sun. For all that, is it a better newspaper? In some ways, it is not. The decline in writing skills that has afflicted the student body as a whole has also hit The Sun. The incessant search for the blockbuster story that has so confounded major newspapers ever since Watergate finds its reflection in The Sun's pages. When a scandal erupts, it is treated in a sensational yet overly facile manner; other scandals remain hidden for want of anyone to do the digging up of facts that a story would depend upon. And, of course, in 1970 there was a lot more spectacular news on campus than there is today. One never knew what type of crazy demonstrations or political developments would take place. In 1971, a Sun editor, believing most of this to be over, warned incoming freshmen, "You are coming to Cornell at a very boring time." He was wrong.

As against that, The Sun today is much more comfortable in its role. It is more consistent from year to year, graphically more pleasing, more interesting to read from cover to cover. The extra space is being used efficiently, with more pictures, more national news, longer reviews, far more letters to the editor. And there is a larger student staff, sometimes more than 100 people, so there is even more local news coverage from time to time. Fewer stories are missed entirely.

But it is ridiculous to make such comparisons. Obviously The Sun has varied from year to year, from decade to decade; these fluctuations hardly matter over the course of a century. On the whole, The Sun has been a good and a successful newspaper. Editors are always promising "improvements" in their product, and no doubt The Sun will continue to change. Whatever the next century holds, those who run The Sun would do well to aspire to a future as distinguished as its past.

The Year There Were Two Cornell Suns

By Charles C. Rosewater '94

Students returning to Cornell in the fall of 1893 were astonished by the discovery of a remarkable astronomical and journalistic phenomenon. There were two *Cornell Daily Suns*. Never before or since has there been such a heat of commotion at the University as resulted from this abnormal occurrence. The real story of this event has never before been written. For many years, no one who knew the inside facts through having had an active part in the controversy could write about it without partisanship, but it would seem that enough time has now elapsed to tell a plain, uncolored story of just how it all happened.

It was late at night, one of those breathless, stagnant June nights. The windows in the back room of Andrus & Church's book-store which served as the editorial sanctum of *The Cornell Daily Sun* were wide open, but the flames of the two gas burners did not flicker. From the pictures on the walls, former Sun and *Era* editors looked down upon eight very serious, almost belligerent faces. Eight stern-visaged young men sat coatless, some of them collarless, upon eight hard wooden chairs. It was not the first time that they had sat there for hours, but this was the last time. Voices and nerves had become tense. They had argued. They had pleaded. Again and again, they had heard the chairman announce, "The vote is a tie. Four votes for Slater. Four votes for Ahern." Each man was still of the same opinion. It was as though they had turned into eight blocks of granite, primitive boulders with rough unhewn edges.

Years have rolled away—thirty-five years. The two most conspicuous actors in the drama have passed to their final rewards. Such an interval makes a true perspective possible and clears the vision so that both sides may be seen clearly. Time even causes blocks of granite to lose their rough edges, when it covers them with moss and lichens and vines. Then, however, the dead-lock of the Ninety-four Sun board, which gave birth to two *Cornell Daily Suns,* thoroughly disrupted the peace of the autumn campus and all who trod its paths and highways.

The original cause goes back to the very beginning of The Sun. Fifteen years previous, some enterprising students started a daily, partly for glory and partly for profit. By mere accident, the board of editors consisted of eight members. Note the number, for the fact that it was even became the cause of all the trouble. Nothing had ever come of this before, because The Sun was a private enterprise and the board was a law unto itself. While it allowed a few positions to be filled by election, most of the men were chosen by what was termed a competition. In the main, it chose the best candidates but the fact remained that the control of the board and succession was in the hands of those who were in power.

As to my own selection on the board, I think it was Artie Howland, the '93 editor-in-chief, who suggested that I compete. I covered a few news stories and then was told that I had been duly elected. It was a proud event for me when I was invited by the outgoing board to a feast and punch-bowl to welcome the new board. The two seniors who had served on the old board were John L. Ahern and Samuel Scott Slater. By custom and precedent these two were expected to fill the positions of editor-in-chief and business manager. But each decided that he wanted to be business manager, and it was their names that have been connected with the rival papers, which have gone down in history as the *Slater Sun* and the *Ahern Sun.*

Those two men were wonderful fellows, each in his own way. Slater was usually referred to as Samuel Scott Slater. Ahern was Johnnie Ahern to all who knew him. Slater, brilliant, handsome, energetic and proud, worked his way through college, but few except his intimate friends knew it. He was a clerk at a summer hotel during vacations and also earned money while in college as correspondent of the New York *World* and other papers. A native of New York City, Slater won some oratorical honors and earned both his bachelor and law degrees in four years. This he accomplished by prodigious work, although he was a delicate chap and never in complete good health. By the time he was out of college three years, he was made managing attorney of the largest New York law office. Later he headed an important law firm and as

state senator was prominent in New York politics and a close friend of Theodore Roosevelt.

Ahern was a big, brawny son of the farm. Like Slater, he had to earn his way through college. It was his grit and determination and Gaelic good humor that carried him through four years of the hardest kind of mostly menial work. He made no secret of it. While Slater was a fraternity man, Johnnie belonged to "the other crowd" and neither wore society pin nor indulged in any of the frivolities of college life. The ruddy, big-boned Irish lad from the farm and the delicate, city-bred, somewhat debonair Slater were as widely different types as one would find in all the throng at Cornell. Ahern after graduation made his way to a responsible position on the business side of one of the Buffalo papers.

Slater, Charlie Young, the '95 member of the board, now publisher of the San Francisco *Call,* and I all belonged to the Kwill Klub, a close little club of men who expected to write for a living. We naturally got together before the organization of the new board and annexed Ormsbee, who was a fraternity brother of Charlie's. We figured that we could control the board with our four votes. We counted on Sanderson, a fraternity man, being with us and possibly Berden, the '96 member, who was an unknown quantity. Leighty was one of "the other crowd" and a friend of Ahern's.

Slater had too much work ahead of him to get his two degrees to take on the duties of editor-in-chief, although quite able to fill the position. He wanted to be business manager. So did Ahern, who realized that he was not equipped for the editorship. Besides, Slater did not want to team with Ahern in the management of the paper, for they had clashed before, on the old board.

The new board met and the first ballot elected me editor-in-chief unanimously. Then came the vote for business manager and to our surprise, Sanderson and Berden voted for Ahern. These two could not be won over to our way of thinking and so the dead-lock continued night after night for 147 ballots.

That final dramatic night came. When we adjourned, the venerable Mr. Andrus and the quiet, smiling Mr. Church, owners of the printing plant that had always printed The Sun, were awaiting the outcome. Most of the students had left Ithaca and the board was not organized. To our delight, we found that they were willing to enter into a contract to print the paper for *us,* without the Ahern four. That settled it as far as we were concerned. Slater stayed in Ithaca to round up advertising contracts and the rest of us went our several ways to spend the summer vacation.

It is not easy to analyze the motives of four youths, after 35 years, and why we attempted the coup, yet it is much easier now to be frank about it. Ahern, the plodder, was not our ideal of the man we wanted as business manager. We bolstered our desires by the fact that The Sun was a private enterprise and we cherished the notion that we had a monopoly of the brains of the board. The long sessions put a spirit of fight in us and when we found that the printers were with us, we calmly ignored some very important elements in the situation as well as the rights of our adversaries. We counted, for one thing, on Andrus & Church being the only shop where The Sun could be printed. We did not understand the fighting qualities of Johnnie Ahern. We did not realize that although The Sun had been run as a private enterprise, the University did not regard it as belonging to a few men. We did not understand the democratic spirit of Cornell and that it wanted no high-handed methods to prevail in the administration and control of The Sun.

We were, therefore, more surprised than anyone, when we found that the Ahern members had made preparations to come out with the only *bona fide* edition of The Sun. But they had, and with the opening of the University two *Cornell Daily Suns* made their astonishing appearance. Now read a portion of the editorial that I wrote in the first issue of the *Slater Sun:*

"Here was the situation. What was to be done? Compromise was impossible. There were but two solutions to the problem. We could either leave The Sun in the hands of a body of men whom we did not consider competent to conduct the paper, or adopt the course which we believe to be the final answer to the question.

"We went to Messrs. Andrus and Church, the publishers of The Sun since its establishment, and stated our case as we have stated it here, and asked them to give us a contract to publish the paper. Their reply was that while they wished to side with neither faction, they agreed with us that it was the only way to avoid the present and the future difficulties, and believing we had the ability to edit a paper, concluded the contract."

In the first number of the *Ahern Sun,* the opposing case was stated as follows:

"This board of editors has made every effort to settle the differences existing between themselves and their former associates, but without success. We have therefore prepared for the publication of The Sun with a view to lifting it out of the control of cliques and placing it on a fair and permanent basis in the control of the student body.

"In this effort we ask the help of every fair-minded student of Cornell University who is willing to make The Sun a paper truly representative of the student body."

That was not all by any means. In each issue of both papers there were vigorous editorials incriminating and reincriminating the other side. As the controversy raged, most everyone began to have an opinion and expressed it freely. It was the talk of the campus, the fraternity houses and faculty meetings. Factions were forming and then President Schurman got into the scrimmage and soundly bumped our heads together. That is hardly true, because, with an intimation of the skill he was to display later as a diplomat, quietly but insistently he forced a culmination of the situation.

At his summons we met in the library of the president's house at half-past seven; it was two-thirty when the eight actors in the drama walked out across the still, dark campus. Too much water has run under the bridge to recall just what was said in the arguments and pleas of both sides that autumn night, but the vivid picture of the scene of this next to the last act in the drama can never be forgotten. Here were eight journalistic cubs, earnest and serious in the belief that this was the most important moment in their careers, a matter of life and death, and a president of a great university, who never once intimated that he felt that it was all a tempest in a tea-pot, listening courteously, patiently and apparently oblivious to the unnecessary inroad into the hours of his well-earned night's rest. That we could have argued our cases for seven hours is not so difficult to understand, but why we should have been *permitted* to do so is beyond my present imagination. The president must have had a wonderful understanding of our youthful minds, as well as a remarkable fund of patience —and possibly a genuine sense of humor.

He made it clear in the very beginning that we must come to a complete agreement before we left, if it took all night. At first he made an effort to have us consolidate by reorganizing the original board. That proved hopeless. There was a too great feeling of self-righteousness and the justness of our respective causes on both sides. We no doubt felt that it would have been humiliating to work with our enemies, after such a clash, and perhaps we had the good sense to know that we could not work together harmoniously. The conclusion finally reached was that the deci-

---

From the Competing Suns:

A Matter of Merit; A Matter of Student Pride

In view of the approaching SUN election it may be well to consider the condition of the SUN first if the "private enterprise" is successful and secondly if the student paper is endorsed.

In the first case the SUN will again become the property of private individuals, controlled by a clique, and will in no true way express student sentiment or reflect student opinion. Its elections will be controlled by wire-pulling, and merit in competition will count for nothing in the case of a man who is not in the ring. In the second case the SUN will be a real student paper under student control and will be published *six* days in a week. It will be in the closest possible touch with the student body. It will be devoted to the interests of the University and the editors will feel a stronger sense of responsibility than they possibly could were they answerable to no one for their actions. The statement that "it is as ridiculous to elect men to the editorial board of a college paper as to elect them to the Glee Club" is itself too ridiculous to require refutation. The editorial board of nearly every college paper published shares with the student body the appointment of their successors. Competition is an excellent method of determining journalistic ability, but competition becomes a mere farce when the electing board feels no responsibility to any body but itself. Is a mock competition better than a fair election? The Slater *Sun* board says, yes, and is endeavoring to bring the student body to entertain the same opinion. The style of competition which they declare will bring out the best material is strikingly illustrated by their action at the present time. Last spring after they had broken away from the regularly elected SUN board the Slater party elected two new men to their board and announced the men as editors through the columns of the commencement SUN. These two men are well known to be parties to the private contract with Andrus & Church. At the present time these two men are, in the words of one of them, "temporarily suspended." This is the competition by which the Slater party are to bring out the highest journalistic ability.

—editorial, "Ahern Sun," October 10, 1893

Now that the time is close when one of the two Suns will drop below the horizon, it may be of interest to compare the work and appearance of the two sheets from a journalistic standpoint. A record has been kept of what is known in newspaper slang as "scoops," that is, news printed in our paper and not in the other. A brief résumé is all which can be given.

In the first issue this paper published exclusively an account of the anniversary program, fraternity house changes, Miss Marlow's return in the spring, Kappa Sigma's losses, and three columns on the season's football prospects. In the second number our contemporary failed to find out Commodore Hagerman's resignation, the arrangements for a new military band and a column and a half of news about the freshman class.

Our third issue contained six columns on the crew races, accompanied by portraits of the oarsmen, and on Monday we printed three-quarters of a column on football practice, the new heating station, changes in the Law School, a review of Johanson's book, and a number of short items. On Wednesday we gave a complete account of the new Sibley building, the doings of the botanical department, the graduate students' club and a half column of Barnes Hall notes.

On Thursday we covered the following news which our friends failed to get: the athletic club meeting, where our base ball players played this summer, junior law meeting, Canadian Club meeting, Cross Country Club run, intercollegiate tennis tournament, and physiological department notes. On Friday we printed a long letter from C.S. Francis on the crew situation, and the program of the anniversary exercises, and Monday's anniversary number covered the celebration in every detail.

Improvements over last year's sheet have been made in a typographical way, the new system of headlines, the exclusion of editorial opinion and advertising from news columns, the dropping of all italics from the "dress" of the paper, and uniformity of capitalization, punctuation and abbreviation have brought the SUN to a higher journalistic level.

And that the journalistic ability of the staff is recognized by the newspaper world, it may be of interest to give a list of papers for which the staff act as correspondents:—New York World, Philadelphia Press, Chicago Tribune, Omaha Bee, Philadephia Ledger, Chicago Record and News, Philadelphia Call, Boston Transcript, Minneapolis Tribune, and Buffalo Express. Furthermore it may be said that in accomplishing what has been done, it has not been necessary to call for assistance on members of the old SUN board, the foot-ball coach, or to have an old Era man act as editor-in-chief.

—news story, "Slater Sun," October 10, 1893

sion should be left to a special election, in which all connected with the University should have a vote. There was to be a mass meeting at which each faction was to present its case, to be followed by a referendum. The terms were agreed upon, set down in a memorandum, signed by all present and then we filed out into the night.

Throughout the days that followed, the two Suns were filled with editorials. There was a lining up of the friends of both sides and all of us and the college politicians who joined sides were busy day and night. Fraternities and boarding houses were visited and addressed; little groups on the campus and at the building entrances could be seen in excited discussion; even the faculty members were becoming partisans. The mass meeting heard orators chosen to represent the factions as well as Slater and Ahern personally. Slater had the advantage of being a fine speaker, but Ahern presented his case quite as vigorously and earnestly.

Then came the election day, only two weeks after both papers had begun publication. It might have been made a complete holiday, for few attended classes. There were long lines of voters. Freshmen and seniors stood in the same line. The faculty and the president himself deposited their ballots in the same boxes. Never was there such a percentage of the whole University represented in a campus vote. And when the votes were counted, the *Ahern Sun* had received an overwhelming majority. There was no doubt as to the verdict.

The *Slater Sun* issued its last paper and was no more. It was generally supposed that the adventure cost our fond fathers a painfully large sum, but the fact was that we paid our own bills and were short less than a hundred dollars. It made a great deal larger dent in our pride than in our pocket-books. I presume that I played fewer games of billiards and missed a few football games, and the others practiced similar economies, but the bills were not sent home.

The *Ahern Sun* became just *The Sun* before long. They com-

–Photo by Howes Gallery
CHARLES C. ROSEWATER '94
Editor-in-Chief of the 'Slater Sun'

pleted their board with some capable fellows and got out a most creditable paper; in fact, by reason of the stimulation of events, a better newspaper than their predecessors. Of course we felt that we could have done a far more capable job, but that may be attributed to our youthful conceit and the compliments of our friends. The smoke of battle cleared away, the football season was on, the campus assumed its normal peace and quiet and before long some enterprising sophomores tried to smoke out a freshman banquet with chlorine, with fatal results, and the little world on top of the hill completely forgot that there had been a time when two *Daily Suns* disrupted the serenity of the vicinity.

* * *

There was a valuable return for all the turmoil. The verdict showed plainly and unmistakably that Cornell University believed and will always believe in democracy. It wanted no autocratic domination in anything that belongs to Cornell. There was also a feeling, mistaken though it happened to be, that some men with a "better-than-thou" attitude were trying to put something over a member of the plain people, represented by John Ahern. John typified Cornell democracy, and the rights of that democracy were being abused.

It also had another significance. A newspaper is a quasi-public institution. The Sun had been founded and had been run as a private enterprise. As a private enterprise, the Slater faction were possibly within their rights, but the University had a different opinion. Regardless of history or any status, it held that *The Cornell Daily Sun* belongs to no group of men, but to the University as a whole. That was settled beyond any controversy or argument for all time on that autumn day at the ballot boxes on the Cornell campus. It wrote down in history that *The Cornell Daily Sun* belongs to Cornell University as its daily means of information, and expression of opinion. And that is as it should be.

—from A HALF-CENTURY AT CORNELL, 1930

The Sun in the Twenties:

Who Cares About Influence?

BY HARRY L. CASE '29

Looking back on The Sun's place at Cornell during the second half of the third decade of this century, I would have to say that it was not a very influential place—nowhere as influential or important as it might, many years later, be nice to think it was.

In fact, I do have one reference that I might cite, which reference merely serves to show that my opinion on this subject was the same then as it is now. In my "Trite Notes on the Contemporary Cornellian," one of the essays in *A Half-Century at Cornell*, I wrote as follows: "No one would be so bold as to say that The Sun enjoys much influence on the Cornell campus; nor would anyone venture that Sun editors care a damn whether it does or not." Of course, that is the kind of statement that can be neither proved nor disproved, in the absence of surveys or polls or computers, none of which were in use in those days. However, I think that few if any of us working for The Sun were there because we had causes that we wanted to espouse. We were there because we were reasonably literate, we liked to write, and in some cases at least, were being pressed by the brothers to satisfy the House's "obligations to the Hill." I suppose that anyone who likes to write likes to see his stuff in print. I am not speaking about the men

on the business side of the paper; I didn't then and wouldn't now speculate on what motivated them. Whatever it was, some very competent men worked on advertising and circulation, and The Sun was a paying proposition in its small way.

Young people then didn't get stirred up about causes as they do now. True, women in some ways were definitely subordinated on the Cornell campus. Thus although The Sun had a women's "representative" and a women's page, women were not considered a part of the staff; no women appear in the picture of the Sun staff in the 1929 *Cornellian*. The idea of a woman as editor-in-chief or business manager would have been preposterous. The more élite fraternities discouraged social association with coeds. And so on; but no women (or no men) so far as I know, were protesting.

Blacks? I don't think there was one black in the Class of 1929; if there was, he or she didn't appear in the class list in the *Cornellian*. No one apparently saw anything strange or wrong about this. There were of course poor and underprivileged people in the United States but they weren't our problem.

You might say that these evidences of discrimination and indifference were evils. There may or may not have been those who thought so, but they weren't writing editorials for *The Cornell Daily Sun*. Occasionally an editor might pick up a cause and work it over, as Jervis Langdon did with the General Strike in Britain in 1926. I can't remember whether Jerv was for it or against it, but whichever it was, it was at considerable length. We came out for Herbert Hoover over Alfred E. Smith in the fall of '28, on the grounds that Smith was too socialistic, or just socialistic—no difference. But there weren't any real issues in those days as far as we were concerned—or maybe I should say there weren't any that I have any recollection of. We got a paper out six days a week mainly because it was fun and exciting—much more fun and exciting than anything else going on up the Hill or down in the Valley.

Yes, The Sun was one of my true loves. Most of us had a strong attachment to our fraternities too, and to our "brothers." The letters of mine stood for, in Greek, "We believe in the divinity of friendship," and I think that, in a sense, we all did. We also, I think, loved Cornell. It was easy for me, as I was raised on the Cornell bottle "before we came here," my father having been a fervent Cornellian. Exactly what we meant by "Cornell" was probably a bit fuzzy—that indefinable something commonly referred to as The Hill, to which we belonged and to which we had our loyalties and our obligations.

Somewhere in the background was the academic part of the University: the professors, the examinations, the grades, and so on. As I look back these 50 years I am aware that the faculty in my college, arts and sciences—and I am quite sure this is true of other colleges—was a distinguished one. Probably the main thing I learned from this distinguished group, however, had little or nothing to do with the subjects that they "taught," but was my perception that men of this caliber could devote their lives to scholarly pursuits. Remember that in those days there was virtually no such thing as a male elementary or high school teacher, so that, unless we were the children of professors or preachers, we had had no exposure to this kind of man. Remember too that the University faculty was 100 percent male, except for the seven Home Economists.

I recall these professors, every one, with great respect, but except as just noted, I doubt that they "taught" me anything about the matters that they were supposedly teaching. I only can think of one exception: I learned something that has stayed with me in Prof. Slichter's course in labor relations, but Mr. Slichter rewarded this accomplishment by giving me an F. There may be a lesson here somewhere, but I don't know what it is.

It is perplexing that Rym Berry '04, who wrote a nice piece for *A Half-Century* entitled "The Primrose Path to Learning," thought that in the good old days at the turn of the century Cornellians didn't have to work very hard and so had time to think and muse and talk philosophy, whereas in 1930 they had to work like dogs to stay in school and had no time for such idle pursuits; yet the editor of *A Half-Century* put it down that "we can pass the faculty's indifferent examinations with a few

hours of concentration in February and June." The same editor, however, didn't think that we spent our leisure time the way Rym said they spent theirs, but rather in a maze of more or less formalized "activities."

The one thing that these two pundits of succeeding generations seem to have agreed on was that the formal part of undergraduate education wasn't as important as the other parts. However, my opinion on this latter has changed markedly. I now think that the formal part of education is a lot more important than the faculty or the administration seem to think, judging by the way they establish their priorities, and that some major reforms in undergraduate education are urgently needed if the American dream of the free citizen in a free society is not to go down the drain of massive impersonal institutions, including the institution of education itself.

It is really quite remarkable, when you come to think about it, how many different cultures thrived concurrently on top of this small Hill. The dominant undergraduate culture, the male fraternity culture, managed the sports, journalism, the big blow-outs such as Junior Week and various lesser events; had probably more than its proper influence on the morés and sartorial styles; and managed to keep very busy indeed, without wasting much time on studies or women or such distractions. There was also the coed culture, about which I know nothing or say nothing, except that it turned out some very fine women, as I learned *post facto*. Then there was the New York State College of Agriculture, with dominion over everything east of East Avenue except the Drill Hall and Bailey Hall and the sporting fields. There was the Jewish culture, with its own fraternities. There was the mini-culture of the foreign students, with their base in the Cosmopolitan Club. Some of the well-defined professionals, including the engineers and the architects, maintained a certain identity, though diluted by their fraternal and possibly other relationships with more articulate groups. And there were several hundred, maybe a couple of thousand, who inhabited the Hill as just students trying only to get a degree and possibly an education, whatever that was. Some of these—I have no idea how many—were persons of genuinely scholarly interests and would naturally develop relationships with the faculty on an intellectual and possibly to some extent a social basis.

Finally there was the "community of scholars," which is what a university is sometimes said to be. I don't think that they were really a community, in any meaningful sense. There were too many of them, and too many fields of specialization—though nothing, God knows, compared with the specialization that has since evolved. Even then, I believe, the historians talked mainly with the historians, the soil scientists with the soil scientists, and so on. But within their respective fields,

The Perils of Sun Politics: A Few Words of Thanks

The staff elections are generally the funniest part of the year to Sun people, at least to those who are not candidates. This annual seriocomic drama normally features things like egregious egos, smarmy sycophants, recondite resignations, and devastating dark horses.

We do not know whether the elections in Spring 1936 were particularly bitter, but we do know that in January the

outgoing editors of the Berry Patch ran an entirely blank column—that is, entirely blank except for a notation that this represented the work of those competing for their position.

So, in April, when the new editors of the Berry Patch were installed, one of them offered the following piece of poetry to his two predecessors, who had supervised his accession.

Thank you for your competition,
Gentlemen;
Thank you for my new position,
Gentlemen;
Thank you for the toil and pain,
Thank you for my wabbling brain,
Thank you, now that I'm insane,
Gentlemen.

Thank you for the fun I've had,
Gentlemen;
Slowly, surely, going mad,
Gentlemen;
Thanks for printing all my hooey;
Thanks for such remarks as, "Phooie!"
Thank you, now that I am screwy,
Gentlemen.

Thanks, although I can't expect,
Gentlemen;
That you'll reward a mind you've wrecked,
Gentlemen;
I don't expect that you'll bestir
Yourselves to murmur, "Thank *you*, sir."
Because, you see, you never were
Gentlemen.
—*berry patch, April 7, 1936*

and conceding some probable exceptions they were a distinguished collection of scholarly gentlemen, and gentlemanly scholars. Yet their culture was not ours, and ours not theirs. I think I was more or less typical; I had no personal relationship with any member of the faculty except in an extra-curricular capacity. One was a close friend of my father. Two others were fraternity brothers; and that sums it up. As editor of The Sun I had a few other contacts, of a more or less business nature, and occasionally did clink glasses with Morris Bishop in Book and Bowl. We didn't really appreciate Morris adequately, though.

In subsequent years I began to get a feeling of what these men, and what Cornell, stood for. I think Cornell has stood for critical, hard-headed thinking; for a sophisticated approach to the questions of what is true and what is false and what is unknown; for freedom and for responsibility; for loyalty to an ideal; and perhaps because Cornell is where it is, for a feeling of beauty. These things, however ill-understood

while we were there, probably have a lot to do with the affection most of us hold for Alma Mater.

This brings us back to the starting question: what influence did The Sun have at Cornell? Well, in my day The Sun belonged to only one of the several cultures I have been speaking of. For that culture it probably was something of a spokesman. To the extent that there was a common denominator of feeling for being a Cornellian, it probably played a role there too. It had, however, very little knowledge or interest in the other cultures. Perhaps it should have, but it didn't. But then, the University didn't interest itself either in the complexities of undergraduate cultures, nor their relations with faculty culture or cultures. So far as I can see, it doesn't now.

HARRY L. CASE '29 PH.D. '34, Sun editor-in-chief 1929-30, was editor of The Sun's 50th anniversary book, A *Half-Century at Cornell*. His interesting postgraduate career included 30 years with the Tennessee Valley Authority and 13 with the United Nations. He is author or editor of several books and plans another, *Commencement Address: A Talk to University Freshmen, and Other Heretical Essays in Education*, for 1981.

After Three Years of War, The Sun Resumes Publication

"The SUN resumes its place on the Cornell Horizon." That was the first sentence of the lead editorial in *The Cornell Daily Sun* on Friday morning, Oct. 11, 1946. Assertiveness with a touch of presumption, the inalienable right of all Sun editorial writers, was reaffirmed. The *Cornell Bulletin*, "Wartime Successor to *The Cornell Daily Sun*," was no more. The *Bulletin* served well for four years, keeping a weekly news and editorial vigil throughout World War II.

During the 1945-46 University year, the stragglers returned from the armed services. One by one old Sun hands clambered up the steep stairs to the former Sun offices over Atwater's Market on State Street. The musty smell and the old-fashioned stamped tier ceiling had not changed at all, but The Sun was not there. Some came to look and go on about their private concerns. Others were drawn in to help the *Bulletin*. Before long, there were plans for the second coming of The Sun.

Melba Levine '47 and Sara H. Beeler '47, editors of the *Bulletin*, were strong, capable and kindly to the stragglers, encouraging participation. Clearly, they knew their business. More than that, they too were ready for the Return of The Daily Sun.

A multitude of decisions had to be made, many by a patient and tolerant board of directors headed by Foster Coffin '12. He led a group of five local citizens (some from Town and some from Gown) who gave The Sun its proper corporate identity, separate and apart from Cornell University, thereby providing the independence cherished by Sun editors, reporters and business managers from the beginning. Surely each of these Sun corporate board members must have opened "Ithaca's Only Morning Newspaper" each day with fear and trembling, wondering what friend or organization might be on the dissecting table now. But not once did a member of the board of directors do anything but support resumption of publication. The two big questions they asked were: "Can you publish *The Daily Sun* again?" and, "When do we start?"

The answer to the first question was a firm "yes." Total confidence, even in the face of insuperable odds, has always been a requirement for election to The Sun. In response to the second question, publication date was set for Registration Day, 1946. All that remained was to do it.

Sun and *Bulletin* staffers merged their talents. The first edition was 24 pages in the familiar tabloid format. The following day, it was 20 pages and then down to 16, and 12, as The Sun settled into the daily routine.

In the newsroom, the frenzy of unfamiliar activities

simmered down to a nightly boil. There was Associated Press copy to be edited, headline counts, layouts, must runs, late local sports, and the flurry of activities which command the attention of neophyte night editors.

In the editorial rooms, the great debates raged every afternoon. The editorial page deadline to the composing room was 6 p.m. It was never easy to settle the fate of the world in two hours. But we did it six days a week. The world was on its own on Sunday.

There was all the idealism of returning veterans made almost wise before their time, captives of hope, and inspired by the Charter of the United Nations. John Hersey's *Hiroshima* helped to shape editorial concerns for peace in the atomic age. Reports of the suicide death of Hermann Goering and the hanging of the convicted Nazi war criminals came in the fall of 1946, along with a national coal strike led by John L. Lewis. The veto had not yet become a pattern of behavior in the newly-formed United Nations Security Council. Hopes turned to fears later when Russian forces crushed Czechoslovakia's efforts to return to the ways of Jan Masaryk. Eduard Benes plunged to his death from an open window in Prague.

The pace was exhilarating on campus and away. The Red Sox lost to the Cardinals in the seventh game of the World Series not long after President Day welcomed Cornell's largest entering class to a university that now numbered 9,000 students. Compets for The Sun came out in droves. Circulation continued to grow and advertisements swelled the pages. More coeds joined the Sun staff than ever before, some to change the editorial policy, others to beat the curfew, and all to breathe more life into the happy enterprise.

Two years later The Sun was solidly reëstablished as a town and campus institution. Senior editors and managers cut the annual cash melon in larger slices than ever before. Staff members had mastered the night editorship in sufficient numbers to assure only one assignment at the desk every two weeks. Wendell Kent '49 and his colleagues had made the business side hum with activity. The rough edges were worn smooth, and The Sun rose brightly every morning.

There was more to be learned in those dusty cluttered offices over Atwater's Market than in many an 8 o'clock class, judging from the number we cut. It was no microcosm of life, but life itself.

—Harold Raynolds Jr. '48
editor-in-chief, 1946-47 and 1947-48

TOP TO BOTTOM: *An Extra Edition of Sunday, December 7, 1941 (one of only a handful of Suns in which the normal front and back pages were combined into a single broadsheet Page One); a "regular" issue of Tuesday, November 22, 1949 (prior to a Thanksgiving Day football game with Pennsylvania); and an Extra Edition of Saturday, November 23, 1963.*

The Sun in the Forties:

A Renaissance of Righteousness

By John Marcham '50

The Sun staff for which I competed in the fall of 1947 reflected changes wrought on the campus by World War II. Women, who dominated extracurricular activities during wartime, did not fall away, but went on after "VE" and "VJ" days to compete for top jobs that had not been open to them before the war. Non-fraternity men, too, had improved chances of becoming Big Men on Campus. The Sun news staff, in the past limited in numbers, grew and grew as part of a general democratization of campus activities.

We were told The Sun of our years set some records: Harold (Ron) Raynolds '48 became the paper's first editor-in-chief to serve two terms, Eve Weinschenker '50 the first woman associate editor, and I the first non-fraternity editor-in-chief (though at least the third faculty son and fourth Ithacan in the job).

Whether our firsts were really firsts or not, we thought The Sun of our time was pretty hot stuff. At least part of the campus agreed. In a rating system used in the late 1940s to determine which fraternity was most active in extracurricular activities, being captain of football or editor-in-chief of The Sun garnered the most BMOC points. (That was before women had a chance at either position.) The Sun drew from the best fraternities and sororities on the Hill, from Telluride, and included National Scholars and junior Phi Betes, pre-meds and pre-laws

in considerable numbers. Board members were bright, attractive, and sociable. The staff partied together on occasion, dated, and sometimes even married.

The Sun reflected a campus swept by conflicting currents during the late 1940s. From one side a student Spirits and Traditions Committee strove mightily to get returning veterans and other individualistic types to wear frosh beanies and adopt other practices that had gone out with the arrival of service cadets during World War II. On another, liberal veterans lobbied against a New York State bonus for veterans so effectively that Tompkins County was the one county to vote "no" when the matter came to referendum. Leftist students worked in the '48 election for Henry Wallace, Progressive Party candidate for president. A Marxist Discussion Group met openly and a scattering of students joined the Communist Party covertly. Alumni were upset, particularly by the radicalism of students in the I&LR school.

Our editorial page was sympathetic to the Soviet Union until the Soviets crushed Czech independence efforts in 1948 (a compositor at The Journal refused to set a piece for our editorial page one night because of its pro-Communism). One year's Sun board blasted both the athletic department for its football ticket policy, and the University administration for plans to build a home for the I&LR school on Hoy Field. The Sun joined forces with athletic team

managers, players, and the honoraries to lobby the Board of Trustees on the Hoy issue. (Three of us on The Sun and one on the *Cornellian* had fathers on the Board of Trustees, which didn't hurt our cause.)

Next year The Sun went after discriminatory membership clauses in fraternity and sorority charters, which split our staff and made us many enemies among other students. We were so sure of our rightness that we asked editor-in-chief Howie Loomis '49, who was also vice president of the Interfraternity Council, to step aside as editor, but he didn't, and The Sun did not achieve any great changes that I can recall. The paper's righteousness brought it into direct and not surprising conflict with the *Cornell Widow*, a student humor magazine, which was defender of the status quo, the good life.

When The Sun spoke of minorities, chances are it was thinking of Jews rather than Negroes as the people primarily aggrieved. As far as its own staff was concerned, ag students were the minority. The upper-lower campus gulf was such that few aggies competed.

Twice The Sun went after student drinking practices—once when the early morning initiation party of the men's senior honoraries led some brothers into an arts classroom where they jostled an elderly professor teaching his class. The other was when a prospective member nearly died during a drinking club initiation. The Sun also got on its high horse

On Writing an Editorial About Christmas

BY JAY CUNNINGHAM '58

Dear Editor:

I am eight years old. Some of my little friends say there is no Santa Claus. Papa says "If you see it in The SUN *it's so." Please tell me the truth, is there a Santa Claus?*

Virginia O'Hanlon

Sixty years ago this pathetic little note was written to the editor of The New York Sun. Being preoccupied with other, more pressing even if less vital world crises, the editor assigned one of his subordinates to the task of taking a stand on the young reader's plea.

The article which this man wrote was printed September 21, 1897, and has emerged as perhaps the most popular editorial in U.S. newspaper history. It is known as the "Yes, Virginia, there *is* a Santa Claus" piece, and it ends with a stirring tribute which stands as a final slam at all scoffers, past present and future: "No Santa Claus! Thank God, he lives, and he lives forever. A thousand years from now, Virginia, nay, ten times ten thousand years from now, he will continue to make glad the heart of childhood."

Another editorial writer for another SUN in another century recently sat down to the same task at his typewriter: what was his paper going to say about Santa Claus? This was a real toughie.

He looked out his window. All he could see was a line of cars jammed in a hopelessly snarled crazy-quilt of traffic. They inched forward fitfully, and many were honking raucously. They had all started out early to beat the vacation rush.

Nope, he said to himself. Not much out there that's like Santa Claus.

He didn't know what to say. Or rather he didn't dare say what he thought he knew: that there probably wasn't a Santa Claus except in kids' storybooks. But you can't say *that* on the editorial page.

He glanced over at his shelf of reference books. He knew them all, chapter and verse: no help there. The complete cynic would say flatly, "Of course there's no Santa. He's absurd."

The skeptic would say, "Well, what if there were?"

The fearful pulpit-pounder would ask, "What (Heavens!) if there *weren't?*"

The curmudgeon would say, "There is if you believe in him, which depends, if you're over 14, on whether you've ever seen him or not."

And the moralist (logical soul) would end up with, "Well, even if there weren't a Santa, somebody would always come up with some other symbol. All relative to the place and the times, you know."

Books! Always trying to dispel myths. Newspapers! Always trying to foster myths. Why couldn't somebody just say, "Yes, dammit! Virginia, there *is* a Santa Claus. Now go and play and wait until Christmas morning and then look in your stocking! What more proof do you need?" Why do we always have to have this ceaseless YMCA platitudinizing about the Spirit of Christmas, and dear old St. Nick (jolly bowl of jelly) and all that stuff!

Santa Claus...What is he? the editorial writer pondered. Then he began to pound away at his typewriter.

Man, myth, or monstrous hoax perpetrated by Macy's and Gimbel's? A huckster genius with thousands of little guerrillas in red and white suits ringing bells? An annual opiate-of-the-people drummer, who comes around once a year to sell people on the idea that it is a good thing for everyone to be a good guy to everyone else for at least 10 days out of every 365?

Or even worse, a giant façade erected by the scribes of Madison Avenue and the pharisees of big business to tinsel over the profitable facts of Yuletide life? Who could say? It seemed on the surface, when he looked out his window, to be an ecstatic carnival tinted with a kind of green—the folding kind.

But he couldn't just leave it at that. You've got to decide about Santa Claus. Is he, or isn't he? The writer asked himself.

He didn't want to dispel any myths. But he couldn't just say yes, either.

He wanted to say something about the people who wish for a white Christmas and then drive their cars through the snow and mess it up; or the people who write Christmas cards only to those who sent them one last year. Or the people who spend money on gifts in accordance with the social status of the receiver. Or the old guys in department store Santa Claus suits who get kids' candy stuck in their false beards while they're trying to cajole the little monsters into selling some toys to their parents. Or the thousands of feet of evergreen timber lost each December for Christmas trees in lobbies and such, where no one lives. Or the carolers who wake you up Christmas night with 40 choruses of "The 12 Days of Christmas." Or the holly wreaths which writhe on mantles and doors and look so unnatural. Or the mistletoe against which girls since the time of Dickens have developed an instinctive radar warning system.

No, I guess you can't really call Santa a gift-wrapped hidden persuader. After all, unlike pajamas or a used car, you can't exchange him. Strip him of his collection pot and his chrome-plated sleigh and his toybags and he has no cash value. He's reduced to feelings and light and the currency not of dollars but of sensitivity.

He is a symbol, all right, a symbol not of the publican charity of those who give but the samaritan charity of those who share. As long as there is a Santa Claus—and because there is—men and children can say, "God Bless us every one—even the Santa-scoffers." The editorial was done.

And if you read it in The SUN, it will be so—not *because* you read it in The SUN, or anywhere, but *in spite of* the reading or writing or telecasting or selling or milksopping of Christmas cheer by those who dwell only in Westinghouses.

—berry patch, December 19, 1957

—Sun Photo by David S. Brown

'LULLAY, MY LIKING, MY DEAR SON, MY SWEETING': *Christmas lights bedeck downtown Ithaca near the Sun office in photographs taken before and after a section of State Street was transformed into the Commons mall in 1975.*

about the availability of stolen final exams one year. All this preaching was too much for The Widow, which in 1949-50 presented a series of "Green Banana" awards for those it thought were oppressive influences on campus. The Sun earned one and I another as editor.

The Widow and Sun agreed on at least one *cause célèbre*, however. When the proctor walked into the Collegetown apartment of a male student and found a coed with him, both were thrown out of school, and The Widow and Sun joined to attack the University for its Victorianism.

Organization of the newspaper at the time was similar to that of today, with separate business and news boards, and the news board had separate subgroups for sports, editorial, women's news, features, and photography.

The boards admitted new members three times a year, at the end of competitions. I tried out for the news board as both a news writer and sports writer, covering frosh football and basketball, doing the required desk work and building up "inches" of clippings—articles and headlines—pasted into my compet book, a spiral scrapbook that was turned in for a measurement at the end of the competition.

I literally stumbled onto my biggest story, walking across the baseball field toward Schoellkopf one day and tripping over surveyors' stakes in the infield. Thus began a great exposé and campaign to save Hoy Field. The land had been given by alumni "in perpetuity" for athletics, along with Upper and Lower Alumni Fields.

My father was a faculty trustee at the time. Years later I learned that President Edmund Ezra Day had accused me in a staff meeting at the time of using Dad's connection to get confidential information about the plans to build an I&LR building on Hoy Field. Ray Howes '24, then secretary of the University, defended me—saying he'd seen me gathering information on my own. In truth, the athletic department eagerly fed us the facts. President Day was roundly embarrassed before the state government, because the state had already approved the project. We won, though later generations of ill-housed I&LRies did not consider us their heroes.

This was the start of three lively years on The Sun for me. One's day began each weekday morning, checking a "must run" list posted by the managing or assistant managing editor in Goldwin Smith, near the south entrance to the central lecture room. Star staff members had beats—certain offices, clubs, or other student activities—and others took general assignment, lectures, and occasional interviews. The separate sports, women's, feature, and photo editors made their own assignments.

Miss Jessica Holland and Mrs. Helen Bell ran the business office downtown,

on the second floor above Atwater's grocery, part of the present home of The Sun. Upstairs was a studio for heavy-footed dancers. The editor and edit board had the next-to-last office, and the news board the far office off the hall. One summer three of us built a darkroom at the head of the stairs.

The business board delivered page layouts in early afternoon. The editor, associate, and managing editors arrived by 3 and the M.E. doled out press releases and other early copy, plus the pages, to the news board member who was that day's "night edit." The night edit arrived by 4:30 or so as I recall it. Two staff members were "assist" each night, so every three weeks you served as night edit once and assist twice.

Compets helped out with the endless rewriting that was a rule, and were given a chance at headline writing, as well. One byproduct of constant rewriting was what became an almost stereotyped way of starting a Sun story: "Speaking before a Bailey Hall audience . . . ," "Hoping to get back its winning touch . . . ," etcetera. We were *The Cornell Daily Gerund*. We had our own language, too. The noun "compet" was also a verb. Thus one "competted" for The Sun.

The sports editor of the day usually arrived after supper to assemble stories based on practice-session interviews with coaches. The days when women's or feature staff were allotted pages, they generally got their jobs done early. The editor-in-chief's editorial for the left-hand column, and the other edit page columns put together by the associate editor and edit board, were done by suppertime.

We went across the street to the Normandy Restaurant and ate triple decker sandwiches and milkshakes for supper. Reporters covering meetings and lectures turned up throughout the evening. AP copy was torn from the wire machine, culled, and rewritten. Compets ran copy and layouts down the street to *The Ithaca Journal* and returned with galley proofs of stories as the night wore on.

Most pages were closed by 11 or so. The night edit and a few hangers-on might go down to the Journal composing room to work out any problems fitting pages. By midevening, one of the top three or four editors was already on hand as proofreader, and stayed to close the edition. A "wet sheet" of each page of type was produced by placing a dampened sheet of paper across the inked form full of type, placing a wooden block on top of the paper and hammering it to transfer the ink to the paper. Thus did we read the contents of the paper one final time.

As jobs were completed, the staff gradually made its way up the Hill in groups, in cars owned by the more fortunate staff members, or by bus until buses stopped running for the night. Coeds had to be sure to get into their dorms before curfew. The last souls might head

down State Street at 1 or later to Les and Wes Diner for a Tullyburger and a shot at the pinball machines before finally starting home. (John Tully '46 himself, father of the burger, was still a student in '48.)

By my senior year, when I was editor-in-chief, I was putting in 70 hours of work a week on the paper. Some nights I got overnight parking tickets because I was still doing a school paper or whatever at 109 E. State as the sun rose. My studies were not done well: In order to earn an A.B. I had to pack an entire economics major of 30 hours into my senior year and from time to time still have the classic nightmare that Freud described, of appearing for an exam totally unprepared.

Our class on The Sun was quite large, and as a result we seniors divided the year's earnings many ways. One Sun man from the Class of '49 who was an active leftist was denied a share by his class, and we added him to the '50 distribution because we liked him, and one more person was not going to diminish our shares very much. The $300 share I got as editor hardly covered the cost of gas and milkshakes for three years, and was less than editors normally received. Even so, it was at least six times what I recall the non-editors received.

By way of a footnote, I was part of a short-lived tradition at The Sun. In 1951, I married the woman's editor of the year following mine, Jane Haskins '51; and in short order my successor as editor-in-chief Chad Graham '51 married Jane's successor as woman's editor, Alison Bliss '52. Though the pressure must have been intense to do the same, *their* successors did not follow suit.

I gained confidence gradually from the Sun experience. In high school I was too shy to serve in a color guard at school assemblies. By junior year in college I could get up before an audience in Bailey Hall to introduce a speaker. I got insights into the workings of elected bodies and institutions while serving on Student Council* and trying to move and shake Day Hall and the student body with my editorials that would later help me as a journalist and as an elected official.

By the spring of 1950, Ron Raynolds, editor my sophomore year, had done very well as a correspondent with *Life* magazine, and the editors asked him to recommend someone else from Cornell for their staff. Which is how I got my first job out of college at what was then the most glamorous working place for a journalist in all the world.

Thus did The Sun provide one townie with a great opening job, $300, a wife, and a career. An alumnus would be churlish to ask anything more of Alma Mater.

JOHN MARCHAM '50, Sun editor-in-chief 1949-50, is currently editor of the *Cornell Alumni News*.

*The Sun had not yet renounced the editor-in-chief's *ex officio* seat on Student Council.—Ed.

The Sun in the Sixties:
The Burden of Forming Opinions

By R.V. Denenberg '64

I owe a good deal to *The Cornell Daily Sun*. In its office I learned how to type ambidextrously and met my future wife. Both these experiences proved useful later on. But perhaps The Sun's most distinctive contribution to my ultimate well-being was to impress upon me the importance of having opinions.

If I did have opinions before taking on the task of writing daily editorials, they were casual, restricted to matters of intense personal interest (like the *je ne sais quois* of the Barf Bar's regimen*), and qualified by normal human doubt. The Sun's editors, however, had cultivated a long tradition of offering bold pronouncements, stiffened by Old Testament conviction, not only on campus controversies but on subjects far beyond the ken or care of the man with the bookbag. The editorial We was an awesome responsibility. Did We approve of the activities of the Syrian Ba'athists? India's policy toward Goa? Federal subsidies for sorghum farmers?

The burden of having so many opinions was made heavier by the necessity of having them by 6 p.m. each day, from Sunday to Thursday. (Opinions sometimes cropped up spontaneously on Fridays and Saturdays and could be stored for later use, but it always seemed like a waste.) At times not even an attitude had developed by late afternoon, engendering fears of an opinion famine. Many of the best opinions evolved during the stroll to the office; the steep angle of Buffalo Street offered a different perspective on the world.

The process of banishing doubt was also hindered by the knowledge that Peruvian peasant revolts or pollution of the ionosphere were hardly the talk of Olin Reading Room. It was, after all, still the pre-dawn hours of the Age of Aquarius, and consciousnesses of all sorts had not even been awakened, much less raised. "Environmentalism" would have been taken for a sociology course, and "Third World" for a club headquartered in Anabel Taylor Hall. The Vietnam conflict was still just a speck on the horizon. No one seemed to need opinions.

The first bona fide political demonstration that I witnessed at Cornell gave some indication of the state of awareness. A group of about a dozen marchers slowly circled the arts quad at lunchtime, carrying placards that denounced the killings of Patrice Lumumba in the Congo. The passersby stared uncomprehendingly, and an oblivious—or malicious—bell ringer in the library tower chimed "Old Black Joe."

Unosticising the Proofreader

The editorial in yesterday's Sun contained a line which commented on the editors of the *National Review*, who make a habit of returning from Spain "...imbued with the virtues of medieval Christianity and the evils of *unosticising*." Those who spent hours thumbing through their copy of Krafft-Ebing in order to find the definition of such an interesting-sounding derivation were not rewarded. For unosticising arose through a proofreader's error. The word used should have been *Gnosticism*—a good old-fashioned Christian heresy.

Normally the proofreader is a competent chap, but whenever he comes across words of historical significance he is knocked galley-west. Only last week on seeing the word *polis* he immediately rushed to change it to *police*.

So it has been resolved that teams of fanatical Dostoevskian monks will continually read chapters of R.R. Palmer to the proofreader until he understands.

—editorial, April 30, 1964

There were some stirrings of dissatisfaction and concern, however, about matters closer to home. The advance cadres of the sexual revolution had begun infiltrating the bastion of the old morality known as parietal hours. Women were not yet liberated; in fact, they were incarcerated. Like a regiment of Cinderellas, the female population disappeared at the stroke of midnight. The curfew was also irritating because it created traffic jams. In the few minutes before the bewitching hour, the Donlon-Dickson-Balch-Risley† complex resembled a bumper car arena.

The curfew finally fell under the hammerblows of editorial ridicule (including comments on a study group dubbed the Petting and Intercourse Commission). The Sun also contributed a spoof edition, announcing that Spring Weekend curfews had been abolished rather than just extended, as was customary. Spoof editions had always aimed for temporary deception, not permanent confusion. But this curfew story had been over-designed for credibility. The Sun's phones were flooded with calls from perplexed dormitory counselors, and Proctor George, the chief keeper of the peace, implied that we had seriously disturbed it and would be held responsible for any coeds missing at check-in time.

The Sun's faith in democracy was severely tried, though, when in the women's referendum on abolition of the curfew, more than a third of the voters cast ballots in favor of retention. Could it be possible, we asked, that people would actually vote to have themselves locked up? Lamenting the fear of freedom, a Sun editorial compared the complacency of many of the women with the contentment of a dairy herd, a reference that proved that even complacent persons could be moved to write nasty letters.

Fraternities also aroused strong feelings. It was the heroic era of the big houses, awash in good cheer and free beer. My first contribution to The Sun was a piece about the superficiality of freshmen rushing "smokers." I was threatened with ostracism, and it was predicted that I would lead a friendless existence until I graduated. But a growing number of non-joiners were braving the perils of unsociability because of conscientious objections to fraternities. The animal houses were the least of the problem; more fundamentally objectionable were the often discriminatory membership rules, written and unwritten, which invidiously divided the "community of scholars" along racial, ethnic and even geographical lines. The University Admissions Office's careful attempts to put together a stimulating diversity of students were defeated by, for example, a house full of nothing but Midwestern engineers of Slavic origin.

The Sun's trumpeting did not make the fraternal walls come tumbling down, but it probably did help change the climate of opinion. In the early 1960s fraternities were self-confident citadels of social exclusiveness; by the mid-1960s they defended their existence on no higher grounds than that they provided housing.

There were also painful moments. The Sun published an extra edition one Saturday to report the assassination of President Kennedy. Since the news arrived on Friday afternoon, the Sun office was empty. But instinctively the staff members gravitated to State Street. We could tell from the

---

*Barf Bar was the popular name for the snack bar formerly in the Baker dorms before Noyes Center was built —Ed.

†This was before the days of coed dormitories. These north campus residence halls were exclusively female—Ed.

Mr. Denenberg Says Good-bye

One of the sad duties that befalls every Sun editor is the task of saying good-bye to his readers. Due to the annual turnover of Sun editors, there is a "farewell edit" every year. The result is that almost everything that could possibly be said on such an occasion has already been said by one editor or another. Normally, then, these editorials are long on triteness, cliches and sentimentality and short on original thinking; a collection of Sun editors' farewell editorials would be a guaranteed cure for insomnia.

But out of this tenebrous group, one or two gems glisten, and one of them is by our present essayist: below, R.V. Denenberg's farewell editorial.

"The Sun also ariseth and goeth down" it is said in Ecclesiastes, and the cyclical rhythm is as characteristic of this publication as it is of the celestial orb. Once a year, every year the people who are The Sun give up their places to a new generation, as it were, of editors and managers. Nothing unusual perhaps for a college organization, but The Sun as a dispenser of opinion as well as a purveyor of news has a certain character. And with the regular change in staff there comes a change of character. And just as successive winters and summers differ, some milder, some harsher; some warmer, some cooler—the successive characters of The Sun, perceptibly or imperceptibly, differ from each other. When you pick up the paper Monday morning it will not be the same newspaper you are reading now.

And so these are some final thoughts, the fruits, bitter and sweet, of a year as professional observer and critic of the campus scene.

To begin with, perhaps the bitterest thing we have to say is that this campus cannot tolerate criticism. It prides itself on an openness of mind, on a liberality of spirit which exists nowhere but in the realm of the abstract—and there only precariously. We like to think we breed the man who can discuss and debate an issue with his sights set on truth and his energies devoted to discovering it. On moot points, on questions without actual consequence, the climate of discussion is salubrious. But let the discussion wander to some topic in which someone has a personal interest, whether it be his fraternity, his activity, or his politics, and suddenly a venom is injected into the controversy. Rather than give and take, we have attack and defense, and all the intellectual impurities, from vengeful personal animosity, to proud self-interest, begin to corrupt the quality of debate.

The pantheon of deadly sins assuredly is rife in the outside world, but according to the mythology of academe, it is not supposed to intrude into the scholastic cloisters. But somehow the same person who can quietly discuss The Fate of Western Civilization or the Good Life, altogether loses his equanimity when the discussion closes in upon his own life. The severest of intellectual challenges will not rouse him so much as the slightest hint that the committee he chairs is ineffective. The same reaction syndrome, on a larger scale, explains why the annual fraternity "debate" becomes a knock down-drag out bludgeon battle filled with vindictiveness, vituperation, and outright character assassination. After all the waters have been churned up, a layer of blue vitriol is all that is left floating on the top. If students react to criticism with all the blind passion of vested interest, how successfully have they been grounded in the intellectual virtue of the open mind? Arguing about Plato is no indication of the tolerant intellect; the things that hit close to home are the real acid tests.

The same is true in the realm of politics. Students come here with fixed ideas on the subject and leave with those same ideas, not because they have not been challenged. They are, but students would rather respond with name-calling than answer the arguments proffered by the other end of the spectrum. Indeed, few are those, at either end, who are in the habit of offering arguments; the great mass in the middle goes on blissfully apathetic, sure that its stock of epithets adequately sums up all political questions. Perhaps the basic reason for this conscientious abstention from political discussion is that politics is considered gauche—especially in comparison to such energy outlets as committee chairman or orientation counselor. Either of these occupations is the approved road to status and prestige, while there is nothing lower in the pecking order than a campus political leader.

Perhaps the underlying evil is precisely that—that this campus is so concerned with prestige and success. Students consider college a training ground for the struggle ahead. Here they practice the arts of social competition, and here they begin to acquire their taste for substantial symbols of success. College is the starting point of a career, and evidences of success look good in the wedding announcements.

* * *

If this is so, then the cause of this malaise is that Cornell is a supremely middle class institution, whose goals, values, and orientation reflect middle class attitudes. We must face the fact that we have this one pervasive, stifling atmosphere. And so before we begin to search our souls about intellectual environment, liberal arts versus multiversity, and so forth, let us first try to realize what it is that makes us all run. And then, when we stop running, perhaps we can liberate our minds from that mental framework which makes this university not a force in society but a thin shadow image of it.

—*editorial, March 20, 1964*

expressions on each other's faces that we wanted to put out an extra. As the edition was gotten together that evening and night, the bustle of activity in the newsroom belied the sense of numbness that everyone felt. I locked myself in the office and wrote an editorial which said that the Kennedys were the closest thing that the country had to a royal family and which urged that the search for the perpetrators not turn into hysteria.

Other sobering events were beginning to disturb the campus. The civil rights movement was gathering momentum in the South and provoking savage resistance. Segregated lunch counters, the poll tax and seats at the back of the bus seemed less tolerable to students of the early 60s than they had to students of previous generations. Cornell's most notable contribution to the movement was the Committee for Free and Fair Elections in Fayette County, Tennessee, which conducted voter registration activities among blacks in the summer of 1964. The student government voted a contribution to the group. By later standards, it was certainly a mild gesture of protest against the status quo, but the decision was challenged on the grounds that it brought "outside" politics into tranquil academia.

A referendum was held. The Sun, in a front page editorial, congratulated the student government for having "climbed out of the sandbox" and urged the voters to approve. The majority took that advice. The result was partly a tribute to the influence of The Sun, but it was also an indication that national political and social issues were beginning to impinge more seriously on the student mind.

Later in the decade, of course, there was no shortage of students ready to voice serious concern about national and international events. One was *expected* to form strong opinions. By then, of course, I was ready. I had had a whole year of practice.

R.V. DENENBERG '64, Sun editor-in-chief 1963-64, is now a free-lance author and journalist.

What Made The Sun Different in 1967

What made The Sun different from other campus groups was our fierce independence and the resulting paranoia it inspired: of the justifiable and not-so varieties.

Mostly, the fear turned out to be an all-too-appropriate response. The IFC was, as always, upset by the anti-fraternity line The Sun espoused, despite the fact that the eloquent series of articles by Al Sisitsky '64, who's now chairman of the Massachusetts State Senate judiciary committee, and R.V. (Dick) Denenberg '64, a superb editor-in-chief, later on *The New York Times*, resulted in more frosh pledging than ever. So, the fraternities started a rival weekly paper.

The University administration, too, found The Sun unwilling to run unretouched press releases, so they also decided to start a rival weekly paper. Being the administration that was doing this, the paper got off the ground about five years later, long after my graduation. I saw it the last time I visited Cornell. It reads like the company rag it is: boring.

Of course we were particularly panicky the night we put out our extra on how the district attorney tried to suppress the *Trojan Horse* lit mag as obscene. Any moment, we figured, squads of Ithaca cops and Tompkins County sheriff's deputies would come storming in like "gang-busters."

The most fun of working on The Sun was trying out something new, a different angle or two. Lots of stories had never been covered, it seemed.

For all the editorial sniping, the news pages had normally ignored fraternity hazing incidents, or soft-pedaled them. So when we front-paged a serious one, everyone (in that fraternity) screamed unfair. And our report on a house that never pledged a black disclosed that they weren't admitted to parties there, either. So the house took a full-page ad to run a two-faced reply. And when an underage girl was found in an animal house at 5 a.m. Sunday sans clothes on or teacup in hand, we ran that too. And we also noted administration grimaces—at us—for covering the news.

A recent glance through the 1966-67 volumes surprised me. Were we really that callow? And so recently? We couldn't even decide whether to use "Black" or "Negro" in headlines. Didn't we know there was a war on? We did, and we covered it in the same offhanded way that the rest of the press did. But with the campus antiwar movement at its peak, Cornell was one place where you were unlikely to forget the war's existence.

But many things haven't changed. William Sloane Coffin was a visiting preacher at Sage Chapel. Ronald Reagan won his first race for governor of California. The Campus Store asked, in an ad two weeks before exams, "Have you put off buying a text or two until later in the term?" Someone on the staff is explaining to someone else, as Phyllis Kaye '67, AME our year, did to me, what the difference is between the Faculty Council and the FCSA. The Straight still tries to restrict entry of canines.

And in some greasy spoon—in 1967 it was Obie's or Bud's or the State Diner or the Rosebud—a Sun M.E. is biting into a boburger at 5 or 6 a.m. after a press run, joined by some compet with a crazed glint in the eye: the sure sign of a future managing editor.

—Richard B. Hoffman '67
Managing Editor, 1966-67

—Sun Photo by Kirk A. Shinsky

Disgruntled Readers

To the Editor:

I observe that Cornell University has erected signs reading: ROAD CLOSED TO THRU TRUCK TRAFFIC. This is the end. I invite the English Department to lie down on East Avenue, before Day Hall. Perhaps tonite.

Morris Bishop '14
—letter, April 5, 1955

To the Editor:

I was going to write you one more letter reinforming you of my disgust with your unethical letters-to-the-editor policy, my disdain for your shoddy, shallow news coverage, and my contempt for your inept advertising board (among other complaints). But...

Four years of subscription to your yellow rag was too much! Save for those issues you failed to deliver, I shall burn all four volumes of The Sun in effigy on Commencement Day.

With great Scorn and Animosity,
David R. Korn '73
—letter, May 4, 1973

Where The Sun Stands
(for the Moment)

During the trying days of the early 70s, it was sometimes difficult to figure out just what The Sun's editorial policy was. An irate professor sent a letter to the editor saying that The Sun's positions were incomprehensible and self-contradictory. He accused the editor of "Orwellian double-think," provoking the following clarification, if that's what you want to call it. It was titled *Laundry List*.

In order to clear up any confusion that may exist as to where The Sun stands, we present the following scorecard of our positions.

We are in favor of liberalized abortion laws. We are pleased by the abortion of Judge Carswell by the Senate. We endorse the lives of the three Apollo astronauts. We oppose the public-relations thinking that made manned moonflights necessary. We deplore firebombings and bomb scares as dangerous, and threatening to any rational political program. We also deplore the violence perpetrated on our inner city residents as being all too closely tied to a rational political program.

We like good food, we do not like fast food. We praise good architecture, we cannot praise defacements like the new Campus Store. We dislike guilt that is used as a denial of responsibility; we also dislike "responsibility" that is used as a denial of guilt. We are in favor of guilt when it serves to enrich an otherwise all-too-wholesome relationship.

We are against compulsory ROTC, we are against a draft that makes non-compulsory ROTC look like a reasonable alternative, we are against a policy that rescues a dying ROTC from deserved oblivion. We laud communication. We hold in disfavor "injunction," "complicity," or any other long word that makes one think of excrement.

We endorse the coming of spring. And we approve of the birds and flowers of the realm.

—editorial, April 15, 1970

Ithaca's Two Daily Newspapers

BY WILLIAM J. WATERS '27

The Cornell Daily Sun and *The Ithaca Journal* have had a long relationship—and will continue to do so, one must assume, until newspapers can be printed by laser beams on a desktop machine in the home or issue from a slot in the wall.

The Sun is now 100 years old—a glorious figure. The Journal is in its 165th year. They became newspaper cousins in 1900, when—and this may be stretching a point—The Sun took its printing to the press of *The Ithaca News*, which was later acquired by The Journal.

They are cousins today because The Journal owns the only newspaper web press in town—a Goss Urbanite offset press installed in 1964.

The Sun started life as a daily; The Journal was a weekly until 1871, when it was renamed *The Ithaca Daily Journal*.

Commercial firms did the printing at several stages of The Sun's early life. The first was Andrus & Church, then Gregory & Apgar, and, after the interlude at The News, Atkinson & Mitchell. By 1912 The Sun's offices were located in The Journal Building, and The Sun's printing was moved to the Cayuga Press, which was described in The Sun's 50th anniversary edition as "the printing plant of *The Ithaca Daily Journal*."

There is also a reference in the anniversary edition to the printing being "returned to the cylindrical press owned by The Journal" in 1917. In that same year The Sun's offices were moved to 147 East State Street.

When this writer appeared on the Ithaca scene in 1923 as a Cornell freshman and became, in January 1926, The Journal's Cornell campus correspondent, The Sun was both composed and printed in The Journal plant. This arrangement continued until the technological revolution of the 1960s and the development of the offset press.

The revolution extended to the composing room. The hot metal method of setting type—slugs of a lead alloy pro-

A Long-Running Production

The Sun's Composing Room Follies

The Sun's purchase of its own composition equipment in 1975 did not change its external appearance very much, although the financial impact soon meant that many more pages were printed in each issue. The advent of the new composing room did bring about some internal changes, however. Two former editors became full-time Sun employees to head the production staff when not editing and designing books. The presence of such talent in the composing room made the proofreader's job, traditionally one of the most important at The Sun, much less so. Today, new Sun staff members become proofreaders first, and editors thereafter; ten years ago, one would be a night editor before becoming a proofreader.

The ex-editors are supposed to keep their paws out of current editorial decisions, which they do with some exceptions. The Sun's joke issues now usually feature a hoax advertisement, prepared by the composing room, lampooning various editors. One year, when The Sun was torn apart by feuding between the student editors, the composing room took revenge by replacing the traditional staff list in the final issue of the year with *two* lists, one for each faction.

Occasionally, the full-time employees and the students squabble. It has been scientifically demonstrated that these fights are always the students' fault. But wars between the editorial and business staffs and the composing room have been standard practice throughout The Sun's history, as these comments from past editors indicate.

In reading over these tidbits, you should be aware that the modern "cold type" system at The Sun dates back only to the mid-1960s. Before that, the type was cast on linotype machines in hot lead. This accounts for some of the arcane terms; "hell box," for example, is where they threw the used type to be melted down for future use.

The Reign of an Absolute Monarch

Having been an Ithacan from age four, I was on at least not totally unfamiliar turf when I ran "copy" from the Sun newsroom to the composing room of *The Ithaca Journal-News* my first night as a compet. In fact, all the printers knew who I was, and I was to learn that to be in their good graces (just, as later, on a "real-life newspaper" to exhibit proper respect and modesty toward photographers) was to earn valuable help. The composing room foreman then for The Sun's nighttime use of the facilities, the absolute monarch, was John Ryan, later to become a movie-theater-chain co-owner and a few times Ithaca mayor. And John decided early I should have the advantage of being given a nickname, to make me known and give me distinction in comparison with other compets. I was dubbed "Flash," and ever since have profited/suffered with it (in junior and senior high school I had been The Journal's Boy Scout column editor, and for 45 years now have been unable to determine whether the metamorphosis from that to compet was a promotion or demotion in the eyes of John and associates).

* * *

Now, in those days anyway, The Sun paid so-many dollars for so-many pages of a printed paper each issue, and Foreman Ryan's duty was to his employer, *The Journal-News*, not to The Sun. And every Sun man (in those days women just wrote and edited their tidy little corner of news, never being on the main board of editors) went through the agony of the first fearsome assignment of being "night editor" and undergoing the persuasion of John that the senior editors would be overjoyed the next morning to see a full page of pictures. The truth was something entirely different, because a full page of pictures meant the mass use of metal printing—plates made from cardboard "mats" (patterns) that had been received in the mail from The Associated Press; and many a senior editor has suffered the first stirrings of an ulcer when, unfolding his Sun, he was faced by a full page of pictures (far less expensive to produce than having printers set a full page of news on Linotype machines), and the seniors knew that John Ryan had pressed his nefarious cost-cutting urging again on some unsuspecting sophomore—so once more would go forth the command, "Don't listen to Ryan about pictures!" until, shortly thereafter, John would work his mystical charms on another night editor.

—Fred Hillegas '38
editor-in-chief 1937-38

duced by Linotype machines—gave way to the photographic image, with letters, words, sentences, and paragraphs recorded on punched tape, then produced on negative film and positive paper by a computer.

In 1975 the composing room arrangement came to an end. The Sun bypassed The Journal's composing room by pasting up its own pages, which were sent directly to the camera in the press room and etched on offset press plates. That was the end of The Journal's composing room night shift.

Sun staffers will remember these night composing room foremen (with apologies to anyone who might be missed): Eugene Bradford, John Ryan (later a three-term mayor of Ithaca), Frank Carman, Ralph "Spatter" Willsey, Don Ostrander, Floyd Ferris, Harvey Royce, Jim Murphy, Dave Sprague, Fred Kruckow, and—at the obsequies in 1975—John Murray.

The Journal's press crew continues to serve The Sun at night and early morning. (Historical note: It took The Sun 20 years to become a true morning paper in 1900.)

The night press foremen were (this list is pretty much in chronological order starting in the 1920s) Bob Angell, Charley

—Sun Photo

MEET THE PRESS: 1968 Sun staff members show their affection for The Ithaca Journal's 1964-vintage Goss Urbanite web press. Although staffers' familiarity with The Journal's press room has lessened since The Sun set up its own composing room in 1975, it is still customary for editors to "stay up for the press run" after special issues have been "put to bed." This provides a perfect excuse for dispatching a cheese omelette at the all-night State Street Diner before witnessing huge, whirling rolls of paper being miraculously transformed by cylinders and blades into a trim procession of Ithaca's only morning newspapers.

The Man Who Ate Night Editors

When World War II came to a close and Sun veterans straggled back to Ithaca, a number of problems, mainly technical, stood in the way of publication.

Could the Ithaca Journal composing room and pressmen do the job? Without doubt! The well-known pre-war composing room foreman, Tig Ferris, was ready and willing. You could tell he longed for the opportunity to intimidate night editors again. His blood was up for terrorizing compets. But even with all of that, we knew he wanted to make The Sun shine again. He helped us all immeasurably to establish the discipline and get the paper out. With Tig presiding over the composing stones, all mechanical and technical problems were solved. There was the smell of printer's ink and hot lead, the sight and sound of Master Ferris' unerring aim firing strike after leaden strike at the Hell Box (O ye compets, stand back when Ferris fires); and, for the night editors, the ultimate joy when the cherished wet sheet of the front page was peeled from the type and laid out on the stone for final corrections.

—Harold Raynolds, Jr. '48
editor-in-chief 1946-47 and 1947-48

An Introduction to Proofreading

Proofreading at The Ithaca Journal was an extremely important job, reserved mainly for seniors. A newcomer was introduced, first, to "type lice" (looking at a stick of hot type, getting closer and closer trying to see the non-existent creatures, and then having one's nose pushed gently into the ink) and, second, to having his tie clipped with scissors, and, third, to having warm type scraps poured down the back of his leg by one of the compositors (who usually mentioned that he had to go to the bathroom shortly before).

And Ellen Shapiro, our managing editor, was for various offenses discreetly folded in half and gently placed butt down in a large waste bin with wheels on the bottom.

—Bob Beyers '53
editor-in-chief, 1952-53

The Foreman Does His Bit

Now that The Sun owns its own composing room, I hear there is little respect for deadlines. When we were composed at The Ithaca Journal midnight was the deadline or else. When I was managing editor, I had a fine sports editor and could usually give him enough space so that we never had problems. But some sports night editors had the annoying habit of going to an evening game and then coming back at 10 or 11 and sending down wire copy that had come over the Associated Press wire at 7 or 8. This infuriated The Journal's foreman, John Murray. He was the guy who decided how much overtime we were going to get. I promised him I'd stop the practice. I'd run white space, I vowed, if stories came down late. I ranted at the sports board. Somebody didn't listen.

A few days later, Murray called me and said he was running white space. I said fine, figuring the hole was four or five inches. I hung up, and the proofreader called, hysterical. "Come down and see what you have done," she said.

The hole was two holes—about 40 inches. I knew if I gave in we would get overtime for days whether we deserved it or not. As I gave the okay, Murray took out of the processor his contribution, in large letters: THIS SPACE RESERVED FOR SPORTS.

The next day, every two-bit intramural team on campus was calling saying if you have so much space how would you like to cover our team. Sports was never late again. But I wondered if I was right to air our dirty laundry in print.

—Cathy Panagoulias '75
managing editor, 1974-75

−Photo by Barrett Gallagher

HOT TYPE TO COLD: *Under a since-vanished procedure, a Sun staffer compares a galley proof sheet with a completed "truck" of lead type which an Ithaca Journal composing room employee has assembled into its final form, except for any necessary corrections the staffer might request. Sturdy eight-wheeled metal carts—the literal "trucks"—were necessary to move the heavy metal "pages" about. The revolutionary arrival of computerized photocomposition in the late 1960s—permitting pages to be composed with scissors, paper and adhesive wax—rendered this traditional process obsolete.*

Terwilliger, Ed Bergsten, Hank Anthony, Harry Banfield (formerly the day foreman and head pressman), Ed Drake, Bill Toth, Mike Van Orman, Dick Carlton (now The Journal's production manager), Terry Camilli, Gary Travis, and John Mikula, the present foreman.

Bob Angell's predecessor was Harry Clark. He later operated the Happy Hour Theater (motion pictures) in the old Cornell Library Building at Seneca and Tioga Streets (the University's first class was graduated there) and built the Temple Theater in the 100 block of East Seneca Street. Both sites are now bank drive-ins.

* * *

When The Sun first appeared on Sept. 16, 1880, its welcome was hardly tumultuous. Morris Bishop '14 wrote this in his history of the University: "The Cornell Sun, one of the first college daily newspapers, appeared on 16 September 1880, to the fury of the *Era.*"

The *Era*, Prof. Bishop explained, was "established by the secret societies. The name was chosen to indicate that with the founding of Cornell a new era, like the Elizabethan Era, had begun. Its early issues consisted largely of news of the campus, announcements and editorials, with fillers in the form of learned articles by faculty members, and the poetry which undergraduates produced in much greater volume than they do today."

The *Daily Journal's* notice of the birth of The Sun was laconic. On Sept. 16, 1880, it reported: "Cornell has now three publications—a quarterly, a weekly, and a daily, the latter having made its first appearance this morning."

Not even the name!

The weekly was the *Era*, the quarterly the *Cornell Review.* The *Review*, dubbed by Prof. Bishop "a pretentious, and worthy, literary magazine," lived from 1873 to 1886, when it became the *Cornell Magazine.* Fourteen years later the *Era* and the *Magazine* were merged. Meanwhile, the *Widow* first

appeared in October, 1894, and the *Cornell Alumni News* began publication in 1899.

* * *

There were other than purely mechanical relationships between The Sun and The Journal over the years. In the spring of 1882 Walter G. Smith '83 was elected The Sun's editor-in-chief. In the fall he resigned to join the staff of The Journal. He later became its associate editor.

Without a complete check of the list of Sun editors, it appears that only one editor-in-chief later became a news executive of The Journal. He is John Marcham '50, now editor of the *Cornell Alumni News* and for a time director of University relations. After stints with *Life* magazine and a weekly newspaper in Connecticut, he returned to Ithaca at the invitation of this writer and became The Journal's city editor. John's wife, Jane Haskins Marcham '51, also a former Sun editor, is now The Journal's City Hall reporter.

The Sun's editor-in-chief in 1926-27 was Jervis Langdon, Jr. '27. His son, Jervis Langdon III '59 (known in interoffice memos as JL3), was editor of The Journal in the late 1960s and early '70s. He is now managing editor of Gannett News Service in its Washington office.

In *A Half-Century at Cornell*, Robert Quick '29 wrote about a "difference of opinion, coupled with charges of political influence, which led to The Sun's losing her most famous graduate": Frank E. Gannett '98.

In 1896 Gannett, who later founded what is today this country's largest newspaper group, both in numbers and in total circulation, was reëlected to the Sun board over W. A. Ross '98.

To quote Quick again:

"In the same election the choice of W. D. Howell '97 as editor over C. D. Clinton '97 was contested. A committee was appointed to arbitrate on both these cases, and brought in the recommendation that the election of Howell should stand,

−Sun Photo by Liza Jones

WHERE'S JUNIOR? *Casper George and Fred Kruckow man a 1969 night shift in the old Ithaca Journal composing room after The Journal's conversion to cold type. George composed The Sun's ads, while Kruckow pasted up its news pages.*

but that Ross should replace Gannett. Gannett resigned as soon as he heard of the committee's decision."

Gannett then became campus correspondent of The Journal, at a salary of $6 per week. Later he edited the *Alumni News* and was managing editor and manager of *The Ithaca Daily News* before he bought, with a partner, what is now the *Elmira Star-Gazette*. That was in 1906. Six years later he acquired *The Ithaca Journal*. In 1919 he bought the paper he once managed, *The Ithaca Daily News*.

The two newspapers were merged into *The Ithaca Journal-News*. The old title, *The Ithaca Journal*, was restored in 1934.

Gannett wrote "Fifty Years of Progress in Journalism" for The Sun's 50th anniversary edition. He correctly forecast the coming of offset printing and photo-composition, with film replacing unwieldy metal type.

Three men who were connected in a curious numerical sequence worked for Frank E. Gannett on The Journal. Harry G. Stutz '07 became managing editor of The Journal in 1915

and editor and publisher in 1927. William E. Seely '17 worked for Stutz on The Journal as an undergraduate. As managing editor of the *Poughkeepsie Eagle-News* he advised this writer, William J. Waters '27, who was in 1922-23 the high school correspondent and later a summertime reporter for the *Eagle-News*, to attend Cornell. He did more than that. He wrote a letter of recommendation on my behalf to Stutz, and in 1926 I joined The Journal as Cornell campus correspondent. Twenty-eight years later I succeeded Stutz as editor of The Journal. Seely became editor and publisher of another Gannett newspaper, the *Mount Vernon Argus*.

One final note, just to show that I did have some tenuous connections with The Sun. I contributed some very light verse to the Berry Patch, edited by my first cousin, Theodore C. Kuhn '27, and my son, William F. Waters '54, was The Sun's sports editor in his senior year.

WILLIAM J. WATERS '27 *was for many years editor of* The Ithaca Journal.

After The Sun: A Choice of Lifestyles

The Sun is notorious in the newspaper industry for the high percentage of its graduates going on to be professional journalists. Sun people are also well represented in other professions: for example, every Sun managing editor in the '70s but one is now either a lawyer or has a job in journalism; the one exception is in business school.

During the counterculture days of the late '60s and early '70s, there was a stigma attached to working in the "establishment," and Cornell graduates had many fights with their consciences over what course in life to pursue. The following is a tale of two answers to the question; two members of the Class of '71 meeting again nine months after graduation. The author, who had been editor-in-chief of The Sun, represents the unshaven; his lunch companion, a former senior editor of The Sun, had become a reporter for the *Daily News*. Sun alumni will doubtless recognize Richard Warshauer.

And now, A *Visit to the Club*.

BY HOWARD A. RODMAN '71

"Why don't you meet me for lunch?" asks Bowtie. "At the Club."

"What club?" The Kid wants to ask, if possible without appearing gauche. But there is no way.

"Cornell Club, of course," says Bowtie.

The Kid arms for the occasion. On the morning of the expedition, he dons purple velvet bells—Levis are too subtle, he feels, might be mistaken for mere poverty instead of true scorn—, an uncoordinated deep blue shirt, brown jacket (well-tailored, but leather nonetheless), and a tie which clashes with all of the above. The Kid is a member of the Class of '71, attended school during the

troubled '60s. No cop-out activist he, no fair-weather freak gone straight upon graduation. I will not wear their double-knits! he says to the mirror, almost aloud.

The Cornell Club of New York is on 50th Street between Lex and Park, just a stone's throw from Hornblower, Weeks, Hemphill, Noyes. Corporateland, thinks The Kid. Artificial complex hydrocarbons, computer read-outs, Mies van der Rohe. A uniformed black man greets The Kid as he enters, directs him to a desk. The deskman inquires of his business.

"I'm supposed to meet a friend, a classmate, here. Upstairs. In the lounge." The Kid is surprised at the servility in his voice. The deskman, with no loss of aplomb, directs him to the stairwell. The Kid is disturbed. He fluffs his hair to make it look raunchier.

The Meeting

He meets Bowtie, who steers him to the dining room. The *maitre d'* greets Bowtie by first name. The—admit it—incongruous pair are given a fine window table, best in the house. Jesus, thinks The Kid. My own classmate, and he has pull at the Club.

The two have not seen each other since what Bowtie would probably refer to slyly as "undergraduate days." Bowtie, currently working as a reporter for a daily metropolitan newspaper, tells The Kid small anecdotes about police reportage. The Kid flounders. He counters with mumbled badinage about his, ahem, literary agent. What this really means is that The Kid's novel has been sitting on the desk of some honcho at Knopf for a long time now and The Kid is getting nervous, and his second novel is going well but goddam if he sees how he's ever going to finish it, and he works in a mailroom at a tall and broad women's fashion house part-time—$47.50 a week takehome—to support his care and feeding, and the Broadway Local is a bitch of a train to have to take during rush hours. None of which The Kid says, of course. But he wonders why he, with his pimp bellbottoms and his

gommint district shoes, should find himself so suddenly concerned with the keeping up of appearances. (Bowtie, his classmate, pulls down a solid Newspaper Guild salary, takes cabs, lives on the East Side and walks to work in good weather.)

Crisp Peas

The Kid orders an open-faced hot turkey sandwich on white; peas, cranberry sauce. Fancying himself the possessor of a keen nose for nuance, The Kid places a small bet with himself that the peas will be from a steam table, all mushy. He loses. They are surprisingly crisp. Those million-dollar club stomachs may be sensitive to anything spicier than HoJo fare but, The Kid concedes, they like crisp peas.

The Kid is getting apprehensive. His hair and *habille* are outrageous, yet not one of the businessmen seated at nearby tables parts with so much as a stare. The cigar which Bowtie proffers is lit, and found to be quite tasteful. There is no denying that the Club coffee beats, hands down, the instant crap he gulps in the mailroom to keep himself awake on the job after white nights of writing and not writing.

It hits The Kid all of a sudden: *we have come of age.* The City ain't C-Town. And it's hurting.

Then again, as the pair proceeds through the library, there is an old man sitting in an overstuffed chair. The old man has fallen asleep. He is even snoring audibly. Ashes from his cigar are on the brink of dribbling down his vest. The Kid thinks, "you gotta be putting me on," fails to suppress a chuckle, even laughing audibly. Bowtie discreetly leads him away from the stereotype but it is too late. The Kid is out the door with a grin. Out on the Streets. Where, he knows, he belongs.

The weather is unseasonably beautiful outside. Bowtie strolls back to his East Side bachelor pad, and The Kid hurries to work, where his boss, Mr. B., tells him how he feels about mailroom boys who take two hour lunches.

—*column, March 10, 1972*

INTERLUDE: Just for Fun

A Great American: Hugo N. Frye

BY WILLIAM C. BANTA '30

In the spring of 1930, while The Sun was marking its first half-century, Berry Patch editors* Lester A. Blumner '30 and Edward T. Horn '31 issued invitations to a memorial dinner at Ithaca. Their stated purpose was to commemorate the 150th birthday anniversary of one Hugo N. Frye of Elmira, a man described as "a pioneer Republican" and "a little-known patriot" who had organized his political party in his state.

On May 26, 1930, the Berry Patch celebration took place. Among those who sent messages of greeting and praise to the faithful Sun celebrants were U.S. Vice President Charles Curtis, Secretary of Labor James J. Davis, Congresswoman Ruth Pratt, Senator Joseph Grundy of Pennsylvania and Claudius H. Huston, Republican national chairman.

Next day the artful dodge was unmasked. In a page-one story, The Sun revealed to the world that "pioneer patriot" Frye was a flim-flam. Further, that Frye was none other than the Hugo N. Frye (You-go-and-fry) whose name was signed to many Berry Patch items carefully pasted into columns of copy in the State Theatre Building city room. In short, some of our leading politicians had been deflated, some unworthy shirts had been stuffed.

Overnight, The Sun's startling scoop became perhaps the most famous of its epoch for its sharp exposure of the foibles of politicians. It showed up their general proclivity to endorse or praise indiscriminately. Other news media applauded it as a timely act of public service, exposing the pomposity, demagoguery, false learning and lack of astuteness of prominent figures in civic life. Sun editors had rightly concluded that men in the high places of government know little and care less about those whom they are called upon to extol.

Press reaction to the Sun-created Republican founder was prompt and laudatory. First metropolitan daily to get the story was the New York World. It is likely that Prof. C.L. Durham '99, a memorial dinner guest with Democratic and journalistic flair, had wired an immediate report for the a.m. edition, May 27, 1930.

Our story had listed the dinner guests, in addition to Blumner and Horn, as R.J. Wallace '30 and E.R. Pope '31 (all Patch editors) and six professors: Julian P. Bretz, H.W. Briggs, Harry Caplan '16, G.A. Shipman, William Strunk '91 and Durham.

* * *

Later in the week, concerning the Frye endorsements, the New York Telegram commented: "Ask a statesman for anything from a package of garden seeds to a testimonial to the lineage of a Holstein heifer, and he will come through without a quibble, a whimper or a bat of an eye."

About this time I visited New York, looking for a post-graduation job amid the early distress signals of nation-wide economic depression. I stepped through open doors of interested employers who beamed at me and said: "So you were with the Cornell Sun, where they originated the Hugo N. Frye caper. Let's talk."

Labor Secretary Davis, "Puddler Jim," had offered the Berry Patch celebrants this message: "It is a pleasure to testify to the career of that sturdy patriot who first planted the ideals of our

—From The Cornell Widow

IS CHICKEN LITTLE A RELIABLE SOURCE? *This February 1949 cover of The Cornell Widow humor magazine roasts The Sun for its drive that year against discriminatory practices by Cornell fraternities. An "editorial" on an inside page, entitled "The Widow Statement on Blanket Discrimination," contained topic headings such as "Just what IS discrimination?" followed by the word "Blah" repeated 315 times.*

party in this region of the country. If he were living today he would be the first to rejoice in evidence everywhere present that our Government is still safe in the hands of the people."

But in the New York Herald Tribune (Republican) I read an editorial warning to "Puddler Jim": "He should be aware of college boys, or at least warn his hard-working secretaries against them. These imps are often expert at the cruel sport of making their elders look foolish."

The Democratically-inclined and since defunct World, however, was unsympathetic with Davis and his frailties. Editorially, it said: "Why did he feel it necessary to go through with this gratuitous piece of flummery? Simply, one imagines, because some politicians feel it necessary to go beyond the bounds of sensible decorum in everything they do: in their speeches, they laud causes that were explained to them only five minutes before they entered the hall; in their personal contacts, they claim acquaintances they never had; in their letters, they pretend admiration for 'sturdy patriots' they never even heard of...."

Meanwhile, the New York Evening World came out with forthright applause: "Cornell is to be congratulated on having added a new star to the galaxy of Republican heroes."

The New York Sun also congratulated the Cornell Sun editors, saying that they "did well to blow away the mists of antiquity that so often surround a national hero in the twilight of fable."

* * *

Press reports about the mythical Frye were read in a U.S. Senate session by Democrat Pat Harrison, who recognized the sound value of a name, causing it to be read as "You go and fry." Vice President Curtis in his high chair was reported to have grinned sheepishly, rubbing his hand over his red face. Congresswoman Pratt said: "I'll admit the joke was on me."

President Herbert Hoover had been among the uninvited. Nevertheless, the White House spokesman got into the act. He issued a denial of having been invited to wire Hoover's appreciation of the non-existent Frye. The statement pointed out that the President stood in no danger of biting at this kind of exploiters' bait as he had protected himself by an efficiency system involving a literary research secretary. (Blumner and Horn had foreseen this.)

How did the Patch editors avoid unsolicited communications and undesired requests for tickets to the memorial banquet? Blumner told me that they simply interchanged mailing addresses in Ithaca. This switch proved of considerable aid in putting the inquisitive and the undesirable off the track.

On campus, numerous students had been *au courant* with the caper before The Sun broke the news. In Prof. Martin Sampson's modern drama course, I sat with Blumner as he nearly broke up the session chuckling over Claudius Huston's attribution to Frye: "far-seeing vision... to discover the fundamental principles on which the future greatness of our country could only be founded."

Throughout, on campus and in the Sun city room, Blumner and Horn maintained low profiles. They mutually agreed to write or say nothing for personal exploitation. For a three-day spell they were constantly bombarded by a host of newspapermen and photographers from New York and elsewhere. Blumner suffered from the misspelling of his name in Time magazine. No photographs were obtained, however, until the Syracuse American canvassed White's and other Ithacan studios. This paper was the first to print pictures of the Berry Patch men.

*The Berry Patch was The Sun's humor column from 1917 until it died out gradually in the 50s.

Were Blumner and Horn disciplined by the University? No indeed. The *Ithaca Journal-News* slanted its news account by stating: "individual members of the faculty have questioned the good taste of the perpetrators." But I recall that several members of the faculty committee on student affairs had been consulted in advance about the expediency of the project and had assured Blumner and Horn that no committee censure would follow. The committee chairman placed the caper on his next meeting's agenda mainly as a matter of form.

During these days, Louis C. Boochever '12 was University director of public relations. After consultation with him, Horn and I (as retiring managing editor) closed the affair by dispatching to each gulled guest the following: "We regret that what was intended as a campus prank should have been given such wide publicity. We intended no disrespect to you, your office or the Republican party and sincerely apologize for any annoyance we may have caused. We appreciate your good sportsmanship."

*   *   *

Somewhat to Blumner's surprise, he landed an immediate summer job on a daily paper with Republican leanings. Later in New York, I encountered him frequently during his coverage of the Wall Street beat for the old International News Service.

Ed Horn, my fraternity brother, became a Lutheran clergyman and at last report is now in retirement.

While perusing a document on hoaxes during the economic depression of the 30s, I was attracted by a reference to "the famous case of Hugo N. Frye." This encouraged me to dramatize the caper in a three-act comedy entitled *Think of a Number*. In 1940, it was produced on stage by the Joe Jefferson Players of Ridgewood, N.J., and directed by my collaborator, the late Walter Wines (a non-Cornellian). Several characters in the play bore faint and disguised resemblances to Blumner, Horn, other Sun editors, compets, Livingston Farrand, Jessica Holland (Sun secretary) and Lew Boochever. One bit of stage action involved tossing a fully clothed dress mannequin through an open city-room window onto the pavement of what could have been State Street below.

In the audience at one performance was Ezra Stone, a Broadway and radio performer of the day. He was interested in a professional production to be retitled *Hugo N. Frye* and asked for some play-doctoring on the script. Meanwhile, the nation had entered World War II and all concerned in the enterprise were called up for military service. That ended Frye's stage career.

The success of the Hugo N. Frye affair lay in the Sun's editors' careful simulation of a familiar situation and in the recognition of its instant newsworthiness. The respondents to the bait acted rationally upon suggestions to which theirs were normal reactions for politicians. The fun-loving public enjoyed its biggest laugh since the "discovery" of the famed Cardiff Giant in 1889 and its subsequent imitation by Phineas T. Barnum.

Could such an event happen again? It's very likely. Let still another generation of politicians appear on the national scene and you could see a similar onthrust of willing testimonials. If it is said of a man that "he pulled a Hugo N. Frye," many persons still know what is meant.

For those who base their dabblings in greetings upon correct information, however, all could pass smoothly. Politicians ought to be wary of a flim-flam by Sun-style humorists like Les Blumner and Ed Horn. The fundamental precaution for a man in the limelight is to have on his office wall a small neatly framed plaque simply printed with the name: Hugo N. Frye.

WILLIAM C. BANTA '30, Sun managing editor 1929-30, is now a professional fundraiser for various worthy causes.

The Luminary . . .

By Joey Green '80

"What makes the Sun *so heavy today?" asked the lonesome boarder, as a copy of that poor but honest luminary dropped to the floor with a dull thud.*

"Oh, that's just the editorial," answered the Widow, "It's always that way."

—The Cornell Widow, 1895

Most editors of *The Cornell Daily Sun* would prefer that this esteemed bastion of college journalism be remembered as a permanent fixture of integrity in the annals of Cornell. Few are willing to admit that rivalries with The Sun have been as prevalent as the paper's typographical errors, and that meddling contemporaries have kept the paper's editors in their proper place through the years.

For The Sun's first 14 years, its most persistent rival was the *Cornell Era*, established by members of the secret societies in 1874 as the first weekly student paper. For a brief time, the *Cornell Times* appeared, but after questions regarding the manner for choosing editors were resolved in 1878, the *Times* folded. However, the selection process and the need for a daily newspaper gave birth to *The Cornell Daily Sun* on September 16, 1880. Contesting the *Era*'s supremacy was not an easy task, as shown by the *Era*'s "Editorial of Welcome" of September 20, 1880, which pointed out that the *Era* was "published by editors elected by their classmates to represent them and the University" while the motives of those on The Sun were primarily self-serving. The *Era* commented that while there was "no desire to injure the *Sun*," the *Era* would chastise it occasionally "if the editors thought it best." But The Sun proved to be a persistent rival and since a daily can always outdo a weekly news bulletin, The Sun slowly forced the *Era* into becoming a literary magazine.

On October 4, 1894, *The Cornell Widow* appeared as an illustrated bi-weekly. Instructor William Strunk proposed "The Widow" as the humor magazine's name, alluding to what was then known as the college widow or the girl who bowled over class after class of freshmen without really landing one. Strunk also proposed the slogan, "Freshmen come and seniors go, but I go on forever." Walter Wilder '96, in designing the masthead for the first issue, was in a more classical mood when he quoted Tennyson directly: "Men may come and men may go, but I go on forever." The widow, first drawn by Wilder as a Gibson girl, was a charming and fashionably dressed young woman who graced the cover of many issues, appeared among its pages, and made editorial comments throughout the years. And while The Widow told her readers in the first editorial "her only desire is that the meeting may afford them as much pleasure as she, herself derives from it," there was one task that had brought The Widow to campus and which always seemed unfinished—to make *The Cornell Daily Sun* a readable newspaper.

The animosity between The Widow and The Sun differed greatly from the bitter resentment between The Sun and the *Era*, since The Widow shared The Sun's contempt for the *Era* and a humorous bi-weekly posed little threat to a daily newspaper.

Two chaps were standing in front of the Ithaca. "Aw, I say," said one, breaking the silence. "I believe I forgot to tell you that I was elected to the Sun board last night."

The other seemed unmoved. "It might have been worse," he offered.

A moment's silence. Then the first one began again. "Pardon me,

A Century at Cornell

. . . and the Lady in Black

old chap, but I don't believe you heard what I said. I said I was elected to the Sun Board,—the Cornell Daily Sun, *you know?"*

"It might have been worse," this time a bit stolidly.

"Now really, you exasperate me, old fellow. I don't understand the significance of your reply. I tell you I was elected to the Sun Board and you reply 'It might have been worse!' What on earth do you mean?"

"Why, you boob, you might have been elected to the Era," called out the other as he jumped on a car.

—The Cornell Widow, *March 1913*

———————————◆———————————

Certainly, The Widow proved herself a persistently acid contemporary, and the two publications were forever taunting each other editorially. While The Widow would poke fun at The Sun's editorial self-righteousness, inaccurate news reports, and innumerable plagiaristic atrocities, provoking The Sun to fight back by panning her issues or debunking her irreverent editorial stance, the opposition served to keep each honest and never turned sour. The Sun had welcomed The Widow with open arms in an editorial on the Little Lady's

THE CORNELL WIDOW
*As Envisioned by A.T. Farrell '99
(the frame has been added)*

—From *The Cornell Widow*

arrival to campus on October 4, 1894.

"Our new contemporary, 'The Widow,' is on the carpet. She is just a bit giddy and carries herself in that don't-care fashion common to widows. Her nonchalance at once charms and astounds. She taps you gently beneath the chin or soundly boxes your ears with a familiarity that would be quite shocking, did you not remember that she is a widow. Sometimes, though, she seems to presume a bit on the privileges of her position, but then, she is only a new-comer and a new-comer at college is very liable to have peculiarities. All things considered, however, she seems to be quite charming and will no doubt be well received if she is a bit careful. Here's wishing her success."

The antagonism toward the *Era* was shared by nearly every publication on campus. When the *Cornell Alumni News* first appeared on April 5, 1889, as the alumni journal, there was a proposal to amalgamate the *Era* with the *Alumni News* under the name *Alumni Era*. An editorial in The Sun of April 21, 1899, shows clearly the status of Cornell publications at that

time and is descriptive of a movement to exclude the *Era* from their ranks. While The Sun was trying to force the *Era* out of the publishing field, the editors supported The Widow when she announced in 1896 that she would cease publication unless students gave their support through subscriptions and literary contributions. "Many have enjoyed the Widow at the book stores, or in their neighbor's rooms...but the college paper does not seem to enter their life, nor do these people seem to feel that they are called upon to offer it their support. The fact of the matter is, the college magazine is doing a work fully as great, though in a different line, as that of the team or the crew, and it deserves, in consequence, an equal support, both financially and in personal, active work."

Despite the support, The Widow would attack The Sun's editorial stance whenever the opportunity arose. At the turn of the century The Sun actually came out against cheering at baseball games on the grounds that such partisan displays afforded the home team an unfair advantage. The Little Lady went a step further and suggested that the baseball manager write to every team on the home schedule to ascertain "whether they prefer a grass or skinned diamond, where they would like the solar system to be stationed, and whether they are accustomed to a baby-blue, cerise, or London Smoke background."

When The Sun advertised for a proofreader later that year, The Widow congratulated the editors on their awakening and noted that she was aware of this crying need two months before. "Still, cheer up, old moss-back! 'Better late than never,' you know. Besides, this—in coincidence,—is all of a piece with your usual news-getting speed."

The Widow's incessant needling during those years most likely provoked The Sun to jump in on her contemporary for an editorial misjudgment. In her May 18, 1906 issue, The Widow named members of the Executive Committee of the Cornell Board of Trustees who were also directors of the Ithaca Street Railway Company, and asserted they had used their influence to place car tracks in an advantageous position in a recent decision by the full Board to allow the railway to operate an electric road along Central Avenue. After making an investigation into the accusation, The Sun asserted that The Widow's suspicions were "foolishly unfounded." The individuals named by The Widow had never been directors of the Ithaca Street Railway Company, nor had they ever held office or owned stocks or bonds in the company, and, as members of the Executive Committee, they never had charge of the questions regarding street railways. Additionally, their past voting records showed they opposed such a decision.

While The Sun believed The Widow's editorial and article to have been written in the best of faith, the paper chastised its misguided and unstudied attack. Noting that "satire and frivolity...may be directed to the most serious purposes," The Sun admonished, "serious matters do not belong in the columns of a comic paper, when levity and presumption take the place of true humor backed by sound argument."

Perhaps The Sun's editorial against The Widow provoked Widow editor Kenneth Roberts '08 to produce the Little Lady's first full-scale parody of The Sun for the 1906 Spring Day festivities. *The Cornell Deadly Sin* was purportedly written by Roberts in one night. Over the years, The Widow published at least seven full-length Sun parodies and several smaller parodies among the pages of the magazine. An accurate account of the full-scale parodies is difficult to assemble since a complete collection does not exist. Prior to the 1906 *Deadly Sin*, The Widow had published but one Sun parody in the magazine of May 1901. Entitled *The Cornell Daily Fun*, the two-page parody featured numerous typographical errors, corrections for the previous day's mistakes, and announcements that "today's mistakes will be corrected tomorrow."

Roberts started a tradition which was repeated for Spring Day 1909 in *The Cornell Daily Bun*. The four-page *Cornell Daily Shine* for Spring Day 1912 jibed at The Sun's annual tradition of giving page one coverage to the paper's annual banquet, and its self-indulgent coverage of its newly elected board of editors. *The Shine* lampooned The Sun's incorporation with the subtitle "Foundered 1880, Incapacitated 1911," and mocked The Sun's advertisements for campus events. The cover photo of the newly elected editors was replaced by a caricature of the new board captioned "As Modest As Ever," and the page one story on the annual banquet read: *"The Shine* held a banquet last night which was by far the best banquet any *Shine* editors were ever invited to. Only those who never said anything bad about *The Shine* were invited so the affair was very exclusive. The banquet proved conclusively

–Scrapbook of Richard Evett Bishop '09

ITHACA'S ONLY MOURNING NEWSPAPER: The Cornell Deadly Sin, *The Widow's first full-scale spoof edition of The Sun, is promoted on a covered wagon during the festivities of Spring Day, 1906.*

that *The Shine* is by far the best college daily by that name, as all the *Shine* editors that made speeches were strong for the paper."

The Cornell Nightly Bun, which appeared in the pages of the 1918 Widow as a one-page spoof is not worthy of comment, and the eight-page *Cornell Deadly Bun* for Spring Day 1919 and the eight-page *Cornell Wrongly Run* for Spring Day 1921 are filled with silly news stories that now are hopelessly dated.

During these years the editorial haranguing between the publications continued. Perhaps in the holiday spirit, The Sun of December 1906 condescended to admit that The Widow's Christmas issue had "an unusually attractive cover."

In October of 1907 The Widow commented on *The Cornell Daily Sun*'s circumlocutious editorials by calling the editors' attention to a new rotating barber pole. "The *Sun* can well afford to comment upon it because it is new," wrote The Widow. "The editorial writers may display their ability by telling us where the stripes go when it revolves. They may remonstrate with it for going around all the time. It is an unequaled oppportunity for their new linotype man to splash type. Go to it, *Sun.*"

The Sun recounted by throwing in a snide comment. When discussing why the paper had abandoned the tradition of reporting June crew results in the first issue in September, The Sun observed that when the decision was made, "The

Widow was forced to scratch off one of its seven stock jokes from the 'when-in-need' list over the editor's desk."

On many occasions the two organizations would band together. Every year The Sun would play *The Daily Princetonian* and The Widow would play *The Princeton Tiger* in baseball. On May 14, 1910, The Sun explained a double Princeton victory by stating that the Widow and Sun boards had agreed at a special joint meeting "to let the Princeton pen shovers win, in order that good feeling might be further promoted."

The Widow's attitude toward The Sun is perhaps best summarized in a Widow editorial of 1911 by the outgoing editorial board advising its successors to "spank The Sun when it gets seriously stricken with the sense of having the world on its shoulders." To that bit of advice the outgoing board of 1912 added that the Widow board should "put a tack on *The Sun's* seat. Stir it to the realization that besides being a remarkably good newsgetter, it has important editorial functions to perform here. Laud it when it comes out with flood stories rivaling the metropolitan dailies; but roast it when it wastes three days chasing the deadly question 'Should the Vassar girls go to the movies?' to its lair, meanwhile neglecting important issues."

The Widow's suitors followed the advice with great diligence. They spanked The Sun for harping on the topic of "Intellectual Languor" among arts students rather than going after important topics, and put a tack on its seat for trying to reconstruct society by editorially attacking the chimemaster for playing too much ragtime, which, according to The Sun, was not suited for the chimes. By October 1912, The Widow felt The Sun had vastly improved, and complained, "This isn't fair. What right has the *Sun* to step forth without a word of warning from the Camembert category and thus rob *The Widow* of one of her most loyal jokes? The new and up-to-date six–count 'em–column daily turned out now enables *The Widow*, as she sits down to her *déjeuner* to make this one of the happiest parts of her day. As she rambles through the *Sun*'s pages, reading 'everything that's fit to print' and maybe a Hygiene lecture or two besides, she is very proud of her contemporary. For the *Sun* to be a thriving, eight-page member of the Associated Press is some stunt, and a thing about which Cornellians may justly be a bit inflated. From *The Widow*'s point of view the only detrimental feature of this giant stride forward is that there are now only two standard, well-oiled University jokes left,–the gym tank and the *Era.*"

We have always, we believe, adopted a rather charitable policy toward the Sun. *To establish this fact uncontrovertibly, the* Widow *is now starting a fund to buy a nice new copy of the World Almanac and put it on the night editor's desk, where he can have it real handy. Of course nobody expects the* Sun *boys to have the same general fund of information that regular newspaper men are supposed to have; but at least you wouldn't expect them to refer to Princeton day after day in their headlines as the "Gold and Black;" you'd think they'd have learned in geography that the late emperor of China was one Kwangsu and not one Mr. K.W. Augsu. They don't label people "Karl William" in China. And also they might be expected to know that the person who is about to pay a young lady's bills is her fiancé and not her "finance" as the boy who wrote up the recent story about Miss Ethel Roosevelt seemed to have it.*

Despite the petty antics, The Sun stood by its contemporary when the Little Lady's suitors got backed into a corner in November 1913 with the "Temptation Number." The issue, while tame by today's standards, was considered exceptionally risqué in its time. Its cover depicted a Polynesian girl coquetting a professor. The Local Women's Christian Temperance Union and the Women's Federation of Clubs found the issue "highly subversive to the public morals" and sought to have it barred from the mails for such obviously off-color jokes as

> *He: I'll bet you are chicken. Aren't you now?*
> *She: Yes, I'm chicken all right, but I'm not scratching for you.*

and an easily misconstrued

> *She: Outside of a girl, what is the most beautiful thing?*
> *He: Her face.*

The Widow's editor, Austin Parker '14, was suspended for a semester, and the artistic editor, Archibald Johnson '14, was placed on probation. By today's standards it seems almost unforgivable that The Sun editorially said the Temptation features "placed the University in a bad light where it was circulated outside of Ithaca," and that "the number warranted a reprimand." But The Sun added, "it was the first offense, there had been no warning, and it was only a step in the wake of *Life* and *Judge* which, unfortunately, are becoming looser and looser every week. Those responsible for it deserved a reprimand, but they did not deserve the harsh punishment given them."

By now the *Era* had undergone several facelifts and despite its appearance as a muckraking magazine, it still received little attention from students on campus. When The Sun attacked the *Era* for not being able to publish more often than on a monthly basis and for lacking quality content, The Widow, calling herself the "real editorial authority on student affairs," chastised The Sun for trying to make a bigger splash than The Widow in this matter, and modestly advised The Sun to "keep your hands off of that little fellow, you *great big stiff.*"

A Widow editorial in February 1916 lambasted an editorial that had appeared in *The Cornell Daily Sun* entitled "Thoughts on Spring." The Widow was upset that "the editorial mentioned that spring was one of the four seasons of the year, and further, that it always had been, but gave absolutely no conclusive proof that it always would be, which is after all the important thing to consider, in our estimation. Had it not been for this doubt raised in our mind by the writer of the editorial, we should probably have proceeded as we always

                                    —From *The Cornell E-Rah*

NEATLY SO-ING IT ALL UP: *An advertisement of one of the oldest establishments in Ithaca reflects the rivalries between Cornell's leading publications. The ad appeared in The Cornell E-Rah, a 1912 spoof of the Era, a literary magazine which was the butt of ridicule from both The Sun and The Widow. Common animosity to the Era, however, did not prevent the latter two journals from incessantly debunking each other.*

have at this period of the year; purchasing a stock of low shoes while they were cheap (only $8.50); pawning our mackinaw, our roommate's galoshes, etc. With the possibility brought to our attention, of winter continuing or the introduction of some new season, we have neglected the above seasonal duties, have taken our flannels out of camphor and wrapped our summer unmentionables in the pages containing the stirring article. Thus does the press mould public opinion and affect actions. Never have we been so upset by an editorial in the 'Sun.'"

When The Sun opened competition to women in 1917, the Little Lady, "far from it for her to decry her own sex or cast aspersions upon her esteemed contemporary, had to have her little snicker," and predicted that opening competition to women would leave no men on the paper by 1935 and would result in a subsequent change into a fashion paper.

In 1918 The Widow congratulated The Sun on its recent addition of a humor column, the Berry Patch. "She has always considered *The Sun* one of the most amusing of publications, and is very glad that they too realize it, and are going to be frank about it," The Widow said. "Of course many people will confuse the Berry Patch with the Editorials but with a careful scrutiny this difficulty may be easily overcome, as the Patch is broken up into short paragraphs." From then on, The Widow criticized the humor in the column as being suspiciously like that of her own pages. In several issues, The Widow compiled lists of jokes and poems that had been reprinted verbatim in the Berry Patch with the issue and page numbers where they could be found in The Widow, *Variety* and *Reader's Digest.*

The enmity between the organizations eventually led to their annual baseball game. Both publications always threatened each other in advance with massacre in editorials, and each reported an overwhelming victory in articles after the games. On many occasions The Sun apparently failed to show up. In 1913, The Widow claimed that "The *Sun* aggregation could not muster up the necessary pep to produce a team worthy of even the lowly *Era*, and the game had to be called off. We have had our little daily bluffed out now for many years but never quite so badly as this. It is reported that when our challenge was received at their offices a meeting of the board was held to determine on some excuse that would allow them to decline to play and still not disgrace them in the eyes of the university." The Widow renewed her challenge for the next year.

"What, what shall we say to the *Sun* board?" taunted the Little Lady's suitors in June 1923. "Can words express our contempt, our scorn, our disdain toward an adversary which failed to put in an appearance at the annual baseball classic,

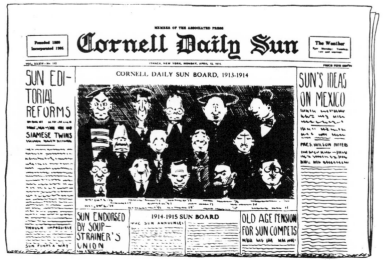

—From *The Cornell Widow*

'A TOTAL ECLIPSE OF THE SUN BY ITSELF'

A Challenge Accepted . . .
We Deign to Answer

—Scrapbook of James Irving Clark '12

On the bulletin board of the SUN office there reposed for a few brief moments the other day a dirty scrap of paper bearing a message poorly typed and evidently written by a seven-year-old child. It bore at the bottom the name of the Cornell Widow, but that such a puerile missive could have indeed been issued by even the lowliest of alleged humor magazines was beyond our comprehension. Further, the message was in black type, and it had been our belief that the Widow office harbored nothing but red ink and some old files of other magazines.

Thus this sleazy document, purporting to be a challenge from the Widow to the Sun to a baseball game on Spring Day, was ruthlessly stripped from the wall for marring the entrancing tidiness and artistic beauty of our offices. Soon, however, an anguished voice over the telephone informed us that the document was in reality the official missive of the Widow. All our illusions that the Widow still had a modicum of pride were rudely dashed. We saddened at the thought that our fair alma mater should harbor such a disreputable trollop.

On second thought, however, we realized that though Time cures all things and will shortly cure the Widow once and for all, there was nothing we could do immediately but condescend to answer the boorish brayings from Cornell's monthly. Herewith we set forth to an admiring world our manifesto.

Realizing the pitiable and unmitigated shortcomings of the Cornell Widow and especially their ludicrous athletic ineptitude and also aware of our own strength, intelligence, and grace abounding, We, the CORNELL DAILY SUN, do hereby so lower ourselves and divest us of that aristocratic fastidiousness that is our birthright to engage in actual tactile combat on the baseball field with those renegades of the Widow, feeling as we do that we shall be no more soiled than was the flower of Irish chivalry in disdainfully crushing the heathen Dane. The time shall be the morning of Spring Day. Details shall be arranged through some menial whom we shall delegate to meet the abject emissaries of the Widow's barbarian rabble.

—editorial, May 14, 1936

the Sun-Widow game on Spring Day? *The Widow* points a withering finger of scorn at such yellow-livered cowards. Such conduct cannot be laughed off, and brands them forever for what they are."

The Sun countered by printing a bogus score, a practice carried on through the magazine's history.

Simply without bounds is the joy of the Widow; *at last the* Sun *has condescended to notice her. She had been almost brazen in her attempts to get some attention from the great journal, Hearst's Boy Scout paper, which does at least one good deed every day. The Little Lady presents the following bit from the decisions of the Cornell Supreme Court—beg pardon, meant the editorial column of the Sun—without comment:*

"The repeated and increasing mention of The Sun *in the* Widow *this year opens these two Cornell publications to the charge, occasionally made against New York dramatic critics, of systematically puffing each other. We rejoice to be able to tell our readers that any such suspicions are, in this case, entirely without foundation."*

The Widow *regrets that she is a* Low-Brow *and a provincial up-starter, because in cases like this she is at a loss to know what is being said about her. For the best interpretation and proof of appropriateness, in less than six volumes, she will offer a spotless 1923 calendar. When the Big City Men start picking on her, the Little Lady feels so helpless, won't somebody please tell her what the Big Boys are saying about her?*
—The Cornell Widow, February 1924

"It has been several years since we have had a raincoat on in the rain," admitted Widow editors in 1935, befuddled over just where The Sun picked up its weather reports. "Do they hand out pieces of litmus paper?" asked the Little Lady. "Can these reports come from the same place the crossword puzzles evolve?...The whole thing is written in sort of a code. Just what this is has never been fully revealed....But it suffices to say that the key of the matter is the word opposite."

The Sun vented its wrath by attempting to perpetrate a prank against The Widow in December 1937. A Sun editor, laboring under the delusion that The Widow was scheduled to be published a week before its actual publication date, decided to steal the entire issue, which, he assumed was already printed and ready for circulation. Enlisting the aid of two cohorts, he invaded the plant of the Norton Printing Company under cover of darkness, searched the place high and low, but found no trace of The Widow. Disconcerted but undaunted, the conspirators decided that the magazine must already have been delivered to the Widow office. They started prowling around the rear of the Strand Theatre, hoping to find a mode of entry. They didn't find one, but they did find, much to their surprise, a policeman waiting with open arms. The Little Lady's suitors reported in the very issue the culprits had hoped to steal that "the long and short of the story is that the little adventure netted the police department a cool 150 bucks, and that we were no worse off on account of it. Will you pardon us while we stifle a grin?"

When The Widow published her "Contemporaries Number" in 1933, she parodied *The Cornell Daily Sun* along with every other Cornell publication. The Sun parody's headline, "Sun to Present Rare Opportunity to Underclassmen; Unusual Interest Aroused on Campus" mocked The Sun's habit of announcing its own editorial competitions in page one stories.

In January 1938 The Sun had developed a new tabloid format, and the Little Lady devoted an entire issue to mocking it. Not only was The Sun pirating jokes from The Widow to fill the Berry Patch, but the editors of the daily had stolen the idea for a Candid Camera feature, which had become one of The Widow's more popular features. The 1938 Sun parody was filled with typographical errors concluding each news story and serving as advertisements; headlines with senseless abbreviations; and juvenile prose and logic in the editorials.

In 1943, despite The Widow's fears that there was "some paper czar withholding our twenty glazed pages to aid in the manufacture of machine gun barrels," she continued publishing six months after *The Cornell Daily Sun*'s presses were brought to a halt.

When the weekly *Cornell Bulletin* replaced *The Cornell Daily Sun* during World War II, The Widow inserted a 16-page newsprint parody, the *Cornell Blotto*, in the March 1945 issue.

The annual baseball game tradition continued. In May 1937, when advertising the Sun-Widow baseball game, The Widow warned fans, "when throwing pop bottles at *Sun* players please be careful of spectators in front of you." During the 1940s, The Sun would print a letter in January challenging The Widow to a baseball game to be played in June, and from then on, "seventy-five percent of the paper would be devoted

to speculation as to how many runs The Widow would lose by, the other twenty-five percent being shared by Li'l Abner and a Swedish crossword puzzle. These immodest ravings would continue unabated until the day of the game, at which time," according to The Widow, "the *Sun* would be stricken with mass amnesia and go off to Watkins Glen for a beer party instead."

But games were occasionally played, and after the 1943 event, The Sun reported it had donated The Widow's blood to the Red Cross. In 1948, The Widow pointed out "a few minor discrepancies that appeared in the November 22 story on the annual Widow-THE CORNELL DAILY SUN game." The Widow alleged, "The game ended with the score 203-6, in favor of THE CORNELL DAILY SUN! THE CORNELL DAILY SUN's tally of 131-1, as it appeared in their article, is a gross injustice to the SUNMEN."

In 1949 the rivalry between the two publications became fierce as The Sun crusaded to end discrimination at frater-

...A Challenge Defended

✒ A Necessary, Though Irksome, Recapitulation ✒

WIDOW	423	861	Didn't bat these innings to let Sun catch up			1,027	2,361	Entrained for Olympic Games	43,682
SUN	o	o	o	o	o	o	O	O	O	O

—From The Cornell Widow, June 1938

There are, despite the triteness of the phrase, some people who never seem to learn. The wiser ones among us, we think, realize and admit when they are defeated; but, alas, there are always those who keep coming back for more. And, believe us, they usually get it.

The point of all this deep philosophy is this: once again the worthy gentlemen who publish a newspaper known as the CORNELL DAILY SUN (come, come now—surely you've heard of it) have signified their intention of engaging in mortal combat with the doughty forces of the WIDOW on Spring Day. And this despite the fact that never in history, despite the use of hired athletes, paid referees and umpires, and unethical methods of play, has the SUN been able to win. Let us, gentlemen of the SUN board, skim back through the well-thumbed pages of history, and attempt to gain some evidence of the disaster that will befall you on this memorable Saturday.

Here are written the records of innumerable baseball games, each one of which has resulted in an overwhelming victory for the WIDOW. Only twice, in fact, in all those games, has the SUN been able to score any runs at all. In one game, the Widow's first baseman dropped dead from a stroke of apoplexy in the middle of the seventh inning, and while he was being carried from the field the opposing team managed to sneak three runners across the plate. Another time, a SUN man, being chased by a pink elephant, ran around the bases so fast that he was not noticed. He was found a week later in Trumansburg almost sober. But despite this unfortunate occurrence, the score of that game was WIDOW-2543, SUN-1. Then there was the year that the Sun board hired the New York Yankees, who, masquerading as Sun men, took to the diamond against the Widow. By some sort of coincidence that was the same year that the Widow brang in the Detroit Tigers, so there was no difficulty after all.

Perhaps history will reveal also those wonderful crew races between the rival boards. There was the one in which the

Sun men sawed the bottom out of the Widow's shell, causing it to sink. Here, indeed, was a predicament, but it presented no problem to the expert navigators of the Widow board. When the shell sank, the crew merely picked it up and ran along the bottom of the lake carrying it, swimming up to the surface at the finish line, and winning the race by some 42 lengths. There was also the memorable year in which the Sun had its shell towed by a submarine, and the Widow discovering this vile plot at the last moment, had to enlist the services of a sea serpent to win the race. But the Little Lady in Black remained, as always, triumphant.

Gentlemen of the Sun board, the facts of history lie on the table before you. If there is any conclusion to be drawn from this, it seems to us that it is that the best team will always win, mind will always triumph over matter, and the right will

always be victorious. You know, gentlemen, that history repeats itself, and yet you apparently take no heed. Do not say, after it is all over, that you weren't warned. You are going into this with your eyes open.

Only one minor point remains. What will it be this year, gentlemen? Well, let us make a suggestion. Let us, for the sake of tradition, have a baseball game. It may be played with a football, a baseball, a basketball, a polo-mallet, or a set of dice, but it's still baseball. And the WIDOW, as always, will win. Eat, drink, and be merry, gentlemen, for the time is not far off when you will be ground into the dust of Upper Alumni Field, and your bones left there to serve as a warning to all future generations of Cornellians, a warning that the WIDOW is, has been, and will continue to be, the greatest of all Cornell publications.

—*from the* WIDOW, *May 20, 1936*

—Scrapbook of James Irving Clark '12

−From *The Cornell Widow*
'WHO ARE ALL THESE LITTLE PEOPLE?'
*This Widow cartoon of February 1949 ridicules The Sun for its
editorial campaign against fraternity discrimination.*

permission for sales in front of Willard Straight Hall only, but The Widow continued sales in front of Schoellkopf. Later, in a letter to The Sun, Widow editor Alan Brown '50 said the magazine was protesting against the official programs being oversized and over-priced, although *The Cornell Daily Sun* later scolded The Widow for having "flung itself into the middle of a grand and glorious crusade against the Athletic Association, with little regard for ethics, but a shrewd eye to public appeal." The Sun further criticized The Widow for "failure to go through the regular channels."

When the Christmas 1949 Widow was criticized as antireligious and not in keeping with any true concept of Christmas, The Sun editorially came to its defense: "If anything, we'd dig the widow for not being stronger in its condemnation of those merchants who quote Bible passages and exude joy in their breakneck run at the average Christmas buyer." That same month, the near death of a student during an initiation had caused the suspension of two drinking societies, Beth L'Amerd (Mummy) and Majura Nolanda. The Widow asserted that The Sun sensationalized the incident to force acting President de Kiewiet to suspend the two societies. The Little Lady crossed The Sun's editors off her list of suitors for a lack of judgment, since "news is responsibility, too." Since national coverage had culminated in a *Daily News* headline, "Cornell Student Quaffs Quart," general student opinion sided with The Widow. But the news had actually gone over the wire services before The Sun had come off the presses. Since the national coverage had tarnished Cornell's reputation, "In the meantime, the Little Old Lady will hide her head for the University, talking quickly and bravely in its defense when the occasion demands. And she will hope quietly, not fervently, to see the clubs, reformed, smiled on once again with good grace."

By the next fall the rivalry slipped back to tongue in cheek, although the Little Old Lady of that October could not excuse The Sun for removing the last source of international news from the paper which "might in any manner remind Cornellians that the battle for Democracy in the outside world is a long and hard one." *Bugs Bunny* had been substituted for *Terry and the Pirates* and The Widow viewed the change as "diametrically opposed to any informative, educational principles that might be held by an institution of this nature," since "Terry was the only indication given by our buckskin journalists that there *was* an outside world."

The heated rivalry had been cooled, and The Widow issued another full-scale parody of the daily, this time another *Cornell Deadly Sin*—"Ithaca's Only Morning Fishwrapper."

When The Widow issued her parody of *The New Yorker* in April 1951, even The Sun paid a grudging lower-case editorial compliment to the issue, calling it "as one of our beloved profs has surprisingly noted, one of the funniest we've seen since we were freshmen . . . a long step in the humorous direction."

The Sun began panning each issue of The Widow in facetious editorial exaggerations, labeling the campus humor magazine "another piece of subversive literature—worse than *The Daily Worker, The Communist Manifesto* or even *Mad Comics*" whose "innocuous title, *the widow* . . . belies its true social significance." The Sun described the Little Lady as "stressing revolution and overlooking our constitutional processes," and "fervently pray[ed] that mothers and children will refrain from reading the widow until the day of conversion" to seeing the light and abandoning the communist fold. "And to cap it off," read one Sun editorial, "the editor's unintelligible phonetic jokes are actually secret messages to a student communist spy ring."

In December 1954, when The Widow's suitors put together a special 60th anniversary issue, The Sun editorialized that "sixty years of effort have produced a good issue." The Sun commented, "When the presses whirred and groaned out the

nities, cheating on examinations and excessive drinking. The Widow stood up for the vices. Editorial fights swung back and forth between the publications. The Sun panned The Widow's issues monthly and referred to the magazine as the widow in editorials and news stories, while the Little Lady picked up her little axe and swatted noisily at The Sun's damfoolishness. The *Cornell Alumni News* reported to its readers that "Pickets appeared on State Street before the *Cornell Daily Sun* offices on February 22, 1949, to protest the paper's 'minimizing' The Widow by printing notices about it in agate type. Placards bore slogans such as 'Has Free Speech Left America?' and 'The *Sun* is Unfair to the Privileged Class!' The *Widow* picketers later paraded across the Quadrangle and through the Willard Straight Hall Ivy Room where morning coffee and bridge addicts paid scant attention."

The February 1949 Widow continued the feud with a cartoon cover picturing a red-faced Sun spokesman with soap box and megaphone, cranking a continuous stream of Suns from a hand-organ. The banner headline read "Chicken Little Asserts Sky is Falling." As self-righteous editorials on fraternity discrimination frequented The Sun's pages, the rivalry had become less friendly. In November 1949, The Widow, speaking for the debunkers, awarded the Green Banana to those people who had made the campus a miserable place to live. Among others, the award went to *The Cornell Daily Sun* "for its daring and courageous editorial assumption, and its intuitive stands on interesting issues," and to The Sun's editor, John Marcham '50, "because he had never seen a world situation, or a banana, except through a cage."

Perhaps the antagonism between the publications brought on by their disagreements led The Sun to come out against The Widow's parody of The Syracuse-Cornell football program in November 1949. The Un-OFFICIAL FOOTBALL PROGRAM, at 15 cents a copy, outsold the University-sponsored edition, much to the dismay of the Athletic Association. The Campus Patrol rounded up the Widow salesmen and stopped the sale of the program because The Widow failed to request permission from the University to solicit. Cornell later gave motto, 'Men may come and men may go, but I go on forever,' it hardly seemed possible that this forever would last more than a few months at the most. But since six decades have now passed without any definite signs of senility, we take this opportunity to demurely split an infinitive and tip our hats to the Little Old Lady. . . ."

By 1955 relations had been so well ironed out that The Sun came to The Widow's aid when her suitors found themselves backed into a corner by their questionable taste. Complaints about The Widow's 1955 Sorority Issue had been received from the Faculty Committee on Student Conduct, faculty members, and members of the administration. Robert Schermer '56 and Edward Berkowitz '56, co-editors of The Widow, and the magazine's managing editor, Peter Liebert '56, were given unofficial reprimands (attached to the student's permanent record but removed at graduation) from the Men's Judiciary Board. But the faculty committee objected more vigorously to the tone of the issue, and substituted the harsher penalty of official reprimands.

The next night, the Faculty Committee on Student Activities declined to take definitive action against The Widow, but issued a strong warning of serious penalties should a similar "offense" be repeated in the future. The committee threatened to deprive The Widow of its status as a recognized student organization, forbid publication of the magazine, or direct that it be disbanded if The Widow "again abused its privilege."

The Sun called the activities committee's resolution "adding insult to injury." The Sun wrote that "Although humor may be so grossly done as to be grotesque, and caricature so ponderous as to appear insulting, these remain ideally high forms of art, and misunderstanding of humor from time to time must be regarded as such and not as deliberately irresponsible malice." The Sun argued that "the difficulty with the activities committee's decision is that it acts as an axe held over the head of editors who learned whatever lesson there was to be learned simply from campus reaction," adding that the unofficial reprimands ". . . may conceivably have been in order, but certainly any stronger punishment of individuals or of organizations is patently unfair."

The Sun's support for its sister publication during the Sorority Issue incident provided the groundwork for a Sun prank against The Widow. In May 1955, Sun staffers, posing as Widow editors, walked out of the printshop with all the copies of the Spring Day Widow the night before it was to go on sale. In a secret hideaway, they pasted stickers on every cover which read, "This issue of the widow, a campus humor magazine, comes to you through the courtesy of *The Cornell Daily Sun*." Overstamped in red were the words *Quality Control*. The copies were left at the Clinton House for the surprised Widow staff to pick up and sell with the humiliating label. A Sun editorial warned purchasers to buy only the copies stamped *Quality Control*.

In the 50s the annual baseball tradition became a football tradition, and although The Widow had long been a victim of 108-0 defeats, according to reports in The Sun, the Little Lady wrested from The Sun the coveted Gallons-Imbibed Trophy in 1955. The reports of the games became more entertaining than the games themselves. In a page one story in 1959, The Sun reported that they had outwitted "a herd of wild oxen imported by their opponents," and that brain had triumphed over brawn for the 80th consecutive year, by a score of 109-0. According to The Sun, the oxen had been "ruled eligible for play when the widowcoach affirmed that the bulls had written the first two issues this year."

But as The Widow went into her sixth decade at Cornell, she began to lose her energy. The Sun helped out by mentioning that "a weak little old lady seeks assistance in rejuvenating her health and circulation" in an editorial. "Despite eighty

years of evidence to the contrary, we believe it is possible for Cornell to have a humor magazine," The Sun said, and urged students to compete for the magazine. When the Little Lady's suitors failed to spank The Sun for inaccurately aging The Widow by some 14 years, it became evident that she was never to reach that age.

In 1962, The Widow returned to the newsstands with a Winter Party issue. Financial woes had delayed the first issue of the school year, which promptly came under fire from The Sun for typographical sloppiness, and for not having writing on a par with its cartoons. The Widow had finally had it. Publication ceased in 1962. The Widow came back for a short time in 1965 only to die again.

When The Widow was temporarily resurrected in 1975 by a group of misdirected students more eager to pad their resumés than they were to bring humor to campus, the editors published a puerile but full-scale parody of The Sun—the only slightly amusing aspect being the title, *The Illegitimate Sun*, which reflected the nature of the editors more than it spoofed the paper.

After the scoundrels killed The Widow in 1975, leaving behind an odiferous trail of unpaid bills, withered alumni support, and skeptical advertisers, I came to campus with hopes of cleaning up after the bastards and reviving interest in campus humor. After much organizing and fundraising, the *Cornell Lunatic* was born, inheriting nothing from The Widow but a fresh start. And in the fall of 1978, amid the pages of the *Lunatic*, we presented an eight-page pull-out, *The Cornell Daily Scum*.

JOEY GREEN '80, a member of The Sun's editorial board while an undergraduate, was founder and editor of the *Cornell Lunatic*, The Widow's successor as campus humor magazine. He plans a career in humor, assuming he can stay out of jail.

LUNATIC'S DELIGHT: *The Widow's 1955 Sorority Issue, which featured unflattering suggestions as to the appearance and demeanor of typical members of the several houses, landed three editors before the Faculty Committee on Student Conduct, and The Widow itself before the Faculty Committee on Student Activities.*

Two-Timing, Three-Legged, Four-Flushed, Five-Ply Fakes: *On three occasions The Sun has concocted complete ersatz editions of rival college newspapers, and successfully substituted the fakes for the true papers on the victim's own turf. Perhaps the best two were the* Syracuse Daily Orange *of 1954 and the* Daily Princetonian *of 1965. Both pranks required scouting forays and meticulous, intricate planning.*

Having the Last Laugh

By Roberta Moudry '81

It is a crisp November morning. Indian summer has been kind to the trees, and patches of fall leaves still color the hills around Ithaca. It is a clear morning and the sun is warm — a good sign for Fall Weekend. But the freshmen of U-Hall 4 are in an uproar. Expecting to grab The Sun from the doorway while still clad in underwear, one sleepy freshman, hoping to catch Doonesbury, is faced with impending crisis — and before eight o'clock yet.

A banner headline has just sent our innocent and still groggy subject running to the hall bathroom to tell others that their U-Hall 10-by-12 foot doubles are to be converted into triples over Intersession, to accommodate 800 unexpected transfer students entering in January.

"Wait," another freshman blurts, pointing to a box in the bottom right hand corner of the front page. "We gotta get up to Barton Hall to get our new room assignments." The freshmen throw on their clothes and head for Barton, having forgotten to even glance at Doonesbury.

Meanwhile, somewhere in a dingy Collegetown apartment, a Sun editor leans out the front door in her bathrobe, squinting at the warm sun. Picking up her Sun, she trudges up the hallway stairs, perusing the front page of the year's joke issue. "This'll fool a couple, anyway," she mutters, heading for the shower. A cup of coffee and a shower are musts. Doonesbury will have to wait.

* * *

Sun joke issues have ushered in special weekends on campus for about 40 years. Recently, they have marked Fall and Spring Weekends. Before the mid-50s, however, issues chock-full of bogus news appeared on the February Junior Weekend, and Spring Weekend in early May.

Whatever the time, be it a special weekend or a random date, some joke — ranging from a believable hoax story to the outrageous *Cornell Inquirer* — has graced the front page. Surprise visits by the President of the United States, sex and drug scandals among administrators, the sale of the arts college to SUNY, and even the revelation that the *Cornell Chronicle* prints on human flesh have flashed across the news pages on fall Fridays.

The Sun's first joke issue, in 1909, told of President Taft's surprise visit to an agriculture college exhibit. Parodies of The Sun put out by *The Cornell Widow* were common at the time, but The Sun itself did not make a habit of printing hoax issues until the mid-30s.

One 30s hoax, *The Cornell Daily Sin* of 1937, had the crossword puzzle top center of Page One. It referred to the two rival senior honoraries, Sphinx Head and Quill and Dagger, as Drinks Fed and Swill and Stagger.

Amidst these frivolities, the editors urged students to compete for the Sun board, repeating no less than eight times that financial remuneration was indeed possible. This is regrettably more ludicrous today than 40-odd years ago. "Besides possible financial remuneration," the story droned, "the competition leads to positions of Editorial Director and Managing Editor with the accompanying prestige or what have you."

This appeal must have been successful, for The Sun continued its daily outpouring of news and editorials. In 1940,

A CENTURY AT CORNELL

another unusual sight greeted Cornellians — in place of The Sun, the *Cornell Daily Worker*, "Ithaca's Only Voice of the People." The *Worker* revealed that the House Un-American Activities Committee, having discovered subversive activities on the Cornell campus, had nabbed President Day as he returned from the Navy Ball, and whisked him off to Washington. Day was quoted as saying, "I've just been dancing to raise money for Cornell's ROTC Band. How could a foreign agent do that?"

This joke was very much a product of the times. Russia and Germany had just concluded a friendship pact, the Nazis had invaded Poland, and World War II, though for the present without the United States, had begun. The humor holds up well now, but later The Sun would come up with some joke issues that today seem not only hopelessly but disgustingly crass and tasteless. The Sun's hostility to the Women Students' Government Association led to one such joke in May 1950.

The front page story announced Cornell's secession from the United States, in a revolt sponsored by the WSGA and led by — are you ready — Adolf Hitler. The five-year-old Hitler mystery was solved as the "political and military genius" was found to have spent the last five years in Goldwin Smith Hall as an English teacher, The Sun reported.

The editors also directed what they doubtless thought were witticisms at the WSGA, which they felt was puritanical. They announced the WSGA had recommended turning the Main Library (now Uris) into a mass sterilization plant for frustrated males. The Sun suggested that the cavernous main reading room could best be used to accommodate the bleachers of Hoy Field, a reputed site for necking.

When joke issues began to appear with some regularity in the mid-50s, they were highly sensational, and filled with stories revolving around those things that played chief roles in fraternity weekends: sex, curfews, houseparty rules, and liquor. For example, the 1955 joke issue on Fall Weekend features a story on the University's Greek statue collection. It bears the title "Sin at C.U. — Find Naughty Art, Red Plots in Subterranean G-S Den" and the descriptive phrase "culturally sexational."

So entangled was the concept of a joke issue with a fraternity weekend that when Fall Weekend was cancelled in 1957, The Sun offered an obituary editorial for the missing weekend in lieu of a joke.

* * *

It was in the 50s, though, that Sun editors conceived of and executed a hoax that made national news. Like the Hugo N. Frye caper of 1930, a Sun prank that humiliated national political figures, this plot was neither part of a fraternity weekend nor aimed at Cornellians. In the fall of 1954, Sun editor-in-chief Dick Schaap '55, managing editor Philip Levine '55, and reporter Charles Bernstein '56 hit upon an exciting and mischievous plan — to spoof the *Syracuse Daily Orange*.

It is no easy task to be a student and produce a daily simultaneously. To mastermind a hoax edition of another paper at the same time verges on lunacy. But where there is a will a way cannot be far behind, and so a group of Sun people and senior honorary members hatched their plot in a new, ultra-exclusive, super-secret society with the mysterious initials IOSN.

The group, 21 in all, set about producing a fake *Daily Orange* to commemorate the end of the long-time football rivalry between the two schools, caused by the schedule of the newly formed Ivy League.

Schaap and Levine drove to Syracuse in mid-October to visit the *Orange*, whose editors were more than willing to show another college paper their set-up. The Sun folks returned to Ithaca with complete notes of schedules and procedures gleaned from the thorough and thoroughly enjoyable tour. Meanwhile, an inside conspirator plotted all delivery points

on a map for the visiting editors.

A week later, the editors returned to Syracuse — this time in the early hours of the morning. Crawling through wet grass at 3 a.m. and peering through windows, the editors took notes on the pressmen's activities and delivery schedules. Perhaps they felt a bit like spies in the movies.

In any case, the plan began to crumble. As the semester's work began to pile up, IOSN enthusiasm faded like a summer tan. Schaap headed for New York City to cover the Cornell-Columbia game and the scheme became just another unemployed great idea. Until Schaap received a telegram in New York. Levine had found a printer who could create an exact typographical copy (none in Ithaca or Dryden could do it). With demonic will, the fictitious edition was churned out, and on Thursday, November 5, 6,500 copies rolled off the press of the *Cortland Standard*.

Friday morning, the gang of 21 arrived in Syracuse, hoax issues in hand. While the stronger, more muscular of the group went to the *Orange*'s pressroom to delay the press run, others dropped bundles of the phony *Orange* at the delivery sites. (Unlike The Sun, the *Orange* was dropped in bundles across campus, for first come, first serve pick-up.)

And so, when students on the Syracuse campus grabbed papers on their way to classes or breakfast, they read that the NCAA "late last night tossed Syracuse University out of the NCAA 'for an indefinite period pending completion of investigations concerning apparent recruiting violations at the University." This may have justifiably caused panic, but a glance at the dateline, which read Black Friday, or the editorial on Page Two which declared that the NCAA's expulsion of Syracuse was "an obvious move to divide the American society into distinct class-conscious groups," should have quelled readers' fears.

And, should these hints not prove sufficient, in small type on the editorial page there appeared the legend: "Published whenever we get a chance during the athletic year by the members of IOSN — Ithaca's Only Syracuse Newspaper."

The real *Orange* eventually came out, having been delayed a mere three hours by the Cornell pranksters. But the hoax *Orange* was the success of the day. Once the prank was discovered, the bogus *Oranges* were snatched up, and 3,000 copies were sold on Ithaca newsstands. Later that day, fake *Oranges* were going for as much as a dollar a copy in Syracuse.

That same day, The Cornell Sun ran a story about a group of incoherent pranksters who hijacked the *Daily Orange*. The story itself was silly, but its very appearance had been a risk. As the hoax had not yet come to fruition by the time The Sun went to press, the editors had gambled. And won.

The hoax *Orange* made news across the country. The Associated Press, United Press International, the *Daily News* and the *New York Herald Tribune* recorded the Cornellians' caper.

Good ideas seldom go unrepeated, and five years later, in the Fall 1959, a pseudo-*Crimson* appeared at the dormitory doors of Harvard and Radcliffe College students, courtesy of a group of Sun people and Cayuga's Waiters. In IOSN fashion, students stalled the printing of the *Crimson* on the Saturday of the Cornell-Harvard football game and delivered the phony papers to all of Radcliffe and to seven of the eight Harvard Houses.

Alerted by a *Crimson* staffer who was pulling an all-nighter, the University Police and members of the *Crimson* tried to halt deliveries of the bogus issue, but with little success.

Thus, as Harvard woke that Saturday morning, they read — and believed — that ten players and the *Crimson* editors had been arrested for conspiring to fix a football game. And while 14 University students were each being released on $5000 bail, Ivy League presidents were meeting to determine the future status of the University.

The Sun only manufactured a hoax issue of another college's paper once more. This time in February 1965, with a fake *Daily Princetonian*, printed at *The Ithaca Journal*.

The *Princetonian* hoax, the perpetrators having the *Orange* and *Crimson* for reference, was undoubtedly the most daring, and most celebrated of the three. From shadowing the delivery trucks to meeting in an all-night bowling alley, the tale of the 1965 hoax reads like a James Bond mystery.

The plan was over a year in the works, having been conceived by Richard V. Denenberg '64 and Bart Mills '64, the editor-in-chief and managing editor of The Sun the year before the hoax was carried off.

The idea for the parody of the Princetonian was born at a Sun dinner where tales of the *Orange* and *Crimson* hoaxes were being recounted. When the younger staff members asked "Why don't we do it to Princeton?," managing editor Sol Erdman '65 agreed to explore the possibility of a phony paper.

A reconnaissance mission to New Jersey revealed that pulling off the caper would be tricky because of delivery procedures. After a 3:30 press run, the Princeton routine was to count the papers, then bundle and mark them for a 5 a.m. delivery to 25 drop points on and around the campus. But unlike the *Orange*'s first come, first serve method, delivery boys picked up Princetonian bundles from the drop sites within 45 minutes and distributed the paper door to door. The conspirators reluctantly agreed that the switch would have to be made at the drop sites.

The delivery map had been procured when Sun editors visited the *Princetonian*. As a double-check, six of the pranksters drove to Princeton on a weekend and spent the wee

---

╔══════════════════════════════════════╗

The New Traditionalism, *Princetonian* Style

The revelation yesterday of unprovoked attacks by Winston Churchill and Arthur Mizener on two important figures in the Princeton tradition creates an opportunity to discuss the role of traditionalism in the life of any institution of higher learning. Regardless of the validity of the attacks by Professor Mizener '30 and the late Sir Winston (regrettably not an alumnus), each serves to underline the need for a re-evaluation.

Any academic institution must live in the present and particularly in the future, and the past can only serve as an aid to the creation of proper guidelines for action. A Woodrow Wilson (the target of Churchill's memoirs) or an F. Scott Fitzgerald (Prof. Mizener's victim) is important not because of his individual identity but because of the things for which he stood. Wilson epitomized a dream and Fitzgerald represented an age, and neither the President's vision nor the author's period is particularly relevant to the present.

Thus Princeton must seek a new past to serve as its guideline, a past which is appealing but which also has relevance to the future. It must seek a middle road between the fragile, "do not touch" traditionalism of a Harvard or a Yale on the one hand, and the phony, forced traditionalism of a Cornell or the blustering red-brickishness of a Brandeis on the other. It must attempt to give expression to the American ambivalence of reverence for the past combined with excitement of the present and the future.

Thus we must thank Prof. Mizener and the great Sir Winston for leading us down the first painful step towards a fuller relationship between our traditionalism and our future progress. It is unfortunate that the push towards this realization has to come from outsiders, but possibly that is an illustration of how dangerous the old traditionalism was becoming, of how it was stagnating the objectivity of academic thought. A new wave of thought is coming, and the new thought is of such a nature that it calls upon us to reject those very ideas which would hinder acceptance of a new, antitraditional approach. Let us welcome the new traditionalism.

—*column from the bogus* DAILY PRINCETONIAN, *February 26, 1965*

╚══════════════════════════════════════╝

hours of the morning following a delivery truck across the Ivy League campus. After a final briefing a week later, the Ithaca version of the *Princetonian* was driven to the New Jersey campus.

The paper was composed as carefully as the mechanics of the plot were devised. The material was written with high scorn for the holier-than-thou and too often pointless traditionalism of the Ivy League. As there was to be a Cornell-Princeton basketball game that weekend, a story whose headline screamed "Bill Bradley Sprains Right Ankle; Hopes for Ivy League Title Sink" filled most of the top half of Page One.

A matching edit entitled "The Loss of Bradley" used hilarious reasoning. The editorial makes a strong, albeit stupid, statement that "The loss of Bill Bradley will undoubtedly hurt Princeton's hopes for the Ivy League basketball title...[but] Bradley's loss may be an aid to education at Princeton as a whole, as well as to sports at the University." The editorial revels in the brilliance of working like an editorial, in which reasons lead to a final statement. In this case, the conclusion was worthy of the reasons: "It would be nice to win the Ivy League basketball title, but if we maintained the correct perspective, we would have to say that we couldn't care less."

To round out Page One, The Sun appointed Princeton President Robert Goheen to a national advisory committee, and dragged the reputations of two celebrated Princetonians, Woodrow Wilson and Arthur Mizener '30, a noted Fitzgerald scholar, through the mud.

The report of a fictitious lecture by Cornell professor Mizener dripped with sarcasm. "Dangling his Phi Beta Kappa key solemnly over the podium, Mr. Mizener said that Fitzgerald's works are flawed and sloppily constructed," it said, and quoted Mizener: "'Compared to authors like Hemingway or Faulkner...Fitzgerald is but a minor hack.'"

To add the finishing touches to the trashing of the ivy-covered Princetonian pride, a brilliant column on the "New Tradition" presented a good six inches of meaningless, but impressive sounding sentences that elaborate on a new breed of traditionalism.   *   *   *

The conspirators' final rendezvous was an all-night bowling alley on U.S. 1. The pranksters had thought of everything. They had even devised a list of alibis, one for each prankster whose mission would send him onto campus before dawn with a briefcase or pile of papers in hand.

At 5:30 a.m., the Ithaca invaders simply walked to their assigned location and switched their bundles for the real *Princetonians*.

Some difficulties arose as Sun staffers crept across Princeton quadrangles in broad daylight to smuggle their fakes onto campus. The hardest routes to make switches on were the eating clubs and at the Nassau Street stores just off campus. Charles Both '65 walked into two stores which had already placed the real *Princetonian*s on the newsstands, and explained that they had somehow gotten the wrong papers. How *does* one get "the wrong papers?" Being understanding sorts, both store owners apologized and traded papers.

The eating clubs presented similar problems, but the switches went smoothly, although Erdman had to wrest two copies of the real paper from kitchen workers in one instance.

The hoax had gone off without a snag. It was an amazing feat and the Sun pranksters knew it, judging by the coverage they gave it on the pages of The Sun. As with the other two hoax issues, there were no hard feelings and the pranksters helped to distribute the real *Princetonian* shortly before noon that day.

So carefully engineered was the plot that even Cornell President James Perkins (Princeton '37) was in on it. Having been informed of the impending stunt, he decided to contribute to the escapade should it succeed. It so happened that Princeton President Goheen was staying at Perkins' house, having come to Ithaca to participate in an International Weekend. Thus, when the call signalling success came from Princeton, a Sun staffer brought copies of the phony issue to Perkins' house. Goheen came down to breakfast with a gleeful President Perkins and a *Daily Princetonian* that claimed that Goheen had been appointed to the national Advisory Committee on Foreign Affairs. Surprise.

Four years later, the childish abandon that so marked the *Princetonian* caper was purged from the campus. Racial tensions and anger at U.S. involvement in Southeast Asia triggered incidents of violence on campuses across the country.

Just two weeks after the Straight takeover in 1969, Spring Weekend passed, unmarked by celebrations. The following Monday, The Sun explained why no joke issue had appeared, in a bitter editorial entitled "Lots of Laughs." It gave two reasons. In a time of crisis, The Sun felt that valuable time could not be spared to dream up a hoax. "Keeping the campus informed had to be our first priority," it said.

A hoax at such a time would be nearly impossible, anyway. "Any hoax, to be all timely, would have had to deal with recent campus events, and if it were a good hoax, it would have made participants in those events laugh at themselves. But Cornell's crisis has been bitterly tinged with cries and counter-cries of 'racist' and 'anarchist,'" The Sun reflected. "Among the casualties of Cornell's crisis was its sense of humor. It was a tangential loss, but a sad one." Other absurdities had captured the limelight that spring weekend. SDS demonstrators climbed onto an old naval deck gun in Barton Hall and painted "End ROTC" on its barrel. The demonstrators were arrested and charged with criminal trespassing although no charges had been filed against any perpetrators of campus violence the entire semester. And it had been a violent spring.

But the campus survived the spring of 1969, and the fall brought another joke issue. The joke issues of the 60s had been for the most part outrageous sex and scandal sheets. Those Suns had played many different roles: the *Daily Booze* in '61, the *Cornell Mirror* in '65, and *Truth* in '63. For the most part, the sex-scandal editions were low on creativity, big on racy comments and sexual allusions, and full of suggestive snapshots, slang, and large, unintelligible headlines.

The most notable of these papers were the joke issues of Spring and Fall 1967. The two issues, both modeled carefully after the *Daily News*, were the brainchildren of managing editor Sam Roberts '68. Today Roberts is city editor of the real *Daily News*. His work with The Sun had prepared him for a career better than he knew.

In Spring 1970, The Sun concocted a parody of the University's newest publication, the *Cornell Chronicle*. Basically a puff job of University press releases interspersed with pretty pictures, the *Chronicle* was a direct result of the Straight takeover. The Sun's version, the *Cornell Comical*, was inane and a close replica of the real *Chronicle*. The editors in the spring of 1970 had a model joke to work with, courtesy of the Office of Public Information. A front page picture of the base of Ezra Cornell's statue with no Ezra in sight accompanied a story lamenting student vandalism. The statue, noted as a vital landmark, would not be replaced though, the *Comical* reported. It would cost too much.

The joke issues of the 70s are of a generally subtler breed of humor. The garish issues of the 60s were designed to amuse, or scandalize: the plots of the 70s were engineered to deceive and to criticize the administration.

To help achieve this end, joke issues beginning in the late 60s added a vital feature not found in earlier years: the what-number-to-call-for-information or where-to-report location. Invariably, the telephone numbers direct the worried to the Office of Public Information and/or an assortment of

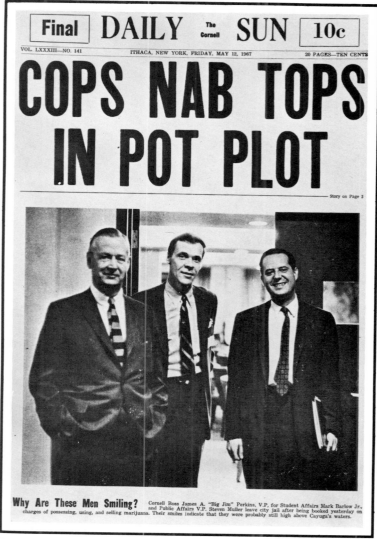

Final DAILY The Cornell SUN 10c

VOL. LXXXIII—NO. 141   ITHACA, NEW YORK, FRIDAY, MAY 12, 1967   20 PAGES—TEN CENTS

COPS NAB TOPS IN POT PLOT

Story on Page 3

Why Are These Men Smiling? Cornell Boss James A. "Big Jim" Perkins, V.P. for Student Affairs Mark Barlow Jr., and Public Affairs V.P. Steven Muller leave city jail after being booked yesterday on charges of possessing, using, and selling marijuana. Their smiles indicate that they were probably still high above Cayuga's waters.

THALER COLLARS DAY HALLERS: *A 1967 Sun spoof issue closely patterned after the New York* Daily News *scooped the nation's press in reporting a stunning development—that President Perkins and other top Day Hall administrators had been arrested by District Attorney Richard Thaler for marijuana dealings. For a reason why The Sun's editors might have felt especially eager to lampoon Thaler, simply turn the page to Chapter V.*

Day Hall offices. It is the Sun editor's way of thanking those especially hard-to-get along with vice presidents, professors and administrators. And it is a documented fact that the numbers get called and the lines form. The jokes may be subtle, but no one ever said they didn't have a sting.

Sometimes, however, the joke is not as preposterous as it first seems. In 1969, a Sun Fall Weekend issue falsely reported that Cornell's Gannett Clinic had decided to begin prescribing oral contraceptives — the Pill — to female students. It was funny, and unthinkable, at the time — but ten years later it was no hoax.

But history can also throw a joke into the laps of plotters. In Fall 1979, when the exiled Shah of Iran entered the Cornell Medical School Hospital, the editors had a ready-made spoof, and two weeks later the banner headline "Iran Offers $15M for Shah" stretched across the top of Page One. And of course The Sun, in a straightforward editorial endorsement, proclaimed "Sell the Shah."

There will always be new jokes in years to come. Regardless of the plot or punchline, the Fall Weekend joke issue acts as a release. It is fun, just once a year, to know something others don't, to make the reader, as well as the victim of the joke, laugh.

For Sun people, the inevitable small box on the following Monday's Page One, denouncing once reliable sources or bemoaning "mechanical errors," is the only correction box that is written with a grin. The box may be entitled "Oops!," but the finer print tells all: "The Sun enjoyed the error."

ROBERTA MOUDRY '81 is associate editor of *The Cornell Daily Sun.*

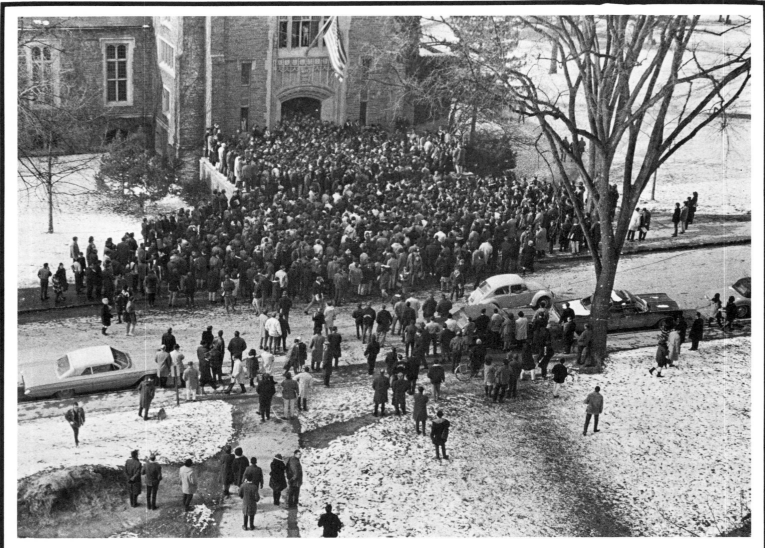

Chapter V: Of Freedom and Responsibility

Are not five sparrows sold for two farthings, and not one of them is forgotten before God?

—Luke 12:6

Contemplation of the bearing of increased liberty on increased virtue, and of struggles, of great good men with great bad men, strengthens a man's heart; study of the sure lines of justice between noble thoughts and noble victories strengthens a man's conscience; contemplation of great lines of purpose running through all that blooms or decays, struggles or suffers in the world-history, connecting all with the great goal which God has set, strengthens a man's soul. This is the higher discipline which gives mental discipline its worth; this repays all discouragement among old books, all buffeting among rugged men.

—Andrew Dickson White

Of all the wise words written and spoken about Cornell University, none have received more of a workout from posterity than "Freedom and Responsibility." The phrase is so hackneyed now that it has nearly lost all meaning, but in this chapter we will examine what it has meant, and what meaning it still has, if any.

Considering how often most Cornellians have heard the phrase, one would suppose that it had been coined by either Ezra Cornell or Andrew Dickson White, or that it was engraved in stone somewhere, possibly at the entrance to a library. This is not the case. As nearly as can be determined, it dates from no earlier than 1938. It was used then, in reference to Cornell's tradition, by a history professor named Carl Becker. Becker expanded on the theme, however, in a speech in April 1940 on the occasion of Cornell's 75th birthday, and it was this speech that was entitled, and popularized the notion of, *The Cornell Tradition: Freedom and Responsibility.*

It was truly an outstanding speech, and well worth the reading even 40 years later. We will, in fact, present the original text later on in this chapter, but it seems somewhat inappropriate to do so now. This is because of another Cornell tradition: the tradition of taking words out of context and then using them to support whatever position we choose. "Freedom and Responsibility" is just such a marvelously pithy, high-sounding and quotable phrase that the temptation to seize and ravish it is almost irresistible, particularly, it seems, among those who have never read the speech. For that matter, among those who have never heard of Carl Becker.

One of the phrase's most attractive qualities is that it can be warped to meet almost any requirement, since *responsibility* qualifies *freedom*, but nobody can be sure how much. Thus, in the early 1970s, the radical groups that were busy shutting down the teaching function of the University were also busy quoting Becker, stressing *freedom* and the expense of *responsibility*. This, however, was no more a perversion than President Malott's earlier use of the phrase (stressing *responsibility*, naturally) in defending restrictions on a variety of student and faculty *freedoms*.

As we will see, when Becker said *freedom* he did not mean political freedom or social freedom or even academic freedom as the concept is now known; when he said *responsibility* he did not mean that Cornellians have made it a habit to behave like sober adults. But this is beside the point after 40 years: history has put its own gloss on the phrase. Any discussion of the meaning of Becker's locution, therefore, might well start by forgetting about Becker and just wonder-

ing whether "freedom and responsibility," as those words are generally understood, is in fact a Cornell tradition.

All things considered, it probably is, more so than at other universities. But Cornell's record is not spotless. Neither is The Sun's. We will now pay a visit to the year 1921 for an example of this.

* * *

The case of Fred Morelli is explained fairly well by The Sun's news stories of the time, which are reproduced here with their original headlines. The only thing you may not follow is just what his offense was, so here is a brief description of the "freshman rules," a Cornell tradition in their own right, although lapsed now, of course.

"Freshman rules" were supposed to unify the freshmen, not to humiliate them; whether they did either is debatable. The rules, normally set up by a group of upperclassmen, varied slightly from year to year, but they always included the provision that freshmen had to wear an official freshman cap, or "dink," grey in the 1920s, red later on. Freshmen usually were also forbidden to wear any insignia of their high school or prep school, to smoke on campus, to walk on the grass, or to patronize certain restaurants and bars such as Zinck's. The rules stayed in effect all year, and during the spring there was, amid great festivity, a bonfire at which the freshmen would burn their caps. Eventually the rules would apply to freshman women also, but in 1921 they were enforced only against males. The enforcement, naturally, was up to the students, for the rules were not official University policy. The traditional penalty for noncompliance was head-shaving, normally carried out under the supervision of a sophomore "vigilance committee." In this case, however, it seems that the freshmen themselves were the enforcers.

One final word: 1921 being part of the interregnum between Presidents Schurman and Farrand, the Cornell president referred to in these stories is actually an acting president, Albert W. "Uncle Pete" Smith '78.

—Sun Photos by Daniel Smith and Paul R. Weissman
A QUESTION OF FREEDOM: *In January 1967, Cornell Safety Division chief James M. Herson confiscated 130 copies of the* Trojan Horse, *a student literary magazine he declared was obscene. In response, student leaders formed the Ad Hoc Committee for Free Expression at Cornell, and sold the Horse, despite the University ban, at a mass rally in front of the Straight (top photo). Tompkins County District Attorney Richard B. Thaler '53 arrived that afternoon with two plainclothesmen, and he used a bullhorn to warn the growing crowd that the Horse's explicit language violated the state penal code (bottom photo). Sales persisted even as Thaler spoke. Five students were then arrested and led to a waiting car, but the students would not allow it to leave. After an hour of argument, Thaler struck a deal with the protesters. The five arrestees would be released and sales would continue, but all those buying or selling the Horse would be morally bound to sign a sheet acknowledging their culpability, should a grand jury decide to act. That afternoon, Thaler obtained a temporary injunction prohibiting the magazine's sale, but Justice Harold E. Simpson '21 ultimately refused to issue a permanent ban. By that time, however, almost every copy of the Horse—whose sales had been sluggish before Herson's confiscation — had been snatched up. The Horse incident is discussed on Page 202. To the left of Thaler in the bottom photo, partly obscured, is Prof. Ralph Bolgiano '44, and to the right of Thaler are Sun editor-in-chief Ronald Thwaites '67, Student Government president David Brandt '67, and Horse editor James Moody '66.*

1912
BURN
Those Frosh Caps and Military Collars
TO-NIGHT
Meet at Sibley Dome at 7:15

Every Frosh bring a Red Light Torch for the
PEE-RADE!
ALL OUT!

—Scrapbook of James Irving Clark '12
BURN, BABY, BURN: *The exhilarating finale to a year of wearing grey felt beanies was the spring evening when every soon-to-be sophomore would gather to build a bonfire fueled with the stigmatizing haberdashery.*

A Freshman Is Taught a Lesson

—Photo by John P. Troy

FROSH OFF THE FIELD: *An ocean of grey fresh-man beanies fills the frosh section of Schoellkopf Crescent during the reign of football coach Gil Dobie, who led the Red from 1920 to 1936.*

Wearing the Grey Cap

Elsewhere in this issue appears a note telling of a freshman who has flatly refused throughout the entire year to wear the prescribed headgear. Such a case should not have been allowed to go on for months, but having done so it should not be allowed to continue another day. A flagrant violation of a rule which is understood by every freshman from the day he enters the University reflects directly upon the attitude of Cornell toward any traditions of long standing. If the other classes leave it to the freshmen to wear or not to wear the grey caps, it is not surprising that the yearlings take advantage of this fact.

There is no single body which can deal with such cases as that mentioned. It is up to public opinion to make it quite evident to the offender that he cannot continue in his ways, and there are plenty of means that can be resorted to in case it comes to a show down. Every student who knows of such violation of rules, and declines to take action, is failing in his duty.

The individual case is not of great importance; but if it is in any sense typical, it is time the student body is waked up to the point of taking drastic action.

—*editorial, April 19, 1921*

IN WHICH 1924 APPLIES MORAL

Sub-conscious Freshman Believes He Could Break a Time-honored Custom.

HIS DREAM EXPLODED

A Self-styled Committee Administers the Proper Antidote Yesterday Morning.

Moral: Wear a frosh cap. Such read the placard hanging from the neck of its worthy wearer, that greeted the eyes of thousands of undergraduates yesterday morning. For the usually quiet quadrangle was the scene of pandemonium for more than half an hour when several hundred members of the 1924 class took it upon themselves to preach the doctrine of the placard. They did so, effectively, efficiently and thoroughly, in fact so rapidly was the chastisement administered that the throng of undergraduates that had

scurried to the scene hardly realized what had taken place.

Obstinacy on the part of the offender was quickly subdued, for despite protests, the freshman headgear was securely fastened to his head. Pushed and shoved, the radical-minded freshman was hurried from Rockefeller Hall, the scene of the first outburst, to the campus, where he was justly made the object of merited ridicule and comment.

This course soon seemed to lose its effectiveness, and so the recalcitrant one was hauled to the drinking fountain in front of McGraw Hall, where the first application was tried. But the committee, adept in the tonsorial arts, knew this was but the beginning, for the next application was administered on the shore of Beebe Lake. The treatment appeared to be a success for chagrin marked the face of the violator of Cornell traditions and customs, as he was escorted back across the campus to his rooming house.

—*news story, April 21, 1921*

Healthy Reaction

Cornell showed a very healthy reaction yesterday morning when the student body devoted the better part of an hour to teaching a wayward freshman that rules are not laid down for a laughing stock. It was one of the most hopeful signs of animation that the University has shown in some months, and was of a more wholesome sort than some of the incidents which have stirred the community this year. In the words of one well-known alumnus, "it looked like the good old days before the war."

—editorial, April 21, 1921

DEFIANT MEMBER OF 1924 IS GIVEN FINAL WARNING

Two Alternatives Made Plain For Freshmen Refusing to Wear Class Cap.

1924 CLASS AGAIN ACTS

President Smith Rescues Morelli From Hands of Class-mates.

UPPERCLASSES INDIGNANT

Drastic Action Is Threatened Should Freshmen Persist in Defying Traditions.

Undergraduate indignation rose to a high pitch yesterday morning when F. Morelli, a member of the freshman class, again appeared on the campus minus his headgear.

The defier of Cornell traditions and customs had hardly appeared on the quadrangle, but that he was discovered, and pandemonium broke loose. Angry members of the 1924 class rushed from all parts of the quadrangle and in a few seconds Morelli was at the mercy of his classmates. But for the prompt action of President Smith, who rushed to the scene, the unruly member of the 1924 class would

—Cornell University Archives

CRACKED BASIN: *Freshmen soaked classmate Fred Morelli '24 with water from this Class of 1873 memorial fountain, which stood until recently before McGraw Hall. In 1980, this beautiful, hand-carved fountain lies broken and forgotten in a grounds division storage area in upper Collegetown.*

Chapter V: Of Freedom and Responsibility

—Cornell University Archives

RAISING CANE: *Members of the Class of 1886 pose before the old Ithaca Hotel to celebrate their victory in an interclass "cane rush" battle. However, not one individual of this glum group can manage so much as a smile. Upperclassmen frequently declared the Ithaca Hotel off limits to freshmen during the University's first half-century. The landmark hotel was torn down in 1967, leaving behind a gaping pit in the downtown shopping district that was finally filled by a new Rothschild's department store in 1975.*

We are informed that some of the first year men are not wearing the freshman caps. That even a few persons are committing this offense is occasion for shame to the freshman class and to all the undergraduates as well.

We would like to know just why these individuals are breaking this University custom. Is it because they are ashamed of their class and their classmates? Is it because of a bull-headed stubbornness or an exaggerated idea of insulted dignity at a supposed humiliation? What is the reason? Perhaps it is because they do not understand the value of the Freshman Rules or the respect with which the upperclassmen regard these regulations. Possibly they feel it would be a disadvantage to wear the caps and to be pointed out as freshmen, but if so, their ideas are wrong and should be corrected very forcibly.

We are tired of explaining to freshmen that the wearing of the cap is a great advantage; that it helps them to become acquainted with each other; that it promotes democracy. We would like them to know what *the failure to wear the cap means*. It occasions the disgust of all who are aware of the offense, both upperclassmen, sophomores and the freshmen's own classmates. It also occasions the wrath of the Vigilance Committee.

This is a matter in which every undergraduate should be vitally interested. It is a custom which all of us would endeavor to maintain throughout the entire freshman class. It is an affair which the Vigilance Committee can remedy as it has done in the past.

Right-minded freshmen, those amenable to reason, are wearing the caps now. But the men who are committing the present offenses are not the reasonable kind. Whenever one is found, who is committing this offense, or any offense against the rules, his name and address should be sent at once to the Vigilance Committee. A list of the members of this committee appears today in another column. They can be depended upon to correct the matter.

We again print the freshman rules today and hope that the upperclassmen and sophomores will be as diligent in seeing that they are enforced hereafter as all right-minded freshmen now are in living up to these precepts.

FRESHMAN RULES

1.—A freshman in contemplation of the rules shall be any student spending his first year at any college or one who would be considered eligible to represent the class in any manner. This applies to three year as well as four year courses.

2.—No freshman shall smoke at all on the Campus, nor shall he smoke a pipe on the streets of Ithaca.

3.—No freshman shall be allowed down stairs in Zinck's or in the Dutch Kitchen under any circumstances; nor shall he be permitted to lounge about the lobby of the Ithaca Hotel at any time; nor shall he be allowed to enter Jay's, the Senate or the Office after 7 p.m. No freshman shall be allowed upstairs in Zinck's or the Senate unless accompanied by an upperclassman.

4.—Each and every freshman shall wear at all times, except on Sundays, a cap of the following description: An official gray cap with a small visor and a black button, or an official gray toque with a black tassel. He shall not at any time while in college wear a pin representing his preparatory school in any manner, nor shall he wear any emblem or insignia of that institution.

5.—No freshman shall be allowed to go without a coat or a cap on the Campus.

6.—No freshman shall be allowed under any circumstances to sit in the first three rows or in boxes at the Lyceum.

—editorial, October 19, 1906

have met with serious injury.

President Smith then took Morelli to his office, and although what transpired is not definitely known, it is the consensus of authentic opinion that the present head of the University lectured to Morelli on the seriousness of defying time-honored customs and traditions.

Prominent members of the faculty, professors and deans, and upperclassmen, declare that but two courses of action are open to Morelli. They point out that he must either abide by the rules prescribed for him, or leave the University and go to some place where his "freedom" will be unrestrained.

Should the unruly member of the freshman class persist in his refusal to don the 1924 headgear, he is likely to meet serious injury as a result. Upperclasses and underclasses alike are highly indignant at the attitude of Morelli and threaten drastic action, to which the first punishment would be mild in comparison, should he persist in appearing on the campus without his grey cap.

At an early hour this morning it was unknown whether Morelli had decided to remain in the University and follow custom and tradition, or to leave and follow his own unmolested "bent" in some other institution.
— *news story, April 22, 1921*

MORELLI GIVEN ABSENCE LEAVE

Freshman, Unwilling to Observe Cap Tradition, Given Leave Yesterday.

ACTION IS VOLUNTARY

Student From Utica May Again Resume Studies at Cornell.

With the issuance of an indefinite leave of absence to F. Morelli '24, who during the past few days caused considerable confusion on the campus because of his refusal to wear a frosh cap, the violator of Cornell traditions is no longer a member of the student body. The first year man decided that he would rather leave the University than to submit to legitimate regulations prescribed for his class.

The action of Morelli was entirely voluntary and came as a result of a long talk with President Smith on the matter. It was evident to both the faculty and undergraduates alike that but two courses of action were open to the freshman in question: either to abide by tradition and custom, or to leave the University, and Morelli selected the latter course.

Whether Morelli will return to the University in the future is a matter of conjecture. He, however, has that right under the leave of absence granted him, and can, should he so elect, return next fall or even for the summer school, and then complete his education, for the matter is one of Cornell custom and tradition and not of a University rule.
— *news story, April 23, 1921*

—*Utica Observer-Dispatch*
FRED MORELLI '24
Morelli finally graduated in 1926, and went on to become a prominent figure in his home town of Utica, N.Y., where the above photograph was taken. Morelli was killed by two shotgun blasts on December 8, 1947 while leaving his night-club, the Ace of Clubs. The previous year he had threatened to blow the cover on local underworld gambling, and police mentioned vengeance as a possible motive for the slaying.

—*Cornell University Archives*
ALBERT W. "UNCLE PETE" SMITH '78
Popular acting president Smith rescued Morelli from an angry mob on April 21, 1921 and apparently urged the individualistic freshman to take a leave of absence (popular opinion would have favored his expulsion). Smith, the father of Sun editor-in-chief Alpheus Smith '19, was one of three students selected to attend Ezra Cornell's wake after the Founder's death on December 9, 1874.

Is Cornell Intolerant?

A serious indictment of Cornell is that made by Professor Burr in connection with the Morelli incident when he charged that the University is intolerant of the "radical-minded," and is tending toward a reign of lynch law. Coming from a Cornellian of long standing, the charge is not one to be cast lightly aside.

Of all places a university should be that where freedom of opinion reigns unquestioned. From the most reactionary to the most radical, all should there find the right to self-expression. If Cornell is intolerant, it is high time there were a change.

Liberty of opinion and of expression there should be; but complete liberty of action has never been recognized by any but avowed anarchists. Granting the validity of the law, there can be no charge of intolerance in the enforcement of it.

Professor Burr bases his contention on two points: that the students had no right to demand the wearing of the cap; and that they were not justified in resorting to "lynch law." In proof of the first he recounts the comparatively brief history of the freshman cap as a Cornell tradition, and continues with an argument against traditions in general as a part of Cornell's make-up.

No matter how many or how few years the grey cap has been the symbol of the first year student, it has become an unwritten law that every freshman is to wear it—a law which is no secret to the prospective Cornellian. With a constantly changing undergraduate body it does not take long for a custom to become firmly planted. Every student now in the University entered under this rule and if he entered as a freshman, wore the cap. The origin of the rule is of little significance.

It is true that the rule makes a requirement that is rather trivial, and it is also true that it dictates in a matter in which no political body would dare to lay down the law. So also do other freshman rules concern somewhat trivial matters, and matters that lie without the ordinary jurisdiction of the law. By what right, then, does a student body impose such rules?

Does every institution that places restrictions on freshmen trespass on the sacred rights of the individual?

The authority for such law is that of precedent, of tradition, of custom, of public opinion. Professor Burr goes to the bottom of the matter when he attacks the existence of such tradition, and the compulsion which makes it binding upon freshmen. "Cornell too," he says, "is growing old;" and he points with approval to the time when the only tradition of which she was proud was that she had no traditions.

"In Heaven's name be men," Dr. White exhorted his first great student audience. "Is it not time that some poor student traditions were supplanted by better?" Perhaps Cornell is growing old. But if the existence of a few traditions to which her sons fondly cling is the criterion of old age, we welcome old age as the healthiest time of life.

As far as the reign of "lynch law" is concerned, there is little room for dispute. Few are those who would soberly advocate it as the means of enforcement of Cornell traditions. That the principle has been mildly overstepped in a single instance, however, is hardly a proper basis for the conclusion that Cornell is governed by "lynch law." Even the most rabid proponent of the wearing of the cap would hardly take issue with the stand adopted by the faculty, who have merely passed a resolution on a rainy day expressing their approval of fair weather.

That Cornell as an institution is intolerant is a generalization scarce warranted by the incident in question. She has shown herself on a number of occasions this year quite reasonable in regard to individual liberty of self-expression. But open defiance of a rule which the students conceive to be well grounded by tradition of long standing, she will not tolerate. "Lynch law" is not a part of Cornell traditions, and never will be; but the enforcement of law, written or unwritten, by legitimate means, must continue.
— *editorial, April 25, 1921*

What became of Fred Morelli? Well, he eventually returned to Cornell and graduated in 1926. You might think he would have become a noted civil libertarian, but he did not. He became a gangster. In 1947, he was shot to death in Utica, N.Y. by some rivals in his chosen field of endeavor.

And what became of the freshman rules? They stayed alive only slightly longer than Morelli. During the late 30s, they were largely ignored, and for a time during World War II they disappeared altogether as military training hopelessly disrupted the normal University schedule. After the war, however, they returned with a vengeance, and caused more controversy than ever before. Many of the new "freshmen" were in fact returning war veterans. Some of these made it entirely clear what their feelings were about shedding one uniform and being asked to don another, particularly by a bunch of pipsqueak sophomores.

By 1949, compliance with the rules had become so sporadic that a group of vigilantes, with the tacit consent of some Student Council officers, broke into the dorms early one morning and kidnapped four freshman offenders. Two of them had their heads shaven; one was given an icy shower; and one had a "v" (for vigilante) branded into his forehead with silver iodide.

This time, The Sun took a different view than it did during the Morelli episode. Calling rule enforcement "a hypocritical jumble," the editor said, "The frosh cap and rules have not come to be a healthy influence in the development of class spirit. They have been given and taken in an atmosphere of bullying, of resentment and of ill-feeling. They are, it is apparent, not the answer if handled with the prevailing attitudes."

This incident was the last straw, and in 1950 the "freshman rules" officially became "freshman traditions." The little red caps faded away almost immediately.

But the 50s presented threats to freedom next to which having to wear a cap looked like very small potatoes. The advent of McCarthyism did not have any spectacular manifestations at Cornell, but it did have some quiet ones. Students and professors had to be careful of what they said and what they taught. Various faculty members were summoned to Washington and asked to name former associates. Alumni and the government pressured Cornell to keep a low profile.

To condense a complicated decade into a sentence, let us say that Cornell's response to McCarthyism was neither particularly reprehensible nor outstandingly progressive.

Joseph McCarthy's efforts to cleanse the academic community of un-Americans were strictly minor league compared to the activities of—yes, even Cornell alumni, after World War I. One group of alumni, headed by Myron H. Van Auken '73, a lawyer, passed the following resolution at a meeting in Utica.

"Whereas, Our war with Germany disclosed the fact that in nearly all of our colleges and universities there was one or more professors who were avowedly or secretly un-American in their views and their teachings;

Resolved, That it is the sense of the college men and women here assembled that the employment of persons whose Americanism is denied or questioned as professors or instructors of any kind should be discontinued, and that educational authorities everywhere in the United States should promptly dismiss every person now employed to instruct the young men and girls, who is tainted with anti-Americanism or un-Americanism, or whose Americanism can be doubted.

Resolved, That it is the sense of this assemblage that college, university and school authorities everywhere should confer no honors, and should not extend any official courtesy to any person who, by word or act during our war with Germany, obstructed any law of our country, or who was not in accord with our country's purpose in entering upon the war, and who is not now a 100 per cent American."

The Sun responded to this resolution as follows.

The Die-Stamped 'American' Professor

When a college graduate like Myron H. Van Auken draws up and secures the passage of a resolution calling upon the trustees of every college and university in the country to discharge from their faculties un-American professors and instructors and not to honor others of this kind it is time to call a halt, and consider.

Has the panic caused by Bolshevism and socialism so befuddled the college graduate that he can urge the investigation of the beliefs of every member of the Cornell faculty, and the discharge of every man whose views do not coincide with his own?

Since when, may we ask, has any group of citizens been granted the power of determining what a man may think in order that he may secure a livelihood?

Mr. Van Auken, and those associated with him, by their own statement are guilty of gross un-Americanism when they would attempt to take from a professor his profession because he thinks as he pleases. The rights of free speech and free thought are inherent in the democratic principles on which this country was founded, and they were curtailed several years ago as a war measure only. If Mr. Van Auken would set himself up as opposed to freedom of thought that is his own business, but he can hardly assume the role of an apostle of Americanism in so doing.

And if some university proceeded to investigate its faculty by what standard would it judge the Americanism of its professors? Does the violent waving of the flag when a band plays the "Star Spangled Banner" automatically constitute an American? Does blind belief in the work of the Administration make a man a dyed-in-the-wool American? Does the wholesale adoption of the beliefs of the majority, most of whom have no real beliefs because they have no thoughts, entitle a citizen to pedestal himself as the ideal American?

We don't believe so, and Americans with an interest in preserving this country as a great democracy will agree. They would be loath to see all thought stifled and the individual shaped to the common mold from which he would emerge as an "American." We are sure even Mr. Van Auken and his associates would regret seeing America "Prussianized" and every man the prototype of his fellow.

With Mr. Van Auken's system in vogue it does not require any great stretch of imagination to picture a board of trustees sitting on the cases of students toward whom suspicion pointed as not measuring up to the arbitrary rule of thought. Why not? They might enter into conversation with other undergraduates and set their minds in motion with effects as disastrous as those attained by the professor.

With Mr. Van Auken in the seat of power no distinguished teacher of a foreign nation might find a place in the universities of the United States unless he would swear he saw no good in his fatherland.

Mr. Van Auken's resolution would hardly attract or deserve notice if it had not been seconded by a group of Cornell graduates.

Their consent to the movement causes one to wonder how so many college graduates, assembled in a body, can sign a resolution whose discrepancies are easily apparent after a little thought. With the resolution in force there would be no difficulty in replying to the question. Even a little thought would be impossible, because thought would be prohibited to college men and women.

—*editorial, November 19, 1919*

President Malott's reaction when a zoology professor, Marcus Singer, was indicted for contempt of Congress more or less typified things. The indictment of Singer, who had admitted his own past left-wing affiliations but refused to name anyone else, took place in the middle of the 1955 fall semester, two years after his testimony. Singer was immediately suspended from Cornell; other professors took over his classes. The Sun, which in 1953 had spent a large amount of money reprinting the entire text of Singer's testimony, objected strenuously to Malott's handling of the case, in a rare front-page editorial.

Nevertheless, Malott did not remove Singer from the payroll, and when it became clear that the legal process would take some time, he allowed him to resume research. But Singer was not permitted to teach again at Cornell until he was cleared on a technicality some three years later.

Malott's actions were considerably less severe than those at certain other universities, where professors were fired routinely for less heinous offenses. On the other hand, Harvard faced an exactly similar situation at exactly the same time, and refused to take any action at all against the professor involved.

The McCarthy period has received so much attention that it is easy to forget an earlier time when things were just as bad: the World War I era. The Second World War was supported by virtually all Americans; the first was a different story. There was a small but not insignificant minority that believed the U.S. should not have gotten involved. But

heaven help any members of this minority who were professors! The depredations against free speech during this war have been well documented; fortunately, Cornell escaped most of them. A euphemistic account of one incident was given in 1930 by Frank Hiscock '75, chief judge of the New York State Court of Appeals during the war—and chairman of Cornell's Board of Trustees.

Writing in A *Half-Century at Cornell*, Hiscock said, "There has been . . . only one occasion in my time when trustees and faculty have found themselves in a quite persistent deadlock and that interestingly enough resulted not from any desire of the trustees to curtail the power of the faculty, but rather from the conviction that the dean of one of the larger colleges should exercise greater powers. Once during the war the University was being criticised for and injured by the utterances of a professor which to put it mildly were extremely unwise. When the matter came to the Board, as it did very urgently, it was referred to the faculty of which the offender was a member with the fortunate result that further offending was stopped with the least amount of disturbance."

Judge Hiscock's views of what took place at other universities were more adamant. Here is what he said about Cornell's main football rival, and remember this was written not during the war but twelve years after it ended.

"I judge it is pretty well conceded now that when the trustees of the University of Pennsylvania during the war dealt with a professor who was making himself notorious by utterances which affronted common judgment, they were

Baiting a Red-Baiter

One of my Sun career's highlights was what's been known ever since as "the McNaboe rallies." First, in Albany, State Sen. John McNaboe, for whatever his own reasons of sincerity or political hype, announced he would vote for no further state appropriations for Cornell because he had proof the Ithaca campus was rampant with marijuana. Today it may sound preposterous, but when the A.P. dispatch from Albany about the senator arrived at the Sun office, other editors and I had to scurry to our Webster's to ascertain details of what we vaguely guessed to be some kind of strange drug, like opium or peyote. The best part of what Noah's tome told us (at least, best for our journalistic purposes) was that some people believed marijuana an aphrodisiac (and I imagine some of us had to surreptitiously look up that word, too). In any event, the next morning's Sun banner headline announced a "marijuana merry-go-round" on the Straight steps that evening. A hurried call to Ithaca police had produced the chief's report there'd been only one marijuana arrest in Ithaca's recorded history, and that a charge against a resident non-Cornell "sheik" (also read "smoothie" or "hipster") who'd obtained said substance from a visiting dance-orchestra musician years before.

So that evening in front of the Straight, a grubby-looking be-derbied Yours Truly was smoking a (tobacco-containing) banquet-length cigarette held in a sinister-looking Turkish-looking water-pipe, while a public-address system blared forth some music and then the sarcastic description of what should happen to Sen. McNaboe—all this in front of a student throng filling the Straight's frontal exterior. A few days later in the Albany session, Mr. McNaboe again swore he'd approve no more Cornell aid, this time because the campus was "a hotbed of Communism." Actually, the campus had a handful-size gaggle of undergraduates in a chapter of the Young Communist League, and up till then they'd bothered no one and no one'd bothered them.

Once again, a Sun front page bannered notice of a "rally," and as fickle fate would have it there was, indeed, a YCL chapter-meeting in the Straight that night. The Sun men's front-door "Big Red red-red rally" was addressed in the light of flickering (red, natch!) railroad flares by "Comrade Flashovitch"* amid the cheers of onlookers and the plaintive but unsuccessful appeals of YCL members please to

—*Cornellian*

'NEWSPAPER TAXIS APPEAR ON THE SHORE': *Fred Hillegas '38 smokes a Turkish water pipe in front of the Straight during a "McNaboe rally." For another McNaboe rally photo, please turn to Page 106.*

be allowed into their scheduled meeting room already overflowing with curious bystanders craning to see a real, live Communist even if an adolescent one.

News photos of the spoof-rallies were published nationwide in newspapers always thirsting for proof of how deleterious youth was/is, and the quality of the farcical rhetoric was as good as possible considering the ages of all of us—no orator ever had better (even though still-to-be-proven) script-writers: two '37 Sun men, Melville Shavelson, now a longtime Hollywood film and network TV scriptwriter-producer-director, and today's New York-based playwright Arthur Laurents—both of them, after the Straight rallies, to work with lesser leading men like Gable, Sinatra, Redford, Kirk Douglas, Bob Hope, and Henry Fonda (with leading ladies like Lucille Ball, Loren and Streisand).

—*Fred Hillegas '38*
editor-in-chief, 1937-38

*To find out how Mr. Hillegas got the nickname "Flash," please turn to page 174.—Ed.

not interfering with any legitimate academic freedom but were exercising an obligatory duty to protect the reputation of the University for which in the last analysis they were responsible. A University doesn't escape damage because a professor who makes obnoxious and condemnable utterances steps across the campus boundary when he makes them."

Despite these threatening words, the most interesting freedom of expression case of the time came at Cornell not during the war but after it, when the famous composer and violinist, Fritz Kreisler, scheduled a concert for Bailey Hall. Kreisler had played at Bailey in 1917 without incident, but he was an Austrian, and the local post of the American Legion was deuced if it could see any reason to allow such a dangerous person to perform in placid Ithaca. The mayor of Ithaca, Frank Davis, added some sour notes with a proclamation requesting "the patriotic citizens of Ithaca to refrain from patronizing or attending the concert to be given by Fritz Kreisler, the enemy alien artist."

This sort of thing was happening all over the country at

Americanism and Ohio State

During the McCarthy years, many campus newspapers—and almost all the rest of the press—retrenched. And with good reason. At colleges all over the country, editors were being expelled, newspapers were being taken over by the administration or shut down entirely, and students and professors would not speak up for them, all because of articles that could conceivably be labeled leftist, socialist, or disloyal.

The Sun was fortunate to escape this, although President Malott made an abortive suggestion in 1953 that all campus publications, including The Sun, should come under the control of the administration.

In this poisonous political atmosphere, the courageous editorial policy of the 1951-1952 Sun editors was a pocket of fresh air. They not only castigated McCarthy; they did extensive research on the trends of the day, indulged in careful analysis, and correctly identified most of the developments in freedom of expression. All this was at least a year before the national press began to do the same thing.

It is true that a college newspaper has little influence on national politics, but nevertheless this series of editorials should stand as one of The Sun's proudest achievements. It is impossible to pick one piece of the 50 or so that ran as standing above the rest, or as representative; it is impossible to fail to recognize the achievement by not printing any. Here, then, is an editorial from 1951, not offered as the best one, or the most significant one but as, like Joseph McCarthy, a symbol. It is called *Who is Un-American?*

Since September 4, no speaker has appeared on the campus of Ohio State University without the personal approval of the president of the university. And the OSU Board of Trustees has made it abundantly clear that it will not stand for the approval of a speaker bearing any trace of Communist or Socialist sympathy. So "free speech" at Ohio State is now defined as freedom to agree with the basic political views of the university's Board of Trustees.

These are the facts of the situation. The events leading up to this unhappy state of affairs tell the story of how a sensation-seeking press can excite hysterical anti-communism to the point where our basic freedoms are infringed.

The trouble began in July, when the graduate students and faculty members planning the annual Boyd H. Bode Conference on Education at Ohio State presented as their main speaker Dr. Harold O. Rugg, emeritus professor at Columbia and a long-time associate of John Dewey in the field of education. Dr. Rugg spoke on each of three days to moderate-sized audiences composed largely of elementary school teachers taking summer courses at Ohio State.

Dr. Rugg's appearance was bitterly attacked in the editorial columns of two local newspapers, the *Columbus Dispatch* and the *Ohio State Journal*, which are under a single ownership and whose political approach is perhaps best indicated by their editorial approval of the actions of Senator Joseph McCarthy. It appears that the editors of these sheets would have overlooked Rugg's appearance entirely except that one of the *Journal*'s readers took the occasion to write a fiery letter to the editor, branding Rugg as a virtual traitor, and the university as a hotbed of Communist teaching.

The Columbus papers reached back to 1934 in their attempt to discredit Rugg. They quoted at length from a series of elementary school textbooks which he wrote at about that time, to show that the professor was a sworn enemy of the American way of life.

Having thus convinced themselves that Rugg was a red-eyed socialist determined to bring about the overthrow of the government, the papers concluded that since the Ohio State University is supported by tax money earned under the capitalist system, it had no right to sponsor speakers who did not believe in the system. The papers "called for an investigation" and viewed the university through pink-tinted glasses, determined to find Communists behind every clump of ivy.

Dr. Rugg took the whole thing fairly calmly. From the platform, he commented that it was "too bad the local press had to go back 17 years to find a controversy" when there are so many things going on today. But otherwise he devoted himself to a discussion of educational aims, with most of what he said, to judge by the comments from the audience after-wards, going well above the heads of his listeners. Even the reporters straining eagerly for a phrase which could be made to sound like the Communist line in the morning edition, uncovered just one doubtful quotation: Dr. Rugg said that he was hoping for a depression to jar the American people out of their complacency. This figure of speech was given prominent coverage, both in the news and editorial columns.

The OSU trustees investigated. Out of their investigation came the ruling that all speakers had to receive prior approval by the president before appearing on campus.

This brought an immediate howl of protest from the faculty, which has some concept of academic freedom and its implications. The Ohio State student newspaper, the *Lantern*, also spoke out bitterly against the trustees' action. The Board met to reconsider on Monday. Out of that meeting came this statement: "As trustees of the Ohio State University, we encourage the fullest academic freedom consistent with national security.

"The facilities of the University will not be made available to known Communists or members of other groups who seek to undermine basic liberties of America."

So Dr. Harold Rugg, an authority on children's education whose liberal views have been called Socialist by people like those who publish the *Ohio State Journal*, may not appear at Ohio State. His appearance before undergraduate and graduate students, and faculty members, would not be "consistent with national security," because the people in his audience are so incapable of thought that they would rush out and spread the Socialist gospel over the capitalist state of Ohio.

So Ohio State, where 16,000 students attend classes to learn to become educated, thoughtful men and women, prepared to make their own decisions in life, will not permit its students to hear the opinions of men whom the trustees think are seeking "to undermine the basic liberties of America."

Just who, we wonder, is being un-American at Ohio State? Is it the speakers who may not agree with the Republican or Democratic parties but have some new ideas of their own? Or is it, rather, the trustees, who—in protecting the campus from those "who seek to undermine basic liberties of America"—have themselves undermined the most basic liberty of all, free speech.

—editorial, October 17, 1951

the time. It was impossible, for example, to hear German-language opera in New York City. And yet President Schurman's response to the brouhaha showed a singular lack of fortitude. The Kreisler concert would go on, he explained, because it was just too late to cancel the violinist's contract.

The Sun, happily, saw things this way: "Fine music owes allegiance to no flag. It is international. It recognizes no boundaries. And the same applies to a great artist. A man of the ability of Fritz Kreisler is not a citizen of Austria any more than he is a citizen of the United States. His is an international citizenship, for his art has carried him beyond the borders of any one country."

The editorial concluded, "The only real objection to Kreisler's coming to Ithaca is that of hate, carried to an extreme."

The Kreisler affair climaxed in astonishing fashion. The public ignored the boycott and jammed Bailey Hall, but some 80 persons opposed to his appearance attempted an invasion, during which the lights were cut off. A pitched battle ensued, and, as described by Morris Bishop, "Kreisler, unperturbed, played on in the din of the Battle of Bailey Hall. President Schurman took his stand beside the performer. A volunteer leaped on the stage with a flashlight for the accompanist. The invaders were magnificently repelled, to the strains of Viotti's Concerto in A minor. No tumult since Nero's time has had such a fine violin accompaniment."

Bishop's prose here is as entertaining as always, but one cannot help objecting to his final allusion. Nero was a notoriously poor fiddle player. I have heard Kreisler play, thanks to the magic of the Victor Talking Machine Company. Only a Bolshevik would compare the two.

Students, also, have enjoyed some of the benefits of the freedom-and-responsibility tradition. The administration has generally left them alone to behave and express themselves as they see fit. *The Cornell Daily Sun* is a good example. Its tone over the last 15 years or so has been so anti-administration that no one can doubt that it is an independent body today; but as a matter of fact it has been independent for a century, and the administration has rarely tried to do anything about it. Other than an occasional touch of gentle persuasion, that is. In A *Half-Century at Cornell*, former

Dash It All!

Rain, rain, go away...
Friday afternoon.
It will no doubt be a severe blow to the intellectual community, but we haven't anything particular to say for Saturday morning. Please don't think that our inefficiency is due to laziness, or to a lack of interest in the world-shaking events going on around us. Senator McCarthy's latest guttersnipe tactics call for comment, the Korean truce talks are apparently at another impasse—we'll leave it to *The New York Times*. We aren't in the mood.

Damn rain, damn rain, go away...
There are two of us who usually contribute the words of wisdom appearing in these columns. At the present moment one is in New York City—the writer has little over 17 minutes to dash home and put on his tux.

A long-distance call to New York City is out of the question. A reprint of an editorial from an old issue seems to be in fashion this week, among magazines as well as newspapers. Or we could leave the space blank and let you fill it with autographs, lipstick prints, or what have you.

Goddam rain, goddam rain, go away...

* * *

Has apathy hit The SUN? Has that demon of all organizations sent its plague upon East State Street at a time when admonishment to remain decorous, analysis of mass dissipation, and interpretation of the immature pedagogical attitude of college youth is called for in these columns?

Call it apathy if you will. At present, though, we're looking out the window, and we're more concerned with the weather than with mass dissipation or even pedagogical attitudes. Why, WHY, we're asking in unison with some 10,000 others...

Perspective, Searching Analysis, or even a glance through *The Ithaca Journal* for typographical errors usually comes up with some sort of answer, or at least copy enough to fill a page. But a glance out the window and a quick rifling through the Associated Press file for the weather report give us an answer which we refuse to accept—which we, with our naïve hopes still high, refuse to admit it's within the narrow realms of possibility.

Please, come another day...
—*editorial, Saturday, May 16, 1953*

Sun editor-in-chief Charles B. Howland '26 recalled, "There were mornings when the editor received a message to stop at Dean Hammond's office to consider whether the Berry Patch Editor had not best be advised to confine himself to humor and leave to the *Police Gazette* and *La Vie Parisienne* their chosen fields."

But it has not always been this way. There was a time when the administration threatened to take over The Sun and every other campus publication; in one year the faculty committee supervising student discipline instituted proceedings against three periodicals, including The Sun, because of "improper" language. And, surprisingly, it was less than thirty years ago.

The Sun's Spring Day 1953 issue contained two items which proved objectionable to the Faculty Committee on Student Conduct, and both pertained to the activities of that houseparty weekend. A third noxious piece ran a few days later. One was a cartoon, which depicted a couple necking on a couch, with the caption, "Gee, honey, it's great seeing you again." Another was a poem that featured the exploits a drunken student, presumably male, who appeared in public wearing panties. The third, an editorial, is reproduced on this page. It told of the editor's annoyance with the rainy weather and the threat it posed to the weekend's activities. The particular editor whose pluvial prose the professors perused with paranoia, Stuart Loory '54, went on to a fine career in journalism, and is now managing editor of the *Chicago Sun-Times*. This editorial gave some hint of future promise for its author. However, it did contain a profanity. Today, the most pristine and cloistered Balch resident uses this particular profanity ten or twelve times a day, but in 1953 it was evidently scandalous. The FCSC demanded to know the authors of the offending pieces, and The Sun obliged with the names.

The committee, however, refused to tell The Sun who was doing the complaining, and a jurisdictional wrangle ensued. The committee asked for an official apology from The Sun; the editors offered to apologize to the persons actually offended, but not to the faculty committee. Loory gave the chairman of the committee a statement to be conveyed to the complainants, saying, "*The Cornell Daily Sun* is sorry if it has offended anybody with its editorial of Saturday, May 16, 1953. The staff of The Sun sincerely hopes that it will not offend these persons again." However, at the insistence of the Sun board of directors, which included three professors, this apology went to the committee with the condition that it could not be made public unless the committee took no action against The Sun.

The committee mulled this proposition over for two weeks, perhaps consulting with the complainant, then discarded the apology and summoned the editors to an official hearing, at which the dean of the faculty, a committee member, issued an ominous warning. The committee avoided dealing with The Sun as a whole by the fiction that its grievance was against the individual editors only; but the dean said, "Although you realize that the committee is now dealing with individuals, it does have the power to call The Sun before it as a corporate body and to, in effect, dissolve The Sun." The editors, of course, did not accept this theory, but they did not press the point, and eventually Loory, a reporter, and The Sun's associate editor were given unofficial reprimands, the lightest possible punishment. Meanwhile, some *Cornell Widow* editors received official reprimands, which were recorded on their transcripts, for similar offenses in The Widow's Spring Day issue.

In October, The Sun transgressed again, and this time found out who the blue-nose was who had been so horrified by the *goddam*. This time, the word in question was not even spelled out in Loory's editorial: it appeared H---. This provoked a letter to Loory from the dean of the faculty, who revealed he had been sent a clipping of the offending editorial. "Accompanying the clipping," the dean wrote, "was a memorandum initialed by the president which read as follows: 'I still see no reason for profanity or implied profanity in The *Cornell Sun*. No other first class *news*paper seems to require it.' During a conversation I had with the president this morning I understood him to agree with me that the use of the "H---" was not a matter which required the attention of the Committee on Student Conduct. I told him that you had stated to that Committee when you appeared before it last spring that the Sun editors would always be willing to give careful consideration to criticisms; and he asked me to approach you on that basis in this instance."

So far, President Malott's ire had only been aimed at things written in fun—but he next took on what purported to be a serious literary work. In November, a new campus literary publication, the *Cornell Writer*, came out with its first edition, which the Sun critic liked, and which The Sun praised editorially. "The most interesting prose piece," according to the Sun critic, "was Ronald Sukenick's serio-comic 'Indian Love Call.' Mr. Sukenick's short story suffered from sketchy characterization and unevenness of tone, but was often perceptive and amusing, and sometimes even hilarious. Mr. Sukenick's skill at satire and parody is abundantly apparent . . . "

The Sun took no notice, but "Indian Love Call" contained a mild vulgarity, one found in Shakespeare. It was employed as a descriptive rather than an expletive, and in a context where no easy euphemism exists. In short, the usage was wholly defensible—but two faculty committees called the *Writer* editors in for possible disciplinary action. The complainant in both cases: Deane Malott.

The Sun fulminated, and so, apparently, did the rest of the campus. Droves of letters to the editor defended the use of the vulgarity, and said that no matter what action the two committees took, it amounted to censorship: all writings would be subject to the editorial review of the faculty.

The Faculty Committee on Student Conduct, chaired by the popular Prof. Jeremiah Wanderstock '41, took a courageous stand, considering who was doing the complaining. The committee voted to take no action, according to an official statement, "after being convinced that the students genuinely believed the story in question to represent a *bona fide* effort in the field of modern realistic writing." However, the statement added, "the Committee voted to caution students that while there are differences of opinion as to the acceptability of the particular story, there are limits set not only by law but also by the standards of good taste on the freedom enjoyed by creative writers, and voted further to urge students to be conscious of these

limits in their literary efforts."

This caveat seems inoffensive enough—but The Sun was furious that the committee would make any statement at all on the merits of the piece. An editorial sneered, "The campus is now graced by a committee which judges the suitability of material appearing in publications officially recognized by the University. May the tenure of this committee be long and healthful; may its meetings be pleasant; may its judgments reflect good discretion, well tempered by the opinions not only of the many commitee members but the assumed opinions of 'a sufficiently large segment of society.'"

If The Sun was unhappy with the *Writer's* exoneration, so was Malott. He suggested to the trustees and others that all publications on campus, including The Sun, should be brought under direct administration control, and three years later he pushed through trustee legislation taking away the faculty's power over student conduct—and giving it to himself. Later in this chapter, we will see what disastrous consequences this led to when puritanism ran amok in 1958.

* * *

The Cornell Widow got into hot water again two years later with a "sorority issue." This 1955 issue was objectionable not so much for obscene words *per se*, as for a general lack of taste. Most sororities were stereotyped as to the appearance of members, sexual proclivities, and average IQ. A great number of the generalizations were not all that amusing. When the issue came out, The Sun advised readers not to buy it, and added perceptively, "As a matter of fact, we are betting against this issue passing the careful scrutiny of the Faculty Committee on Student Activities. If you want a souvenir copy, you will probably have to get yours early before the masked campus patrolmen confiscate all available copies."

The Sun was right. The Men's Judiciary Board, a student group, called three Widow editors before it and handed them unofficial reprimands. In an unprecedented move, however, the FCSC, using its supervisory powers, upgraded the penalties to official reprimands.

Then (I apologize for the acronyms, but what can be done?) it was the turn of the FCSA, the group The Sun had been referring to. The FCSA did not have the power to penalize the individual editors, but it did issue a "strong warning" that it might disband the magazine "if the committee after due consideration finds the Widow has again abused its privilege."

The FCSA used the following rationale: "Under the Cornell tradition of freedom with [sic] responsibility, student organizations which abuse their freedom by violating the student code of honor stand responsible for such abuse." The mild-mannered Carl Becker would have torn out his hair upon reading this, had he been alive.

The FCSA concluded by adjudging The Widow guilty of violating "1. The rights of individual women students who might conceivably have been identified with the cruel and inhuman verbal caricatures contained in the issue;

"2. The rights of the sororities against which unfounded imputations of grave misconduct were laid;

"3. The rights of the faculty member to whom vulgar remarks were imputed; and

"4. The rights of the University upon which general discredit was cast without excuse or justification by the printing of the name *Cornell* on the cover of a magazine containing vulgar material."

The Sun, although disapproving of the issue's content, was furious at The Widow's treatment, as the editorial reprinted here attests. But the 1955 Widow fracas was the last student-publication wrangle for a long time, and marked the end of the University judicial system's attempts to enforce journalistic propriety. The following year, the U.S.

1955: The Sun Sticks Up for the widow

As *The Cornell Widow's* 1955 sorority issue sank deeper and deeper into the judicial bog, The Sun, which had previously panned it, turned defender of free expression. For those who have somehow followed the jumble of initials designating all the committees, this editorial was written after the MJB had taken action and been overruled by the FCSC, but before the FCSA had provoked The CDS to further fulminations by threatening to disband the CW. The editorial is titled—what else—*Freedom and Responsibility*—Ha! Note the lowercasing of the poor widow's name; this was a standard part of the longtime Sun-Widow rivalry, about which you can read more elsewhere in this book.

S-F-A has been somewhat of a minor slogan at the University. Of course, it doesn't rate with "Freedom and Responsibility" or "I would found an institution," but it supposedly has meant something. The letters denote Student-Faculty-Administration, a mythical triumverate which, according to ancient lore, governs student body affairs.

Like so many superstitions and fables, this triumverate has been shattered by reality. Hidden behind the scenes is the real ruler—the Board of Trustees—and the triumverate stands revealed as three subsidiary outposts of bureaucracy.

Not too long ago, the widow came out with a nasty attempt at humor; the issue wasn't in particularly good taste. The editors of the magazine soon discovered the reaction; indignant letters piled up in The SUN office as rapidly as used beer cans stack up in the widow headquarters.

And, as if the violent student reaction was not enough to convince the widowers of the error of their ways, the Men's Judiciary Board took time off from guiding drunks and lunatics to tag the three widow editors with unofficial reprimands. And, just to make things official, the Faculty Committee on Student Conduct was to review the decision and to apply its usual rubber stamp.

But, for the first time since the MJB was initiated, the Faculty Committee did not wave its wand of approval over the decision. Why? Because new facts were discovered. Of course not. Rather, several members of the Board of Trustees made verbal complaints to the Faculty.

The complaints were enough to set off a chain reaction. From all indications, the Faculty Committee agreed that the MJB had uncovered the facts—whatever facts there may be to a case like this. But, the Faculty felt a little stronger than the MJB about the seriousness of the offense.

So, with the whip of the Board of Trustees slashing in the background, the Faculty Committee handed out official reprimands to replace the unofficial reprimands meted out by the MJB. Thus, the Trustees were vindicated, the Faculty made an unnecessarily harsh decision, the students involved were more severely punished and nothing constructive was accomplished.

Aside from the mark which will remain on the students' records until they graduate, we can see nothing that has been accomplished by the greater penalty—not that there was any call for a penalty in the first place. This official reprimand will not do anything to improve the quality or taste of the widow. Supposedly, that was the goal of the trial or inquisition.

Student opinion alone was enough to move the widow to mend its ways. The MJB added another touch which was not even necessary. Now, the Faculty has moved a step further. "Freedom and Responsibility"—Ha!

By the way, another Faculty Committee—this one on Student Activities—gets its opportunity to please the Trustees today.

Getcha widow

By the way, while we're on the topic, the widow is putting another vile issue on sale today. This one is guaranteed 100 percent okay. Every page has been approved by the Faculty Committee on Student Conduct. It's got the Good Housekeeping Seal...besides, it's all about the tuition increase. No professor or dean jokes...good, clean fun...it's boring...

—editorials, March 17, 1955

Supreme Court handed down the first in a long series of decisions defining the sorts of things that could be punished as obscene, and while it was not clear whether these legal principles applied to Cornell, it was obvious that faculty and administration had no more taste for restricting expression.

By the mid-1960s bad language of all kinds was far more acceptable, and many student newspapers nationwide began to use phraseology that would make even returning Vietnam veterans blush. The Sun resisted this national trend, as an episode in late 1966 illustrates. A story arose—it is too complicated to explain in full—where the words *a horse's ass* played a vital role, and simply could not be omitted. The first day, The Sun ran two stories with the inelegant euphemism, "A (similar to horse's hindquarters)." However, it immediately became obvious that the story was an important one and would be covered for many weeks, and the phrase would have to appear every day. The editors gave up and decided to print the offending words in all their splendor from then on.

This piece of prudery served as a fascinating prologue to the January 1967 events involving a second equine, the literary magazine *Trojan Horse*.

Trojan Horse, founded in 1963 to critical applause, was by 1967 in financial difficulties. According to The Sun, it was also dominated by a small clique, and published too much indifferent material by alumni and non-students.

The focus of all the *Horse's* 1967 trouble was "Selections From a Journal by David Murray," the longest work in a short magazine. After reading this piece 13 years later, one can understand why so many people were offended. Offensive it was, and still is. It purports to be a diary of a young man with many sexual hang-ups. It contains graphic depictions of sex acts, unpleasant sexual fantasies, acts of excretion. It reveals the author's fascination with sex organs. It repeatedly employs a great number of our language's least acceptable words. Measuring on a scale of impropriety, if all the Sun, Widow and *Writer* stuff that caused alarm in the 50s amounted to a mud puddle, this was Cayuga Lake. The *Horse's* printer actually refused to handle it. It had to be typed out, mimeographed, and stapled into the magazine.

Then, as now, the college community was familiar with all the words Murray used, and had heard them too many times to claim shock. Therefore, it was and is feasible to ignore the vulgarities and to make a judgment as to the merits of the piece as a whole, which is unfortunate, because it then becomes even more offensive, if possible. The writer simply has nothing to say. The characters are developed abysmally. The dirty words are inserted, it seems, to prove that they can be, not to serve any literary purpose. The stream-of-consciousness style the author affects is a difficult one to keep control of. Murray demonstrates this quite well.

The Sun's literary critic agreed with the foregoing assessment. In a generally negative review of the *Horse*, he said, "One can wonder at the censorship exercised by the printer who would not reproduce Murray's piece; but one questions equally the judgment of the editors in bothering to print it at all. It is not that it is erotic or lewd; the bookshelves of three Ithaca bookstores have much better passages. But it is tedious and superfluous. The obscenity is offensive not for what it says, but because it consistently ruins what could have been nice lines. One comes out of the piece knowing almost nothing about the narrator except that he is fascinated with his own debauchery."

What happened next has never been satisfactorily explained. There have been a thousand different devil theories, some with President Perkins a behind-the-scenes Beelzebub directing the suppression of the *Horse*, others featuring various law-enforcement officials in the same role. There were a lot of strange coincidences, and the actions of the campus police were inexplicable. Perhaps some day the real story can be told. Here, at any rate, are the superficial events.

The magazine went on sale on a Wednesday. On Thursday, the campus police raided the Straight and Noyes Lodge and confiscated 130 copies of the *Horse*. The putative force behind the raid was the top campus cop, James M. Herson, who said the issue was obscene.

The situation that day was chaotic, for two reasons. First, the *Horse* editors still had about a thousand unseized issues in their possession. Second, practically every Cornell administrator was in New York City for a meeting of the Board of Trustees; the acting president was the dean of the graduate school, who clearly had no idea what he had done to deserve such a mess. Nevertheless, he agreed to issue an official statement forbidding further *Trojan Horse* sales, pending a final hearing.

The editors (remember, this was an age of civil disobedience, not the quiet 50s) announced they would defy the ban and sell the *Horse* Friday in front of the Straight, and they invited all students to come support them. The president of Student Government, for one, announced he would help sell.

But the best was yet to come. As it became clear that there would indeed be a large, angry demonstration in front of the Straight, the Faculty Committee on Student Affairs, which would have the ultimate say as to whether the *Horse* could be sold, met and expressed "grave concern" over the manner of the seizures. What a liberalization of faculty committees in only 13 years—from disciplining students for merely suggestive remarks, to tacit approval of the *Trojan Horse*!

Meanwhile, the student scheduling board met in emergency session and voted 8-0 to allow *Horse* sales, although it said the issue was "in violation of commonly accepted standards of decency and taste." The dean of students then told the *Horse* editors that Cornell would permit the sale to proceed.

Friday's sale and anti-seizure rally brought a remarkable turnout of 1,500 students—and an uninvited guest. County District Attorney Richard Thaler '53 appeared and arrested five *Trojan Horse* salesmen. Once having told them they were under arrest, however, he faced the problem of what to do next, since he had not brought along the battalion of police that would have been necessary to get the five students through the angry crowd. The Law—Thaler and one plainclothesman—managed to escort the students to a waiting car in front of the Straight, but that was as far as it got. Push came to shove.

Thaler, suddenly noticing that things were not going his way, offered the crowd a deal: he would leave without the five students, provided those in the crowd who had sold the *Horse* would agree to sign notarized statements to that effect, so that *they* could be prosecuted. Rally leaders agreed, and Thaler left, without his car. The protesters celebrated by letting the air out of its tires.

The community closed ranks. Nearly everyone agreed that the Murray piece was garbage, but that neither Cornell nor Thaler should have played sanitation worker. There were a few dissenters: Baxter Hathaway said the piece had merit; Walter Berns said it was so horrendous that the University should do nothing to protect it.

The Sun printed an extra edition Saturday to chronicle

Thaler's invasion, and editorially called for all Cornell students to thwart him by signing the statement admitting they had sold the *Horse*. By Monday, nearly 200 had done so. Five literature professors addressed a letter to the acting president, requesting his views on the advisability of teaching Hemingway, Sartre, Grass, Garcia Lorca and Cleland in light of the *Trojan Horse* incident.

And on Tuesday, Herson resigned. He did, however, go on to bigger and better things. Today, he is Ithaca's chief of police.

* * *

The *Trojan Horse* affair marked the last time there was an important effort to stifle student expression at Cornell. The groups that have had trouble since then are the faculty and outside speakers. The most notorious incident involving an outsider took place in December, 1975.

Spiro Agnew once boasted that he would not be allowed to speak at any Ivy League university. But he would have gotten a hero's welcome next to that accorded to the former South Vietnamese leader, Nguyen Cao Ky, a man who many Cornellians believed had the blood of their friends on his hands. When the Interfraternity Council announced it was sponsoring Ky's appearance, and paying him $1,500 at that, The Sun used some of its most violent editorial language, wondering why "people in responsible positions would actually consider inviting a bandit like Ky to speak here."

The audience that packed Bailey Hall did not come to

'FASCIST KY, SELL-OUT TO THE BOURGEOISIE': *Former South Vietnamese premier Nguyen Cao Ky attempts to speak on "Vietnam's Fatal Twenty Years" in Bailey Hall on December 9, 1975.*

—Sun Photo

hear Ky as much as to be heard by him. There were banners calling him a fascist and a killer; the cursing and catcalling was continuous. Ky did not even attempt to deliver a speech but instead opened the floor to questions, virtually all of which were diatribes. Within a few minutes the moderator, deciding the event could not continue, led Ky from the stage, and a year-long controversy over whether anyone's rights were violated, and if so, by whom, ensued. President Corson issued a statement condemning the disruption (The Sun called him a hypocrite on the ground that some years earlier he had banned radical leader David Burak from campus), a special faculty investigating committee was formed, and eventually, charges were filed in the campus judicial system against a philosophy professor, Richard Miller, who had been one of the more vocal anti-Ky questioners.

The Ky case, however, was not a black-and-white one. There were just too many questions. Did Ky really have to leave the stage? Did the sponsors do enough to ensure order? Was Miller's role really crucial? Was Ky's well-paid appearance entitled to the same protection a professor's lecture would have? A year later, a judicial hearing board acquitted Miller.

Since that time, a few speakers have been heckled, but there have been no incidents as serious. Both Presidents Corson and Rhodes have pledged with grim determination to see that all speakers are given a hearing.

In many ways, the faculty has not been as fortunate. In the late 60s, several classes were disrupted, mostly due to offended racial, and occasionally political, sensibilities. More than one professor described this period as a "new McCarthyism." There were, of course, some differences. The community as a whole opposed McCarthy. If professors had spoken out against the loyalty crusade, they would have been in the majority, at least at Cornell. But during the late 60s, the views that were suppressed were genuinely unpopular ones. In the 50s the pressures came from outside; in the 60s they were internal. It should also be said that the pressure for faculty to conform in the 50s must have been more effective. In the 60s there were a number of angry incidents. The 50s were quiet. Professors knew better than to step out of line.

In the early 70s, not only teaching methods but the sort of research individual faculty members were doing, especially if war-related, provoked some challenges to "academic freedom." Things have quieted down since then; today, it is even possible for a professor to broach racial matters without too much fear.

Still, it would be otiose to state that academic freedom on the Cornell campus is an absolute. A professor who goes sharply against prevailing views in any one of many subjects is still asking for trouble. I leave you with one example, which occurred less than two years ago.

The issue, a popular one today, was sexism. The speaker, a popular, usually conservative government professor named Werner Dannhauser, took an unpopular view. Addressing a group of women, he attacked the sponsor of his talk, Cornell's relatively new Women's Studies Program, because he said it was too dogmatic. He said women are "patently different" from men, and it should not be assumed that they are men's equals. Instead, he said that the possibility of women being superior or inferior should be considered, and that the Women's Studies Program refused to do this.

Dannhauser went on to construct a hypothetical argument for women's inferiority, and he said the most serious accusation concerned his own specialty, philosophy. Here is The Sun's summary:

> "Philosophy, the way of the philosopher, is the highest way of life. Women have performed absolutely badly in that field," Dannhauser said . . .
> "If on the highest level of the intellect, women do not function as well as men, that is a difference that ultimately has to be understood in terms of inferiority or superiority," he said.
> Arguments concerning "opportunity and socialization" are not important when applied to philosophy because "it takes less equipment to be a philosopher than any other field," Dannhauser said.
> He referred to the aristocratic women of 17th and 18th century France as a prime example. Such women had more leisure time than men. They had contact with the great minds of the time and nothing came of it, he said.

Now, this is quite a bold argument, and there are several possible rebuttals to it. To confine two of the best to one sentence, one could first say that there are a variety of other factors that account for the relative paucity of prominent female philosophers; and second that even if it were shown that women as a class were intellectually unfit to be philosophers it would not be nearly such a big deal as Dannhauser thought. But the point is not whether it was a good argument, but that Dannhauser was taking pot shots at a sacred cow.

Consequently, the rebuttal, when it came, pursued neither of the approaches I have suggested. Instead, it was seriously argued that Dannhauser's facts were incorrect and that women *do* have a good record in philosophy! A letter to The Sun signed by no less than eleven Cornell philosophy professors charged that Dannhauser's statements proved that he "is illiterate in contemporary philosophy, to which the contributions of women have been numerous and distinguished. The writings of Elizabeth Anscombe, Philippa Foot, Judith Jarvis Thompson, and Ruth Barcan Marcus, to name only four, by now form part of the assumed background for any serious discussion in areas as diverse as metaphysics, theory of knowledge, philosophy of mind, ethics and modal logic; and any university in the world would be honored to have one of these philosophers on its faculty."

Replying the following day, Dannhauser said, "I am delighted to have stirred up controversy and especially pleased to have awakened eleven members of the philosophy department from their dogmatic slumbers so that they could issue a dogmatic manifesto. They suffer from a dangerous inability to tell the difference between philosophers and professors of philosophy."

As to the four women named by the philosophy department, Dannhauser said, "In my remarks, I myself had mentioned Hannah Arendt and others. It is my contention, however, that the leading philosophers of our century—Wittgenstein, Russell, Whitehead, Heidegger, Husserl, Sartre, Bergson, etc.—have been and are men."

And there the argument died. Not one person wrote in to accuse the emperor of going naked; not a single Cornellian was willing to defy the philosophy professors by saying he, or she, had never heard of any of the famous women philosophers they had named.

Now when twelve specialists argue about their specialty, it is very difficult for the layman to contribute anything. But to summarize: a professor in 1978 took an unpopular position on a politically touchy subject. He was immediately castigated by eleven colleagues who in essence called him a charlatan and an academic fraud. Were they sincere? I honestly cannot even guess; perhaps you can do better. After all, the readers of this book will almost all be Cornellians, and most will have had at least some exposure to philosophy. So here are four questions for you: How many names on Dannhauser's list are you familiar with? How many on the philosophy department's? Does the Cornell faculty have Freedom today? Does it have Responsibility?

* * *

And now, let us drop the cliches. Here is what "Freedom and Responsibility" was meant to mean; here is Carl Becker's original address.

To get you in the proper frame of mind for this sudden time switch: we are now in Spring 1940. It is the 75th anniversary of the signing of Cornell's charter. Cornell is expanding rapidly; enrollment has just hit the staggering total of 7,000, which has many of the faculty upset. Cornell's fifth president, Edmund E. Day, has been in office less than three years, and he is clearly not as popular as his predecessor. There is a war going on in Europe, and a lot of people suspect it will some day embroil the United States.

The speaker, Professor Becker, specializes in the history of ideas. Although his field is officially modern European history, he is the author of *The Declaration of Independence*, written in the 20s and still, in 1940, the leading work on the subject. Becker is a small, shy man, generally considered to be a brilliant writer but only a fair lecturer. He is not a Cornell alumnus (Wisconsin '96), but he is known as a student of Cornell traditions and as a particular admirer of some of the early Cornell professors.

The Cornell Tradition: Freedom and Responsibility

By Carl L. Becker

Seventy-five years ago today Reuben E. Fenton, the Governor of the State of New York, signed a charter for Cornell University. The founding of the University was made possible in great part by the generosity of Ezra Cornell, a citizen of Ithaca. The first faculty was assembled, the University was organized, and instruction was begun under the farsighted leadership of the first president, Andrew D. White; and in a relatively short time, as such things go, the new institution, as a result of the distinguished achievements of its faculty and the high quality of instruction offered to its students, acquired a reputation which placed it among the leading universities of the country.

In the process of acquiring a reputation Cornell acquired something better than a reputation, or rather it acquired something which is the better part of its reputation. It acquired a character. Corporations are not necessarily soulless; and of all corporations universities are the most likely to have, if not souls, at least personalities. Perhaps the reason is that universities are, after all, largely shaped by presidents and professors, and presidents and professors, especially if they are good ones, are fairly certain to be men of distinctive, not to say eccentric, minds and temperaments. A professor, as the German saying has it, is a man who thinks otherwise. Now an able and otherwise-thinking president, surrounded by able and otherwise-thinking professors, each resolutely thinking otherwise in his own manner, each astounded to find that the others, excellent fellows as he knows them in the main to be, so often refuse in matters of the highest import to be informed by knowledge or guided by reason—this is indeed always an arresting spectacle and may sometimes seem to be a futile performance. Yet it is not futile unless great universities are futile. For the essential quality of a great university derives from the corporate activities of such a community of otherwise-thinking men. By virtue of a divergence as well as of a community of interests, by the sharp impress of their minds and temperaments and eccentricities upon each other and upon their pupils, there is created a continuing tradition that gives to a university its corporate character or personality, that intangible but living and dynamic influence which is the richest and most durable gift any university can confer upon those who come to it for instruction and guidance.

Cornell has a character, a corporate personality, in this sense, an intellectual tradition by which it can be identified. The word which best symbolizes this tradition is freedom. There is freedom in all universities, of course—a great deal in some, much less in others; but it is less the amount than the distinctive quality and flavor of the freedom that flourishes at Cornell that is worth noting. The quality and flavor of this freedom is easier to appreciate than to define. Academic is not the word that properly denotes it. It includes academic freedom, of course, but it is something more, and at the same time something less, than that—something less formal, something less self-regarding, something more worldly, something, I will venture to say, a bit more impudent. It is, in short, too little schoolmasterish to be defined by a formula or identified with a professional code.

And I think the reason is that Cornell was not founded by schoolmasters or designed strictly according to existing educational models. The founders, being both in their different ways rebels against convention, wished to establish not merely another university but a somewhat novel kind of university. Mr. Cornell desired to found an institution in which any person could study any subject. Mr. White wished to found a center of learning where mature scholars and men of the world, emancipated from the clerical tradition and inspired by the scientific idea, could pursue their studies uninhibited by the cluttered routine or the preoccupations of the conventional cloistered academic life. In Mr. White's view the character and quality of the university would depend upon the men selected for its faculty; devoted to the general aim of learning and teaching, they could be depended upon to devise their own ways and means of achieving that aim. The emphasis was, therefore, always on men rather than on methods; and during Mr. White's administration and that of his

immediate successors there was assembled at Cornell, from the academic and the non-academic world, a group of extraordinary men—erudite or not as the case might be, but at all events as highly individualized, as colorful, as disconcertingly original and amiably eccentric a group of men as was ever got together for the launching of a new educational venture. It is in the main to the first president and this early group of otherwise-thinking men that Cornell is indebted for its tradition of freedom.

Many of those distinguished scholars and colorful personalities were before my time. Many of those whom I was privileged to know are now gone. A few only are still with us—worthy bearers of the tradition, indefatigable in the pursuit of knowledge, in the service of Cornell, in the promotion of the public good, young men still, barely 80 or a little more. Present or absent, the influence of this original group persists, and is attested by stories of their sayings and exploits that still circulate, a body of ancient but still living folklore. It is a pity that some one has not collected and set down these stories; properly arranged they

Carl Lotus Becker
Coiner of the Classic Phrase

would constitute a significant mythology, a Cornell epic which, whether literally true or only characteristic, would convey far better than official records in dean's offices the real significance of this institution. Some of those stories I have heard, and for their illustrative value will venture to recall a few of them.

There is the story of the famous professor of history, passionate defender of majority rule, who, foreseeing that he would be outvoted in the faculty on the the question of the location of Risley Hall, declared with emotion that he felt so strongly on the subject that he thought he ought to have two votes. The story of another professor of history, who, in reply to a colleague who moved as a sense of the faculty that during war time professors should exercise great discretion in discussing public questions, declared that for his part he could not understand how any one could have the Prussian arrogance to suppose that every one could be made to think alike, or the Pomeranian stupidity to suppose that it would be a good thing if they could. The story of the eccentric and lovable professor of English who suggested that it would be a good thing, during the winter months when the wind sweeps across the hill, if the university would tether a shorn lamb on the slope south of the library building; who gave all of his students a grade of 85, on the theory that they deserved at least that for patiently listening to him while he amused himself reading his favorite authors aloud, and for so amiably submitting to the ironical and sarcastic comments—too highly wrought and sophistically phrased in latinized English to be easily understood by them—with which he berated their indifference to good literature.

* * *

There is the story of the professor who reluctantly agreed to serve as dean of a school on condition that he be relieved of the irksome task at a certain date; who, on that date, although no successor had meantime been appointed, cleared out his desk and departed; so that, on the day following, students and heads of departments found the door locked and no dean to affix the necessary signature to the necessary papers. A school without a dean—strange interlude indeed, rarely occurring in more decorous institutions, I should think; but one of those things that could happen in Cornell. And even more characteristic of the Cornell tradition is a story of the first president, Andrew D. White.

It is related that the lecture committee had brought an eminent authority to give, in a certain series, an impartial presentation of the Free-Silver question. Afterwards Mr. White, who had strong convictions on the subject, approached the chairman of the committee and asked permission to give a lecture in that series in reply to the authority. But the chairman refused, saying in substance: "Mr. President, the committee obtained the best man it could find to discuss this question. It is of the opinion that the discussion was a fair and impartial presentation of the arguments on both sides. The committee would welcome an address by you on any other subject, or on this subject on some other occasion, but not on this subject in this series in reply to the lecture just given." It is related that Mr. White did not give a lecture on that subject in that series; it is also related that Mr. White became a better friend and more ardent admirer of the chairman of the committee than he had been. It seems that Mr. White really liked to have on his faculty men of that degree of independence and resolution.

These stories are in the nature of little flash lights illuminating the Cornell temper. A little wild, at times, the Cornell temper; riding, not infrequently, as one may say, high, wide and handsome. Some quality in it that is native to these states, some pungent tang of the soil, some acrid smell of the frontier and the open spaces—something of the genuine American be-damned-to-you attitude. But I should like to exhibit the Cornell tradition in relation to a more general and at the same time a more concrete situation; and I will venture to do this, even risking a lapse from good taste, by relating briefly my own experience in coming to Cornell and in adjusting myself to its peculiar climate of opinion.

My first contact with the Cornell tradition occurred in December 1916, at the meeting of the American Historical Association at Cincinnati, when Professor Charles Hull invited me to come to his room in the hotel to meet his colleagues of the history group. Intimations had reached me that I was, as the saying is, being considered at Cornell for a position in European history, so that I was rather expecting to be offered a job, at a certain salary, on condition that I should teach a certain number of courses, assume certain administrative duties, and the like. I took it for granted that Cornell would handle these matters in the same businesslike way that other universities did. But I found that Professor Hull had a manner and a method all his own. He did not offer me a job—nothing as crude as that; he invited me, on behalf of his colleagues, to join the faculty of Cornell University. The difference may be subtle, but I found it appreciable.

On the chance that I might have formed a too favorable opinion of Cornell, Professor Hull hastened to set me right by itemizing, in great detail, the disadvantages which, from a disinterested point of view, there might be in being associated with the institution, as well as, more doubtfully, certain possible advantages. Among the disadvantages, according to Professor Hull, was the salary; but he mentioned, somewhat apologetically, a certain sum which I could surely count on, and intimated that more might be forthcoming if my decision really depended upon it. By and large, from Professor Hull's elaborate accounting, I gathered that Cornell, as an educational institution, was well over in the red, but that, such as it was, with all its sins of omission upon it, it would be highly honored if I could so far condescend to its needs as to associate myself with it.

There apparently, so far as Professor Hull was concerned, the matter rested. Nothing was said of courses to be taught, minimum hours of instruction, or the like mundane matters. In the end I had to inquire what the home work would be—how many hours and what courses I would be required to teach. Professor Hull seemed surprised at the question.

"Why," he said, "I don't know that anything is *required* exactly. It has been customary for a Professor of Modern History to give to the undergraduates a general survey course in modern history, and sometimes if he deems it advisable, a more advanced course in some part of it in which he is especially interested, and in addition to supervise, to whatever extent may seem to him desirable, the work of such graduate students as may come to him. We had rather hoped that you would be disposed to do something of this sort, but I don't know that I can say that anything specific in the way of courses is really *required*. We have assumed that whatever you found convenient and profitable to do would be sufficiently advantageous to the University and satisfactory to the students."

Well, there it was. Such a magnification of the professor, such a depreciation of the university, had never before, in similar circumstances, come my way. After a decent interval I condescended to join the faculty of Cornell University. And why not: To receive a good salary for doing as I pleased—what could be better? The very chance I had been looking for all my life.

* * *

And so in the summer of 1917 I came to Cornell, prepared to do as I pleased, wondering what the catch was, supposing that Professor Hull's amiable attitude must be either an eccentric form of ironic understatement or else a super-subtle species of bargaining technique. Anyway I proposed to try it out. I began to do as I pleased, expecting some one would stop me. No one did. I went on and still no one paid any attention. Personally I was cordially received, but officially no one made any plans to entertain me, to give me the right steer, to tell me what I would perhaps find it wise

to do or to refrain from doing.

There was about the place a refreshing sense of liberation from the prescribed and the insistent, an atmosphere of casual urbanity, a sense of leisurely activity going on, with time enough to admire the view, and another day coming. No one seemed to be in a hurry, except Mr. Burr, of course, and sometimes perhaps Mr. Ranum. But that was their affair—a response, no doubt, to the compulsion of some inner daemon. At least I saw no indication that deans or heads of departments were exerting pressure or pushing any one around. Certainly no head of the history department was incommoding me, for the simple reason, if for no other, that there didn't seem to be any history department, much less a head.

There were seven professors of history, and when we met we called ourselves the "History Group," but no one of us had any more authority than any other. On these occasions Professor Hull presided, for no reason I could discover except that we met in his office because it was the largest and most convenient. Whatever the History Group was it was not a department. If there was any department of history, then there were six; in which case I was the sole member, and presumably the head, of the department of Modern European History. The only evidence of this was that twice a year I received a communication from the president: one requesting me to prepare the budget, which consisted chiefly in setting down the amount of my own salary, an item which the president presumably already knew more about than I did; the other a request for a list of the courses given and the number of students, male and female, enrolled during the year.

I always supposed, therefore, that there were six departments of history, each manned by one professor, except the department of American history, which ran to the extraordinary number of two. I always supposed so, that is, until one day Professor Hull said he wasn't sure there were, officially speaking, any departments of history at all; the only thing he was sure of was that there were seven professors of history. The inner truth of the matter I have never discovered.

But the seven professors were certainly members of the Faculty of Arts, the Graduate Faculty, and the University Faculty since they were often present at the meetings of these faculties. They were also, I think, members of the Faculty of Political Science, a body that seemed to have no corporeal existence—since it never met, but that nevertheless seemed to be something—a rumor perhaps, a disembodied tradition or vestigial remain never seen, but lurking about somewhere in the more obscure recesses of Goldwin Smith Hall. I never had the courage to ask Professor Hull about the University—about its corporate administrative existence, I mean—for fear he might say that he wasn't sure it had any: it was on the cards that the university might turn out to be nothing more than 40 or 50 professors.

At all events, the administration (I assumed on general principles that there was one somewhere) wasn't much in evidence and exerted little pressure.

There was a president (distinguished scholar and eminent public figure) who presided at faculty meetings and the meeting of the Board of Trustees, and always delivered the Commencement address. But the president, so far as I could judge, was an umpire rather than a captain, and a Gallup poll would have disclosed the fact that some members of the community regarded him as an agreeable but purely decorative feature, his chief function being, one of my colleagues said, "to obviate the difficulties created by his office." I never shared this view. I have a notion that the president obviated many difficulties, especially for the faculty, that were in no sense created by his office. There were also deans, but not many or much looked up to for any authority they had or were disposed to exercise. Even so, the general opinion seemed to be that the appointment of professors to the office was a useless waste of talent. "Why is it," asked Professor Nichols, "that as soon as a man has demonstrated that he has an unusual knowledge of books, someone immediately insists on making him a bookkeeper?"

* * *

The rules were not many or much displayed or very oppressive —the less so since in so many cases they were conflicting, so that one could choose the one which seemed most suitable. The rules seemed often in the nature of miscellaneous conveniences lying about for a professor to use if he needed something of the sort. An efficient administrator, if there had been one, would no doubt have found much that was ill-defined and haphazard in the rules. Even to a haphazard professor, like myself, it often seemed so, for if I inquired what the authority for this or that rule was, the answer would perhaps be that it wasn't a rule but only a custom; and upon further investigations the custom, as like as not, would turn out to be two other customs, varying according to the time and the professors. Even in the broad distribution of powers the efficient administrator might have found much to discontent his orderly soul. I was told that according to the Cornell statutes the University is subject to the control of the Board of Trustees, but that according to the laws of the state it is subject to the Board of Regents. It may or may not be so. I never pressed the matter. I was advised not to, on the theory that at Cornell it always creates trouble when anyone looks up the statutes.

The general attitude, round and round about, seemed to be that the university would go on very well indeed so long as no one paid too much attention to the formal authority with which anyone was invested. And, in fact, in no other university that I am acquainted with does formal authority count for so little in deciding what shall or shall not be done.

In this easy-going, loose-jointed institution the chances seemed very good indeed for me to do as I pleased. Still there was an obvious limit. The blest principle of doing as one pleased presumably did not reach to the point of permitting me to do nothing. Presumably, the general expectation would be that I would at least be pleased to do something, and the condition of doing something was that I alone had to decide what that something should be. This was for me something of a novelty. Hitherto many of the main points—courses to be given, the minimum hours of instruction, the administrative duties to be assumed—had most been decided for me. I had only to do as I was told.

This might be sometimes annoying, but it was never difficult. Mine not to question why, mine not to ask whether what I was doing was worthwhile or the right thing to do. It was bound to be the right thing to do since someone else, someone in authority, so decided. But now, owing to the great freedom at Cornell, I was in authority and had to decide what was right and worthwhile for me to do. This was not so easy, and I sometimes tried to shift the responsibility to Professor Burr, by asking him whether what I proposed to do was the right thing to do. But Professor Burr wasn't having any. He would spin me a long history, the upshot of which was that what I proposed to do had sometimes been done and sometimes not, so that whatever I did I was sure to have plenty of precedents on my side. And if I tried to shift the responsibility to Professor Hull I had no better luck. He too would spin me a history, not longer than that of Professor Burr, but only taking longer to relate, and the conclusion which he reached was always the same: the conclusion always was, "and so, my dear boy, you can do as you please."

In these devious ways I discovered that I could do as I pleased all right. But in the process of discovering this I also discovered something else. I discovered what the catch was. The catch was that, since I was free to do as I pleased, I was responsible for what it was that I was pleased to do. The catch was that, with all my great freedom, I was in some mysterious way very much bound. Not bound by orders imposed upon me from above or outside, but bound by some inner sense of responsibility, by some elemental sense of decency or fair play or mere selfish impulse to justify myself; bound to all that comprised Cornell University, to the faculty that had so politely invited me to join it without imposing any obligations, to the amiable deans who never raised their voices or employed the imperative mood, to the distinguished president and the Board of Trustees in the offing who every year guaranteed my salary without knowing precisely what, if anything, I might be doing to earn it—to all these I was bound to justify myself by doing, upon request and in every contingency, the best I was capable of doing.

And thus I found myself working, although without interference and under no outside compulsion, with more concentration, with greater satisfaction, and, I dare say, with better effect, than I could otherwise have done. I relate my own experience, well aware that it cannot be in all respects typical, since it is characteristic of Cornell to permit a wide diversity in departmental organization and procedure. Yet this very diversity derives from the Cornell tradition which allows a maximum of freedom and relies so confidently upon the sense of personal responsibility for making a good use of it.

I should like to preserve intact the loose-jointed administrative system and the casual freedoms of the old days. But I am aware that it is difficult to do so in the present-day world in which the complex and impersonal forces of a technological society tend to diminish the importance of the individual and to standardize his conduct and thinking, a society in which life often seems impoverished by the overhead charges required to maintain it. Universities cannot remain wholly unaffected by this dominant trend in society. As they become larger and more complicated a more reticulated organization is called for, rules multiply and become more uniform, and the members of the instructing staff, turned out as a standardized article in mass production by our graduate schools, are more subdued to a common model. Somewhat less than formerly, it seems, is the professor a man who thinks otherwise. More than formerly the professor and the promoter are in costume and deportment if not of imagination all compact; and every year it becomes more difficult, in the market place or on the campus, to distinguish the one from the other at ninety yards by the naked eye. On the whole we all deplore this trend toward standardization, but in the particular instance the reasons for it are often too compelling to be denied. Nevertheless, let us yield to this trend only as a necessity and not as something good in itself. Let us hold, in so far as may be, to the old ways, to the tradition in which Cornell was founded and by which it has lived.

But after all, one may ask, and it is a pertinent question, why is so much freedom desirable? Do we not pay too high a price for it in loss of what is called efficiency? Why should any university pay its professors a good salary, and then guarantee them so much freedom to follow their own devices? Surely not because professors deserve, more than other men, to have their way of life made easy. Not for any such trivial reason. Universities are social institutions, and should perform a social service. There is indeed no reason for the existence of Cornell, or of any university, or for maintaining the freedom of learning and teaching which they insist upon, except in so far as they serve to maintain and promote the humane and rational values which are essential to the preservation of democratic society, and of civilization as we understand it. Democratic society, like any other society, rests upon certain assumptions as to what is supremely worthwhile. It assumes the worth and dignity and creative capacity of the human personality as an end in itself. It assumes that it is better to be governed by persuasion than by compulsion, and that good will and humane dealings are better than a selfish and a contentious spirit. It assumes that man is a rational creature, and that to know what is true is a primary value upon which all other values depend. It assumes that knowledge and power it confers should be employed for promoting the welfare of the many rather than for safeguarding the interests of the few.

In the long history of civilization the rational and humane values have sometimes been denied in theory, and persistently and widely betrayed in fact; but not for many centuries has the denial in theory or the betrayal in fact been more general, more ominous, or more disheartening than in our own day. Half the world is now controlled by self-inspired autocratic leaders who frankly accept the principle that might makes right, that justice is the interest of the stronger; leaders who regard the individual as of no importance except as an instrument to be used, with whatever degree of brutality may be necessary, for the realization of their shifting and irresponsible purposes; leaders who subordinate reason to will, identify law and morality with naked force as an instrument of will, and accord value to the disinterested search for truth only in so far as it may be temporarily useful in attaining immediate political ends. If these are indeed the values we cherish, then we too should abandon democracy, we too should close our universities or degrade them, as in many countries whose most distinguished scholars now live in exile they have been degraded, to the level of servile instruments in the support of state policy. But if we still cherish the democratic way of life, and the rational and humane values which are inseparable from it, then it is of supreme importance that we should preserve the tradition of freedom of learning and teaching without which our universities must cease to be institutions devoted to the disinterested search for truth and the increase of knowledge as ends in themselves desirable.

These considerations make it seem to me appropriate, on this memorial occasion, to recall the salient qualities which have given Cornell University its peculiar character and its high distinction; and, in conclusion, to express the hope that Cornell in the future, whatever its gains, whatever its losses, may hold fast to its ancient tradition of freedom and responsibility—freedom for the scholar to perform his proper function, restrained and guided by the only thing that makes such freedom worthwhile, the scholar's intellectual integrity, the scholar's devotion to the truth of things as they are and to good will and humane dealing among men.

—*speech, April 27, 1940*

The Background to Becker's Speech

As you can see, the "freedom" Becker was talking about had little to do with the "freedom" so dear to all those who take his name in vain. What Becker valued was freedom from an oppressive administration. He wanted to be left alone, to be allowed to teach and do research as he saw fit.

Now this kind of freedom has some similarities to the kinds of freedom we have discussed in the preceding pages, but there are also some considerable differences. Becker writes about how pleased he was by his freedom to teach what he wanted in 1917. If, however, he had wanted to teach that the British were principally responsible for the outbreak of World War I (which is what Cornell students in 1980 are taught) he would have found that his freedom did not extend quite so far. That is perhaps an inappropriate example; it is unlikely Becker would have been called upon to express a view on it in 1917. He did, however, teach modern European history, and in that course he could no more have blamed the French for the Franco-Prussian War than he could have suggested that the sun revolves around the earth. It would have cost him his job immediately. It might well have landed him in jail.

Becker's remarks sound a lot like the political rhetoric of 1980. Get government out of our hair, the candidates say, and we will be more efficient, more excellent; our system will work by itself. Unlike a lot of political tirades, though, what Becker says rings true. There actually were fewer rules at Cornell, less supervision; the faculty really was more powerful, and the administration less so, than at other schools. Although Becker did not mention this, Cornell's students were freer also: more free to set their own curriculum, to spend their time as they pleased, and, for that matter, more free to bust out. There is no doubt that Becker was right when he said this freedom was a major reason for Cornell being as fine an institution as it was in 1940.

In 1940, however, one could sense, and Becker did sense, a change. The atmosphere was frostier under President Day. In looking at the careers of Cornell's first eight presidents (I omit President Rhodes, who has not been in office long enough to generalize about) the difference between the first four and the last four is very striking. More than anything else, it is a difference in personal character. Most of what has been written about former Cornell presidents is so saccharine and banal that it is difficult to make any judgment as to their strengths and weaknesses. But one bond unites the first four: almost every portrait of them says something about their warm, engaging personalities; each one is described as thoughtful, considerate, and urbane. It is absolutely clear that the first four presidents all got more than professional respect and admiration from their constituency; that they were genuinely liked as individuals. Firsthand accounts of how the students and faculty felt about Schurman and Farrand, and even White, are to be found elsewhere in this book.

Of the second four, only James Perkins had a brief burst of personal popularity, and by the time he was forced out of office he was despised. President Corson is a shy man; he was almost unknown to the student body during his term. Presidents Day and Malott both presented a frigid exterior. Here is how Morris Bishop describes Day: "He was a man of power and dominance, keen in his judgment of men and things, serious of purpose. . . He was also impatient, sometimes tactless in dealing with opposition, inclined to rely rather on statistical evidence than on intuition. He lacked

the grace of President Farrand in attaining his ends. Some professors of the humanities complained that he never really understood the aims of humane education, recalcitrant to statistical analysis. This was a misconception, to which President Day deliberately lent himself." One can understand why Becker was so uneasy.

When we read Becker's address, and also Paul O'Leary's essay earlier in this book, we are struck by their admiration for the simpler times when rules as rules were unnecessary. Let common sense be the guide, they say. If a student or professor does something wrong, correct or punish him. Otherwise leave him alone. This system, in fairness, seemed to work well at Cornell.

Day and Malott, both primarily businessmen rather than educators, were uncomfortable with this concept. Many more standards and rules were set up, not necessarily to restrict freedoms but because it was felt that there had to be some easily-understood regulation to cover every situation. Teaching loads for faculty became strictly defined; a much closer watch was kept on budgets; the number of administrators was sharply increased. These trends were firmly ensconced when Becker made his speech. During Malott's term new regulations governing student life were issued at a bewildering clip. When students protested the new rules, they frequently made it clear that they objected more to the fact of the rules than to their content.

The administration's seeming fascination with expanding the number of regulations was the cause of the last event we will look at in this book. The 1958 apartment party fracas makes good reading now, especially since the administration behaved so foolishly throughout that it is impossible not to sympathize with the underdog students.

*   *   *

But before we leave the erudite Carl Becker, who spent so much time studying the institution he loved, it might be enlightening to read some more of his prose. These three quotations are from *The Declaration of Independence*.

1. "Apart from the peculiar felicities of phrasing, what strikes one particularly in reading the Declaration as a whole is the absence of declamation. Everything considered, the Declaration is brief, free of verbiage, a model of clear, concise, and simple statement."

2. "In truth the Declaration is built up around a single idea, and its various parts are admirably chosen and skilfully disposed for the production of a particular effect. The grievances against the king occupy so much space that one is apt to think of them as the main theme. Such is not the case. . . It is difficult to justify rebellion against established political authority. Accordingly, the idea around which Jefferson built the Declaration was that the colonists were not rebels against established political authority, but a free people maintaining long established and imprescriptable rights against a usurping king."

3. "The framers of the Declaration were not writing history, but making it. They were seeking to convince the world that they were justified in doing what they had done; and so their statement of 'causes' is not the bare record of what the king had done, but rather a presentation of his acts in general terms. . ."

"Freedom and Responsibility" is the most misconstrued and inappropriately employed phrase in Cornell's history. At least, though, you now know what it was that Becker actually said. I suspect you now also know why.

A VISION IN A DREAM: *Spring Weekend floats glide over Triphammer Bridge in 1954, heading for the central campus and State Street downtown. The cartoon character Pogo rows on Delta Upsilon's foreground float, as Cinderella's pumpkin coach draws near. Besides parades of tissue-paper fantasies (a tradition which died out in the 1960s), each 1950s Spring Weekend featured beauty queens, fraternity "anything that floats" naval competition on Beebe Lake, and formal dances to the Big Band sound. When many of the outdoor events of Spring Weekend 1957 were canceled due to torrential rain, an astonishing bacchanalia ensued which went beyond mere drunken rowdiness—there were instances of vandalism and theft, many minor injuries, one accidental death and two near-deaths. The administration subsequently cracked down on students' social lives, which in turn sparked the legendary "apartment party" upheaval of Spring 1958.*

The Granddaddy of All Student Protests

We now turn to an incident as bizarre as it is amusing. Throughout this book the reader has had to exercise great imagination to try to understand what things were like at certain times in Cornell's history. Frequently, this is not too difficult. We cannot imagine a 1980 freshman being forced to leave Cornell because he refuses to wear a beanie, yet it makes sense when set in 1921; we read with awe of the 1940 standards of ethics that induced Cornell to forfeit a football game it had already won; we can visualize a Straight take-over in the chaotic days of 1969 and yet sense that it could not happen today.

This story, though, is different. It is a story of sex, and how the Cornell administration tried valiantly to ban it from campus. If this happened when The Sun was founded in 1880, we would smile and understand. Possibly we might even accept its happening in the neo-Victorian days of 1910.

But the events you are about to read of took place in 1958!

Some historians have found this controversy significant because it culminated in the nation's first big "student power" demonstration, and so served as a prologue to the tempestuous 1960s. To a certain extent, this view is correct. In November 1957, *Time* magazine characterized college

students of the time as "The No-Nonsense Kids" and quoted a "typical" student as saying "Such irrational actions as riots are too much of a risk. Anything you do out of the ordinary brings ridicule."

Cornell, to be sure, did have a "riot" in 1958, but as riots go it was unimpressive. The dean of men was hit by an egg (apparently thrown by his daughter); the president was heckled, burnt in effigy, and had eggs and stones thrown at his house; and some students cursed in public; but that was the extent of the damage. There have been 30 or 40 better demonstrations at Cornell since then, if what you like is screaming or violence.

There also was a certain amount of rhetoric that could be construed as calling for more student power, but this was really a side issue, a gratuitous assertion that the administration had no idea what students were thinking.

It is far easier to explain the 1958 events as a result of two local factors: first, there was a brilliant and incisive student leadership, for which The Sun was the major platform, and in which the editor-in-chief of The Sun, Kirkpatrick Sale '58, was the dominant force. Sale and another leader, Richard Farina '59, went on to success as writers, Sale as a social and political commentator, Farina as author of *Been*

1956: Should Students Have a Voice?

In Fall 1956, Cornell suddenly banned liquor at football games. Not too alarming, perhaps, but it raised the same sorts of issues of administration high-handedness over moral matters that would lead to the 1958 fracas, and The Sun's editorial response was also similar.

It is difficult to understand the reasoning which went into the University's action barring drinking in Schoellkopf stadium. Indeed, the motivation, the timing, the method of formulation and the construction of the order seem entirely out of keeping with the liberal aims of the Administration.

We recognize that a drinking problem exists on campus; of this there can be little doubt. We believe, however, that such an arbitrary, unannounced and radical move can do nothing to solve this problem.

There is a broad gulf fixed between the aims of the University's rule—to stop disorder and drunkenness in the stands—and the method of approach. So much so, that the antagonism and resentment over the means almost negate the acknowledged value of the end.

Of primary importance here is the apparent departure from the customary deliberation in controlling student activities. Students at the University have learned to respect the Administration for allowing student participation in policy-making in areas of campus social activity. This action all but cancels that privilege.

We feel that the authorities had little understanding of the feelings of the student body when this rule was passed. The haste and bad-timing of the order, for one thing, and the arbitrary manner in which it was promulgated, for another, show clearly the lack of contact with student opinion prevalent in the Administration groups which discussed the matter.

Hesitating to pick at old bones of contention, we nevertheless wonder whether the removal of authority in student activities and discipline from the Faculty may have indirectly contributed to the unfortunate bungling of the "no drinking" order.

But whatever the cause of the radical change in the University's approach to student activities, it is now perfectly clear that this rash action has met with almost unanimous student resentment. And this, we feel, with some justification.

First, the reasoning to the desired end is at once fallacious. Because of an age-old history of instances of drunkenness at football games, the University feels the only solution is to ban alcohol from Schoellkopf. But without inspection of personal effects, the rule will obviously be broken. Anything short of personal searches can do little to stop the parade of hip flasks, canteens and small bottles of alcoholic beverages which will reach Schoellkopf on any normal Saturday. By making the possession of intoxicants in itself an offense, the University is encouraging the "smuggling" of drinks.

If drinking is allowed outside of Schoellkopf, as we trust it still is, two points of the University's argument become invalid. For students will still be able to enter the field in various stages of concealed intoxication, and will be able to drink just as heavily after the game is finished. Also, the possible notion that the University is turning "dry" is thus invalidated.

So, in truth, the University is unequipped to stop the parade of liquor into Schoellkopf; it is actually encouraging "underground" carrying of flasks; it is not stopping the incidents of drunken disorder, more numerous outside of Schoellkopf than within; and it cannot stand on a "prohibitionist" platform.

Where the idea for the drinking ban arose is still a mystery. Presumably, the Office of the Dean of Men may be absolved from blame. It maintained, so far as can be determined, a respectable reluctance to sanction the timing of, and the approach to, the proposal.

Neither is the President's Committee on Student Conduct directly responsible. They refused, it is now believed, to issue any kind of "law" to ban drinking. Rightly, they considered the matter out of their jurisdiction.

And the fact that the law, as it was finally written, was announced by the Board of Physical Education and Athletics proves nothing except that the Board was forced to act as a "front" for the real powers which motivated the ruling. Who those powers are, again, is unknown. By elimination, however, one might easily be able to discover in which offices of Day Hall the plan originated.

Second, we question the timing of the announcement. Two days before Fall Weekend is hardly the time to prepare students for a dramatic re-orientation of the University's attitudes on what amounts to a "moral" problem. But this negligence may be attributed, probably, to ignorance rather than malice.

Third, we resent the fact that the students were not allowed an attempt at solution through their own agencies. If the University felt, as they did, that outsiders as well as students are involved in the problem, it nevertheless remained for the Administration to appraise the students of the seriousness of the situation, and wait for student-supported action for its correction.

It is now plain that the University has alienated most of the student body on this issue, and, if for no other reason than public relations, the announcement has proved unsuccessful. It is amusing that, concerned about the reception students would give, the Dean of Men's office hastily (within one day) assem-

−Sun Photo by Steven Fox

bled a small group of "student leaders" to be witnesses *ex post facto*. By marshalling the support of these leaders, the Dean and the Assistant Dean felt, student opinion would emerge in sympathy with the rule. Such, we are happy to report, was most wonderfully not the case.

Finally, the absence in the stated rule of any system of penalties is seriously damaging both to student morale and to the University's purpose.

* * *

We wonder, as we have heard others wonder during the last 24 hours, if this latest action is but another step in "tightening the reins" of University control over student activities. Sensibly or not, we have felt, over the last few years, a certain strictness of policy emerging from Day Hall, as more and more the freedom-part of "freedom and responsibility" slips out of reach.

It is certainly not our intention, however, to charge the Administration of seeking, by some treacherous intrigue, to rob the students of their freedom. Rather must we admit that students have become increasingly unwilling to carry the responsibilities of social organization which are naturally theirs. When these are neglected, the Administration must enter the picture.

But, far from any pious lecture on "the Cornell tradition of freedom and responsibility," what this campus needs is a renewed effort to explain the University's policy on student participation in important decisions affecting the students themselves. We feel the disturbance caused by the "no drinking in Schoellkopf" rule could have been avoided if the students were, for once, given a chance to solve a difficult problem by themselves.

—*editorial, October 25, 1956*

Down So Long It Looks Like Up to Me, a novel based on his 1958 experience.

Second, the potential for a student uprising is always there, although it may be hard to trigger: all it takes is for the administration to be sufficiently obtuse. And if ever an administration deserved what it got, if ever a bureaucracy became entangled in a net of its own making, it was the 1958 Cornell administration.

This is a funny story, and part of the reason is that there are clearly heroes and villains. In almost all of Cornell's other controversies, arguments could be made for one side or another: what should have been done about the Straight takeover, for example, still provokes spirited debate. But in this case, the enormous silliness of the administration is beyond cavil. President Malott started a war that was lost before the first shot was fired; most people knew this even as hostilities commenced. In a scintillating appeal to history, Sale predicted, "Could this really have happened? posterity will say. What must the Administration have been like? What the students? Did our Cornell ever think that it really had a role in morality?. . . and then posterity will smile wryly. . ."

And, 22 years later, we do.

*   *   *

Like many funny stories, this one begins tragically. Few things can be more tragic than the needless death of a student, and there was one during the 1957 Spring Weekend, one of the two big fraternity weekends of the school year. A sophomore, apparently drunk, fell off a second-floor patio at a fraternity house, fracturing his skull and dying three hours later.

If this had been some ghastly freak, it might have been easier to accept, but, sadly, it was just another incident in what seems to have been the wildest weekend in Cornell's history, before or since.

Cornellians are wont to blame things on the weather, and indeed much of the blame must be laid to it: unending, torrential rain, cancelling almost all of the scheduled outdoor events, and obliging the celebrants to stay inside the fraternity houses, where there was an excess of liquor.

The weather also closed down Tompkins County Airport, so that many of the men's "import" dates never arrived. There was also unusual confusion concerning sleeping arrangements. This was one of the rare weekends during the year when women were permitted to sleep overnight at fraternities (in separate quarters, it goes without saying.) But in some houses where men's beds were reserved for the exclusive use of female guests, no provision had been made for where the evicted males would sleep. Because of these two factors, a large number of "stag" men, including several uninvited guests from Hobart and Ithaca College, roamed the campus at all hours, crashing party after party. Apparently, the revelry did not stop before dawn.

The results were predictable. A surfeit of public fights; four automobile accidents, including one head-on collision that injured three students; around $5,000 worth of property stolen, purportedly by stags. A woman fell out of a tree, injuring her ankle, and a man in a fraternity house suffered a broken leg when, according to the official report, "a piano fell on him."

Furthermore, according to the President's Committee on Student Activities, "Noisy parties were reported to the campus patrol and to Ithaca Police. Garbage and eggs were thrown at paraders and policemen during the float parade. Rowdiness and public drinking were exhibited. A large tree stump was put on the Stewart Avenue bridge.

"There was a sharp rise in number of visits and admissions to the Infirmary for injuries and inebriation. There were lacerations from broken glasses with or without

severance of tendons of fingers and hands. Incidents occurred with every conceivable degree of injury. Many of these were automobile accidents, others fights when boys got inebriated."

By rights there should also have been two other deaths. A second sophomore fell out of a third-floor fraternity window; he was in critical condition for several days. More interesting, an intoxicated Ithaca College freshman, attempting to jump out of the way of an oncoming car in a fraternity parking lot, overdid it slightly and ended up at the bottom of Fall Creek Gorge. His fall was measured at 175 feet, but he escaped injury when it pleased Providence to have him land fanny-first inside an abandoned tire at the bottom of the chasm.

*   *   *

Events like these would call for action even in 1980, so it is no shock to learn that President Malott called in the leaders of the Interfraternity Council and demanded to know what they were going to do about it. He also flatly stated that there would be no further party weekends until decisive measures were taken to prevent a recurrence.

In response, the IFC drew up a revised social code that restricted drinking, prohibited roving stags, and increased the number of chaperones at parties. All in all, a reasonable effort, and, that done, the IFC started to plan for the 1957 Fall Weekend.

Stunningly, the administration, through the President's Committee, rejected the new code, and cancelled the weekend. At first, the campus was mystified, since it seemed the committee agreed with most of the proposals, and the proposals seemed to attack all the problems of the preceding spring, excepting the rain, which was resistant to legislation.

It soon became clear, although many people refused to believe it, that the committee's main goal was not the elimination of alcohol, but the control of sexual expression! Whether the committee simply had an attack of Victorianism or somehow suffered the hallucination that sexual activities rather than drinking had caused the spring events, we do not know. We do know that it systematically began turning back the clock by eliminating mixed company as much as possible, and pushing social rules back 20 years or more, bucking every social trend.

This sounds inconceivable; it *is* inconceivable, but to even try to understand we need some background. First, to believers in equality of the sexes, forget it. This is 1958 we are talking about, when double standards were *really* double standards. Women had to live in dormitories while men could live in apartments (this was not changed until 1965); a dress code of sorts survived, for women; women had curfews and chaperonage requirements, men had none. In the event of any sexual peccadillos, women were subject to far more severe punishments: the normal penalty for an unmarried woman student discovered to have had sexual intercourse was expulsion. As a matter of fact, one woman *was* expelled in January 1958 for "moral reasons," along with two men who were merely suspended indefinitely.

While there is little data on the subject, rules and penalties like these probably prevented excessive promiscuity. If we assume that students were basically virtuous at that time, the rush with which the sexual revolution arrived on campus is amazing. Without attempting to date the high-water mark of sex on campus, suffice it to say that ten years after these events, cohabitation was in vogue; twenty years afterward, the University which had tried so hard to exterminate illicit sex was dispensing contraceptives and prescribing The Pill at Gannett Clinic.

But we are ahead of ourselves again.

Who Will Enforce the New Social Rules?

When the President's Committee handed down its fraternity social code in December 1957, The Sun reacted with two of the most biting editorials in its history. The first one called the new code a "dangerous and foolhardy action," a "supreme folly," etc. More important, it attacked the whole concept of the administration regulating student conduct, and called for the power to be returned to the faculty. Noting that the committee members were directly responsible to President Malott, the editorial asserted that "a great many qualified Faculty members refuse to sit on this Committee, knowing that their first dissent may be their last, and so the composition of the Committee may consist of only those who slavishly agree with Administration dicta." Here, the second editorial of the series.

Once it is recognized that the conception and formulation of the University's Social Events Standards are in most respects unfortunate, it is necessary to determine the specific aspects of the code which might—indeed must—be improved in order to produce the "desirable social climate on the campus" which is sought by the President's Committee on Student Activities. For the student body, like it or not, is going to have to live under these regulations, and their actions should therefore be directed to improving and perfecting the standards as much as possible.

To us, and to much of the campus, the two most errant regulations are those concerning the elimination of room parties and the elimination of single overnight parties. Perhaps it is most natural to react to those things which are "eliminated," but we feel that the dissatisfaction with these two rules goes deeper than that.

First, the committee has chosen to abolish room parties—i.e., individual parties in fraternity rooms—since "reports from people attending these parties and from chaperones indicate that room parties have been one of the main problem areas in the past." We do not quite know what "problem areas" are, but it cannot be denied that there is a certain amount of intimacy that goes on in private rooms: this may be what the committee opposes.

But let us face facts. No amount of legislating is ever going to prevent society—much less students—from "necking." And it must be recognized that at any kind of a weekend, necking will play a significant part. Maybe it's unfortunate, maybe it leads to evil, maybe the committee doesn't like it—but there it is. Therefore the abolition of room parties and the institution of "Commons Areas" in which necking is forbidden will only succeed in making students leave the fraternity houses, where supervision is possible, and go out alone to cars and apartments, where supervision is not possible.

Moreover, despite what the committee may think, there are many students who simply want to be away from the crowd for awhile, who may wish to talk or play bridge or rest. The abolition of room parties deprives them to a large extent of this right, and succeeds in eliminating an area for personal, private conversation on a campus which has altogether too few such areas.

Second, the committee has chosen to abolish single overnights—although, it is true, the committee chairman has suggested that changes might be forthcoming if this is the students' major bone of contention. The committee gave two reasons for their action: 1) Single overnights tend to extend beyond their specific limits so that students cut classes and their academic work suffers; 2) if fraternities are given the privilege of holding parties until 3 a.m. as on single overnights, then any other group may have this privilege even if the latter groups do not have facilities.

Our objection to these arguments is that they, like the rest of the code, leave many things unconsidered. First, once single overnights are restricted to Saturday nights, presumably not conflicting with classes, there is nothing more that the committee can do to insure that students will attend classes. Second, we see no reason why fraternities should be discriminated against for 3 a.m.

parties, when they can provide overnight facilities and various other groups cannot.

In addition, the committee is errant in requiring women to go to "assigned areas" at 1:30 a.m. Sunday and keeping them there until 8 a.m. Sunday. After all, women can just as easily go back to their rooms at 1:30, letting the men sleep in their own beds, and legally come out of the dormitories at 6 a.m.—two hours earlier than the committee would have them. Obviously, the whole reasoning of the committee is ridiculous here, and unless it reconsiders this area with haste, it will put itself into even deeper holes than it has already constructed, if possible.

There are other areas of the code which must also be revised. Attention must be given to the entire question of regulations concerning imported women who are housed in hotels and motels either on a houseparty weekend or on a normal weekend. Are they required to be in their rooms at 1:30 a.m. on a normal Saturday night and 4 a.m. on a houseparty Saturday night? Will the Campus Patrol arrest a Cornell man and his imported date if they walk across the campus at 2 a.m. during the year? If so, it would be a disastrous blow to the freedom of the Cornell student, and an entirely indefensible policy. We can only assume that the committee blindly failed to consider this matter, and will make clear its position on it soon.

The other major problem which the committee must face is how to enforce the regulations which it has imposed on the student body. It will be a very difficult problem, and there will be no easy solution. But we do not sympathize with the committee. It has chosen its path and it must stick to it: as long as it disregards student responsibility for obeying the code, as it does, it must disregard student responsibility for enforcing it. The job of enforcement, like the job of imposition, should be up to the Administration.

Of course the committee could not set up efficient police enforcement of the code, even if it wanted to; it must depend to a large extent on student cooperation, the kind of cooperation which it ignored so summarily in the formulation of the code, but which it needs so badly now. To this cry of need we feel sure the students will respond. Interfraternity Council is sure to appreciate the problem of the committee and aid it as much as possible in enforcing the rules.

But there is a point beyond which IFC cannot, and must not, go. It cannot be expected to enforce the three or four points with which it disagrees, even if it agrees to enforce the many points which it accepts. We believe that IFC should go as far as it honestly can in aiding the University in the enforcing of its improper code—but it must not be compelled, by coercion or persuasion, to enforce illogical and unjust provisions which it does not accept.

Thus the problem of enforcing such things as room party provisions, bed checks, and "Commons Area" regulations may well remain for the University to solve. Perhaps it will ignore enforcement and depend upon student spirit and judgment to follow the rules, perhaps it will establish an efficient dean's force with spyglasses—but whatever it does it must remember that once student cooperation is ignored the problem is much greater.

Thus it appears that the Administration put itself into a very unfortunate situation. It has, in the larger sense, negated student responsibility in handing down a social code in which the student groups had little real voice, in which student provisions were never given a try, in which the moral sense and judgment of the student body was ignored. Once any body—governmental or educational—takes an action of this sort it must recognize two concordant facts: the rules must be carefully and explicitly formulated with few or no areas of weaknesses and imprecision, and the enforcement of the rules is the action of that body and not of those upon whom the rules are pressed. The President's Committee did not recognize these facts, and has thereby created a dangerous and improper situation. It can only remain for the students to attempt to alleviate this situation—and once this is done, ensure that it will never happen again at this university.

—editorial, December 17, 1957

The Great Student Uprising of 1958

BY CARL P. LEUBSDORF '59

In the aftermath of the nation's sexual revolution of the 1960s and 1970s, it almost seems laughable to recall that the great student uprising that rocked the Cornell campus in the spring of 1958 revolved around whether women should be allowed to visit men's off-campus apartments.

But that was an age in which virtually every undergraduate woman lived in a dormitory, when there were strict sign-out and curfew rules that applied to all of them, and when key officials in the administration took seriously their efforts to serve *in loco parentis*—in place of the student's parents.

In retrospect, what happened at Cornell that term, the spring of my junior year, seems almost like a forerunner of the more significant student revolts of the 1960s. While this may be true, it is safe to say that the goals of those who resisted the administration's heavy-handed efforts were more narrowly focused; students wanted to maintain an open social atmosphere at Cornell that was in accord with the University's long tradition of "freedom with responsibility."

Until 1953, it had been illegal for any Cornell woman to visit off-campus apartments of male students. Then, in the face of widespread violations, new rules were issued permitting women—in groups of at least two—to visit apartments, provided the apartment was registered with the University. Freshmen were still barred unless chaperones were present. Whether the purpose of such visits was academic or social, they quickly acquired the somewhat inaccurate name of "apartment parties."

At the same time, campus social life was governed only by a general code of conduct. There was no specific set of rules. But when Spring Weekend 1957 was marked by an unusual degree of vandalism and drunkenness—plus the death of a student who fell from a fraternity porch and broke his neck—Deane W. Malott, the University president, called in student leaders and demanded they take action to curb excesses.

* * *

That fall, student leaders sought to write new rules. But the administration spurned their attempts. Instead, taking advantage of a 1955 action by the Board of Trustees that transferred control over student activities from the faculty to the president, it imposed strict new rules.

By a vote of 11 to 4, with all four student members dissenting, the President's Committee on Student Activities voted in December 1957 to impose a new Social Code. Instead

---

Carrie Nation and Deane Malott

As Miss Humphreyville's committee met secretly to deliberate tightening restrictions on apartment parties, a survey of women's reactions to the *existing* rules was released in March. About 26 percent of upperclasswomen were polled, and 56.1 percent admitted that within the past year they had violated the apartment regulations, meaning that they had entered a man's apartment without a second woman being present. 61.7 percent said the existing rules were too severe, and about half felt they should be eliminated entirely. 15 percent said they had occasionally refused to go to a man's apartment alone because it would have violated the rules; 63.8 percent said they had never refused on these grounds; perhaps the others had never been asked.

Sun editor Sale, well aware of the ominous prospects of a total ban, seized the opportunity to call for abolition of the rules instead, with a deft allusion to the Volstead Act.

It took three months and seven days, but the Women's Student Government Association finally released the results of its apartment party survey Wednesday. Since only 346 women were polled, since the questionnaire was somewhat faulty, and since WSGA's mathematical calculations leave some room for improvement, the findings should be taken with a grain or two of salt. And yet they do illustrate some points which may be significant.

The number of violations of the rulings—more than half the women admitted violating—does not indicate that the apartment party regulations should be stiffened or changed, but rather that they should be eliminated. Furthermore, approximately one-half of the women indicated that they felt women should be allowed in apartments "under any circumstances."

Quite clearly, there is something wrong with the present rulings. (At present, the University graciously allows upperclasswomen to visit an apartment when it is registered with Day Hall and when at least two women are present.) When half the people violate a provision, there is more likely something wrong with the provision than with the people.

We do not remember Prohibition ourselves, but we are given to understand that there was some law passed that did not meet with great favor. And when no one paid any attention to the law, it was finally decided to eliminate it. Now, while the University does not stand in the same position as the federal government, it might well learn a lesson from this: that a ruling universally broken is worse than no ruling at all. Better have women going to men's apartments honorably than have them sneaking in under cover of night.

Let not the Administration argue that the apartment provisions are "privileges," that the students are lucky to have had the opportunities they have had since 1953, when the rulings were put into effect. Since when is it a privilege for a woman to go to a man's apartment? If the Administration wants students to follow the behavior patterns of society, it cannot refuse them this basic right.

Let not the Administration say that it needs apartment party rules for "public relations," to assure the handwringing parent that his daughter will be unsullied for four years. For it is not the apartments which are at fault if someone becomes sullied, it is not even the apartment regulations—it is, most probably, the person involved. The act of going to an apartment, moreover, is not a terribly significant one, and it cannot be called evil in itself. That immorality may take place is not a reason to keep women from them—next you would have to prevent women from riding in cars. Finally, it would seem to be worse "public relations" to have a ruling broken by half the women on campus than to have no ruling at all.

Lastly, let not the Administration act surprised that so many people violated the apartment provisions. We would be surprised if they were surprised. There is nothing surprising in the fact that women want to go to a man's apartment for privacy, comfort and hospitality. They always have wanted to, they always will. And we think it is a good thing, rather. This is something which should be available for everyone, and no one should be shocked that people desire it.

In short, all signs seem to indicate that the apartment rules are generally useless. It is all very kind of the University to offer this privilege, but this is not really a privilege, it is more of a right that should be offered to everyone. The apartment party regulations cannot be strengthened or changed, they must be eliminated altogether, and students must be left to go freely.

—editorial, February 28, 1958

THE IMPORTANCE OF ART: *Former Sun editor-in-chief Kirkpatrick Sale '58 was daubing at a canvas in Prof. H. Peter Kahn's painting class one May morning, shortly after Theresa R. Humphreyville—the chairman of an administration committee charged with regulating student activities—had announced her displeasure with situations "conducive to petting and intercourse." While editor, Sale had consistently sought to marshal popular opposition to administrators like Humphreyville. Quite recently, he had joined his roommate Richard Fariña '59 in declaring that "action among the students themselves" was crucial to thwarting Day Hall's drive to "define morality for the undergraduate." But it was only now, with brush in hand, that the decisive inspiration struck. What if a small group of students banded together, instead of complaining and lobbying individually? What if they used art department pigments to paint large, colorful protest posters, and displayed them between classes in front of the Straight? Sale called his friends, and at 10 o'clock on the sunny morning of May 23, 1958, ten or fifteen students stood with placards on the Straight steps. Soon there were 100 people . . . then 150. Sale decided it was necessary for someone to get up and speak. "We're here not only to protest the apartment ban," shouted Sale: "We're here to protest the social code, deferred rushing and crushing the faculty. Today is a day for action! We don't need people who are going to chicken out!" At Sale's suggestion, the swelling throng of protesters marched on Day Hall—the first march on the administration building in Cornell's history—chanting "We want Malott shot!" Packs of students bolted for the arts quad to lure others from their classes. When the reinforced ralliers returned to Day Hall, they were 1,500 strong. Carol N. Lipis '59 captured the crowd's imagination when she announced that a group of Sage Hall women would stay out one half hour beyond their 12:30 a.m. curfew that night; suddenly it was obvious that there would be another demonstration that evening in front of Sage. Sale, fearing that things were getting out of hand, asked the crowd to sing the alma mater, and then disperse. Dean of Men Frank C. Baldwin chimed in that it would be nice if everyone went to get coffee at Willard Straight. To this, a lone firebrand replied, "We don't want coffee, we want freedom." A dozen eggs were then lobbed at Day Hall, a number of which splattered Baldwin. It was said that at least one of the eggs was thrown by Baldwin's own daughter Polly, who had been among the original picketers that morning in front of the Straight. Below left: Sale, his arm in a bandage, holds a large sign while addressing the rally from the west steps of Day Hall. Below right: Demonstrators carrying "No Ban" placards mill with fresh protest recruits on the arts quad.*

of the previous generalized standards, it set a 3 a.m. curfew for parties in fraternities and other living units on party weekends, and a ban on mixed company between the hours of 3 a.m. and 8 a.m. Other provisions closed parties to non-members and required the serving of soft drinks and snacks.

The Sun, which played a key role in the entire year-long episode, both on its editorial pages and in the University community at large, called the action "a black mark" against the administration. Resentment was widespread, but there seemed little hope of a reversal.

* * *

Then, having set these University-wide social standards, the President's Committee began to look into the question of apartment parties. A poll taken by the Women's Student Government Association showed the dimensions of the problem. Almost one in every four women was polled, and, of these, 56.1 percent admitted breaking the rules. The majority view clearly favored removal of the existing, unenforceable rules.

But the width of the gulf between students and the administration quickly became evident. Commenting on the poll, The Sun noted that "when half the people violate a provision, there is more likely to be something wrong with the provision than with the people." It called for elimination of the rules.

Frank C. (Ted) Baldwin '22, the dean of men, reacted in an opposite manner. Expressing distress at the number of violations, he said that "a lot of people thought in 1953 that the rules were too liberal, and maybe they were right."

And while students, and most notably The Sun, continued

Morning Rally . . .

—Photo by Sol Goldberg

—Sun Photo

A CENTURY AT CORNELL

to urge relaxation of the rules, it soon became evident that the administration intended to move in the opposite direction.

Matters came quickly to a head that spring. On the morning of May 12, The Sun reported that the President's Committee was considering "a general ban on unchaperoned apartment parties," and that a clear majority of the committee had indicated at a meeting the previous week that it favored such a ban.

"This action does not befit a liberal university which has always boasted of student freedom," The Sun said, calling on the committee to take a "more moderate" course.

Resentment built quickly on campus. In a letter printed in The Sun, J. Kirk Sale '58, who had been the paper's editor until that March, and Richard Fariña '59 called for student action to fight the impending ban. The Student Council passed a resolution calling for the retention of apartment parties as an "essential, right and moral part of the educational atmosphere."

Petitions opposing the ban were drafted, as The Sun's editorial pages continued to be filled with letters from outraged students.

On the evening of May 20, leaders of the President's Committee appeared before the Student Council to give their rationale for the proposed ban. What they said that night virtually assured the trouble that quickly followed.

Lloyd H. Elliott, executive assistant to President Malott and the man seen by many as the architect of the restrictive policies, said that "apartment entertaining was not in the best interests of an educational environment." Theresa R. Humphreyville, a professor of home economics who was the chairman of the committee, said that the "apartment situation is conducive to petting and intercourse."

Those statements produced a Sun editorial accusing the administration of trying to subject thousands of Cornell students "to a group standard in conformity with the morals of middle class, small town America." And they led to the student demonstrations of Friday, May 23, 1958.

Ironically, the tide had probably turned already. Mr. Elliott was on his way to become president of the University of Maine, and his replacement, already selected, was Dr. John Summerskill, an authority on student psychology and far more liberal. (He later gained national prominence as president of San Francisco State University during the 1960s.) The President's Committee had started to back away from a total ban on apartment parties.

* * *

But it was too late. That morning, about 1,000 students demonstrated in an orderly, good-natured way in front of the administration building, Day Hall. Sale addressed the group, making clear the demonstration was aimed at more than just the apartment parties issue but rather at the entire pattern of restrictive actions by the administration. Though a few eggs were thrown at the end, the tenor of that first demonstration was peaceful.

To underscore the protest, a number of upper-class women who lived in Sage Hall, in the middle of the campus, decided to stay out beyond the 12:30 a.m. curfew. A second protest demonstration was organized in support of their protest. At about 11 p.m. that night, a crowd formed in front of Sage, and the mood was far more angry than that of the morning. When

...Anger at Midnight...

—Sun Photo

THE MOMENT MEETS THE MAN: *By midnight, 3,000 enthusiastic demonstrators—about one quarter of the student body—filled the open area in front of Sage Hall women's dormitory, now Sage Graduate Center. Blazing oil torches and flashes from cameras illuminated the throng, which held freshly painted placards and the Cornell class pennants of previous generations ("Let's Go Back to the Good Old Days," explained the signs). Clusters of women watched from Sage's upper windows (above). They could not join the crowd, since administrators had taken the precaution of locking the dorm's doors to exiting traffic at 11:30, one hour before curfew. Early in the protest, Student Council president K. Peter Kellogg '59, equipped with a little toy bullhorn, sought to inform his impatient constituents of an apparent softening of the administration stand, but he was shouted down with cries of "Puppet! Puppet!" and "We want Sale!" The masses were not disappointed. Kirkpatrick Sale began to speak, and his performance (left) was magnificent. "What we need now is less Student Council and more student body!" he barked at the top of his lungs. Using the steps of Sage as a platform, and flanked by demonstration leaders Robert M. Perry '59, David W. Seidler '59 and Richard Fariña '59, Sale fired the horde with a series of questions. Did they like the University's decision to ban alcohol at Schoellkopf Crescent? Came the reply—a thundering "No!" Did they like Theresa R. Humphreyville? A louder "No!" —and laughter. Sale's speech was targeted against the administration in general, and when he concluded, hundreds joined in chanting "We want a new president!" — a chorus which had never before been heard at Cornell.*

—Sun Photo

—Sun Photo

'THANKS A LOT, DEANE MALOTT': *Although men supplied the noise and the numbers at the midnight Sage Hall demonstration, women supplied the courage. The thousands of males outside were not violating any University rules, but females planning to stay out beyond the 12:30 a.m. curfew faced certain judicial action and an uncertain punishment. With Sale's speech ended and the deadline approaching, leaders of the women's protest took over the megaphone. When figures were totaled the next morning, it was disclosed that 129 women had been late in entering their dorms or sororities; the average for a normal Friday night was ten or less. Of the 129, some 40 explicitly stated that their lateness was intentional, and eventually received unofficial reprimands. About ten minutes after the women's curfew passed, the Sage Hall ralliers strung up an effigy of President Malott from an American elm. The mannequin (bottom left) was labeled "No Ban" and "This Ain't Ezra." Students moved in with their torches to set it ablaze (top), and cheered as it burned (bottom right). Demonstration leaders Perry and Seidler then asked the crowd to disperse. Most did, including Sale, who headed to The Palms for a beer. But several hundred others were in a dangerous mood, and began marching and driving their cars across the arts quad. Their goal was the Cayuga Heights home of Malott, one mile away.*

...An Effigy Burns...

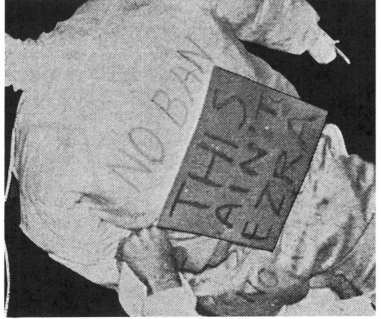

—Sun Photo

—Sun Photo

A CENTURY AT CORNELL

the president of the Student Council, K. Peter Kellogg '59, tried to get the rowdy crowd's attention to say that Elliott had decided to oppose the total ban on apartment parties, he was shouted down. The crowd, which eventually numbered about 3,000, yelled for Sale, and the former Sun editor declared that "what we need now is less Student Council and more student body."

At 12:40 a.m., an effigy of President Malott was burned in front of Sage. Eventually, the crowd broke up, but several hundred students began to march to the president's house in Cayuga Heights, perhaps one and a half miles away. Malott met the group on the front steps and told them, "This university will never be run by mob rule." Eggs and rocks were thrown, and obscenities shouted.

The episode produced nationwide headlines, along the lines of this one that appeared in the New York *Journal-American*: "Four Suspended by Cornell after 2-Day Riot Over Girls." Four demonstration leaders, including Sale, were promptly suspended, though they later got off with light, or no penalties.

President Malott invited student leaders to confer with him, and the Student Council called for a return of control over student activities to the faculty. By the middle of the 1958-59 school year, with Mr. Summerskill taking advantage of the climate for change that clearly was evident, the entire course of the previous three years had been reversed. Power was returned to the faculty, the student government was revamped and given new authority, and the machinery was created for liberalization of Cornell's social rules.

* * *

It had scarcely seemed possible in the tension and anger of the previous May.

In no place did that tension and anger show more clearly than in the pages of The Sun. The newspaper had played a key role in mobilizing student dissatisfaction, both under

Sale's editorship in 1957-58 and under that of David A. Engel '59, who took over that March. But the events of May 23 produced a sharp split.

"The remarkable demonstrations of Friday smacked strongly and unpleasantly of vengeance," The Sun editorial declared on Monday, May 26. It went on to say that administration officials had begun to be impressed with the extent of student opposition and that, after the peaceful demonstration of that Friday morning, "they were more impressed than ever with the depth of student feeling."

But it came down sharply against the second demonstration as misdirected and potentially counter-productive, concluding that "Under the circumstances Friday, however, the demonstrations did more harm than good."

* * *

Three weeks later, the senior staff of The Sun, headed by Sale, resumed control of the paper for the traditional graduation issue. "We feel that the demonstrations were right, and that they succeeded in their purpose," Sale wrote. "They have prodded the students, faculty and alumni from their lethargy...."

As is often the case, the truth lay somewhere in between. The degree of student resistance that was manifest even before that Friday had certainly slowed, and perhaps reversed, the restrictive administration mood. But the demonstrations also had the effect of dramatizing the dispute, and making liberalization inevitable.

The students of the late 1950s were in step with the forward march towards greater sexual liberalization, while the Cornell administration was trying to stay with an era that, even then, had passed. In that sense, Cornell's student activists were the forerunners of those who led the even more significant movements for civil rights and student freedom in the 1960s.

CARL P. LEUBSDORF '59, Sun associate editor 1958-59, now is chief Washington correspondent for *The Baltimore Sun*.

—Sun Photo

...And a 'Riot'

SMOKE BOMBS, ROCKS AND EGGS: *The leaderless mob of 1,000 males arrived at Malott's 205 Oak Hill Road home at 1 a.m., jamming his and neighbors' lawns. The crowd clamored for the president to appear, and demanded his resignation. Catcalls and obscenities—and black clouds from two smoke bombs—filled the air. Malott finally emerged, backed by a crescent of Safety Division officers. A chant of "Go Back to Kansas" greeted his arrival. The besieged president (circled, above) said he was aware the students "meant business" about the apartment party issue, but insisted he would not be pressured by street tactics. Eggs splattered Malott as he spoke, and rocks were thrown at his home, shattering a window. Helpless to do otherwise, he withdrew. The students—many of whom were embarrassed by Malott's humiliation—grew silent, and dispersed. Staying overnight at the Malott home was trustee chairman John L. Collyer '17, donor of a $250,000 crew boathouse to be dedicated the following afternoon. Upon seeing the demonstrators, Mrs. Collyer reportedly remarked to her husband, "Are these the boys you're giving the boathouse to, John?"*

An Appeal to Posterity
The Monument Stands

We received in the mail the other day the final and official version of the Cornell University Social Events Standards. A neat little document it is, concise and rippling, but it made us a little sad to know that this paper will go into the files of The Sun and rest open to the merciless gaze of posterity. Somehow we rather picture posterity picking the virginal code out of the files in another few decades, blowing the dust off the top, and regarding it with a poignant mixture of amusement and disbelief.

How absurd! a code to make people moral, posterity will say. To think that back then they tried to legislate morality! Listen to this: "The University does stand in the role of parents"—how strange, how fantastic. Could this really have happened? posterity will say. What must the Administration have been like? What the students? Did our Cornell ever think that it really had a role in the morality of students?

And then posterity will smile wryly and return the relic to its proper place, gathering dust in the files.

But today, the code has no dust on it. It stands pure and white, untainted by time and fingerprints. It stands as a monument to one of the worst acts of the Cornell University Administration in recent years, one of the most erring acts of the '50s. It stands high, today, for all to see.

But we can hope that someday it will not be high, someday, after the diligent efforts of intelligent students, after a new committee and perhaps a new Administration, it will crumble. We hope that the student and the administrator alike in future years will come to understand the social bounds of this our life, and will let the Cornell undergraduate regain his proper stature as a mature and responsible individual.

We can hope, posterity, we can hope.

—*editorial, February 27, 1958*

The evolution of student response to the administration's delusion is instructive. When the President's Committee, chaired by the redoubtable Miss Humphreyville, originally tabled the reformed IFC code in Fall 1957, The Sun foresaw what was to come. "Now it seems clear that the President's Committee has moved from the problem of how to control houseparty behavior to the much wider scope problem of the whole social situation at Cornell, with all that includes and connotes," it commented editorially. "Figuratively speaking, the committee more or less cleared the field instead of going on with the game."

The most striking thing about the code the committee substituted, other than its aversion to sexuality, was its length. The prolixity of some of the regulations disguised their close resemblance to the IFC rules the committee had rejected. But this was par for the Malott administration's course. The president was noted for his expansion of the number of regulations, based on his feeling that people should know where they stand and not be guided by vague generalities.

The very existence of the President's Committee was also symptomatic of the way Malott ran Cornell. He had a propensity to centralize things, to shorten chains of command, to increase the authority of the University administration. You may recall that the student editors who used vulgar language in 1953 and 1955 were haled before faculty conduct committees. The faculty then, as throughout Cornell's history, had final say over student disciplinary matters.

In 1956, however, the Board of Trustees, at Malott's behest, took this power away from the faculty and handed it to the president. The Faculty Committees on Student Activities and on Student Conduct were abolished, replaced by *President's* Committees.

In 1957-58, the President's Committee on Student Activities consisted of six administrators; five faculty members, of whom Miss Humphreyville was one; and four students. Final control, however, rested with Malott. One marvels at the courage shown by Kirk Sale in criticizing the administration so vehemently: Malott could have expelled him; or, more probable and more painful, could have put him on disciplinary probation, which would have forced him to resign his editorship. No Cornell president before or since has ever had these powers.

Unsurprisingly, The Sun repeatedly and stridently called for authority over student conduct to be returned to the faculty. It pointed out that committee members served at the pleasure of the president, and, as Sale put it, "their first dissent may be their last." Sale's father, a Cornell English professor, no doubt played a significant role in his son's

In the Building: A Pleasant Tale

We heard about the new decree, but knowing how easily these rumors get around we didn't give it too much credence until one day we happened to be sauntering by G.S. and noticed a ladder propped up against the north entrance. We approached a little nearer and, squinting against the glare of Ithaca sunlight, we made out a little man perched on top of the ladder hacking away at the stone with a chisel. Upon closer scrutiny, we discerned a half-completed letter B. A bit puzzled at what we had seen, we proceeded southward to investigate the situation further. Upon reaching the end of G.S. we mounted the stairs and glanced upward. We stood transfixed. There, chiseled in the masonry above the door, were five massive Gothic letters — GIRLS. We hurried back to the other end of G.S. just in time to witness the finishing touches of the letter O.

Our faith in rumor having been restored, we decided to stroll over to The Building to find out the background of its latest decree. We didn't hurry; we had no expectation of changing things. We had learned by now that although the wheels grind slow, once they had been set in motion there was just no stopping them. No, we just wanted to see what aspect of the students was being protected this time.

We passed through the entry to The Building, walked up the stairs, were received in the reception room, passed on through the outer outer office, into the inner outer office, through the outer inner office and finally sank, panting for breath, into the plush carpeting of the inner inner office.

The Dean smiled. "Glad you dropped in, yes indeed, glad you dropped in. Always have time to 'shoot the breeze' with the students. Yes sir."

"The entrances," we said, "the Gothic letters . . ."

"Yes, sir, the wheels grind slow, but once they've started . . ."

"Yes," we smiled, "but why?"

—Sun Photo by Hall Hutchison

SNAKES, SNAILS, PUPPY DOG TAILS: *This decoration on the west facade of the downtown DeWitt Building (formerly Ithaca's high school) seems to resemble the stone carvings the editorialist envisions.*

"University policy. Been that way for years—can't understand why students are so surprised. You know, youngsters are funny." The Dean gave a patronizing, but unmistakably hearty laugh. "They're here four years and say 'things were *never* this way.' Now, we've been here ten years and know they've *always* been this way. Students come and go, you know, but we here in The Building

are the permanent members of the university community."

"What," we queried, "is the need that the new decree will fill?"

"Oh, that's easy—Morality, of course, Morality. After all, how would it look if boys and girls . . ."

"Yes," we agreed, "terrible, terrible. Both using the same door, yes indeed, terrible."

"And the trustees, the alumni. There are so many things a corporation—uh, er—a university, yes, university has to contend with. Things a student would never think of. Of course, we always have the good of the corporation—uh, no, university—no, no, students, yes that's it, the students—we always have the good of the students uppermost in our minds."

"What do you think of the decree?" we asked.

"Think, think—oh yes,—er—think, yes, think. Well, you know, we, all of us think these moral-type situations are good, don't we now?"

"Yes," we agreed, "good. Do you further think," we meekly inquired, "that there will be any reconsideration of the decree in the light of any new developments?"

"Well, of course there are committees working on these things all the time. Constantly considering them. But, uh, look here, for any further information you'd better see The Man Upstairs."

So we left, puzzled but resigned—as usual—and decided to wait another day before we went upstairs.

—editorial, March 19, 1958

views, not only on this subject, but when the question of Malott's dedication to excellence and to his faculty came up.

Whether written by Malott, Miss Humphreyville, Lloyd Elliott, or some other member of the President's Committee, the new administration social code contained a big surprise for the IFC: women in fraternity houses were to be restricted at all times to "commons areas."

A commons area, according to the code, was "a space which, by reason of its size, location, appointments and associated use, invites unrestricted use by all guests and members of the host organization. It is intended that all these considerations should identify the commons areas as places with activities of a nonretiring and impersonal nature."

Elucidating, the committee pointed out, "this provision eliminates room parties. Reports from people attending these parties and from chaperones indicate that room parties have been one of the main problem areas in the past."

The committee members thus enacted a blunderbuss ban on all mixed gatherings in private rooms, although, it is to be surmised, they were chiefly concerned about parties involving only two persons.

Furthermore, during the few "overnight" weekends, when visiting women had extraordinary permission to sleep in fraternity houses, women were to be restricted to their sleeping quarters after 3 a.m., and such quarters had to be separated from the rest of the house by a commons area, which was to be patrolled by a night watchman. Houses that could not meet these requirements were forbidden to have overnight guests.

All this must have been quite startling to the student leaders. Remember, sex had not been a problem the raucous previous spring—if anything, the lack of women caused by the closing of the airport created difficulties that would not otherwise have been there.

The committee, however, had charted its course. Eventually, the students were able to get it to compromise on certain things. A couple of curfew times were liberalized, more "overnights" were permitted than first envisioned; but on the question of "room parties," Miss Humphreyville was adamant. So, when her committee announced it was going to deal next with off-campus apartment regulations, no great imagination was necessary to foresee what steps it might deem necessary.

The administration's social code for fraternities was announced on a Thursday night in December, and the IFC and Student Council leaders were quoted in Friday morning's Sun as approving of it. Over the weekend, however, they reconsidered. On Monday, the IFC announced that it would refuse to enforce the code, its president saying "it is quite unreasonable and would prove extremely inefficient to ask students to enforce rules that they did not believe in." The Sun added two vicious editorials, and the considerable sarcasm at Kirk Sale's disposal was thereafter aimed squarely at the administration. In January the Student Council chimed in, "rejecting" the newly-imposed code by a vote of 16-0, and it was joined in its resolution by Panhellenic, the IFC, and the Women's Student Government Association. The Sun clapped and whistled.

Given this unprecedented display of student defiance, the administration backed down somewhat. Miss Humphreyville, who had earlier said it was the committee's code or nothing, now offered to reconsider specific provisions, and President Malott agreed to hold an open meeting to discuss student rights.

The IFC responded to these overtures by hinting that a compromise could be reached, but The Sun was a holdout. "Perhaps the demands of the students were too great, and

FRANK C. BALDWIN '23,
DEAN OF MEN
*Splattered by His Own
Daughter's Egg?*

LLOYD H. ELLIOTT,
AIDE TO MALOTT
*If It's Not Educational,
It Ought to Be Curbed*

perhaps the IFC is merely being realistic in its willingness to compromise. But we feel that if the students are really behind the specific proposals made, if they believe these are the revisions necessary for student enforcement of the social code, then they should fight for them," an editorial stated.

On January 19, 1958—the day before Malott's open meeting with Student Council—the IFC capitulated, agreeing to a modified code that nevertheless forbade room parties. Miss Humphreyville, no doubt as part of the bargain, said publicly that

THERESA R. HUMPHREYVILLE,
HOME EC PROF
*Crusader Against Petting
and Intercourse*

the room party ban would be reconsidered at a later time. Sale was incensed, and his response was very interesting. He eliminated The Sun's editorial page and instead ran the complete text of Becker's "Freedom and Responsibility" address. The united student front had shattered; from now on Sale and The Sun would lead.

It did not take long to see that they had followers. The audience facing Malott was a bitter one, heckling him as no Cornell president had ever been heckled before. Toughing it out, Malott blamed the IFC for not having produced an acceptable code, said "Students should conform to the mores of the society in which we live," and added, "it takes about four years for anything to be done, since it sometimes takes four years to get students to change their opinions." Editorially, The Sun termed these remarks "inaccurate and unjust."

The student body's opposition to the new moral crackdown was virtually unanimous, and it was a committed opposition. All four student members of the President's Committee voted against the new fraternity code. The Sun printed scores of letters to the editor on the issue and *not one* supported the administration; not one faculty member spoke up in the committee's defense.

By now it should have been obvious to even the most mulish administrator that the President's Committee was driving at top speed down the wrong lane of a superhighway. And yet the committee did not have to turn around to avoid a cataclysm; it only had to pull off the road for a while. The new fraternity code caused much rancor, but it did go into effect without incident. Those advocating defiance were still a minority. This might have been a good time for the administration to stop the car; instead, however, it stepped on the gas.

And so, when Miss Humphreyville foolishly made it official that the committee was indeed contemplating a general ban on *apartment* parties, the student body was united again. In a letter reprinted here, Sale, whose term as editor was over, and Farina advocated ignoring established channels such as the Student Council, but there was actually no need for this because Student Council, in its boldest action to date, resolved that it was "mandatory" that the administration not ban the presence of women in apartments. It called apartment parties "an essential, right and moral part of the educational atmosphere."

There were a host of good reasons not to enact the ban even in the absence of student protest. Unenforceability was certainly one, but consider, also, the plight of the "independent"—the male who did not belong to a fraternity. Under the rules enacted by Miss Humphreyville's

committee, women could not venture inside men's rooms in fraternity houses, but they *were* permitted inside the house proper. Off-campus, however, if Miss Humphreyville had had her way, they would not have been able to enter apartments *at all*. The meaning of this, simply, is that independents could not socialize with women *anywhere*, except outdoors and at public events such as concerts. (Of course, this being 1958, men were not permitted in dorm rooms, nor could women live off campus.)

Even in 1980, when we pride ourselves on our advanced moral standards, we can look back and sympathize with those who pointed out to Miss Humphreyville that there actually are some activities that can take place between young men and women without supervision; that some people need, as the Student Council put it, "some degree of privacy in an atmosphere other than that of a party situation"; that "apartment entertaining is the only present means of fulfilling this need and even this is not adequate."

Continued on Page 224

A Call to Action

After the fraternity social code was imposed, the President's Committee turned its attention to "apartment parties," and few suspected it would look on them with approval. When Miss Humphreyville confirmed that the committee was indeed contemplating a general ban on women in men's apartments, two of the students who would eventually be suspended for leading the riot wrote The Sun and rejected any further "going through channels." (Kirk Sale's term as editor of The Sun had expired two months previously.)

To the Editor:

Puritanism has long been the chief characteristic of American morality, for reasons yet unfathomed by either God or the rest of the world. Sanity, and H.L. Mencken, have been fighting against this notion since its inception, yet in those final rest-homes for outmoded theories, the college campuses, puritanism still struggles along.

On this campus, the President's Committee on Student Activities does all it can to uphold the value of puritanism. Under the guise of looking morally at the entire social framework of life at Cornell—a job which it has neither the right nor ability to undertake, of course—it has chosen to make a rigid and virtually indefensible social code, and, as the juggernaut rolls along, a move to tighten the apartment party regulations and perhaps eliminate apartment parties altogether.

* * *

First, we ask the Committee to state positively its specific objections to the present behavior of undergraduates in connection with apartments. In other words, *exactly* what does the Committee find wrong or immoral with what it feels to be the present state of affairs. If the members object to sexual intercourse, let them voice this objection explicitly, for this is a question which involves a great deal more than the single question of parties in apartments.

Second, we urge other students, who feel that any tightening of the rules is improper, demeaning and unjustified, to act on this conviction. Let Cornell students not sit passively by once more while the President's Committee takes away privileges and attempts to define morality for the undergraduate. If there is resistance to the elimination of apartment parties, let it be formulated now.

* * *

Action among students themselves is crucial—not through the ineffectual and idealistic student "government" groups, whose members adopt an affected sense of morality for the duration of their meetings, but through informal and constant discussion and argumentation. Students should also talk to the members of the Committee and make known their objections

'IF YOU WOULD ONLY PACK UP YOUR SORROWS': *Although Richard Fariña joined roommate Kirkpatrick Sale in urging "action among the students themselves" in the accompanying letter, Fariña decided he would rather sleep late than attend the May 23 morning demonstration in front of the Straight. That evening, however—after the full drama and color of the day's events had become apparent—Fariña stood among the demonstration's leaders on the steps of Sage Hall. While in France in the early 1960s, Fariña would marry Joan Baez's sister Mimi, with whom he recorded two acclaimed folk albums, including "Reflections in a Crystal Wind" (the above portrait of the Fariñas is from this album's cover). A fictionalized account of the 1958 protests—now bass drums rumble and skyrockets explode—climaxes Fariña's 1966 novel Been Down So Long It Looks Like Up to Me. With perfect romantic timing, Fariña died in a motorcycle accident outside Carmel, California just two days after the novel's publication.*

to the misguided puritanism which will probably take away their apartment party privileges.

Finally, we would ask the members of the committee to stand back from the archaic campus trees and look with real objectivity at the forest of the modern world. Viewing campus life narrowly, as it does now, the committee succeeds only in making a dangerously wide gap between the actual behavior of American society and what it would like to have at Cornell—a gap already too wide.

Richard Fariña '59
J. Kirk Sale '58
—letter, May 13, 1958

The Students Condemn the Committee

The May 20 "P&I" remarks of Miss Humphreyville, and, to a lesser extent those of Lloyd Elliott, Malott's assistant, provoked a blizzard of letters to the editor. Normally, when there is a blizzard, the wind blows in several directions at once. But one need not be a weatherman to know which way the students were going: it was a shutout; every single letter attacked the administration, although, to be sure, a few later letters did not condone the rock-and-egg throwing.

The letters were of an astonishingly high standard, and are well worth reading today. In terms of vigor, logical analysis, and careful style they far surpass what was written by students about the Straight takeover, for example. It is easy to say that students now simply do not write as well as they used to; then again, if they had an issue of such overriding importance to write about, they might surprise us.

Here, then, are seven of the best letters: vicious, perhaps, but hardly unfair.

Rather Inexperienced

To the Editor:

The "explanation" of the President's Committee on Student Activities of their basis for revising apartment party regulations is an insult to every Cornell student, male or female, of age or not. Personally I cannot imagine how such notions ever took hold of these usually mature, wise and experienced minds. How can Dr. Elliott assert that "Apartment entertaining is not in the best interests of an educational environment"?

The stupidity of this statement is overwhelming. What do the living units of the parties therein have to do with an educational environment? Cornell, its faculty, its libraries, and its academic pressures are my educational environment, which definitely does not include my kitchen, bathroom, or living room. After studying all week, I like to entertain my chosen friends, male or female, in my own way and my own place, during the weekend. Or be entertained by them, and interchange ideas and news, and enjoy our privacy.

* * *

Miss Humphreyville, who seems to be rather inexperienced in these matters, asserts that "the apartment situation is conducive to petting and intercourse." Are the automobile-back-seat situation, the grass-in-back-of-Balch situation, the rooms-in-Collegetown situation, the empty-classroom-at-night situation and all other such situations also conducive to the same situation?

Perhaps she should eliminate the student body!

How can the executive assistant to the President have such an idiotic concept of this great University, as to place it even remotely close to a "carefully chaperoned boarding school"? That is the kind of place I wanted to get away from when I came here in 1953. I wanted to come to the place the critic Nathan called the educational institution most resembling a European University. The place where I could train my mind and educate my self, where I could really begin to live my own life, according to the rules so carefully taught me in church and at home.

* * *

The President's committee is seeking to destroy a basic tenet of all society—the right to privacy and freedom of action. So long as there are no violations of the rights of others, or the law, every University student should be able to do as he pleases, and he must defend this right. Many of the blunders of the present Administration can be ignored or laughed at, but this proposal and its "explanations" are too inane, and far too dangerous to be allowed to pass unnoticed.

There has got to be some mass protest action from the whole student body. We must defend ourselves from dictatorial prudishness and real stupidity with all available resources!

> —**Juan Felipe Goldstein '59**
> —*letter, May 23, 1958*

The Student and the Machine

To the Editor:

What is the aim of a University? This question, at least to the students, somewhat less to the faculty, and rather ambiguously to the administration, lies at the heart of the recent prohibitions and limitations leveled at this campus by those who profess to be acting *in loco parentis*.

We of the immature, adolescent, somewhat confused standards are at present still allowed to speak. Whether we have the ability to act upon our value judgments is another question. But what are words, since from "babes" they no longer bring appreciated "gems"? But speak we must or else we are doomed to be the "silent generation."

Room parties, over-night parking and apartment parties are the causes of intellectual apathy, petting and intercourse! Cornell will abolish all distractions and diversions and return the lamp of scholarship to its domain. Gone the concept of the well-rounded individual. Gone the dream of a University community. Gone the ideal of closely bound students, faculty and administration. It is time to herald the Thinking Machine. No emotion, no benefit of experience—just an enormous brain—reading, listening to scholars, writing papers, taking exams. Learning about democratic ideology, but not having the terrible conflict of acting. Just a machine—not life-like, not terribly animate! And if the machine lasts four years without breaking apart or running down, Cornell will give it a piece of paper and make it a man or woman, prepared to assume its role in a much less bright society.

We machines can be the leaders of tomorrow, and we will be pure. Vice has not touched us, and personal morality was never our problem. We will be the most educated babies around. Thank you, Cornell. That's a wonderful goal you have set for yourself. And you are owed a lot of credit for having the courage to balk the whole American way of life.

* * *

Where communism, anti-semitism, and segregation have failed in America, Cornell may succeed. But if you succeed, Cornell, you will succeed because we are not mature enough to teach you that men and women are not made in a library. Evidently, your experience in apartments has taught you much more than ours in our limited stay in your warped environment. Maybe we can justify your fears when we leave here and find the society you have condemned. We certainly haven't found it here.

But we do have one question to ask you before you embark upon your monumental task—how do you turn real live people into machines—and then, how do you turn them back into people again without somewhere along the line breaking the machine?

> —**Barbara Lebhar '58**
> —*letter, May 22, 1958*

A Great Leveller

To the Editor:

At a time when a uniform ban on unchaperoned apartment parties, or their virtual elimination through hidebinding rules, would seem to be Phase Two in the steamroller process of social re-evaluation and strait-jacketing of personal decision (whether one is of age or not), there are a few things that need to be said, briefly and to the point:

First, the main objection to a social code, as several have already pointed out, is not that it is puritanical so much as that it is a Great Leveller, contracting the wide spectrum of behavior to one level of expectation—and a rather artificially decorous middle-class one, at that. Those of us who would like to be pluralists and eclectics cannot abide by the kind of "educational experience" the social code pretends to foster, nor can we understand anyone who has the Prussian arrogance to suppose that everyone can be made to behave alike, or the Pomeranian stupidity to suppose that it would be a good thing if they did, to paraphrase Carl Becker.

* * *

Second, perhaps a few words of mingled glee and rancor from Mencken are apropos:

Talking about another kind of prohibition from that which looms over us now, the late H.L. said that in the case of "all things sinful and charming . . . if these deviltries were equally open to all men, and all men were equally capable of practising and appreciating them, their unpopularity would tend to wither . . ."

On Comstockery: "It is argued against certain books, by virtuosi of moral alarm, that they depict vice as attractive. This recalls the king who hanged a judge for deciding that an archbishop was a mammal."

* * *

Currently it is argued against certain kinds of student parties, by our campus Committee on Un-Cornellian Activities (those same virtuosi of moral alarm), that they promote vicious excesses in matters of taste and conduct. This recalls the ship's captain who wouldn't enter port because none of the harbor pilots had ever been on the rocks and therefore didn't know where they were.

Or the Italian Cardinal, who replied, when a companion refused some proferred cigarettes, saying "I have no vices," with the riposte "It is not a vice, or doubtless you would have it."

—**Jay Cunningham '58**
—*letter, May 21, 1958*

—*Photo by Sol Goldberg*

SILENT GENERATION? *Students gathered behind Sage Chapel listen to a protest leader during the afternoon demonstration of May 23, 1958.*

The Apotheosis of Group Activity

To the Editor:

The imminent apotheosis of the group and canonization of group activity have been blessed with strong support by Mr. Malott's Committee on Student Activities.

Although it is true, as several commentators have pointed out, that the main rationale for the committee's action is a Victorian belief in the fundamental immorality of sex, there is another noteworthy assumption underlying its reconsideration of apartment party rules. Not only is privacy regarded as bound to encourage immorality, but privacy is regarded as in itself immoral. Completely engrossed in the organization and the group, our society views any attempt by the individual to enjoy himself by himself with suspicion. Any activity which is not a group activity requires special justification.

When such thinking invades University campuses, the death knell for privacy has probably been sounded. Professors are continually affirming that the chief purpose of higher education is the development of the individual to the point where the college graduate possesses sufficient internal resources to be able to think and evaluate for himself. The President's committee is implying that this is not possible, nor even desirable.

Several "educators" at this University and others have bemoaned the increasing necessity for factory-like mass academic institutions. How sincere can their regrets be when they are determined to destroy the few remaining opportunities for private interchange?

We are convinced that there is nothing sinful in privacy. If it is the purpose of the University or American society to support and encourage a high valuation of intellectual independence, it must do the same for personal privacy. It is a severe indictment of the University that while the importance of the individual is publicly lauded in the lecture halls, it is quietly condemned and destroyed in the committee rooms.

—**Dorothy Heller '60**
Muriel F. Rosenthal '60
—*letter, May 21, 1958*

The Perfect Model

To the Editor:

Dr. Lloyd H. Elliott's defense of the apartment party ban has deeply touched this reader. Since I feel that education is the sole purpose of the University, and since I represent a small minority on the campus, I present the following plan, which Dr. Elliott so succinctly introduced to the Student Council, to the campus at large.

Dr. Elliott declared that "apartment entertaining is not in the best interests of an educational environment leading to educational achievement. . . . Since the purpose of the University is education, any factors which subvert this purpose should be curbed." Any factors! Oh, what a pregnant, practical idea to make Cornell the most educational university the world has ever known! What an opportunity lies before us to establish Cornell as the perfect model for institutions of higher learning!

Pause for a moment from your studying to recall the factors which detract from the educational environment at Cornell. Picture the football player hurrying through his chemistry lab to reach Schoellkopf promptly at 5 p.m. Imagine the crewman rising at dawn for morning practice, then returning to the boat house again the early evening. Think of the miler missing Friday classes to run in the Heps at Annapolis. What segment of present campus life could more detract from an educational environment? Athletics must be curbed.

And the Straight! Here students spend countless evening study hours at committee meetings for exhibits, for auctions, and for teas. Here students congregate to drink coffee, to listen to music, and to buy tickets. The Straight must be curbed.

Musical organizations require rehearsal time, and Student Council, Pan Hellenic Council, and the Interfraternity Council require long meetings every week. The Outing Club leaves the campus on weekends, WVBR must be staffed every evening, and Sphinx Head holds midweek banquets. Activities detract from an educational environment. Activities must be curbed.

* * *

How practical these measures would be! The University annually spends thousands and thousands of dollars on these diversions. What improvements could be effected with the money saved from coaches' salaries, equipment expenses, and activity budgets! Buses could be purchased to replace cars, which have served for years as rolling apartment parties. Study halls could be erected on deserted parking lot and tennis courts.

Spotlights could be added to eliminate the enticing darkness on Libe Slope and in the gorges. Bewitching locations such as Beebe Lake could be drained, and the suspension bridge and Libe Tower razed. All the nostalgic Cornell traditions must be sacrificed for the cause of an educational environment; every student must admit, for example, that a kiss on the suspension bridge inevitably leads to "petting and intercourse."

Traditionless, athleticless, activityless, Cornell University could be on the threshold of a new era in higher education, an era where the educational environment will be protected from any factors which might subvert it. Dr. Elliott deserves strong praise for sparking this revolution.

—**David B. Howell '60**
—*letter, May 23, 1958*

No Morals?

To the Editor:

I'm not much with words, and I never thought I'd be prompted to express my views to a newspaper, but I have never been so humiliated in my life as I was upon reading Miss Humphreyville's statement concerning the conduciveness of apartments to petting and intercourse. I am almost ashamed to walk across campus for fear of someone's thinking, "There goes a coed. She has no morals." It's a terrible feeling not to be able to hold your head up with pride, knowing you are trusted and respected.

My parents have always trusted me in any situation. When I came to Cornell they gave me "blanket permission" to go wherever I felt it necessary or wherever I wanted to go. They put their trust in the job they had done as parents and in me. I hardly think the University well placed to imply that my parents' trust is misdirected and their daughter does not deserve the respect of the University.

—**Bonnie L. Bowen '60**
—*letter, May 26, 1958*

—Photo by Sol Goldberg

DUMP THE HUMP: *Student signs ridicule Prof. Theresa R. Humphreyville for her antediluvian attitudes about undergraduate sexuality.*

The Ban Will Be Unsuccessful

To the Editor:

Next year there will be a ban on apartment parties. This is as certain as death and eight o'clock classes. Once the University "discusses" adding another restriction to the many already fettering the freedom of the student, there is little the student governments can do to prevent it, for all their committee meetings, debates and election promises. The University has the impregnable weapon of time. When enacting a new regulation, it need only graduate those who might remember "the good old days" to see student agitation fade like the ripples surrounding a rock tossed in a pond. And the ripples have always faded, no matter how big the rock. And so, because the University stands firmly upon its past successes with manipulating the liberties of the student body as it pleases, next year there will be a ban on apartment parties.

There have been stringent regulations thrust upon the student before. But past regulations were promulgated principally to prevent the students from engaging in activities, which, while pleasurable to them, could not honestly be considered natural.

For some, it may be enjoyable to drink past the point of sobriety, but we are hardly born with a genetic thirst for alcohol. It may have been fun to omit sleep from our Spring Weekend schedule, but it is hardly an innate characteristic that enables us to go for 48 hours without rest. And so it was with party hopping and block parties; the University deprived us of activities, which, with a little more maturity we probably wouldn't miss too much anyhow.

Not that any rational being can fathom the logic of these regulations. For that vociferous minority which abuses its privileges before regulations have been effected, continues to abuse them afterwards. People whose personal moral codes are so low that they engage in crimes the regulations seek to prevent certainly have no qualms about breaking a few University rules.

Ironically, it is only those who have conducted themselves properly who are affected by these regulations; they lose much of their sense of responsibility. But while social regulations of the past few years leave much to be desired (both meanings intended), the University may rest assured that they will have (and have had) no trouble in seeing that they stick, or in enforcing them.

But, shortly after enacting the apartment party ban, the University will wish it never had. No institution, no matter how big its endowment, no matter how tough its police force, no matter how obstinate its administration, no matter how obsolete its social mores, no matter how narrow-minded its trustees, and no matter how numerous its regulations, can prevent a large group of people from doing something fundamentally natural and healthy, unless this group of people chooses to give it up voluntarily.

And it is fundamentally natural and healthy for women to share dinners, study sessions and social diversion with men in the latter's homes; and while those who

seek to achieve this ban may have had regrettably few opportunities to realize it themselves, sex too is considered natural and healthy. But so that occasional abuse by the smallest of minorities can be eliminated, the democratic, sensitive, tactful, freedom-loving, student-conscious minds behind the proposed ban will, in one swift slice, excise both an exceptional opportunity for students to develop a responsible social maturity, and the last sizable piece of student freedom left. The ban will be unsuccessful.

*   *   *

The ban will be unsuccessful, simply because, as the prohibitionists found out, you cannot eliminate by legislation something which is a natural part of a people's everyday life. The ban will be unsuccessful because the students consider social life to have more meaning than just that found at a fraternity party or in a parked car. The ban will be unsuccessful because those who perform immoral deeds will continue to do so, ban or not. The ban will be unsuccessful because the University can only guide its students toward maturity by instilling within them a sense of responsibility, not by dissolving that which they already possess. The ban will be unsuccessful, but in failing, it will teach the University what many of its courses have been teaching its students for years: that you cannot limit the license of the few by eliminating the freedom of the many.

—**Martin G. Blinder '58**
—*letter, May 23, 1958*

Continued from Page 220

* * *

In short, although responding to a situation that clearly required some response, the administration for over a year had been following a course of unexampled stupidity. But the best was yet to come. The remarks of Elliot and Miss Humphreyville at Student Council's May 20 meeting must rank as among the most anserine in Cornell's history. In particular, Miss Humphreyville's homily that "the apartment situation is conducive to petting and intercourse" provoked a frenzied reaction among students. The Sun was deluged with angry letters. Three days later, during the peaceful afternoon demonstration, students raised banners glorifying "P&I" and waved posters proclaiming "Queen Victoria Is Dead—Theresa Reigns Instead." That evening, as a quarter of the student body gathered before Sage Hall, chanting for Sale to speak, the fuse ran out.

The Silent Generation had passed on.

* * *

Overnight, it seemed, the omnipotent President's Committee was a dead letter. Malott immediately appointed the popular John Summerskill vice president for student affairs, and also expressed concern over "the lack of understanding which exists of the objectives of the University." Furthermore, Malott invited student leaders to come to his office to discuss the problems. He also beat down an effort by the trustees to have Sale expelled, although Sale did miss a day of classes when he was temporarily suspended by the dean of men, along with Farina and two others, the day after the demonstration.

And, as soon as he took office, Summerskill announced a moratorium on any further social regulations. The apartment ban was never heard of again.

Student Council responded to the riot with some non-negotiable demands. While deploring certain "regrettable incidents," the council said, "Because of the Administration's continued disregard for the students' voice, student opinion could find expression only in mass demonstrations of protest.

"Therefore:

"We, the members of Student Council, request evidence that the Administration has re-evaluated its position. To affirm its faith in the ability of the individual student to control maturely his social behavior, the President's Committee on Student Activities must, at its next meeting, issue a statement affirming its conviction that unchaperoned apartment parties are a desirable part of the Cornell social situation . . .

"The President's Committee must realize that disregard-

—Sun Photo by Richard A. Shulman

'WOULDN'T IT BE NICE?': *Only a decade after the 1958 protests—when students sought to uphold the "privilege" of campus-bound women to visit off-campus apartments during the day—it had become perfectly acceptable for a couple to share a Collegetown apartment, like the 1971 roommates above.*

The Fall of Women's Curfews

March 14, 1962—The Women's Student Government Association votes overwhelmingly to remove senior women's curfews.

April 2, 1962—The Faculty Committee on Student Affairs approves the WGSA measure, on a trial basis only for one year.

Spring, 1964—Agitation starts for abolition of junior women's curfews, but FCSA vetoes the proposal. The committee agrees, however, to reconsider the measure "some time in the future."

November 8, 1964—WGSA again passes a measure abolishing junior women's curfews.

January, 1965—After some shuttling between committees, FCSA approves the measure, with the stipulation that it will not consider ending sophomore women's curfews for at least a year.

April 28, 1967—WSGA passes a resolution supporting abolition of curfews for second semester sophomore women and FCSA approves the proposal.

April 12, 1968—First semester sophomore women's curfews are abolished by FCSA, after a March WSGA referendum.

December 13, 1968—FCSA eliminates curfews for currently enrolled freshmen women. Within a few months, curfews for future freshmen women would be abolished as well.

---

ing Council's request may leave the student body no alternative but to revert to mass protest methods."

The last word, appropriately enough, came from some other academic administrators. After the spring disturbances, Malott named the deans of all the undergraduate colleges a committee to report on what should be done about student conduct. The deans' report, as you might expect, was written in dignified language, which at least differentiated it from the student statements on the same issue. If Malott was expecting support from the committee of deans, however, he was quite mistaken. Remember how Miss Humphreyville's Social Conduct Standards for fraternities reminded us: "We believe in conformance with the standards of society . . . since the University does stand in the role of parents . . ."? Now read this:

"In the Deans' considered opinion, the University cannot undertake to act *in loco parentis*, if this means maintaining concern for and supervision over all aspects of the student's life—social, moral, and religious as well as intellectual. The University should not attempt to spell out rules, regulations, and codes governing student behavior beyond the bare minimum necessary in any society. It would be difficult to produce evidence to show that a proliferation of rules and codes is conducive to the observation of order, morality, personal honor, and the rights of others."

And Kirk Sale, wherever he was at the time, must have smiled as he read, "The Deans strongly recommend that the concept of a . . . President's Committee on Student Activities be abolished at Cornell . . . the central challenge for all segments of the university community is the development and maintenance of a stimulating spirit of learning at Cornell. The Deans believe that concerted, intensive effort in this direction will be the most effective means of improving student and faculty morale and reducing the dissatisfaction, restlessness, and disturbance which have been so widespread."

* * *

If this story seems like it had a happy ending, consider this. Returning control of student disciplinary matters to the faculty led fairly directly to the Straight takeover. Eleven springs after the apartment party crisis, the faculty-controlled judicial system could not handle a racial crisis, and the faculty itself was forced, in humiliating fashion, to nullify the reprimands its judicial system had meted out. Could an administration committee have done better? If what President Perkins said at the time and later is to be believed, yes.

Things at Cornell are never static, or at least they have not been over the last hundred years. New systems, new solutions, new personalities are always being tried out. In the first chapter of this book, President Rhodes asserted that Cornell has and seeks a diverse student body. This may or may not be so, but nobody can argue that Cornell's *history* is not diverse.

Yet, somehow, it all fits together. One of the lessons the format of this book teaches us is that no such format is valid. Trends can be established, themes can be isolated, but in the end we can no more put the 1958 riot in a different chapter than the Straight takeover than we can separate comments on social life and housing from the administration's enrollment policy.

Consequently, a great number of theories about the course of Cornell's history are possible. If you dislike students, you can think of how they forced poor Fred Morelli off campus for his insolence in refusing to wear his freshman cap in 1921; of the inexcusable actions of Spring Weekend 1957, which led to the even more inexcusable administration actions of 1958; or of some of the more irresponsible political actions of the last 20 years. The faculty has countenanced numerous violations of academic freedom almost from the time the University was founded, and has not asserted its power recently to prevent any of the ruinous cuts in academic budgets. If you do not care for the administration, consider the indefensible rises in tuition and enrollment of the last 30 years, and how one administration blamed tuition hikes on enrollment increases and only 15 years later another called for enrollment increases in order to keep tuition hikes to only slightly over the rate of inflation. Or, if this topic is too grim, chuckle at the thought of President Malott and Miss Humphreyville, gallantly trying to hoist an umbrella against the typhoon of the sexual revolution.

On the other hand, Cornell's history has more heroes than bad guys. Andrew White, Anna Comstock, Carl Becker, Liberty Hyde Bailey, Robert Cushman, Hendrik van Loon, and Morris Bishop (to speak only of the dead) are predecessors every Cornellian can be proud of.

And so, we learn from the past. The actors change; the production goes on. Yesterday's radicals become today's sober citizens. Sometimes they even become Cornell's most loyal alumni.

This book has focused on events rather than generalities, and so it may give the impression that Cornell's history is largely one of lurching from crisis to crisis. Even if this were true, it would tell more about the alumni who have continued to support Cornell than it does about the people who cause the crises. For example, any number of people who thought the Perkins administration was wicked or spineless or incompetent or some combination continued to stand up for the University during the time of the Straight takeover, secure in their idea that Cornell would come back some day, perhaps stronger than ever. Cornell survived, just as it has survived all manner of challenges and idiocies over the last hundred years. It must say something for the place's character. We can always strive for improvement, but in the present we can take comfort in both the knowledge of the past and the hope of what the future can bring. Call it Freedom and Responsibility or whatever you like, the Cornell tradition endures. The angry young man of the 50s, Kirk Sale, said it best in his final editorial.

> The graduate must realize that, although the reign of administrative values is still unfortunately present, there may in the future be an opportunity for change, a change that will make him even prouder to be a Cornellian. He will then know that future graduates will become more useful to their country and to mankind, and that Cornell's greatness is the kind of greatness that can be halted but never ended.
>
> Thus the student of the Class of 1958 can assess his part as a member of a major university, can determine what his place was and what it will be, can discover what Cornell has meant and what it will mean to him. And it is likely that every graduate, no matter how much he may have been educationally injured by the inadequacy of his liberal education, by the lack of intellectual atmosphere, and by the reign of administrative values, can still say,
>
> "I have entered and have become more learned and more thoughtful; I am departing and I will become more useful to my country and mankind."

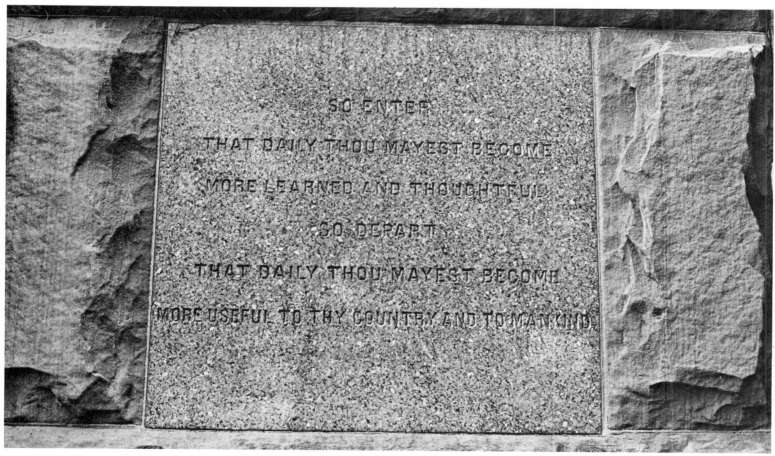

—Sun Photo by Carin Ashjian and Hall Hutchison

BENEDICTION: *Andrew Dickson White addressed these words to future Cornellians when he built his white sandstone and red limestone gateway on Eddy Street. White translated the lines from a portal of the centuries-old University of Padua.*

Chapter V: Of Freedom and Responsibility

To Remember
a Friend

Newly-elected Sun bigwigs pose in April, 1974. From left: Cathy Panagoulias, managing
editor; Jennifer Sprague, editor-in-chief; Dennis Arnsdorf, business manager.

*Jennifer Sprague '75, one of The Sun's most talented and popular editors-in-chief, died in 1979 at the age of 25. She
was a person of great dedication and strong opinions, and to honor her memory and to advance what she stood for,
The Sun is establishing a permanent memorial fund in her name. This is the formal announcement of that fund.*

A transplanted Brooklynite, Jennifer adopted Ithaca as her own and made a commitment to preserving its environment through her writing. Long after leaving The Sun, she held to its standards and taught them to others, calling
them the best guidelines in a sometimes imperfect profession.

The purpose of the Jennifer Sprague Fund will be to promote high standards of journalism at Cornell and at The
Sun. The Fund's trustees intend to do this through such measures as annual prizes for excellence in writing and
reporting; scholarships; and support of internships.

Five close friends of Jennifer Sprague are the Fund's trustees: Prof. Joseph Bugliari, ag ec and B&PA; Daniel Margulis
'73, the editor of *A Century at Cornell*; Prof. Richard Polenberg of the history department; Deborah Schoch '75 of *The
Ithaca Journal*; and John Schroeder '74, the designer of *A Century at Cornell*. While some of these people have Sun
affiliation and while The Sun has made a substantial contribution to the Fund, the trustees will administer the
Fund independently of The Sun.

Now, we solicit your support, personal or financial. If you would like to contribute money, serve on a judging panel,
or assist the Fund in some other way, please write any of the trustees, or to The Jennifer Sprague Fund, c/o *The
Cornell Daily Sun*, 109 East State Street, Ithaca, New York 14850.

CODA

The Forty-Ninth Greatest University

BY KURT VONNEGUT, JR. '44

Good evening, fellow Cornellians.

You should have invited a more sentimental speaker, I think. This is surely a sentimental occasion, and I am sentimental about faithful dogs sometimes, but that is as far as it goes.

The most distinguished living writer who was also a Sun man is, of course, Elwyn Brooks White of the Class of 1921. He will be 81 on July 11th. You could send him a card. His mind is as clear as a bell, and he is not only sentimental about dogs but about Cornell. I myself liked only two things about this place. The Sun and the horse-drawn artillery. Yes—there was horse-drawn artillery here in my time. I suppose I should tell you how old I am, too. I will be 58 in November of this year. You could send me a card. We never hooked up the horses to caissons, because we knew that was no way to frighten Hitler. So we just put saddles on the horses, and pretended we were at war with Indians, and rode around all afternoon.

It was not Cornell's fault that I did not like this place much, in case some dean or alumni secretary is about to burst into tears. It was my father's fault. He said I should become a chemist like my brother, and not waste my time and his money on subjects he considered so much junk jewelry—literature, history, philosophy. I had no talent for science. What was infinitely worse: all my fraternity brothers were engineers.

I probably would have adored this hell hole, if I had been allowed to study and discuss the finer things in life. Also: I would not have become a writer.

I eventually wound up on academic probation. I was accelerating my course at the time—because of the war. My instructor in organic chemistry was my lab partner in biochemistry. He was fit to be tied.

And one day I came down with pneumonia. It is such a dreamy disease. Pneumonia used to be called "the old people's friend." It can be a young person's friend, too. All that you feel is that you are sleepy and that it is time to go. I did not die, so far as I know—but I left Cornell, and I've never come back until now.

Good evening, fellow Cornellians. I am here to congratu-late The Cornell Daily Sun on its 100th anniversary. To place this event in historical perspective: The Sun is now 40 years younger than the saxophone, and 60 years older than the electric guitar.

It was a family to me—one that included women. Once a week we allowed coeds to put together a woman's page, but I never got to know any of them. They always seemed so burned up about something. I never did find out what it was. It must have been something over at the sorority house.

I pity you Sun people of today for not having truly great leaders to write about—Roosevelt and Churchill and Chiang Kaishek and Stalin on the side of virtue, and Hitler and Mussolini and Emperor Hirohito on the side of sin.

Oh, sure, we have another world war coming, and another great depression, but where are the leaders this time? All you have is a lot of ordinary people standing around with their thumbs up their ass.

Here is what we must do, if glamour is to be restored to those who lead us into catastrophes, out of catastrophes, and then back into catastrophes again: We must outlaw television and set an example for our children by worshipping the silver screen in motion picture palaces every week.

We should see moving and talking images of our leaders only once a week in newsreels. This is the only way we can get leaders all balled up in our heads with movie stars again.

When I was a freshman here, I didn't know or care where the life of Ginger Rogers ended and the life of General Douglas MacArthur began. The senior senator from California was Mickey Mouse, who would serve with great distinction as a bombardier in the Pacific during the Second World War. Commander Mouse dropped a bomb right down the smokestack of a Japanese battleship. The captain of the battleship was Charlie Chan. Boy, was he mad.

What a shame that there are so many young people here who never saw J. Edgar Hoover on the silver screen. There was a man 14 feet high who could not be bribed. Imagine a man who loved this country so much that he could not be bribed, except for some minor carpentry on his house. You can't imagine such integrity without the magic of the silver screen.

Was The Sun any good when I was here? I don't know, and

I am afraid to find out. I remember I spelled the first name of Ethel Barrymore "E-T-H-Y-L" one time—in a headline.

In preparation for this event, I had lunch last week with the best editor-in-chief I worked under here. That was Miller Harris, who is one year older than I am. I would sure hate to be as old as he is. I wouldn't mind being as old as E.B. White, if I could actually *be* E.B. White. Miller Harris is president of the Eagle Shirt Company now. I ordered a shirt from him one time, and he sent me a bill for 1/144 of a gross.

He said at lunch that The Sun in our day was without question the finest student newspaper in the United States of America. It would be nice if that were true. Eagle shirts, I know, are the greatest shirts in the world.

I was shattered, I remember, during my sophomore year here, when a world traveler said that Cornell was the 49th greatest university in the world. I had hoped we would at least be in the high teens somewhere. Little did I realize that going to an only marginally great university would also make me a writer.

That is how you get to be a writer, incidentally: you feel somehow marginal, somehow slightly off-balance all the time. I spent an awful lot of time here buying gray flannel. I never could find the right shade.

I finally gave up on gray flannel entirely, and went to the University of Chicago, the 48th greatest university in the world.

Do I know Thomas Pynchon? No. Did I know Vladimir Nabokov? No. I know and knew Miller Harris, the president of the Eagle Shirt Company.

Well—I am more sentimental about this occasion than I have so far indicated. We chemists can be as sentimental as anybody. Our emotional lives, probably because of the A-bomb and the H-bomb, and the way we spell "Ethel," have been much maligned.

I found a family here at The Sun, or I no doubt would have invited pneumonia into my thorax during my freshman year. Those of you who have been kind enough to read a book of mine, any book of mine, will know of my admiration for large families, whether real or artificial, as the primary supporters of mental health.

And it is surely curious that I, as an outspoken enemy of the disease called "loneliness," should now remember as my happiest times in Ithaca the hours when I was most alone.

I was happiest when I was all alone—and it was very late at night, and I was walking up the hill after having helped to put The Sun to bed.

All the other university people, teachers and students alike, were asleep. They had been playing games all day long with what was known about real life. They had been repeating famous arguments and experiments, and asking one another the sorts of hard questions real life would be asking by and by.

We on The Sun were already in the midst of real life. By God, if we weren't! We had just designed and written and caused to be manufactured yet another morning newspaper for a highly intelligent American community of respectable size—yes, and not during the Harding Administration, either, but during 1940, '41 and '42, with the Great Depression ending, and with World War Two well begun.

I am an atheist, as some of you may have gleaned from my writings. But I have to tell you that, as I trudged up the hill so late at night and all alone, I knew that God Almighty approved of me.

KURT VONNEGUT, JR. '44, Sun assistant managing editor 1942, also served briefly as Sun associate editor during the war years. He has since been noted chiefly as a novelist. This piece is the speech he gave at The Sun's traditional end-of-year banquet on May 3, 1980.

—Photo by D. Ruether

TREKKING UP THE HILL: A MISTY DAWN ON LIBE SLOPE, OCTOBER 1965